WHAT IS DANCE?

WHAT IS DANCE?

READINGS IN THEORY AND CRITICISM

ROGER COPELAND

MARSHALL COHEN

OXFORD UNIVERSITY PRESS
Oxford   New York   Toronto   Melbourne
1983

Oxford University Press

Oxford   London   Glasgow
New York   Toronto   Melbourne   Auckland
Delhi   Bombay   Calcutta   Madras   Karachi
Kuala Lumpur   Singapore   Hong Kong   Tokyo
Nairobi   Dar es Salaam   Cape Town

and associate companies in
Beirut   Berlin   Ibadan   Mexico City   Nicosia

Library of Congress Cataloging in Publication Data
Main entry under title:
What is dance?
Bibliography: p.   Includes index.
1. Dancing—Addresses, essays, lectures.
I. Copeland, Roger.   II. Cohen, Marshall.
GV1599.W47   1983   793.3   82-14366
ISBN 0-19-503217-9
ISBN 0-19-503197-0 (pbk.)

Printing (last digit): 9 8 7 6 5

Printed in the United States of America

To
Michele Gross
and
Margaret Dennes Cohen

PREFACE

Those looking for a widely diversified collection of good writing about dance will, we are certain, find it here. In fact, we would like to think that *What Is Dance? Readings in Theory and Criticism* contains much of the best writing about dance currently available in English. But—as the subtitle implies—this anthology was conceived with a somewhat more specific purpose in mind. The essays in this book have been selected and organized so as to identify and examine the basic issues of dance aesthetics, the questions and problems that arise when one thinks about the art of dance in a sustained and rigorous manner (e.g., questions about the underlying nature of dance, its unique properties, the ways in which movement conveys meaning, the relationship of dance to the other arts, etc.).

But at the same time, we have no intention of artificially isolating theoretical approaches to dance from those of more immediate concern to the performer, choreographer, critic, or historian. For example, questions about genre distinctions and the nature of style are obviously of consequence to the student of dance history, as well as to the philosopher. Questions about the varying ways in which movement may represent the world beyond the dancer's body or express emotions are essential to any critic or reviewer who wishes to use words such as "representation" or "expression" in an informed and philosophically

responsible manner. The difference, then, between this anthology and other existing dance collections is that the articles have
been selected not only for their merit, but for the representative
positions they take and the problems they raise. In other words,
we have selected articles that will ask the same sorts of questions
about dance that philosophers have traditionally asked about the
other arts.

Anthologies of this sort have long been available in the other
arts, even those such as cinema and photography that have
acquired cultural respectability more recently than dance. Thus,
a dance collection of this sort is, we believe, long overdue. Dance
is surely among the most vital of the contemporary arts, especially in America. In fact, for some time now it has been fashionable to speak of a "dance boom" in this country. But the impulse
to theorize about dance continues to meet with considerable
resistance, not only from dancers and choreographers, but also
from many dance critics and historians who tend to dismiss theory as either an irrelevance or an impertinence.

According to this view, dance writing should be primarily
descriptive; and writers who stray from the immediate, palpable
surface of the dance commit an act of sacrilege against the art
itself. Some, no doubt, would go even further and argue that of
all the arts, dance is the most resistant to theoretical consideration, the art that continually re-directs our attention to the concrete and the immediate. In their view, one of the functions of
dance is to keep us firmly rooted on earth, to prevent us from
floating away into the heady atmosphere of "pure" thought.

But the dance community pays a considerable price for this
bias against theory. It rarely enjoys the sort of vigorous intellectual debates that enlivens discussion of the other arts. And now
that academic dance programs have largely declared their independence of physical education departments, it is essential that
they find ways of integrating the study of dance into the liberal
arts curriculum. Why should dance be immune to modes of
inquiry that are routinely applied to the other arts? Those who
criticize dance theory for not retaining the sensory vitality of the
dance experience, or for failing to resemble the dance under discussion, are asking theory to perform a function it was never
designed to undertake. The poet and critic Baudelaire once spoke
of his desire to " . . . transformer ma volupté en connaissance"—
that is, to transform voluptuous, sensory pleasure into knowledge of how that pleasure was produced. This strikes us as a perfect description of what many of the theoreticians represented in

this book have attempted to do. Theory is the mind reflecting on sensory experience, uncovering the general principles that govern (and make possible) that experience.

Furthermore—and this is something that critics of theory often fail to understand—theories answer to experience. They stand or fall according to how well they account for individual cases. This is one of our reasons for including in this book a chapter of practical criticism largely focused on individual dances or the work of particular choreographers. We believe that at their best, theory and criticism exist in a mutually beneficial relationship with one another. The best theory can always be brought to bear upon particular works. The best criticism will be informed by general principles and will not simply express intuitions or subjective reactions.

Whenever possible, the essays in this book have been arranged dialectically, so that significant areas of disagreement can be brought into sharper focus. The chapter introductions are intended not merely to summarize the articles but to clarify the issues they raise and to test their theoretical assertions against actual choreographic practice. Frequently, the introductions refer to essays that for one reason or another are not included in the book. We hope, thereby, to situate the book's contents in a broader intellectual context and at the same time to suggest additional, related readings. We have tried to limit our selections to articles not readily available in other existing collections, but several widely anthologized articles by writers such as Noverre, Ellis, and Valéry are so essential to our purposes that it would be unwise to exclude them.

As for the book's format: In the first section—"What Is Dance?"—we examine attempts to define the art of dance and to distinguish it from other sorts of rhythmic, patterned movements performed by human beings, other animals, and inanimate objects. Here, we have selected articles by theoreticians of dance that most clearly parallel the classic definitions of art in general (e.g., the theory that art is an imitation of nature, the expression of emotion, or the embodiment of form).

Section II—"The Dance Medium"—explores the inherent limitations of the dance medium. What sorts of tasks is dance uniquely well equipped to perform? At what point does dance begin to exceed its competence and encroach on the domain of the other arts? In the next section—"Dance and the Other Arts"—we expand this line of inquiry, exploring not only the similarities and differences among dance and the other arts, but also the means by which movement can (or cannot) be united with related arts in performance. Several writers in this section also discuss the ways in which dance has influenced—and been influenced by—the other arts.

The fourth section—"Genre and Style"—examines the genres or categories into which individual dances have traditionally been classified. In other words, what sets of shared properties enable us to refer to some dances as examples of ballet, others as modern dance, still others as post-modern, etc. And ultimately, how adequate and how necessary are such systems of classification?

In Section V—"Language, Notation, and Identity"—some of the articles consider the question of whether or not a system of movement can be thought of as a "language" in any meaningful sense. Other articles examine the problems that arise when one attempts to notate choreography and to reconstruct older dances from written notation. Section VI—"Dance Criticism"—is devoted to examples of practical criticism organized so as to illustrate the historical development of dance criticism. The introduction to this section discusses the special difficulties that the critic of dance must contend with. The final section—"Dance and Society"—contains articles that analyze dance sociologically. Some of these essays examine the non-aesthetic, utilitarian functions that dance performs in various societies. Others explore the ways in which particular dances—especially social, non-theatrical dances—reflect and illuminate the cultural mores of the societies in which they are created.

Obviously, many significant issues go unexplored in this book. But we hope that these essays and the manner in which they have been organized and introduced will stimulate a more rigorous approach to the subjects the book does address. The introductions to Sections II, III, IV, and VI were written primarily by Roger Copeland; those to Sections I, V, and VII were written primarily by Marshall Cohen. The editors would like to thank Michele Gross, Margaret Dennes Cohen, John Wright, Curtis Church, Natalie Tutt, and the staff of the Dance Collection, New York Public Library, for their invaluable advice and assistance. Photographs not otherwise credited are used by courtesy of the Dance Collection, The New York Public Library at Lincoln Center.

Oberlin, Ohio   R. C.
Princeton, N.J.   M.C.

November 1982

CONTENTS

IV   GENRE AND STYLE   225

Ballet

Modern Dance

CONTENTS

WHAT IS DANCE?

I

What Is Dance?

What is dance? Can we formulate a definition comprehensive enough to cover the wide variety of activities routinely referred to as dance? Unfortunately, the theoretical literature of dance provides only limited help in answering this question. Dance is sometimes defined as any patterned, rhythmic movement in space and time. A broad definition of this sort, which refuses to distinguish between human and non-human motion, enables us to describe as "dances" the movements of waves or the orbits of the heavenly bodies. In addition, this usage enables biologists like Karl von Frisch (in *The Dancing Bees*) to describe the movement patterns of non-human creatures, like bees, as dances. Even if we consider this usage metaphorical and reject such a broad conception of the dance on the ground that dance is an exclusively human activity (and perhaps necessarily a learned or an intentional one) serious problems still arise. For there are other patterned rhythmic movements performed by humans—marching in parades for example, or sawing trees—which are generally thought to differ from dancing. If we are to arrive at a satisfactory conception of dance we have much to gain by appealing to the most influential traditional theories of art and the dance literature that is informed by them.

Three of these traditional theories may prove especially useful: the theories of art as imitation, expression, and form. If, as the imitation theory suggests, art is an imitation of nature, or of human actions or passions, then parades will not be dances because they do not in general imitate anything. Nor, if the expression theory is correct, will sawing trees or rowing boats be forms of dancing because these activities are not generally expressions of emotion or attempts to communicate emotion.

Some approaches to artistic activity, such as the theory that it is essentially the creation of form, may not seem to help in distinguishing parades from dances; for, even if we concede that dances must have form, it may be that parades (and even that tree-sawings) do so as well. Form may be a necessary though not a sufficient condition of art. But it may be that, by combining elements from different theories, we can achieve a more adequate one. Perhaps dances, unlike parades, must create forms that express emotion. Or perhaps, unlike tree-sawings, dances must be undertaken for purely aesthetic (as opposed to utilitarian) purposes. Let us, then, turn our attention to some of these traditional theories in the hope that they can help us to formulate a more adequate definition of "dance."

The dominant theory of art in the Western tradition, deriving from Aristotle's *Poetics*, assumes that art is a form of imitation. This doctrine received its most influential statement in the literature of dance in the letters of the great eighteenth-century choreographer and theorist J.-G. Noverre, who claimed that dancing is, or should be, "a faithful likeness of beautiful nature." As with many other theorists, Noverre's failure to adhere to the distinction between "is" and "should be" often makes it unclear whether he is offering a real definition of dance, or expressing a principle of preference or taste. Clearly, Noverre's taste in dance led him to reject the empty acrobatics of his day in favor of a more pantomimic and accurate "representation of nature." But he and others might argue that what is not "true" dance is not in fact dance except in a trivial and uninteresting sense.

Despite the fact that the mimetic theory began to be challenged in the late eighteenth and the early nineteenth century by formalist and expressionist views, the idea that art is a form of imitation has retained its influence up to the present time. The American dance historian Selma Jeanne Cohen examines Aristotle's contention that the dancer can imitate human character as well as what people do and suffer. In her opinion, however, it is only in the last three hundred years that the technical achievements of classical ballet and of modern dance have permitted dance actually to represent characters as well as their action and suffering. In the original version of her article, which she has revised and expanded for this anthology, Cohen accepted the Aristotelian tradition's conception of the dance and did not ask, with the modern formalist, whether dance needs to serve any imitative function at all. The formalist might argue that the technical advances she mentions have in fact permitted dance to elaborate its purely formal potential more convincingly and therefore to renounce extrinsic imitative concerns. Alternatively, the expressionist might ask whether some of the techniques of modern dance and of twentieth-century ballet that Cohen describes do not serve the purposes of greater expressiveness rather than of more accurate imitation. Both Noverre, an imitation theorist, and Fokine, who speaks mainly of expression, reject what they consider empty spectacle and meaningless virtuosity. But they do so in the name of significantly different ideals.

The theory that art is a form of self-expression, or an expression of emotions, has been especially influential since the romantic era and has been given elaborate philosophical defenses in such works as Croce's *Aesthetic* and Collingwood's *The Principles of Art*. It is a theory that has been especially influential with advocates of modern dance, and one of the most influential of these was the *New York Times* critic John Martin. For Martin the art of dance is the expression and transference through the medium of bodily movement of mental and emotional experiences that the individual cannot express by rational or intellectual means. According to Martin, the dancer's movements are intentional. The movements of the dancer's muscles are transferred by kinesthetic sympathy to the muscles of the spectator; and because he is used to associating movements with intentions, the spectator is able to arrive by induction at the intention that lies behind the original movement. This thought-conveying quality of movement, Martin, following the Greeks, calls "metakinesis." Martin's account of metakinesis is highly questionable, especially so because he does not pay sufficient attention to the conventions presupposed in the conveying of meanings. More generally, his theory is open to the objection that all dance is not in fact an expression of emotion (many works of Balanchine's and Cunningham's are not) and that even when dances are expressions of emotion they do not communicate these emotions by arousing them, or their kinesthetic correlates, in the spectator.

Susanne K. Langer, the American philosopher, taught for many years at Connecticut College for Women and was closely associated with that institution's historic role in the development of American modern dance. She possesses a detailed knowledge of the dance that is rare among aestheticians and has developed one of the most elaborate and influential twentieth-century theories of the dance. Langer's complex theory of art is in part a version of the theory of art as expression. But she specifically rejects the doctrine which she thinks is widespread in the dance literature, and especially in the literature of modern dance, that dance arises in the emotions of the artist, emotions which are then directly "expressed" in the work of art. In her view, the gestures of the dance express feelings, but not what the dancer feels. They are virtual or illusory gestures which are logically or symbolically expressive but not self-expressions.

For Langer it is crucial to distinguish between the rhythmic motions or patterns in space that constitute the materials of dance and the dance itself. These physical materials (which might constitute a parade) must be transformed by the choreographer into an illusion; and following the great eighteenth-century poet, dramatist, and aesthetician Friedrich Schiller, she thinks it is this illusion that constitutes the work of art. Each art form creates its own distinctive illusion, and dance creates the illusion of "interacting forces" or dynamic Powers that seem "to move the dance itself." These powers create "the illusion of a conquest of gravity, i.e., of the forces that are normally known and felt to control the dancer's body." To the primitive or mythic mind, these powers are realities, not illusions or symbols, and they are not believed to be created by the dancer at all. Rather, they are thought to be powers which must be invoked, adjured, challenged, or placated as the case may be. Dance does not become an art, however, until these magical and practical beliefs are replaced by what the tradition descending from Kant and Schopenhauer calls an "aesthetic attitude." When this attitude is adopted these dynamic powers are perceived not as superpersonal realities but as artistic illusions or images. This doctrine permits Langer to make a clear distinction between ritualistic and artistic or theatrical dance. Langer differs from those who insist on the necessity of intentionally adopting an aesthetic attitude or of achieving "psychical" distance, in suggesting that the art work or aesthetic object itself demands and, indeed, imposes this relationship on the perceiver.

In his essay "Primitivism, Modernism, and Dance Theory," which appears in Section II, Marshall Cohen criticizes Langer's commitment to the expression theory, even in the attenuated form in which she maintains it. He also questions whether it is necessary to identify the dance with an illusion created by physical movement rather than with the physical movements themselves (as, indeed, post-modernists like Yvonne Rainer have tried to do). Finally, he questions whether dance creates the sorts of illusion, and especially the illusion of the conquest of gravity, that Langer and many balletomanes allege. This claim is especially paradoxical in view of Langer's special admiration for modern dancers like Mary Wigman who celebrate the qualities of weight and gravitational pull in their dances.

André Levinson, the exiled Russian critic who later pursued a journalistic career in Paris, argues that dance is neither imitation nor expression. In Levinson's more formalistic view both these theories (which, like Selma Jeanne Cohen, he does not carefully distinguish) assign dance a function outside itself and treat dance as a "sign." But dance, he argues, is pure form and it is wrong to think of the dancer's steps as gestures imitating character or expressing emotion. It is understandable, then, that Levinson endorsed the ideals of classical ballet and resisted the innovations of Duncan, Diaghilev, and Fokine. He attributed to Mallarmé the crucial theoretical distinction between gestures through which the mime gives expression to emotions or character, and what he regards as fundamental, the dancer's steps. In his essay, "The Spirit of the Classic Dance," Levinson observes that "it is as though everyone piles upon dance supplementary burdens in his effort to redeem—even if only in a small way—the actual movements of the dance." These anti-formalists fail to appreciate that the beauty of the dance consists precisely in the contours of the movement itself. Levinson's brand of formalism provides a compelling theoretical rationale for the work of a choreographer like George Balanchine, but his ideas remain unpersuasive to those who look upon ballet and modern dance as a narrative art, a form of emotional expression, or a vehicle for interpreting the natural or social world.

The great twentieth-century poet and critic Paul Valéry develops a conception of the aesthetic nature of dance in a manner significantly different from both Langer and Levinson. For Langer the origins of dance are intensely practical. Dance is the envisagement of a world beyond the spot and the moment of one's animal existence. As we have seen, for the mythic consciousness this creation is a reality, not an illusion, and the Powers that inhabit it must be "invoked, adjured, challenged, and placated. . . ." It is only with the rise of philosophic and scientific thought that a secularized consciousness recognizes the world as

the choreographer's creation, as an illusory world of "romance."
This relatively late historical development transforms dance into
an art and renders the spectator's response "aesthetic." For Valéry, by contrast, dance is in its origins and essence impractical.
What may look like dancing in animals is in his view actually a
useful activity and therefore not dancing at all. Man, however,
possesses surplus energy, more energy than his vital organs
require, and he soon discovered that certain of his movements,
by their frequency, succession, or range, gave him a pleasure
equivalent to intoxication. Valéry's dancer creates a "world," but
unlike the world of Langer's primitive dancer, it is not one in
which the dancer interacts with superpersonal powers. Rather, it
is a self-contained world, radically opposed to the practical
world. In it the dancer's actions are without aim or conclusion,
and his function is, as Levinson says, "pure." But unlike Levinson, Valéry does not insist that the dance itself be purely "formal" rather than representational or expressive. Even narrative
movement sequences qualify as "dance" provided that they
serve no direct, practical function in the real world.

Langer's theory raises a question that it fails to answer persuasively. Why, without motives of worship or magic-making did
moderns go on dancing at all? Her strained answer is that the
image of Powers is an important legacy and still, in a sense, provides them with a world image. For Valéry the question does not
arise because the dance has always been non-utilitarian. Dance
creates an inner life consisting of sensations of time and energy
which respond to one another and form a closed world of "resonances." It is this intrinsically valuable world of self-contained
resonances that has always been communicated to the aesthetic
spectator. The problem with Valéry's view is, of course, that his
intense anti-utilitarianism makes it impossible to classify the ritual movements of primitive tribes as dance or to acknowledge
the moral or political aims of many dances that are, nevertheless,
plainly artistic and theatrical. He might argue, however, that
when we view such dances from a purely "disinterested," aesthetic point of view, we see them as merely beautiful, rather than
practical movements.

The selections from Nelson Goodman, the Harvard philosopher, analyze some of the main types of symbolization or reference that occur in dance as well as in the other arts. In particular,
he distinguishes between representation and expression, which,
as we have seen, other writers often confuse. He distinguishes
both of them from exemplification, a type of symbolization that

he feels is important in the arts but that has been neglected by traditional writers. (Exemplification may be illustrated by the tailor's swatch which functions as a sample of a bolt of cloth, and as a symbol of certain properties that the bolt possesses like its color and its weave.) Goodman does not single out any of these types of symbolization as the essence of art, or of dance. Indeed he thinks that the presence of one or another of them varies with the art, the artist, and the work. In the "Afterword" which Goodman has written especially for this volume, he shows how each of these features characterizes different aspects of his own multimedia work "Hockey Seen." Goodman's searching analyses are, however, by no means uncontroversial. He repudiates the traditional notion that imitation is the essence of representation, or even of realistic representation (and by implication, therefore, the view that dance is an art of imitation). Rather, in his view, the core of representation is denotation and he believes that (given an appropriate system of representation) almost any image can represent anything. Representation is relative and realism a matter of cultural conventions not natural correspondence. Whereas anything can denote, or even represent, anything else, a thing can *express* only what it possesses or exemplifies and, in particular, what it possesses or exemplifies metaphorically. Thus, Goodman's own dance expresses conflict and frustration, features which an art work (as opposed to a person) can possess only metaphorically. But "Hockey Seen" *exemplifies* certain abstract patterns which, like a game of hockey, it literally possesses.

Some will find unduly narrow the restriction of expression to exemplification that is metaphorical, and others will object to treating expression purely as a matter of exemplification, whether literal or metaphorical. For they will think that whether a work of art is expressive has something to do not only with properties of the work of art but also with the emotions and feelings of the artist who created it or with the experiences of the audience that receives it. However that may be, Goodman has given a more precise account of Langer's distinction between the logically expressive and self-expression. At the same time, as we have seen, he resists Langer's claim that the dance is necessarily or essentially expressive as well as the claim that works of art are characteristically approached with an aesthetic attitude, if by this is meant one that is aimless from a practical point of view or that is sharply contrasted with an attitude that is cognitive or scientific.

We have observed that the philosophical literature of the dance is from some points of view a disappointing one. David Michael Levin, the young American philosopher and dance theorist, attributes this inadequacy in part to the fact that dance has been traditionally associated with the female principle and that Western philosophers feel an aversion to it because they suffer from patriarchal biases. Indeed, to the extent that philosophy has reflected the West's religious and ethical biases generally, it has tended to deny the body's sensuous presence. But Levin suggests that phenomenology may provide the resources for correcting the inadequacies of our philosophical tradition because it calls attention to the sensuous human body as it is actually experienced in living. The phenomenological method, first expounded by the German philosopher Edmund Husserl, places great importance on elucidating the *Lebenswelt,* or world of lived experience as it is immediately and directly known through prereflective consciousness.

This approach encourages the dance writer to view the performer as a unified "consciousness-body" and to bypass all considerations of the dance's objectivity or subjectivity (in contrast to Langer's distinction between the objective materials of the dance and the illusion these materials project). For example, Maxine Sheets, in her book *The Phenomenology of Dance,* writes that "when we see a dance, we do not see separate objective factors with no unifying center. What we see is something which perhaps can only be empirically written as forcetimespace; an indivisible wholeness appears before us." The phenomenological method can, as Levin and Sheets suggest, help produce more exact descriptions of dance as it is actually experienced in live performance, but its emphasis on non-divisible wholeness also presents very real problems for the critic eager to distinguish the dancer from the dance.

Francis Sparshott, the Canadian aesthetician, offers a quite different explanation for what he takes to be the paucity and inadequacy of the philosophical literature on dance. If an art is to generate a significant philosophy, it is necessary, in his view, that the art occupy a culturally central position, or that it be capable of being absorbed into a culturally prevalent ideology. He argues that dance has never held a culturally central position in the West, and that the main ideologies available to the other arts have not been available to it. Neither the system of the fine arts that was developed from the sixteenth to the early eighteenth century nor the Hegelian system that dominated European thinking about the arts in the nineteenth century found a significant place for the art of dance. The system of the fine arts, deriving ultimately from Aristotle, insisted on the importance of imitation. But, despite Noverre's attempt to argue that dance was in fact an art of imitation, Sparshott thinks it was generally regarded as mere movement and not accepted as a form of representational theater. Furthermore, he thinks that the Hegelian system, which takes beauty to be ideas embodied in forms adequate to them, could easily have found a central place for dance. However, because Hegel refused to acknowledge a split between the rational and the real he always based his schematizations on something closely observed in history. The lamentable state of the art of dance in Hegel's lifetime is therefore sufficient explanation for his failure to assign dance a significant place in his system. The romantic ballet was born in Paris soon after Hegel's death but in Sparshott's astringent view neither the romantic ballet nor any subsequent developments have enabled dance to assume a privileged place alongside the other major arts. Philosophers, he says, cannot bestow seriousness; they can only explain it. Those who think that the dance has in fact assumed an increasingly important role in our culture since Hegel's time will look for other explanations of philosophy's inadequacies. Or they may think that the gravity, brilliance, and resonance of dance as we now have it are in fact beginning to generate a literature that will allow us to reverse Sparshott's severe judgment. The pages that follow are offered in that hope.

JEAN-GEORGES NOVERRE
From LETTERS ON DANCING AND BALLETS

LETTER I

Poetry, painting and dancing, Sir, are, or should be, no other than a faithful likeness of beautiful nature. It is owing to their accuracy of representation that the works of men like Corneille and Racine, Raphael and Michelangelo, have been handed down to posterity, after having obtained (what is rare enough) the commendation of their own age. Why can we not add to the names of these great men those of the *maîtres de ballet*[1] who made themselves so celebrated in their day? But they are scarcely known; is it the fault of their art, or of themselves?

A ballet is a picture, or rather a series of pictures connected one with the other by the plot which provides the theme of the ballet; the stage is, as it were, the canvas on which the composer expresses his ideas; the choice of the music, scenery and costumes are his colours; the composer is the painter. If nature has endowed him with that passionate enthusiasm which is the soul of all imitative arts, will not immortality be assured him? Why are the names of *maîtres de ballet* unknown to us? It is because works of this kind endure only for a moment and are forgotten almost as soon as the impressions they had produced; hence there remains not a vestige of the most sublime productions of a Bathyllus and a Pylades.[2] Hardly a notion has been preserved of those pantomimes so celebrated in the age of Augustus.[3]

If these great composers, unable to transmit to posterity their fugitive pictures, had at least bequeathed us their ideas and the principles of their art; if they had set forth the laws of the style of which they were the creators; their names and writings would have traversed the immensity of the ages and they would not have sacrificed their labours and repose for a moment's glory. Those who have succeeded them would have had some principles to guide them, and the art of pantomime and gesture, formerly carried to a point which still astonishes the imagination, would not have perished.

Since the loss of that art, no one has sought to re-discover it, or, so to speak, to create it a second time. Appalled by the difficulties of that enterprise, my predecessors have abandoned it, without making a single attempt, and have allowed a divorce, which it would appear must be eternal, to exist between pure dancing and pantomime.

More venturesome than they, perhaps less gifted, I have dared to fathom the art of devising ballets with action; to re-unite action with dancing; to accord it some expression and purpose. I have dared to tread new paths, encouraged by the indulgence of the public which has supported me in crises capable of rebuffing one's self-esteem; and my successes appear to authorize me to satisfy your curiosity regarding an art which you cherish, and to which I have devoted my every moment.

From the reign of Augustus to our days, ballets have been only feeble sketches of what they may one day become. This art, born of genius and good taste, can become beautiful and varied to an infinite degree. History, legend, painting, all the arts may unite to withdraw their sister art from the obscurity in which she is shrouded; and it astonishes one that *maîtres de ballet* have disdained such powerful assistance.

The programmes of the ballets which have been given, during the past century or so, in the different courts of Europe, incline one to believe that this art (which was still of no account), far from having progressed, is more and more declining. These kinds of traditions, it is true, are always strongly suspect. It is with ballets as with entertainments in general; nothing so grandiose and so alluring on paper, and often nothing so dull and ill-arranged in performance.

I think, Sir, that this art has remained in its infancy only because its effects have been limited, like those of fireworks designed simply to gratify the eyes; although this art shares with the best plays the advantage of inspiring, moving and captivating the spectator by the charm of its interest and illusion. No one has suspected its power of speaking to the heart.

If our ballets be feeble, monotonous and dull, if they be devoid of ideas, meaning, expression and character, it is less, I repeat, the fault of the art than that of the artist: does he ignore that dancing united to pantomime is an imitative art? I shall be tempted to believe it, because the majority of composers restrict themselves to making a servile copy of a certain number of steps and figures to which the public has been treated for centuries

past; in such wise that the ballets from *Phaéton*,[4] or from another
opera, revived by a modern composer, differ so little from those
of the past that one would imagine they were always the same.

In fact, it is rare, not to say impossible, to find genius in the
plans, elegance in the forms, lightness in the groups, precision
and neatness in the tracks which lead to the different figures; the
art of disguising old things and giving them an air of novelty is
scarcely known.

Maîtres de ballet should consult the pictures of great painters.
This examination would undoubtedly bring them in touch with
nature; then they should avoid, as often as possible, that symmetry in the figures which, repeating the same thing, offers two
similar pictures on the same canvas. That is not to say that I con-
demn in general all symmetrical figures or to think that I claim
to abolish the practice entirely, for that would be to misinterpret
my views.

The abuse of the best things is always detrimental; I only dis-
approve of the too frequent and too repeated use of these kinds
of figures, a practice which my colleagues will feel to be vicious
when they essay to copy nature faithfully and to depict on the
stage different passions with the shades and colours which
appertain to each in particular.

Symmetrical figures from right to left are, in my opinion, only
supportable in the *corps d'entrées*,[5] which have no means of
expression, and which, conveying nothing, are employed simply
to give the *premiers danseurs* time to take breath; they can have a
place in a *ballet général* which concludes a festival; further, they
can be tolerated in *pas d'exécution, pas de quatre, pas de six*, etc.,
although, to my mind, it would be ridiculous, in these fragments,
to sacrifice expression and feeling to bodily skill and agility of
the legs; but symmetry should give place to nature in *scènes d'action*. One example, however slight it may be, will make my meaning clear and suffice to support my contention.

A band of nymphs, at the unexpected sight of a troupe of
young fauns, takes flight hurriedly in fear; the fauns, on their
side, pursue the nymphs with eagerness, which generally suggests delight: presently, they stop to examine the impression
they have made on the nymphs, at the same time the latter suspend their course; they regard the fauns with fear, seek to discover their designs, and to attain by flight a refuge which would
secure them against the danger which threatens; the two troupes
approach; the nymphs resist, defend themselves and escape with
a skill equal to their agility, etc.

That is what I term a *scène d'action*, where the dance should speak with fire and energy; where symmetrical and formal figures cannot be employed without transgressing truth and shocking probability, without enfeebling the action and chilling the interest. There, I say, is a scene which should offer a ravishing disorder, and where the composer's art should not appear except to embellish nature.

A *maître de ballet*, devoid of intelligence and good taste, will treat this portion of the dance mechanically, and deprive it of its effect, because he will not feel the spirit of it. He will place the nymphs and the fauns on several parallel lines, he will scrupulously exact that all the nymphs be posed in uniform attitudes, and that the fauns have their arms raised at the same height; he will take great care in his arrangement not to place five nymphs to the right and seven to the left, for this would transgress the traditions of the *Opéra*, but he will make a cold and formal performance of a *scène d'action* which should be full of fire.

Some ill-disposed critics, who do not understand enough of the art to judge of its different effects, will say that this scene should offer two pictures only; that the desire of the fauns should express one, and the fear of the nymphs depict the other. But how many different gradations are there to contrive in that fear and that desire; what oppositions, what variations of light and shade to observe; so that from these two sentiments there result a multitude of pictures, each more animated than the other!

All men having the same passions, differ only in proportion to their sensibilities; they affect with more or less force all men, and manifest themselves outwardly with more or less vehemence and impetuosity. This principle stated, which nature demonstrates every day, one should vary the attitudes, diffuse the shades of expression, and thenceforth the pantomimic action of each person would cease to be monotonous.

It would result in being both a faithful imitator and an excellent painter, to put variety in the expression of the heads, to give an air of ferocity to some of the fauns, to others less passion; to these a more tender air, and, lastly, to the others a voluptuous character which would calm or share the fear of the nymphs. The sketch of this picture determines naturally the composition of the other: I see then the nymphs who hesitate between pleasure and fear, I perceive others who, by their contrasting attitudes, depict to me the different emotions with which their being is agitated; the latter are prouder than their companions, the former mingle fear with a sense of curiosity which renders the picture more seductive; this variety is the more attractive in its likeness to nature. You must agree with me, Sir, that symmetry should always be banished from dances with action.

I will ask those who usually are prejudiced, if they will find symmetry in a flock of stray sheep which wish to escape from the murdering fangs of wolves, or in a band of peasants who abandon their fields and hamlets to avoid the fury of the enemy who pursues them? No, without a doubt; but true art consists in concealing art. I do not counsel disorder and confusion at all, on the contrary I desire that regularity be found even in irregularity; I ask for ingenious groups, strong but always natural situations, a manner of composition which conceals the composer's labours from the eyes of the spectator.

As to figures, they only deserve to please when they are presented in quick succession and designed with both taste and elegance.

I am, &c.

(1760, rev. 1803)

Notes

[1]As a general rule, whenever Noverre uses the term *maîtres de ballet*, he employs it in its old sense of meaning the person who composes the dances in a *divertissement* or ballet. Nowadays, such a person is termed the *chorégraphe*, while the designation *maître de ballet* is applied to the individual responsible for the training of the dancers and the maintenance of their technique at the requisite standard of efficiency. [Notes in this article are by the translator, Cyril Beaumont, 1930.—Eds.]

[2]Bathyllus and Pylades were two celebrated mimes famous about 22 B.C. Bathyllus of Alexandria, the freedman and favourite of Mæcenas, together with Pylades of Cicilia and his pupil Hylas, brought to a fine degree of perfection, during the reign of Augustus, the imitative dance termed *Pantomimus*, which was one of the most popular public amusements at Rome until the fall of the Empire. Bathyllus excelled in the interpretation of comic scenes, while Pylades was unsurpassed in the representation of tragic themes. At first, the two actors gave performances in common, then, becoming jealous of each other's fame, they quarrelled and established rival theatres. Each founded a school and each had a numerous band of followers whose fierce partisanship led to many brawls and sometimes bloodshed.

Some account of these actors will be found in Castil-Blaze. *La Danse et les Ballets*, 1832, Chapter I. For a description of their performances, consult Smith (W.). *A Dictionary of Greek and Roman Antiquities*. 2 Vols. 1891. Vol. 2, p. 334, *Pantomimus*.

[3]The first Emperor of the Roman Empire. Born Sept. 23rd, 63 B.C. Died Aug. 29th, A.D. 14.

[4]A lyrical tragedy in five acts and a prologue, with libretto by Quinault and music by Lully. It was first played before the Court on Jan. 6th, 1663. The first public performance was given at the Académie Royale de Musique, on April 27th of the same year. It had an immense success due to its many charming airs and the wealth of the mechanical effects introduced. Its theme was the return of the Golden Age, and it was intended as a panegyric in honour of Louis XIV.

[5]An *entrée* is a *divertissement* executed by a number of dancers.

Compan, in his *Dictionnaire de Danse* (1787) gives the following definition: "The usual division of all kinds of ballets is five acts. Each act consists of three, six, nine, and sometimes twelve *entrées*. The term *entrée* is given to one or more bands of dancers who, by means of their steps, gestures and attitudes, express that portion of the whole theme which has been assigned to them."

SELMA JEANNE COHEN
DANCE AS AN ART
OF IMITATION

In the thirty years since this piece was written, both the author and the art of dance have changed considerably. The paragraphs set in italics constitute a sort of critique of what the writer now perceives as some of the more egregious misstatements in this early effort.

"Rhythm alone, without harmony, is the means of the dancer's imitations," wrote Aristotle, who then added—a bit grudgingly—"for even he, by the rhythms of his attitudes, may represent men's characters, as well as what they do and suffer." (*Poetics*: 1447a).

Yet, until recently, that is just what dance did not do. Aristotle had dropped the subject without arguing his assertion, and, for many centuries, the potentialities of his statement were ignored in both theory and practice. The trouble was that dance was only potentially capable of imitation; technically its means were inadequate.

"Until recently." Only if we insist that Bathyllus and Pylades were mimes and not dancers. And if we interpret "recently" rather broadly.

When, in the sixteenth century, some serious thinking about dance technique had started, theories of the art as imitation began to stir. But they advocated only the lesser part of Aristotle's claim—that the dancer imitates what men do and suffer. Even when given an allegorical significance, the closest the contemporary ballets came to the imitation of character was the depicting of generalized classes of men distinguished by a single trait, such as desire for power or delight in intrigue.

Père Claude Ménestrier, who wrote in 1682, distinguished a ballet from a "danse simple" by its imitation of men's actions, of animals, or inanimate things. Get something composed of several parts, like kinds of music or hours of the day, he told the choreographer, and then select the most pleasing items, for these will make the prettiest dances. In suiting the means of imitation to its object, Ménestrier was dogmatic: a dance of winds should be quick, one of drunkards irregular. Beyond this, he had little to say about the use of technique—there was so little of it to use. Since this limited dance vocabulary could not alone tell the audience that a dancer represented "faith" or "philosophy," Ménestrier recommended appropriate costumes, in addition to the conventional aid of spoken verses, to define the intention.

There was not, in the seventeenth century, enough codified range of body movement to make dance itself the means of imitation of character. Stereotyping was the simple answer for this, and further theorizing was unnecessary. Consequently, apart from the works of a few aestheticians who wrote on dance only incidentally to their concern with the other arts and from the isolated case of John Weaver whose main interest was pantomime, the practice and idea of dance as imitation slumbered quietly till the middle of the eighteenth century.

Actually John Weaver was a most important choreographer and dance theorist, who pre-dated Noverre in using plots drawn from Greek drama. Weaver's works contained what he called dances "of a pantomimic kind." Where does pantomime end and dance begin? A good question.

Dance itself, however, had never been more awake. The five positions of the feet, the foundation of modern ballet, were named and recognized by 1700; Beauchamps, Pécour, Rameau, and Feuillet, through France's Royal Academy, established officially the principles of classic technique which dancers absorbed, enhanced, and turned into a vehicle for virtuoso display. Soon after Camargo had called attention to the brilliance of the complicated entrechat over the simple sauté and even before Heinel had done what was apparently the first double pirouette, some people began to wonder if dance was really meant to develop simply by multiplication and ornamentation. In 1741 Rémond de Saint-Mard claimed that dance had once depicted something and not just sparkled. His complaints were soon followed by those of Batteux, Bonnet, Cahusac, Diderot, and Noverre. The call was for the return of dance to its true function—imitation.

Noverre's demands on the choreographer were far greater than those of his predecessors. The seventeenth century had assumed the presence of spoken verses and had depended on telling costumes to explain the meaning of its ballets. Now Noverre wanted dance itself to be sufficient for expression. Whereas Ménestrier was satisfied with the imitation of species of things, Noverre saw ballet in terms of individuals, the actors in a mute play. His ballets were based, not on the revue-type plan recommended by Ménestrier, but on stories derived from the classics and especially from Greek tragedy.

Noverre was also concerned with the techniques available for imitation:

> I am of the opinion, Sir, that a maître de ballet who does not possess a complete knowledge of dancing can compose in a mediocre manner only. By dancing I mean the serious style which is the true foundation of ballets. If he ignore its principles, his resources will be limited, he must renounce the grand style, abandon history, mythology and national dances, and confine himself solely to ballets founded on peasant dances with which the public is surfeited and wearied . . . ." (Jean-Georges Noverre. *Letters on Dancing and Ballets.* Tr. Cyril W. Beaumont, C. W. Beaumont, London: 1930.)

For some time following, choreographers accepted Noverre's line of thought. A danger, however, beset the path of this literary dance genre. It could be carried to such an extreme (as Vigano was said to have done) that ballets became mere pantomime, practically devoid of dancing. Encouraged by the current growth of professionalism in dance, a fresh concern with the attractions of technique dimmed interest in the ballet d'action.

In 1820 Carlo Blasis wrote several lengthy treatises which, while they assented to the idea of dance as imitation, contributed little to the development of its theory. Yet Blasis on dance technique? Here was a tremendous advance over the practical manuals of the 1700's. Blasis described a greater diversity of body positions, and, with him, the pirouette was found to have a multiplicity of possible forms. The lag in theory had again been accompanied by advance in practice. And again the solidification of technical innovations was followed by fresh theoretical insights.

But this time the period of technical growth was of longer duration. The advent of women's dancing on pointe was stimulated by the tastes of the Romanticists for ethereal, ghost-like maidens. The newly enriched ballet technique gave the impression of supernatural lightness and grace, and the white-clad sylph, a type rather than an individual character, was the era's most popular figure. But when the fashion for Romanticism had run its course, dance was left with a rich technique—and almost nothing else. Since the technique itself offered so vast a field for quantitative development, little effort was made to invest it with quality, with meaning.

But in the early twentieth century Michel Fokine mourned that the only difference between a dancer doing thirty-two pirouettes and an acrobat who did twice as many was that the acrobat did his with more certainty. The aim of the dancer, he cried, is not to establish a record; it is to express feeling beautifully.

Fokine's audience was, for the most part, lethargic, satisfied with ballet as display. The St. Petersburg productions contained pretenses of drama, for they were composed of alternating scenes of conventional mime, which told the story, and divertissements, which stopped the story to introduce dancing. Dualism had resulted from the ballet's using means other than dance to depict sentiments or characters alien to the balletic style. Dainty feet in pink satin slippers pattered lightly over the stage while hands signified "I am poor and unhappy."

The problem was not only with sentiments or characters alien to the style. Even more basic was the problem of conveying ideas by means of movement. The ballerina wants to say: "You are a prince and I am a peasant, and because our society forbids the mingling of classes, our romance is doomed, and you know it." Can any dance style serve her needs?

Fokine set out to destroy this firmly entrenched dualism. A ballet, he argued, must have complete unity of expression. The choreographer must know many styles so that he may select the one that will tell his story without the aid of extraneous, non-dance devices. "The best form is that which most fully expresses the meaning desired, and the most natural that which most closely corresponds with the idea to be conveyed" (C. W. Beaumont, *Michel Fokine and his Ballets*. C. W. Beaumont. London: 1945, p. 137).

Noverre had suggested that the choreographer who did not know all styles of dance would be limiting his potential range of imitation. Fokine went a step further to claim that the choreographer should not only know all styles which he may then employ as needed, but that he should be able to create new ones. "Not to form combinations of ready-made and established dance-steps, but to create in each case a new form corresponding to the subject, the most expressive form possible for the representation of the period and the character of the nation represented—that is the first rule of the new ballet" (*Ibid.*, p. 146).

In these last two paragraphs Fokine moves beyond the demand for identifiable representation to urge the importance of expressive form. The distinction should have been noted. The latter, in the words of Rudolf Arnheim, produces "the kind of stirring participation that distinguishes artistic experience from the detached acceptance of information." (Art and Visual Perception, Berkeley, 1954, pp. 363–64.)

The modern trend follows the line of Fokine but has become far more explicit regarding the nature of expressive movement. Fokine wrote mainly in terms of styles, periods, and national characters. Contemporaries go further by analyzing the movement signs of particular emotional qualities.

No. Fokine was already concerned with signs of emotional states, as was Noverre, for that matter. What changed was the idea of what kinds of emotion could or should be signified by dance. The "how" of signifying was equally important. In 1916 Fokine referred to dance as "the development and ideal of the sign." In 1931, this attitude involved him in an argument with Martha Graham whose movement impressed him as lacking in idealization. For Fokine, dance should be at once significant and beautiful, the latter in both a moral and a pictorial sense. For Graham, dance should be a revelation of experience, regardless of how unpleasant the result might be.

The theory of Rudolf von Laban, for instance, is, because of its systematic classifications, one of the most important for modern dance thought.

The moods or expressions of movements have a double source. It will be easily understood that a body and arm stretched high wide has a different expression from that of a body huddled up on the floor. It would be wrong, however, to speak of definite moods expressed by positions, because the dancer can move into any position in very different ways. Suppose he reaches the highly stretched position one time with a soft floating movement and another time with an energetic thrust. It is obvious that the mood of the movement will be different each time. The expression of movement depends therefore on several factors—space, location, including shape, and dynamic content, including effort. (Rudolf von Laban. *Modern Educational Dance*. London: 1948, p. 44.)

Laban has stimulated much contemporary thought on dance as imitation.

The dance language has been expanded as choreographers began to utilize a greater range of movement (e.g., higher extensions, inward as well as outward rotation), learned to employ heretofore neglected parts of the body (e.g., torso, hips), and when they experimented with factors of timing and dynamics, effort, tension. This enriched vocabulary has provided dance with an enlarged capacity for expressiveness. There was little cause for the early critics to praise dance for its powers of characterization, since its scope was then so restricted. The artificiality of the balletic codification, in which the limbs are always turned out, developed for a number of good reasons, physical and aesthetic, but its prevalence tended to discourage the concept of dance as imitation by limiting the kinds of subjects susceptible to adequate representation. The expansion of the dance vocabulary has had a humanizing effect. To be sure, the balletic moods are human. But when isolated from their natural context, a world in which other moods coexist, they present a picture of a narrowly contrived society. The classic world was a beautiful and elegant one and it deserved all the praise allotted to it. But it could represent few forms of emotional conflict. The technical scope, the vocabulary of movement, had to be enlarged before dance could imitate the diversity of real characters with all the complexity of the emotional drives that make people dramatically interesting. However, the classic language has been supplemented; it has not been eliminated.

The limitation of the dance vocabulary was not the only factor affecting the range of characters represented by early ballet. Nor was the extension of that vocabulary necessarily the cause of the latter's growing breadth. New concepts of what is socially or artisically acceptable (or needed), and therefore worthy of imitation, have often stimulated the expansion of the dance vocabulary, as new ideas lead to the invention of new words to convey them.

From Beauchamps to Fokine, ballet, invariably turned out in the limbs, rigid in the torso, with its emphasis on long, unbroken line, on lightness and ease, was the only fully developed technique available for use. But in the twentieth century, a new group appeared to construct a contrary language, devoid of turn-out, and employing a writhing torso, angular line, and the floor plane of movement instead of the air which the outmoded sylphs had inhabited. In violent reaction to the nineteenth century abuses, the moderns rejected the entire ballet vocabulary.

"Ballet . . . the only fully developed technique." Not at all. The Orient had quite a few developed techniques to offer, as Ruth St. Denis, Fokine's contemporary, was to discover.

But they had established another set of limitations. The new vocabulary made possible the representing through dance of the less refined emotions that ballet could not handle. But it voluntarily eliminated the moods that ballet could represent so well. True, the world does contain neurotics who look especially neurotic when crawling about on the floor. But it also contains well-adjusted individuals (and they are human individuals, not supernatural types) who best express themselves by leaping into the air with turned out limbs and pointed toes. Aristotle did not limit the kinds of characters that dancers could represent. Now that the emotionalism of the revolt is settling, contemporary dance can be inclusive. It can represent in its own medium a multitude of characters if it refuses to reject any useful part of the dance medium either because it is untraditional or because it belongs to an old tradition.

I'm no longer so sure abut those well-adjusted individuals. Since 1953, many choreographers have rejected the demands of representing any kind of characters at all, thus freeing themselves for wide-ranging movement inventiveness. What this paper failed to do, however, was to take note of the riches of non-imitative dance already in existence (e.g., Petipa's formally structured variations).

I think I was in my "modern dance" phase when I wrote this. I no longer subscribe to such exclusiveness.

Dance's sphere of imitation is that of men's characters as well as what they do and suffer. Within its sphere, the possibilities for expression are great. Today, for the first time, growth in technique has been accompanied—not followed—by growth in theory of imitation. Dance has found a movement means sufficient to portraying real diversity of character. It remains for the art to explore the full potentialities of its known resources.

(1953 and 1982)

JOHN MARTIN
From THE DANCE

DANCE AS A MEANS OF COMMUNICATION

Indubitably no other art form has been so inaptly named as the "modern dance." Not only is the phrase non-descriptive, but it is markedly inaccurate, since there is absolutely nothing modern about modern dance. It is, as a matter of fact, virtually basic dance, the oldest of all dance forms. The modern dancer, instead of employing the cumulative resources of academic tradition, cuts through directly to the source of all dancing. He utilizes the principle that every emotional state tends to express itself in movement, and that the movements thus created spontaneously, though they are not representational, reflect accurately in each case the character of the particular emotional state. Because of the inherent contagion of bodily movement, which makes the onlooker feel sympathetically in his own musculature the exertions he sees in somebody else's musculature, the dancer is able to convey through movement the most intangible emotional experience. This is the prime purpose of the modern dance; it is not interested in spectacle, but in the communication of emotional experiences—intuitive perceptions, elusive truths—which cannot be communicated in reasoned terms or reduced to mere statement of fact.

This principle is at least as old as man himself; primitive societies, as we have seen, have found it so potent that they have called it magic and based religious and social practices on it. But it had never been consciously utilized as the basis of art, so far as any record exists, until the turn of the present century when

Isadora Duncan made it the very center and source of her practices, and the so-called modern dance was born.

(1946)

JOHN MARTIN
From THE MODERN DANCE

METAKINESIS

Movement, then, in and of itself is a medium for the transference of an aesthetic and emotional concept from the consciousness of one individual to that of another. This should not be as strange an idea as it seems to be. Back as far as Plato, and perhaps farther, it has been toyed with by the metaphysical philosophers. Kinesis is the name they gave to physical movement; and in an obscure footnote in Webster's Dictionary—so common a source of reference as that!—we find that there is correlated with kinesis a supposed psychic accompaniment called metakinesis, this correlation growing from the theory that the physical and the psychical are merely two aspects of a single underlying reality.

We are not here concerned with theories of metaphysics, and it makes very little difference what we may choose to believe about the relation in general between the physical and the psychical. It is extremely important, however, that we see in the dance the relation that exists between physical movement and mental—or psychical, if you will—intention. Metakinesis is perhaps a formidable word, but it is the only one the dictionary yields for the expression of one of the vital points of the modern dance.

A few minutes ago, it was said that the discovery of movement as the substance of the dance in the same sense that sound is the substance of music, was one of the four important discoveries of the modern dance. The second of these discoveries is that of metakinesis. Nobody invented it, it has always been true. It was true when the early man of savagery conveyed his sense of the mystery of death, and when he stirred a whole tribe into warlike frenzy by leading them into a particular kind of dance. It was true, and recognised in a degree, in the great days of the Greek theatre, where movement was an important feature of drama. Indeed, the Greek tragic chorus, which at moments of highest tragedy sought refuge in chanting songs of deep fervour and dancing to them, was used, as Gilbert Murray has said somewhere, to express the "inexpressible residue of emotion" which mere rationality—words and pantomime—could not convey. It was also true during the many years of the classic ballet. Without it audiences would have had no more delight in watching a ballerina balance herself on one toe in defiance of gravity than they would have had in watching feathers float on the air. It was their own consciousness of gravity which held them to the earth that made them applaud the feat of some one else in defying it. But no conscious artistic use was made of metakinesis until the modern dance arose. You will still find many dancers who will laugh at it—while their audiences slip rapidly away into the performances of their colleagues who have not such keen senses of humour.

The Germans have realised the value of it to such an extent that they have named their type of dancing in general "expressionistic," or the kind of dancing which expresses through movement the dancer's feeling.

Because of this close relationship between movement and personal experience, temperament, mental and emotional equipment, it is manifestly impossible for every one to be taught to do the same type of movement. The ideal dance education, therefore, is that which trains the student to find his own type of movement. Rudolf von Laban, the German theorist, has divided all people into three general types, according to their style of movement, much as singers are divided into such general types as soprano, tenor, bass, etc. He has arrived at certain interesting conclusions, based on physiological and psychological research, and coloured always with a sense of metakinesis. Certain individuals, he has found, are tall and thin and move in a certain manner, always more or less alike. These he calls "high dancers." Others are short and squat and move in another manner. These he calls "low dancers." Between them are the "middle dancers." Now the reason they move in certain fashions is not that they are of a certain stature, and their stature is not what it is because of their type of movement. Both are the result of some personal, mental, psychological characteristics. This is a complete verification, as far as it goes, of the metaphysicians' theory that kinesis and metakinesis are two aspects of a single underlying reality.

EXTENSION OF RANGE

It is easy to see what this metakinetic concept did in the way of extending the range of the dance. So long as the entire emphasis was laid upon design, the colour of dancing was exceedingly limited. Design, no matter how well wrought and ingenious, can never as an abstract element be productive of anything even at its best beyond pleasure to the eye, a certain aesthetic satisfaction which results from contact with completeness of form, and to a degree of kinesthetic satisfaction in vicarious muscular experience for its own sake.

These ingredients obviously wear thin very easily. By the time Noverre came upon the scene in the middle of the eighteenth century they had already worn so thin that he bent his every effort toward restoring their lost substance. This he felt could be done by making the dance an "imitative art" like the drama. Almost everybody who has come after him has accepted his theory and continued the campaign of likeness to acting, until the theory was finally exploded in the experiments of the modernists, among them Diaghileff.

The added range which was so greatly needed was supplied by these innovators in a measure by the introduction of pantomime in a more emphasised manner. This theoretically allowed for the expression of every human emotion and every conceivable dramatic situation which did not depend upon words. But the incongruousness of such a theory is apparent. To attempt to express dramatic ideas and personal experiences while standing with the feet in the fifth position, moving the arms in arbitrary arcs, is likely to be absurd. It is like trying to combine pure decoration and portraiture; to the extent that the result is pure decoration it is not portraiture and vice versa. Stereotyped movements can only express stereotyped concepts of emotion. As the highly individual shadings and gradations of personal emotion begin to colour these movements, they lose their classical perfection and become bad dancing. Thus the canvas has been marred two ways: to a certain extent we have limited the integrity of the emotion to conform to an arbitrary code, and at the same time we have deviated from the arbitrary code in order to conform to emotional integrity.

Diaghileff evidently realised the fallacy of this theory very clearly and up to the time of his death worked incessantly to supplant it with something sound. The glory of the Ballet Russe in 1909 was not due to the discovery of any final form, of any permanent rule of procedure; it was only one more step in the endless progression which constitutes the history of every art. Though there are those who maintain that the dance has gone steadily downward since the days of "Scheherazade" and "Cleopatra" and "The Fire Bird," Diaghileff knew better. His later productions employed the services of choreographers, artists, musicians, who would aid him in the discovery of new forms suitable to the expression of new ideas. His experiments never achieved their goal and many of them remained tentative, and what the possibilities may be in his method of procedure we can only surmise. Certainly they would seem worth the effort of further pursuit, if any artist can be found capable of pursuing them.

In the meantime, the modern dancer has answered the riddle by discarding completely the theory of arbitrary forms and building on the principle that emotional experience can express itself through movement directly. Thus for the first time it has become possible to have a creative tragic dance as well as an abstract lyrical one. The theatre has its tragedies as well as its comedies, music is full of tragic compositions; but until Isadora Duncan convinced the world against its will, there was never a vision of a tragic dance such as the Greeks and their forebears knew. If she did not see clearly through to its creation, she at least saw its possibilities and made many glorious, unruly, lawless efforts at achieving them.

FORM AND METAKINESIS

Thus far we have discussed purely physical aspects of dance form. With metakinesis we come to the most intangible as well as the most important of its considerations. The dancer's ability or inclination to use the overtones of movements to convey his intention determines to a very large extent—indeed, almost entirely—his type of dancing.

At its highest point of development we find the so-called expressionistic dancing with Mary Wigman as an outstanding practitioner. This class of dance is in effect the modern dance in its purest manifestation. The basis of each composition in this medium lies in a vision of something in human experience which touches the sublime. Its externalisation in some form which can be apprehended by others comes not by intellectual planning but by "feeling through" with a sensitive body. The first result of such creation is the appearance of certain entirely authentic movements which are as closely allied to the emotional experience as an instinctive recoil is to an experience of fear. In this process are evolved movements which may never have been seen before in a dance but which are nevertheless the inevitable material for this particular composition. When these movements have been arranged in rhythmic relation to each other, the arrangement dictated still by the logic of the inner feeling but at the same time productive of an aesthetic reaction in an onlooker, the composition is complete. This type of dance is generally of the utmost simplicity. It cannot permit of ornamentation, for that would only defeat its purpose of expression. Frequently it establishes its rhythms with great clarity and thereafter touches only the high spots of its design, leaving it to you to fill in the space and complete the form. When this is accomplished, the highest type of aesthetic reaction has been produced.

It has sometimes been said of dancing of this sort that it lacks variety, but this is a misstatement of the case. It may not reveal its variety to certain spectators who are not equipped to see it. The man who is looking for routines, for "steps" and "tricks," of course will not find them, and because he does not know how to look for anything else he will naturally miss the almost unlimited variety which is before him.

Metakinesis is sometimes applied literally through pantomime, generally in dances with a literary program. The pantomimic or literary dance is not a pure type of dancing, but is a leaning toward that subdivision of dancing which we call acting. In dances of this description the considerations of time and space patterns are of minor importance. The process of composition develops through a series of incidents generally concerned with external agencies. Its form is governed by dramatic laws, and movement serves a secondary purpose.

At the farthest extreme from the purely pantomimic dance we find that type of composition which seeks its effects through abstractions and ignores as far as may be all metakinetic considerations. Between these types there are to be found any number of variations, and any of them is good when it produces its effect.

To be sure, no dancer when he sets out to make a dance sits down and calculates all the various types of patterns and rhythms and dimensions he must work with. The technique of

composition, like other techniques, is of no use until it is learned
and forgotten and some of it has stuck in the process. The part
that is retained is the part that is of service to him; the rest he
need not bother to carry about with him, for he has not made it
his own.

(1933)

SUSANNE K. LANGER
From FEELING AND FORM

VIRTUAL POWERS

. . . What, then, is dance? If it be an independent art, as indeed
it seems to be, it must have its own "primary illusion." Rhythmic
motion? That is its actual process, not an illusion. The "primary
illusion" of an art is something created, and created at the first
touch—in this case, with the first motion, performed or even
implied. The motion itself, as a physical reality and therefore
"material" in the art, must suffer transformation. Into what?—
Thiess, in the passage just quoted, has given the answer: "Everything becomes expression, *gesture*. . . ."

All dance motion is gesture, or an element in the exhibition of
gesture—perhaps its mechanical contrast and foil, but always
motivated by the semblance of an expressive movement. Mary
Wigman has said, somewhere: "A meaningless gesture is abhor-
rent to me." Now a "meaningless gesture" is really a contradiction in terms; but to the great dancer all movement in dance was
gesture—that was the only word; a mistake was a "meaningless
gesture." The interesting point is that the statement itself might
just as well have been made by Isadora Duncan, by Laban, or by
Noverre. For, oddly enough, artists who hold the most fantastically diverse theories as to what dancing is—a visible music, a
succession of pictures, an unspoken play—all recognize its gestic
character. *Gesture* is the basic abstraction whereby the dance illusion is made and organized.

Gesture is vital movement; to the one who performs it, it is
known very precisely as a kinetic experience, i.e., as action, and

somewhat more vaguely by sight, as an effect. To others it appears as a visible motion, but not a motion of things, sliding or waving or rolling around—it is *seen and understood* as vital movement. So it is always at once subjective and objective, personal and public, willed (or evoked) and perceived.

In actual life gestures function as signals or symptoms of our desires, intentions, expectations, demands, and feelings. Because they can be consciously controlled, they may also be elaborated, just like vocal sounds, into a system of assigned and combinable *symbols*, a genuine discursive language. People who do not understand each other's speech always resort to this simpler form of discourse to express propositions, questions, judgments. But whether a gesture has linguistic meaning or not, it is always spontaneously expressive, too, by virtue of its form: it is free and big, or nervous and tight, quick or leisurely, etc., according to the psychological condition of the person who makes it. This self-expressive aspect is akin to the tone of voice in speech.

Gesticulation, as part of our actual behavior, is not art. It is simply vital movement. A squirrel, startled, sitting up with its paw against its heart, makes a gesture, and a very expressive one at that. But there is not art in its behavior. It is not dancing. Only when the movement that was a genuine gesture in the squirrel is *imagined*, so it may be performed apart from the squirrel's momentary situation and mentality, it becomes an artistic element, a possible dance-gesture. Then it becomes a free symbolic form, which may be used to convey *ideas* of emotion, of awareness and premonition, or may be combined with or incorporated in other virtual gestures, to express other physical and mental tensions.

Every being that makes natural gestures is a center of vital force, and its expressive movements are seen by others as signals of its will. But virtual gestures are not signals, they are symbols of will. The spontaneously gestic character of dance motions is illusory, and the vital force they express is illusory; the "powers" (i.e., centers of vital force) in dance are created beings—created by the semblance gesture.

The primary illusion of dance is a virtual realm of Power—not actual, physically exerted power, but appearances of influence and agency created by virtual gesture.

In watching a collective dance—say, an artistically successful ballet—one does not see *people running around;* one sees the dance driving this way, drawn that way, gathering here, spreading there—fleeing, resting, rising, and so forth; and all the motion seems to spring from powers beyond the performers.[1] In a *pas de deux* the two dancers appear to magnetize each other; the relation between them is more than a spatial one, it is a relation of forces; but the forces they exercise, that seem to be as physical as those which orient the compass needle toward its pole, really do not exist physically at all. They are dance forces, virtual powers.

The prototype of these purely apparent energies is not the "field of forces" known to physics, but the subjective experience of volition and free agency, and of reluctance to alien, compelling wills. The consciousness of life, the sense of vital power, even of the power to receive impressions, apprehend the environment, and meet changes, is our most immediate self-consciousness. This is the feeling of power; and the play of such "felt" energies is as different from any system of physical forces as psychological time is from clock-time, and psychological space from the space of geometry.

The widely popular doctrine that every work of art takes rise from an emotion which agitates the artist, and which is directly "expressed" in the work, may be found in the literature of every art. That is why scholars delve into each famous artist's life history, to learn by discursive study what emotions he must have had while making this or that piece, so that they may "understand" the message of the work. But there are usually a few philosophical critics—sometimes artists themselves—who realize that the feeling in a work of art is something the artist *conceived* as he created the symbolic form to present it, rather than something he was undergoing and involuntarily venting in an artistic process. There is a Wordsworth who finds that poetry is not a symptom of emotional stress, but an image of it—"emotion recollected in tranquillity"; there is a Riemann who recognizes that music *resembles* feeling, and is its objective symbol rather than its physiological effect; a Mozart who knows from experience that emotional disturbance merely interferes with artistic conception. Only in the literature of the dance, the claim to direct self-expression is very nearly unanimous. Not only the sentimental Isadora, but such eminent theorists as Merle Armitage and Rudolf von Laban, and scholars like Curt Sachs, besides countless dancers judging introspectively, accept the naturalistic doctrine that dance is a free discharge either of surplus energy or of emotional excitement.

Confronted with such evidence, one naturally is led to reconsider the whole theory of art as symbolic form. Is dance an exception? Good theories may have special cases, but not exceptions. Does the whole philosophy break down? Does it simply not "work" in the case of dance, and thereby reveal a fundamental weakness that was merely obscurable in other contexts? Surely no one would have the temerity to claim that *all* the experts on a subject are wrong!

Now there is one curious circumstance, which points the way out of this quandary: namely, that the really great experts—choreographers, dancers, aestheticians, and historians—although explicitly they assert the emotive-symptom thesis, implicitly contradict it when they talk about any particular dance or any specified process. No one, to my knowledge, has ever maintained that Pavlova's rendering of slowly ebbing life in "The Dying Swan" was most successful when she actually felt faint and sick, or proposed to put Mary Wigman into the proper mood for her tragic "Evening Dances" by giving her a piece of terrible news a few minutes before she entered on the stage. A good ballet master, wanting a ballerina to register dismay, might say: "Imagine that your boy-friend has just eloped with your most trusted chum!" But he would not say, with apparent seriousness, "Your boy-friend told me to tell you goodby from him, he's not coming to see you any more." Or he might suggest to a sylph rehearsing a "dance of joy" that she should fancy herself on a vacation in California, amid palms and orange groves, but he probably would not remind her of an exciting engagement after the rehearsal, because that would distract her from the dance, perhaps even to the point of inducing false motions.

It is *imagined feeling* that governs the dance, not real emotional conditions. If one passes over the spontaneous emotion theory with which almost every modern book on the dance begins, one quickly comes to the evidence for this contention. Dance gesture is not real gesture, but virtual. The bodily movement, of course, is real enough; but *what makes it emotive gesture*, i.e., its spontaneous origin in what Laban calls a "feeling-thought-motion,"[2] is illusory, so the movement is "gesture" only within the dance. It is *actual movement*, but *virtual self-expression*.

Herein, I think, lies the source of that peculiar contradiction which haunts the theory of balletic art—the ideal of a behavior at once spontaneous and planned, an activity springing from personal passion but somehow taking the form of a consummate artistic work, spontaneous, emotional, but capable of repetition upon request. Merle Armitage, for instance, says: ". . . Modern dance is a point of view not a system. . . . The principle underlying this point of view is that emotional experience can express itself directly through movement. And as emotional experience varies in each individual, so will the outer expression vary. *But form, complete and adequate, must be the starting point if the modern dance as an art-form is to live.*" How form can be the starting point of a direct emotional reaction remains his secret. George Borodin defines ballet as "the spontaneous expression of emotion through movement, refined and lifted to the highest plane." But he does not explain what lifts it, and why.

The antinomy is most striking in the excellent work of Curt Sachs, *A World History of the Dance,* because the author understands, as few theorists have done, the nature of the dance illusion—the illusion of Powers, human, daemonic or impersonally magical, in a non-physical but symbolically convincing "world"; indeed, he calls dancing "the vivid representation of a world seen and imagined" (p. 3). Yet when he considers the origins of the dance, he admits without hesitation that the erotic displays of birds and the "spinning games" and vaguely rhythmic group antics of apes (reported by Wolfgang Köhler with great reserve as to their interpretation) are genuine dances; and having been led so easily to this premise, he passes to an equally ready conclusion: "The dance of the animals, especially that of the anthropoid apes, proves that the dance of men is in its beginnings a pleasurable motor reaction, a game forcing excess energy into a rhythmic pattern" (p. 55). . . .

The reason why the belief in the genuinely self-expressive nature of dance gestures is so widely, if not universally, held is twofold: in the first place, any movement the dancer performs is "gesture" in two different senses, which are systematically confused, and secondly, *feeling* is variously involved in the several sorts of gesture, and its distinct functions are not kept apart. The relationships among actual gestures and virtual ones are really very complex, but perhaps a little patient analysis will make them clear.

"Gesture" is defined in the dictionary as "expressive movement." But "expressive" has two alternative meanings (not to mention minor specializations) it means either "self-expressive," i.e., symptomatic of existing subjective conditions, or "logically expressive," i.e., symbolic of a concept, that may or may not refer to factually given conditions. A sign often functions in both capacities, as symptom and symbol; spoken *words* are quite normally "expressive" in both ways. They convey something the speaker is thinking about, and also betray *that* he is (or sometimes, that he is not!) entertaining the ideas in question, and to some extent his further psycho-physical state.

The same is true of gesture: it may be either self-expressive, or logically expressive, or both. It may indicate demands and intentions, as when people signal to each other, or it may be conventionally symbolic, like the deaf-mute language, but at the same time the *manner* in which a gesture is performed usually indicates the performer's state of mind; it is nervous or calm, violent or gentle, etc. Or it may be purely self-expressive, as speech may be pure exclamation.

Language is primarily symbolic and incidentally symptomatic; exclamation is relatively rare. Gesture, on the contrary, is far more important as an avenue of self-expression than as "word." An expressive word is one that formulates an idea clearly and aptly, but a highly expressive gesture is usually taken to be one that reveals feeling or emotion. It is *spontaneous* movement.

In the dance, the actual and virtual aspects of gesture are mingled in complex ways. The movements, of course, are actual; they spring from an intention, and are in this sense actual gestures; but they are not the gestures they seem to be, because they seem to spring from feeling, as indeed they do not. The dancer's actual gestures are used to create a semblance of self-expression, and are thereby transformed into virtual spontaneous movement, or virtual gesture. The emotion in which such gesture begins is virtual, a dance element, that turns the whole movement into dance-gesture.

But what controls the performance of the actual movement? An actual body-feeling, akin to that which controls the production of tones in musical performance—the final articulation of *imagined* feeling in its appropriate physical form. The conception of a feeling disposes the dancer's body to symbolize it.

Virtual gesture may create the semblance of self-expression without anchoring it in the actual personality, which, as the source only of the actual (non-spontaneous) gestures, disappears as they do in the dance. In its place is the created personality, a dance element which figures simply as a psychical, human or superhuman Being. It is this that is expressing itself.

In the so-called "Modern Dance" the dancer seems to present his own emotions, i.e., the dance is a self-portrait of the artist. The created personality is given his name. But self-portraiture is a motif, and though it is the most popular motif of solo dancers today, and has become the foundation of a whole school, it is no more indispensable to "creative dancing" than any other motif. Quite as great dance may be achieved by other devices, for instance by simulating necessary connection of movements, i.e., mechanical unity of functions, as in *Petroushka*, or by creating the semblance of alien control, the "marionette" motif in all its varieties and derivatives. This latter device has had at least as great a career as the semblance of personal feeling which is the guiding principle of so-called "Modern Dance." For the appearance of movement as gesture requires only its (apparent) emanation from a center of living force; strangely enough, a mechanism "come to life" intensifies this impression, perhaps by the internal contrast it presents. Similarly, the mystic force that works by remote control, establishing its own subsidiary centers in the bodies of the dancers, is even more effectively *visible power* than the naturalistic appearance of self-expression on the stage.

To keep virtual elements and actual materials separate is not easy for anyone without philosophical training, and is hardest, perhaps, for artists, to whom the created world is more immediately real and important than the factual world. It takes precision of thought not to confuse an imagined feeling, or a precisely conceived emotion that is formulated in a perceptible symbol, with a feeling or emotion actually experienced in response to real events. Indeed, the very notion of feelings and emotions not really felt, but only imagined, is strange to most people. . . .

The almost universal confusion of self-expression with dance expression, personal emotion with balletic emotion, is easy enough to understand if one considers the involved relations that dance really has to feeling and its bodily symptoms. It is, furthermore, not only induced by the popular conception of art as emotional catharsis, but is aggravated by another, equally serious and respected doctrine (which is, I think untenable on many counts, though it is the theory held by Croce and Bergson) namely that an artist gives us insight into actualities, that he penetrates to the nature of individual things, and shows us the unique character of such completely individual objects or persons. In so-called "Modern Dance" the usual motif is a person expressing her or his feelings. The absolutely individual essence to be revealed would, then, be a human soul. The traditional doctrine of the soul as a true substance, entirely unique, or individual, meets this theory of art more than halfway; and if the person whose joys and pains the dance represents is none other than the dancer, the confusions between feeling *shown* and feeling *repre-*

sented, symptom and symbol, motif and created image, are just about inescapable.

The recognition of a true artistic illusion, a realm of "Powers," wherein purely imaginary beings from whom the vital force emanates shape a whole world of dynamic forms by their magnet-like, psycho-physical actions, lifts the concept of Dance out of all its theoretical entanglements with music, painting, comedy and carnival or serious drama, and lets one ask *what belongs to dancing,* and what does not. It determines, furthermore, exactly how other arts are related to the ancient balletic art, and explains why it is so ancient, why it has periods of degeneration, why it is so closely linked with amusement, dressing-up, frivolity, on the one hand and with religion, terror, mysticism and madness on the other. Above all, it upholds the insight that dance, no matter how diverse its phases and how multifarious, perhaps even undignified its uses, is unmistakably and essentially art, and performs the functions of art in worship as in play. . . .

The writings of the most thoughtful dancers are often hard to read because they play so freely across the line between physical fact and artistic significance. The complete identification of fact, symbol, and import, which underlies all literal belief in myth, also besets the discursive thinking of artists, to such an extent that their philosophical reflections are apt to be as confused they are rich. To a careful reader with ordinary common sense they sound nonsensical; to a person philosophically trained they seem, by turns, affected or mystical, until he discovers that they are *mythical.* Rudolf von Laban offers a perfect instance: he has very clear ideas of what is created in dance, but the relation of the created "tensions" to the physics of the actual world involves him in a mystic metaphysics that is at best fanciful, and at worst rapturously sentimental.[3]

The chief source of such abortive speculations is the failure to distinguish between what is actual and what is virtual in the making of the symbol, and furthermore, between the "virtual" symbol itself and its import, which refers us back to actuality. But this telescoping of symbols and meanings, word and world, into one metaphysical entity is the very hallmark of what Cassirer has termed "the mythical consciousness"; and that is *structurally* the same as the artistic consciousness. It is metaphorical almost from first to last. But as one remembers that the statements Laban makes about emotions refer to *body feelings,* physical feelings that spring from the *idea* of an emotion and initiate symbolic gestures

which articulate this idea, and that his "emotional forces" are
semblances of physical or magical forces, one can turn his spacious physical account of the world and its energies into a
description of the illusory realm of "powers," and then his analyses all make sense.[4] Especially his treatment of objects as complexes of intersecting forces in balletic space[5] is a piece of bold
logical construction, for it lets one conceive the entire world of
dance as a field of virtual powers—there are no actualities left in
it at all, no untransformed materials, but only elements, living
Beings, centers of force, and their interplay.

The most important result, however, of recognizing the primary illusion of dance and the basic abstraction—virtual spontaneous gesture—that creates and fills and organizes it, is the
new light this recognition sheds on the status, the uses, and the
history of dancing. All sorts of puzzling dance forms and practices, origins, connections with other arts, and relations to religion and magic, become clear as soon as one conceives the dance
to be neither plastic art nor music, nor a presentation of story,
but a play of Powers made visible. Form this standpoint one can
understand the ecstatic dance and the animal dance, the sentimental waltz and the classical ballet, the mask and the mime and
the orgiastic carnival, as well as the solemn funeral round or the
tragic dance of a Greek chorus. Nothing can corroborate the theory of artistic illusion and expression here advanced, so forcibly
as an authoritative history of dancing, re-read in the light of that
theory; the following chapter, therefore, will present at least a
few significant facts, historical or current, to substantiate the conception of dance as a complete and autonomous art, the creation
and organization of a realm of virtual Powers.

THE MAGIC CIRCLE

All forces that cannot be scientifically established and measured must be regarded, from the philosophical standpoint, as
illusory; if, therefore, such forces appear to be part of our direct
experience, they are "virtual," i.e. non-actual semblances. This
applies to chthonic powers, divine powers, fates and spells and
all mystic agencies, the potency of prayer, of will, of love and
hate, and also the oft-assumed hypnotic power of one's mind
over another (hereby, I do not mean to call in question the *phenomenon* of hypnotizing a subject, but only the concept of a
psychical "force" emanating from the "master mind").

The assumption of mysterious "powers," or concentrations of forces not theoretically calculable in mathematical terms, dominates all prescientific imagination. The world picture of naive men naturally stems from the pattern of subjective action and passion. Just as the envisagement of spatial relations begins with what Poincaré called our "natural geometry," so the comprehension of dynamic relations starts from our experience of effort and obstacle, conflict and victory or defeat. The conception of "powers" in nature operating like impulses, and of force inhering in things as strength is felt to be in the body, is an obvious one. Yet it is a myth, built on the most primitive symbol—the body (just as most of our descriptive language is based on the symbolism of head and foot, leg and arm, mouth, neck, back, etc: the "foothills" of a range, the mountain's "shoulder," the "leg" of a triangle, the "bottleneck," the "headland," etc.). This envisagement of the world as a realm of individual living forces, each a being with desires and purposes that bring it into conflict with other teleologically directed powers, is really the key idea of all mythical interpretations: the idea of the Spirit World.

Ernst Cassirer, in his voluminous writings on the evolution of symbolic forms,[6] has traced this principle of "spiritualizing" (which is not really "anthropomorphizing," since it affects the image of man himself in strange ways) through the entire fabric of language, and has shown how human minds thinking with words have built up their whole world out of "powers," which are modeled on subjective feelings of potency. Religion, history, politics, and even the traditional abstractions of philosophy reflect this fundamental *Weltanschauung* which is incorporated in language. The formulation engendered by the subjective model is really a great metaphor, in which our "natural" conception of the world is expressed; but where the human mind has only one symbol to represent an idea, the symbol and its meaning are not separable, because there is no other form in which the meaning could be thought and distinguished from the symbol. Consequently the great metaphor is identified with its meaning; the feelings of power that serve as symbols are attributed to the reality symbolized, and the world appears as a realm of potent Beings.

This conception of nature characterizes what Cassirer calls the "mythic consciousness." But, as mythic thinking determines the form of language and then is supported and furthered by language, so the progressive articulation and sharpening of that supreme instrument ultimately breaks the mythic mold; the gradual perfection of *discursive form,* which is inherent in the syntax of language as metaphor is inherent in its vocabulary, slowly begets a new mode of thought, the "scientific conscious-ness," which supersedes the mythic, to greater or lesser extent, in the "common sense" of different persons and groups of per-sons. The shift is probably never complete, but to the degree that it is effected, metaphor is replaced by literal statement, and mythology gives way to science.[7]

The primitive phases of social development are entirely dom-inated by the "mythic consciousness." From earliest times, through the late tribal stages, men live in a world of "Powers"— divine or semidivine Beings, whose wills determine the courses of cosmic and human events. Painting, sculpture, and literature, however archaic, show us these Powers already fixed in visible or describable form, anthropomorphic or zoomorphic—a sacred bison, a sacred cow, a scarab, a Tiki, a Hermes or Korê, finally an Apollo, Athena, Osiris, Christ—the God who has a personal appearance even to the cut of his beard, a personal history of birth, death, and glorification, a symbolic cult, a poetic and musi-cal liturgy. But in the first stages of imagination, no such definite forms embody the terrible and fecund Powers that surround humanity. The first recognition of them is through the feeling of personal power and will in the human body and their first representation is through a bodily activity which abstracts the sense of power from the practical experiences in which that sense is usually an obscure factor. This activity is known as "dancing." The dance creates an image of nameless and even bodiless Powers filling a complete, autonomous realm, a "world". It is the first presentation of the world as a realm of mystic forces.

This explains the early development of dance as a complete and even sophisticated art form. Curt Sachs, in his compendious *World History of the Dance,* remarks with some surprise: "Strange as it may sound—since the Stone Age, the dance has taken on as little in the way of new forms as of new content. The history of the creative dance takes place in prehistory."[8] Dance is, in fact, the most serious intellectual business of savage life: it is the envisagement of a world beyond the spot and the moment of one's animal existence, the first conception of life as a whole— continuous, superpersonal life, punctuated by birth and death, surrounded and fed by the rest of nature. From this point of view, the prehistoric evolution of dancing does not appear strange at all. It is the very process of religious thinking, which begets the conception of "Powers" as it symbolizes them. To the "mythic consciousness" these creations are realities, not symbols; they are not felt to be created by the dance at all, but to be invoked, adjured, challenged, or placated, as the case may be. The symbol of the world, the balletic realm of forces, *is* the world, and dancing is the human spirit's participation in it.

Yet the dancer's world is a world transfigured, wakened to a special kind of life. Sachs observes that the oldest dance form seems to be the *Reigen*, or circle dance, which he takes to be a heritage from animal ancestors.[9] He regards it as a spontaneous expression of gaiety, non-representative and therefore "introvert," according to his (rather unfortunate) adaptation of categories borrowed from Jung's dynamic psychology. But the circle dance really symbolizes a most important reality in the life of primitive men—the sacred realm, the magic circle. The *Reigen* as a dance form has nothing to do with spontaneous prancing; it fulfills a holy office, perhaps the *first* holy office of the dance— it divides the sphere of holiness from that of profane existence. . . .

. . . What is created is the image of a world of vital forces, embodied or disembodied; in the early stages of human thought when symbol and import are apprehended as one reality, this image is the realm of holiness; in later stages it is recognized as the work of art, the expressive form which it really is. But in either case, the several dance elements have essentially constructive functions. They have to establish, maintain, and articulate the play of "Powers." Masquerading and miming alone cannot do this, any more than naturalistic representation of objects can of itself create or shape pictorial space. But histrionic motifs assure the illusion, the "dance ecstasy." "It aims simply at ecstasy," says Dr. Sachs, "or it takes over the form of the mystic circling, in which power jumps across from those on the outside to the one on the inside or vice versa . . . the people encircle the head of an enemy, the sacrificial buffalo, the altar, the golden calf, the holy wafer, in order that the power of these objects may flow across to them in some mysterious way."[10]

Whatever motifs from actual life may enter into a dance, they are rhythmicized and formalized by that very ingression. Within the Magic Circle every action grows into balletic motion and accent: the lifting of a child or of a grail, the imitations of beasts and birds, the kiss, the war whoop. Free dance movement produces, above all (for the performer as well as the spectator) the illusion of a conquest of gravity, i.e. freedom from the actual forces that are normally known and felt to control the dancer's body. Frank Thiess remarked this fact in his excellent book, already quoted in the previous chapter. After some pertinent comments on the excessive use of stretching, leaping, and balloon-bouncing techniques in otherwise quite empty performances, "in which the ballerinas seek to demonstrate that the earth's gravitation has practically no hold upon them," he adds: "None the less, this demand for conquest of gravity was based on a correct conception of the nature of dance; for its main tendency is always to surmount the bonds of massive weight, and lightness of movement is, perhaps, the cardinal demand one has to make on a dancer. . . . It is, after all, nothing but the conquest of material resistance as such, and therefore is not a special phenomenon at all in the realm of art. Consider the triumph of sculpture over the stone, of painting over the flat surface, of poetry over language, etc. It is, then, precisely the material with which any particular art has to work that is to be overcome, and to a certain degree is to be rendered no longer apparent."[11] Somewhat later, still in this connection, he designates the toe dance as "the frozen symbol of this ideal," especially intended to show that the body has lost nearly all its weight, so that it can be supported by the tips of its toes. And here he adds a comment significant for the theory of semblance: "In actuality," he says, "the toes are securely boxed, the support of the body is the instep. But that is neither here nor there; the body is supposed to *appear* weightless, and thus, from the artistic standpoint, to *be* so."[12]

Even the toe dance, so much despised by Isadora Duncan and by the schools she inspired, is essentially creative, not athletic. The art of dancing is a wider category than any particular conception that may govern a tradition, a style, a sacred or secular use; wider than the cult dance, the folk dance, the ballroom dance, the ballet, the modern "expressive dance." Isadora, convinced that the exhibition of personal feeling was the only legitimate theme for terpsichorean art, could not understand her own reactions to the dancing of Kschinsky and Pavlova, which captivated her despite her beliefs and ideals.

"I am an enemy of the Ballet," she wrote, "which I consider a false and preposterous art, in fact, outside the pale of all art. But it was impossible not to applaud the fairylike figure of Kschinsky as she flitted across the stage more like a lovely bird or butterfly than a human being. . . . Some days later I received a visit from the lovely Pavlova; and again I was presented with a box to see her in the ravishing Ballet of Gisèle. Although the movement of these dances was against every artistic and human feeling, again I could not resist warmly applauding the exquisite apparition of Pavlova as she floated over the stage that evening."[13]

How a ballet could be "ravishing," in which every movement was contrary to art and human feeling, was a problem that she evidently did not pursue in her theoretical musings. Had she thought more deeply about her own words, she might have found the answer, the key to the loveliness of Kschinsky and Pavlova and their entire "false and preposterous art," and the very thing her own dance seems to have lacked most grievously: the dancer as an apparition.

The play of virtual powers manifests itself in the motions of illusory personages, whose passionate gestures fill the world they create—a remote, rationally indescribable world in which forces seem to become visible. But what makes them visible is not itself always visual; hearing and kinesthesia support the rhythmic, moving image, to such an extent that the dance illusion exists for the dancer as well as for the spectators. In tribal society some dances include all persons present, leaving no spectators at all. . . .

But a new demand is made on the dance when it is to enthrall not only its own performers, but a passive audience (rustic audiences that furnish the music by singing and clapping are really participants; they are not included here). The dance as a spectacle is generally regarded as a product of degeneration, a secularized form of what is really a religious art.[14] But it is really a natural development even within the confines of the "mythic consciousness," for dance magic may be projected to a spectator, to cure, purify, or initiate him. Tylor describes a savage initiation ceremony in which the boys solemnly witnessed a dog dance performed by the older men. Shamans, medicine men, witch doctors and magicians commonly perform dances for their magical effects not on the dancer, but on the awed spectators.

From the artistic standpoint this use of the dance is a great advance over the purely ecstatic, because addressed to an audience the dance becomes essentially and not only incidentally a spectacle, and thus finds its true creative aim—to make the world of Powers visible. This aim dictates all sorts of new techniques, because bodily experiences, muscular tensions, momentum, the feelings of precarious balance or the impulsions of unbalance, can no longer be counted on to give form and continuity to the dance. Every such kinesthetic element must be replaced by visual, audible, or histrionic elements to create a comparable

ecstatic illusion for the audience. At this stage, the problems of
the tribal or cult dance are practically those of the modern ballet:
to break the beholder's sense of actuality and set up the virtual
image of a different world; to create a play of forces that *confronts*
the percipient, instead of engulfing him, as it does when he is
dancing, and his own activity is a major factor in making the
dance illusion.

The presence of an audience gives dance its artistic discipline;
and where this audience commands great respect, for instance
where the dancers perform to royal spectators, choreographic art
soon becomes a highly conscious, formalized, and expert presentation. It may, however, still be religious; in the Orient it has
never entirely lost its cult significance, although its long tradition has brought it, by this time, to a state of technical perfection
and cultural sophistication that our own balletic efforts cannot
match, and indeed, our balletic thinking probably cannot
fathom. "In southeastern Asia," says Dr. Sachs, "where the
wrench dance has moved into a more restricted province, the
limbs are methodically wrenched out of joint. . . ."

Be that as it may, the separation of stage dancing from the
purely ecstatic took place long ago—probably much longer ago
in some parts of Asia than in Europe—and ever since this schism,
the two kinds of dance have followed different lines of development, and each has been affected in its own way by the great
trauma that Western civilization has of necessity inflicted on all
the arts—secularization.

Why, without motives of worship or magic-making, did people go on dancing at all? Because the image of Powers is still, in
some sense, a world image to them. To the "mythic consciousness" it presents reality, nature; to a secular mind it shows a
romantic world; to the knowing psychologist this is the infantile
"world" of spontaneous, irresponsible reactions, wish-potency,
freedom—the dream world. The eternal popularity of dance lies
in its ecstatic function, today as in earliest times; but instead of
transporting the dancers from a profane to a sacred state, it now
transports them from what they acknowledge as "reality" to a
realm of romance. There are quite genuine "virtual powers" created even in social dance; artistically they may be trivial—
merely the magnetic forces that unite a group, most simply a
couple, of dancers, and the powers of rhythm, that "carry" the
body through space with seemingly less than its usual requirement of effort—but they are convincing. For this reason even
social dancing is intrinsically art, though it does not achieve

more than elementary forms before it is put to non-artistic uses—
delusion, self-deception, escape. The dream world is essentially
a fabric of erotic forces. Often the dance technique serves merely
to set up its primary illusion of free, non-physical powers, so that
a daydream may be "started" by the dancer's ecstatic removal
from actuality, and after that the dance becomes confused and
makes way for self-expression pure and simple. Dancing which
ends in making actual indecent passes at the girl, like the Bavarian *Schuhplattler*, in hugging and kissing, as the early waltz usually did, or even quite innocently in a game of genuine competition—trying to catch a ring, trying to escape from a circle,
etc.—such dancing is merely instrumental. Its creativity is the
lowest possible, and as soon as it has served a practical purpose
the dance itself collapses.

But this is an extreme picture of the degeneration of dance due
to secularization. Its normal fate is simply the shift from religious
to romantic uses. Undoubtedly the artistic virtues of some reli-
giously ecstatic dances, practiced year in, year out by dancing
sects, are no greater than those of the saraband, the minuet, the
waltz, or the tango. In fact, the divine Powers contacted in traditional mystic dancing are often but vaguely distinguishable
from the erotic forces, the bonds of love and the communing
selves, or the freedom from gravity, which enthusiastic ballroom
dancers experience.

The most important, from the balletic standpoint, is the last—
the sense of freedom from gravity. This ingredient in the dance
illusion is untouched by the shift from cult values to entertainment values. It is a direct and forceful effect of rhythmicized gesture, enhanced by the stretched posture that not only reduces the
friction surfaces of the foot, but also restricts all natural bodily
motions—the free use of arms and shoulders, the unconscious
turnings of the trunk, and especially the automatic responses of
the leg muscles in locomotion—and thereby produces a new
body-feeling, in which every muscular tension registers itself as
something kinesthetically new, peculiar to the dance. . . .

To make the dance a work of art requires that translation of
kinesthetic experience into visual and audible elements, which I
mentioned above as the artistic discipline imposed by the presence of passive spectators. The dancer, or dancers, must transform the stage for the audience as well as for themselves into an
autonomous, complete, virtual realm, and all motions into a play
of visible forces in unbroken, virtual time, without effecting
either a work of plastic art or of "melos." Both space and time, as

perceptible factors, disappear almost entirely in the dance illusion, serving to beget the appearance of interacting powers rather than to be themselves apparent. That is to say, music must be swallowed by movement, white color, pictorial composition, costume, décor—all the really plastic elements—become the frame and foil of gesture. The sudden effects of pure time or perfect space that sometimes occur are almost immediately merged again into the life of the dance.

The primary illusion of dance is a peculiarly rich experience, just as immediate as that of music or of the plastic arts, but more complex. Both space and time are implicitly created with it. Story runs through it like a thread, without linking it at all to literature; impersonation and miming are often systematically involved in its basic abstraction, virtual gesture, but dance pantomime is not drama; the mummery of masks and costumes, to which its thematic gestures belong, is depersonalizing rather than humanly interesting. Dance, the art of the Stone Age, the art of primitive life par excellence, holds a hegemony over all art materials.

Yet like all art it can harbor no raw material, no things or facts, in its illusory world. The virtual form must be organic and autonomous and divorced from actuality. Whatever enters into it does so in radical artistic transformation: its space is plastic, its time is musical, its themes are fantasy, its actions symbolic. This accounts, I think, for the many different notions which dancers and aestheticians have held as to what is the essence of dance. Every one of its secondary illusions has been hailed as the true key to its nature, assimilating the whole phenomenon of dance to the realm wherein the given illusion is primary; dance has been called an art of space, an art of time, a kind of poetry, a kind of drama. But it is none of those things, nor is it the mother of any other arts—not even drama, as I think a study of dramatic creation will presently show. . . .

Today, in our secular culture, those artists are the dancers of the stage, of the Russian ballet and its derivatives, of the various schools of "Modern Dance," and occasionally of the revue, when some number in its potpourri of good and bad entertainment rises to unscheduled heights, through the inadvertent engagement of a genius. The work of dance composition is as clear and constructive, as imaginative and as contrived as any plastic or musical composition; it springs from an idea of feeling, a matrix of symbolic form, and grows organically like every other work of art. It is curious to compare the further words of Mary Wigman, in the essay from which I have just quoted, with the testimonies of musicians on the creative process:

"All dance construction arises from the dance experience which the performer is destined to incarnate and which gives his creation its true stamp. The experience shapes the kernel, the basic accord of his dance existence around which all else crystallizes. Each creative person carries with him his own characteristic theme. It is waiting to be aroused through experience and completes itself during one whole creative cycle in manifold radiations, variations and transformations."[15]

The substance of such dance creation is the same Power that enchanted ancient caves and forests, but today we invoke it with full knowledge of its illusory status, and therefore with wholly artistic intent. The realm of magic around the altar was broken, inevitably and properly, by the growth of the human mind from mythic conception to philosophical and scientific thought. The dance, the most sacred instrument of sorcery, worship, and prayer, bereft of its high office, suffered the degeneration of all cast-off rituals into irrational custom or social play. But it has left us the legacy of its great illusions, and with them the challenge to an artistic imagination no longer dependent on delusions for its motive powers. Once more human beings dance with high seriousness and fervor; the temple dance and the rain dance were never more reverent than the work of our devout artists.

Serious dance is very ancient, but as art it is relatively new, except possibly in some old Asiatic cultures. And as art it creates the image of that pulsating organic life which formerly it was expected to give and sustain. "The image which has assumed form gives evidence of the primary vision conceived through the inner experience. That creation will ever be the most pure and forceful in its effect, in which the most minute detail speaks of the vibrating, animated unity which called forth the idea. The shape of the individual's inner experience . . . will also have the unique, magnetic power of transmission which makes it possible to draw other persons, the participating spectators, into the magic circle of creation."[16]

(1953)

Notes

[1]Compare Cyril W. Beaumont's account of a rehearsal of the Alhambra Ballet: "The pianist renders the theme of the movement . . . while the dancers perform evolution after evolution which Nijinska controls and

directs with dramatic gestures of her arms. The dancers swirl into long, sinuous lines, melt into one throbbing mass, divide, form circles, revolve and then dash from sight." (Published in *Fanfare*, 1921, and quoted in the same author's *A Miscellany for Dancers*, p. 167.)

[2]Rudolf von Laban, who constantly insists that gesture springs from *actual* feeling (cf. *Welt des Tänzers: Fünf Gedankenreigen*, especially p. 14), understands nonetheless that dance begins in a *conception* of feeling, an apprehension of joy or sorrow and its expressive forms: "At a stroke, like lightning, understanding becomes plastic. Suddenly, from some single point, the germ of sorrow or joy unfolds in a person. Conception is everything. All things evolve from the power of gesture, and find their resolution in it."

[3]Cf. *op. cit., passim.*

[4]Cf. *op. cit. Zweiter Reigen*, where a pseudo-scientific discussion of physical nature ends with the paragraph: "The tensions which we experience, suddenly, everywhere, in motionlessness, in the sudden sensation of falling, of swinging, are the sparks, the organic parts of a great, invisible, and for us perhaps terrifying world, of which we are little aware."

[5]Tension *(Spannung)* he describes as "a harmonious, simultaneous self-awareness, self-perception, self-exploration, self-experiencing of the infinite transformations and potentialities of transformation in the world with relation to each other." After this heroic effort at cosmic definition, he continues: "From this universal process arises something physically perceivable, a form of being which in this work I call nucleation *(Ballung)*. This nucleation arises, endures, expires and begets by this play of tensions the impressions of Time, Space, Power, and the like. . . . A nucleation derived from the special modes of sympathetic vibrations of the homogeneous infinite will be sensibly and coarsely received by the eye. 'Sensibly,' that is to say, is 'making sense.' Our experience interprets that phenomenon as a space-filling nucleation, a Thing." (p. 6.)

[6]See especially vols. I and II of *Die Philosophie der symbolischen Formen;* also *Spache und Mythos (Language and Myth)*, and *An Essay on Man*, part I, *passim*, especially chap. 2, "A Clue to the Nature of Man: the Symbol."

[7]Cf. his *Substance and Function.*

[8]*World History of the Dance*, p. 62.

[9]"The origins of human dancing . . . are not revealed to us either in ethnology or prehistory. We must rather infer them from the dance of the apes: the gay, lively circle dance about some tall, firmly fixed object must have come down to man from his animal ancestors. We may therefore assume that the circle dance was already a permanent possession of the Paleolithic culture, the first perceptible stage of human civilization." (*Ibid.*, p. 208.)

Dr. Sachs certainly oversimplifies the problem of art and overestimates the evidence (from Köhler) for the solution he accepts. We do not know that the apes experience only lively fun as they trot around a post; perhaps some fickle forerunner of mystical excitement awakens in them at that moment. Perhaps their antics are merely playful. Perhaps the tendency to rhythmic tramping was set off by Prof. Köhler's example, and would never have developed in the jungle unless they watched human dancers somewhere. We know too little to infer anything from "the dance of the apes."

[10]*Ibid.*, p. 57.
[11]*Der Tanz als Kunstwerk*, p. 63.
[12]*Ibid.*, p. 67.
[13]*My Life*, p. 164.
[14]Cf. Rudolf Sonner, *Musik and Tanz*, p. 9: "In the last analysis dance always goes back to a religious-ceremonial practical motive. Only in a late stage do dances descend to a sphere of purely aesthetic hedonism, in which they lose all serious meaning."

Also Curt Sachs, *op. cit.*, p. 6: "As early as the Stone Age, dances became works of art. As early as the Metal Ages, legend seizes the dance and raises it into drama. But when in higher cultures it becomes art in the narrower sense, when it becomes a spectacle, when it seeks to influence men rather than spirits, then its universal power is broken."

[15]"The New German Dance," p. 21.
[16]*Ibid.*, p. 23.

ANDRÉ LEVINSON
THE IDEA OF THE DANCE: FROM ARISTOTLE TO MALLARMÉ

"The French are not sufficiently artistic," complained Théophile Gautier in *La Presse* in 1848, "to be satisfied with the plastic forms of poetry, painting, music and the dance. They need, in addition, a concrete significance, action, a logically worked out story. . . . If they had the courage they would quote Aristotle apropos of a well-taken or a bungled cabriole." A complete history of choreographic thought as well as an explanation of those periodic upheavals through which the dance of the theatre has passed can be found in these jesting words of Gautier. Ever since the students of the Renaissance created the ballet, inspired by the *Orchesis* of the Greeks, there have been two elements vying for supremacy in the dance: movement and story, abstract form and pure expression, execution and pantomime. Down to our own day the balance between these two tendencies remains unstable. From the first treatises of the Italian dancing masters of the *Quattrocento* to Isadora Duncan swaying in the empty orchestra of the theatre of Dionysus, the influence of the ancients has dominated and often confused the study of the subject. The Renaissance fashioned the ballet on classic models and went back to the Greeks for rules to govern it. In the palimpsests they found a key to choreographic beauty. The story about Julius Caesar Scaliger, humanist philosopher, performing for the Emperor Maximilian the Pyrrhic war dance which he had reconstructed from ancient sources is an instance of how the archeologists and scholars have monopolized the study of the mysterious Greek *Orchesis*.

Since the only work which could have given us accurate and technical information about this baffling *Orchesis* has long been irrevocably lost (the work of Aristoxenes, who developed the theory of rhythm), the humanist philosophers were forced to turn to the rhetoricians and historians for the quotations concerning the dance that adorn their pages. One constantly encounters the same passages from Plato, Xenophon, Cassiodorus and from that sparkling account of the Roman pantomime in which Lucian of Samothrace set down his personal comments without any attempt at a critical approach to the subject. But the final authority is always Aristotle, who, in the first chapter of his *Poetics* formulated his ideas of the dance, whose purpose he says is "to imitate character, emotion and action, by rhythmical movement." This fatal text assigns to the dance an aim *outside of itself* and creates confusion between saltatory motion and expressive or descriptive gesture, using the dance as a substitute for words. The dance ceases to be a thing in itself. Aristotle declares that it interprets and imitates life. Lucian repeats his dictum. For the soaring of the dancer through space, for the inherent beauty of this divine sport, the philosophers substitute the concrete excellences of the sign language. From Plutarch to Cassiodorus, there is little mention of anything but "speaking hands" and "eloquent fingers." Aristotle's definition is at the root of all the battles the ballet has fought from Jean-Georges Noverre (1760), who terms it an art of imitation designed to "copy nature faithfully and to delineate the emotions upon the stage," down to Michel Fokine, who, in his turn, championed the dramatic ballet against the great formal ensembles, stylized and abstract, arranged by Marius Petipa, the French ballet-master who reigned for half a century over the Russian dance.

One needs only to open at random the books of Fabrisio Caroso or Rinaldo Corsa, or the *Orchesography* of Canon Thoinot Arbeau (translated into English and edited by C. W. Beaumont) to find the Aristotelian doctrine arbitrarily superimposed upon the technical analysis of the branles and pavanes of their time. Thus Arbeau, having defined the relation between music and dancing, cannot refrain from adding "but first and foremost, all experts agree that the dance is a sort of silent rhetoric"; it is "a speech in dumbshow" which the dancer executes with "her own feet" (1588). During the reign of Louis XIV, Father Ménestrier attempted to outline an aesthetic of the dance in his treatise *On the Ancient and Modern Ballet, According to the Rules of the Theatre* (1682), relying on the same sources. He does, however, attack the conclusions of his predecessors and when he proceeds, in accordance with the Aristotelian method, to study the quantitative and qualitative elements of the ballet, the learned Jesuit actually gives an account of the essential attributes of the dance of the theatre. After the manner of the ancients, he distinguishes three kinds of movement in the ballet: the motion of the body, the patterns of the dance and the expression of emotion—in other words, the dance steps, the path of the dancer upon the plane surface of the stage and the gestures "for the purposes of imitation." Ménestrier refuses to consider the ballet as mute tragedy or danced comedy. He understands that it is a composite art that obeys its own particular rules.

During the 18th century, the style of the *danse noble*, or court dance, as it was elaborated by the disciples of Lully, such as Beauchamps and Pécourt, achieved the extreme of splendor and refinement. In this "age of the minuet," the masked dancer, with his wig and flaring hips, was a living symbol of the taste of the times. His movements were as stylized as his costume. He embodied the spirit of the rococo. But at the same time a violent reaction began to stir in the breasts of the Encyclopedists against the pure dance, which they termed an art of ostentation, a stilted show, a mere social accomplishment. They inveighed against the fixed and "meaningless" rhythms of the sarabande or gavotte. The whole clan of the philosophers went on the warpath against the ballets of Rameau, which they said were only a collection of dance suites, displayed on some allegorical pretext in a pompous decor. Jean-Jacques Rousseau burst forth against the opera, as

Tolstoi did a century later. This "art for art's sake," whose beauty is pure form, seemed to him a mere routine. Dancing for dancing's sake, with no purpose, either instructive or constructive, seemed a futile diversion, while ballets, in which the different episodes were connected merely by some metaphysical relation, bored him. Saint-Mars in his *Ideas on the Opera* enlarged upon the superiority of pantomime that speaks to the heart, over the dance that addresses itself merely to the eye. And Cahusac in his treatise, *The Ancient and the Modern Dance*, sets out to prove the superiority of the ancient dance,and particularly the Roman pantomime, over the French dance. For him, the dancers of the *Opéra*, in spite of the perfection of their mechanical equipment were no more than bodies without souls. It remained, however, for Diderot, in his discourses following *The Natural Son*, to formulate most emphatically the point of view of the philosophers (1757). For him the dance is to pantomime what poetry is to prose; it is rhythmic pantomime. Diderot maintains that to dance a minuet, even with infinite grace, where the dancer follows a path previously laid out, without expressing or imitating anything, is not dancing any more than to run through solfège is singing. "A dance is a poem," he concludes, "although, to be sure, it is the imitation of one through movement." The dance was still awaiting its genius.

This genius, Voltaire discovered and acclaimed in the person of Noverre, the greatest French choreographer of history, a dancer who was at the same time a thinker. His famous *Letters on the Dance* (1760), that are at once a satiric pamphlet and a plan of action, a manual and a profession of faith, confirm the triumph of the ancient doctrine of Aristotle, the great misconception that confuses the dance with pantomime and the dance step *(le pas)* with gesture. In this work, which Diderot praised as being full of ideas and written with fire, the theory of the "ballet of action" is developed. Noverre, in the name of nature and supported by the example of the Greeks, arrays himself against everything in the traditional ballet which represents stylization, symmetry, abstract or decorative arrangement. Twenty years later this master who was a forerunner of the modern ballet in the same sense that Gluck was the precursor of the music-drama took up the cudgels again with these words:

> Shatter the hideous masks, burn the ridiculous periwigs, do away with the awkward hoop-skirts, substitute taste for routine; let us have a costume more distinguished, more accurate and more pic-

turesque; demand action and movement on the stage, soul and expression in the dance; indicate the abyss that separates the mechanics of the craft from the creative spirit that would place it among the imitative arts.

In such words does Noverre define his own course. Through him the ballet becomes a "living tableau of the emotions, customs and manners of all the peoples of the world;" through every form of pantomime it addresses itself to the soul through the medium of the eye. It is interesting to note that in this descriptive and psychological definition all idea of the dance itself, even to the very word, is absent. What had become of it? It had simply become a means to an end; it was no longer an end in itself. Its independence, its intrinsic aesthetic value had been sacrificed to the expression of character and sentiment, to the *ethos* and *pathos* of Greek philosophy. To be sure, in the writings of his old age, Noverre, mellowed by half a century of experience and reflection, resigned himself to the idea that "the dance, in the strict sense of the word, is no more than the art of forming patterns with grace, precision and facility, to the rhythm and beat of the music" (1804).* But the impetus had already been given; all the theatres of the old school, from Naples to Saint Petersburg adopted the "ballet of action," accepting the Aristotelian sophistry. A new tradition was founded in which emotion prevailed over the play of pure form, psychological motivation over the dynamics of movement. And when at the Scala in Milan Salvatore Vigano, a nephew of Boccherini, produced his celebrated choreodramas, *The Titans* and *The Prometheus*, which Stendhal preferred to the plays of Shakespeare, he was doing no more than developing upon a somewhat more elaborate musical foundation the ballet-pantomime of Noverre.

It was not until the great romantic renascence of 1830, of which Marie Taglioni is the supreme incarnation, that the dance came into its own again. In *The Sylphide*, the dance instead of being subservient to expressive gesture, itself became the interpreter of the emotions and their symbolic equivalent. The classic step, which even Noverre had called the mechanical and mate-

---

*It is amusing that the veteran Noverre should end by denying the authority of the Greek theatre, invoked by him in his youth, and should come to pride himself on having substituted a natural gesticulation for the ignoble sign language of the Romans and the "foolish and unnatural" conventions of the ancients.

rial part of the dance, the severe discipline of stylized movement, which he termed "sterile academic routine," in short the dancer's technique came to express the highest things of the soul. In a constant approach to a geometric purity of design, making a pattern in space of straight lines and sweeping perfect curves, idealizing the dancer's body and dematerializing her costume, the *ballet blanc* is able to transmute the formal poses of the slow dance movement—the *Arabesques* of the *Adagio*—as well as those aerial parabolas outlined by seemingly imponderable bodies (technically known as the *grands temps d'élévation*) into a mysterious and poetic language. Those words from *Faust*, *"Alles Vergängliche ist nur ein Gleichnis,"* seem particularly applicable to this highly spiritualized art. And in the same way it is easily understood why the contemporaries of Taglioni called her a Christian dancer.

The romantic ballet and the spiritual impulse back of it found no adequate literary expression. Carlos Blasis, who codified the new laws of the dance, augmented by the great furor of 1830, remained faithful to the poetics of the 18th century. The only great critic who commented on the dance spectacles for a period of thirty years was Théophile Gautier, the librettist of *Giselle,* and he was consistently opposed to what he called the "metaphysics of the ballet." At bottom a pagan, this leader of the "plastic school of poetry" defended the cause of pure dance. For him the true, the unique, the eternal subject of a ballet is the dance. It remains to define exactly what he meant by the word. "The dance is nothing more than the art of displaying elegant and correct designs in positions favorable to the building up of patterns in line"; it is "essentially materialistic and sensual." Gautier, moreover, preferred the *Cachucha* of Fanny Elssler, "the Andalousian of the North" to the seraphic lyricism of Taglioni, "Marie, pleine de grâce." And so it happened that the romantic ballet had to wait until the period of its decline, when it was on the verge of falling into an academic routine, to find its philosophic expression and its aesthetic evaluation in the writings of a great Symbolist poet, Stéphane Mallarmé.

Mallarmé was a man of exalted spirit, who devoted his life to a dream of achieving a definitive work that would be an orphic explanation of the world and would give to our obscure existence a clearer meaning. Vainly he sought some clue to this great work in the dramas and the music of Richard Wagner. But he caught a glimpse of it in the ballet.

I should like to try to penetrate the thought of Mallarmé through his notes—"pencilled in the theatre" in a prose as obscure as it is elusive—and to estimate something of the "visionary accuracy" of his ideas. To do this, I shall have to transcribe faithfully his laconic and isolated words and arrange them in some sort of order. "The theatre is a higher spirit," he declares, and "the ballet is the supreme theatrical form of poetry." The ballet's function is "symbolic"; each step is "a metaphor," a hieroglyph of a mysterious writing, which one must be inspired to read. The illiterate ballerina can be the unconscious revealer of something which she symbolises without understanding what it is. Only our poetic instinct can decipher her "writing of the body." Her dance is a "poem freed of all the apparatus of writing." The dance steps, *pointes* and *taquetés, allongés* or *ballons*, are the rites, through which the idea is enunciated, expressing that which would be inexpressible in any other language. Mallarmé does not neglect pantomime; it also "emanates from the dream." But he recognizes that there is an essential difference between the gestures through which the mime expresses his emotion and the dancer's steps, the alphabet of the inexpressible. Pantomime and ballet are for him two different and separate forms of art. The hero of a ballet, who is an object of rivalry between a woman who walks and a fairy who flies, lives in a double world.

Mallarmé reveals to us here at once the typical material of the romantic ballet and the inspiration of his own poetry. Man in conflict between reality and his dreams or (to put it in other words) the mime and the dancing star, the woman who walks and the dancer who moves on the tips of her toes, or soars in the air, whichever way it is expressed we have the essence of the myth, the subject of all the hand-books in turn from Philip Taglioni's *Sylphide* to Marius Petipa's *Bayadera*. Mallarmé recognized in the ballet the distinct attributes of two different forms of the theatre, of two methods of being, placed in juxtaposition or opposed one to the other. "The dancer who expresses herself by dance steps understands no other eloquence, even that of gesture." Her body, almost unclothed in its cloud of tulle, her legs in their silken sheaths, are no more than "the direct instruments of an idea." The dance becomes for the spectator with imagination the "mysterious and holy interpretation" of universal life and of our inmost being. These ideas of Mallarmé restore to the opera ballet something of that ceremonial grandeur and exaltation that the dance rituals of the ancient Orient or the "astronomic dances" of Egyptian priestesses must have had.

And finally it is once again a poet—the most celebrated of contemporary France—who has described and defined with incomparable verbal perfection and rare penetration this "mixture of flesh and spirit" which is the dance. *The Soul and the Dance* by Paul Valéry is written in the form of a Platonic dialogue between Socrates and his disciples.* In spite of the fact that the scene is supposed to represent a Greek festival, the individuals who appear before the banquet guests present a classic ballet—the steps of the ballerinas are described with a precision that leaves no doubt of that. Indeed in mentioning *entrechats* and *battements* Mr. Valéry borrows deliberately from the vocabulary of Vestris. The banquet hall in which Socrates and his friends are feasting seems to overlook, in spite of the anachronism, the stage of the *Opéra*. The spectacle opens with an ensemble entrance, half gay, half solemn. Then Athnikté (who might just as well be called Pavlova) appears, commencing with a simple march encircling the stage, which is, however, "altogether divine," calling into play the highest expression of her art. To queries as to why this simple march becomes the perfect prototype of all solemn processions, it is explained that the dancer follows an invisible pattern, and that the number and length of her steps are coordinated with her height, which threefold relationship "of these measurable graces" transforms each movement into a high artistic accomplishment. Then follows what the ballet dancer would call the "variation on the points" in which Athnikté gives herself over to complete movement. She dances a scherzo, running and jumping upon the "extreme tips of her toes" and then whirls into the finale, performing a series of great turns. She spins upon herself, before falling exhausted. The guests demand the meaning of these "beautiful, harmonious motions," the goal towards which these "deliciously firm, inexpressibly supple limbs" are striving, the purpose of this fairy-like gymnastic of the ballet, this dream implicit with symmetry, order, action and resulting reaction. One of the interlocutors is bound, at all costs, that the dancer should represent something. But Socrates answers in decisive words which are the keystones to the whole arch of the dialogue. "Do you not realize that the dance is the pure act of metamorphosis?" Marvellous words! In dismissing, summarily, this common misapprehension, they go straight to the foundation, to the scheme of the dance and its meaning, which is neither expression nor imitation but pure function. In these imag-

---

*I have written a brochure analyzing this dialogue from the point of view of the choreographer (André Levinson. *Paul Valéry, Philosopher of the Dance*. Paris, 1927).

ined words of Socrates, the famous and unhappy paradox of Aristotle seems at last to be reduced to nothing.

(1927)

PAUL VALÉRY
PHILOSOPHY OF
THE DANCE

Before Mme Argentina captivates you and whirls you away into the sphere of lucid, passionate life created by her art; before she demonstrates to you what a folk art, born of an ardent and sensitive race, can become when the intelligence takes hold of it, penetrates it, and transforms it into a sovereign means of expression and invention, you will have to resign yourselves to listening to a few observations on the art of the dance by a man who is no dancer.

You will have to wait a little while for the moment of the miracle. But you are quite aware, I am sure, that I am no less impatient than you are to be carried away by it.

Let me begin at once by telling you without preamble that to my mind the dance is not merely an exercise, an entertainment, an ornamental art, or sometimes a social activity; it is a serious matter and in certain of its aspects most venerable. Every epoch that has understood the human body and experienced at least some sense of its mystery, its resources, its limits, its combinations of energy and sensibility, has cultivated and revered the dance.

It is a fundamental art, as is suggested if not demonstrated by its universality, its immemorial antiquity, the solemn uses to which it has been put, the ideas and reflections it has engendered at all times. For the dance is an art derived from life itself, since it is nothing more nor less than the action of the whole human body; but an action transposed into a world, into a kind of *space-time*, which is no longer quite the same as that of everyday life.

Man perceived that he possessed more vigor, more suppleness, more articular and muscular possibilities, than he needed to satisfy the needs of his existence, and he discovered that certain of these movements, by their frequency, succession, or range, gave him a pleasure equivalent to a kind of intoxication and sometimes so intense that only total exhaustion, an ecstasy of exhaustion, as it were, could interrupt his delirium, his frantic motor expenditure.

We have, then, too much energy for our needs. You can easily observe that most, by far the most, of the impressions we receive from our senses are of no use to us, that they cannot be utilized and play no part in the functioning of the mechanisms essential to the conservation of life. We see too many things and hear too many things that we do nothing and *can* do nothing with: the words of a lecturer, for instance.

The same observation applies to our powers of action: we can perform a multitude of acts that have no chance of being utilized in the indispensable, or important, operations of life. We can trace a circle, give play to our facial muscles, walk in cadence; all these actions, which made it possible to create geometry, the drama, and the military art, are in themselves useless, useless to our vital functioning.

Thus life's instruments of relation, our sense, our articulated members, the images and signs which control our actions and the distribution of our energies, co-ordinating the movements of our puppet, might be employed solely for our physiological needs; they might do nothing more than attack the environment in which we live or defend us against it, and then their sole business would be the preservation of our existence.

We might lead a life strictly limited to the maintenance of our living machine, utterly indifferent or insensitive to everything that plays no part in the cycles of transformation which make up our organic functioning; feeling nothing and doing nothing beyond what is necessary, making no move that is not a limited reaction, a finite response, to some external action. For our useful acts are finite. They carry us from one state to another.

Animals do not seem to perceive or do anything that is useless. A dog's eye sees the stars, no doubt, but his being gives no development to the sight. The dog's ear perceives a sound that makes it prick up in alarm; but of this sound the dog assimilates only what he needs in order to respond with an immediate and uniform act. He does not dwell on the perception. The cow in her pasture jumps at the clatter of the passing Mediterranean Express; the train vanishes; she does not pursue the train in her thoughts; she goes back to her tender grass, and her lovely eyes do not follow the departing train. The index of her brain returns at once to zero.

Yet sometimes animals seem to amuse themselves. Cats obviously play with mice. Monkeys perform pantomimes. Dogs chase each other, spring at the heads of horses; and I can think of nothing that suggests free, happy play more fully than the sporting of porpoises we see off shore, leaping free of the water, diving, outracing a ship, swimming under its keel and reappearing in the foam, livelier than the waves amid which they glisten and change color in the sun. Might we not call this a dance?

But all these animal amusements may be interpreted as useful actions, bursts of impulse, springing from the need to consume excess energy, or to maintain the organs designed for vital offense or defense in a state of suppleness or vigor. And I think I am justified in observing that those species, such as the ants and the bees, that seem to be most exactly constructed, endowed with the most specialized instincts, also seem to be those most saving of their time. Ants do not waste a minute. The spider does not play in its web; it lurks in wait. But what about man?

Man is the singular animal who watches himself live, puts a value on himself, and identifies this value with the importance he attaches to useless perceptions and acts without vital physical consequence.

Pascal situated all our dignity in thought; but the thinking that raises us—in our own eyes—above our sensory condition is precisely the kind of thinking that has no useful purpose. Obviously our meditations about the origin of things, or about death, are of no use to the organism, and indeed, exalted thoughts of this kind tend to be harmful if not fatal to our species. Our deepest thoughts are those that are the most insignificant, the most futile as it were, from the standpoint of self-preservation.

But because our curiosity was greater than it had any need to be, and our activity more intense than any vital aim required, both have developed to the point of inventing the arts, the sciences, universal problems, and of producing objects, forms, actions that we could easily have dispensed with.

And moreover, all this free, gratuitous invention and production, all this play of our senses and faculties, gradually provided itself with a kind of *necessity* and *utility*.

Art and science, each in its own way, tend to build up a kind of utility from the useless, a kind of necessity from the arbitrary. Ultimately, artistic creation is not so much a creation of works as the creation of *a need for works;* for works are products, a supply presupposing a demand, a need.

Quite a bit of philosophy, you may think . . . and I admit that I've given you rather too much of it. But when one is not a dancer; when one would be at a loss not only to perform, but even to explain, the slightest step; when, to deal with the miracles wrought by the legs, one has only the resources of a head, there's no help but in a certain amount of philosophy—in other words, one approaches the matter from far off, in the hope that distance will dispel the difficulties. It is much simpler to construct a universe than to explain how a man stands on his feet—as Aristotle, Descartes, Leibnitz, and quite a few others will tell you.

However, it seems perfectly legitimate for a philosopher to watch a dancer in action, and noting that he takes pleasure in it, to try to derive from his pleasure the secondary pleasure of expressing his impressions in his own language.

But first, he may derive some fine images from it. Philosophers have a great taste for images: there is no trade that requires more of them, although philosophers often hide them under dull-gray words. They have created famous ones: the cave; the sinister river you can never cross twice; or Achilles running breathlessly after a tortoise he can never overtake. The parallel mirrors, runners passing on the torch to one another, down to Nietzsche with his eagle, his serpent, his tight-rope dancer. All in all quite a stock of them, quite a pageant of ideas. Think of the metaphysical ballet that might be composed with all these famous symbols.

My philosopher, however, does not content himself with this performance. What, in the presence of the dance and the dancer, can he do to give himself the illusion of knowing a little more than she about something that she knows best, and he not at all? He is compelled to make up for his technical ignorance and hide his perplexity under some ingenious universal interpretation of this art whose wonders he notes and experiences.

He embarks on the task; he goes about it in his own fashion. . . . The fashion of a philosopher. Everyone knows how his dance begins. . . . His first faint step is a *question*. And as befits a man undertaking a useless, arbitrary act, he throws himself into it without foreseeing the end; he embarks on an unlimited interrogation in the interrogative infinitive. That is his trade.

He plays his game, beginning with its usual beginning. And there he is, asking himself:
"What then is the dance?"

What then is the dance? At once he is perplexed, his wits are paralyzed. He is reminded of a famous question, a famous dilemma—that of St. Augustine.

St. Augustine confesses how he asked himself one day what Time is; and he owns that he perfectly well knew as long as he did not think of asking, but that he lost himself at the crossroads of his mind as soon as he applied himself to the term, as soon as he isolated it from any immediate usage or particular expression. A very profound observation. . . .

That is what my philosopher has come to: he stands hesitant on the forbidding threshold that separates a question from an answer, obsessed by the memory of St. Augustine, dreaming in his penumbra of the great saint's perplexity:
"What is Time? But what is the dance?"

But, he tells himself, the dance after all is merely a form of time, the creation of a kind of time, or of a very distinct and singular species of time.

Already he is less worried: he has wedded two difficulties to each other. Each one, taken separately, left him perplexed and without resources; but now they are linked together. Perhaps their union will be fertile. Perhaps some ideas may be born of it, and that is just what he is after—his vice and his plaything.

Now he watches the dancer with the extraordinary, ultra-lucid eyes that transform everything they see into a prey of the abstract mind. He considers the spectacle and deciphers it in his own way.

It seems to him that this person who is dancing encloses herself as it were in a time that she engenders, a time consisting entirely of immediate energy, of nothing that can last. She is the unstable element, she squanders instability, she goes beyond the impossible and overdoes the improbable; and by denying the ordinary state of things, she creates in men's minds the idea of another, exceptional state—a state that is all action, a permanence built up and consolidated by an incessant effort, comparable to the vibrant pose of a bumblebee or moth exploring the calyx of a flower, charged with motor energy, sustained in virtual immobility by the incredibly swift beat of its wings.

Or our philosopher may just as well compare the dancer to a flame or, for that matter, to any phenomenon that is visibly sustained by the intense consumption of a superior energy.

He also notes that, in the dance, all the sensations of the body, which is both mover and moved, are connected in a certain order—that they call and respond to each other, as though rebounding or being reflected from the invisible wall of a sphere of energy within the living being. Forgive me that outrageously bold expression, I can find no other. But you knew before you came here that I am an obscure and complicated writer. . . .

Confronted by the dance, my philosopher—or a mind afflicted with a mania for interrogation, if you prefer—asks his usual questions. He brings in his *whys* and *hows*, the customary instruments of elucidation, which are the apparatus of his own art; and he tries, as you have just perceived, to replace the immediate and expedient expression of things by rather odd formulas which enable him to relate the graceful phenomenon of the dance to the whole of what he knows, or thinks he knows.

He attempts to fathom the mystery of a body which suddenly, as though by the effect of an internal shock, enters into a kind of life that is at once strangely unstable and strangely regulated, strangely spontaneous, but at the same time strangely contrived and, assuredly, planned.

The body seems to have broken free from its usual states of balance. It seems to be trying to outwit—I should say outrace— its own weight, at every moment evading its pull, not to say its sanction.

In general, it assumes a fairly simple periodicity that seems to maintain itself automatically; it seems endowed with a superior elasticity which retrieves the impulse of every movement and at once renews it. One is reminded of a top, standing on its point and reacting so sensitively to the slightest shock.

But here is an important observation that comes to the mind of our philosopher, who might do better to enjoy himself to the full and abandon himself to what he sees. He observes that the dancing body seems unaware of its surroundings. It seems to be concerned only with itself and one other object, a very important one, from which it breaks free, to which it returns, but only to gather the wherewithal for another flight. . . .

That object is the earth, the ground, the solid place, the plane on which everyday life plods along, the plane of walking, the prose of human movement.

Yes, the dancing body seems unaware of everything else, it seems to know nothing of its surroundings. It seems to hearken to itself and only to itself, to see nothing, as though its eyes were jewels, unknown jewels like those of which Baudelaire speaks, lights that serve no useful purpose.

For the dancer is in another world; no longer the world that takes color from our gaze, but one that she weaves with her steps and builds with her gestures. And in that world acts have no outward aim; there is no object to grasp, to attain, to repulse or run away from, no object which puts a precise end to an action and gives movements first an outward direction and co-ordination, then a clear and definite conclusion.

But that is not all: in this world nothing is unforeseen; though the dancer sometimes seems to be reacting to an unforeseen incident, that too is part of a very evident plan. Everything happens as if. . . . But nothing more.

Thus there is no aim, no real incidents, no outside world. . . .

The philosopher exults. No outside world! For the dancer there is no outside. . . . Nothing exists beyond the system she sets up by her acts—one is reminded of the diametrically contrary and no less closed system constituted by our sleep, whose exactly opposite law is the abolition of all acts, total abstention from action. He sees the dance as an artifical somnambulism, a group of sensations which make themselves a dwelling place where certain muscular themes follow one another in an order which creates a special kind of time that is absolutely its own. And with an increasingly *intellectual* delight he contemplates this being who, from her very depths, brings forth these beautiful transformations of her form in space; who now moves, but without really going anywhere; now metamorphoses herself on the spot, displaying herself in every aspect; who sometimes skillfully modulates successive appearances as though in controlled phases; sometimes changes herself brusquely into a whirlwind, spinning faster and faster, then suddenly stops, crystallized into a statue, adorned with an alien smile.

But this detachment from the environment, this absence of aim, this negation of explicable movement, these full turns (which no circumstance of ordinary life demands of our body), even this impersonal smile—all these features are radically opposed to those that characterize our action in the practical world and our relations with it.

In the practical world our being is nothing more than an intermediary between the sensation of a need and the impulse to satisfy the need. In this role, it proceeds always by the most economical, if not always the shortest, path: it wants results. Its guiding principles seem to be the straight line, the least action, and the shortest time. A practical man is a man who has an instinct for such economy of time and effort, and has little difficulty in putting it into effect, because his aim is definite and clearly localized: *an external object.*

As we have said, the dance is the exact opposite. It moves in a self-contained realm of its own and implies no reason, no tendency toward completion. A formula for pure dance should include nothing to suggest that it has an end. It is terminated by outside events; its limits in time are not intrinsic to it; the duration of the dance is limited by the conventional length of the program, by fatigue or loss of interest. But the dance itself has nothing to make it end. It ceases as a dream ceases that might go on indefinitely: it stops, not because an undertaking has been completed, for there is no undertaking, but because something else, something outside it has been exhausted.

And so—permit me to put it rather boldly—might one not—and I have already intimated as much—consider the dance as a kind of *inner life*, allowing that psychological term a new meaning in which physiology is dominant?

An inner life, indeed, but one consisting entirely in sensations of time and energy which respond to one another and form a kind of closed circle of resonance. This resonance, like any other, is communicated: a part of our pleasure as spectators consists in feeling ourselves possessed by the rhythms so that we ourselves are virtually dancing.

Carried a little further, this sort of philosophy of the dance can lead to some rather curious consequences or applications. If, in speaking of this art, I have kept to considerations of a very general nature, it has been somewhat with the intention of guiding you to what we are now coming to. I have tried to communicate a rather abstract idea of the dance and to represent it above all as an action that *derives* from ordinary, useful action, but *breaks away* from it, and finally *opposes* it.

But this very general formulation (and that is why I have adopted it today) covers far more than the dance in the strict sense. All action which does not tend toward utility and which on the other hand can be trained, perfected, developed, may be subsumed under this simplified notion of the dance, and consequently, *all the arts can be considered as particular examples of this general idea*, since by definition all the arts imply an element of action, the *action which produces*, or else manifests, the *work*.

A poem, for example, is *action*, because a poem exists only at the moment of being spoken; then it is *in actu*. This act, like the dance, has no other purpose than to create a state of mind; it imposes its own laws; it, too, creates a time and a measurement of time which are appropriate and essential to it: we cannot distinguish it from its form of time. To recite poetry is to enter into a verbal dance.

Or consider a virtuoso at work, a violinist, a pianist. Just watch his hands. Stop your ears if you dare. But concentrate on the hands. Watch them act, racing over the narrow stage that is keyboard. Are they not dancers who have also been subjected for years to a severe discipline, to endless exercises?

Remember that you can hear nothing. You merely see the hands come and go, stop for a moment, cross, play leapfrog; sometimes one waits, while the five fingers of the other seem to be trying out their paces at the other end of the racecourse of ivory and ebony. You begin to surmise that all this follows certain laws, that the whole ballet is regulated, determined. . . .

Let us note in passing that if you hear nothing and are unfamiliar with the music being played, you have no way of knowing what point in his piece the performer has come to. *What you see* gives you *no indication* of the pianist's progress; yet you are quite certain that the action in which he is engaged is at every moment subject to some rather complex system. . . .

With a little more attention you would discover that this system puts certain restrictions on the freedom of movement of these active hands as they fly over the keyboard. Whatever they do, they seem to have undertaken to respect some sort of continuous order. Cadence, measure, rhythm make themselves felt. I do not wish to enter into these questions which, it seems to me, though familiar and without difficulty in practice, have hitherto lacked any satisfactory theory; but then that is true of all questions in which time is directly involved. We are brought back to the remarks of St. Augustine.

But it is easy to note that all automatic movements corresponding to a state of being, and not to a prefigured localized aim, take on a periodic character; this is true of the walker; of the absent-minded fellow who swings his foot or drums on a windowpane; of the thinker who strokes his chin, etc.

If you will bear with me for a few minutes more, we shall carry our thought a little further: a little further beyond the customary, immediate idea of the dance.

I was just saying that all the arts are extremely varied forms of action and may be analyzed in terms of action. Consider an artist at work, eliminate the brief intervals when he sets it aside; watch him act, stop still, and briskly start in again.

Assume that he is so well trained, so sure of his technique that while you are observing him he is a pure executant whose successive operations tend to take place in commensurable lapses of time, that is to say, with a certain *rhythm*. Then you will be able to conceive that the execution of a work of art, of a work of painting or sculpture, is itself a work of art and that its material object, the product of the artist's fingers, is only a pretext, a stage "prop" or, as it were, the subject of the ballet.

Perhaps this view seems bold to you. But remember that for many great artists a work is never finished; perhaps what they regard as a desire for perfection is simply a form of the inner life I have been speaking of, which consists entirely of energy and sensibility in a reciprocal and, one might say, reversible exchange.

Or think, on the other hand, of those edifices that the ancients built, to the rhythm of the flute commanding the movements of the files of laborers and masons.

I might have told you the curious story related in the *Journal* of the Goncourt brothers, about the Japanese painter who, on a visit to Paris, was asked by them to execute a few works in the presence of a little gathering of art lovers.

But it is high time to conclude this dance of ideas round the living dance.

I wanted to show you how this art, far from being a futile amusement, far from being a specialty confined to putting on a show now and then for the amusement of the eyes that contemplate it or the bodies that take part in it, is quite simply *a poetry that encompasses the action of living creatures in its entirety:* it isolates and develops, distinguishes and deploys the essential character-istics of this action, and makes the dancer's body into an object whose transformations and successive aspects, whose striving to attain the limits that each instant sets upon the powers of being, inevitably remind us of the task the poet imposes on his mind, the difficulties he sets before it, the metamorphoses he obtains from it, the flights he expects of it—flights which remove him, sometimes too far, from the ground, from reason, from the aver-age notion of logic and common sense.

What is a metaphor if not a kind of pirouette performed by an idea, enabling us to assemble its diverse names or images? And what are all the figures we employ, all those instruments, such as rhyme, inversion, antithesis, if not an exercise of all the pos-sibilities of language, which removes us from the practical world and shapes, for us too, a private universe, a privileged abode of the intellectual dance?

And now let me give you over, weary of words but all the more eager for sensuous enchantment and effortless pleasure, to art itself, to the flame, to the ardent and subtle action of Mme Argentina.

You know what prodigies of comprehension and invention this great artist has achieved, what she has done for Spanish dancing. As for me, who have spoken to you only of the dance in the abstract—and too abundantly at that—I cannot tell you how much I admire the labor of intelligence with which Argen-tina, in a noble and deeply studied style, has revived a type of folk dance that has been so much cheapened lately, especially outside of Spain.

I think she has achieved her aim, a magnificent aim, since it meant saving an art form and regenerating its nobility and legit-imate power, by an infinitely subtle analysis both of the resources of this type of art, and of her own resources. That is something very close to me, that concerns me passionately. I am a man who has never seen a contradiction—indeed, I cannot conceive of one—between intelligence and sensibility, conscious reflection and its raw material, and I salute Argentina, as a man who is precisely as pleased with her as he would like to be with himself.

(1936)

NELSON GOODMAN
From LANGUAGES OF ART*

MODES OF SYMBOLIZATION

1. Though this book deals with some problems pertaining to the arts, its scope does not coincide very closely with what is ordinarily taken to be the field of aesthetics. On the one hand, I touch only incidentally on questions of value, and offer no canons of criticism. No mandatory judgments are implied concerning any work I cite as an example, and the reader is invited to substitute his own illustrations. On the other hand, my study ranges beyond the arts into matters pertaining to the sciences, technology, perception, and practice. Problems concerning the arts are points of departure rather than of convergence. The objective is an approach to a general theory of symbols.

"Symbol" is used here as a very general and colorless term. It covers letters, words, texts, pictures, diagrams, maps, models, and more, but carries no implication of the oblique or the occult. The most literal portrait and the most prosaic passage are as much symbols, and as 'highly symbolic', as the most fanciful and figurative.

Systematic inquiry into the varieties and functions of symbols has seldom been undertaken. Expanding investigation in structural linguistics in recent years needs to be supplemented by and integrated with intensive examination of nonverbal symbol systems, from pictorial representation on the one hand to musical notation on the other, if we are to achieve any comprehensive grasp of the modes and means of reference and of their varied and pervasive use in the operations of the understanding. "Languages" in my title should, strictly, be replaced by "symbol systems". But the title, since always read before the book, has been kept in the vernacular. The nonreader will not mind, and the reader will understand.

---

*Selections from *Languages of Art* included in this anthology have been adapted by Professor Goodman, who has also added supplementary footnotes and supplied an Afterword. The supplementary footnotes are marked with an asterisk. The note, section, and figure numbers often differ from those in the book.

2. Whether a picture ought to be a representation or not is a question much less crucial than might appear from current bitter battles among artists, critics, and propagandists. Nevertheless, the nature of representation wants early study in any philosophical examination of the ways symbols function in and out of the arts. That representation is frequent in some arts, such as painting, and infrequent in others, such as music, threatens trouble for a unified aesthetics; and confusion over how pictorial representation as a mode of signification is allied to and distinguished from verbal description on the one hand and, say, facial expression on the other is fatal to any general theory of symbols.

The most naive view of representation might perhaps be put somewhat like this: "A represents B if and only if A appreciably resembles B", or "A represents B to the extent that A resembles B". Vestiges of this view, with assorted refinements, persist in most writing on representation. Yet more error could hardly be compressed into so short a formula.

Some of the faults are obvious enough. An object resembles itself to the maximum degree but rarely represents itself; resemblance, unlike representation, is reflexive. Again, unlike representation, resemblance is symmetric: B is as much like A as A is like B, but while a painting may represent the Duke of Wellington, the Duke doesn't represent the painting. Furthermore, in many cases neither one of a pair of very like objects represents the other: none of the automobiles off an assembly line is a picture of any of the rest; and a man is not normally a representation of another man, even his twin brother. Plainly, resemblance in any degree is no sufficient condition for representation.[1]

Just what correction to make in the formula is not so obvious. We may attempt less, and prefix the condition "If A is a picture, ...". Of course, if we then construe "picture" as "representation", we resign a large part of the question: namely, what constitutes a representation. But even if we construe "picture" broadly enough to cover all paintings, the formula is wide of the mark in other ways. A Constable painting of Marlborough Castle is more like any other picture than it is like the Castle, yet it represents the Castle and not another picture—not even the closest copy. To add the requirement that B must not be a picture would be desperate and futile; for a picture may represent another, and indeed each of the once popular paintings of art galleries represents many others.

The plain fact is that a picture, to represent an object,[2] must be a symbol for it, stand for it, refer to it; and that no degree of resemblance is sufficient to establish the requisite relationship of reference. Nor is resemblance *necessary* for reference; almost anything may stand for almost anything else. A picture that represents—like a passage that describes—an object refers to and, more particularly, *denotes*[3] it. Denotation is the core of representation and is independent of resemblance.

If the relation between a picture and what it represents is thus assimilated to the relation between a predicate and what it applies to, we must examine the characteristics of representation as a special kind of denotation. What does pictorial denotation have in common with, and how does it differ from, verbal or diagrammatic denotation? One not implausible answer is that resemblance, while no sufficient condition for representation, is just the feature that distinguishes representation from denotation of other kinds. Is it perhaps the case that if *A* denotes *B*, then *A* represents *B* just to the extent that *A* resembles *B*? I think even this watered-down and innocuous-looking version of our initial formula betrays a grave misconception of the nature of representation.

3. "To make a faithful picture, come as close as possible to copying the object just as it is." This simple-minded injunction baffles me; for the object before me is a man, a swarm of atoms, a complex of cells, a fiddler, a friend, a fool, and much more. If none of these constitute the object as it is, what else might? If all are ways the object is, then none is *the* way the object is.[4] I cannot copy all these at once; and the more nearly I succeeded, the less would the result be a realistic picture.

What I am to copy then, it seems, is one such aspect, one of the ways the object is or looks. But not, of course, any one of these at random—not, for example, the Duke of Wellington as he looks to a drunk through a raindrop. Rather, we may suppose, the way the object looks to the normal eye, at proper range, from a favorable angle, in good light, without instrumentation, unprejudiced by affections or animosities or interests, and unembellished by thought or interpretation. In short, the object is to be copied as seen under aseptic conditions by the free and innocent eye.

The catch here, as Ernst Gombrich insists, is that there is no innocent eye.[5] The eye comes always ancient to its work, obsessed by its own past and by old and new insinuations of the ear, nose, tongue, fingers, heart, and brain. It functions not as an instrument self-powered and alone, but as a dutiful member of a complex and capricious organism. Not only how but what it sees is regulated by need and prejudice.[6] It selects, rejects, organizes, discriminates, associates, classifies, constructs. It does not much mirror as take and make; and what it takes and makes it sees not bare, as items without attributes, but as things, as food, as people, as enemies, as stars, as weapons. Nothing is seen nakedly or naked.

The myths of the innocent eye and of the absolute given are unholy accomplices. Both derive from and foster the idea of knowing as a processing of raw material received from the senses, and of this raw material as being discoverable either through purification rites or by methodical disinterpretation. But reception and interpretation are not separable operations; they are thoroughly interdependent. The Kantian dictum echoes here: the innocent eye is blind and the virgin mind empty. Moreover, what has been received and what has been done to it cannot be distinguished within the finished product. Content cannot be extracted by peeling off layers of comment.[7]

All the same, an artist may often do well to strive for innocence of eye. The effort sometimes rescues him from the tired patterns of everyday seeing, and results in fresh insight. The opposite effort, to give fullest rein to a personal reading, can be equally tonic—and for the same reason. But the most neutral eye and the most biased are merely sophisticated in different ways. The most ascetic vision and the most prodigal, like the sober portrait and the vitriolic caricature, differ not in how *much* but only in *how* they interpret.

The copy theory of representation, then, is stopped at the start by inability to specify what is to be copied. Not an object the way it is, not all the ways it is, nor the way it looks to the mindless eye. Moreover, something is wrong with the very notion of copying any of the ways an object is, any aspect of it. For an aspect is not just the object-from-a-given-distance-and-angle-and-in-a-given-light; it is the object as we look upon or conceive it, a version or construal of the object. In representing an object, we do not copy such a construal or interpretation—we *achieve* it.[8]

In other words, nothing is ever represented either shorn of or in the fullness of its properties. A picture never merely represents *x*, but rather represents *x* as a man or represents *x* to be a mountain, or represents *the fact that x is* a melon. What could be meant by copying a fact would be hard to grasp even if there were any such things as facts; to ask me to copy *x* as a soandso is a little like asking me to sell something as a gift; and to speak of copying something to be a man is sheer nonsense. We shall presently have to look further into all this; but we hardly need look further to see how little is representation a matter of imitation.

The case for the relativity of vision and of representation has been so conclusively stated elsewhere that I am relieved of the need to argue it at any length here. Gombrich, in particular, has amassed overwhelming evidence to show how the way we see and depict depends upon and varies with experience, practice, interests, and attitudes.

4. Brothers and sisters are alike siblings and the difference between being a brother and being a sister depends solely upon whether the sibling is male or female. Is it similarly the case that what is represented and what is expressed are alike denoted, and that the difference depends solely upon whether what is denoted is a particular or a property? Or is there some more radical difference between the two relations?

Offhand, expression may appear to be less literal than representation. Most often the feeling or emotion or property expressed is remote from the medium of expression: a painting may express heat, a musical composition may express color or fragility. Surely any sort of copying is out of the question here. Expression is by intimation rather than by imitation. But we have seen that representation is not imitation either, that no degree of similarity is required between even the most literal picture and what it represents.

Perhaps, then, a difference is to be sought in the opposite direction: perhaps expression is more direct and immediate than representation. Consonant with this is the idea that an expression is causally linked with what is expressed. The expression on a face, for example, may be the effect of the fear or anger or sorrow a person feels, the facial configurations at once arising from and showing forth that emotion; or James-Lange-like, the emotion may arise from perception of the bodily expression. In neither version will this stand up very long. A pleased expression may be due to politeness and endured with discomfort; and fear may give rise to an expression of abject approval that drains rather than bolsters confidence. An actor's facial expression need neither result from nor result in his feeling the corresponding emotions. A painter or composer does not have to have the emotions he expresses in his work. And obviously works of art themselves do not feel what they express, even when what they express is a feeling.

Some of these cases suggest that what is expressed is, rather, the feeling or emotion excited in the viewer: that a picture expresses sadness by making the gallery-goer a bit sad, and a tragedy expresses grief by reducing the spectator to virtual or actual tears. The actor or dancer need not feel sad, but succeeds in expressing sadness just to the extent that he makes me feel sad. If this view is any more plausible than the first one considered, it is hardly more defensible. For one thing, whatever emotion may be excited is seldom the one expressed. A face expressing agony inspires pity rather than pain; a body expressing hatred and anger tends to arouse aversion or fear. Again, what is expressed may be something other than a feeling or emotion. A black and white picture expressing color does not make me feel colorful; and a portrait expressing courage and cleverness hardly produces such qualities in the viewer.

These confused notions of expression are entangled with the popular conviction that excitation of the emotions is a primary function of art. Let me enter here a parenthetical protest against this idea, and against aesthetic theories—such as that of emotional catharsis—dependent upon it. But I shall come back to this later in Section 8.

If expression does not differ from representation in being less a matter of imitation or in being more a matter of causation, is expression nevertheless a more nearly absolute and invariable relation? We saw that representation is relative—that any picture may represent any object. In contrast, it seems that a smiling face can hardly express grief, a drooping figure elation, a slate-blue picture express heat, or a staccato and presto passage calm. If the connection is not causal, at least it seems constant. But this distinction evaporates too. When the first fine Japanese films reached us, Western audiences had some difficulty in determining what emotions the actors were expressing. Whether a face was expressing agony or hatred or anxiety or determination or despair or desire was not always instantly evident; for even facial expressions are to some extent molded by custom and culture. What the insular and amateur spectator may take to be instinctive and invariable, the professional actor or director knows to be acquired and variable. If we prejudicially regard the gestures of a foreign dance as highly artificial, and those of our native dances as more innate, the perceptive performer or teacher harbors no such delusions; an eminent choreographer and director writes:

Along the way I have often been obliged to teach young men how to make love, and young girls how to be predatory or flirtatious or seductive, and I've had to advise everybody how to express anxiety, alarm and endless other emotional states. They may have felt these things, but the movements for them are complete strangers.
    ... gestures are patterns of movement established by long usage among men.... There are many feelings which can be expressed in so many ways that there is really no one pattern for them. For example, hope has no shape, nor do inspiration, fear, or love.[9]

And the anthropologist concurs:

Insofar as I have been able to determine, just as there are no universal words, sound complexes, which carry the same meaning the world over, there are no body motions, facial expressions or gestures which provoke identical responses the world over. A body can be bowed in grief, in humility, in laughter, or in readiness for aggression. A "smile" in one society portrays friendliness, in another embarrassment and, in still another, may contain a warning that, unless tension is reduced, hostility and attack will follow.[10]

With representation and expression alike, certain relationships become firmly fixed for certain people by habit; but in neither case are these relationships absolute, universal, or immutable.

5. A gesture, too, may denote or exemplify or both. Nods of agreement or dissent, salutes, bows, pointings, serve as labels. A negative nod, for instance, applies to without normally being among things disapproved. An orchestra conductor's gestures denote sounds. They may indeed have and even exemplify some properties—say of speed or cadence—of the music, but the gestures are not among their own denotata. The same is true of such activities in response to music as foot- and finger-tappings, head-bobbings, and various other minor motions. That these are called forth by the music, while the conductor's gestures call it forth, does not affect their status as labels; for labels may be used to record or to prescribe—"strawberry", "raspberry", "lemon", and "lime" may tell us what *is* in or what *to put* in the several containers.
    Why, though, do these negligible activities become so significant when related to music? Their significance is simply that of labels applied in analyzing, organizing, and registering what we hear. *Contra* theories of empathy,[11] these labels need not themselves have any particular properties in common with the music. Psychologists and linguists have stressed the ubiquitous partici-

pation of action in perception in general, the early and extensive use of gestural, sensorimotor, or enactive symbols, and the role of such symbols in cognitive development.[12] For Jaques-Dalcroze, the use of these activities for grasping music is a fundamental factor in musical education.[13]

The dance director unlike the orchestra conductor, gives samples. His demonstrations exemplify the requisite properties of the actions to be performed by his class, whereas his oral instructions prescribe rather than show what is to be done. The proper response to his knee-bend is a knee-bend; the proper response to his shout "lower" (even if in a high voice) is not to shout "lower" but to bend deeper. Nevertheless, since the demonstrations are part of the instruction, are accompanied by and may be replaced by verbal directions, and have no already established denotation, they may—like any sample not otherwise committed as to denotation—also be taken as denoting what the predicates they exemplify denote, and are then labels exemplifying themselves.

The action of a mime, on the other hand, is not usually among the actions it denotes. He does not climb ladders or wash windows but rather portrays, represents, denotes, ladder-climbings and window-washings by what he does. His miming may indeed exemplify activities involved in climbing or window-washing, as a picture may exemplify the color of a house it represents; but the picture is not a house, and the miming is not a climbing. The mime's walks, of course, may exemplify walking as well as denoting walks, just as "short" exemplifies shortness as well as denoting short words; but such self-denoting and self-exemplifying symbols are in the minority in pantomime as in English and in painting. The word "bird" or a picture of a bird, not being itself a bird, exemplifies no label denoting all and only birds; and a miming of a flight, not being a flight, exemplifies no label denoting all and only flights. A word or picture or pantomime does not often exemplify any label coextensive with it.*

Some elements of the dance are primarily denotative, versions of the descriptive gestures of daily life (e.g., bowings, beckonings) or of ritual (e.g., signs of benediction, Hindu hand-postures).[14] But other movements, especially in the modern dance, primarily exemplify rather than denote. What they exemplify, however, are not standard or familiar activities, but rather

---

*Labels are coextensive if and only if they apply to just the same things.

rhythms and dynamic shapes. The exemplified patterns and properties may reorganize experience, relating actions not usually associated or distinguishing others not usually differentiated, thus enriching allusion or sharpening discrimination. To regard these movements as illustrating verbal descriptions would of course be absurd; seldom can the just wording be found. Rather, the label a movement exemplifies may be itself; such a movement, having no antecedent denotation, takes on the duties of a label denoting certain actions including itself. Here, as often elsewhere in the arts, the vocabulary evolves along with what it is used to convey.

6. What is expressed is metaphorically exemplified. What expresses sadness is metaphorically sad. And what is metaphorically sad is actually but not literally sad, i.e., comes under a transferred application of some label coextensive with "sad".

Thus what is expressed is possessed, and what a face or picture expresses need not (but may) be emotions or ideas the actor or artist has, or those he wants to convey, or thoughts or feelings of the viewer or of a person depicted, or properties of anything else related in some other way to the symbol. Of course, a symbol is often said to express a property related to it in one of these ways, but I reserve the term "expression" to distinguish the central case where the property belongs to the symbol itself—regardless of cause or effect or intent or subject-matter. That the actor was despondent, the artist high, the spectator gloomy or nostalgic or euphoric, the subject inanimate, does not determine whether the face or picture is sad or not. The cheering face of the hypocrite expresses solicitude; and the stolid painter's picture of boulders may express agitation. The properties a symbol expresses are its own property.

But they are acquired property. They are not the homely features by which the objects and events that serve as symbols are classified literally, but are metaphorical imports. Pictures express sounds or feelings rather than colors. And the metaphorical transfer involved in expression is usually from or via an exterior realm rather than the interior transfer effected in hyperbole or litotes or irony. A pretentious picture does not express the modesty that may be sarcastically ascribed to it.

Properties expressed are, furthermore, not only metaphorically possessed but also referred to, exhibited, typified, shown forth. A square swatch does not usually exemplify squareness, and a picture that rapidly increases in market value does not express the property of being a gold mine. Normally, a swatch exemplifies only sartorial properties while a picture literally exemplifies only pictorial properties and metaphorically exemplifies only properties that are constant relative to pictorial properties.[15] And a picture expresses only properties—unlike that of being a gold mine—that it thus metaphorically exemplifies as a pictorial symbol. Daumier's *Laundress* so exemplifies and expresses weight but not any metaphorical property dependent upon the physical weight of the picture. In general, a symbol of a given kind—pictorial, musical, verbal, etc.—expresses only properties that it metaphorically exemplifies as a symbol of that kind.

7. Expression, since limited to what is possessed and moreover to what has been acquired at second-hand, is doubly constrained as compared with denotation. Whereas almost anything can denote or even represent almost anything else, a thing can express only what belongs but did not originally belong to it. The difference between expression and literal exemplification, like the difference between more and less literal representation, is a matter of habit—a matter of fact rather than fiat.

Yet the habits differ widely with time and place and person and culture; and pictorial and musical expression are no less relative and variable than facial and gestural expression. Aldous Huxley, upon hearing some supposedly solemn music in India, wrote:

> ... I confess that, listen as I might, I was unable to hear anything particularly mournful or serious, anything specially suggestive of self-sacrifice in the piece. To my Western ears it sounded much more cheerful than the dance which followed it.
>
> Emotions are everywhere the same; but the artistic expression of them varies from age to age and from one country to another. We are brought up to accept the conventions current in the society into which we are born. This sort of art, we learn in childhood, is meant to excite laughter, that to evoke tears. Such conventions vary with great rapidity, even in the same country. There are Elizabethan dances that sound as melancholy to our ears as little funeral marches. Conversely, we are made to laugh by the "Anglo-Saxon attitudes" of the holiest personages in the drawings and miniatures of earlier centuries.[16]

The boundaries of expression, dependent upon the difference between exemplification and possession and also upon the difference between the metaphorical and the literal, are inevitably

somewhat tenuous and transient. An Albers picture may pretty
clearly *exemplify* certain shapes and colors and interrelations
among them, while it merely possesses the property of being
exactly 24½ inches high; but the distinction is not always so easily drawn. Again, the status of a property as metaphorical or literal is often unclear and seldom stable; for comparatively few
properties are purely literal or permanently metaphorical. Even
for very clear cases, ordinary discourse only sporadically
observes the difference between expression and exemplification.
Architects, for instance, like to speak of some buildings as
expressing their functions. But however effectively a glue factory
may typify glue-making, it exemplifies being a glue factory literally rather than metaphorically. A building may express fluidity or frivolity or fervor,[17] but to express being a glue factory it
would have to be something else, say a toothpick plant. But since
reference to a possessed property is the common core of metaphorical and literal exemplification, and the distinction between
these is ephermeral, popular use of the term "expression" for
cases of both kinds is not very surprising or pernicious.

Music and dance alike may exemplify rhythmic patterns, for
example, and express peace or pomp or passion; and music may
express properties of movement while dance may express properties of sound. With respect to verbal symbols, ordinary usage
is so undiscriminating that a word or passage may be said to
express not only what the writer thought or felt or intended, or
the effect upon the reader, or properties possessed by or ascribed
to a subject, but even what is described or stated. In the special
sense I have been discussing, though, a verbal symbol may
express only properties it metaphorically exemplifies; naming a
property and expressing it are different matters; and a poem or
story need not express what it says or say what it expresses. A
tale of fast action may be slow, a biography of a benefactor bitter,
a description of colorful music drab, and a play about boredom
electric. To describe, as to depict, a person as sad or as expressing
sadness is not necessarily to express sadness; not every sad-per-
son-description or -picture or every person-expressing-sadness-
description or -picture is itself sad.And a passage or picture may
exemplify or express without describing or representing, and
even without being a description or representation at all—as in
the case of some passages from James Joyce and some drawings
by Kandinsky.

Yet though exemplification and expression are distinct from,
and run in the opposite direction from, representation and

description, all are intimately related modes of symbolization. In these varied ways, a symbol may select from and organize its universe and be itself in turn informed or transformed. Representation and description relate a symbol to things it applies to. Exemplification relates the symbol to a label that denotes it, and hence indirectly to the things (including the symbol itself) in the range of that label. Expression relates the symbol to a label that metaphorically denotes it, and hence indirectly not only to the given metaphorical but also to the literal range of that label. And various longer chains of the elementary referential relationships of labels to things and other labels, and of things to labels, may run from any symbol.

To exemplify or express is to display rather than depict or describe; but as representation may be stereotyped or searching, and exemplification trite or telling, so may expression be platitudinous or provocative. A property expressed, though it must be constant relative to certain literal properties, need not coincide in extension with any easy and familiar literal description. Finding a disjunction of conjunctions of ordinary literal properties of pictures that is even approximately equivalent to metaphorical sadness would give us a good deal of trouble. The expressive symbol, with its metaphorical reach, not only partakes of the greenness of neighboring pastures and the exotic atmospheres of farther shores, but often in consequence uncovers unnoticed affinities and antipathies among symbols of its own kind. From the nature of metaphor derives some of the characteristic capacity of expression for suggestive allusion, elusive suggestion, and intrepid transcendence of basic boundaries.

Emphasis on the denotative (representative or descriptive), the exemplificatory ('formal' or 'decorative'), and the expressive in the arts varies with art, artist, and work. Sometimes one aspect dominates to the virtual exclusion of the other two; compare Debussy's *La Mer*, Bach's *Goldberg Variations*, and Charles Ives's *Fourth Symphony*, for instance; or a Dürer watercolor, a Jackson Pollock painting, and a Soulages lithograph. In other cases two or all three aspects, fused or in counterpoint, are almost equally prominent; in the film *Last Year at Marienbad*, the narrative thread, though never abandoned, is disrupted to let through insistent cadences and virtually indescribable sensory and emotional qualities. The choice is up to the artist, and judgment up to the critic. Nothing in the present analysis of symbolic functions offers any support for manifestos to the effect that representation is an indispensable requirement for art, or is an insuperable barrier to it, or that expression without representation is the highest achievement of the human spirit, or that representation and expression alike corrupt exemplification, or so on. If representation is reprehensible or revered, if expression is exalted or execrated, if exemplification is the essence of poverty or purity, this must be on other grounds.

8. A persistent tradition pictures the aesthetic attitude as passive contemplation of the immediately given, direct apprehension of what is presented, uncontaminated by any conceptualization, isolated from all the echoes of the past and all the threats and promises of the future, exempt from all enterprise. By purification rites of disengagement and disinterpretation we are to seek a pristine, unsullied vision of the world. I need hardly recount the philosophic faults and aesthetic absurdities of such a view until someone seriously goes so far as to maintain that the appropriate aesthetic attitude toward a poem amounts to gazing at the printed page without reading it.

I have held, on the contrary, that we have to read the painting as well as the poem, and that aesthetic experience is dynamic rather than static. It involves making delicate discriminations and discerning subtle relationships, identifying symbol systems and characters within these systems and what these characters denote and exemplify, interpreting works and reorganizing the world in terms of works and works in terms of the world. Much of our experience and many of our skills are brought to bear and may be transformed by the encounter. The aesthetic 'attitude' is restless, searching, testing—is less attitude than action: creation and re-creation.

What, though, distinguishes such aesthetic activity from other intelligent behavior such as perception, ordinary conduct, and scientific inquiry? One instant answer is that the aesthetic is directed to no practical end, is unconcerned with self-defense or conquest, with acquisition of necessities or luxuries, with prediction and control of nature. But if the aesthetic attitude disowns practical aims, still aimlessness is hardly enough. The aesthetic attitude is inquisitive as contrasted with the acquisitive and self-preservative, but not all nonpractical inquiry is aesthetic. To think of science as motivated ultimately by practical goals, as judged or justified by bridges and bombs and the control of nature, is to confuse science with technology. Science seeks knowledge without regard to practical consequences, and is concerned with prediction not as a guide for behavior but as a test of truth. Disinterested inquiry embraces both scientific and aesthetic experience.

Attempts are often made to distinguish the aesthetic in terms of immediate pleasure; but troubles arise and multiply here. Obviously, sheer quantity or intensity of pleasure cannot be the criterion. That a picture or poem provides more pleasure than does a proof is by no means clear; and some human activities unrelated to any of these provide enough more pleasure to render insignificant any differences in amount or degree among various types of inquiry. The claim that aesthetic pleasure is of a different and superior *quality* is by now too transparent a dodge to be taken seriously.

The inevitable next suggestion—that aesthetic experience is distinguished not by pleasure at all but by a special aesthetic emotion—can be dropped on the waste-pile of 'dormitive virtue' explanations.

This clears the way for the sophisticated theory that what counts is not pleasure yielded but pleasure 'objectified', pleasure read into the object as a property thereof. Apart from images of some grotesque process of transfusion, what can this mean? To consider the pleasure as possessed rather than occasioned by the object—to say in effect that the object is pleased—may amount to saying that the object expresses the pleasure. But since some aesthetic objects are sad—express sadness rather than pleasure— this comes nowhere near distinguishing in general between aesthetic and nonaesthetic objects or experience.

Some of these difficulties are diminished and others obscured if we speak of satisfaction rather than pleasure. "Satisfaction" is colorless enough to pass in contexts where "pleasure" is ludicrous, hazy enough to blur counterinstances, and flexible enough to tolerate convenient vacillation in interpretation. Thus we may hope to lessen the temptation to conjure up a special quality or kind of feeling or to indulge in mumbo-jumbo about objectification. Nevertheless, satisfaction pretty plainly fails to distinguish aesthetic from nonaesthetic objects and experiences. Not only does some scientific inquiry yield much satisfaction, but some aesthetic objects and experiences yield none. Music and our listening, pictures and our looking, do not fluctuate between aesthetic and nonaesthetic as the playing or painting varies from exalted to excruciating. Being aesthetic does not exclude being unsatisfactory or being aesthetically bad.

The distinguishing feature, some say, is not satisfaction secured but satisfaction sought: in science, satisfaction is a mere by-product of inquiry; in art, inquiry is a mere means for obtaining satisfaction. The difference is held to be neither in process performed nor in satisfaction enjoyed but in attitude maintained. On this view the scientific *aim* is knowledge, the aesthetic *aim* satisfaction.

But how cleanly can these aims be separated? Does the scholar seek knowledge or the satisfaction of knowing? Obtaining knowledge and satisfying curiosity are so much the same that trying to do either without trying to do the other surely demands a precarious poise. And anyone who does manage to seek the satisfaction without seeking the knowledge will pretty surely get neither, while on the other hand abstention from all anticipation of satisfaction is unlikely to stimulate research. One may indeed be so absorbed in working on a problem as never to think of the satisfaction to be had from solving it; or one may dwell so fondly on the delights of finding a solution as to take no steps toward arriving at one. But if the latter attitude is aesthetic, aesthetic understanding of anything is foredoomed. And I cannot see that these tenuous, ephemeral, and idiosyncratic states of mind mark any significant difference between the aesthetic and the scientific.

None of this is directed toward obliterating the distinction between art and science. Declarations of indissoluble unity— whether of the sciences, the arts, the arts and sciences together, or of mankind—tend anyway to focus attention upon the differences. What I am stressing is that the affinities here are deeper, and the significant differentia other, than is often supposed. The difference between art and science is not that between feeling and fact, intuition and inference, delight and deliberation, synthesis and analysis, sensation and cerebration, concreteness and abstraction, passion and action, mediacy and immediacy, or truth and beauty, but rather a difference in domination of certain specific characteristics of symbols.

(1968)

AFTERWORD—AN ILLUSTRATION

One illustration in terms of a particular theatre piece involving dance may help relate these selections to each other and to the whole undertaking of *Languages of Art*. In the author's multimedia *Hockey Seen: A Nightmare in Three Periods and Sudden Death,* the second period is a fast, high-energy movement based on the swift actions and conflicts of the game.[18] The referee's struggle to keep things under control is a major theme in this period. He starts and stops the play, separates fighting players, banishes some to the penalty box, and signals to players and watchers the infractions committed and the consequent penalties. At one point, he performs a solo based on these signals.

In terms of the types of reference distinguished in *Languages of Art*, this period denotes—depicts, represents—incidents in a hockey game; not, of course, incidents in any particular game, but incidents common to hockey games. Representation, contrary to a prevalent opinion, may be either particular, as in a portrait, or general, as in the eagle-picture in a dictionary.

The work as a whole, however, hardly depicts either any particular hockey game or hockey games in general but is rather, like a centaur-picture, a fictive representation. We often say that such a representation depicts a game or an animal that never did and never will exist. Less inconsistently, we may say that the picture or the dance does not represent or denote at all but rather is *denoted* by such a predicate as "centaur-picture" or "hockey-representation".

Of greater import, the work *exemplifies*, as does a purely abstract dance, certain movements and patterns of movement, changes of pace and direction, configurations and rhythms. Many of these are derived from both the action of hockey and the vocabulary of dance, but the reference by the work to such properties is a matter of exemplification not representation.

Moreover, the second period *expresses* various aspects of competition, conflict, violence, frustration, and the struggle between aggression and authority. These properties are not literally exemplified: no fights, no defeat or victory, no punishment, no (intended) violence or injury occur on the stage. These are properties possessed metaphorically, and referred to, by the work, and thus expressed by it. The slow-motion third period, with all the players wearing goal-tender's masks, expresses taut and long-drawn defensive tensions and perhaps an effort to fend off an unknown fate by fearsome visages.

The three elementary species of reference: denotation, exemplification, and expression often interact. The representation of hockey affects the way the action is organized in our perception, and this influences the features that the work comes to exemplify and express. Much the same action, divorced from the reference to hockey, might be seen as exemplifying and expressing quite

Photograph by William J. Rynders

"Hockey Seen" (2nd Period). "The second period expresses various aspects of competition, conflict, violence, frustration, and the struggle between aggression and authority." (Goodman)

other properties. Furthermore, reference is often through chains such that each link is reference of one or another of the three elementary types. For example, the work represents hockey, which in itself exemplifies ferocity of competition. Thus the representation of hockey refers via hockey to such ferocity. This indirect reference is not itself denotation or exemplification or expression but a complex of the first two and is altogether different from the direct expression of the same ferocity—an expression that may be missing from an ineffectual work or a listless performance.

I am not attempting to instruct choreographers or performers or dance critics, but to provide a framework for a philosophical account of what they do, and to relate that to what goes on in the other arts, in the sciences, and in all our activities of making and remaking our worlds.[19]

(1981)

Notes

[1]What I am considering here is pictorial representation, or depiction, and the comparable representation that may occur in other arts. Natural objects may represent in the same way: witness the man in the moon and the sheep-dog in the clouds. Some writers use "representation" as the general term for all varieties of what I call symbolization or reference, and use "symbolic" for the verbal and other nonpictorial signs I call nonrepresentational. "Represent" and its derivatives have many other uses, and while I shall mention some of these later, others do not concern us here at all. Among the latter, for example, are the uses according to which an ambassador represents a nation and makes representations to a foreign government.

[2]I use "object" indifferently for anything a picture represents, whether an apple or a battle. A quirk of language makes a represented object a subject.

[3]Not until the next chapter will denotation be distinguished from other varieties of reference.

[4]In "The Way the World Is," *Review of Metaphysics*, vol. 14 (1960), pp. 48–56, I have argued that the world is as many ways as it can be truly described, seen, pictured, etc., and that there is no such thing as the way the world is. Ryle takes a somewhat similar position (*Dilemmas* [Cambridge, England, Cambridge University Press, 1954], pp. 75–77) in comparing the relation between a table as a perceived solid object and the table as a swarm of atoms with the relation between a college library according to the catalogue and according to the accountant. Some have proposed that the way the world is could be arrived at by conjoining all the several ways. This overlooks the fact that conjunction itself is peculiar to certain systems; for example, we cannot conjoin a paragraph and a picture. And any attempted combination of all the ways would be itself only one—and a peculiarly indigestible one—of the ways the world is. But what is *the world* that is in so many ways? To speak of ways the world is, or ways of describing or picturing the world, is to speak of world-descriptions or world-pictures, and does not imply there is a unique thing—or indeed anything—that is described or pictured. Of course, none of this implies, either, that nothing is described or pictured. See further my *Ways of Worldmaking* (Hackett, Indianapolis, 1978).

[5]In *Art and Illusion* (New York, Pantheon Books, 1960), pp. 297–298 and elsewhere. On the general matter of the relativity of vision, see also such works as R. L. Gregory, *Eye and Brain* (New York, McGraw-Hill Book Co., 1966), and Marshall H. Segall, Donald Campbell, and Melville J. Herskovits, *The Influence of Culture on Visual Perception* (Indianapolis and New York, The Bobbs-Merrill Co., Inc., 1966).

[6]For samples of psychological investigation of this point, see Jerome S. Bruner's "On Perceptual Readiness," *Psychological Review*, vol. 64 (1957), pp. 123–152, and other articles there cited; also William P. Brown,

"Conceptions of Perceptual Defense," *British Journal of Psychology Monograph Supplement XXXV* (Cambridge, England, Cambridge University Press, 1961).

[7]On the emptiness of the notion of epistemological primacy and the futility of the search for the absolute given, see my *Structure of Appearance* (2nd edition; Indianapolis and New York, The Bobbs-Merrill Co., Inc., 1966—hereinafter referred to as *SA*), pp. 132–145, and "Sense and Certainty," *Philosophical Review*, vol. 61 (1952), pp. 160–167.

[8]And this is no less true when the instrument we use is a camera rather than a pen or brush. The choice and handling of the instrument participate in the construal. A photographer's work, like a painter's, can evince a personal style.

[9]Doris Humphrey, *The Art of Making Dances* (New York, Rinehart & Co., Inc., 1959), pp. 114, 118.

[10]From a talk by Ray L. Birdwhistell, "The Artist, the Scientist and a Smile," given at the Maryland Institute of Art, December 4, 1964.

[11]See, for example, Theodor Lipps, *Raumaesthetik und Geometrisch-Optische Täuschungen* (Leipzig, J. A. Barth, 1897), translated by H. S. Langfeld in *The Aesthetic Attitude* (New York, Harcourt, Brace & Co., Inc., 1920), pp. 6–7: "The column seems to brace itself and raise itself, that is to say, to proceed in the way in which I do when I pull myself together and raise myself, or remain thus tense and erect, in opposition to the natural inertness of my body. It is impossible for me to be aware of the column without this activity seeming to exist directly in the column of which I am aware."

[12]See, for example, Burton L. White and Richard Held, "Plasticity of Sensorimotor Development in the Human Infant," in *The Causes of Behavior*, ed. J. F. Rosenblith and W. Allinsmith (2nd ed., Boston, Allyn and Bacon, Inc., 1966), pp. 60–70, and the earlier articles there cited; Ray L. Birdwhistell, "Communication without Words," prepared in 1964 for publication in "L'Aventure Humaine," and the articles there cited; Jean Piaget, *The Origins of Intelligence in Children* (New York, International University Press, Inc., 1952), e.g., pp. 185ff, 385; and Jerome S. Bruner, *Studies in Cognitive Growth* (New York, John Wiley & Sons, Inc., 1966), pp. 12–21. I cannot accept Bruner's trichotomy of symbols into the enactive, the iconic, and the symbolic, since the latter two categories seem to me ill-defined and ill-motivated. A classification of symbols as enactive, visual, auditory, etc., may be useful for some purposes of developmental psychology; but for our purposes here these distinctions cut across what seem to me more consequential differences among modes of reference.

[13]He understands very clearly and takes full advantage of the uses of muscular movements as elements of teachable symbol systems implementing the comprehension and retention of music. See especially *The Eurhythmics of Jaques-Dalcroze* (Boston, Small, Maynard, & Co., 1918), articles by P. B. Ingham (pp. 43–53) and E. Ingham (pp. 54–60).

[14]The dancer's act of benediction, like its replicas on the stage and in the church, denotes what is blessed. That the addressee of the dancer's

gesture is not thereby among the blessed means only that the dancer, like the novelist, is making fictive use of a denoting symbol. But of course a gesture may, like the word "centaur", be denotative in character even though it denotes nothing.

[15]A property is thus constant only if, although it may or may not remain constant where the pictorial properties vary, it never varies where the pictorial properties remain constant. In other words, if it occurs anywhere, it also occurs whenever the pictorial properties are the same. The constancy here in question obtains within a given symbol system between the metaphorical extension of the expressed property and the literal extension of the basic pictorial properties; but a property thus constant also itself qualifies as a pictorial property.

[16]In "Music in India and Japan" (1926), reprinted in *On Art and Artists* (New York, Meridian Books, Inc., 1960), pp. 305–306.

[17]A building may "express a mood—gaiety and movement in the whirly little Comedy Theatre, Berlin—or even ideas about astronomy and relativity like Mendlesohn's Einstein tower, or nationalism like some of Hitler's architecture", according to Richard Sheppard in "Monument to the Architect?" *The Listener*, June 8, 1967, p. 746.

[18]First performed in August 1972 in Cambridge, Mass., and most recently in August 1980 in Knokke, Belgium, sponsored by the Belgian radio-television system in conjunction with the Ghent University conference *Art in Culture*. Drawings by Katharine Sturgis; author and producer, Nelson Goodman; choreographer, Martha Gray; composer, John C. Adams; television director, Jozef Cassiers; film director, Jacques Dubrulle; performers, Arthur Bridgman, Dante del Guidice, Tom Grunewald, Leslie Koval, Nusha Martynuk, Carter McAdams, Myrna Packer, Harry Streep III.

[19]See *Ways of Worldmaking* (Hackett, Indianapolis, 1978).

DAVID MICHAEL LEVIN
PHILOSOPHERS AND
THE DANCE

I have occasionally been asked for references to philosophic works that deal with the dance. When I reply that philosophers, especially the older and better-known philosophers of our tradition, have had very little to say about dancing, I am asked why this is so. I would like to address myself here to that very difficult question.

The question "Why?" possibly calls for an interpretation of the intrinsic nature of the philosophic discipline—an account which would make it understandable, if not forgivable, why so many philosophers, even those who have chosen to write on the arts or in the field of aesthetics, have ignored the art of dance. I would like to concentrate on this possibility. In so doing, however, I realize that, in a certain very precise sense, I am not answering the whole question.

A "causal" explanation of why philosophy in general has ignored the dance would necessarily involve me in issues which are of a broadly scientific nature: political issues, sociological issues, issues in cultural anthropology, and psychological issues. Although these matters are not within the compass of my professional competence, neither are they entirely beyond my understanding. Consequently, I would like, very briefly, to indulge in some speculations. I offer them for whatever they are worth.

To begin with, I think it is important to bear in mind the fact that our Western civilization is fundamentally patriarchal. That means, in effect, that it is necessarily organized around male dominance and a corresponding (well-hidden) aversion to the female principle (in Jungian terms, the *anima*). What does this mean? Well, of course, we might notice that most choreographers and dance critics (both of whom represent the hidden power of the "intellectual" side of dance) have been male, while the dancers themselves (representing the "physical" side), and also the majority of balletomanes (representing the intuitive and appreciative side), have been either females or males who are female-oriented. This is interesting and important, especially with regard to our "modern" times. But, rather than elaborating this point, which may in part explain the neglect of philosophers (most of whom have been male), I would like to delve a little deeper into the anthropological roots of dance. For there, in those ancient beginnings of dance, we will find, I think, a much deeper explanation for this state of affairs.

What I want to suggest is that the origin of dance lies in the female principle. Before it was cultivated as an art (dance for the sake of dance), dance took place in a ritually consecrated space. Dance was originally an ecstatic, mystic celebration, a form of worship intended to invite the manifestation or embodiment of primordial and supernatural powers. More specifically, dance was in its origin an essential part of the ancient fertility rites. As such, it related the participants to the generosity of Mother Earth and the spacious, open, benevolent, female side of Father Sky.

The dancers involved in these rites were not ordinary mortals; they were sacred vessels, inspired and possessed by the various deities, both wrathful and peaceful. Over the centuries, this sacred female principle in dance became increasingly repressed. Folk dancing, though still vaguely recalling the origins of dance, sublimated the principle in socially conventional (and more patriarchally acceptable) styles. Meanwhile, in the courts of Europe, dance was cultivated, first as a show of social grace (sublimated courtship and flirtation, and regulated communication between the sexes), and later as a pure spectacle of skill and style. Eventually (perhaps in the nineteenth century), dance developed into an art enjoyed entirely for its own sake. (Could it be that the possibility of enjoying it for its own sake depended on its being separated from its disturbing origins?) Dance, as a form of art, as a spectacle, was put on the stage. Thus it was returned to its own special space, but by this time the space was secular, not sacred. So we see that, in the end, the patriarchy won out. A somewhat compromised victory, of course, since dance not only has continued to enthrall, but has even flourished. However, it has continued, I think, more or less on patriarchal terms.

Well, so much for my speculations. Whether they are fantasy or truth, or perhaps a mixture of the two, they set the stage for a point which I regard as less controversial but no less thought-provoking: namely, that the religious and ethical foundations of our Western civilization are fundamentally hostile to the vital and intrinsic "demands" of the human body. This hostility takes many different forms; every dimension of our civilization expresses and reinforces it, often in disguised and not easily identifiable ways. Consider, for example, the primary symbol of the Christian religion—the cross. This powerful symbol presents as clearly as any symbol could the crucifixion of the human body. It is not enough that the body is visibly emaciated and starved (in accordance with the patriarchal ascetic ideal of self-mastery); no, it must also be visibly punished, finally destroyed. To be sure, the *doctrine* of Christianity asserts the resurrection of Christ's body. But two things need to be acknowledged: first, that there is no correspondingly visible symbol of the resurrection; and second, that the resurrected body exists not on Earth but only in Heaven. I take these points to mean that, in effect, we do not really believe in the resurrection of the human body. That is to say, we do not really believe in the *holiness* of the human body as it is here and now on Earth. Or, in more practical terms, we do not really accept the human body. And certainly, we do not allow ourselves fully to recognize the real possibility of "perfecting" it, or bringing it closer to the state of being in which its intrinsic holiness, its sublime beauty and grace, will manifestly shine through.

Perhaps you will want to argue that we do, in fact, entertain some ideal of perfection, and that, moreover, we do attempt to actualize this ideal. I would agree. But I also want to point out that this ideal is not at all what I am talking about. For, however it may appear, it is, in its deepest significance, an instrumental ideal, a patriarchal and dualistic ideal of mastery, power, and manipulation. As such, it involves a deep-seated suspicion of, and an aversion to, the spontaneous libidinal sensuousness of the human body. (This is the true sense, I believe, of Freud's "death instinct.") The instrumental perfecting of the body is entirely in the service of our Western technology. Far from working toward the liberation of the body, it is, in its essence, just another, more advanced (and therefore, too, a more carefully disguised) form of crucifixion. Why this patriarchal rejection of the sensuous body? What could be the connection between patriarchal aversion to the female principle (an aversion implicit in mastery and instrumentality) and our cultural rejection of the body? I suspect that the rejection arises because, somehow, the body in its sensuousness (thus, above all, in its play and dance) is identified with the female principle. More specifically, it is associated with the intolerable pain and frustration we experience over the loss of Mother, the primordial sensuous female body. The instrumental approach to the body, which emerges as our cultural ideal, would thus represent an apparently necessary cultural stage of reaction-formation.

The ideal I have in mind, which radically contrasts with our instrumental ideal, is perhaps most clearly presented in the symbol of the healthy bisexual Buddha-body, serenely seated on an opened lotus flower and radiating neutral (non-dualistic) warmth, compassion, inner vitality and resolve, and the wisdom of a matriarchal power which is beyond the dualist aggression definitive of patriarchal power. Unlike our Christianity, Buddhism recognizes the intrinsic liberating wisdom of the body— a wisdom which is supremely manifest in the beauty and grace of its spontaneous, fully opened, and harmoniously attuned presence.

Furthermore, Christianity inherited from Judaism a mind/body (spirit/flesh) dualism, which it decisively intensified and even enshrined in religious and ethical doctrine. Already, in the stern Judaic code of ethical law, there was a fundamental aversion both to direct, spontaneous libidinal *expression* and to its correlative—the direct, mature *reception* of experience. Postponement of gratification, which was a necessary defense during the early stages of libidinal existence, gradually developed into a habit and stayed a habit long after its necessity was left behind. It became, as Freud correctly saw, the internalized rule of the stern patriarchal superego. Judaism, or at least its dominant ecclesiastical side, installed the implicit dualism of moral conscience on the throne of power, turned shame into guilt, and aversion into gratification. Henceforth, the ethical life was to be a life of spiritual discipline; and the body, denied its own intrinsic spirituality, had to be subjugated by the masterful power of the ethical mind.

It is time that we turn to the substance of philosophy. I want to show why it is that philosophers could not have written satisfactorily about dance even if they had chosen to do so. Western philosophy down through the ages reflects this uncompromising dualism. In fact, our philosophy does more than reflect it; in the course of time, philosophers have systematically defended and exalted it, either by espousing some sort of explicit dualism (Descartes) or else by advocating some form of reductionism (the idealism of Berkeley, the materialism of Holbach, the behaviorism of Quine) in which the dualism is not transcended but merely suppressed.

Regardless of their school, philosophers have traditionally misunderstood the nature of the human body. (From what I have said above, it may be gathered that I do not regard this fact as accidental!) Broadly speaking, I think we may say that philosophers have, in one way or another, denied the reality of the body's sensuous presence. Thus the idealists and many of the rationalists hold that the sensuous body is reducible to, or generated by, or somehow absorbed in, the functioning of mind (mind in a certain peculiarly "pure" and non-sensuous state). And when we examine the theories of the materialists, the classical empiricists (David Hume, for example) and their descendants the behaviorists, we find the human body more or less reduced to the status of a mere thing obedient to purely physical laws. Nor does the body fare any better among rationalists like Descartes, whose dualism separated the wayward body so completely from the enlightened mind that he was able to assert, with perfect composure, that the body is nothing more than a complicated machine. In the rationalism of philosophers like

Spinoza, we may be pleased to learn that mind and body are substantially identical. But we are also told that the sensuousness of
the body is, in reality, a "confused idea."

If philosophers cannot even develop an adequate account of
the human body, how can they be expected to say anything true
and interesting about dance? Dance is the fine art and perfection
(or perfect presencing) of the moving human body. This means
that any philosophy of the dance must begin with a satisfactory
understanding of the nature of human movement. As a starting
point, we require a conception which distinguishes the movement of things from the purposive action, or spontaneously self-
generated movement, of the human body. But, until fairly
recently, philosophers have had a very distorted conception of
such movement.

Better late than never, the time now seems ripe for a new
approach to the problem. And indeed in keeping with the new
atmosphere of "liberated consciousness" and, in particular, our
heightened cultural awareness of the experienced body, the so-
called analytic philosophers in England and the United States
have begun to concentrate on problems which they usually
group under the appropriately scholastic heading, "theory of
action." However, we have yet to see the fruits of their endeav-
ors, and we shall have to wait a very long time before they get
around to looking at and talking sensitively about the dance.
Fortunately, there exists another, far more promising coterie of
philosophers—the phenomenologists. Starting with Edmund
Husserl, who fathered phenomenology in the early years of this
century, an extremely revolutionary and profoundly humanistic
philosophical movement got under way. Of those pioneers who
were able to understand what Husserl was doing and who were
able to learn from him, I would distinguish, above all, Martin
Heidegger, Jean-Paul Sartre, and Maurice Merleau-Ponty.
Thanks to these three giants, each one making his own very special contribution, the human body is finally beginning to receive
its due.

This is not the place to elaborate and defend my bold remarks.
Perhaps it will suffice if I say here first, that phenomenology is
unique in putting an understanding of the human body right in
the center of its field of vision; and second, that the phenomenological approach is so far the only approach which has truly
appreciated the sensuous human body just as it is actually lived,
and which has seriously attempted to articulate this appreciation
as faithfully, as rigorously, and as sensitively as it possibly could.

The phenomenology of dance ought to be viewed as absolutely fundamental to our philosophical understanding of the body. That it does not seem to have been viewed in this light is, however, painfully obvious. All I can say here, by way of explanation, is that phenomenology is still a young discipline whose latent resources of radicality it takes great insight—and no small measure of courage—to use providentially.

In no other civilization and in no prior age, has the human body been so technologized, reified, and endangered in so many uncontrollable ways. At the same time, the health and material comfort of the body have never before been so amazingly ensured. Here and there, the dialectic of these extremes is encouraging some very deep thinking and therapeutic experimentation. I see the dance as a treasury of the body's much-needed wisdom. It is a treasury we have only begun to cherish.

One other factor in the philosophers' neglect of dance should be noted here. And once again, our attempt to understand refers us to the larger and more pervasive conditions of our civilization. Philosophers writing in the field of aesthetics have traditionally ignored the subject of aesthetic perception in order to concentrate on the problem of judgment ("good taste") and the cognitive nature of aesthetic values. Such concentration can, of course, be justified. Nevertheless, it is too close to the predominant concerns of the masterful superego to be free of supervision and unconscious censorship. Since the art of dance is, ontologically speaking, the art of the human body; and since what is most interesting about the human body primarily concerns perception and its ontology, we can readily understand the neglect. But we should not tolerate persistent aesthetic blindness. From this standpoint, phenomenology appears to be especially attractive. Its adherence to the discipline of "neutralized" (non-dual?) description, together with its recognition of the fundamental ontological importance of perception, make it uniquely well-suited to provide dance with the appropriate ontologically grounded critical aesthetics.

The question of an appropriate aesthetics for dance prompts me to a brief delineation of the philosopher's calling, as I see it, in this regard. The critical task as I conceive it makes strenuous demands upon the sensibility, the intelligence, and the erudition of the philosopher. What else do we philosophers deserve to expect?

An adequate philosophical approach to the work of art should centrally involve three interdependent and reciprocally enriching levels of critical appreciation and interpretation. The first level is that of a phenomenological description of the perceptually visible. This sort of description is neither scientifically objective nor viciously subjective. But it is objective in the sense that it articulates what is experienced with maximum rigor and care. And it is also subjective inasmuch as it always insists on confining itself to the experiential standpoint of the subject. Among those who have written about dance, Edwin Denby seems to have achieved something very close, at times, to the ideal of phenomenological description. Here, for example, is his description of the Adagio in Balanchine's *Concerto Barocco:* "At the climax, . . . against a background of chorus that suggests the look of trees in the wind before a storm breaks, the ballerina, with limbs powerfully outspread, is lifted by her male partner, lifted repeatedly in narrowing arcs higher and higher. Then at the culminating phrase, from her greatest height, he lowers her. You watch her body slowly descend, her foot and leg pointing stiffly downward, till her toe reaches the floor and she rests her full weight at last on this single sharp point and pauses. It has the effect at that moment of a deliberate and powerful plunge into a wound, and the emotion of it answers strangely to the musical stress. . . ." (See "A Balanchine Masterpiece," in Denby's *Looking at the Dance.*)* In another piece, "Flight of the Dancer" (reprinted in the same volume), Denby gives us a stunning account of the leap in classical ballet. (Compare it to Kierkegaard's in *Fear and Trembling.* The similarities are unsettling.) I wish I could quote the Denby, but its length and intricacy resist the fragmentation that would result. It must be read to be believed, for in Denby we have a critic with discriminating sensibility and two mathematically precise eyes to match.

The second level engages us in historical interpretation; it is "criticism" in the fullest and truest sense. Every form, or medium, of art is simultaneously involved in two historical processes. First, there is the immanent dialectic of the history of the art form itself. Lincoln Kirstein's *Movement and Metaphor* and Richard Buckle's *Nijinsky* are superlative illustrations of studies in this field. Both of them consider particular dance works in the light of the history of the dance art in order to make explicit, through their interpretation, the implicit logic of this unique history in its bearing on the works under examination. Fundamental to this interpretation is the insight that each distinct art form

---

*In this anthology. Eds.

is defined by the historical unfolding of a unique configuration of technological, epistemological, and ontological problems. At each point in the endless history of the art, these problems will take the articulate form of certain specifically appropriate questions and difficulties—challenges, if you like. That is, at each point, these challenges will be faced, made explicit, and somehow resolved. But every resolution is only partial: not merely because art, like perception itself, can never approach these problems except in terms of a certain perspective, but also because every solution generates further problems, which are bequeathed, along with the more felicitous resolutions, to the next generation of artists. However, beyond the immanent dialectic there is the cultural context of art, which likewise has a history. This—which I will call the transcendent dialectic—is the historical ground within which the art form emerges and distinctly figures. The adequate (ideal) historical interpretation of an art form must take the historical ground into account. It should interpret this ground itself and articulate the dialectic of its relationship to the historical figure of the art in question. Good criticism thus consists in providing works of art with an interpretation that gives them a place in the living history of our world. Consequently, it is the responsibility of the critic to be at one and the same time profoundly conservative and irrepressibly radical. The critic keeps the work in the cherishing openness of memory; but in the very act of discovering its dialectical place—or really, in fact, articulately creating its place—he also irrevocably surrenders it, problematic and incomplete as it necessarily is, to the critical judgment of history still in the making.

The third level of interpretation makes manifest the ontology of the work of art in question. This level is metaphysical, in that (1) it concerns the very being of the work—that which most fundamentally underlies its presence, its phenomenological modes of givenness—and (2) it articulates the invisible. What I mean may perhaps be clarified analogically by reference to linguistics. According to Noam Chomsky, the object of linguistics is to construct an adequate theory which will explain the multitude of natural languages in terms of a deep (transcendental) structure of grammar, from which the natural languages may be shown to be derived according to a finite set of transformation rules. Now, this deep transcendental structure is certainly manifest in the phenomenon of our natural languages; on the other hand, it is not immediately accessible: it is, in other words, invisible. Thus we must ultimately recognize a difference between the visibility of the phenomenon and the invisibility of the noumenon. This is the ontological difference, I want to suggest, in which the work of art is eternally kept and treasured.

Hegel's *Lectures in the Philosophy of the Fine Arts,* Nietzsche's *The Birth of Tragedy,* Heidegger's essay, "The Origin of the Work of Art," and Jean Paris' three Carnegie-Mellon lectures on painting are paradigms of the sort of interpretive approach I have in mind. What these paradigms share is a rare concern for the *being* of the work of art; the concealed story of its invisible origin and promise, which is always waiting to be told and retold. For that telling is the true receiving of the work of art; it is a mindfulness which understands the work's mute presence and gives to it, in return, the present of breath.

Dance seems to be especially needful in this regard. Dance is a very reticent art. It is a sublime art whose fleeting presence is the gift of an instant infinitely greater than the phenomenal interlude that so often conceals its treasure. In my essay, "Balanchine's Formalism" *(Dance Perspectives 55),** I started to tell the concealed story of classical ballet, which Balanchine's radical "deviations" helped me to read. That is a story about the invisible sense—or origins—of beauty and grace, the two conditions which define the essence of the classical ballet art. But the story is not complete. And because dance is very much alive today, many more stories remain to be told.

(1977)

FRANCIS SPARSHOTT
WHY PHILOSOPHY
NEGLECTS THE DANCE

The 1960's saw an immense increase of interest in dance in the United States—an interest soon reflected in sociological and anthropological studies that now begin to be plentifully published. This situation drew attention to a strange state of affairs in aesthetics. A venerable tradition regards dance as one of the

---

*In this anthology. Eds.

most basic of arts, and this tradition was strengthened in the early years of the present century by evolutionary notions that remarked the ubiquity of dance in primitive cultures and singled out dance-like behavior among primates as one of the principal animal antecedents of human art. But philosophers of art, contenting themselves with this lip-service, had done little work on the aesthetics of the art thus determined as fundamental. Examples of general points in aesthetics were and are seldom drawn from dance, and separate articles and monographs on dance aesthetics are few. Moreover, though there is an extensive early literature on dance, that literature is little known to the learned and literary worlds at large. One wonders why this should be so.

One suggestion is that dance is a female art, and our civilization has been patriarchal. But that is not so. World-wide, men dance as much as women do, and sometimes more. To assert that, despite this, dance is somehow an expression of the truly feminine aspects of the human psyche is to remove oneself from the domain of responsible discourse. And if dance here and now is in some respects institutionally associated with femininity, that is a contingent phenomenon calling for historical explanation rather than itself an explanation for the larger currents of thought.

Another explanation is that dance is corporeal, and philosophers fear and hate the body. That may explain why philosophers are seldom athletes, but dance as an art or arts is not, from the standpoint of observer or critic, significantly more bodily and less spiritual than other arts tangibly embodied.

A third suggestion is that examples of dance have not until the advent of TV and videotape been generally accessible, so that few philosophers could acquaint themselves with much dance or rely on such acquaintance in their readers; and that the lack of a generally readable dance notation rendered dances themselves ephemeral. That is true, but does not explain what needs explaining, for aesthetics has never depended on a common stock of specific instances.

To be surprised that little has been written on the philosophy of dance is to be naive about the conditions in which philosophies of specific arts get written. That an art exists, and that admired works are created in it, has never sufficed to generate a philosophy of that art. It is necessary that the art should occupy at the relevant time a culturally central position, or that the ideology of the art could be integrated with a culturally prevalent ideology. Thus, theories of literature abound because poets have been thought crucial figures in the culture of their times, and because vernacular literatures played key ideological roles in the rise of European nationalism. Philosophies of music reflect an era when music was allowed so central a role in education that its importance became not something to be established but a datum to be explained. Theories of cinema were developed in acknowledgement of the fact that the movies for some decades dominated even sophisticated imaginations, and this domination needed to be explored from within. But when we turn to dance we find, first, that for various reasons the ideologies available to the other arts have not been available to it, so that philosophers could not bring it into their general theories of the arts; and second, that dance has at no convenient time been a culturally central art. It may attain centrality in small non-literate ("primitive") societies, but their ways of doing things are not imaginatively accessible to us—nothing like them belongs anywhere in our imagined heritage. Dance was also a focus of interest in the personal monarchies of the sixteenth and seventeenth centuries, but this association with courts has itself sufficed to remove it from centrality in any contemporary western society. Attempts to find other contexts in which dance as an art might achieve the centrality one might expect it to possess have not yet succeeded. For instance, Isadora Duncan and others in the early years of this century thought dance might be the natural expression of Whitmanian democracy, the spirit of the healthy individual in open spaces; but the replacement of the frontier mentality by a disillusioned one-small-world-ism has woken us from that dream. Again, Diaghilev's Ballets Russes nearly succeeded in tearing ballet (still the only highly developed dance in the west) loose from its monarchical associations and making it a *Gesamtkunstwerk* that would rival Wagnerian opera, but in the end it did not come about. World War I shifted the balance of artistic acceptability towards less opulent forms; Wagner was in any case there first; and, perhaps most important, Diaghilev failed to establish a strong choreography at the core of his enterprise, which never fully established itself as dance rather than miscellaneous spectacle. Most recently, a new dance associated with such names as John Cage and Merce Cunningham has offered itself as the pure and necessary art of the moving body. But it turned out that there was no place for it to fill. As art for an alternative culture its place was preempted by the artistically unprecedented and unexpected outbursting of popular musics, a worldwide cultural revolution whose measure we have yet to take; and within its own solemn circle of art, as the name of John Cage reminds us, it did not establish a cultural presence and function separate from that of avant-garde music, para-theater, and "art" generally.

The upshot of the history summarized above is that there has been nothing for a philosophy of the dance to be about. Indeed, the very idea of an art of dance as such, distinct from mime and pageantry, is new and perhaps unstable. The prestigious court ballet of Louis XIV and his predecessors was less like anything we would call dance than like a pageant or a homecoming parade. The dances available from classical antiquity as imaginary exemplars for those who would dignify the dance were either pure mime, whose values were entirely those of expression and communication, or choric maneuverings whose value lay in the ceremony of which they formed part. The *ballet d'action* of Noverre and his contemporaries was again mimetic in its emphasis. Even Isadora Duncan at one time denounced the idea of a pure dance, saying that the value of her dances lay in their fidelity to the music for the sake of which they were created. Dance as dance, the rhythmically patterned movements of the body, was at all these times decried as a mere capering. The objection was not to its physicality but to its lack of meaning. Natural movements of the living body are motivated; unmotivated movements are mere swingings, jerkings, twitchings. The invention of a pure art of dance depends on the development of a characteristic system of motivation of its own, or something that will do duty for that. Till then, however many beautiful dances we have, there can be no philosophy of dance, because their significances remain indefeasibly miscellaneous. Only their beauty unites them. Beauty justifies dances, dancers, dancing, and the dance, but little can be said about it.

In order to vindicate a place for an art (such as dance) among the serious cultural concerns either of mankind or of our civilization, one must define a place that only it can fill, or that it fills in a distinctive way. To do that convincingly, it is advisable to construct a survey of real or possible arts among which the art in question is determinately located. Many such "systems of the arts" have been constructed. Some of these cover the whole range of human skills or a large part of that range, and others confine themselves to anatomizing the practices and skills that we lump together as "art" without relating art as a whole to any similarly articulated scheme for other areas of human activity.

Many such systems, notably that of S. K. Langer, do make a place for dance. But only two such systems have been so widely accepted that our own spontaneous thinking still shows their influence, because they form part of the tradition within which our minds work. And neither of these two preferred systems assigns a place to dance. Since philosophers of art, like other philosophers, spend most of their time (and most of them spend all their time) examining particular problems within unexamined frames of reference, these omissions go far to explain why philosophers neglect the dance. Of course, the prevalence of these two schematisms is not itself an ultimate datum, but demands explanation. Such explanation would include a demonstration of how each schema articulated the most pressing relevant concerns of the most influential ideologists of its age, and an explanation of that influence. No such explanation can even be sketched here; we will only note that the successful promulgation of a system of the arts from which dance was omitted shows either that dance was felt to lack significance at the relevant time or that its significance was not felt to lie within the proper scope of the system.

The two prevailing schemata of the arts to which I refer are the system of the "fine arts" as arts of imitation, derived via Aristotle from the Platonic *Epinomis* and developed in the sixteenth to early eighteenth century, and the system of the arts articulated by Hegel in his lectures on aesthetics and found at the basis of much nineteenth-century writing. Neither scheme commands the assent of serious thinkers today, but no other scheme of comparable mesmeric power has displaced them, so that they remain detectable as unquestioned operative assumptions in shaping the ways we still frame our questions.

The system of the "Fine Arts" is, for our purposes, best examined in the shallow but sophisticated version presented by D'Alembert in his "Preliminary Discourse" to Diderot's *Encyclopédie* (1751), where it forms part of a classification of the kinds of human knowledge.[1] "Another kind of reflective knowledge," he writes, ". . . consists of the ideas which we create for ourselves by imagining and putting together beings similar to those which are the object of our direct ideas" (p. 37). Among these arts of imitation painting and sculpture are primary because "it is in those arts above all that imitation best approximates the objects represented and speaks most directly to the senses" (ibid.); architecture does the same sort of thing only not so well; "Poetry, which comes after painting and sculpture, . . . speaks to the imagination rather than to the senses"; and music "holds the last place in the order of imitation" because it lacks a developed vocabulary, though it is nowadays evolving into a "kind of discourse" expressing the passions of the soul (p. 38). But, significantly from our point of view, "Any music that does not portray something is only noise" (p. 39). All these arts that "undertake the imitation of Nature" are called the Fine Arts "because they have pleasure for their principal object" (p. 43); they could all be included "under the general title of Painting" because they differ from that art only in their means (p. 55), or could be considered forms of poetry if "poetry" is taken in its old broad sense of "invention or creation." In the whole of this discussion, D'Alembert never mentions dance. Why not? Presumably because what he is classifying is forms of *knowledge*. Any dance which is not a variety of representational theater, and hence a form of "Painting," is mere movement in the same way that non-expressive music is "only noise," hence not a branch of knowledge and not to be included among the arts. What makes D'Alembert's exclusion of dance particularly remarkable is that his enumeration of great artists gives pride of place to those active at the court of that passionate practitioner and devotee of dance, Louis XIV; he even mentions Lully, Louis' great ballet impresario, but mentions him only as a musician. Yet the ballets of Louis' court were great public occasions, assigned high symbolic importance by their devisers and commentators. How could D'Alembert have overlooked them? A possible explanation is that opera (in which dance interludes were a normal component) was originally devised as a re-creation of Greek tragedy and inherited tragedy's traditional place among arts that "imitate Nature"; but the court ballet, in which Prince and nobility took part, found its ancestry in a different region of Platonic thought, in the choric dances in which the city expressed its unity and its symbolic equivalence with the hierarchy of the cosmos. Thus its strictly choreographic component (always subsidiary in the whole design) was as such below the level of art, its theatrical component is categorized as a continuation of painting by other means, and its inner significance lies in a mode of imitation radically other than that which the fine arts exemplify. There was thus no way in which the court ballet could be assigned a distinctive place among the fine arts, and its successors suffered the same difficulty.

In face of this exclusion it is easy to see what apologists of dance should do: they should say that dance stands alongside painting and poetry as an independent mode of imitation. And

so they did. Noverre, among others, took just that line.[2] But the
move never won general acceptance, because it was not as "imitation of Nature" that significant dance was significant.

The other schematism of arts that has dominated our minds is
Hegel's. It goes like this. The fine arts are arts that produce
beauty. Beauty is the adequation of a form to an idea, so that a
fine art embodies ideas in forms adequate to them. As civilization
advances, arts become more refined. Symbolic arts in which
spirit partly informs matter give way to classical arts in which
spirit and matter are perfectly fused, and these in turn yield to
romantic arts in which spirit dominates its material embodiment.
After that, spirit assumes autonomous forms and art as a whole
is superseded. The paradigm of a symbolic art is architecture; of
a classical art, sculpture; the romantic arts are typically painting,
music, and poetry. Sculpture is the central art, the most artistic
of the arts; among romantic arts music is central, the most romantic, but poetry is the most spiritual and the most advanced.

One might have looked for dance in two places in Hegel's
scheme. On the one hand, since the central place assigned to
sculpture rests on the old thesis that of all natural forms only the
human body, the favorite subject of sculpture, gives natural
expression to "the Idea" because it is the body of the only theorizing animal, one might have expected dance, which sets actual
human bodies in graceful motion, to join sculpture at the center.
That place had been prepared for it by the Fine Arts schematism,
but Hegel leaves it empty. On the other hand, dance might have
been set alongside architecture as the primitive art, in which the
actual materiality of the body is partly infused with formally significant properties in the same way that an architect gives a significant form to actual materials in all their solid strength. Why
does Hegel refuse to make either of these obvious moves?

So far as Hegel knew, architecture of the appropriate heavy
and symbolizing sort did dominate the early civilizations of
Egypt and India; and sculpture, since Winckelmann, was taken
to epitomize Greek civilization. But no civilized era had
expressed its characteristic orientation in dance. Dance belonged
to savages, and to primitive men whose expression was inarticulate. As a means of expression it is subhuman and pre-artistic.
Apes and peacocks dance. Long after Hegel's death, as we have
seen, such animal behavior would be assigned to the ancestry of
art.

The supposed facts of history may have sufficed, but another
thing that might make dance an unlikely partner for sculpture

would be that the body made by God in His own image must already be expressive in the only way in which it can be expressive. The dancer as dancer can express no idea higher than the personality and full humanity his life should already more fully and perfectly show. An idealization of gesture could not be more eloquently expressive of humanity, but only an attenuation and trivialization.

What, then, of the analogy of architecture? The dancer's agility and grace imperfectly animate his real corporeal presence, the sweating and straining body, as an architect imparts an illusory lightness to the vault that sustains and is confirmed by the loads imposed on it. Even if no advanced civilization has taken dance as its central expression, should we not recognize that dance, like architecture, is an inevitable and basic art—that human beings will always build, and will always dance, and it will always matter to them how they do so? If the origins of dance are prehistoric and even prehuman, what is at the origin is not necessarily superseded, or if it is so is superseded only by losing its place at the focus of concern. It was in this sense that Hegel thought all art was superseded: science and philosophy must from now on always be more central to the concerns of humanity, but art has by no means completed its mission.

Hegel's relegation of architecture to the past corresponds to a historical fact. The architecture of his day was bankrupt, reduced to exploiting a repertory of forms of which the original significance was lost, in desperate search for any sort of authentic or persuasive style. Similarly, nothing in Hegel's day suggested any inevitable importance for an art of dance. The *ballet d'action* of Noverre and his contemporaries had quickly relapsed into the formalism they had protested against, and the dance of Hegel's day had nothing more significant to show than Vigano's *choreodrammi* at Milan—magnificent spectacle, but mere spectacle. In Hegel's terms, spectacle is not art. A modern art, a living art, had in Hegel's day to be a romantic art; and it was not until the year of Hegel's death (1831) that the dance of the nuns in *Robert le Diable* revealed the possibilities—quickly followed up—of a romantic art of dance.

Hegel will acknowledge no split between the rational and the real, and therefore always bases his schematizations on something very solid and closely observed in history. Dance in his place and time offered no such basis to observation, and to have claimed for it any systematic significance would have been pure ideology.

Dance as romantic art is born in the romantic ballet of Paris immediately after Hegel's death, and it is this ballet that still typifies the art of dance in the general mind. Such a dance, culturally prestigious and ideologically significant, might have won a posthumous place in the Hegelian system. But it did not. As Ivor Guest shows, the inner meaning of that ballet was a yearning for the unattainable as symbolized in a man's hopeless love for a fairy being, an etherealized woman.[3] But not only is that sort of "idealism" a weak escapism, incapable of bearing any but the most vapid symbolism; more seriously, the artistic fact it corresponded to was the cult of the ballerina, of Marie Taglioni and her rivals and successors down to Pavlova—and of the ballerina as kept or keepable woman, whose body was central only as fetish for the Jockey Club. The idealization of the feminine is the degradation of the female. So far from vindicating for ballet a place among the arts in which the human spirit finds its defining form, this social attitude excludes ballet from art and confines it within the luxury trades. Association with ballet has meant the stigma of spiritual sickness, and for a while it seemed that the only hope for a serious art of dance was to repudiate ballet utterly. Unfortunately, no technique of comparable development, and no tradition of comparable weight, existed in the west or (because of the rigors of training, if nothing else) was importable from the east.

What this all amounts to is that there has not yet been any available basis for a philosophy of dance. Nor can such a basis be invented by philosophers. Philosophers cannot invent or bestow seriousness; they can only explain it.[4]

(1981)

Notes

[1]Jean Le Rond D'Alembert, *Preliminary Discourse to the Encyclopedia of Diderot*, trans. by Richard Schwab and Walter Rex, Indianapolis, Bobbs-Merrill, 1963.

[2]Jean-Georges Noverre, *Letters on Dancing and Ballets* (1760), trans. by Cyril Beaumont, New York, Dance Horizons, 1966.

[3]Ivor Guest, *Romantic Ballet in Paris*, Middletown, Conn., Wesleyan University Press, 1966.

[4]Most of this essay is condensed from a longer paper, "On the Question: 'Why Do Philosophers Neglect the Aesthetics of the Dance?'" to appear in *Dance Research Journal*.

II
The Dance Medium

In his essay "Degas, Dance, Drawing," Paul Valéry recounts a now legendary conversation between the painter Degas and the poet Mallarmé. Degas—who also wrote poetry on occasion—complained to his friend that writing was an extremely painful experience for him despite the fact that he was never at a loss for ideas. "But Degas," replied Mallarmé, "you can't make a poem with ideas. . . . You make it with words."

Mallarmé was not denying that poems can express ideas; he was merely insisting that for the poet, ideas can only be expressed through the *medium* of words. As Aristotle was the first to point out, every artist works in a particular medium: composers in the medium of sound, painters in the medium of canvas and pigments, etc. G. Baldwin Brown, in his classic study *The Art of the Cave Dweller*, argues that serious pictorial art began when the primitive artist first grappled with the problem of accommodating his mental image of an animal to the actual, physical surface on which he intended to paint it. Presumably, the properties of each medium will determine to a great extent what can be expressed or represented in that medium. If this is so, it follows that some media will be better suited to certain tasks than others.

What then is the *medium* of dance and what sorts of subjects, ideas, and experiences is that medium best equipped to embody?

Most people would say simply that the medium of dance is the human body. That sounds plausible enough; but unfortunately, the matter cannot be resolved quite so easily. For if we define the dance medium simply as the body, what are we to make of the other theatrical elements—costumes, scenery, lighting—that traditionally have both adorned and concealed the dancer's body?

Most of the questions examined in this section center on the nature of the dancer's body. How does it differ from the inanimate raw materials of painting and sculpture? Paul Taylor, for example, has noted that "dancers are not exactly like tubes of paint with which to cover the canvas of space. They have character and personality which they assert." Havelock Ellis distinguishes between dance and architecture on the ground that the choreographer often uses his own body as a medium, but the architect creates an object external to himself. Does this mean that the choreographer's relationship to his medium is inherently less objective than that of the architect? Another question that engages a number of writers in this section is whether or not choreographers should reveal and acknowledge the basic properties of their medium.

We've already seen that, for Susanne Langer, the actual physical movements of the body are not in and of themselves sufficient to constitute a work of art; the dancer's body must project an illusion of "virtual force." Stéphane Mallarmé, writing about the dancer La Cornalba, appears to agree with Langer when he insists that "the ballerina is not a girl dancing . . . she is not a girl, but rather a metaphor which symbolizes some elemental aspect of earthly form: sword, cup, flowers, etc." Clearly, for Mallarmé, the dancer must transcend the natural body in order to represent something impersonal and metaphorical.

Thus, it makes perfect sense that Mallarmé was a great admirer of the pioneer modern dancer Loïe Fuller who manipulated billowing silks through brightly colored lights so as to generate the illusion that her body had vanished into these free-flowing materials. And far from constituting an isolated phenomenon in the history of dance, Fuller represents a major choreographic tradition: the concealment or transformation of the human body. Martha Graham's body-concealing costume of stretch jersey for "Lamentation" and Alwin Nikolais's frequent use of the body as a sort of mobile projection screen also belong to this time-honored tradition. We might even include the earliest court ballets such as the "Ballet Comique de la Reine" in which the performers were costumed in floor-length dresses, arranged into allegorically evocative floor patterns, and viewed from above—all of which had the effect of deemphasizing the actual physical properties of the individual dancers' bodies. In his review of the original "Le Sacre du Printemps," Jacques Rivière, the French editor and essayist, credits the choreographer Nijinsky with having initiated a counter-tradition in which the dancer's body is liberated from all such artifices and encumbrances. Rivière discusses two different sorts of artifice that choreographers have traditionally employed to conceal the body. The first, he associates, appropriately enough, with Fuller: "the play of lights, floating draperies, veils that envelop the body and disguise its shape, the blurring of all contours, the dancer's chief aim is to lose herself in her surroundings."

But even when the dancer has been stripped of these theatrical accessories, there is still no guarantee that the actual, physical body will become visible and theatrically legible. For example, Rivière complains that, in Fokine's "Le Spectre de la Rose," "Nijinsky's body literally disappears in its own dance. The only things that remain visible of that muscular being with its so strong and prominent features are exquisitely fleeting contours, constantly evanescing forms."

By contrast, he argues that the angular, geometric severity of "Le Sacre" reveals the true contours of the dancers' bodies. It is, he insists, the first choreographic work capable of countering the vague, amorphous aesthetic of Impressionist painting. Rivière's description of "Le Sacre" may be difficult to reconcile with the accounts of other commentators who tend to stress its primal energy rather than its visual clarity. Many of Rivière's comments may seem more applicable to a work like Balanchine's "Agon." Be that as it may, Rivière was one of the first writers to praise choreographers for revealing rather than concealing the body.

In fact, he accurately anticipates what Lincoln Kirstein would later write about Balanchine: "He has not been troubled how to dress dancers, but to undress them so their nudity is most intelligible. It almost amounts to an anti-theatrical bias." Of course, the nudity Kirstein speaks of is only metaphorical. The "undressed" dancers in Balanchine's formalist ballets are dressed in practice clothes rather than theatrical costumes; but Rivière's anti-theatrical bias, his desire to reveal the body either as unadorned object or as sensuous presence, has probably been carried to its ultimate extreme by the post-modern minimalists like Yvonne Rainer whose work has on occasion employed complete nudity.

Some would argue that choreographers who share this "anti-theatrical" bias are being truer to the underlying nature of their medium than those who don't. This "purist" doctrine is derived in large part from the *Laocoön*, a theoretical treatise by the eighteenth-century German dramatist and aesthetician, Gotthold Lessing. Subtitled "An Essay on the Limits of Painting and Poetry," *Laocoön* attempts to define the essential nature of these two arts and to distinguish between them accordingly.

Poetry, Lessing argued, is a temporal art because words are perceived consecutively, in time. Painting, by contrast, is an art of space, not time, because its images are assimilated all at once, in a single "spatial" whole. According to this doctrine, it is the responsibility of the painter, the poet (and by implication, all other artists as well) to recognize and work within the *limiting conditions* of the medium. This purist doctrine led Lessing to inveigh against painters who depict allegorical subjects—stories that unfold in a temporal sequence. Equally objectionable to him were poets whose imagery was static and "pictorial," rather than temporal. Thus, according to Lessing, artists must work within the constraints of their own media and not trespass upon the domain of the other arts.

What then, according to this purist doctrine, are the *limits* of dance? George Balanchine has said that "there are no mothers-in-law in ballet," suggesting that dance lacks the means of indicating certain sorts of complex relationships between characters. In fact, Balanchine even argues that the realm of story and character is better left to literature altogether: "The ballet is such a rich art form that it should not be an illustrator of even the most interesting, even the most meaningful literary primary source. The ballet will speak for itself and about itself. . . . I am always sorry when an excellent ballerina depicts with her movements only some literary theme. The human body, and in particular the female body, carries in itself true beauty. And one really does not want to know whom this or that ballerina represents but only to see the pure beauty of her body, her movements."

But is Balanchine expressing a general truth about the art of dance or only his own preference for plotless, formalist ballets? As Selma Jeanne Cohen points out, one of the characters in Agnes de Mille's "Fall River Legend" is, if not a mother-in-law, at least a stepmother. But de Mille cannot accomplish this feat of characterization without the assistance of a theatrical property. (The father places a white shawl, already associated with the

mother who has died, around the shoulders of another woman
while his daughter watches.) But even if de Mille *had* found a
way of characterizing the stepmother through pure movement,
does the Lessing doctrine still imply that her ballet is "impure"
because it attempts something that might have been more easily,
if not more compellingly, evoked in words?

The problem comes down to this: What is a legitimate aspira-
tion for an artistic medium? Must the medium confine itself to
what it and it alone can do or is that being unnecessarily dogmatic and restrictive? Isn't there something to be said for the
pleasure of contrasting the way Martha Graham treats the myth
of the House of Atreus with the very different way Aeschylus
dramatizes these same stories in the *Oresteia*? Doesn't some of the
magnificence of Limón's "The Moor's Pavane" derive from the
abstract, economical way he distills the sprawling complexity of
Shakespeare's *Othello*? Some would go further and say that any
effects the medium is capable of generating are legitimate to it.
Why in a more general sense, must only one art tell stories,
depict character, etc.?

It is also worth noting that some modernist artists appear to
believe that each medium has discernible limits, but that peculiarly compelling aesthetic effects may be achieved by intentionally violating them. Yvonne Rainer for example, once wrote,

> I remember thinking that dance was at a disadvantage in relation
> to sculpture in that the spectator could spend as much time as he
> required to examine a sculpture, walk around it, and so forth—but
> a dance movement—because it happened in time—vanished as
> soon as it was executed. So in a solo called "The Bells" I repeated
> the same seven movements for eight minutes . . . in a sense allow-
> ing the spectator to walk around it.

André Gide once said that Lessing's book presents one of those
seminal theories that should be either re-affirmed or contradicted
every thirty years. The writings of Clement Greenberg, the contemporary art critic, constitute one of the most adventurous re-
statements of this purist aesthetic. According to Greenberg, the
quest for purity is one of the hallmarks of modernism. The true
modernist art work must not only conform to the underlying
principles of its medium; it must also actively acknowledge those
limiting principles and jettison anything that might obscure its
essential nature. In the case of painting, this essential nature is
flatness. Therefore, painters must not only refrain from creating

an illusion of three-dimensional space (which would trespass on the domain of sculpture); they must also find ways of calling attention to the flatness of the canvas.

In his essay "Balanchine's Formalism," the American philosopher David Michael Levin relies on Greenberg's theory of modernism to illuminate George Balanchine's singular accomplishments. According to Levin, the concealed essence of ballet is an exquisitely delicate tension between weight and weightlessness. This essence can only be revealed by stripping away the theatrical and representational elements that have traditionally concealed it. (Hence, Balanchine's "anti-theatrical" bias.) In the formalist ballets that result, Balanchine acknowledges the tangible weight of the body, but only to "suspend" that weight, rendering the body magically weightless.

Needless to say, not all modernists have followed this austere, purist path. In fact, any comprehensive account of modernism would have to acknowledge an opposing tendency toward the re-unification of dance and the other arts. One of the major discontents of modernity is the pervasive feeling of isolation and fragmentation; and many artists have turned toward the rituals of "primitive" societies in search of holistic models. The best known and most influential proposal for re-capturing the presumed unity of primitive ritual through modernist art is Wagner's theory of the *Gesamtkunstwerk*, an ideal synthesis of music, dance, and speech.

As Frank Kermode, the contemporary British literary critic, argues in his essay, "Poet and Dancer Before Diaghilev," it was a fascination with this ideal of re-unification that led so many turn-of-the-century poets to rhapsodize over Loïe Fuller and the early productions of Diaghilev's Ballets Russes. Compared with these multi-sensory spectacles, the poet's medium, language, appeared bloodlessly abstract, longwinded, and "dissociated" from the objects it represents. Contrasting dance with written language, Mallarmé insists that the dancer "writing with her body . . . suggests things which the written work could express only in several paragraphs of dialogue or descriptive prose."

Dancing, Kermode argues, was thought to "achieve naturally that 'organic unity' which . . . modern poetry can produce only by a great and exhausting effort of fusion." Loïe Fuller, as we've already seen, appeared to become "one" with her materials, and Diaghilev's ballets were often glamorous and presumably seamless collaborations among the leading painters, composers, and choreographers of his era. ("Parade" for example, had settings and costumes by Picasso, a score by Satie, choreography by Massine.) Thus, we might say that primitivist "wholeness" and modernist purity constitute two very different conceptions of the dance medium.

Marshall Cohen, in his essay, "Primitivism, Modernism, and Dance Theory," argues that neither of these extreme positions provides an accurate account of the contemporary dance events we most value. He challenges the claim that the work of the Ballets Russes constitutes a true realization of the Wagnerian *Gesamtkunstwerk* because it excludes the art of speech. Indeed, in many of Diaghilev's best-known works, the dancing was clearly of lesser importance than the costumes and scenery, thereby undermining any claim of unity and equality among the arts. And even if these ballets were to achieve the desired degree of synthesis, they would still be perceived by modern "dissociated" sensibilities, transforming them into one more eclectic variety of contemporary art rather than a full-fledged restoration of primitive wholeness.

Cohen is equally critical of David Levin's attempts to impose Clement Greenberg's theories on the work of George Balanchine. Levin, he points out, mistakenly argues that Balanchine's ballets achieve a state of simultaneous weight and weightlessness by disguising the three-dimensionality of the body. Levin takes Greenberg's ideas about the flatness of contemporary visual art and applies them much too literally to ballet. But dancing, Cohen argues, has at least as strong a claim on the third dimension as does sculpture. In fact, one of the most characteristic features of Balanchine's choreography is the way it exhibits the dancer's body in three-dimensional space. And Balanchine's art, even though it leans in the direction of modernist purity, always derives its primary inspiration from the music to which it is choreographed, thus denying it the absolute autonomy that the doctrine of modernist purity seems to demand.

Whether or not this ideal of purity has ever been achieved by a choreographer is arguable. Mary Wigman created what she called "absolute" dances performed in silence with a bare minimum of theatrical support. But these dances were conceived of as representations of inner realities. Merce Cunningham often creates movement that is self-contained, and neither representational nor directly dependent upon music. Yet music and decor remain essential components of Cunningham's *mise-en-scène*, even if each maintains its autonomy.

Balanchine, as we have seen, suggests that one of the limita-

of the dance medium is its inability to represent character. Heinrich von Kleist, the nineteenth-century German playwright and essayist, suggests that another very real limitation of the medium—and this presumably applies to all of the performing arts—is the self-consciousness of the human performer. Kleist's essay is really a meditation on the relationship between grace and self-consciousness, framed in the form of a parable about the marionette theatre. One of the speakers in Kleist's tale is a dancer who greatly admires the movement of puppets. "It is true," he says, "that the range of their movements is rather limited, but those which they can command they accomplish with a grace and ease which every thinking person can only wonder at." The puppets, unlike the dancers, are "without affectation," their bodies obey only the law of gravity, "an admirable quality which one looks for in vain among the majority of our dancers." According to Kleist, human beings are less graceful than puppets because "we have eaten of the tree of knowledge." In other words, self-consciousness prevents us from regaining a state of grace.

Kleist's parable may seem too abstract at first to be immediately applicable to theatrical dance; but one need only think of works like "Coppélia," "The Nutcracker," and "Petrouchka"—not to mention Oskar Schlemmer's "Triadic Ballet"—all of which celebrate the movement of puppets or inanimate objects. But, more important, Kleist helps us to understand more precisely the nature of the dance medium by examining the differences between the dancer's body and other sorts of bodies, both animate and inanimate. Unlike the puppet's inanimate body or the bodies of other animals, the dancer's body is infected with self-consciousness, and the dancer's training consists at least in part of learning how to control self-consciousness in order to approach more closely Kleist's ideal of grace (although, as we have already seen, John Martin takes a more positive view of the matter, arguing that the conscious, *intentional* nature of the dancer's movement is both different from and superior to mere inanimate motion).

But the performer need not actively imitate a puppet, doll, or machine in order to approach Kleist's ideal. Dalcroze's eurythmics, which both Nijinsky and Mary Wigman studied, attempts to alleviate the performer's self-consciousness by minimizing the reaction time between musical stimulus and bodily response. We might also think here of André Levinson's definition of the ideal ballerina as "a machine for manufacturing beauty."

In a sense though, all of these attempts by human beings to rival the unselfconsciousness of the puppet are—at least according to Kleist—misguided, because human beings cannot return to innocence; we have no choice but to increase our knowledge and self-awareness.

STÉPHANE MALLARMÉ
BALLETS

La Cornalba delights me; she seems almost naked in her dance. For in an effortless rise and fall, this creature now in flight, now drowsed in veils, is summoned into the air and seems to hang there, purely Italian in the soft stretching of her body.

Is that, for lack of any other Poetry, the only memory remaining from the performance at the Eden theater? By no means! For what we call Poetry is, on the contrary, abundant there (a most pleasant interlude for a mind now free of characters in costumes and dresses, reciting immortal verse). But the magic spell of the libretto does not come out in the performance. I leaf through the program and learn that the very stars themselves—which, I am firmly convinced, should be but rarely disturbed, and even then only for high reasons of meditative gravity (in this case, according to the accompanying explanation, it is Cupid who moves and assembles them)—the very stars are present! And now the incoherent, haughty absence of meaning which twinkles in the alphabet of Night yields and, with a few starry pin-pricks in a blue curtain, spells out VIVIANNE, the tempting name of the fay and title of the poem. For, of course, the *corps de ballet*, grouped in its entirety around the *star* (what name could be more suitable to her!), cannot figure the ideal dance of the constellations. No! and you can see what a plunge this meant into other worlds, straight to the depths of art! The snow, too: no dance of whiteness back and forth, no waltz can keep each flake alive; and so it is with the vernal thrust of blossoms. All that which is Poetry—nature brought to life—leaves the libretto and freezes in cardboard equipment and in the glittering stagnancy of purple and yellow muslin. Then again, as far as stage movement goes, I saw a magic circle which was certainly not drawn by the fay's own endless round or by her silken cords. Innumerable little clever details, yet none of which assumes any normal, established function in the reproduction. Going back to the "starry" example just mentioned, has there ever been a more heroic refusal of the temptation to understand not merely analogies of high seriousness, but also this law: that the chief goal of the dance, apart from its mechanics, is a mobile, unending, ubiquitous synthesis of the attitudes of each dance group, a synthesis which they must fraction ad infinitum? Hence an equal exchange resulting in the deindividualization of the coryphée, of the group, of the dancing entity, which is therefore always a symbol, never a person.

Here is a judgment, *here* is an axiom for the ballet!

I mean that the ballerina *is not a girl dancing;* that, considering the juxtaposition of those group motifs, *she is not a girl,* but rather a metaphor which symbolizes some elemental aspect of earthly form: sword, cup, flower, etc., and that *she does not dance* but rather, with miraculous lunges and abbreviations, writing with her body, she *suggests* things which the written work could *express* only in several paragraphs of dialogue or descriptive prose. Her poem is written without the writer's tools.

Following a legend came the Fable: not at all in the classical or *deus ex machina* tradition, but in a more limited sense: simply the transposition of human character and gesture to the purely animal level. This involved a rather facile re-translation of the human feelings which the fabulist had attributed to his enamored and wingèd creatures; here the characters were, indeed, more perfectly instinctive in their silent leaps than those who are given a conscious language to speak on the stage. The dance must be all wings; there must be birds, flights to the never-never land, and quivering descents like those of arrows. That, precisely and ideally, is what one should see in a performance of *The Two Pigeons:* namely, the predetermined sequence of the fundamental motifs of the Ballet. It should not be difficult for the imagination of the spectator to find such connections; but in this case it was difficult to find even a slight resemblance, and in art it is the result that counts. Delusion! except for the first act, in which we saw the love-birds turned, in an attractive incarnation, into mimicking, dancing human beings.

Two pigeons loved with a tender love,

two, or rather several pairs on a roof-top which could be seen, like the sea, through the archway of a Thessalian farm; and they were alive, not painted, which made for depth and exquisite taste. Each love-bird points to the others, then to himself, thus awakening to language through comparison. And so, little by little, the couple recalls the dove-cote with its pecking, flitting, swooning little ways; and at last the others, in delightful imitation, come invading, gliding down upon them from their frolics in the air. Now the two are children, now birds, now children once again, depending on our vision of this game of doubles and exchanges which male and female play henceforth and play forever—nothing more nor less than the game between the sexes! But now I must avoid any further consideration suggested by the Ballet—that catalyst and paradise of all spirituality—because after this simple prelude, nothing deserved even a momentary backward glance; absolutely nothing, save the perfection of the dancers. It would be tiresome to point out the foolish nothingness which followed the graceful motif of the prelude. One might mention the wanderer's flight which did, at least, conjure up that heavenly inability to disappear that keeps the ballerina's toes delightfully on the stage. And then when home calls once again, when the sweet, poignant hour of the prodigal has come (including a celebration), and when the heartrent lovers, all flight and forgiveness, reunite, there will be . . . well, you can imagine the final triumphant dance hymn, with the fiancés together again in drunken joy after the space between them, brought about by that unavoidable flight, has been gradually reduced to nothing! It will be . . . why, as if the whole thing were taking place right in your own home, ladies and gentlemen, with an appropriate kiss (quite inappropriate in art); for the Dance is only the mysterious and sacred interpretation of such a scene. But then, if we take that view, a little run on the flute will remind us that our vision is ridiculous in the eyes of our vulgar contemporaries, whom we must allow for, after all, out of consideration for the theater's tickets.

There was a very clearly discerned relationship between the usual lines of the dancer's flight and several choreographic effects; and there was the (not entirely ingenuous) fitting of the Fable to the Ballet. Apart from these, there was simply a love story. During the interlude of this uniquely shreds and patches performance, the wondrous and matchless virtuosa Mlle. Mauri summed it up, mingling her divination with pure and trembling animality. At every point she indicated the allusions which had not yet been brought into perfect focus; and with a touch of her fingers, just before she took a step, she would call a shimmering fold forth from her skirt and seem to fly up to the Idea on impatient wings.

The historical scenic art form is the Drama. The Ballet, on the contrary, is a symbolic form. The two should be allied, but not confused. You must not give brusque and common treatment to two attitudes which are jealous of their respective gifts of silence. Acting and dancing become suddenly hostile whenever they are forcibly brought together. For example: when the attempt was made just now to show forth the single essence of a bird through twin performers, it was decided (you will remember) to pair a mime and a ballerina. But they are too unlike! If one is a dove, why, the other will be . . . Lord knows! perhaps the breeze. Fortunately, at the Eden theater, the exclusive qualities of the two art forms were most judiciously observed: the hero living in his twin worlds—a child still, and yet a man—was set in thematic opposition to the rival heroine who was both a woman *walking* toward him on royal carpets and also the original fay, equally important with her flutterings. This distinction of each scenic genre, in contact or opposition with the other, becomes the controlling feature of the work, and the resulting disparity is used for its very structure. But a communication between the two still remains to be found. Ordinarily, the librettist fails to understand that the ballerina expresses herself with steps, and that beyond this she has no eloquence, not even that of gesture.

Even if genius should say: "The Dance is a figuration of caprice in rhythmical flight. Here, with their numbers, are the few basic equations of all fantasy; and the human form in its most excessive mobility, in its truest development, cannot escape them, insofar, of course, as they are a visual embodiment of the idea"— and now take a glance at any choreographic ensemble, and compare!—there is still no one who would accept this method of setting up a ballet. The modern cast of mind is well known, and even in the case of those whose faculties are exceptional when used, it must be replaced by some nameless, impersonal, glittering glance of absoluteness, like that lightning which has in recent years enveloped the ballerinas at the Eden theater, fused its naked electricity with paints of a whiteness beyond the ken of flesh, and surely made of her that wondrous being who has drawn back beyond all conceivable living worlds.

At those times when we ordinarily watch the Dance with no special object in mind, the only way to lead our imagination on is to stand patiently, calmly watching each of the dancer's steps, each strange pose—toeing, tapping, lunge, or rebound—and then ask ourselves: "What can the meaning of it be?" Or, better still, find inspiration suddenly and interpret it. Doubtless that will mean living entirely in the world of revery. World sufficient, nonetheless; nebulous or clear, spacious or limited—any of these, so long as that illiterate ballerina, flutteringly engaged in her profession, encloses it with her circlings or bears it off in flight.

Oh, stranger to me and yet a Friend, as you sit hidden some evening in the theater: if, at that sorceress' feet (she! all unaware of sorcery), you will but humbly place the Flower *of your poetic instinct* (like those roses which are thrown off and up into visible higher worlds by a flick of her pale and dizzying satin slippers), drawing from this alone the true light and revelation of your numberless secret imaginings, then (in an exchange which seems to be the secret and revelation of her smile), through her always ultimate veil, she will give you back your concepts in all their nakedness, and silently inscribe your vision as would a Symbol—which she is.

(1886–97)

JACQUES RIVIÈRE
LE SACRE DU PRINTEMPS

The great innovation of *Le Sacre du Printemps* is the absence of all "trimmings." Here is a work that is absolutely pure. Cold and harsh, if you will, but without any glaze to mar its inherent brilliance, without any artifices to rearrange or distort its contours. This is not a "work of art" with all the usual little contrivances. Nothing is blurred, nothing obscured by shadows; there is no veiling or poetic mellowing, no trace of aesthetic effect. The work is presented whole and in its natural state; the parts are set before us completely raw, without anything that will aid in their digestion; everything is open, intact, clear and coarse. . . .

Le Sacre du Printemps is the first masterpiece capable of confronting those of the Impressionists. . . .

Innovative as the music of *Le Sacre du Printemps* might be, the fact that it can be compared to that of Moussorgsky shows that it has retained a certain link to our past experience, that it is possible to find its approximate derivation. The same cannot be said for the choreography. It no longer has any ties whatsoever to the classical ballet. Here, everything has been started anew, everything fashioned on the spot, everything reinvented. The innovation is so shocking and so crude that the public cannot be denied the right—of which it moreover has made overly conscientious use—of rebelling against it. Let us therefore try, in the faint hope of accustoming the public to it, to define this innovation in some detail.

Once again, in my opinion, it consists in the absence of all artifices. As regards the dance in general, one might say that there are two types of artifices. First, those of Loie Fuller: the play of lights, floating draperies, veils that envelop the body and disguise its shape, the blurring of all contours; the dancer's chief aim is to lose herself in her surroundings, to blend her own movements with movements that are vaster and less well-defined, to conceal every exact form in a sort of multihued effusion of which she now is nothing but the indistinct and mysterious center. Quite naturally, she has been led to illustrate Debussy's "Nuages."

Against this first type of artifice, the Russians openly declared themselves from the start. They had the body reappear from under its veils and took it out from that billowing atmosphere in which it had been immersed; henceforth, our only impressions were to come from the body's own movements and from the clearly visible and distinctly outlined figure drawn by the dancer with his arms and legs. They brought clarity back to the dance. I well remember those first nights. For me, it was the revelation of a new world. It was possible, then, to come out of the shadows, to let every gesture be seen, to spell out everything in full without any mystery, and yet be profound and pathetic, holding the spectators' attention as by the most intricate and enigmatic tricks. I made a discovery in art similar to that of geometry in the sciences, and the joy that I felt was similar to the satisfaction one experiences when watching a perfect scientific demonstration. At each of Nijinsky's whirls, just after he had closed, kneeling and crossing his hands, the buckle he had opened while soaring into space, I took an immense pleasure in mentally reviewing the entire figure described by his movement: alive, pure, precise, boldly drawn, as if wrenched in one block and by force from the formless mass of possibilities. There remained no doubts, no confusion, nothing that might cause me to hesitate; rather, I felt reassured and content, like a man who takes in at one glance a system of mathematical propositions from which all possibilities of error have been scrupulously eliminated.

Nevertheless, in this dance which to us had seemed so severe, Nijinsky was able to detect yet another kind of artifice, well before we had noticed it ourselves, and he accordingly undertook to cleanse choreography of it. Having experienced a certain unease in executing Fokine's creations, he understood that they still contained a certain artfulness, a certain vacillation, some sort of inner vagueness that would have to be eliminated at any cost. Conciseness such as this could still be refined; such exactness could be carried even further. . . . From that day on, he would not rest until he himself had turned the screw, had tightened the bolts of the choreographic machinery, so that it might function with absolute precision. Those who find the feeling of something being done in a slipshod and so-so fashion extremely disconcerting, will readily understand him.

First, let us determine the nature of this second type of artifice. What is there that still obscures the dancer even after he has divested himself of all accessories? The very intensity of his motion, his passage, his flight across time, the arabesque described by his movement; "he travels along a road which he destroys in the very act of his passing; he follows a mysterious thread that becomes invisible behind him; by his brushing-off gesture, by those hands that he waves in the air, by the thousand slow revolutions of his body, he gives the appearance of a magician busy at obliterating the traces of his handiwork; he will not be caught; we shall not be able to hold him fast and pin his arms to his sides, so as to survey him at leisure from head to foot."* Something interposes itself between him and us; it is that very movement of his; we see him move in a world parallel to ours but different from his; he has lost himself on his own voyage and we perceive him only through a haze formed by the accumulation of his gestures and by his ceaseless to-and-fro motion. More specifically: in the course of his first ten steps, the dancer outlines a figure that immediately thereafter tends to leave him, to escape, to go off on its own, like a melody which, once one has

---

*This passage is taken from a note I wrote last year (July 1, 1912) on Fokine and in which I made several assertions, which today Nijinsky obliges me not to deny entirely, but rather to surpass, just as he himself, without denying it, has surpassed Fokine.

found its first notes, continues by itself, making its own improvisations, until it finally imposes itself on the voice that gave it
birth. There is a spring concealed in it that thrusts it from its
position. No sooner have the first movements been created by
the body than it seems as though, having become aware of themselves, they say to their author, "That's enough! Now we do it by
ourselves!" Unchained, they regenerate each other by repetition,
by redoubling, by variation, drawing from themselves an infinite abundance. The body which at first had dictated their
actions, now serves only as their support; it now is merely asked
to receive and to execute them. Thus, in their hands, the body
loses its own form and articulation. They rearrange it, correct it,
retouch it; they create passages in it where there had been gaps;
they join its members by a graceful and unbroken line; they erase
angles, fill in holes, throw bridges. From head to toe, the body
in some way takes on fluidity and fullness. An added elegance
casually descends and rests upon it. Like a heavily made-up
actor, it is no longer recognizable. The *Specter of the Rose* offers
the best example for this transfiguration. Nijinsky's body literally disappears in its own dance. The only thing that remains
visible of that muscular being, with its so strong and prominent
features, are exquisitely fleeting contours, constantly evanescing
forms. The atmosphere in which he is submerged is dynamic
rather than multicolored, but he is rendered as indistinct by it as
Loie Fuller by her luminous veils. As delightful as the spectacle
may be, there is in the *Specter of the Rose* a certain inner lack of
truth that can no longer fail to trouble me.

The innovation of *Le Sacre du Printemps* thus lies in doing away
with dynamic artificiality, in the return to the body, in the effort
to adhere more closely to its natural movements, in lending an
ear only to its most immediate, most radical, most etymological
expressions. Motion has been reduced to obedience; it is constantly made to return to the body; it is tied to it, caught and
pulled back by it, like someone being caught by the elbows and
prevented from fleeing. This is motion that does not run off, that
has been forbidden to change its own little tune; motion that
must come back to take orders every minute. In the body in
repose, there are a thousand hidden directions, an entire system
of lines that incline it toward the dance. With Fokine, they all
ended in one single movement that joined and exhausted them
all; rather than listening to each one, he listened to them all combined; he expressed them by substitution, replacing their varied
multitude by a simple and continuous arabesque. In *Le Sacre du*

Printemps, on the other hand, as many propensities and occasions as are offered by the body, as many times does the movement stop and start again; as many possible points of departure the dancer discovers in himself, as many times does he rise again. He regains possession of himself at each instant; like a source that must successively drain all its fountainheads, he recovers his strength, and his dance becomes the analysis, the enumeration of all the body's inclinations toward motion that he can find in it. Here we discover in Nijinsky the same preoccupation as with Stravinsky: to approach everything according to its own orientation. His aim is to follow all the inclinations of the body very directly, regardless of their divergence, and to produce movement only through them. He cannot pursue them all at the same time, however, and as soon as he has followed one for an instant, he suddenly leaves it; he breaks with it and returns to seek another. A dance simultaneously faithful and cut off! Similar to our body, all the motions remain in perfect harmony with the members that execute them; they retain their meaning and conciseness; they remain joined to them as if linked to them organically. And the dancer, when we see him again in memory, instead of effacing himself behind his gestures, stands out very clearly among their multitude, like a Hindu deity among its many arms. . . .

Just now we have examined in what sense Nijinsky reacted against Fokine; what he rejected and what he destroyed. Now we must understand the positive aspects of his innovation. What benefit did he derive from doing away with artifice? To what end did he break up choreographic movements and groups? What kind of beauty lies hidden beneath this reduced and dislocated dance? Without taking into account his marvelous adaptation of the subject of *Le Sacre du Printemps*, it is easy to perceive where his innovation constitutes an improvement over Fokine's dance.

The latter is inherently unsuited to the expression of emotion; one can read into it nothing but a vague, entirely physical and faceless joy. Indeed, in the fluid and continuous motions of which it is composed, as in the large arabesques of the Renaissance painters, the emotive power of the gesture, its secret and inner force, is diluted and dissolved. On this undefined road on which the dancer sets out, the emotions find a too easy outlet and spend themselves in vain. Instead of the emotion being the object that the movement tries to describe and make visible, it becomes a mere pretext for erupting into movement, and is soon forgotten amid the abundance of which it is the source; it quickly loses itself among the repetitions it engenders. The body sweeps everything away; its freedom reaches into the soul, demolishing its innermost recesses, its resources, and its reserves.

By breaking up movement and bringing it back to the simple gesture, Nijinsky caused expression to return to the dance. All the angles, all the breaks in his choreography, are aimed only at preventing the escape of emotion. The movement closes over the emotion; it arrests and contains it; by its perpetual change in direction, it deprives emotion of every outlet and imprisons it by its very brevity. The body no longer is a means of escape for the soul; on the contrary, it collects and gathers itself around it; it suppresses its outward thrust, and, by the very resistance that it offers to the soul, becomes completely permeated by it, having betrayed it from without. The restraint imposed by the body upon the soul conveys upon the body a peculiar kind of spirituality that is visible in all its ways. There is a profound and constrained quality in this captivated dance: all that it loses in spirit, in animation, in capriciousness, it gains in meaning.

Fokine's dance had so little power of expression that, in order to make the spectator aware of the performers' changes of mood, they had to resort to facial mimicry; scowls or smiles. By adding and superimposing this upon the gestures, it merely demonstrated their ineffectiveness. It was merely an additional property; another type of resource needed to supplement the poverty of the language of choreography.

In Nijinsky's dance, however, the face no longer plays a part of importance; it is merely an extension of the body—its flower. It is above all the body that speaks. Moving only as a whole, it forms a block, and its language is a sudden leap with arms and legs outspread, or a sideways move with knees bent, the head dropped upon a shoulder. At first glance, it appears less adroit, less diverse, less intelligent. However, by its compact shifts of position, its sudden turnabouts, its ways of coming to a stop and shaking itself frenetically on the spot, it conveys ever so much more than the eloquent, fast, and elegant speaker represented by Fokine. Nijinsky's language consists of perpetual detail; he lets nothing pass; he seeks out all the corners. There is no turn of phrase, no *pirouette*, no preterition. The dancer is no longer being carried away by a trivial and indifferent inspiration. Instead of lightly touching upon things during the course of his flight, he lets his full weight fall on them, marking each by his heavy and complete plunge. He leaps in a bound upon each emotion that he encounters and wishes to express; he flings himself upon it, envelops it, and stays for an instant, to imitate it. He forgets everything so as to assume its likeness for a short while; for some time, he suffocates it with his form, blinds it by his very being. No longer obliged to fashion a link between each successive gesture, nor to think constantly of what is to follow, he leaves nothing of himself in the transition. He completely abandons himself to the invitation of the inner object; he becomes unique like the latter as he designates it by the momentary immobility of his entire body. Let us remember Nijinsky, the dancer! With what eloquence he curled himself, like a cat, around emotions! How he hovered over them closely! How well he knew how to arrange all his limbs in their image and to make himself their faithful effigy! He is both an inventor and interpreter. All that he breaks, all that he takes away from the dance, is done to attain a realistic and complete—as if opaque—imitation of emotion. He takes his dancers, rearranges their arms, twisting them; he would break them if he dared; he belabors these bodies with a pitiless brutality, as though they were lifeless objects; he forces from them impossible movements, attitudes that make them seem deformed. But he does this only in order to draw from them all the expression they are able to give. And at last, they speak. From all those bizarre and twisted forms arises a strange materialization; they distinctly reveal a thousand complex and mysterious objects that now need only to be looked at.

Indeed, it has all become clear and easy; it has taken on the very shape of that which must be understood. Here, before our eyes, has emotion been designated, held fast, and interpreted. Here it is, like a large doll, left behind by the dancer while he goes on. What could be more moving than this physical image of the passions of the soul. How different this is from their expression through articulated language. Not that there is any greater depth, any observance of detail, or any subtleties the spoken word could not render, but by means of this tangible figure we are brought closer to them and put into their presence in a more immediate manner; we are able to contemplate them before the arrival of language, before they are pressed upon by multitudinous and subtly varied but loquacious crowds of words. There is no need for translation; this is not a sign from which the subject must be interpreted. But though our intelligence fails to grasp it, we are there; we are present through our body, and it is the body that understands. A certain predisposition, a certain inner awareness. . . . Each of the dancer's gestures is like a word that I could have said. If at times it seems strange, it is so only in the light of my thoughts, since it immediately enters into my limbs, into the depth of my organism, in a low, complete, and perfect harmony. Just as music had us absorb its narrative in "large, easily manageable pieces," it is thus that we face this extravagant dance with a peculiar barefaced credulity and with a feeling of intimacy that "goes beyond words." We stand before it like children at a puppet show: they don't need to have things "explained to them"; rather, as the show goes on, they laugh, they tremble, they understand.

Nijinsky has given the dance a power of interpretation it had lacked. But would not his effort to relate the dance more closely to the body, to cause the dance to interflow with and confine it to the bodily strength of our limbs ultimately risk depriving it of its beauty and grace? Where, indeed, is there grace in these mean and clumsy gestures, forever held captive, forever brutally interrupted whenever they are about to soar forth? There seems to be something cacophonic in the choreography of *Le Sacre du Printemps*.

However, grace does not signify smooth roundedness; it is not incompatible with angular design. I claim that there is grace here, and one more profound than that of the *Specter of the Rose*, being more closely bound up with its theme. This grace is not of the independent kind; it does not come from above to alight upon objects like a bird; it is merely the outward emanation of an absolute necessity, only the effect of an impeccable inner adjustment. In the choreography of *Le Sacre du Printemps*, all has been perfected with the utmost rigor; in order to arrive at the motions, as we see them, that compose it, Nijinsky had to cultivate and develop them over a long period of time; he chose them from among the confused tangle of our instinctive movements; he preserved them from others; he gave them a slight push and led them a little farther away from the body than they would have gone on their own. In short, he patiently gave them their singular perfection, and from that achievement a new and original harmony was born. As soon as one ceases to confuse grace with symmetry and with arabesques, one will find it on each page of *Le Sacre du Printemps*; in those faces turned in profile over shoulders turned front, in those elbows held tight to the waist, in those horizontal forearms, in those hands held open and rigid, in that trembling descending like a wave from the dancers' heads to feet; in that shadowy, straggling, and preoccupied promenade of the Maidens in the second scene. One will find it even in the dance of the Chosen Maiden, in the short and abortive tremors that agitate her, in her difficulties, in her frightful waits, in her prisonerlike and unnatural gait, and in that arm raised to heaven and waved straight above her head in a gesture of appeal, threat, and protection.

All during my analysis of *Le Sacre du Printemps*, I have considered the means employed by Stravinsky and Nijinsky as though they had an intrinsic value of their own, independent of the subject to which they are applied. This separation may seem artificial, and one may rightfully object that I am trying to see an entirely new technique in something that has been created for and is meaningful only with regard to a very specific work. Some will say that this angular choreography is suited only to represent the still unformed and awkward gesticulation of primitive beings. This muted music can serve only to depict the deep anguish of spring. One as well as the other is well-suited to the chosen theme; neither goes beyond it nor can be separated from it. . . .

(1913)

DAVID MICHAEL LEVIN
BALANCHINE'S FORMALISM

What are the elements that constitute the singular beauty of classical ballet? One might say: Among other things, certainly, a tension between weight and weightlessness. But George Balanchine was one of the first to regard this tension as the concealed essence of the ballet art, and especially as the essence of the phenomenon of grace. Discriminating this essence as the telos of a new ballet aesthetic, Balanchine was also one of the first to demonstrate how it so informs the classical idiom that, when it is properly isolated, exhibited and—in a word—released, it can be exquisitely expressive entirely on its own. The expressivity of classical dance is indeed possible without the various resources of mimetic and symbolic convention. Or, in other words, classical ballet is not essentially mimetic, nor essentially representational; rather, these functions merely enclose what *is* of the essence: the immanent sensuous beauty and grace of the dancing body.[1] Balanchine has mastered the deepest logic of this intrinsic, expressive power of the human body; has followed, in particular, its surprising constraints on costume and stage décor. To release such an essence requires a very delicate touch. For it is most easily presented in concealment. As we shall see, costuming and staging can make all the difference.

Modernism, in this context, is the aesthetic principle that accounts for the privilege being given to the revelation of this essence, this sort of essence. And modernism demands the exclusion of every element that might veil, or mute, or distract from the conditions of the revelation. Formalism is a direct consequence of this chosen aesthetic. It is not, and never has been, for Balanchine, an end in itself. The cherished essence of classical ballet—its syntactical treasures—will remain deeply sublimated, to the extent that there are any semantic elements in the presentation of the dance that must be taken as mimetic or in some other way representational.

The timelessness of Balanchine's miraculous art amounts to this: that he found the possibility of drama in a ballet form, which lets the semantical transparencies of modernism articulate, or heighten, the innermost syntactical treasures of classicism. Or, considering this timelessness in a different focus, it amounts to the tense simultaneity of the body's weight and weightlessness. And in this supernatural instant, a sublime essence is brought to presence: the dancer's capacity to suspend the natural condition of his body in the very act of acknowledging it.

Agon (1957); *Monumentum pro Gesualdo* (1960); *Violin Concerto, Duo Concertant, Symphony in Three Movements* (1972). These are demanding works that offer a difficult and, for many of us, a perplexing pleasure. These are ballets which preserve the classical choreographic syntax of movements and attitudes, yet defy a venerable tradition of staging and costume. Their austere production, so exquisitely reduced and uncomplicated, allows us to perceive the most elementary, immanent expressiveness of the classical ballet forms; and somehow, in this very elusive process of illumination, the phenomenal presence of the forms is richly altered. Formalism, I want to show, can explain some of George Balanchine's most memorable and certainly most innovative ballets.[2]

What is this formalism? What is its particular modernity? We know that the modernist aesthetic has brought to articulation certain long-suppressed resources in painting and sculpture. What, then, does it mean to say that Balanchine's experiments with formalism have similarly demonstrated one of classical ballet's innermost possibilities?

The attempted modernity of *Chopiniana*, the recent issue of a misguided ardor, might seem to provide some grounds for doubting that ballet can tolerate the conditions of formalism. But we must remember that the New York City Ballet's *Chopiniana* is not an original ballet, but only a revised "modern" production of Fokine's *Les Sylphides* of 1909. Still, consideration of its aesthetic infelicities might gain us access to the secret ambition—and clear logic—of Balanchine's art.

In his review of *Chopiniana*, Dale Harris[3] rightly argues that this production purports merely to divest the original ballet of those romantic realms of meaning that constitute its historically right yet—from a metaphysical standpoint—quite "accidental" decorative scaffolding (principally, the décor and costumes), and to reveal thereby the hidden beauty of its simpler, quintessential structure. It has, in fact, robbed the ballet of a most delicate sense and charm.[4] In the case, then, of *Les Sylphides*, the apparently superficial embroidery of the ballet—which Rayner Heppenstall has aptly subsumed under the category "Moonlight and Muslin,"[5] and in which a particular texture and quality of sense are brought to life—cannot be detached from some apparently "hidden" choreographic structure without fatally touching its peculiar aesthetic essence. The hidden beauty is just an illusion, for the essential structure has been so tightly, so rightly, expressed through the immediate, sentimental intelligibility of precisely those "decorations." Costumes and décor, we find, cannot always be subsumed under the category of "mere decoration." (Similarly, the pedestal of a sculpture and the frame of a painting are not invariably added as mere decoration. Michelangelo's statue of Moses requires a pedestal, just as the paintings of Van Eyck and Corot, for example, works constructed in the knowledge of their final condition, quite evidently require their frames. But if we put a pedestal under Robert Morris' polyhedrons or under some of Henry Moore's huge sculptures; or if we put a conventional frame around Monet's *Water Lilies*, we are certainly adding mere decorations, which would actually subtract from their aesthetic quantity. In the case of Anthony Caro's sculptures, the presence of a pedestal would contradict their sculptural essence.)

Let us dismiss, then, the problematic *Chopiniana,* and consider instead the numerous ballets that exhibit the particular innovations of Balanchine's aesthetic. My principal contention is that this master choreographer came to understand, more profoundly perhaps than anyone before him, the possibility of abstracting the pure classical syntax of the mobile human body as the defining condition, or essence, of the ballet art (the essence toward which, he thought, his favorite precursors were variously striving?); and that, consenting to this possibility, he boldly completed the development of a modernist formalism, which would be phenomenologically adequate—as no other possible aesthetic could be—to the consummate release and expression of this sublime, or implicit, essence.[6] (I do not mean to suggest that Balanchine never has chosen to set aside this formalism. He has, indeed, many times preferred to produce ballets in the older, more "theatrical" style. His traditional ballets—such as the narrative *La Valse*— will also be admired and remembered; but simply because they are exquisite inventions, and not because they introduce another possible aesthetic.) More particularly, I would like to concentrate on the striking affinities I am wont to discern between Balanchine's altogether original interpretation of the ballet art and the no less original aesthetic that defines the paintings and sculptures we shall call, after Clement Greenberg, "modernist art."

According to Greenberg, modernist painting and sculpture consummate an intrinsically logical progression of these traditional arts, which have passed through four stages: first, a painterly aesthetic (the theory of Alberti's treatise *On Painting* of 1435), committed to the simplicity of actual *Mimesis,* the faithful representation of the human reality; second, an aesthetic which subordinated the demand for exact representation to the demand for a sensuous yet still lucid figuration (as in Matisse's 1916 *The Piano Lesson* and Klee's 1912 *Actor's Mask*); third, an aesthetic which kept figuration, but distorted and perplexed it and rendered it entirely abstract, so that the expressiveness of the art—powerfully heightened—became a function, not of some discriminable symbol or subject-matter faithfully transcribed, but rather of the sensuous properties of the abstractly presented structure (as in Picasso's 1912 *Torero* and de Kooning's 1957 *Parc Rosenberg*); finally, an aesthetic which demanded the total annihilation—or anyway, the precarious suppression—of all figurative tendencies. We might summarize this progression by saying that an aesthetic of immanence (an aesthetic of self-revealing presence) has come to replace the earlier aesthetic of mimetic connotation and transcendent symbolism. For the modernist aesthetic (exhibited to various degrees, for example, in the paintings of Jackson Pollock, Morris Louis, Barnett Newman, Kenneth Noland, and Frank Stella; the sculptures of Anthony Caro and David Smith) challenges the work of art to reveal, to make present (I do not say: to represent) its defining condition as art. It requires moreover that the work accomplish this in a self-referential, or reflexive, manner—solely in terms of the abstract, sensuous properties residing in, and constitutive of, the structure itself. Thus, for the modernist aesthetic, the "form" of the work and its "content" (prepared for its formal role because of its pure abstractness) are one and the same—identical in the strictest sense of this word. If the modernist painting or sculpture represents nothing, refers to nothing outside itself (refers to nothing transcendent), then the sense that it nonetheless expresses and makes totally present may be fittingly described as a revelation. Modernist art, to speak paradoxically, reveals . . . itself! Less paradoxically, it exists solely for the revelation of its ownmost (and latent, or immanent) defining conditions. (Needless to say, I am bent on purging the term "revelation" of every metaphysical association—using it, indeed, in a specifically Kantian, anti-metaphysical sense. Thus employed, the term implies a repudiation of all symbolism and intellectual interpretation and invokes, rather, the significant qualities that are immanent in the purely sensuous structures of perceptual experience.)[7]

But what are the conditions that define its being and its unique model of phenomenological givenness (or presence)? Greenberg and Michael Fried have suggested the answer. So too has Martin Heidegger, in his *Holzwege* essay entitled "Der Ursprung des Kunstwerkes." And it may be significant that here their lines of thought coincide. A work of art is of course a material object; yet, at the same time, it also is the negation of this objecthood. So what the modernist work of art is meant to reveal, what it must reveal, is precisely this contradiction. And if it suppresses one or the other of these two modalities of its being, it has simply failed to articulate the truth about art which seems logically imperative at this given point in its history.

On Fried's view, the two ineluctable defining conditions of painting are its flatness and its shape. No painting can conceivably exist unless it is reduced to flatness and has assumed a certain shape. But, since material objects are also shaped and may also be flat, painting can defeat, or suspend, its own objecthood if—and only if—it accomplishes what no mere object can possibly do: it must somehow materially acknowledge these conditions, rendering them totally present. Discussing modernist sculpture, Greenberg writes: "To render substance entirely optical, and form, whether pictorial, sculptural, or architectural, as an integral part of ambient space—this brings anti-illusionism full circle. Instead of the illusion of things, we are now offered the illusion of modalities: namely, that matter is incorporeal, weightless, and exists only optically, like a mirage."[8]

Not surprisingly, the role of color has posed a serious problem for the modernist aesthetic. Painters must take care lest their colors create an illusion that would prevent the wholly optical acknowledgment of the painting's flatness. Sculptors risk the danger that their coloring may create a surface bespeaking the objecthood of a sculptural mass whose interior it simply conceals: a surface unable to present itself as a merely optical extension. Robert Morris, we know, simply relinquished the use of color, while those sculptors who have dared to use color (David Smith and Calder) somehow succeeded in negating the very (material) surface, which color must logically also affirm. If the structure itself cannot jeopardize this implict mass behind the color surface, the work will fail to halt its reduction to mere objecthood. Color similarly imperils modernist painting. The work must simultaneously acknowledge, or make present, the flatness and shape which root it in the earth, and yet somehow employ its color in a purely optical way, so that the space of the painting— the "world" created through the act of painting—will be truly accessible (aesthetically intelligible) only to a disembodied eye. (Unlike the visual illusion that emerges in the painting of a representation on a flat canvas, offering the illusion of a tactile accessibility, the modernist illusion offers itself as an illusion accessible only to the eye, hence only to an eye that does not have a tactile and mobile support.)

Fried asseverates, moreover, that the imperative defeat or suspension of objecthood entails that modernist art defeat or suspend its possible "theatricality."[9] Unfortunately, he does not establish the terms of this entailment with compelling clarity. The connection, however, can be made. The possibility of "theatre" requires the situatedness of a spectator with regard to the theatrical object. Thus, the theatricality of the object is possible only insofar as the spectator can be oriented towards it in a temporal and spatial perspective. This means that the spectator/object relationship is to be defined (in part) through a heightened consciousness of the limiting co-ordinates of the spectator's corporeality and the object's objecthood. Now, it is precisely this sort of relationship that the opticality of modernist art is meant to defeat. So Fried is right, after all, in claiming that theatricality and modernist formalism contradict one another.

We may note a parallel progression toward modernism in the history of the ballet. In Europe, ballet originated as a species of court entertainment. Long after it entered the public domain, however, it continued to be, in essence, a divertissement, a merely theatrical event. The early ballet consisted of artificial and rigidly determined dance movements. Gradually, though, it submitted to the desire for a more stylized, but also more "natural," expressiveness.[10] Beyond this stage, the ballet has mainly developed along four distinct routes. Two of these are rather akin to Abstract Expressionism. The one is certainly theatrical and, even in its incipient formal abstractness, it sustains the confident expressiveness of intelligible gestural symbols. (I am thinking, for example, of the works of Antony Tudor, and of the sort of productions we associate with Martha Graham.) The other belongs to those ballets that have tried to mix a formal abstractness of movement with a theatricality which often substitutes the expressiveness of stage décor, lighting, and costumes for the expressiveness of symbols intrinsic to the movements of the dancers. (Here I am thinking of the Joffrey Ballet's *Clowns* and *Astarte*.) A third, and very different sort of route is represented by the dance of Merce Cunningham, Yvonne Rainer, and perhaps Twyla Tharp. This form is entirely abstract; the movement is very expressive, although it rigorously excludes every quality of expression not wholly immanent in the dancers' abstract movements. At the same time, however, the production as a whole does not exclude theatricality, which is latent in the various items (including costumes) that may be employed as props. In addition, the acceptable dance syntax, here, is unlike the classical syntax (however abstract), not only in regard to some of its formal properties, but also in regard to the extent of its vocabulary. (So the inventions of Cunningham, Tharp, and Rainer differ from those of Balanchine, even when they are scarcely more abstract.) The fourth route, of course, is the one paved and traveled by George Balanchine.

As a point of departure, let us refer to what Mr. Harris construes to be the defining condition of that ballet art exemplified in such works as *Les Sylphides*. He writes: "It seems to embody an entire theory about what ballet ought to be, one which, though capable of easy sentimentalization and by no means without its limitations, is nevertheless valid: the belief that ballet is a poetic experience whose purpose is to summon up transcendent longings through graceful movement." And with regard to *Les Sylphides* in particular, he observes that "Fokine's sylphs have evolved into powerful and universal symbols."[11] Whatever one may think about the rightness of the attempt to impose a formalist aesthetic on this venerable ballet, one must surely concede that, from the standpoint of their intention (to release the latent possibilities which "ensoul" the ballet art), the New York City Ballet was logically compelled to violate this Fokine aesthetic.

Viewed against the classical tradition, Balanchine's unique aesthetic can seem exceedingly austere. It calls for a "bare-bones" reduction of the ballet essence. Yes—but only because this asceticism is designed to release a beauty and a grace which the older, seemingly richer essence had in principle to suppress. Whereas the older art sought expressiveness, both in the decorations of stage and costume and in the familiar symbolism of immediately intelligible gestures and postures (a symbolism certainly meant to evoke "transcendent longings"), the new Balanchine art refuses the expressiveness of stage costumes and excludes, too, all those resources of corporeal syntax that cannot achieve their expressiveness without the encumbrance of some mimetic or transcendent symbolism.

The abstractness of dance formalism does not exclude the sensuous expressiveness of the body. Indeed, this is the only truly intrinsic expressiveness that is possible in the formal syntax; what formalism excludes, rather, are such modes of expressiveness and meaning as do not directly reveal their presence through a wholly abstract, a purely syntactic medium. A form, as such, may be either representational or abstract, and if abstract, either abstracted from the semantic materials of a prior representation or else originally abstract. A form may be abstract, and none the less sensuous, insofar as the perception of the form is capable of inducing modes of kinetic and kinaesthetic pleasure. So, odd though it may seem, the Balanchine aesthetic has adopted a profoundly anti-theatrical approach to ballet, amply demonstrating that the theatricality of stage and costume, as well as the theatricality of distinctly allusive movement, are not, in fact, the necessary conditions of drama in a performing art. (I have described the tendency of Balanchine's works as "anti-theatrical." But I am most definitely not suggesting that his ballets mute, or are meant to defeat, the tensions and resolutions of drama.)

If the failure of *Chopiniana* was possible only because the New York City Ballet confused the rightness of sentiment with the wrongness of sentimentality and, in consequence, excluded both, still, in the creation of his own ballets, Balanchine himself has not failed to distinguish between theatrical expressiveness (the semantics of sentiment and allusion) and "classically pure" formal expressiveness (modes of corporeal presence which are latent in, or immanent to, the "classical" syntax of human mobility).

Such formal expressiveness, however, requires not only that he suppress the theatricality of stage and costume, but also that he purge the classical dance syntax of its theatrical allusiveness. In fine, it requires that he reduce the mimetic "content" of traditional ballet movements to the expressive presence of an entirely abstract syntax. Structure and content, then, become identical to the degree that each submits to the process of abstraction. In some Balanchine ballets—extraordinary works such as *Agon* and *Violin Concerto*—a traditionally expressive "content" coincides with the expressive presence of structure. Content *is* structure. For structure has been allowed to refer exclusively to, and to reveal, itself: it can speak—we discover—in its own language, a language by no means less poignant, less expressive than the other, more conventional address. (Sara Leland, who has danced thirteen years for Balanchine, is quoted as saying in an interview: "Mr. B. depends on the movement itself to bring out the quality he wants in a ballet, he does not try to develop 'expression' in the dancers. It is there, he tells us, in the choreography—we have only to dance the choreography to express it."[12]

The kind of movement, then, that can reveal itself is ontologically distinct from the kind of movement that cannot reveal itself. The movements of the human body are different in essence from the movements of inanimate objects. The human body is through and through intentional; even at rest, it transcends its objective actuality towards some immanent and virtual state. So an aesthetic can take it as imperative that, in the art of dance, the movements of the human body shall exhibit precisely this ontological distinction. If it is of the essence of the human body that it is a moving object only in the mode of surpassing (i.e., simultaneously acknowledging and defeating) its own objecthood, then it can be, correspondingly, of the essence of ballet that the movements reveal in dance this essential condition. This is precisely the principle that defines modernism.

To achieve a modernist drama, the syntax of dance must be so presented that it is aesthetically accessible neither as purely literal movement (an objective modification, in Euclidian space, of the dancer's "real" body) nor as wholly figurative movement (a subjective qualification of the dancer's formally expressive "phenomenal" body), but rather as both simultaneously. This possibility derives from the fact that the human body spans a dynamic tension between the objectively actual and the inwardly virtual. Formalism can heighten this tension to the degree that it achieves a disclosure of the body that demonstrates the dancer's objective spatialization, at the same time that it suspends, or annihilates, this condition through the peculiar, deep expressivity of a syntax reduced to pure self-reference. The syntax must utilize and acknowledge the tangible weight, the massive balances of the body, but only in order to defeat or suspend them, and to render the objective body as a magically weightless, optically intangible presence. (Actually, as we shall see, this *presence* of the dancing body is also a sort of *absence*, since the sublimity of grace, unlike the beauty of poise, is up-lifting, and releases the body from the horizontal space-field of the stage.)

The reader of Nabokov's *Ada* will find, near the beginning of the novel, the following curious passage: "Presently the vegetation assumed a more southern aspect as the lane skirted Ardis Park. At the next turning, the romantic mansion appeared on the gentle eminence of old novels. It was a splendid countryhouse, three stories high, built of pale brick and purplish stone."[13] Nabokov, of course, has used language, here, so that it accuses itself. The words create, or posit, a world of representational validity; at the same time, they nullify this world by an acknowledgment of their act of creation. Similarly, George Balanchine sometimes deploys the dancer's weight in a way that especially fits the human body to betray this declaration of objecthood, and indeed to betray this in the very act of declaring it. The drama in the metamorphosis of corporeality (objecthood)—the drama we behold in the sublime immanence of grace—thus replaces the older ballet intention, transcendence through the grace of "longing."

Sartre rather briefly discusses the phenomenon of grace.[14] It is much to his credit that he recognized the relevance of this matter for a complete phenomenology of the human body. And his analysis is certainly fascinating. I am convinced, however, that, in addition to being incomplete, it calls for some rectification. In Sartre's view, grace "refers obscurely to a transcendent Beyond of which we preserve only a confused memory and which we can reach only by a radical modification of our being. . . ." I would like to invoke, here, a grace of whose possibility this most fastidious of phenomenologists seems only dimly sensible: the possibility that, in a graceful disposition of the body, in the radiant immanence of a grace that Balanchine's modernist ballets exquisitely detail, it is the body itself—but as a sublime and sacred presence—that is revealed.

We shall find it helpful, at this point, to make use of Kant's distinction, in *The Critique of Judgment*, between the beautiful and the sublime. To Kant, the beautiful is that which, through the commodiousness of an objectively embodied form alone, can induce a pleasure whose immediate ground is the harmony of the understanding (as the faculty of lawfulness, canons of taste) and the imagination (as the faculty of playful perceptual organization). The sublime, on the other hand, is that which induces a mediated, and more difficult sort of pleasure: that which has its ground entirely within the subjective conditions of productive (imaginative) consciousness itself, and for which the sublime is merely the original occasion. For the sublime, unlike the beautiful, does not offer an immediately commodious (purposive) form; on the contrary, it offers something which is manifestly formless, or which, in any case, defeats the straightforward perception of sensible form. Thus, the sublime challenges the imagination to surpass its perceptual rootedness, summons it to strive for a glimpse of some possible, but very obscure, form. The sublime, then, requires that the imagination strive to produce, entirely out of its ownmost latent (or transcendental) resources, an adequate image of a form that is not at all embodied in the natural or sensible world. According to Kant, the sublime presents the imagination with an occasion to discover, within itself, and beyond the "pain" of its striving for a higher form, its supernatural destination.

Now the art of dance can induce two very different modes of aesthetic sensibility. The one mode is induced by the beauty of the natural, or immediately sensible, form of the dance, while the other mode is induced, rather, by a sublime suspension, or perhaps defeat, of the immediately sensible form of the dance. The beauty of dance is the traditional beauty of the phenomenon of *poise* (Middle English *poisen, peisen*, to weigh). Beauty belongs to the poise, the tensions and equilibrations, of the self-moving body expressing itself through movements and attitudes, tensional vectors of force, within the horizontal space-field of its objective stage relationships.[15] (This field is principally constituted according to the right/left, forwards/backwards, and near/far schemata.) The beauty of dance resides in the classical manner of the body's original spatialization of, and thereby its spatialization within, the horizontal field of the stage; it resides, if you will, in the dancer's poised excursions into the density of an architectural field of space. This field is traditionally staked out, in part, by the surrounding objects (which may include other dancers) in the stage design, and it is around these entities that the dancer pivots; but the field is also "inflected" by the traditional costuming which, in virtue of its circumstantial appropriateness, further installs the dancer within it. The classical beauty of dance requires the equipoise, the lucid presence, of the dancing body.

The sublimity of dance, however, is the sublimity of the phenomenon of grace. Sublimity belongs to the grace of a body whose movements and attitudes make it appear no longer to be inhabiting, no longer to be installed in, the surrounding horizontal field (the object-coordinated, object-pivoted space of the stage.)[16] In the instant of grace, the dancer seems, rather, to be up-lifted, to be released into a purely optical space, weightlessly suspended in the vertical time-field of a supervenient Grace. It is as if the dancer's body, released from its condition of poised objecthood, is being rewarded precisely for its ecstatic, and gratefully disciplined, revelation of this very condition.

The Persian dervish poet Rumi tells us that, "Whosoever knoweth the power of the dance, dwelleth in God."[17] In the myths of cosmology, Grace is a gift from the Sky of God. Grace acknowledges the supernatural destination of the soul, everlastingly released from the circumstantial field of Earth. Through Grace, the soul casts off its autochthonous embodiment (and consequently its objecthood) and returns to the Sky of God. Thus, in beholding the spectacle of Grace, our productive imagination surpasses its sensible ground, and we witness the joining of Earth and Sky.

We have seen that the graceful dancer appears to be weightless. But now we can also see that Grace is the necessary condition for this weightlessness, this unearthly suspension of objecthood. For it is precisely from the Sky of God that the supervenient order of Grace, up-lifting, descends. But why is the

gift of Grace thus bestowed upon the dancer? Is it not—paradoxically—because, through the skillful body, the dancer is so eloquently praising the gravity of the body, acknowledging in gratitude the Earth of the body? And is it not because, in order to
fully acknowledge this, the dancer has skillfully perfected the
releasing possibilities of the body? The dancer's grace-fulness is
a sublime presence (or, more accurately, a presence/absence),
which belongs to the horizontal field of gratitude, of spatialized
skill, but—at the same time—belongs totally and immortally to
the vertical time-field of Grace, the Sky of God. And finally, we
are in a position to understand the costuming and stage requirements for the modernist presentation of grace. For costuming
and staging are elements that constitute the horizontal field of
space within which the dancer must move. But, if modernism is
to reveal the sublime essence of grace, and not just show the
beauty of poise, the stage-space must be cleared of everything
that would locate the dancer within the binding coordinates of
the horizontal field, thus defeating the possibility of a vertical
release in the Time of Grace.

Modernist ballet certainly preserves the innermost resources
of the older syntax; and it still entertains—through the drama of
tension and the grace of release and resolution. But it gives birth
to its aesthetic presence entirely within the syntax of a constant
tension between the phenomenal body yielding itself to objecthood and the same body, at the same time, artfully suspending
its objecthood. In the same interview quoted above, Sara Leland
observed that, "In the Balanchine *plié*, you are perched for
flight." An acute and important point. In the Balanchine *plié*—
which is, after all, an incontestable acknowledgment, or demonstration, of the dancer's objective weight and necessary
effort—the choreography has also made present, but at first only
in the tensed mode of suppressed virtuality, the graceful arc of
flight, which is about to suspend the force of gravity on behalf
of its own phenomenal space.

Concepts such as "simultaneity" and "virtuality," which are
indices of temporality, turn out to be fundamental to an understanding of formalist space. Much, certainly, needs to be said
about the properties of formalist time;[18] but I shall limit myself
to the observation that Edwin Denby made in an interview
recorded by Arlene Croce and Don McDonagh: "Well, to me the
big difference [between gesture in dance and gesture in mime]
is that a dance gesture is like a dance step—it has a limit in time.
If you enlarge on it, you enlarge on it in relation to a definite

time. . . . If the various moves the body goes through to make a step—say it goes through four moves, A-B-C-D, and B, is, say, one and a half times as long as the others—then if you want to diminish B, you diminish it still within that musical time. Or enlarge it. You don't just enlarge it without any relation to anything in time that the rest of the dance has. But in acting gesture, there isn't any [such] time. The time is real, it's everyday time. If you lift up a cup of coffee this way, it means something in everyday time that you do it slowly, instead of grabbing it and pulling it up. But in dance, it might be necessary to lift it up that slowly simply because that is the time [appropriately] choreographed for it." And Denby's next remark explicitly distinguishes "formal" time and "real" time: "When I'm watching dancing, my eye expects a certain time. More than one's eyes, really. If you start to believe in a character and a story, inside yourself you shift to that other time."[19] In Balanchine's modernist ballets, a formal— or abstract—time must replace real time, because it is a factor altogether fundamental to the possibility of an optical space in which weight and mass are suspended at the same time that they are acknowledged.

What made modernist ballet possible, I think, was Balanchine's discovery that there is exquisite drama concealed in the equilibration of corporeal contraries: the virtual position, which almost imperceptibly emerges from an actual movement; the defiant pulse of a self-conscious form, which threatens the objecthood of perfect poise; the mass, which seems—for one tensely magic second—to be stolen from the body, as its very movement denies, through form, the constraints of weight. The drama does not take place, for us, in an always tangible space; it exists, rather, in the tensional revelation of a sublime, precariously optical modality.

Thus, for example, there are moments when we perceive the weight-presence of the dancers in the intricate *pas de deux* of *Violin Concerto* very much the way we must perceive the modernist mass of, say, "Tanktotem IX," a late metal work from the factory of the sculptor, David Smith.[20] At the juncture between plate and tripod, exactly where we should expect the demonstration of weight, we discover that the line of the tripod can become, instead, a purely pictorial element. Opticality has suspended the natural weight of the steel plate! Since "Tanktotem" in fact resembles a human body—resembles, even, a dancer in pose—it is especially rewarding to notice points of correspondence between this phenomenon at the juncture of plate and tripod, and the suspensions of weight that can seem to occur, for vision, in some of Balanchine's ballets.

The possibility of achieving, through formalism, a purely optical reduction of corporeal mass and weight in accordance with the modernist aesthetic is certainly latent in most of the classical ballet positions—the *attitude croisée*, for example, and the height of the *soubresaut*, and the *arabesque allongée*. What so forcefully strikes me about the first and third positions is, first, the fact that in both cases, though in different ways, the dancer's vertical leg is made to seem as if it were carrying a weightless mass. Like the tripod of Smith's sculpture, this vertical leg is metamorphosed, and its one and only role is to present to vision the spectacle of a purely pictorial—no longer material—line. In the *attitude croisée*, this metamorphosis is mainly the harmonic effect of the arms and the raised leg; whereas, in the *arabesque allongée*, the secret of the illusion may be said, rather, to be contained in the extended torso.

In the *attitude*, the raised, turned-out leg inscribes a dynamic plane of space, which reproduces, or translates, and thus enhances, the centrifugally constituted planes inscribed by the two arms, so that the juncture of the torso, the elevated leg, and the vertical leg—a juncture that otherwise would be the center of dramatic energy—becomes, instead, a point on the periphery of a radiant force whose center is suspended above the ground. Thus, the dancer's weight appears to be lifted off the vertical leg (or, more accurately, the weight appears to depart from the leg in a breathtaking instant), producing the illusion that this leg is a pictorial line in a merely optical space. In the *pas de deux* of *Agon*, there is a sustained *adagio*, within which a similar metamorphosis takes place. The male dancer, on his knees, is bending forward and extending his arms upward behind him, while the female dancer executes an *arabesque penchée*, leaning over him from behind and joining her hands to his. This time it is the raised leg, rather than the vertical grounded leg, that creates the optical paradox. The one raised leg, accentuating the trajectory of the two pairs of arms, projects the bodies upward and even seems to lift the dancers off the floor. Thus, the leg steals away the weight of the two floored bodies—it is as if their substance has magically evaporated!—and turns them into a purely abstract structure, itself becoming, within this literally time-less phenomenon, a purely pictorial structural line.

What, now, is the effect of the torso? In the *attitude croisée*, it forms a simple continuation of the line of the vertical leg, so that, in effect, it suppresses one geometric plane and allows itself to appear as an event in only two spatial dimensions—an event in optical space. In the *arabesque allongée*, the torso—visually weightless—certainly touches the vertical leg, but touches without "really" resting upon it. Somewhat as a balloon is connected to its string, the torso seems to float, meeting the leg only to contrive—for a breathtaking interval—an optical, or flat, pictorial symmetry. It is as if the leg/torso juncture were the intersection of two mathematical lines.

And consider the height of the *soubresaut*. This position, too, can prove the modernist possibility—another variation of the optical, or sublime body. The dancer is in a jump-and-fall movement, and this declares her obedience to objecthood; yet, at the same time, the articulation she has imposed on her movement utterly annihilates the body as an object of nature—steals it, I want to say, from tangible space, and then re-creates it, a purer form, in the ether of an optical, vertical field. The arms define the small circular limits of a tilted, but still fairly horizontal plane; while the line from head to feet presents the segment of a very much greater circle, whose approximately vertical plane cuts through the plane of the smaller circle. And we do not reckon these lines, circles, and planes—need I hasten to add?— among the common entities that occupy our tangible universe!

Consider, now the *sus-sous* and the *pirouette à la seconde*. In the first disposition of the body, the dancer's feet are tightly closed and on pointe, and one of the legs hides the other, so that it looks as though the dancer's body is a weightless extension, a mass that somehow is not a mass: the torso and head are not so much a distinct quantity supported by the legs, as they are a qualitative and linear continuation of the legs. In the other example, the dancer moves dramatically from second position *demi-plié* (a disposition of the body that forcefully reveals its weight, its objecthood) into a wondrous turn that seems to suspend this condition. And to these particular figures and modalities of the body, in which the dramatic, tensional possibilities of formalism reside, we should add the great classical leaps, most positions on pointe, and numerous lifts and dives and *portés*, performed in partnering.

My contention is that by means of his choreography (quite subtle, yet daring innovations on the classical syntax), and no less by his choices in costumes and staging, Balanchine has revealed these possibilities in all their lucid beauty, and demonstrated on the stage of history that the modernist illusion is the essence, and even perhaps the perfection, of the classical ballet art.

But, whether or not we hold that the works of Balanchine's modernism represent the perfection of classical ballet, we cannot deny that, in these works, a new mode of spatialization has appeared. That is, we must at least grant that the classical ballet, as a unique art form, has been metamorphosed, in the Hegelian sense of being *aufgehoben*, and that modernist ballets inaugurate a new moment of ballet history. Lincoln Kirstein has divided the history of the spatialization of ballet into two modes: originally, the stage-space was "planimetric" (designed on the flat plane of the floor for the privilege of a bird's-eye view); and subsequently, it became "stereometric" (designed for a frontal spectator's view).[21] This is an accurate history. But modernist ballets oblige us to recognize the emergence of a third mode: I shall call it "optical," for it is akin to the illusionist space of the paintings and sculptures that established modernism. Ballets made according to the older principles of spatialization constitute a field-space which, for the eye of the beholder, always seems to be corporeally accessible. The ballets staged according to the principles of modernism always seem to exist in a forbidden, unearthly field, accessible only to the disembodied eye. Thus we see that the principles of modernism do govern and account for the peculiarities of stage décor and costuming in many of Balanchine's ballets.

From the standpoint of ballet formalism, the presence of color in stage and costume can only be problematic. Balanchine, however, understands the perils of color. (Some of his critics, though, have missed the point of his imperturbably black-and-white logic.) The perils, it may be gathered, are not unlike the ones we have already discussed with respect to modernist painting and sculpture. Unless the colored items (stage décor and costumes, for example) are used with exquisite care; unless they are modalized with great subtlety, they will sacrifice the grace of opticality for the charming diversions of mere "theatre." (I recall, at this point, what Kant had to say, in his *Critique of Judgement*, about the difference between *"Schönheit"* and *"das Reizende."* I do not share, however, the Kantian thesis that the latter is in any way aesthetically inferior; it is simply, I believe, a different sort of art. Likewise, I repudiate Fried's rather Kantian decree that "theatricality" is an aesthetic deficiency, a weakness. I am unable to find any ultimate criteria that would elevate the "formal" above the "theatrical.") Color improperly introduced will simply destroy the formal drama of the body, which charms by means of theatrical illusion—when it is corporeal weight that needs expression; or else it imposes a theatrical presence, a straight-forward corporeal reality—when it is rather the opticality of the sublime suspension of weight that asks to be revealed. So if we allow the possibility of Balanchine's modernism, we must recognize that his color asceticism is a matter of aesthetic principle.

The familiar open stage of the Balanchine production, uncluttered by props and scenery and rather uniformly illumined by a chromatically homogeneous backdrop, is also an aesthetic necessity within the modernist framework.[22] The staging must permit the expressive energies of the dance syntax to condense and disperse as fits. Traditional stage décor, on the contrary, tends either to attract and absorb (into its own reserve of space) such energies as should condense, or else to obstruct the space of energies that should magically disperse and up-lift. In fine, it works by a logic which is independent of the inner imperatives of the dance syntax itself and which, all too easily, can contradict the modernist experience. The chromatically simple backdrop, however, provides a uniform illumination for the dance events. There is no painterly light source to constitute an autonomous surrounding space, possessed of its *own* discriminations and figurative compositions. (You might ponder, here, the lighting of space in Caravaggio and Flemish Renaissance paintings.) Thus, the dance events, instead of being enveloped and partitioned within an *externally* generated (real) space, become the constitutive *source* at the interior of their own total space.

In *Duo Concertant*, a spotlight on the dancers chases away a powerful negative space—darkness—and encloses them in a bright chrysalis that condenses their energies at the same time that it denies the phenomenal space any constructive independence, any aesthetic validity of its own. And if it truly seems that the dancers are dancing into being a space that their bodies occupy exhaustively, it can almost seem, too, that the uncanny causality of this creation is reversible, and the dancers' movements are just the optical inventions of a supervenient luminosity. Such a space—a total, surrounding space, which is truly the invention of the dance movements themselves—will appear as magically dematerialized, optical. It is nothing at all, in effect, since it comes into being only at (and only for) the moment when a human body traverses it. Having in itself neither temporal nor substantial permanence, it can bestow on the feat that traverses and occupies it the sudden grace of eternity.

Such are the necessities of this chosen aesthetic. "Balanchine's formalism!"—Yes, you might wish to say this. But if there is any difference between an artist who produces some formalist ballets and an artist who simply *is* a formalist, then in the art of George Balanchine, we shall find, thank goodness, that his genius soars high above the limits of a *parti pris*.

(1973)

Notes

[1]See André Levinson, "The Spirit of Classic Dance," *Theatre Arts Monthly*, IX/3 (March, 1925), pp. 165–177. Levinson does not fully espouse ballet formalism; but he does wish to repudiate the notion that ballet aesthetics must depend on analogies. Ballet, he asserts, is a distinct and autonomous art form; its aims, principles, and elements cannot be borrowed from the other arts, nor can they be properly interpreted by means of the categories that fit other arts. Rayner Heppenstall, however, was indeed an ardent herald of ballet formalism: "Ballet is not expressive in literary senses. By its nature, it expresses only itself, which is to say, certain general qualities of style." See his *Apology for Dancing* (London, 1936), p. 195. "The dancer," he argues, "must always be concerned, supremely with muscle, not soul, not expression, not literary significance." *Op. cit.*, p. 125. Heppenstall is pleading, clearly, for a formalism in ballet semantics. This is not the same as pleading for a sweeping formalism in syntax. And indeed, he did not warmly welcome the syntactic freedom of modern dance. Ballet must present "the 'significance' of physical movement, in its own right." *Op. cit.*, p. 126. Thus ballet, possessed of its own quite peculiar "expressive functions," must be regarded as altogether distinct from the narrative arts, and especially from theatre. Heppenstall's formalism differs from Clive Bell's more extreme position. For Heppenstall says that, "the whole of life hangs together so completely, and the Dance is so profoundly rooted in the whole of life, that Ballet can be fully understood only by reference to every other order of human activity." *Op. cit.*, p. 147. Compare the foregoing with Bell's chapter called "The Aesthetic Hypothesis" in his *Art* (New York, 1958), pp. 15–34.

[2]I wish to distinguish between the ballets that establish Balanchine's greatness and the ballets that mainly establish the originality of his genius. The latter are those produced in accordance with the principles of formalism, whereas the former certainly include numerous works constructed within the traditional conventions of the art. By no means am I disposed to argue that the formalist ballets, as such, are superior to the traditional ones!

[3]The Harris review, which it is an uncommon pleasure to read in these times of careless reviews, appeared in *Ballet Review*, IV/2 (1972), pp. 25–32.

[4]Just what Fokine wanted to achieve is stated in "Fokine's Theories on the Art of Ballet," in Cyril Beaumont's *Michel Fokine and His Ballets* (London, 1945), pp. 135–152.

[5]See *Apology for Dancing*, p. 51. Note, in this regard, his prophetic statement: "Ballet may well come to dispense with decor altogether, except what the lighting can provide." *Op. cit.*, p. 168.

[6]Balanchine's indebtednesss to Marius Petipa is, of course, well documented. See, for example, Lincoln Kirstein's studies "Balanchine Musagète," in *Theatre Arts* (November, 1947) and "Balanchine and the Classic Revival," *ibid.* (December, 1947). See also Balanchine's own gloss on his *Le Baiser de la Fée* (1928), in *Stravinsky in the Theatre*, edited by Minna Lederman (New York, 1949). I am not saying that Balanchine invented the formalist aesthetic, nor am I claiming that he was the first ballet master to move in the direction of modernism. My point is, rather, that Balanchine was the first to accept it without qualification, and the first to work out the uncompromising demands, the exacting visual logic, of the modernist choice. Balanchine discovered how to accomplish the intentions of modernism.

[7]The precedent for my usage from Jean-Paul Sartre's discussion of perception in *Being and Nothingness* (special, abridged edition, tr. by Hazel Barnes [New York, 1971] and from Maurice Merleau-Ponty's analyses in *Phenomenology of Perception* (tr. by Colin Smith [New York, 1972]) and "Eye and Mind" (in the anthology *The Primacy of Perception* [Evanston, 1964]).

[8]"The New Sculpture" in his *Art and Culture* (Boston, 1961), p. 144. Note Heppenstall's kindred position on the distance between ballet and theatre, *op. cit.*, p. 195.

[9]See "Art and Objecthood," *Artforum* (June, 1967), pp. 12–23.

[10]See "Fokine's Theories on the Art of Ballet," *op. cit.*

[11]*Op. cit.*, p. 25.

[12]*Dance Magazine* (August, 1972), p. 32. In this respect, Balanchine's method resembles the reductive, sparse methods of such film directors as Yasujiro Ozu and Robert Bresson. In *Late Autumn* and *An Autumn Afternoon*, for example, Ozu's method evokes that emptiness, that silence, that serenity, which, in Zen, is called *mu*. (See Donald Richie, "The Later Films of Yasujiro Ozu," *Film Quarterly*, 13 [Fall, 1959], p. 22.) Bresson's method seeks in the visibility of the icon the invisible touch of supernatural grace. Both methods require that the actors sublimate the natural expressiveness of personality, and that they learn, in effect, how to eliminate the drama of acting. Bresson states: "It is not so much a question of doing 'nothing,' as some people have said. It is rather a question of performing without being aware of oneself, of not controlling oneself. Experience has proved to me that when I was the most 'automatic' in my work, I was the most moving [and expressive]." See James Blue, *Excerpts from an Interview with Robert Bresson* (Los Angeles, 1969). See also Roland Monod, "Working with Bresson," *Sight and Sound*, 26 (Summer, 1957), p. 31. Bresson's theory of acting, like Ozu's, is: "For-

get about tone and meaning. Don't think about what you're saying; just speak the words automatically. When someone talks, he isn't thinking about the words he uses, or even about what he wants to say. Only concerned with what he is saying, he just lets the words come out. . . ." Balanchine certainly seems to have given analogous instructions to his dancers. Consider, further, Selma Jeanne Cohen's study, "Antony Tudor. Part Two: The Years in America and After," *Dance Perspectives* 18 (1963). Lucia Chase is quoted as saying: "Tudor does not explain the feeling he wants; he shows emotion by motion, by demonstrating the movement. You have to sense the meaning from him; to find out what he is after, you have to keep doing the movement until you feel it." (p. 73) Thus, the dancer, 'as character,' may contribute movement ideas to Tudor choreography. But as a dancer he is never allowed to 'interpret' a movement. Margaret Black says: "In Tudor's choreography, you never have to superimpose feeling. You don't have to make the movement speak; it does." And Diana Adams elaborates: "Tudor does not want interpretation; he wants simplicity of execution. . . . The movement in itself should suffice, without interpretation being added on to it." (pp. 75–75) But Tudor's approach to dance movement, while technically similar, in some measure, to Balanchine's, has a very different intention behind it. Balanchine's aim is to articulate the maximum degree of sensuousness in form; Tudor's is, rather, to release that maximum of dramatic energy which is contained in the tension between the visible expression of the psyche and its invisible ground.

[13]Vladimir Nabokov, *Ada* (New York, 1969), p. 38.

[14]*Op. cit.*, pp. 376–378.

[15]For my analysis of the horizontal field of poise and the vertical field of grace, I am greatly indebted to my colleague, Samuel J. Todes. See his "Comparative Phenomenology of Perception and Imagination," Parts I and II, *Journal of Existentialism* (Spring and Fall, 1966). It is an exciting fact, though, that Curt Sachs had described the horizontal/vertical axes of dance many years earlier in his *World History of the Dance* (New York, 1937), pp. 25–26.

[16]For a distinction similar to that between the mimetic and the formal, and for a parallel analysis of their respective illusions, see Sachs, *op. cit.*, p. 60 and *passim*. He distinguishes the "image dance" and the "imageless dance." In the first, the dancer, as he correctly observes, seems "bound to the body," whereas in the second, the dancer appears to be "free of the body." This is akin to saying that mimetic dance mainly exhibits qualities of poise, while formal dance is especially suited to the showing of grace.

[17]Quoted by Sachs, *op. cit.*, p. 4. Note that, according to Christianity, the body upon which grace is bestowed becomes "the temple of the Holy" (1 Cor. 6:19).

[18]And ultimately, something should be said, too, about music, since it is in this medium that temporality is most immediately constituted in its sensuous aspect. In his piece on Igor Stravinsky (*Ballet Review*, III/6),

Dale Harris writes: "The reduced importance of extrinsic forms of expressiveness, the parallel emphasis on structure, the identification of subject with form—these Stravinskian qualities have been the chief influences upon ballet in our time." (p. 6) I would like to add that it is these same qualities (which plainly constitute a formalism within the possibilities of the medium of music) that explain, in part, the many successes Balanchine has had in setting his ballets on Stravinsky scores. The formalism of the one complements and heightens the formalism of the other.

Balanchine's *Concerto Barocco*, first performed in 1941, is, in some respects, a modernist ballet. But in two respects it remains mimetic: First, the movement of individual dancers and of partners often provides intimations of the aristocratic manners which were appropriate to Bach's time. Second—and more importantly—the patterns of the dancers in their larger groupings often translate abstract musical space into an aesthetically equivalent corporeal stage-space. Chords, for example, and counterpoint, inversions, and discrete melodic phrases, as well as figures of musical time, or rhythm, have their unique counterparts in both the floor-plane and the frontal spatializations of the dance-groupings.

[19]*Ballet Review*, II/5, p. 5. Denby seems close to pointing out how a choreographer can get theatrical meaningfulness *entirely within a formal time-framework*, simply by means of a sudden modification in tempo (see p.6). For me, one of the most memorable instances of this intention—an instance which also involves an unexpected break in the formal space constructions—occurs in Frederick Ashton's *Enigma Variations* (1968). There is a moment in the "Nimrod" variation when Elgar breaks through the formal space of *arabesques* and *pas de basques*, hesitates, and then moves toward his friend in a delicate demonstration of affection. This sudden shift in tempo, which is not only a shift from formal to real time, but also a moment when the formal space of ballet has yielded to the natural expressive space of sentiment, creates a spectacle of exquisite tenderness and beauty.

[20]See Rosalind E. Krauss, *Terminal Iron Works: The Sculpture of David Smith* (Cambridge, 1971).

[21]*Movement and Metaphor*, (New York, 1970), pp. 10–11. Kirstein's terms are anticipated by those of André Levinson, who distinguishes a "horizontal" choreographing of the dance, "based on outlines and figures marked by the feet of the dancer on the floor" from the later "vertical" choreographing, "the [frontal] configuration of motion in space." *Op. cit.*, pp. 170–171.

[22]In the June 25, 1973, issue of *New York,* Alan Rich asseverates that "the principal reason the City Ballet is losing touch with its audience is that it has been allowed to become a vast blank wall on which Balanchine sketches his infinite variations on a single theme." And, while admitting that there are very "subtle" differences, which make each of his ballets unique, Rich contends that "too many Balanchine ballets look alike." Just how blind can a ballet critic afford to be? To know the con-

summate Hollywood-style showmanship of which Balanchine is capable, one has only to see his *Stars and Stripes* (1958). In the light of such proven genius for the dazzling ballet spectacle, Mr. Rich should have asked himself what aesthetic grounds there could be to explain why Balanchine did not choose simply to multiply the number of such spectacles.

FRANK KERMODE
POET AND DANCER
BEFORE DIAGHILEV

Diaghilev figures in the title simply as a terminus; he arrived in Paris in 1909, and everybody knows what happened. *"Le rêve de Mallarmé se réalise,"* said Ghéon. What dream of Mallarmé? That which found a true theatrical sonority, a stage liberated from cardboard falsities; which emerged from a confluence of the other arts and yet remained, as Wagner did not, theatre. The Ballets Russes demonstrated the correspondence of the arts so wonderfully that in comparison Wagner's effort was, said Camille Mauclair, *"une gaucherie barbare."* Diaghilev arrived, not a moment too soon, in response to prayers from both sides of the Channel. One could trace the developments in taste which prepared his reception—not only in the limited sphere of the dance but in writings on actors (the cult of Duse, for example), in the fashionable admiration for oriental art and theatre, in *avant-garde* agitation for theatrical reform. In March 1908 *The Mask,* a quarterly dedicated to this end and strongly under the influence of Gordon Craig, prayed in its opening editorial for a religion that did not "rest upon knowledge nor rely upon the World" but rather brought together "Music, Architecture, and Movement" to heal "the Evil ... which has separated these three Arts and which leaves the world without a belief." The editor can hardly have expected his prayers to be answered so soon—not precisely by the theatrical reforms he had in mind, but by the Russian dancers, prophets of that Concord and Renaissance he so earnestly requested. Havelock Ellis, with his usual wide view, put the situation thus in *The Dance of Life* (1923): "If it is significant that Descartes appeared a few years after the death of Malherbe, it is equally significant that Einstein was immediately preceded by the Russian Ballet."

Ellis makes Diaghilev a John the Baptist of a "classico-mathematical Renaissance," and the notion that this was a renaissance of some kind or other was evidently in the air. However, such credit as is due to its heralds should not all be awarded to the Russian ballet. There was, obviously, Isadora Duncan; but Isadora doesn't take us to the root of the matter. Where, for my purposes, that lies, I can perhaps suggest in this way: what Camille Mauclair said of Diaghilev was somewhat disloyally said, for he had used almost the same words years before of the American dancer Loïe Fuller. Art, he declared, was one homogeneous essence lying at the root of the diversified arts, not a fusion of them; and Loïe Fuller was *it*, "a spectacle . . . which defies all definition . . . Art, nameless, radiant . . . a homogeneous and complete place . . . indefinable, absolute . . . a fire above all dogmas." The language is Mallarméan; as we shall see, it was all but impossible to write of Loïe Fuller otherwise unless you were very naïve. Still, not even Mallarmé could start a renaissance single-handed, and there has to be a word or two here about whatever it was that predisposed everybody to get excited in this particular way about dancers.

The peculiar prestige of dancing over the past seventy or eighty years has, I think, much to do with the notion that it somehow represents art in an undissociated and unspecialized form—a notion made explicit by Yeats and hinted at by Valéry. The notion is essentially primitivist; it depends upon the assumption that mind and body, form and matter, image and discourse have undergone a process of dissociation, which it is the business of art momentarily to mend. Consequently dancing is credited with a sacred priority over the other arts, as by Havelock Ellis (whose essay is valuable as a summary of the theoretical development I am now discussing) and, with less rhapsody and more philosophy, by Mrs. Langer in the twelfth chapter of *Feeling and Form* and (more flatly) in the opening essay of *Problems of Art*. In view of this primitivizing, it is worth remembering that the increase of prestige was contemporaneous with a major effort by anthropologists, liturgiologists, and folklorists to discover the roots of the dance in ritual of all kinds, and also with the development of a certain medical interest in dancing. We are all familiar with the interest shown by the generation of Valéry and that of Eliot in these matters; and from Eliot, at the time when he was busy with Jane Harrison and Frazer we can get some notion of how they struck the literary imagination. Here, for instance, is a passage from an uncollected *Criterion* review of two books on dancing:

> Anyone who would contribute to our imagination of what the ballet may perform in future . . . should begin by a close study of dancing among primitive peoples. . . . He should also have studied the evolution of Christian and other liturgy. For is not the High Mass—as performed, for instance, at the Madeleine in Paris—one of the highest developments of dancing? And finally, he should track down the secrets of rhythm in the still undeveloped science of neurology.

Mr. Eliot found the Noh plays exciting and praised Massine for providing in the ignorant modern theatre that rhythm regarded as essential by Aristotle. But the peculiar modern view could hardly have been developed before dancing became an accredited fine art; and the date for this seems to be 1746, when Batteux included it among the five with music, poetry, painting, and sculpture. The general and developing Romantic tendency was to give music pre-eminence as being non-discursive, "autonomous" as the word now is, referring to nothing outside itself for meaning; poems would be like that if there were not a basic flaw in their medium, the habit that words have of meaning something in ordinary usage. But some of this prestige was undoubtedly captured by dancing; it is more "natural" and more "primitive" than music, more obviously expressive of what Mrs. Langer calls "patterns of sentience" and "the mythic consciousness." I use this late terminology because it is careful enough to avoid certain radical confusions. The dance, though expressive, is impersonal, like a Symbolist poem that comes off. Miss Deirdre Pridden[1] finds the proper word to be Ortega y Gasset's "dehumanization"; the dancer *"vide la danse, autant que faire se peut, de son humaine matière."* Something might here be said about organicist theories of expressiveness in Modern Dance, opposed not only to conventional ballet (as Fuller and Duncan and Yeats were) but sometimes even to the use of music as irrelevant to the *Gestalt* of the dance; the source of these theories is Delsarte, but they have been much refined. However, there is no disagreement from the fundamental principle that dance is the most primitive, non-discursive art, offering a pre-scientific image of life, an intuitive truth. Thus it is the emblem of the Romantic image. Dance belongs to a period before the self and the world were divided, and so achieves naturally that "original unity" which, according to Barfield for instance, modern poetry can produce only by a great and exhausting effort of fusion.

The nineties poets wrote endlessly about dancers, welcomed foreign troupes and prepared the way for the serious impact of the Japanese Noh in the next decade.[2] But they also enjoyed the dancers themselves, and regularly fell in love with them. Symons and his friends would meet the Alhambra girls after the show and take them along to the Crown for drink and serious talk; serious not because of what Symons called the "learned fury" of these "maenads of the decadence," but in a humbler way. This was the epoch of the Church and Stage Guild, Stewart Headlam's club for clergy and actors. Headlam believed "in the Mass, the Ballet, and the Single Tax" and such was his balletolatry that he wrote a book on ballet technique. But he also believed that the liturgy must not continue to be deprived of dancing, and so laboured to make the stage respectable, that the stigma on dancing might be removed. Among the membership girls from the Empire and the Alhambra preponderated. Headlam was not original in his liturgical views, which may have gained currency from Anglo-Catholic propaganda for ceremonies not explicitly forbidden;[3] however, he gives one a pretty good idea of what must have been a common enough belief in this passage from an article he contributed to his own *Church Reformer* (October 1884) in a series on the Catechism:

> ... to take an illustration from the art of dancing, which perhaps more than all other arts is an outward and visible sign of an inward and spiritual grace, ordained by the Word of God Himself, as a means whereby we receive the same and a pledge to assure us thereof; and which has suffered even more than the other arts from the utter antisacramentalism of British philistia. Your Manichean Protestant, and your superfine rationalist, reject the Dance as worldly, frivolous, sensual, and so forth; and your dull, stupid Sensualist sees legs, and grunts with some satisfaction: but your Sacramentalist knows something worth more than both of these. He knows what perhaps the dancer herself may be partially unconscious of, that we live now by faith and not by sight, and that the poetry of dance is the expression of unseen spiritual grace. "She all her being flings into the dance." "None dare interpret all her limbs express." These are the words of a genuine sacramentalist ...

The poet is T. Gordon Hake. Headlam knew Symons well, and also Yeats and many other nineties poets and painters. He seems, in his Guild and in writing of this kind, to reflect rather accurately the liturgical, poetic, and music-hall aspects of this renaissance of dancing. The liturgical ingredient developed luxuriously in the border country of Anglo-Catholicism; witness R. H. Benson's essay, "On the Dance as a Religious Exercise," an account of the Mass as a dramatic dance:

> The Catholic . . . is not ashamed to take his place with the worshippers of Isis and Cybele, with King David, and with the naked Fijean, and to dance with all his might before the Lord.

The antiquarian interest culminated in G. R. S. Mead's *The Sacred Dance of Jesus* (published in *The Quest* in 1910, but long excogitated.) This was Havelock Ellis's chief source, and it is a work of great and curious learning, written in a long tradition of attempts to explain Matt. xi. 1.7, "We have piped unto you and ye have not danced." Mead was most interested in the second-century *Hymn of Jesus,* but he deals with the Fathers and with medieval church dancing, with the liturgies of the Greek Orthodox and Armenian churches, and so forth. I doubt if Mead is taken very seriously by modern historians—he isn't cited in the large bibliography of Backman's *Religious Dances* (1952)—but for a while he mattered a lot. Yeats, for example, went to his lectures. He was by no means the only zealous dance-historian of the time. Toulouse-Lautrec, who was not interested in these matters, had an English *savant* thrown out of a dance-hall for plaguing him about antiquity; this could have been Mead, but not necessarily. At a time when it was relatively easy for a dancer to acquire a reputation for learning, Loïe Fuller was said on high authority (Anatole France) to be wise in the history of dancing; she took as her prototype Miriam, who, according to Philo, as quoted by Mead, symbolizes perfect sense, as Moses symbolizes perfect mind.

The presence of the *savant* in the *bal* tells us something about the seriousness with which music-hall dancing was taken on both sides of the Channel. From Symons and Goncourt one knows that it was so; and of course this was a period of close relations between London and Paris. Yvette Guilbert often appeared in London, Marie Lloyd and others in Paris; it was fashionable to treat them both as very great artists. This cult of music-hall has been persistent; there is a classic statement of it in Mr. Eliot's essay on Marie Lloyd (1932), and it still goes on in a London which has only one or two feeble surviving halls, constantly threatened with demolition. Nothing distresses some

English intellectuals more than the closing of a music-hall. This attitude is a weakly descendant of a positive *avant-garde* reaction against commercial theatre in the nineties; failing dance-drama or über-marionettes, there were still Marie Lloyd and Little Tich, defying cultural and social division, freely satirical, speaking with the voice of the belly. You could talk of Yvette Guilbert, who, according to André Raffalovitch, sang "the sufferings of those the world calls vile," in the same breath as the Duse.

The Parisian music-halls were certainly not short of a similar intellectual *réclame*, and had their place, as part of the metropolitan experience, with all the other pleasures devised for an élite that took its pleasures seriously—fine clothes, Japanese prints, neurasthenia. They are as important in the early history of modern art as folk-music and primitive painting, with which indeed they are obviously associated. Our received idea of this world owes more to Toulouse-Lautrec than anybody else, and there is no reason to think it very inaccurate. The circus, the vaudeville, the *bal*, were serious pleasures; the primitive, the ugly, the exotic were in demand. The brutal patter of Aristide Bruant, La Goulue coarsely cheeking the Prince of Wales, the emaciated and psychopathic May Belfort, the cherished ugliness of Mme Abdala; all are characteristic. The mood is that of the violent Lautrec drawings of Guilbert and Jane Avril, of dancers calling themselves Grille d'Egout or La Goulue, of café-concerts with such names as Le Divan Japonais and prostitutes with such *noms de guerre* as Outamoro. In this atmosphere all the dancers I am concerned with did their work, and were treated very seriously.

Of a good many of them it was enough to say, as Symons did in his excited lines on Nini Patte-en-l'air, that they possessed

> The art of knowing how to be
> Part lewd, aesthetical in part
> And *fin-de-siècle* essentially.

Symons was one of those Englishmen whose solemn Parisian pleasures were the admiration of Lautrec—Conder, the strangest of them, he often drew, superbly drunk in his fine evening clothes. But Symons was building an aesthetic in which dancing was to have a central place—the climactic essay is called "The World As Ballet"—and so his interest was slightly different from the painter's. Lautrec was equally absorbed by La Goulue and Jane Avril; but for Symons the former, a Messalina who wore her heart embroidered on the bottom of her knickers, was less important than the latter, who demonstrated that the female

Loïe Fuller, radically transforming her shape by manipulating the fabric of her costume with long sticks. " . . . the woman who seemed to be doing almost single-handed what Diaghilev was later to achieve with the help of great painters, musicians, and dancers." (Kermode)

body was "Earth's most eloquent Music, divinest human harmony."

Some time in the thirties a French exhibition, devoted to life under the Third Republic, showed Jane Avril and Loïe Fuller as representing the Dance. . . . Isadora Duncan was a "symbolist" dancer; but it is sometimes forgotten that she derived much that was admirable in her dancing from Loïe Fuller, and this brings me to the most important of all these names, to the woman who seemed to be doing almost single-handed what Diaghilev was later to achieve only with the help of great painters, musicians, and dancers. . . . Consider, for example, the "Fire Dance," a popular item from early days. She told the credulous Mr. Tindall of *Pearson's Weekly* that this dance had its origin in an accident: when she was dancing her Salome at the Athénée (1893) she danced before Herod as "the setting sun kissed the top of Solomon's temple." But it also kissed her garments, and the public, always vocal, cried out and called it "the fire-dance." In fact this was merely another attempt to offset the cold electric calculations of Fuller. The *Danse de Feu* was lit from below stage, by a red lantern directed through a glassed-in trap. The effect was striking *(Pearson's Weekly* has some lurid coloured photographs). Fuller appeared to the music of the "Ride of the Valkyries," shaking, we are told, and twisting in a torrent of incandescent lava, her long dress spouting flame and rolling around in burning spirals. She stood, says Jean Lorrain, in blazing embers, *and did not burn;* she exuded light, was herself a flame. Erect in her brazier she smiled, and her smile was the rictus of a mask under the red veil that enveloped her and which shook and waved like a flame along her lava-nakedness. Lorrain goes on to compare her with Herculaneum buried in cinders (it wasn't, of course), the Styx and its banks, Vesuvius with open throat spitting fire. Only thus, he argued, could one describe her motionless, smiling nakedness in the midst of a furnace, wearing the fires of heaven and hell as a veil. Gustave Fréville called her a nightmare sculpted in red clay. "The fire caresses her dress, seizes her entirely, and, inexorable lover, is sated by nothing short of nothingness." Years later Yeats was pretty certainly remembering this dance as well as Dante and a Noh play when he spoke in his "Byzantium" of the dance as an emblem of art, caught up out of nature into the endless artifice of his Byzantium, the endless death-in-life of the mosaic:

> . . . blood-begotten spirits come
> And all complexities of fury leave;
> Dying into a dance
> An agony of trance,
> An agony of flame that cannot singe a sleeve.

The "Fire Dance" had all the qualities Yeats asked of the art, for not only was the dancer unconsumed, but she also wore the obligatory enigmatic smile. "From his flame which does not burn," says Ménil in his *Histoire de la Dance* (1904), "there leaps, between two volutes of light, the head of a woman wearing an enigmatic smile." Ménil, as it happens, goes on—as Jourdain did—to question whether all this trickery of silk and electric light was really dancing at all, and he wonders how, from the vulgarity of the cheap glare and waving skirt, there could come this hashish-like experience. Goncourt's reaction was similar: "What a great inventor of ideality man is!" he moralized, contemplating this "vision of what is strange and supernatural" yet has its origin in common stuff and vulgar lights.

Other dances were greeted with equal rapture. Georges Rodenbach draws widely on Fuller's repertoire in his poem "La Loïe Fuller," first published in *Figaro* in May 1896, and warmly praised by Mallarmé. It has fifty-eight lines, and is too long to quote in full, but here are some samples:

> *Déchirant l'ombre, et brusque, elle est là: c'est l'aurore!*
> *D'un mauve de prélude enflé jusqu'au lilas,*
> *S'étant taillé des nuages en falbalas,*
> *Elle se décolore, elle se recolore.*
> *Alors c'est le miracle opéré comme un jeu:*
> *Sa robe tout à coup est un pays de brume;*
> *C'est de l'alcool qui flambe et de l'encens qui fume;*
> *Sa robe est un bûcher de lys qui sont en feu. . . .*
>
> *Or, comme le volcan contient toutes ses laves,*
> *Il semble que ce soit d'elle qu'elle ait déduit*
> *Ces rivières de feu qui la suivent, esclaves,*
> *Onduleuses, sur elle, en forme de serpents . . .*
> *O tronc de la Tentation! O charmeresse!*
> *Arbre du Paradis où nos désirs rampants*
> *S'enlacent en serpents de couleurs qu'elle tress! . . .*
>
> *Un repos.*
>   *Elle vient, les cheveux d'un vert roux*
> *Influencés par ces nuances en démence;*
> *On dirait que le vent du large recommence;*
> *Car déjà, parmi les étoffes en remous,*
> *Son corps perd son sillage; il fond en des volutes . . .*
> *Propice obscurité, qu'est-ce donc que tu blutes*
> *Pour faire de sa robe un océan de feu,*
> *Toute phosphorescente avec des pierreries? . . .*
> *Brunehilde, c'est toi, reine des Walkyries,*
> *Dont pour être l'élu chacun se rêve un dieu. . . .*
>
> *C'est fini.*
>   *Brusquement l'air est cicatrisé*
> *De cette plaie en fleur dont il saigna. L'étreinte*
> *De l'Infini ne nous dure qu'un court moment;*
> *Et l'ombre de la scène où la fresque fut peinte*
> *Est noire comme notre âme, pensivement.*

What Mallarmé liked about this was the recognition that Roden-bach restores to dancing its ancient character—it provides its own décor *(elle s'étoffe)*. For Fuller's "imaginative weavings are poured forth like an atmosphere" in contrast with the short-skirted coryphées of the ballet, who have no *ambiance* save what the orchestra provides.

Everything conspires to bring Fuller's performance into the position of an emblem of the Image of art, "self-begotten" in Yeats's favourite word; or like the body of a woman yet not in any natural sense alive *(prodige d'irréel)*, enigmatic, having the power of election. The darkness of the stage at the end of the performance is the natural darkness of the modern soul which only the Image, hardly come by and evanescent, can illuminate: "the embrace of eternity lasts us only a short moment." This power of fusing body and soul, mending all our division, is celebrated even in *Pearson's Weekly*. More completely than any other dancer before her, Loïe Fuller seemed to represent in visible form the incomprehensible Image of art in the modern world,[4] as Mauclair said: "The Symbol of Art itself, a fire above all dogmas." And she remains the dancer of Symbolism, from Mallarmé to Yeats; a woman yet totally impersonal, "dead, yet flesh and bone"; *poème dégagé de tout appareil du scribe.* "Thanks to her," said Roger Marx, "the dance has once more become the 'poem without words' of Simonides . . . above all one is grateful to her for giving substance to that ideal spectacle of which Mallarmé once dreamed—a mute spectacle, which escaped the limits of space and time alike, and of which the influence, powerful over all, ravishes in one common ecstasy the proud and the humble."

In February 1893, Mallarmé went to the Folies-Bergère to see Loïe Fuller. It was an historic evening. André Levinson, complaining in the early twenties of the exaggerated deference paid in literary circles to the music-hall, credits the Goncourts and Huysmans with beginning the vogue, but goes on: "One day Stéphane Mallarmé, aesthetician of the absolute, was seen pencilling, in his seat at the Folies Bergère, his luminous *aperçus* on the so-called serpentine dances of Loïe Fuller, *fontaine intarissable d'elle-même*. Since then the whole world has followed . . ." What Mallarmé was writing emerges as a passage of prose notably difficult even for him, but the centre, indeed the source in most cases, of contemporary poetic comment on Fuller. Concerning her, he says, and the way in which she uses the fabrics in which she is dressed, the articles of contemporary enthusiasts—which may sometimes be called poems—leave little to be said. "Her performance, *sui generis,* is at once an artistic intoxication and an industrial achievement. In that terrible bath of materials swoons the radiant, cold dancer, illustrating countless themes of gyration. From her proceeds an expanding web—giant butterflies and petals, unfoldings—everything of a pure and elemental order. She blends with the rapidly changing colours which vary their limelit phantasmagoria of twilight and grotto, their rapid emotional changes—delight, mourning, anger; and to set these off, prismatic, either violent or dilute as they are, there must be the dizziness of soul made visible by an artifice." He goes on to suggest that in this kind of dancing, in which the dancer seems to have the power infinitely to expand the dance through her dress, there is a lesson for the theatre, in which there is always a banality that rises up between dance and spectator. Loïe Fuller makes one see how the subtleties inherent in the dance have been neglected. "Some restored aesthetic," says Mallarmé, "will one day go beyond these marginal notes"; but he can at least use this insight to denounce a common error concerning staging, "helped as I unexpectedly am by the solution unfolded for me in the mere flutter of her gown by my unconscious and unwitting inspirer." And he speaks of the dancer's power to create on the boards of the stage her own previously unthought-of milieu. The *décor* lies latent in the orchestra, to come forth like a lightning stroke at the sight of the dancer who represents the idea. And this "transition from sonorities to materials . . . is the one and only skill of Loïe Fuller, who does it by instinct, exaggeratedly, the movements of skirt or wing instituting a place. . . . The enchantress makes the ambience, produces it from herself and retracts it into a silence rustling with *crêpe de Chine.* Presently there will disappear, what is in these circumstances an inanity, that traditional plantation of permanent sets which conflict with choreographic mobility. Opaque frames, intrusive cardboard, to the scrap-heap! Here, if ever, is atmosphere, that is nothingness, given back to ballet, visions no sooner known than scattered, limpid evocation. The pure result will be a liberated stage, at the will of fictions, emanating from the play of a veil with attitude or gesture." He sees the dance of Fuller as "multiple emanations round a nakedness" which is central, "summed up by an act of will ecstatically stretched to the extremity of each wing, her statuesque figure strict, upright; made dead by the effort of condensing out of this virtual self-liberation delayed decorative leaps of skies and seas, evenings, scent and foam." And he concludes, "I thought it necessary, whatever fashion may make of this miraculous contemporary development, to extract its summary sense and its significance for the art as a whole."

There is dispute among students of Mallarmé as to the place of dancing in his unsystematic system, and less attention than might be expected is paid to this tribute to Loïe Fuller. But there seems to be no very good reason for discounting what it says: that she represented for him at least the spirit of an unborn aesthetic; that she offered a kind of spatial equivalent of music; that she stands for the victory of what he called the Constellation over what he called Chance, *"le couronnement du labeur humain,"* as Bonniet describes it in his Preface to *Igitur*. Like the archetype of Art, the Book, Fuller eliminated *hasard*. Thibaudet, indeed, believed that the whole concept of the Book owed something to Mallarmé's meditations on the dance; so did Levinson, arguing that Mallarmé glimpsed in the ballet "a revelation of the definitive *Œuvre*, which would sum up and transcend man"; so, more recently, does M. Guy Delfel. The fitness of the dance as an emblem of true poetry is clear. Valéry was expanding the views of Mallarmé when he made his famous comparison between them (poetry is to prose as dancing is to walking). Mallarmé's growing concern for syntax, so irrefutably demonstrated by L. J. Austin, does not militate against this view that the dance took over in his mind some of the importance of music; for syntax is the purposeful movement of language and such movement has, in either art, to be assimilated to the necessarily autonomous condition of the Image. The dance is more perfectly devoid of ideas, less hampered by its means, than poetry, since it has not the strong antipathy of language towards illogic; yet it is not absolutely pure; the dancer is not inhuman. Mallarmé deals with precisely this point in the opening article of *Crayonné au Théâtre* (before 1887) when he discusses the ambiguous position of the dancer, half impersonal; very like the position of the poet ("The pure work requires that the poet vanish from the utterance" in so far as he can). But Fuller was more purely emptied of personality: an apparition, a vision of eternity for Rodenbach; for Mallarmé "l'incorporation visuelle de l'idée."

If it seemed necessary, as it did, for poets to reclaim their heritage from music, the dance provided something more exactly fitting as an emblem of what was aspired to; and in a sense Fuller can stand for the liberation of Symbolism from Wagner. She is much more properly the Symbolist dancer than any orthodox ballerina; and there is a clear discontinuity between the general

admiration for dancers of French poets earlier than Mallarmé
and his praise of Fuller. In Baudelaire the "human and palpable
element" counts for much; in Gautier also. But in the new age,
the age of Mallarmé and Yeats, what matters is that the dancer
"is not a woman"; that she is "dead, yet flesh and bone." The
difference constitutes a shift in the whole climate of poetry, represented by the shift in English poetic from Symons to Pound,
from Symbolism as primarily an elaborate system of suggestion,
of naming by not naming, to the dynamism of the Vortex and
the Ideogram. For Fuller is a kind of Ideogram: *l'incorporation
visuelle de l'idée,* a spectacle defying all definition, radiant,
homogeneous.

Such, at any rate, was the way those people saw Fuller who
saw her with eyes opened to dance as a *majestueuse ouverture* on
a reality beyond flux. They saw in her *"la voyante de l'infini."*
When Diaghilev came, defying the *genres,* overwhelming the
senses with music and colour and movement, one or two people
perhaps remembered her as having been the first to do it. I am
convinced that Valéry did. Again and again he returns to the
dance as a satisfactory emblem of a desirable poetry. It best illustrates what he calls non-usage—"the *not* saying 'it is raining'—
this is the language of poetry; and movement which is not
instrumental, having no end outside itself, is the language of
dancing. Poetry, like dancing, is action without an end." As the
dancer makes an image of art out of the quotidian motions of her
body, so the poet must "draw a pure, ideal Voice, capable of communicating without weakness, without apparent effort, without
offence to the ear, and without breaking the ephemeral sphere
of the poetic universe, an idea of some Self miraculously superior
to Myself." The Dance makes of an activity of the body—sweat,
straining muscle, heaving chest—an idea, a diagram of a high
reality. Valéry called his dialogue, *L'Ame et la Danse,* of 1921, "a
sort of ballet of which the Image and the Idea are Coryphaeus in
turn." The dialogue embodies in language of refined wit and
gaudy elegance the essence of our post-Wagnerian aesthetic.
Athiktè, the central figure, is usually thought of as a conventional ballet-dancer; and she does dance on her points. But, as
Levinson said in his pamphlet on the dialogue *(Paul Valéry, poète
de la danse, 1927)* the *tourbillon,* her ecstatic finale, is not merely a
ballet step, it is the whirling of a mystic's dance. Though Valéry
collected ballet photographs, they were of a special sort, *chrono-
photographies;* the plates were exposed in darkness, the dancers
carrying lights; and the result was a whirl of white lines, a record

of the pattern of aimless poetical acts. In any case, we need not suppose him so devoted to the ballet as to have forgotten Loïe Fuller. He was on the point of refusing the invitation to write the dance dialogue because he "considered . . . that Mallarmé had exhausted the subject" and undertook it finally with the resolve that he would make Mallarmé's prodigious writings on the subject "a peculiar condition of my work." So I believe that when he came to write the passage comparing the dancer with a salamander—living "completely at ease, in an element comparable to fire"—he was remembering Fuller. The passage culminates in a long, rhapsodical speech from Socrates: "what is a flame . . . if not *the moment itself?* . . . Flame is the act of that moment which is between earth and heaven . . . the flame sings wildly between matter and ether . . . we can no longer speak of movement . . . nor distinguish any longer its acts from its limbs." Phaedrus replies that "she flings her gestures like scintillations . . . she filches impossible attitudes, even under the very eye of Time!" Eryximachus sums it up: "Instant engenders form, and form makes the instant visible." And when the dancer speaks, she says she is neither dead nor alive, and ends: "Refuge, refuge, O my refuge, O Whirlwind! I was in thee, O movement—outside all things . . ." A Bergsonian dancer almost, "*révélatrice du réel*" as Levinson says.

The propriety of yoking together Avril and Fuller as I have done here is now, perhaps, self-evident. Avril is a smaller figure altogether, but she demonstrates the strength of the link between dancing and poetry, as well as the important pathological element in the dancer's appeal. Fuller deserves, one would have thought, some of the attention that has gone to Isadora. Levinson who repeatedly declares his faith in classical dancing as the one discipline "*féconde, complète, créatrice*," respected Fuller, but despised Duncan as having no technique, no beauty, no suppleness, her feet flattened and enlarged by years of barefoot prancing, her music primitive. The fact is that Duncan was much more the Tanagra figurine, the dancer from the Pompeian fresco, than Fuller, who earned these descriptions in her early days. And Duncan certainly did not submerge her personality in strange disguises and unnatural lights. The Modern Dance has developed theories sufficiently impersonal to make it intensely interesting to Mrs. Langer, creating a symbolic reality independent of nature. But it depends always upon the body—upon the power of the body not to express emotion but to objectify a pattern of sentience. Fuller with her long sticks, her strange optical devices, her burying the human figure in masses of silk, achieved impersonality at a stroke. Her world was discontinuous from nature; and this discontinuity Valéry, speaking of his Symbolist ancestry, described as "an almost inhuman state." She withdrew from the work; if to do otherwise is human, said Valéry, "I must declare myself essentially inhuman."

This is the doctrine of impersonality in art with which T. E. Hulme and T. S. Eliot among many others have made everybody familiar. "The progress of an artist is a continual self-sacrifice, a continual extinction of personality . . . the more perfect the artist the more completely separate in him will be the man who suffers and the mind which creates." Thomas Parkinson, commenting on Ortega y Gasset's "dehumanization"—"a point can be reached in which the human content has grown so thin that it is negligible"—remarks acutely that the confused reception accorded to Pound's *Pisan Cantos* was due to critical shock at their identification of the sufferer and the creator. Pound, in leaving off his "ironic covering," simply broke with a rule of poetic that he himself had done much to enforce. Mr. Parkinson is glad; he wants to let "the Reek of Humanity" back into poetry, where he thinks it belongs, and he seems to regard the impersonality doctrine as a lengthy but temporary deviation from some true "romantic aesthetic." I am not sure that he is right, or how far he misunderstands the human relevance of what the impersonal artist attempts. Mrs. Langer could answer him, and I am quite sure that there Pound does not show the way back to reeking humanity. In Mr. Eliot, in Valéry, we surely are aware of what Stevens called "the thing that is incessantly overlooked: the artist, the presence of the determining personality."

However this may be, Fuller's progressive extinction of the dancing body was a necessary component of her success as an emblem of the Image, out of nature. The imagination of the spectator fed upon her, independently of what she intended (she once caught sight of herself in a glass when dancing, and was surprised that what she saw bore no relation to her intention). She is abstract, clear of the human mess, dead and yet perfect being, as on some Byzantine dancing floor; entirely independent of normal action, out of time. It is a highflown way of talking about an affected music-hall dancer with an interest in stage-lighting; and, but for the example of Mallarmé, we should hardly venture it. Yet she was not a mere freak; dancers are always striving to become, like poems, machines for producing poetic states; "they labour daily," as Levinson says, "to prevent a relapse into their pristine humanity." Only when the body is objectified in this way does it function, in the words of Whitehead, as "the great central ground underlying all symbolic reference." Also, it dies; and in so far as it is permitted to appear like something that does, it cannot represent victory over *hasard*, perfect being, the truth behind the deceptive veil of intellect. How is this to be overcome? "Slash it with sharp instruments, rub ashes into a wound to make a keloid, daub it with clay, paint it with berry juices. This thing that terrifies us, this face upon which we lay so much stress, is something they have always wanted to deform, by hair, shading, by every possible means. Why? To remove from it the terror of death, by making it a work of art." So William Carlos Williams on primitive ways into the artifice of eternity. Fuller's dehumanization was another way; it is very closely related to a critical moment in the history of modern poetic, but it is also, and this is as we ought to expect, rooted in the terror and joy of the obscure primitive ground from which modern poets draw strength for their archaic art.

(1958–61)

Notes

[1] *The Art of The Dance in French Literature.* London, Adam & Charles Black, 1952.

[2] It is quite untrue, by the way, that Fenollosa and Pound 'introduced' the Noh plays; interest in them is at least as old as this century.

[3] Mr. Ian Fletcher directs my attention to Sabine Baring-Gould's periodical *The Sacristy* (1871–2) where liturgical dancing is discussed with other matters such as liturgical lights and symbolic zoology, and to later ecclesiastical contributions.

[4] I ought to say that this passage will make more sense to anybody who has read my *Romantic Image.* London, Routledge & Kegan Paul, 1957.

MARSHALL COHEN
PRIMITIVISM, MODERNISM, AND DANCE THEORY

> "What a charming amusement for your people this is,
> Mr. Darcy!—There is nothing like dancing after all.—I
> consider it one of the first refinements of polished
> societies."
>   "Certainly, Sir;—and it has the advantage also of
> being in vogue amongst the less polished societies of
> the world.—Every savage can dance."
>
>   *Pride and Prejudice*

The theory of modern art tends toward two sharply contrasting ideals. One, deriving from Lessing's *Laocoön*, insists that each art maintain a proper relation to the medium in which it works. This view often incorporates some version of what may be called the principle of modernism in the arts. According to this principle the most advanced, the most significant, the most self-critically modern, or simply the most valuable, works of art are those that do not dissemble the artistic medium in which they are created, or do not trespass on the domain of other artistic media. In one of its forms the doctrine requires that modernist art confine itself to exploiting or to exhibiting only those properties that are essential to a work in the medium it employs. Sometimes, of course, no special value is attached to works which satisfy the modernist ideal. To describe a work as modernist in that case may simply be a way of referring it to a certain style.

The other ideal, which received its most celebrated formulation in Wagner's notion of the *Gesamtkunstwerk*, looks to an art that will draw on the most potent resources of all the major artistic media. This second ideal is often associated with some form of primitivism. A synthesis of the arts is desirable because, only where it is achieved, can we restore that unity of experience and idea, or re-establish that fusion of image and reality, which characterizes primitive art. To be sure, the ideal of the "total work of art" may rest on other than primitivist foundations—a synthesis of the arts may be desired not because it restores some primitive unity but rather because it manifests a transcendental one, or simply because it is supposed to produce singularly powerful sensory effects (to be "cruel"). And it may, of course, be thought that the usable residue of primitive experience can be recaptured within the confines of discrete artistic media. When this approach is taken it is the art of dance that is most often thought to possess a privileged access to the primitive.

At the present time, the modernist ideals of honesty to materials, purification of the medium and even of artistic minimalism prevail and some of the prestige of the most gifted artists derives from the belief that their art adheres to these principles. Merce Cunningham's modernism may appear to provide a counter-example to these observations, for he deploys the arts of language, music and sculpture in his work and collaborates with other artisits in a way that is unprecedented since the Diaghilev era. His ideal is, nevertheless, firmly anti-Wagnerian, for, like Brecht, he insists on the integrity of the individual arts and rejects the ideal of fusion. Typically, in his works, the various arts are simply juxtaposed and they proceed in relative independence of one another. Indeed, as Roger Copeland has observed, it is not simply that Cunningham's dancers do not perform *to* music. They are required to concentrate in such a way as to be unaffected by it.[1] (This emphasis on the intellectuality of the dancer is, in fact, a central feature of Cunningham's own reaction against the primitivist tendencies of classical modern dance.) Some of Cunningham's followers pursue a more orthodox approach to the ideals of modernism. They insist that, since dance is created in the medium of the human body, dance should confine itself to examining and revealing the qualities of human movement in greater isolation, for its own sake, and often as it is exhibited in the most ordinary, least dance-like "tasks." More importantly, for present purposes, George Balanchine's admirers have attempted to present him as an artist who has successfully freed dance from its dependence on dramatic representation and theatrical *mise-en-scène*. Abstract possibilities that Marius Petipa adumbrated in, say, *Raymonda*, Act III, and *La Bayadère*, Act IV, have been pursued and realized with exemplary brilliance in the most advanced modernist works of Balanchine. In these works, *Symphony in C, Agon, Episodes, Stravinsky Violin Concerto*, the essence of the art of ballet stands revealed.

It has not always been so. Frank Kermode, writing as recently as the early sixties, remarked that during the last sixty or seventy years the peculiar prestige of dance had much to do with "the notion that it somehow represents art in an undissociated and unspecialized form—a notion made explicit by W. B. Yeats and hinted at by Paul Valéry."[2] And Richard Wagner thought the music-drama would, by restoring the undifferentiated unity of the Greek tragic drama, achieve precisely this result. Others looked to something more primitive than Greek tragic drama and were prepared to find a reunification of the arts in places other than Bayreuth. Unquestionably, views such as these influenced the symbolists' reception of Loïe Fuller, and prepared the triumph of the Ballets Russes in Paris in 1909. The idea that an integration of the arts is best met in ballet is influential as late as the mid-thirties. Adrian Stokes, speaking for a significant body of opinion, observed, "Dramatic action or movement and music have consistently inspired the one the other in modern Russian ballet alone. In grand opera, however reformed, they inspire each other at one moment and handicap at the next. Where the work of a Gluck or a Wagner is incomplete, the work of Diaghilev is complete."[3] But it is not ballet alone that is viewed from this kind of perspective. Eric Bentley writes, for instance, that in Graham we find the fullest realization of the magical theater of which Gordon Craig and W. B. Yeats and so many others dreamed.[4] And Antonin Artaud glimpsed his ideal of total theater, embodied in a "language before speech," in the work of the Balinese theater, which he described as "a kind of superior dance."[5]

This complex of ideas is not, I think, persuasive. Even if we found the ideal of the *Gesamtkunstwerk* more compelling than we do, we would have to acknowledge the crucial fact that the art of dance does not, in general, employ the arts of speech. This is one reason why cinema and some extensions of traditional theater have, more often and more reasonably, been looked to for plausible realizations of the ideal of *Gesamtkunstwerk*.[6] To be sure, dance could satisfy this requirement by incorporating sung or spoken language as it has in Diaghilev's *Les Noces* and in Martha Graham's *Letter to the World*. But even the success of these works has not pointed the art of dance—or even Diaghilev's or Graham's conceptions of it—in the direction of total theater. It might, of course, be argued that the arts of speech need not be included in a grand synthesis of the arts. This paradox might be argued for by primitivists (and some symbolists) on the ground that dance's non-verbal language of gesture can express meanings and ideas with greater force, precision and economy than is possible for abstract "verbal" languages. Ideas of this sort are unquestionably reflected in Artaud's search for a non-verbal

theater and in Mallarmé's observation that the ballerina is not
dancing but writing with her body.[7]

But the undifferentiated unity of the primitive world (like the
very existence of an emblematic or a transcendental one, which
does equivalent work in some related theories) is itself a myth—
and a modern one. Even if primitive mysteries are re-enacted,
they are experienced by dissociated modern sensibilities and, as
some say, only as an aesthetic phenomenon. The art of dance as
we know and experience it is one among the arts. It does not
displace or incorporate all the other arts, not even all the other
theatrical arts. Certainly, the claim that Diaghilev realized the
Wagnerian ideal is extravagant and misleading and Diaghilev's
contribution does not, in any case, seem as decisive for the aesthetics of dance as it once did. Little of his repertory remains of
value. *Parade,* for whose special combination of the arts Guil-
laume Apollinaire coined the term "surrealism," is sometimes
invoked as a brilliant synthesis of the arts. But for Jean Cocteau
and his collaborators *Parade* was by design an anti-Wagnerian
statement and a repudiation of the "primitivism" of the earlier
Diaghilev repertory. In any case, Leonide Massine's choreographic contribution compares unfavorably with the contributions of Cocteau, Picasso and Satie and the work remains unsatisfactory from any point of view.[8] This is not to say there is
nothing of value in the Diaghilev inheritance, but what there is
certainly does not confirm the view that Diaghilev is complete
where Wagner is incomplete. *Petrouchka* is certainly an impressive work (though not the fully-realized masterpiece Stokes and
legend suggest) and, like some of the finer works of Graham, it
permits dramatic representation and even outright storytelling.[9]
In this respect such works unquestionably resist a certain kind
of purism, but this is far from showing that they aspire to, or
achieve, a full Wagnerian synthesis. In fact, the most fruitful portion of Diaghilev's legacy, works like *Les Sylphides,* parts of *Fire-
bird,* and *Apollo* point in the direction of Balanchine's achievement. Balanchine's art, at its most characteristic, does indeed lean
toward the purist ideal. In its most original moments it rejects or
attenuates storytelling (though not dramatic implication and
metaphor) and derives its imagery mainly from the music to
which it is set. But this commitment to music in fact provides an
insurmountable obstacle to those who would represent his art,
the greatest realization of the art of dance we know, as an
embodiment of the purist ideal. For the purist ideal requires the
independence (if not necessarily the isolation) of music and

drama (they work in two different physical media and are by nature two separate arts). I would not deny, of course, that dance can exist independently of music. Doris Humphrey's *Water Study* and Jerome Robbins's *Moves* show that dances of this sort can achieve remarkable success. We have not been persuaded, however, that dances of this sort represent the ideal realization of the art of dance. Neither primitivism nor modernism in the formulations with which we are most familiar provides an accurate account of dance as we have inherited it or as we prefer it.

In what follows I do not pretend to offer anything like a full discussion of the theory or practice of primitivism or modernism. Given the many possible forms in which these ideas have been or could be developed, any such account in the present compass is out of the question. I do, however, offer a reasonably full discussion of what are perhaps the two most elaborate philosophical discussions of dance to appear in English in recent years, and these essays are usefully read against the background I have sketched. Susanne Langer is by no means the unqualified primitivist some (like Frank Kermode) have taken her to be, and David Levin (unlike those who inspire him) is not a dogmatic proponent of modernist ideals. Yet primitivist ideas seem to have misled Mrs. Langer as modernist ones have misled David Levin. It is a matter of some interest, I think, that their versions of primitivism and modernism—these two conflicting but intimately related modern artistic options—have led both of them to very similar misinterpretations of the dance as we know it. A criticism of their views should, I believe, contribute to an assessment of the larger body of ideas with which they are associated. And an assessment of modernism and primitivism is, I believe, a central task of contemporary aesthetic theory. T. S. Eliot wrote, "Anyone who would contribute to our imagination of what ballet may perform in (the) future . . . should begin by a close study of dancing among primitive peoples . . ."[10] We have seen that many of the prophets of the *Gesamtkunstwerk* looked into the distant and even into primitive past for a vision of the artwork of the future. Susanne Langer, in the relevant chapters of *Feeling and Form*, goes further. She thinks we must look to primitive dance for an understanding of dance in general. Unlike some proponents of the ideal of total theater, however, she does not hope to recover the primitive experience of dance and is therefore not drawn to the theory of the *Gesamtkunstwerk* as a vehicle of that recovery. Indeed, contrary to Frank Kermode's suggestion, she supposes we can only understand the modern art of dance if we understand that the art of dance functions for us in a manner very different from the way it functions in primitive life.[11] Nevertheless, we shall see that the idea of the primitive misleads Mrs. Langer, as it has misled the proponents of the ideal of the *Gesamtkunstwerk*, although in a different way.

Mrs. Langer locates the origins of dance in the primitive. Indeed, in her view, it is the first art and "the most serious intellectual business of savage life: it is the envisagement of a world beyond the spot and the moment of one's animal existence, the first conception of life as a whole—continuous, superpersonal life, punctuated by birth and death, surrounded and fed by the rest of nature." But to the "mythic consciousness" these creations are "realities, not symbols. They are not felt to be created by the dance at all, but to be invoked, adjured, challenged, placated, as the case may be. The symbol of the world, the balletic realm of forces, is the world, and dancing is the human spirit's participation in it."[12] But Langer does not suppose the present role of dance is to reconstitute the religious and magical properties primitive dance possessed. Rather, she aligns herself with the tradition of Kant and Schopenhauer and insists that, in order to become an object of aesthetic experience, dance must disengage itself from precisely those practical and cognitive—that is, from those non-aesthetic functions—that it served in primitive life. For Langer, the artist guarantees we can take an aesthetic attitude toward a work of art by creating an object of a special sort, a "virtual" object, or an appearance or illusion, that by its very nature can support only an aesthetic, and not a practical, interest. In her view, from the physical materials available to an art, the art creates its "primary" illusion. As the painter creates the illusion of space from pigments and canvas, the dancer, working with movements of the human body, creates "a world of powers, made visible by the unbroken fabric of gesture." But an art can never be identified with the materials from which it is made— for these untransformed materials are not, themselves, the pure appearances or semblances or illusions that alone constitute art, and that are alone the proper objects of aesthetic interest. The aesthetic, as opposed to the mythic consciousness, recognizes these illusions for what they are, and does not take the world of illusory Powers to be a reality. The aesthetic object is, by nature, purely visual.

Critics (the present writer included) have elsewhere objected to Langer's notion of illusion or "virtual" object, and questioned whether it is necessary to suppose each art creates objects of this kind to serve as the target of the aesthetic attitude.[13] But it is worth protesting here against the negative view that nothing which can be characterized in purely physical terms (namely, bodily movements) can constitute a work of art, as well as against the positive view that dance is, in fact, an art of illusory gestures. Langer supposes that real gestures are expressions of emotion. She thinks, correctly, that dance theorists (especially theorists of modern dance) have often falsely supposed dances are really expressions of the dancer's (or of the choreographer's) emotions. But she wrongly supposes the proper way to correct this mistake is to declare these expressions of emotion only apparent or illusory. No doubt, this solution appeals to her because, in her view, dance like every other art must present some illusion or other. Why not suppose, then, that dance creates, if not the reality, then the illusion that emotion is being expressed? Mrs. Langer is undoubtedly correct in thinking dancers do not always express emotions, but it is important to insist that they do not always give the impression of expressing them either. Mrs. Langer has merely sophisticated and attenuated the expression theory of dance. She ought to have rejected it outright.

André Levinson long ago remarked on the confusion of gesture with *le pas*.[14] The Rose Adagio or the Act II *pas de deux* in *Swan Lake* may appear to express Aurora's or Odette's emotion (that is, they may be gestures in Langer's sense) but what emotion does the Bluebird *pas de deux* or the dance of the cygnets express? (To be sure, the dance of the cygnets is designed to relieve emotion.) And, then, what emotions does Merce Cunningham express in *How to Pass, Kick, Fall and Run* or Yvonne Rainer in *The Mind Is a Muscle, Part I (Trio A)?* Indeed, the movements of these contemporary dances are specifically designed to purge movement of its emotional valence and, in Langer's terms, to leave the materials of dance untransformed into gestures, or the illusion of gestures, or anything else. No doubt there are certain kinds of dances in which the inability to transform movements into gestures does, indeed, amount to failure (though not necessarily in the failure to create a dance). Performing movements with the unearned suggestion that they are endowed with emotional significance is empty rhetoric, and performing them with the suggestion that they are endowed with symbolic import is portentousness. These are, respectively, the characteristic vices of certain schools of dance ("modern" dance) and of certain choreographers (Robbins at his worst, Maurice Béjart almost always). I expect it is because we have witnessed these failures and expe-

rienced these vices so often that a taste for non-gestural movement has become very strong. However that may be, there is no
doubt dances can be constructed that are not gestural in Langer's
sense. In fact, we find dances constructed of movements and
actions and even of gestures (like the gesture of warning or of
recognition), which, since they need not express or appear to
express emotion, would not be gestures in Langer's sense—real
ones (Isadora Duncan's?) or apparent ones (of the sort we find in
representational ballets). There is in any case no reason to accept
Langer's residual expressionism, or to suppose that if we concede
that dances can be constructed of non-illusory physical materials,
we will fail to guard against the possibility that someone will
take an impermissible, non-aesthetic interest in them. A more
pertinent worry would be that far too many dances constructed
of pure movement do not support any kind of interest at all.

Even if we waive these objections to the centrality Mrs. Langer
assigns to the role of gesture in dance we shall have to object to
her view that the dance necessarily creates a "world image," and
a world image of a very specific sort. No doubt, her theory marks
an advance on those that would return us to a primitive state of
mind in which we believe the world image is a reality in which
we participate. Mrs. Langer thinks more plausibly that for us
dance merely creates an image of the world, an image to which
we respond aesthetically. But, like her residual expressionism,
her residual primitivisim is unconvincing. For on her view, this
world image descends from, and bears the (sometimes faded)
lineaments of that original primitive world. In Langer's view the
world of dance is a world of "interacting forces" which seem "to
move the dance itself," whether that image is taken for a reality
as by the mythic mind, or acknowledged to be a romantic world
or a world of dreams, as it is by the aestheticizing modern mind.[15]
Mrs. Langer's characterization of this world is not sufficiently
clear for it to be assessed with confidence. But we can wonder
whether Jooss's *The Green Table* or Tudor's *The Echoing of Trumpets*
inhabits a world of romance, or whether Graham's willful heroines or the contestants in Balanchine's *Agon* seem to be moved
by invisible forces rather than to be self-moving. Mrs. Langer's
claim becomes somewhat more precise when she says dance
movement creates "the illusion of a conquest of gravity, i.e. freedom from the actual forces that are normally known and felt to
control the dancer's body." [16] This contention, central to Langer's
view of the dance, is surely questionable. No doubt, this kind of
thing is often said of ballet, especially of the Romantic ballet

which often invokes a supernatural world of anti-gravitational fairies, sylphs and wilis. Even here, of course, this is not the illusion that is always sought. We are all too aware of the pull of gravity on Hilarion as he is danced into the abyss by the wilis. Even more obviously, it was one of the major objectives of the classical modern dance to acknowledge, and even to insist on, the gravitational pull on the dancer's body. Isadora Duncan, no doubt as part of her largely misconceived polemic against ballet, observed that "all movement on earth is governed by the law of gravitation, by attraction and repulsion, resistance and yielding; it is that which makes the rhythm of dance."[17] Graham's floor work was essential to her dance aesthetic, and the relation to earth was a major theme of Humphrey's. (In *Circular Descent*, for example, "she allowed the body to sink into the restful earth and to halt the endless battle against gravitation, and against all opposition.")[18] And it is central in Mary Wigman, the modern dancer whose genius Mrs. Langer paradoxically seems to admire most. (A typical description reports Wigman "tended to kneel, crouch, crowd; her head was often downcast and her arms were rarely lifted high.") Against all this evidence, why does Mrs. Langer persist in her view? Only, so far as I can see, because of her residual primitivism. The world created by the modern dancer, even if it is no longer believed in, must nevertheless present itself as a world of mysterious and invisible "powers," "a Spirit World," free of all physical determination. Mrs. Langer's commitment to her theory seems to overcome her own taste in dance and, one must suppose, the evidence of her senses.

Even in the case of ballet, as I have suggested, Mrs. Langer's theory is unacceptable. There are, to be sure, moments and even sustained passages in which we might want to agree that the dancer appears to defy the laws of gravity. A good example might be the Bournonville dancer's *grand jeté en avant en attitude* in which, after a quick thrust upwards of the front leg, the back leg shifts high in attitude to "ride" the jump in the air before the front leg is lowered to land, giving the illusion of suspension in the air for several seconds.[19] But illusions of this kind are not essential to ballet and they do not even have priority among the illusions and images ballet projects. Many of the images are not illusory at all: we simply see the dancer performing the classical *pas* and *enchaînements* composed of them. We admire the dancer's speed, grace and fluidity; these are non-illusory features of the dancer's movements and poses. And even where the aesthetic effect of a ballet does depend on an illusion, it may not depend on the illusion or on the visual qualities of the image alone. Aesthetic pleasure is not simply pleasure in the contemplation of images, and dance is not a purely visual art. Our pleasure in ballet is often, in part, a pleasure in the dancer's virtuosity and this requires that we have reason to believe the image is created in a certain way. Fred Astaire, dancing on the wall and across the ceiling in *Royal Wedding*, creates the illusion of a more extreme violation of the laws of gravity than anything we know in traditional ballet. But since we do not believe Astaire was actually photographed dancing on a wall (we are not so sure in the case of Donald O'Connor's "Make 'em Laugh" in *Singin' in the Rain*) this anti-Bazinian cinematic trick gives us none of the pleasure we derive from "antigravitational" illusions in classical ballet. It was only when *Giselle* substituted *pointes* for flying wires that Romantic ballet became a sublime art.[20]

Ballet is not, then, a purely visual art and its images are not necessarily illusory. Ballets may, in fact, require nothing more than an arrangement of the special array of movements consecrated by this art and its traditions. This sort of point is often insisted upon by modernism, but modernism in many of its manifestations yields doctrines as unacceptable as those associated with primitivism. It is to one such theory that we now turn.

In his important essay on "Balanchine's Formalism," David Levin attempts to account for Balanchine's peculiar genius by assimilating his achievement to the modernist aesthetic.[21] Levin's conception of modernism is derived from Clement Greenberg's influential account. In Greenberg's analysis, however, modernism is identified with a number of distinguishable ideas and it will be useful to separate them out. Sometimes Greenberg asserts that the identifying feature of modernist art is its refusal to dissemble the medium. Modernism does not use art to conceal art, but rather to call attention to it. Modernism in this sense requires "frankness."[22] Unlike the old masters, Edouard Manet "declares" the surfaces on which he paints, and the Impressionists leave no doubt that the colors they use are made of real paint and come from pots and tubes. Ballets are modernist in this sense when they do not dissemble the movements of the dancer's body (and try to create the illusion that the dancer is really a swan or a bluebird). Modernist ballets would acknowledge that the Swan Queen is really a dancer and that her attempts to free her legs from drops of water are made with *petits battements* as the male bluebird's motions are constructed out of *brisés volés* and *cabrioles* (Langer's non-gestural mere twisting and turning in the air?).

But in this sense it is easy to exaggerate the extent to which ballet ever seriously dissembled the medium. Even in the most representational of traditional ballets one is meant to remain aware that roles are danced by dancers whose movements are drawn from the repertory of classical technique. To be sure, in some of Balanchine's storyless ballets there is little dissembling at all. But, to my mind, this is a less radical innovation than it may seem. How crucial, after all, are the dissemblings in *Raymonda*, Act III, and *La Bayadère*, Act IV? Although Levin sometimes invokes this conception of modernism, it is not the one that seems mainly to concern him.

Sometimes Greenberg means by modernism not a refusal to dissemble the medium, but a refusal to trespass on the domain of another medium.[23] This is the requirement not of frankness, but of propriety. A painting might, for example, meet the requirement of frankness and freely acknowledge the medium in which it is created. But it might be thought to trespass on the domain of literature by telling a story or, as Greenberg thinks traditional painting did, on the domain of sculpture by creating the illusion of three-dimensional space. In order to meet the requirement of propriety, modernist painting had to eschew creating the illusions of three-dimensional tactility and of weight. Painting had to become purely "optical."[24] It is this feature of opticality that Levin fixes on as the distinctive characteritstic of Balanchine's modernism. I shall want to question whether Balanchine's ballets do, in fact, possess this characteristic. But, even if they did, it would not follow that they did so because Balanchine was conforming to the modernist canon of propriety. After all, dancing's claim on the third dimension is at least as strong as sculpture's; there is no plausible reason why propriety requires that dance defer to sculpture and confine itself to the realm of the purely optical. Matters are complicated, if not thrown into a hopeless state of confusion, by Greenberg's announcement that the new "constructivist" sculpture which he admires is, like modernist painting, itself essentially optical. But he admits that insofar as this is so "the prohibition on one art's entering the domain of another is suspended."[25] If modernist ballet is to espouse the ideal of "opticality," the canon of propriety will have to be suspended for it as well, and for the same reason. Plainly, the operative theory here is not that each art must confine itself to its distinctive domain, but rather that sculpture and dancing must investigate further the nature of that "opticality" which painting, the avant-garde modernist art, first pursued. But this is a very different demand from the demand for propriety. Its theoretical foundations are obscure, its credentials in modernist theory dubious and its applicability to ballet, even to Balanchine's ballet, implausible. Something like it may be true of the "two-dimensional" effects Nijinsky sought in *L'Après-Midi d'un Faune*. But this is a very special case and it certainly does not provide a paradigm of Balanchine's practice.

A third characterization of modernism brings us closer to the main body of Levin's essay. Sometimes Greenberg identifies modernism with the requirement neither of frankness nor of propriety (modernism's transformation of the *genre* theorist's decorum) but with what we may call minimalism.[26] This version of modernism excludes, in addition to everything that falls into the domain of another art, everything that is inessential to the art in question. According to minimalism, each art must confine itself to exhibiting its own essential qualities. Modernism in this sense requires that the work of art "reveal," or "make present," the defining conditions for a work of its kind, that is to say, the minimal conditions for being a work in that medium. In what follows we shall identify modernism with minimalism in the sense suggested. In order to understand Levin's view of Balanchine's modernism it will be useful to quote the passage from Levin's essay in which he shows how Greenberg's younger colleague, Michael Fried, applies this modernist doctrine to painting. This will provide the key to Levin's own doctrine of modernist dance. "On Fried's view" he writes, "the two ineluctable defining conditions of painting are its flatness and its shape. No painting can conceivably exist unless it is reduced to flatness and has assumed a certain shape. But since material objects are also shaped and may also be flat, painting can defeat, or suspend, its own objecthood if—and only if—it accomplishes what no mere subject can possibly do: it must somehow materially acknowledge these conditions, rendering them totally present."[27] By revealing this "contradiction" the object establishes its claim to be a work of art.

We may now consider what I take to be Levin's application of this argument to the case of dance. (Some improvisation is necessary, as Levin is not explicit at every point.) The minimal defining condition for dancing is a configuration of physical movements. But, since inanimate objects are also capable of physical movements, dancing must defeat, or suspend, its own physicality and it can do this if—and only if—it accomplishes what no inanimate object can accomplish: it must somehow acknowledge its own physicality and render it totally present. Modernist dance accomplishes this task by acknowledging the tangible weight and mass of the body but only in order to defeat them, to render the objective body as a magically weightless, optically intangible, presence. In this way the work of art is shown to be a material object and at the same time the "negation" of that objecthood. In order to achieve this suspension of objecthood the dancer's space must be cleared of everything that would locate dance within the binding coordinates of the horizontal field. The failure to do so would prevent the unearthly suspension of objecthood and the possibility of a vertical release into "the sky of grace." It is to help in achieving this minimalist illusion of pure opticality and weightlessness (and now, not to achieve frankness or to maintain propriety, though, given an appropriate understanding of minimalism, they may follow of necessity) that the semantic allusiveness and mimetic gestures of traditional ballet are repudiated in favor of a purely abstract, syntactic symbolism, and that the architectural field of space, traditionally staked out with objects and other dancers' bodies and inflected with color and costume, is avoided. For mimesis and architecture tie the dancer to the horizontal field of beauty and prevent the dancer's vertical release into the realm of the sublime. Something very like the freedom from gravity that for Langer has characterized dance from primitive times and that she associates with its invocation of a world of spirits is viewed by Levin as the minimalist essence of the most advanced modernist art, an art whose essence requires a return to "the sky of God." Unfortunately, I do not believe anything like this view is true, even when it is radically restricted as it is with Levin to the single case of Balanchine's art.

I shall not, here, attempt to criticize Levin's philosophical assumptions in any detail, although the question must at least be raised why the exhibition of movements which present themselves as distinctively human should be sufficient to create ballet or why the intentionality that for Levin characterizes human movement should reveal itself in the illusion of weightlessness or of optically intangible presence. After all, Greenberg finds precisely these qualities in modernist paintings and sculptures. Why, then, can they not be engendered by the movements of non-human, or even by the movements of inanimate, bodies (mobiles)? We shall confine ourselves here, however, simply to questioning whether Balanchine's art, even in its purest examples, is in fact endowed, and uniquely endowed, with the qualities Levin discerns.

It is certainly true that Balanchine tends to avoid storytelling—though even in such central "modernist" works as *Apollo* storytelling is crucial. But it is far from true that he avoids mimetic gesture or dramatic implication. Perhaps his most ubiquitous form of mimesis is found in the imitations and transformations of historical forms of dance—*Agon, Liebeslieder Walzer, Stars and Stripes, Who Cares?* and *Square Dance* among others. And it has often been remarked that his *pas de deux* constitute an elaborate examination of the relations between the sexes, presenting us with a highly distinctive view of women.[28] This is hardly accomplished by the exclusion of mimetic gesture. Then, too, Balanchine's allusion to the types of human temperament, to the destiny of individuals, to human isolation, triumph and apotheosis, cannot be and has not been missed.[29] If Balanchine makes little use of scenery it is certainly untrue that he refuses to relate dancers to one another in a space that seems corporeally accessible. A major characteristic of Balanchine's choreography is the lucid articulation of physical space—often by great Petipa-like diagonals or by the positioning of discrete groups of dancers against whose locations the trajectory of other dancers is traced or from whose configurations smaller groups of dancers emerge (his familiar "daisy chains, London bridges and turnstile formations").[30] Often the effect of this organization is precisely to bind the dancer to what Levin calls the horizontal space of the stage that the dancer characteristically assaults with his brilliant attack and devours with his speed.

Indeed, it is the speed and physical presence of the Balanchine dancer, rather than her weightlessness (or the tensions generated by that weightlessness), that has usually impressed Balanchine's commentators. It would perhaps be frivolous, though I think it is significant, to mention that Balanchine found a place in his company for Gloria Govrin, who gave the illusion that she was about to ascend into the sky of God no more than the earthbound figures of *Ivesiana* do. If these examples are thought to be eccentric, no one can, I think, make such an objection to Arlene Croce's observation (offered without philosophical *parti pris*) that in the third statement of the theme in *The Four Temperaments* the weight on the dancer's one supporting *pointe* "looks crushing."[31] I do not want to suggest that crushing weight is a quality Balanchine favors, but neither is the quality of weightless opticality on which Levin himself puts such (crushing) weight.

To these observations Levin would reply it is not his view that the dancer simply creates the illusion of weightlessness or of pure opticality. Rather, the dances create a "tense simultaneity" of weight and weightlessness. He points in one place to the Balanchine *plié* in which, despite the dancer's obvious objective weight and effort, Balanchine makes present "at first only in the tensed mode of suppressed virtuality, the graceful arc of flight, which is about to suspend the force of gravity . . ."[32] Quite aside from the doubts one may harbor about whether the dancer in the "arc of flight" actually appears weightless, it is necessary to ask the following questions: are the characteristics here cited really specific to the Balanchine *plié*, or do they not characterize the Bournonville *plié* equally well? And are they in fact characteristic of the Balanchine *plié*? We should remind ourselves that the third girl in *The Four Temperaments*, turned in deep *plié* with the other foot held in *passé* position, reminded Croce of "the bass fiddle the forties jazz player spins after a chorus of hot licks."[33] Even if we were to accept Levin's description of the Balanchine *plié*, why should we single out this particular moment to carry so heavy a philosophical burden? By what criterion does Levin single it out, or is this a case of selective vision with Heidegger and Clement Greenberg serving as the main selectors? Again, Levin asks us to consider the situation in which the dancer moves dramatically from second position in *demi-plié* (a disposition of the body that forcefully reveals its weight, its objecthood) into a wondrous turn that seems to suspend this condition.[34] In this case we must observe, in the first place, that the alleged impressions of weight and weightlessness are not simultaneous but successive. More important, perhaps, is the fact that even if the wondrous turn is thought to create the impression of weightlessness it certainly does not create the impression of "pictorial flatness" or of "pure opticality." (Roger Copeland has remarked to me that in actual practice the illusion of weightlessness almost invariably induces a kinetic and tactile response in the perceiver that interferes with a purely "optical" appreciation.) Balanchine's dancers are, significantly, turners more than they are jumpers, and these turns establish and insist on the dancer's plasticity, on the fact that the dancer occupies three dimensions. So, too, many of Balanchine's characteristic formations emphasize the three-dimensionality of the dancer. The three muses are posed in arabesque around Apollo and the ballerina's leg, lifted high in attitude, hooks her partner's neck and head in the *Agon pas de deux*. Even Lincoln Kirstein with his talk of "the aria of the aerial"[35] observes that in Balanchine the dancer's silhouette must not be papery, but solid, read in three dimensions. He traces the standards of plastic legibility and expressiveness that govern ballet to that Renaissance sculptural tradition in which "the principle of *contraposto*, a three-quarter view opposition of limbs" dictates "the placement of members as an active spiral, denying any flattening symmetrical frontality."[36] Unquestionably the ideals of Giovanni da Bologna and Jean Goujon have been modified and to some extent displaced by subsequent cultural and artistic developments. But Balanchine is still to be understood in relation to this tradition and not as a balletic equivalent of David Smith and contemporary constructivism.

As I see it, Balanchine does not create the dance equivalent of the purely optical illusions of certain types of modernist painting and sculpture. Rather, Balanchine perpetuates classical ballet's idealization of the human body, though he idealizes it in a specialized, perhaps as many have suggested in a specifically Americanized, way. (It must be admitted, of course, that one man's Americanization is another man's dehumanization.) Indeed, it is reasonable to speculate that a large part of the great popularity film, photography and dance enjoy at the present time derives from the fact that these arts have not "suspended" the objecthood of the human body, or treated it as part of a purely "abstract syntax."[37] Even if Levin were more nearly accurate in his description of Balanchine's dances than I think he is, his interpretation of Balanchine as a minimalizing modernist would be wholly unacceptable for another reason suggested earlier on. The essence of Balanchine is the setting of dances to music. The look of a Balanchine ballet can never be considered in abstraction from the music to which it is set and no consideration of the look of a Balanchine ballet could in itself account for the power of Balanchine's art. Balanchine's dancers do not create the illusion that they are free from the force of gravity; rather they give the impression that their movements are determined by, and reveal the structure of, the music to which they are danced.

Neither the doctrines generated by primitivist commitments nor those elaborated in response to modernist ideals provide an adequate account of the central manifestations and achievements of dance as we know it. Still less, can the character of that art be discovered by considering the nature and possibilities of any particular physical medium, or by imagining how a combination of all the major arts would look. If some of the prestige of twentieth-century dance derives from the assumption that it satisfies one or another of these ideals, its achievements are great enough to survive a more accurate description of its formal nature and its historical qualities. The immensely difficult task of accurate description and adequate theorizing largely remains to be done.

(1981)

Notes

[1]Roger Copeland: "The Politics of Perception," *The New Republic* (November 17, 1979), p. 28.

[2]Frank Kermode: "Poet and Dancer Before Diaghilev," in *Puzzles and Epiphanies* (London: Routledge and Kegan Paul, 1962), p. 2.

[3]Adrian Stokes: *Russian Ballets* (London: Faber and Faber, 1935), p. 114.

[4]Eric Bentley: *In Search of Theater* (New York: Vintage Books, 1959), p. 58.

[5]Antonin Artaud: *The Theater and Its Double* (New York: Grove Press, 1958), p. 58.

[6]Susan Sontag: "Film and Theater" reprinted in Gerald Mast and Marshall Cohen (eds.), *Film Theory and Criticism*, second ed. (New York: Oxford University Press, 1979), p. 375.

[7]Bradford Cook (tr.): *Mallarmé: Selected Prose Poems, Essays and Letters* (Baltimore: The Johns Hopkins Press, 1956), p. 62.

[8]E. T. Kirby (ed.): *Total Theater: A Critical Anthology* (New York: E. P. Dutton and Co., 1969), p. xxiv.

[9]David Vaughan: "Fokine in the Contemporary Repertory," *Ballet Review 7*, nos. 2 and 3 (1978–79), p. 22.

[10]T. S. Eliot: quoted in Kermode, op. cit., p. 3.

[11]Ibid., p. 2.

[12]Susanne K. Langer: *Feeling and Form* (New York: Charles Scribner and Sons, 1953), p. 190.

[13]Marshall Cohen: "Appearance and the Aesthetic Attitude," *The Journal of Philosophy LVI*, no. 23 (November 5, 1959), pp. 921–924. Samuel Bufford, "Langer Evaluated: Susanne Langer's Two Philosophies of Art," reprinted in George Dickie and Richard Sclafani (eds.), *Aesthetics, A Critical Anthology* (New York: St. Martin's Press, 1977), pp. 168–78.

[14]André Levinson: "The Idea of the Dance: From Aristotle to Mallarmé" *Theater Arts Monthly* (August 1927), p. 576.

[15]Langer, op. cit., p. 201.

[16]Ibid, p. 194.

[17]Walter Terry: *The Dance in America*, rev. ed. (New York: Harper and Row, 1971), p. 43.

[18]Ibid, p. 108.

[19]Henry Haslam: "How To Perform Bournonville," *Ballet Review 2*, no. 6, p. 23.

[20]Peggy Van Praagh and Peter Brinson: *The Choreographic Art* (New York: Alfred A. Knopf, 1963), p. 33.

[21]David Michael Levin: "Balanchine's Formalism," *Dance Perspectives 55* (Autumn 1973), pp. 29–48. Reprinted in *Salmagundi*, special issue on *Dance* (Spring-Summer 1976), pp. 216–236.

[22]Clement Greenberg: "Modernist Painting," in Gregory Battcock: *The New Art: A Critical Anthology* (New York: E. P. Dutton and Co., 1966), p. 163.

[23]Clement Greenberg: "The New Sculpture," *Art and Culture* (Boston: Beacon Press, 1961), p. 139.

[24]Ibid., p. 144.

[25]Ibid., p. 143.

[26]Clement Greenberg: "After Abstract Expressionism," *Art International VI* (October, 1962), p. 29. For a fuller discussion of Greenberg's views see my "Notes on Modernist Art," *New Literary History III* (1971–72), pp. 220–23.

[27]Levin, op. cit., p. 33.

[28]Arlene Croce: *Afterimages* (New York: Alfred A. Knopf, 1977), p. 127. My obligations to this work go well beyond the footnotes I have supplied.

[29]Ibid., pp. 185–190.

[30]Roger Copeland: "Balanchine—Ballet's First Modernist," *The New York Times (Arts and Leisure)*, January 15, 1978.

[31]Croce, op. cit., p. 188.

[32]Levin, op. cit., p. 42.

[33]Croce, op. cit., p. 188.

[34]Levin, op. cit., p. 46.

[35]Lincoln Kirstein: "Classic Ballet: Aria of the Aerial," *Playbill* (New York: American Theater Press, Inc., May 1976), pp. 3ff.

[36]Lincoln Kirstein: *"The Classic Ballet: Basic Technique and Terminology"* (New York: Alfred A. Knopf, 1977), p. 5.

[37]Roger Copeland: "Photography and the World's Body," *The Massachusetts Review* (Winter 1978), pp. 797ff.

HEINRICH VON KLEIST
PUPPET THEATRE

During the winter of 1801 which I spent in M. . . I met one evening in the public gardens a certain Herr C., who had recently been engaged as *premier danseur* in the opera there, and enjoyed an extraordinary popularity.

I told him that I had been surprised to see him several times already in a marionette-theatre, which they had rigged up in the market place, and which delighted the crowd with its burlesque plays, songs and dances. He declared that the miming of these puppets gave him great pleasure, and he made it clear that he thought a dancer who wanted to educate himself could learn a great deal from them.

His manner of saying this seemed to me to show that it was more than a passing whim, and I sat down beside him in order to question him more closely as to his reasons for this extraordinary statement. He asked me if I did not think that some of the dance movements of the puppets, especially of the smaller ones, were very graceful. I admitted that it was so; a group of four peasants whom I had seen doing a round dance in quick tempo were as charming as a picture of Teniers.

I questioned him about the mechanism of these figures, and inquired how it was possible to control each separate limb and central point as the rhythm of their movement or the dance rhythm demanded, without holding myriads of strings on your fingers.

He replied that I must not imagine each limb was disposed and moved individually by the puppeteer at every moment of the dance. Every movement, he said, has its own center of gravity; it was only necessary to control this from the inside of the puppet; the limbs were only pendulums which followed mechanically without any further action on the part of the operator. He added that this movement was a very simple one; whenever the center of gravity was moved in a straight line the limbs would describe a curve, and often, as a result of a slight involuntary shock, the whole would achieve a sort of rhythmic movement which resembled dancing.

This remark seemed to me to throw some light on the pleasure which he claimed to find in the marionette-theatre. But I was still far from suspecting the conclusions he was about to draw from it.

I asked him if he thought the puppeteer who operated the puppets ought to be a dancer himself, or at least to have some conception of the beauty of the dance. He replied that however easy the mechanical side of any occupation might be it did not follow that it could be performed entirely without feeling. The line described by the center of gravity was a very simple one, he said, and in most cases straight. In the case of a curved line, the line of the curve would seem to be only of the first or at the most of the second degree, and even in the latter case only elliptical;

a form of movement absolutely natural to the extremities of the human body on account of the joints, and so presenting no great difficulties to the puppeteer. But from another point of view there was something very mysterious about this line. For it was no less than the path of the dancer's soul, and he doubted if there were any other way of discovering it than that the puppeteer should place himself at the marionette's own center of gravity, in other words that he should dance.

I retorted that it had been described to me as a rather dull, mechanical occupation, like turning the handle of a hurdy-gurdy. "Not at all," he said. "I would rather say that the movements of his fingers have a kind of artistic relation to the puppets to which they are attached, almost of the same nature as numbers have to their logarithms or the asymptote to the hyperbola." He admitted, however, that this last fraction of soul might be withdrawn from the marionette, and its dance transposed into the realm of purely mechanical forces and, as I had pictured it, be produced by turning a handle. I expressed my surprise that he should pay so much attention to this mere travesty of fine art, invented for the amusement of the masses. It was not only that he seemed to think it capable of development, but he even seemed himself to take a great interest in it. He smiled and said he ventured to assert that if a mechanic could be found to construct a marionette according to his specifications he would make it perform a dance which not one of their most accomplished dancers, even Vestris himself, would be able to equal.

"Have you ever heard," he went on, while I gazed in silence at the ground, "have you ever heard of the artificial limbs made by English artificers for poor wretches who have lost a leg?" I said I had never come across any such thing.

"That is a pity," he returned, "for if I were to tell you that it is even possible to dance with them I am afraid you would not believe me. Yes, really, they can dance. It is true that the range of their movements is rather limited, but those which they can command they accomplish with a grace and ease which every thinking person can only wonder at."

I replied lightly that in that case he had found his man; for the artificer who was capable of constructing such a remarkable leg would certainly have no difficulty in putting together a whole marionette according to his requirements.

He seemed to reflect on this, and I went on: "What kind of demands would you actually make on his ingenuity?" "Nothing out of the common," he replied: "Symmetry, flexibility, lightness, but all in a higher degree, and above all a more natural disposition of the centers of gravity."

"And what advantage would these puppets have over living dancers?"

"What advantage? First of all, my friend, a negative one, namely, that they would always be without affectation. For affectation sets in, as you know, when the soul, the *vis motrix*, is elsewhere than at the center of gravity, during its movement. Now since the puppeteer can only have control over this center of gravity through the medium of his wires or strings, all the other limbs are, as they should be, inert, mere pendulums, obeying only the law of gravity; an admirable quality which one looks for in vain among the majority of our dancers. . . . Just watch P.," he went on, "when she is playing Daphne, and looks back at Apollo who is pursuing her; her soul is in her vertebral column, and she bends as if she were going to break in two, like a naiad of the Bernini school. Or look at young F., as Paris, standing among the three goddesses and handing the apple to Venus; his soul—it is really horrible to see—is in his elbow. . . ." He broke off, then added: "Such mistakes are unavoidable, since we have eaten of the tree of knowledge. The gates of Eden are barred against us and the angel drives us on. We must make a journey round the world and see whether we can perhaps find another place to creep in at."

I laughed. It is true, I thought, the mind can't go wrong if it is nonexistent. But I noticed he had something more to say and begged him to continue.

"Another advantage of the puppets," he said, "is that they are not subject to the law of gravity. They know nothing of that worst enemy of the dancer, the inertia of matter; for the force which lifts them into the air is greater than that which binds them to earth. What wouldn't our good G. give to be sixty pounds lighter, or to be assisted in her pirouettes by a corresponding weight? Puppets only use the ground as fairies do; brushing it lightly in order that the momentary check may give a new impulse to their bounding limbs. We use the earth to rest on, to recover from the exertions of the dance, a moment which is clearly not in itself dance, and with which there is nothing to be done but to make it disappear as quickly as possible."

I said that however clear his paradox might be he would never persuade me that there could be more grace in a mechanical doll than in the structure of the human body. He replied that a human being was simply incapable of rivalling the marionette in this respect. Only a god could measure himself against matter, in the field of dance; and this was the point, he said, where both ends of the world's circle fit into each other.

I was still more astonished and could think of no answer to such extraordinary statements.

"It seems," said he, taking a pinch of snuff, "that you have not read carefully the third chapter of the first book of Moses, and anyone who is not familiar with that first period of human culture cannot be expected to talk intelligently about a later one, least of all about the last." I said that I recognized what a disturbing effect consciousness had upon the natural grace of human beings. A young man of my acquaintance had, as it were, lost his innocence before my very eyes, in consequence of a simple remark, and despite all his efforts could never get back again into Paradise. "But what conclusions would you draw from that?" I added. He asked what strange occurrence I was alluding to.

"About three years ago," I said, "I was bathing with a young man whose whole person seemed to exhale an extraordinary charm. He must have been about sixteen at the time, and the favor he found with women had as yet only called forth in him the faintest traces of vanity. We happened not long before to have seen in Paris the youth who is pulling a thorn out of his foot; the cast of this statue, as you know, is to be found in most German collections. My young friend caught sight of himself in a mirror just as he was putting his foot up on a stool to dry it, and this reminded him of the statue. He smilingly drew my attention to the resemblance. As a matter of fact I had just made the same discovery myself; but either because I wanted to put his charm to the test, or perhaps to act as a slight curb on his vanity, I laughed and said it was only his fancy. He blushed and lifted his foot again, so as to convince me; but his attempt very naturally failed. After a third and fourth attempt he became quite embarrassed; ten times he tried, but it was no use. He was incapable of reproducing the original movement. Worse still, the movements he made had something so comic about them that I could hardly keep from laughing.

"From that day, indeed from that very moment, a curious change took place in the young man. He would spend the whole day in front of the mirror, and one by one his charms began to fade. An invisible, tangible force seemed to spread itself like an iron net over his free, unselfconscious gestures, and within a year he had completely lost the extraordinary charm which had delighted everyone who saw him. I still know someone who was present on that unhappy occasion and who would confirm every word I have said."

"I think," said Herr C., "that I must take this opportunity to tell you another story: you will readily see the connection. Once when I was travelling in Russia I happened to be staying on the estate of a Lithuanian nobleman whose two sons were great fencing enthusiasts. The elder one, in particular, who had just come back from college, prided himself on his performance, and one morning, directly I went into his room, handed me a rapier. We fought, and as it happened I beat him. Perhaps his excitement got the better of his prudence; in any case every thrust of mine went home, and at last his rapier flew out of his hand into a corner of the room. Half-joking and half vexed, he announced as he picked it up that he had met his master. But, he said, 'everything in the world has its master, and I will now show you yours.' The brothers burst out laughing and shouted: 'Come along, come along to the wood-house,' and taking me by the hand they led me up to a bear which their father was having trained in the yard. I was surprised to see the bear standing on its hind legs with its back against the post to which it was tied, and its right paw raised ready to strike; it was in fencing position. I really thought I must be dreaming, face to face with such an opponent. But Herr von G. cried: 'Make a pass at him! Make a pass at him! and see if you can hit him.' When I had recovered a little from my astonishment I did make a pass at him. But the bear, with a very slight movement of his paw, parried the stroke. I tried to upset him by some feints, but the bear did not stir. Then I made a sudden cunning pass at him, which would have got a man straight in the chest; but the bear with a quick movement of his paw parried the blow. By now I was almost reduced to the condition of young Herr von G. The bear's solemnity robbed me of my presence of mind. Passes and feints followed each other, the sweat poured down; it was all of no use. Not only did the bear parry all my thrusts, as if he had been a world fencing champion; but, unlike any human fencer, he was never taken in by my feints. He just stood gazing into my eyes as if he could read my soul in them. He stood with his paw raised; and if my thrusts were not serious he never moved. Do you believe this story?"

"Absolutely!" I cried, delighted, "I would believe the first stranger who told me so plausible a story, and how much more you!"

"Well, then, my friend," said Herr C., "you have all that you need to enable you to understand me. In the organic world we see that grace has greater power and brilliance in proportion as the reasoning powers are dimmer and less active. But as one line, when it crosses another, suddenly appears on the other side of the intersecting point, after its passage through infinity; or as the image in a concave mirror, after retreating into infinity, suddenly reappears close before our eyes, so, too, when knowledge has likewise passed through infinity, grace will reappear. So that we shall find it at its purest in a body which is entirely devoid of consciousness or which possesses it in an infinite degree; that is, in the marionette or the god."

"You mean," I said rather tentatively, "that we must eat again of the tree of knowledge in order to relapse into the state of Innocence?"

"Certainly," he replied. "That is the last chapter of the history of the world."

(1810)

III

Dance and
the Other Arts

The earliest Italian and French court ballets, the Elizabethan
court masques, the most celebrated works of the Ballets Russes,
and many of the so-called "happenings" of the 1960's all have at
least one thing in common: they all attempted to synthesize several individual arts into a composite whole. Although the dream
of uniting (or, as some writers have claimed, re-uniting) the separate arts can be traced back to Renaissance theories of opera, the
best known and most ambitious proposal for this sort of theatrical synthesis is Wagner's theory of the *Gesamtkunstwerk* or
"total work of art." Wagner called his *Gesamtkunstwerk* the "art
work of the future"; but, ironically, he conceived of it as an
attempt to revive the essence of classical tragic drama, or what
he called "the great unitarian art work of Greece." Wagner, like
the Renaissance neo-classicists before him, takes his cue from
Aristotle's *Poetics* which argued that Greek tragic drama combined six basic elements: plot, character, diction, thought, music,
and spectacle.

Wagner, though, concentrates on the re-unification of three
major elements: music, dance, and speech. In a prose style more
rhapsodic than discursive, he insists that

> The arts of Dance, of Tone, and Poetry thus call themselves the
> three Primeval Sisters. . . . By their nature they are inseparable

185

without disbanding the stately minuet of Art; for in this dance, which is the very cadence of Art itself, they are so wondrous closely interlaced with one another. . . .

Unfortunately, the seamless unity he advocates is more easily achieved in theory than in practice. (Mallarmé complained that, in Wagner's operas, both dance and poetry are give short shrift.) But no matter how far Wagner himself may have fallen short of his own ideal, the theory itself continues to exercise a tremendous fascination for modern artists and intellectuals. Frank Kermode, as we have already seen, points out that both Loïe Fuller and the early Ballets Russes extravaganzas were hailed as "true" realizations of the *Gesamtkunstwerk*, out-Wagnering Wagner.

But neither Fuller nor Diaghilev attempted a reconciliation of dance and speech. Fuller in fact argued that "motion and not language is truthful." And when Cocteau tried to convince Diaghilev that the French and American managers in "Parade" should speak through megaphones, the impresario replied that spoken language had no place in the work of the Ballets Russes.

Of course, it's entirely possible that the sort of unity and equality among the arts that Wagner advocates has never existed, not even in "the great unitarian art work of Greece." Aristotle, after all, lists the six constituent elements of tragic drama in order of descending importance, with music and spectacle (under which dance movement is subsumed) ranked lowest.

But for many twentieth-century figures, the true appeal of the *Gesamtkunstwerk* lies not in the integration of the arts per se, but rather in its promise of a return to primitive origins, to the sort of ecstatic, ritualistic experience from which the separate arts presumably evolved. Dance is often hailed as the oldest and most primitive of the arts (both R. G. Collingwood and Havelock Ellis will make that claim in different ways in this anthology). And thus it is toward dance—especially the modern dance—that many proponents of the *Gesamtkunstwerk* turn. That, certainly, is the way Eric Bentley, one of America's finest critics and theoreticians of the drama, responds to the work of Martha Graham.

Bentley argues that this desire to re-create a theatre of primitive, wordless ecstasy is a peculiarly *modern* impulse. (Presumably, only the inhabitants of urban, secular societies feel the pressing need to re-awaken some sense of wholeness and animal vitality.) "It seems curious at first," notes Bentley, "that the result of 'scraping back' should be a modern style, that you should go to the beginning in order to find the end, but such is the way now to the only true modernity." Writing in the early 1950's, he insists that "Graham is *the* dancer of the age of anxiety. But she is not content, like, say, Jerome Robbins in his ballet on this theme, to discourse about anxiety. . . . We can only express neurosis in art by conquering it, if fragmentarily, if momentarily. . . . And health is found at the very foundation or nowhere. Down through the cerebral nervosities to the primal energies, that is Martha Graham's journey." Sounding more than a bit like a radical Freudian, a Wilhelm Reich, or a Norman O. Brown, Bentley suggests that, for those who wish to correct the "neurotic" character of modern civilization, language itself is part of the problem, and that much of the appeal of modern dance derives from the fact that it often seems not only non-verbal, but anti-verbal.

Of course, Bentley, like many other twentieth-century theatre people, is enthusiastic about modern dance for another, more purely aesthetic reason: it provides a bold, colorful, highly theatrical alternative to the prosaic style of surface realism that dominates the commercial stage. "If we need something to offset our realistic theatre, undoubtedly the dominant theatre of our age," writes Bentley, " . . . then we should thank Martha Graham. She is the fullest realization we know of that magical theatre of which Craig and Yeats and so many others have dreamed." Yeats wrote a number of short dramas that he called "Plays for Dancers" and Gordon Craig, the visionary designer-director who was for a time romantically involved with Isadora Duncan, once wrote that "the actor is for me only an insufferable difficulty. . . . (Actors) must cease to speak, and move only, if they want to restore art to its old place. Acting is action—and dance the poetry of action."

The contemporary distrust of language suggests at least one reason why a complete theatrical synthesis is not likely to be achieved any time soon. But Constant Lambert, the British composer and longtime musical director of the Sadler's Wells Ballet, points out another, very different problem with the Wagnerian ideal. He argues that when the separate arts have fully realized the unique potential of their own media, they cannot be happily or successfully married to one another: "A speech from *Hamlet* or *The Duchess of Malfi* . . . , or one of Keats's odes," he writes, "can only lose by any association with music because they are already complete works of art in themselves. If the music parallels their concentration and richness, it will only distract our attention from the words; if it remains in the background allowing the words to speak for themselves, then it is superfluous.

Exactly the same situation can be observed in the world of ballet."

The greatest dance scores of Tchaikovsky and Stravinsky cannot—should not—attempt to stand on their own in the concert hall. (Many of us would, of course, disagree with this particular claim.) But Lambert does not intend these remarks pejoratively. On the contrary, he insists that the dance scores of Tchaikovsky and Stravinsky are exemplary because they appreciate the difference between direct or present action and recollected or imaginary action. In the dance, he says, we are solely concerned with present action: "Choreography by its very nature is denied the oblique approach to narrative or action open to the writer or (concert hall) composer." Thus, the ideal musical accompaniment for dance will avoid any sense of vagueness, mere suggestion, or recollection; it will create instead a vivid sense of present action.

But is it true that choreography can never take an "oblique" approach to action? What about Balanchine's "Serenade" or Robbins's "Dances at a Gathering," works that hint subtly and indirectly at narrative complications amid an otherwise formal structure? Furthermore, Lambert's insistence that the ideal music for dance convey a sense of present action would seem to rule out many scores by both Debussy and Ravel that have inspired great works of choreography. Certainly, according to Lambert's extremely strict criterion of acceptability, Balanchine should probably never have choreographed "Episodes" to Webern. One also wonders what he would say about the choreography of Merce Cunningham where sound and movement are intended to make (often) conflicting claims on our attention.

Lambert examines one other controversial question: How closely should the dancing follow the music? He takes a firm stand against the tradition of "music visualization" and is opposed to the sort of slavish correspondence between music and movement advocated by Dalcroze. "The dance," he says, "should not be a translation of the music, but an interpretation of it." Even in the early 1930's, when this article was written, it was already evident to Lambert that George Balanchine is the exemplary choreographic interpreter of music, the master of contrapuntal complexity.

Like Lambert, Étienne Decroux, the renowned French mime and teacher of Marcel Marceau, is anti-Wagnerian; in fact, he is an uncompromising advocate of modernist "purity." In his conversation with Eric Bentley included in this section, he argues that "the law of art is not addition, but subtraction. To add is to make a mess, to restore the original 'togetherness' or disorder of the world. What is rich in art? Not a mixture. A purity. A single thing—which penetrates deeply." Thus pantomime should not translate or interpret a preexisting work of dramatic literature: "it should renounce the privilege of sheltering behind the great names of writers."

When Bentley suggested to Decroux that pantomime is often difficult to distinguish from dance, the renowned mime replied that he saw the two arts as virtual opposites. Dance, he said, is abstract and based on music; pantomime concrete and based on the direct observation of daily life. Every one of the mime's gestures must have a real-life counterpart, whereas dance is too abstract to be read in this literal way. The dancer can be compared to a man "out for a walk," someone taking a stroll; but the mime is a man walking somewhere specific, a man with a destination. The dancer, unlike the mime, belongs to a world wholly mastered by man: when dancers on stage pretend to carry a grand piano, they make no attempt to indicate its real weight; but the mime will insist on displaying the strain that the object occasions. Decroux of course, is talking about ballet, not about modern or post-modern dance, both of which often assume an entirely different attitude toward "effort" (indeed, in some post-modern dances, the performers might well be asked to move a *real* grand piano).

But in arguing for the clearest possible distinction between dance and pantomime, Decroux echoes Mallarmé who wrote in *Ballets:* "Acting and dancing become suddenly hostile when they are brought forcibly together. . . . Ordinarily, the librettist fails to understand that the ballerina expresses herself with steps, and that beyond this she has no eloquence, not even that of gesture." Clearly, Decroux and Mallarmé both have reservations about the way mime was employed in nineteenth-century narrative ballets (for example, the sequence at the beginning of the second act of "The Nutcracker" when the Prince describes in mimed gesture the battle between the mice and the lead soldiers).

George Bernard Shaw, who was an extraordinarily perceptive critic of music and drama as well as a great playwright, takes a very different view of the ideal relationship between pure dance and pantomimic gesture. An avowed enemy of both escapist diversion and "art for art's sake"—indeed, of any divorce between "art" and "life"—Shaw detested the "brainless artificiality" of the ballet he saw as a music critic in London during the 1890's. He proposed that self-indulgent displays of technical virtuosity be replaced by a more representational form of dance-drama. "Why not then," he suggests, "call in the services of a dramatic story-teller . . . and make a clean sweep of all the merely habitual business that has no purpose and no meaning?"

Clearly, Shaw has more in common with Noverre, Fokine, or even the early partisans of modern dance than with a formalist like André Levinson—although, to be precise, Shaw is not railing against formalism per se, but rather against "meaningless" displays of technique and the reduction of dancers to the status of trained seals. Granted, he would probably have objected just as vehemently to the most complex, formalist ballet of Balanchine's; but no formalist of Balanchine's stature was at work in London in the late nineteenth century. Put another way, the essential concern of the ballets Shaw wrote about was not shape, line, and color, but rather acrobatic feats. Thus Shaw advises the dancer to "move us; act for us; make our favorite stories real for us; weave your grace and skill into the fabric of our life; but don't put us off for the thousandth time with those dreary pirouettes and entrechats and whatd'yecallems."

It is instructive to compare Shaw's essay with Bentley's, because, as theatre people, both write about dance from the vantage point of dramatic literature. Bentley speaks for those who are dissatisfied with the realistic drama and who propose that the theatre move in the direction of the wordless, more abstract modern dance. Shaw, dissatisfied with the remoteness of nineteenth-century ballet from social reality, encourages it to move in the direction of the realistic drama (that is, toward the sort of drama that he himself would soon be writing). Shaw is suggesting, at least implicitly, that the academic vocabulary of steps be supplemented with expressive and mimetic gesture, although it isn't entirely clear whether he is advocating the sort of conventionalized mime then in use in the Russian Imperial ballets of Petipa or whether he would prefer the sort of gesture derived from Delsarte that found its way into the early modern dance.

In the introduction to Section II, we saw that Lessing insisted on a strict differentiation between the spatial and the temporal arts. Painters were advised to avoid subjects involving the passage of time because their medium is spatial. One might reasonably assume—on Lessing's advice—that dancing would constitute a most unlikely subject for painters. Why, then, does dance figure so prominently in the paintings of Picasso, Toulouse-Lautrec, and, above all, Edgar Degas? Theodore Reff, the art historian and critic, answers this question by examining the many reasons for Degas's life-long infatuation with ballet. Degas, he points out, had always been fascinated by the pictorial potential of beings in motion—whether dancers, pedestrians crossing Parisian streets, or race horses galloping at Longchamp. Degas had studied (and even copied) Muybridge's famous sequence photographs of horses in motion.

But ballet held a particular attraction for him, Reff suggests, because it is in the nature of ballet movement to appear at once dynamic and poised (a quality that reminded Degas of the classical Greek sculpture he so dearly loved). Furthermore, Degas believed passionately that art and conscious effort are inherently superior to nature and spontaneity. And thus, the very artificiality of classical ballet, the dancer's willed triumph over the natural inclinations of the body, confirmed his own prejudices in favor of art over nature. But Degas's keen eye also allowed him to penetrate the artificial aura projected by the dancer in performance, so as to reveal the contrast between the drudgery of the dancer's daily existence and the magic of her momentary glory on stage.

RICHARD WAGNER
From THE ART-WORK OF THE FUTURE

... The three chief artistic faculties of the entire man have once, and of their own spontaneous impulse, evolved to a trinitarian utterance of human Art; and this was in the primal, earliest manifested art-work, the *Lyric,* and its later, more conscious, loftiest completion, the *Drama.*

The arts of *Dance,* of *Tone,* and *Poetry:* thus call themselves the three primeval sisters whom we see at once entwine their measures wherever the conditions necessary for art manifest themselves. By their nature they are inseparable without disbanding the stately minuet of Art; for in this dance, which is the very cadence of Art itself, they are so wondrous closely interlaced with one another, of fairest love and inclination, so mutually bound up in each other's life, of body and of spirit: that each of the three partners, unlinked from the united chain and bereft thus of her own life and motion, can only carry on an artificially inbreathed and borrowed life—not giving forth her sacred ordinances, as in their trinity, but now receiving despotic rules for mechanical movement. . . .

This is Art the free. The sweet and forceful impulse in that dance of sisters, is the *impulse of Freedom;* the love-kiss of their enlocked embraces, the *transport of a freedom won.*

The solitary unit is unfree, because confined and fettered in un-Love; the *associate is free,* because unfettered and unconfined through Love. . . .

Each separate faculty of man is limited by bounds; but his united, agreed, and reciprocally helping faculties—and thus his faculties in *mutual love* of one another—combine to form the self-completing, unbounded, universal faculty of men. Thus too has every *artistic* faculty of man its natural bounds, since man has not *one only Sense* but separate *Senses;* while every faculty springs from its special sense, and therefore each single faculty must find its bounds in the confines of its correlated sense. But the boundaries of the separate senses are also their joint meeting-points, those points at which they melt into one another and each agrees with each; and exactly so do the faculties that are derived from them touch one another and agree. Their confines, therefore, are removed by the agreement; but only those that love each other can agree, and "to love" means: to acknowledge the other, and at like time to know one's self. Thus Knowledge through Love is Freedom; and the freedom of man's faculties is—*All-faculty.*

Only the Art which answers to the "all-faculty" of man is, therefore, *free;* and not the Art-*variety,* which only issues from a single human faculty. The Arts of Dance, of Tone, of Poetry, are each confined within their several bounds; in contact with these bounds each feels herself unfree, be it not that, across their common boundary, she reaches out her hand to her neighboring art in unrestrained acknowledgment of love. The very grasping of this hand lifts her above the barrier; her full embrace, her full absorption in her sister—i.e., her own complete ascension beyond the set-up barrier—casts down the fence itself. And when every barrier has thus fallen, then are there no more *arts* and no more boundaries, but only *Art,* the universal, undivided.

It is a sorry misconception of Freedom—that of the being who would fain be free in loneliness. The impulse to loose one's self from commonalty, to be free and independent for individual self alone, can only lead to the direct antithesis of the state so arbitrarily striven after: namely to utmost lack of self-dependence. Nothing in Nature is self-dependent excepting that which has the conditionments of its self-standing not merely in itself, but also outside of itself: for the inner are first possible by virtue of the outer. That which would separate itself must, necessarily, first have that from which to separate. He who would fain be nothing but himself, must first know what he is; but this he only learns by distinguishing from what he is not: were he able to lop off entirely that which differs from him, then were he himself no differentiated entity, and thus no longer cognisable by himself. In order to will to be the whole thing which of and in himself he is, the individual must learn to be absolutely not the thing he is not; but the thing that is absolutely what *he* is not, is that thing which lies apart from him; and only in the fullest of communion with that which is apart from him, in the completest absorption into the commonalty of those who differ from him, can he ever be completely *what* he is by nature, what he must be, and as a reasonable being, can but will to be. Thus only in Communism does Egoism find its perfect satisfaction.

That Egoism, however, which has brought such immeasurable woe into the world and so lamentable a mutilation and insincerity into Art, is of another breed to the natural and rational egoism which finds its perfect satisfaction in the community of all. In pious indignation it wards off the name of "Egoism" from it, and dubs itself "Brotherly-" and "Christian-" "Art-" and "Artist-Love"; founds temples to God and Art; builds hospitals to make ailing old-age young and sound—and schools to make youth old and ailing; establishes 'faculties,' courts of justice, governments, states, and what not else?—merely to prove that it is not Egoism. And this is just the most irredeemable feature of it, and that which makes it utterly pernicious both to itself and to the general commonalty. This is the isolation of the single, in which each severed nullity shall rank as something, but the great commonalty as naught; in which each unit struts as something special and "original," while the whole, forsooth, can then be nothing in particular and for ever a mere imitation. This is the self-dependence of the individual, where every unit lives upon the charges of his fellows, in order to be "free by help of God"; pretends to be what others *are*; and, briefly, follows the inversion of the teaching of Jesus Christ: "To *take* is more blessed than to give."

This is the genuine Egosim, in which each *isolated art-variety* would give itself the airs of universal Art; while, in truth, it only thereby loses its own peculiar attributes. . . .

. . . Thus the Poetic art can absolutely not create the genuine art-work—and this is only such an one as is brought to direct physical manifestment—without those arts to which the physical show belongs directly. Thought, that mere phantom of reality, is formless by itself; and only when it retraces the road on which it rose to birth, can it attain artistic perceptibility. In the Poetic art, the purpose of all Art comes first to consciousness: but the other arts contain within themselves the unconscious Necessity that forms this purpose. The art of Poetry is the creative process by which the Art-work steps into life: but out of Nothing, only the god of the Israelites can make some-thing—the Poet must have that Something; and that something is the whole artistic man, who proclaims in the art of Dance and Tone the physical longing become a longing of the soul, which through its force first generates the poetic purpose and finds in that its absolution, in its attainment its own appeasing.

Wheresoever *the Folk* made poetry—and only by the Folk, or in the footsteps of the Folk, can poetry be really made—there did the Poetic purpose rise to life alone upon the shoulders of the arts of Dance and Tone, as the *head* of the full-fledged human being. The Lyrics of Orpheus would never have been able to turn the savage beasts to silent, placid adoration, if the singer had but given them forsooth some dumb and printed verse to read: their ears must be enthralled by the sonorous notes that came straight from the heart, their carrion-spying eyes be tamed by the proud and graceful movements of the body—*in such a way* that they should recognise instinctively in this whole man no longer a mere object for their maw, no mere objective for their feeding, but for their hearing- and their seeing-powers—before they could be attuned to duly listen to his moral sentences.

Neither was the true *Folk-epic* by any means a mere recited poem: the songs of Homer, such as we now possess them, have issued from the critical siftings and compilings of a time in which the genuine Epos had long since ceased to live. . . . But before these epic songs became the object of such literary care, they had flourished mid the Folk, eked out by voice and gesture, as a bodily enacted Art-work; as it were, a fixed and crystallised blend of lyric song and dance, with predominant lingering on portrayal of the action and reproduction of the heroic dialogue. . . .

The *Opera*, as the seeming point of reunion of all the three related arts, has become the meeting-place of these sisters' most self-seeking efforts. Undoubtedly Tone claims for herself the supreme right of legislation therein; nay, it is solely to her struggle—though led by egoism—towards the genuine artwork of the Drama, that we owe the Opera at all. But in degree as Poetry and Dance were bid to be her simple slaves, there rose amid *their* egoistic ranks a growing spirit of rebellion against their domineering sister. The arts of Dance and Poetry had taken a personal lease of Drama *in their own way:* the spectacular Play and the pantomimic Ballet were the two territories between which Opera now deployed her troops, taking from each whatever she deemed indispensable for the self-glorification of Music. Play and Ballet, however, were well aware of her aggressive self-sufficiency: they only lent themselves to their sister against their will, and in any case with the mental reservation that on the first favorable opportunity they each would clear themselves an exclusive field. So Poetry leaves behind her feeling and her pathos, the only fitting wear for Opera, and throws her net of modern Intrigue around her sister Music; who, without being able to get a proper hold of it, must willynilly twist and turn the empty cobweb, which none but the nimble play-sempstress herself can plait into a tissue: and there she chirps and twitters, as in the French confectionary-operas, until at last her peevish breath gives out, and sister Prose steps in to fill the stage. Dance, on the other hand, has only to espy some breach in the breath-taking of the tyrannizing songstress, some chilling of the lava-stream of musical emotion—and in an instant she flings her legs astride the boards; trounces sister Music off the scene, down to the solitary confinement of the orchestra; and spins, and whirls, and runs around, until the public can no longer see the wood for wealth of leaves, i.e., the opera for the crowd of legs.

Thus Opera becomes the mutual compact of the egoism of the three related arts. To rescue her supremacy, Tone contracts with Dance for so many quarters-of-an-hour which shall belong to the latter *alone:* during this period the chalk upon the shoe-soles shall trace the regulations of the stage, and music shall be made according to the system of the *leg-*, and not the *tone-*, vibrations; item, that the singers shall be expressly forbidden to indulge in any sort of graceful bodily motion—this is to be the exclusive property of the dancer, whereas the singer is to be pledged to complete abstention from any fancy for mimetic gestures, a restriction which will have the additional advantage of conserving his voice. With Poetry Tone settles, to the former's highest satisfaction, that she will not employ her in the slightest on the stage; nay, will as far as possible not even articulate her words and verses, and will relegate her instead to the printed text-book, necessarily to be read *after* the performance, in Literature's decorous garb of black and white. Thus, then, is the noble bond concluded, each art again itself; and between the dancing legs and written book, Music once more floats gaily on through all the length and breadth of her desire. *This is modern Freedom in the faithful counterfeit of Art! . . .*

Thus supplementing one another in their changeful dance, the united sister-arts will show themselves and make good their claim; now all together, now in pairs, and again in solitary splendor, according to the momentary need of the only rule- and purpose-giver, the Dramatic Action. Now plastic Mimicry will listen to the passionate plaint of Thought; now resolute Thought will pour itself into the expressive mold of Gesture; now Tone must vent alone the stream of Feeling, the shudder of alarm; and now, in mutual embrace, all three will raise the Will of Drama to immediate and potent Deed. For One thing there is that all the three united arts must will, in order to be free: and that one thing is the Drama: the reaching of the Drama's aim must be their common goal. Are they conscious of this aim, do they put forth all their will to work out that alone: so will they also gain the power to lop off from their several stems the egoistic offshoots of their own peculiar being; that therewith the tree may not spread out in formless mass to every wind of heaven, but proudly lift its wreath of branches, boughs and leaves, into its lofty crown. . . .

(1849)

ERIC BENTLEY
MARTHA GRAHAM'S
JOURNEY

What is Martha Graham's place in our theater? It would be idle to pretend that the hopes of ten and twenty years ago have been realized, that modern dance has been accepted and established like ballet, much less that is has made any impact upon the dramatic theater. It is the poor relation among the theater arts; actors are paid at least when they work, but modern dancers have to make their living in some other profession. To the public, modern dance has as yet a hazy existence, is probably confused with gym lessons in girls' colleges, and is certainly associated with a horse-tail hair-do and square shoulders; it is to theater what spiritualism is to religion: a suburban, low-heeled, pretentious, but not really dangerous rival. Judging by a recent experiment in New York—*Mourning Becomes Electra* as a dance drama—I should judge that its procedures cannot be taken over by actors and substituted for dialogue; Decroux's claim that dance is distinct from pantomime was made good. Nor have attempts to use modern dance within the framework of drama been much more successful. No wonder it has been whispered that Miss Graham's art will go down to the grave with her.

I don't know what one can say about this opinion except that it will become true if enough people repeat and believe it. Even so, when a given form of an art dies, there is no knowing what elements from it may nourish other forms and survive in them; the wind bloweth where it listeth. There is certainly a case for trying to define the theater of Martha Graham while it is still there to define. Even if her influence were over, it would remain important that she herself exists.

Havelock Ellis spoke of dances pantomimic and ecstatic, and we may speak of theater generally under the same two heads. The pantomimic theater depicts life, holds the mirror up to nature. The ecstatic theater affirms life and celebrates nature— by awakening in us the vital, natural forces. The one shows life as it has become—what we call psychology and sociology. The other is concerned with life still unlived, unindividuated, primordial, life unfiltered, still in the wellspring. This other theater has been forgotten. Or if not forgotten, remembered only by theorists like Nietzsche or by creative artists like Wagner and O'Neill, who for different reasons never succeeded in reviving it. None of these men was primitive enough, had direct enough access to the depths. Martha Graham has the edge over them in that dance is of itself more primitive than literature or opera. True, dance energy can be sublimated into Mozart operas or even into Shavian discussion plays, but that is only to say you can't banish dance from the theater altogether. It would be natural to suppose it would come back naked after a period in operatic or literary dress. Nearly half a century ago Jane Harrison said that as our life becomes more and more artificial and we live more and more at second hand, we feel a growing need for that direct contact with life which is felt in dance. She had explained in advance the origin of modern dancing—which, translated into the terms of dramatic criticism, is a revival of ecstatic theater. If we need something to offset our realistic theater, undoubtedly the dominant theater of our age, if we need reminding of another possibility, if it is desirable to keep another, *the* other, sort of theater alive, then we should thank Martha Graham. She is the fullest realization we know of that magical theater of which Craig and Yeats and so many others have dreamed.

The ecstatic theater takes the form of modern dance, the pantomimic theater takes the form of realistic drama. But how relative our conception of realism is! Less realistic than our drama, modern dance is more realistic than ballet. Within the field of dance criticism it is the hard realists who defend Graham, the aesthetes who defend Balanchine. Edwin Denby writes:

> Judged by what I look for in ballet, Miss Graham's gesture lacks a way of opening up completely, and her use of dance rhythm seems to me fragmentary. It does not rise in a long sustained line and come to a conclusion. I find she uses the stage space the way the realistic theater does, as an accidental segment of a place; not the way the poetic theater uses the stage—as a space complete in itself.

A realist would reply that theater is indeed a "segment" of the world, though not an accidental one, and that it is both intelligent and "poetic" to suggest that the lines of a stage design continue outside the theater. Here and now I am more concerned with another remark of Denby's. He says that Miss Graham "began with the decorative attitudes and the connecting walks

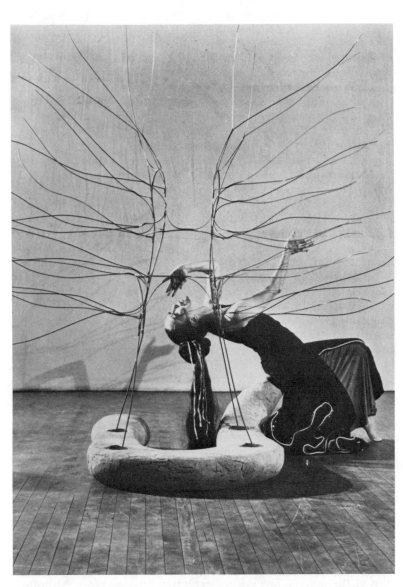

Martha Graham in "Cave of the Heart" (1947). "If we need something to offset our realistic theater, undoubtedly the dominant theater of our age, if we need reminding of another possibility, if it is desirable to keep another, *the* other, sort of theater alive, then we should thank Martha Graham. She is the fullest realization we know of that magical theater of which Craig and Yeats and so many others have dreamed." (Bentley)

of Denishawn 'exotica'; her formal point of departure was an
actor's loose gesture sequence, not a dancer's logically sustained
dance sequence." The *parti pris* here is given away by the ascrip-
tion of the epithet "loose" to an actor's gestures and the epithet
"logical" to a dancer's steps. More serious is the preceding clause.
"Decorative attitudes" and "connecting walks" and "exotica"
suggest triviality. It is for those who have let Graham's art work
on them to report how much more than "exotic" is the unfamiliar element in it; "exotic" is the word we give to originality that
we fail to recognize. How much more her walks do than "connect" is apparent to every sensitive witness of the first minute of
her *Joan*. Ballet-dancers would do well to learn from Miss Graham the virtues of omission: when a plain walk is right and
expresses everything that is to be expressed, more than a walk
would be wrong.

As for "decorative attitudes," what Graham has done for them
is enough in itself to stamp her a genius. She can stand or sit
doing nothing and keep our attention, not by "personality" in
the ruined, everyday sense, not by her private ego, let alone her
sex appeal or charm (also in the ruined sense), not wholly by her
beauty either, but by a personality that she achieves on stage by
sheer concentration of purpose. Admittedly this is in part a matter of beauty. But Graham's beauty is of a formidable sort, enigmatic, ambiguous. Sometimes, especially in photographs, she
looks like the standard glamorous woman of these United States.
Yet above the standard American mouth, set in the unnaturally
motionless mask of her upper face, are the perturbed eyes of the
American intelligentsia, luminous centers of un-American activities. There are times when one hates Martha Graham's face.
Because there is no drama without contrast, beauty has to be
ambivalent to be dramatic.

Martha Graham's attitudes would only seem "decorative" to
someone who does not look for their meaning because he is sunk
in the formalism (or anti-realism) of the ballet. What gives life to
an attitude? Is it not the dramatic quality we call "projection"?
At the crudest level what gives projection is the projecting portion of the body, a fact wittily exploited by Mae West. Although
Miss Graham exploits her physique more fully than Miss West,
it is her peculiar glory to suggest by the physical so much of the
non-physical. Hence the relevance of the most spiritual part of
the body, the face, and of the most spiritual part of the face, the
eyes.

There was a time when the face was not important, even to an actor. He kept it hidden under a mask. In modern times, however, the face has increasingly become the center of theatrical action, and the cinema has offered us faces eighteen feet high, with features as large as our arms and legs. Only the ballet-dancer has kept a semblance of the mask by the impassivity—deliberate or involuntary—of her face. Ballet-dancing evinces one of the leading characteristics of decadence: making one part of an organism develop inordinately while letting the rest fall into desuetude. A race of ballet-dancers would eventually be all legs; the fixed expression on the face would be detachable, as with Cheshire cats. On the nonballet stage, with the spread of realism, attention has come more and more to be focused on the face.

There are, of course, not only degrees of realism, but also kinds. We customarily think of realism as the mimicking of externals, yet Stanislavsky wrote of Chekhov's spiritual realism, and Stark Young has eloquently described a similar inwardness and passion in the realism of Duse. If the opposite of realism is formalism, or love of patterns for their own sake, Martha Graham is rather to be classed with Chekhov and Duse. The nature of her medium makes her—or helps her to be—less psychological. She is concerned with the inner life, but not with individual psychology. Just as music-drama has best been able to project certain instinctual types (Orpheus, Don Juan, the Flying Dutchman), so the dance-drama of Martha Graham approaches female archetypes: Herodias, Judith, Joan. Just as music undercuts psychology and takes us down to the subsoil in which psychology has its roots, so Graham's dance portraits present only the dynamic variations of feeling that underlie our motives and decisions. Hence it is her most nearly perfect compositions, such as *Herodiade*, that most defy analysis. Unless I am mistaken, it would be foolish to read such a piece as allegory and say "this means Herodias is plotting mischief" and the like. Miss Graham is creating an *Urwelt* from which mischief could indeed come, but which has itself no moral or psychological bias; great good could come from it too.

Realistic compared with the ballet, unrealistic compared with modern drama, Martha Graham is certainly—and, at her best, single-mindedly—concerned with reality. Reality is both external and internal, and if it is chiefly the internal that she sees, we shall ask how well she sees it rather than demand that she sees the external too. Of a work of art we demand that it be all true, not that it be all the truth. It must be what the artist sees when looking with all his might through the spyglass of his medium.

There are some who would be happier if Miss Graham would dance more decoratively, just as there must be others who would wish her to drop the larger movements of the dance and limit herself to the smaller movements of life. They wish the one or the other on grounds of style. They want her more realistic or less so. She must refuse to comply, not on grounds of style, but on grounds of meaning. Whatever the resultant style, she must interpret life. Seeing her early career, critics expressed their amazement at her ruthlessness in eliminating movements and postures that said nothing. In modern fashion, she brought back into art much of the unevenness of life; hence her syncopated rhythms and spasmodic moves. By this time her system of contractions and releases is indeed a system, and her wearier works, like *Judith*, are more of an inventory than an invention. None the less, in the *Joan* we still find her, in Stark Young's words, "scraping back to the design," going back to the beginning. And that, in the theater today, is the *unum necessarium*. Such an example, from a great performer and creator—Chaplin, Decroux, Graham—is all we can expect and more than we deserve.

It seems curious at first that the result of "scraping back" should be a modern style, that you should go to the beginning in order to find the end; but such is the way now to the only true modernity. That a sprinkling of false modernities should overlay and to some extent disguise and distort the true meaning of Graham's work is confusing but unavoidable. None of us keeps clear either of infections or of false remedies. Even Martha Graham is not a goddess.

She is a priestess. A present-day priestess of an ancient cult. Notoriously, she is the dancer of the age of anxiety. But she is not content, like, say, Jerome Robbins in his ballet on this theme, to discourse *about* anxiety with the resources of top-drawer ingenuity. Nor is it enough to see neurosis from the vantage-point of neurosis as Robbins, in more earnest vein, occasionally may be said to have done. That is no vantage-point at all. We can only express neurosis in art by conquering it, if fragmentarily, if momentarily. The only vantage-point to view sickness from is health. And health is found at the very foundations or nowhere. Down through the cerebral nervosities to the primal energies, that is Martha Graham's journey. If we accompany her, even part of the way, must we not benefit?

(1952)

CONSTANT LAMBERT
MUSIC AND ACTION

Music, though the most subtle of all arts in its powers of suggestion, is the most clumsy in its powers of definition. It can suggest some nostalgic half-shade of emotion with an almost mathematical precision denied to literature, yet it is incapable of the simple distinction between "He said" and "He thought" without which the art of the novel would be impossible. (Even in the works of writers like Joyce and Faulkner, who exalt the interior monologue at the expense of the action, the distinction between the two is as firmly established as in the case of Dickens.) But although music is incapable of making this distinction in so many words, or rather so many notes, it would be a great mistake to imagine that this distinction does not exist.

We use the word "music" to cover the world of ordered sound in general, often without realising that music can be divided into as many distinct branches as literature—poetic drama, prose drama, novels, belles-lettres, travel books and the like. No one would dream of making a play out of Sir Thomas Browne's *Urn Burial* or Kant's *Critique of Pure Reason*, yet some of the recent choreographic assaults on famous pieces of music have not been less absurd in their misunderstanding of medium. The crude distinction between music actually written for the stage and music written for the concert-hall is naturally appreciated; but it is not so often realised that a similar distinction can exist as regards two pieces of concert-hall music—I mean the difference between what may be called direct or present action, and what may be called recollected or imaginary action.

The difference can most clearly be seen if we compare two pieces apparently in the same genre and sharing certain similarities of style: Rimsky-Korsakoff's *Scheherazade* and Balakireff's *Thamar*, two evocative orchestral works both of which were eventually turned into ballets. I am not alone in considering Balakireff's work greatly superior from the purely musical point of view, and I expect many will agree with me in preferring Fokine's choreography and Bakst's décor in *Thamar* to their work in *Scheherazade*, considered again as separate artistic elements. Yet *Scheherazade*, is to me the more successful and satisfying ballet of the two, for the simple reason that the music has the direct two-dimensional quality of present action, while Balakireff's work has the more subtle quality of imagined or recollected action. The success is all the more remarkable when we remember that the scenario of *Thamar* follows closely the Lermontoff poem round which Balakireff wrote his symphonic poem, while the scenario of *Scheherazade* has nothing in common with the stories round which Rimsky-Korsakoff wrote his symphonic suite. The point, I think, is this: Rimsky-Korsakoff's formal outlook being as simple and direct as the narrative methods of the *Arabian Nights* themselves, his music lends itself to any tale of a type similar to those he actually chose to illustrate. Balakireff, on the other hand, approaches his subject with something of the formal subtlety of a Conrad, and hence even the most painstaking realization of his tale does a certain violence to the musical content. There is in *Thamar* none of the obvious physical climax which lends itself so successfully to action in the closing scene of *Scheherazade*. Instead we are given an emotional summing-up after the action is over. As a result the actual murder of the Prince on the stage is too strong an action for the music, while on the other hand the epilogue is choreographically speaking too weak.

Conrad, to whom I have compared Balakireff, provides us with a particularly good example of the difference between direct and recollected action which it is so important for the choreographer to realise when dealing with music. It is a platitude to point out that although Conrad's plots, considered as a dramatic framework, are melodramatic, his books are never melodramatic because of his oblique approach to the more theatrical incidents. When, however, he tried to turn his novels and tales into plays they became just melodramas and rather bad ones at that. It is as though some one had re-written a Greek tragedy and shown us the messenger's speech in terms of action; made us see Jocasta committing suicide, Oedipus gouging his eyes out. Such a play would be an outrage on taste, but is it less of an outrage when Massine represents the personal tragedy which lies behind the slow movement of Tchaikovsky No. 5 by a bogy-man with pantomime wings breaking in on a pair of lovers? Choreography by its very nature is denied the oblique approach to narrative or action open to the writer or composer. Hence the necessity for the choreographer and scenario-writer to exercise the utmost discrimination and reticence in the choice of a ballet theme.

To return to *Thamar*, which provides a peculiarly apt test-case for our argument. Though less suited to action than *Scheherazade* because of its emotional-cum-formal subtlety, it is, on the other hand, well suited to action because of its narrative time-sense. It cannot be emphasised too strongly that although the composer is forced to adopt time as his medium he does not always approach time in the same way. Sometimes his themes succeed each other in dramatic sequence like the acts of a play, sometimes their sequence and their position in time is dictated by purely formal reasons. In a symphonic poem by Liszt or Strauss the former is the case. The triumphant apotheoses or pathetic death-scenes which end their works are definitely the last act of the play and represent the final word on the subject in hand. But this is not so in the case of a Mozart symphony. We have it on his own authority that Mozart conceived a symphony in its full form in one moment of time. It stands to reason, then, that the return of a theme in his works can have no narrative or dramatic significance. The recapitulation balances the exposition, much as a tree on one side of a picture might balance one on the other. We do not look at a picture "reading from left to right" as in a society photograph, but take in its design as a whole; and though we inevitably have to listen to a Mozart symphony from left to right, as it were, we should try as far as possible to banish this aspect of the work from our minds and try to see it as the composer conceived it, in one moment of time.

The trouble with any choreographic interpretation of a classical symphony (as opposed to a romantic symphonic poem) is that the dancing is bound to emphasise the least important aspect of the music—its time-sequence. Let us suppose that a choreographer wished to set Mozart's G minor quintet as a ballet. (A hideous thought, but not more hideous than many recent choreographic conceptions.) Any one who appreciates this masterpiece must also appreciate the fact that the final movement, though more light-hearted in tone than the rest of the work, represents not a final "winning through" or "triumph over adversity" but a facet of experience only, no more important than the others through its being placed at the end. But if it were presented on the stage we would be bound to feel during the finale that after a *mauvais quart d'heure* the dancers were cheering up considerably. Perverse though the idea may seem, a complicated *tableau-vivant* would actually be a closer interpretation of Mozart's thought than any ballet.

It is true that there are many symphonies of a later date into which narrative element and dramatic time-sequence enter and which therefore are more suited than Mozart's symphonies to choreographic interpretation. In fact it may safely be said that the worse the symphony the more likely it is to make a good ballet. But that does not alter the fact that the symphony, of all musical forms the most concentrated, intellectual, and withdrawn from present action (as opposed to emotional retrospect), is of all musical forms the least suited to physical or dramatic expression.

That certain symphonic movements are "danceable" is really beside the point. A poem may be musical in the extreme and yet be totally unsuited to musical setting (the greater part of Keats for example). The choice of music for dancing may well be compared to the choice of words for music. The most suitable poems for music are either short lyrics definitely written for the purpose, such as the songs in the Elizabethan dramas which impose their own treatment, or rather loosely written poems with more poetic suggestion than form, such as the poems of Walt Whitman. Fletcher's "Sleep" from *The Woman Hater* is a moving poem when read in the study, but it is doubly moving when heard in Warlock's setting. Whitman's poems, or rather rough drafts for poems, become complete works of art only when supported by the music of Delius or Vaughan Williams. In each case the poem gains. But it is obvious that a speech from *Hamlet* or *The Duchess of Malfi*, an intellectual non-lyrical poem by Donne, or one of Keats's odes can only lose by any association with music because they are already complete works of art in themselves. If the music parallels their concentration and richness it will only distract our attention from the works; if it remains in the background allowing the works to speak for themselves then it is superfluous.

Exactly the same situation can be observed in the world of ballet. Tchaikovsky's short dance tunes or *variations* may be compared to madrigal verse. They "dance themselves" in the way an Elizabethan lyric "sings itself." For all their charm they are only heard to full advantage when in collaboration with the dance. (Imagine the flat effect of a concert performance of the brilliantly conceived *Blue Bird* numbers.) The music of the impressionist composers (in which I would include, of course, early Stravinsky) provides the equivalent of the loosely written *vers libre* of the Whitman type, even when it is specifically written for stage action. That is to say it has more pictorial suggestion than form and does not achieve artistic completeness until defined and pinned down by action. *Petrouchka* is meaningless in the concert-hall unless one knows the ballet; *L'Oiseau de Feu* is only possible when reduced to suite form and even then loses half its effect.

One is in no way decrying these composers by pointing this out. Tchaikovsky and Stravinsky are undoubtedly the two greatest composers the ballet has seen, the one representing the classical opera side of ballet, the other the music-drama side. They would indeed have failed as ballet composers were their work to be satisfying in the concert-hall. But a Beethoven symphony, like a speech in *Hamlet* or an ode by Keats, satisfies us completely in its present form. Any action which might accompany it would either be an irritating distraction or a superfluous echo.

That the greatest of stage composers were thoroughly conscious of the difference between real and imagined action, between statement and reflection can be seen clearly if we look at the work of two composers who divided their attention equally between the concert-hall and the theatre, Mozart and Tchaikovsky. While it would not be quite true to say that the essential style of their music changes when they write for the theatre, it is certainly true that the physique of their music changes. I can think of no tune in any Mozart opera which Mozart could have used as the first or second subject in a symphony, and the same is true of the tunes in Tchaikovsky's ballets. In such a dance as the *pas de deux* in *Lac des Cygnes*, Act II, the very shape of the fiddle solo is determined by the "lifts" in the choreography. We find no such melodic figuration in his symphonies, still less in any classical symphonies. It is most interesting to compare the minuets Mozart actually wrote for dancing with the symphonic minuets in which the dance form merely crystallises some phase of emotion and does not call to action. It is even more interesting to compare the valses in Tchaikovsky's ballets with the valses in his Third and Fifth symphonies.

Impure symphonist though he was, Tchaikovsky only once included in his symphonies a movement more suited to the theatre than the concert-hall. I refer to the finale of the Second Symphony, a straightforward peasant dance which, apart from some sequential passages of development, is no more symphonic in style than the *Kazatchok* of Dargomizhky which it emulates. This movement, by the way, was the only piece of symphonic music (technically speaking) ever used by Diaghilev. The phrase "symphonic suite" as applied to *Scheherazade* has very little meaning, and it is worth noticing that the first movement, which most nearly approaches to symphonic style, was used as an overture only.

To say to the choreographer that he should restrict himself to ballet music written specifically as such by a master of the art like Tchaikovsky or Stravinsky is obviously a vain counsel of perfection. To start with, the supply of such music is by no means equal to the demand. The days when the greatest composers turned naturally and easily to ballet seem to be gradually passing (it is a sign of the times that Stravinsky should have written only one true piece of ballet music since the war—*Le Baiser de la Fée*), and a large number of the ballets written by contemporary composers approach the art from far too literary and operatic a point of view. This is particularly true of the miming scenes where the average composer tries to suggest in the score each inflection of the action. He would be well advised to take a leaf out of Tchaikovsky's book. Tchaikovsky's miming scenes are always admirable because he is content to establish only the general atmosphere of the scene, and does not try to emphasise imaginary words in operatic recitative style. How tiresome by contrast is the opening of *The Three-Cornered Hat* where the music underlines every little detail in the scenario. Falla's ballet (admittedly a first-rate work when viewed as a whole) does not get really going until the dance of the neighbours, which though inessential from the dramatic point of view is good theatre for the simple reason that it is good ballet.

The supply of true ballet music, then, being so inadequate it is only natural that at least half the ballet repertoire should be founded on music written for its own sake. When this music is suited to the dance in texture and rhythm, and not too introspective or philosophical in mood, it can often be as satisfactory as ballet music written for the purpose: witness *Les Sylphides* among classical ballets, and *Cotillon* among modern ballets. But the question of arranging ballets to classical or non-dramatic music immediately raises the most important problem of all for the choreographer: How closely should the dancing follow the music?

There seems to be a growing theory that dancing which represents visually the formal devices and texture of the music must of necessity be pleasing to the musical mind. Nothing could be further from the truth. I am sure there must be innumerable musicians beside myself who experience the same feeling of exasperation when the choreographer turns the stage into a vast lecturer's blackboard and, by associating certain dancers with certain themes, proceeds to underline obvious formal devices in the music which any one of average intelligence can appreciate with half an ear. Literal translations from one language into another are always unsatisfactory and usually ridiculous. "Symphonic" ballets are no exception to this rule. Moreover, the choreographer is debasing his art if he thus makes dancing a mere visual *exposé* of the music. The dance should not be a translation of the music but an interpretation of it. It should not slavishly imitate the musical texture but should add a counter-subject of its own. Choreography which does this is truly contrapuntal, whereas choreography which interprets a fugue in the Dalcroze manner is merely a species of choreographical "vamping," far more harmonic than contrapuntal in feeling.

It is significant that Balanchine, who undoubtedly has the greatest technical knowledge of music among present-day choreographers, is also the most free in his treatment of the music. He is one of the few choreographers with the intelligence to realise that visual complexity is not the most suitable accompaniment to aural complexity. The reverse, surely, is the case. (I am not speaking now of dramatic, narrative ballets where the purple patches in the choreography must inevitably coincide with the purple patches in the story and music.) A complicated fugue occupies, or should occupy, so much of our aesthetic concentration that we cannot assimilate an equal elaboration of physical design at the same time. On the other hand a simple valse tune lends itself to the richest and most complex design on the stage.

I hope I may be pardoned a personal reference in pointing to two highly successful examples of the choreographic counterpoint I am trying to define. One was Ashton's treatment of a three-part *fugato* in *Pomona* as a lyrical dance for a *solo* dancer; the other was the astonishing choreographic fugue which Nijinska arranged to a purely homophonic passage in the finale of *Romeo and Juliet*. We can find examples of the same kind of thing even in the ballets of Massine, who for all his brilliant and indeed unsurpassed sense of purely choreographic design shows only a mechanical and superficial appreciation of musical design. The finales of *Amphytrion* and *Le Pas d'Acier*, for example, where he erects a choreographic structure of remarkable complexity on a comparatively simple musical basis, are to my mind far more successful than the finale of *Choreartium*, which rivals the music in complexity but never in intensity. These two ballets, however, were composed before he had started the vogue for "symphonic" ballet, which marks the nadir of the collaboration between music and the dance.

In a brief essay such as this it is impossible to do more than to adumbrate a few lines of approach to a highly controversial subject which as yet has received little serious attention. I have not attempted to propound anything in the nature of an aesthetic theory. The art of ballet is still too young for that. Ballet did not reach its Wagnerian stage until the pre-war Diaghilev days, and though it has made up since for lost time it is still inclined to lag behind. It will lag farther behind if choreographers, instead of finding new forms inspired by their own medium, pin themselves to forms which belong essentially to another medium, forms, moreover, which (save in a few rare instances) have already outlived their period of aesthetic significance.

(1936)

ERIC BENTLEY
THE PURISM OF
ÉTIENNE DECROUX

FIRST POSTULATE.

If a good play releases before me its powerful flow of verbal water, I am in a state of literary receptivity.

Let a mime appear all of a sudden, and I will judge him queer.

If, when he has begun to "lead me into" his performance, the word again has its turn, it is its turn to be queer.

Hence: one must not place Pantomime and the Word side by side in time when both are richly active.

SECOND POSTULATE.

But can one mix them? Yes, when both are thin—for then one completes the other. Deprived of their music the words of a pleasant song seem thin; the same with the music of the same song deprived of its words.

Hence: one can mix words and pantomime on condition that they be thin.

THIRD POSTULATE.

But cannot one of them manifest itself richly? Yes, to the extent that the second manifests itself thinly.

IN OTHER WORDS:

When two arts are active together, the one must retreat when the other advances, and vice versa.

The poems of Verlaine which have most profited from music are precisely those which are least satisfactory when simply read.

The actor should abstain from all gesture when he speaks rich verses. Conversely, a considerable pantomimic activity may happily accompany words, *thin* words.

But instead of its being a man accompanying words with gestures, it will be a man accompanying his gestures with words . . . and hence thin ones.

But not being aware of the possibilities of Pantomime, no actor can write words that are deliberately thin *and good*— that is, whose thinness is proportionate to the envisaged richness of Pantomime.

Hence, for a long time yet, Pantomime should not insinuate itself into works of dramatic literature; it should renounce the privilege of sheltering behind the great names of writers.

—ÉTIENNE DECROUX

It is usually hard to meet the French on anything like intimate terms. They do not wish to have lunch with you. They make an appointment for the midafternoon, perhaps they drink an apéritif; after which they consider their duty done and never see you again.

Barrault is to be seen for a moment in his dressing-room with the autograph-hunters at his heels and the smile of dutiful, harrassed royalty on his lips.

With Decroux it is different. When you are introduced to him after a performance, he assures you that, while shaking hands and passing the time of day are all very well, one must sit down in peace and for a lengthy session if one intends to get anywhere. I went to his small apartment in the *quatorzième* a couple of times and stayed several hours each time.

I was particularly interested in the purism of Decroux, according to which the theater arts should be separated rather than combined. I mentioned his note on Pantomime and the Word as cited above. Decroux appealed to the well-established view that, in Reinhardt's words, it is to the actor and no one else that the theater belongs. Yes, I said, but the actor is not merely a mime, he also speaks. Decroux replied without fuss that this was precisely the trouble. When an actor speaks he shares the responsibility for his performance with the author of his words; in fact, he becomes the author's slave. "The poet's lines follow one another inexorably like the trucks of a freight train. The poor actor can't squeeze himself in between them. You understand, don't you, how in the end the slave revolts? The cry of the actor against literature is the cry of the native against imperialism, of the Indian against England. . . ." Decroux explained to me his view of a theater without words. It will be all acting. Although costume, lighting, and setting cannot, like words, be totally eliminated, they will be drastically cut down. The result will be essential theater.

I asked if there was anything behind this view except an intense love of pantomime. He said there was. He thought that what I called "purism" was the correct view of art in general. "In the world outside, I grant you, in the universe, things are not separated; they exist in a jumble, together. But man does not accept this situation. *L'homme aime la différence*—man likes difference. Man as scientist admits that things are 'together' in the world, but in the laboratory he separates them. Man as artist refuses even to admit things are 'together' in the world. He is Prometheus, and protests against the nature of things. He lives by the pretense that things are separate in the world too. He lives by separation. The law of art is not addition, but subtraction. To add is to make a mess, to restore the original 'togetherness' or disorder of the world. What is rich, in art? Not a mixture. A purity. A single thing—which penetrates deeply. A single thing that leads to all things." A fervor pressed upon the natural gentleness of Decroux's voice whenever he brought before his inner eye the vision of life as "difference." "Think of love, the love of man and woman. How different are the sex organs of man and woman, how wonderful their union, what a miracle of nature, how they fit together! Now think of the union of like and like—homosexuality! It exists—but it is inconceivable!" And when his American pupil Alvin Epstein came into the room, Decroux said: "Didn't we decide, Ahlveen, that the law of difference is a law of economy? That life is too economical to repeat itself? That even a machine never repeats itself, one part never duplicates the work of another?" The thought would wander all round the intellectual globe before returning to theater and pantomime. The idea was plain. Each art has its own territory and should stick to it. The opposite of Wagnerism.

I raised the objection that the art of dance, for example, was by its very nature dependent on another art (that of music). And, secondly, wasn't dance very close to pantomime, couldn't the two be said to overlap? Decroux was firm. "I will take your first point first. Your 'example' is too carefully chosen: it is the only one you could find. And what must we conclude? Only that dance is the weakest of the arts, the one that can't exist alone—like potatoes, the weak vegetable, a parasite on meat! As to your second point, you have fallen into a cardinal error in thinking of pantomime and dance as akin. They are opposites. Dance is abstract and based on music. Pantomime is concrete and based on life. Dance flows like a stream; pantomime moves with the natural plunge and lunge of the muscles. Dance is soaring and vertical, pantomime earth-bound and horizontal. The dancer works with the leap, the mime with the walk. The dancer deals in symmetric patterns, exact repetitions, regular rhythms, as music enjoins; the mime in asymmetry, variation, syncopation, the rhythmic patterns of speech and natural body movement. Dance comes from excess of energy. When a bear paces to and fro in his cage, he is finding the symmetric patterns of the dance in the usual way. A dancer is a man taking a walk—because his energies are not used up by his work—whereas a mime is a man walking *somewhere*, to a destination. Pantomime is the energy it takes to turn the water-wheel; dance is the gay, spectacular splash of the excess water, the water the wheel does not need. Watch dancers on the stage pretending to carry a grand piano. They rejoice in the hollowness of the pretense. They trip along. The piano has no weight. Now watch mimes going through the same act. They present precisely the weight of the piano by indicating the strain it occasions." As his way is, Decroux let the subject broaden out. The classic dancer and the mime, he maintained, belonged to two diametrically opposite types of man: *l'homme du salon* and *l'homme du sport*. The former belongs to a world that has been mastered by man. Things are done *to* him. Thus, he does not walk, he *is walked:* all the normal symptoms of the adventure that walking is are eliminated; what we see is an imposed pattern. "When a sportsman walks, on the other hand, you see what walking is. Just watch his legs and the way his arms move in concert with them! Your ballet-dancer, like your *homme du salon* in general, has been trained *not* to make these movements; your mime is trained, on the other hand, to display, exploit, and accentuate them—that is, to give them style."

I found these remarks pertinent to the general reconsideration of realism which is afoot today, but when I suggested that pantomime was a more realistic art than dance, Decroux was not particularly pleased. He hastened to state a case against realism (or what he takes for such). "You remember Flaubert's *choisir pour simplifier?*" he asked. "Art should not be too present. Poetry is absence. That is why memory is a good poet. Memory is at a distance, subtracting, adding, assembling. Art is like a dream." I recalled that when Decroux's troupe presents a factory, they make out of it a tenuous abstract beauty, deliberately forgoing the grease and sweat, the human concreteness of it. I recalled that, in one of his demonstrations, Decroux had made much of the rendering of spiritual facts by physical means. "It is the mind's dearest luxury," he said, "to imagine a world without causality—to defy gravity, for instance. The law of life is shock, impact—thus unbroken fluidity of movement suggests the unreal, the spiritual." And instead of leaving this realm to the dancers, Decroux has worked out ways of eliminating contractions—and all jerks and thrusts—from body movement. This is his contribution to that transfiguration of life on the stage which is the professed aim of "magical" theater. As Decroux talked, I thought of Gordon Craig's conception of a stage on which the entrances and exits of characters would be unremarked. A world without causality.

From time to time I returned to the topic that interested me most, Decroux's purism. I sought new points of attack. For instance: "What do you do with Shakespeare, Racine, and the rest?" Decroux did not wish to be so crude. "Let's not talk about sheer good and sheer bad," he said. "There is a hierarchy of the higher and lower. We need the lower in art because the higher is so good we can't stand much of it. Mixed works of art are certainly to be classified as lower. As theater men Shakespeare and Racine are too literary. A work of high art is suited only to its own proper end. Thus a theatrical work is suited to acting and not to reading. A play should be unreadable." A further complaint of Decroux's against language was that it consists of arbitrary noises and symbols that have to be learned. "What we could use on the stage is vocal mime—sounds like cries and sighs—only more highly developed—which are in themselves expressive."

This is Decroux at his most uncompromising. At other times he makes concessions. "There is more fundamental Pantomime," he has written, "in the diction of a Lucien Guitry than in the gesticulations of a pupil of the Youth Hostels or in the *cabrioles* of a dancer." At the end of the statement introducing this article, the mime's renunciation of literature is said to be indicated "for a long time yet," but not forever, not in principle. In a relenting mood Decroux said to me: "History is a zigzag. There are times to be rebellious and *avant-garde*, times to hold on and be conservative; times when one should argue for synthesis, times when

one should argue for separation. ..." The slave's *cri de coeur*
against the master, he conceded, is no objective statement of the
facts.

As I left for the last time, he pressed my hand and smiled. "I
fear that there has been *un petit peu d'égoisme* in my talk to you,"
he said. "I wanted to deposit my thought in you as in a museum."
I reminded him that what I wrote would be simply my impressions and not a scientific record. (No notes had been taken during the conversations. If they had been, the talk would have
been different, and probably inferior. The letter killeth.) "The
only way you'll get your views into print as you want them is by
writing them down yourself," I said. "Why don't you do so?"

"You remember what Lenin said when he broke off *The State
and Revolution* in the middle?" Decroux said, acknowledging the
pretentiousness of the analogy with a twinkle. "'It is better to
make the revolution than to write about it.' Some day, perhaps.
For the present I am busy with my troupe."

(1950)

BERNARD SHAW
From MUSIC IN LONDON
1890–94

... What is wanted to make the ballet more popular is not its
wholesale adulteration with comic opera, but its internal reform.
It should be recognized that the stock of movements out of
which the principal dancers make up their solos is so limited that
the frequent playgoer soon learns them off by heart, and comes
to regard the solo as a dreary platitude, only to be endured when
the dancer has extraordinary charm of person and brilliancy of
execution. In order to get even a very conventional round of
applause, and that, too, from people who obviously have no
more sense of dancing than the oratorio audiences who applaud
interpolated high notes have of music, a principal dancer must
spoil her solo by a silly, flustering, ugly, teetotum spin, which

no really fine dancer should condescend to. Then there is the *corps de ballet*, consisting of rows of commonplace dancers, individually uninteresting (from the artistic point of view), but useful for the production of lines and masses of color in rhythmic motion—for realizing, in short, the artistic conception which was in Mr. Swiveller's imagination when he described the dance as "the mazy." Now in planning the evolutions of the *corps de ballet*, nothing is easier than to ring the changes on mere drill, or harder than to devise really artistic combinations and developments. The natural result is a tendency to give us an intolerable deal of drill with each halfpennyworth of poetic color and motion. The last scene of a ballet is generally a bore, to which some sort of non-artistic interest is occasionally imparted by such desperate devices as making successive squads of girls represent different nations, or different uniforms in the services, or different periods of civilization, or what not, with the result, generally, of making the whole affair twice as stale and tedious. All such mechanical efforts to make lifeless entertainments attractive invariably lead to frightful expenditure, the last thousand pounds of which rarely produce sixpenn'orth of effect. Why not, then, call in the services of a dramatic story-teller, with the requisite sense of the poetry of motion and movement and spectacle, and make a clean sweep of all the merely habitual business that has no purpose and no meaning? The monotony and limitation of the dancer's art vanishes when it becomes dramatic. The detestable bravura solos which everybody hates, and which belong to the same obsolete phase of art as the eighteenth-century florid arias written for the singing virtuosi of the Italian stage by Hasse, Porpora, and Mozart in his boyhood, would soon fall into disuse and ridicule; and we could say to our prima ballerina assolutissima, when she attempted a "variation," "Spare us, dear lady. Dont do it. Our cherished Cavallazzi, a superb dancer, never does it. It was not that sort of thing that made the success of Yolande, of Asmodeus, of Excelsior, or of any of the ballets that are still borne in mind years after their withdrawal. Hundreds of forgotten assolutissimas have done it just as well as you are going to do it; and none of them are remembered save those who stamped themselves on our memories in their dramatic moments. Move us; act for us; make our favorite stories real to us; weave your grace and skill into the fabric of our life; but dont put us off for the thousandth time with those dreary pirouettes and entrechats and arabesques and whatd'yecallems."

That is the cry of humanity to the danseuse, the ballet-master, and the manager. . . .

(1893)

THEODORE REFF
EDGAR DEGAS AND
THE DANCE

. . . If the evolution of Degas' vision of the dance is relatively easy to trace, the reasons for his attraction to it in the first place are more complex and obscure. Surprisingly, though this was by far the most important of his themes, no searching explanation of its interest and meaning for him has been offered; and he himself seemed to discourage further thought, maintaining that the dance was merely "a pretext for painting pretty costumes and representing movements." Yet such an explanation, however incompletely it is given here, inevitably sheds light on both the social and the personal grounds of his art.

To a nineteenth-century Parisian, especially one with Degas' middle-class background, the ballet was a familiar part of the contemporary scene. His father, a wealthy banker, was an enthusiastic patron of the Opera and introduced him to it at an early age. Some of the Opera's musicians were good friends of Degas, who portrayed them in 1868–69 in L'Orchestre de l'Opéra, the earliest picture in which he showed dancers in traditional costume. Thus the ballet was an appropriate choice for a young artist drawn to themes of modern urban life; and it was in this sense that Edmond de Goncourt, a pioneer in the literary depiction of such themes, understood Degas' pictures when he first saw them. "Yesterday I spent the whole day in the studio of a strange painter called Degas," he noted in his journal for February 13, 1874. "After a great many essays and experiments and trial shots in all directions, he has fallen in love with modern life, and of all the subjects in modern life he has chosen washerwomen and ballet dancers. When you come to think of it, it is not a bad choice. It is a world of pink and white, of female flesh in lawn and gauze, the most delightful pretexts for using pale, soft tints." Characteristically, Goncourt dwells on the aesthetic aspects of Degas' dance pictures, ignoring their content and meaning; aristocratic in manner and elegant in taste, he responds solely to their subtle coloring and delicate textures. Yet for this very reason he is able to appreciate the novelty of a complex design like the Corcoran Gallery's *Ecole de danse*, a variant of which he saw in Degas' studio that day: "There was the green room with, outlined against the light of a window, the curious silhouette of dancers' legs coming down a little staircase, with the bright red of a tartan in the midst of all those puffed-out white clouds. . . ."

What Edmond de Goncourt failed to note in Degas' rehearsal pictures, Ludovic Halévy, a different kind of writer and a close friend of the artist, certainly grasped. This was the pictorial wit and irony with which Degas observed the world behind the scenes at the Opera, a world inaccessible to the public but much frequented by writers, journalists, and men-about-town. It was this smart world that Degas, alone among the Impressionists, though he was soon followed by Forain and others, made his own both socially and artistically, identifying this insider's view of the reality behind the theatrical illusion with his own disillusioned brand of urban realism. Here he could observe the young dancers struggle for professional success or maneuver, at the prompting of ambitious mothers, to capture a husband or "protector" among the gentlemen who circulated freely backstage. And like Halévy himself, in the novel *La Famille Cardinal*, which he illustrated in numerous monotypes about 1878-79, Degas conceived of such observations as the very essence of his wordly realism, a little heartless, yet just. . . .

The struggles of the young dancers—or "rats," as the very young ones were commonly called—their unceasing efforts to master a difficult art, their daily round of exercises and lessons, clearly fascinated Degas, who must have compared these strenuous efforts with his own as an artist. In literally hundreds of paintings, drawings, and prints, he shows dancers straining and twisting at the practice bar, or rubbing aching muscles and joints, or bent over double to tie a slipper, or in unguarded moments of fatigue stretching or yawning or scratching themselves. . . . It was just this dichotomy in Degas' vision of the ballet and the theater that appealed to his wordly contemporaries, writers such as Champsaur who, in *L'Amant des danseuses*, describes pictures based on Degas of the dancer on stage "in the splendor of her somewhat artificial beauty, in her glorification under electric lights," but also backstage, "breathless with fatigue, her features sagging, the muscles of her calves and thighs bulging, the lines of her body graceless and almost brutal. . . ." Like the laundress pressing down hard on her iron or yawning, overheated and exhausted, like the street-walker waiting on the café terrace in a torpor, the dancer in Degas' work is often an embodiment not of feminine charm but of the lower-class woman's struggle for survival, burdened and deformed by her labors. Yet nothing is more characteristic of his achievement than the way in which he extracts from such scenes of awkwardness and distress—and here the pictures . . . of a bather precariously balancing herself as she washes or lying in a strangely undignified position on the floor also come to mind—images of transcendent beauty. To create beauty out of urban dreariness was essential to his naturalist conception of modern art.

The ballet, then, had a dual attraction for Degas: it was at once realistic and artificial, like the Opera or the theater itself. He could respond with equal interest to the pathos of the dancer's daily existence and the magic of her momentary glory on stage. This double-edged awareness is, of course, implicit in any understanding of the theater as a social milieu and also informs images of it by other artists—among his predecessors, Daumier and Gavarni; among his followers, Forain, Lautrec, and the early Picasso. Throughout the nineteenth and early twentieth centuries, artists and writers found inspiration in the vivid forms of urban entertainment, delighting in the transformations wrought by decors, costumes, and artificial lights, and at the same time identifying themselves with the entertainers as talented performers who, like themselves, led a marginal and precarious existence. What is unique in Degas' art is his emphasis on the dance. Though he also created memorable images of the theater, the orchestra, the *café-concert*, and the circus, he is above all "l'amant des danseuses," and this more specialized interest, too, reveals important features of his artistic personality.

The classical ballet was for Degas a supreme example of formal, disciplined, even artificial beauty. The dancer's steps, the movements of her body and arms and legs, down to the smallest inflections of her hands and feet, were part of an elaborate ceremony, mastered through years of exercise and rehearsal, and were thus a living demonstration of the superiority of art to nature. To the creator who never tired of saying, "No art is less spontaneous then my own; what I do is the result of reflection and study of the great masters," the classical ballet, whose steps had been invented and named at the court of Louis XIV and had changed little in the following two centuries, despite the innovations introduced in the Romantic period, was bound to seem an ideal source of inspiration. It is the conventional and classical aspect of the ballerina's appearance and performance that distinguishes Degas' *Danseuses à la barre* of 1876 from the young couples in modern dress dancing informally in Renoir's exactly contemporary *Moulin de la Galette*. In their stylized, almost ceremonial movements, Degas' dancers are in fact closer in spirit to the Salomé who moves like a toe-dancer before Herod in Gustave Moreau's famous picture, also of 1876. That Degas had been influenced by Moreau in the 1850s, long before he became a colleague of Renoir's, merely confirms biographically what is evident visually in his dramatic conception of the dance.

So convinced was Degas that art is essentially artifice, an emblem of the mind triumphant over mere matter, that he could paint even those pictures of the ballet which seem most naturalistic, the pictures of exercise, instruction, and rehearsal, entirely from memory and imagination. Despite their appearance of authenticity, they were created in the studio, with a few notebook sketches, some drawings made from models, and a prodigious visual memory as his sole source of documentation. . . . According to Degas himself, he did not always possess even that much visual information; writing to Albert Hecht, an influential friend, about 1882, he asks: "Do you have the power to have the Opera give me an admission pass for the day of the dance examination? . . . . I've done so many of these dance examinations, without having seen them, that I'm feeling a little ashamed about it." We are uncertain how literally to take such a confession, coming from an artist who enjoyed saying provocative things and who seems not to have painted a dance examination either before or after 1882. But at the very least it hints at the distance between appearance and reality in even the most seemingly authentic of his dance pictures.

However appealing as a spectacle of formal, stylized character, the ballet would never have interested Degas if its essence were not the human figure in motion. The wax-work dancers he saw at the Musée Grévin, though life-size and utterly realistic in attitude, costume, and setting, could hardly have satisfied him, though they may well have inspired his own subtly modeled and realistically clothed figurine, the *Petite danseuse de quatorze ans,* which he showed in 1881, one year before the Musée Grévin opened. It was because the living dancers moved, and in rhythmic patterns determined by the music and a long choreographic tradition, that he was so much drawn to them. All beings in motion fascinated him, from pedestrians crossing streets in Paris to race horses galloping at Longchamp; and when, at the end of his long life, virtual blindness forced him out of his studio, he spent hours walking or riding on omnibuses, finding consolation in sensations of ceaseless change. The movements of horses particularly interested him, and he was one of the first artists to grasp the significance of Eadweard Muybridge's instantaneous photographs of them, which he copied and used as models for his equestrian paintings from about 1880 on. Even in his earlier pictures, . . . he displays an uncanny ability to capture the phases of a horse's walk or canter. But as in the case of the dancers, it was because these were harmonious movements, orderly and rhythmic as a result of long training, that they appealed so much to Degas. We have only to compare the patterns of repeated movement in the *Danseuses se baissant* and in *Trois jockeys* of the same date to realize how closely related the two phenomena were in his mind. In many ways the thoroughbred race horse was the ballet dancer's natural counterpart; as Paul Valéry put it, "No animal is closer to a *première danseuse,* a star of the corps de ballet, than a perfectly balanced thoroughbred, as it seems to pause in flight under the hand of its rider, and then trips forward in the bright sunshine. Degas painted it in a single line of a poem: 'Tout nerveusement nu dans sa robe de soie.'" That the poem Valéry quotes, a sonnet entitled "Pur sang," is one of eight, of which almost all the others are devoted to dancers or the dance, confirms the close association of the two themes in Degas' imagination.

The ballets Degas saw at the Opera of his day were rarely classical in content, but despite their exotic or folkloric subjects and settings, he invariably showed the dancers in their traditional white *tutus,* which had been introduced in the Neoclassical period. (Only in *Le Ballet de "Robert le Diable"* does he show them in the nuns' habits they wore in that production.) And in treating the lessons, exercises, and rehearsals that were his principal motifs, he naturally portrayed the young "rats" in their required practice costumes, with somewhat longer white *tutus* and flesh-colored tights, to which he added colorful sashes and black velvet chokers as accents. This time-honored aspect of the ballet undoubtedly also appealed to the mature Degas, a man of strongly conservative character who cherished old customs and attitudes. More than that, the classical ballet had for him the deeper significance of resembling and thus evoking the truly classical art of ancient Greece. In the modern dancers' movements, daringly expanded as they had been by the great stars of the Romantic period, he could hardly have seen many traces of those noble, stately rhythms he so much admired in ancient statues and reliefs, yet he persuaded himself that he did. When he was asked by the American collector Mrs. Havemeyer, "Why, monsieur, do you always do ballet dancers?" he replied at once, "Because, madame, it is all that is left of the combined movements of the Greeks." If we substitute "synthetic" for "combined," a better translation of the word "combiné" that Degas probably used, we understand more easily what he meant: he could find in the ballet—and transpose into his own art—those images of the human body in motion, at once dynamic and poised, that seem to synthesize the very essence of a movement, as in classical statues. And if we examine a pastel such as *Danse grecque. . .* , with its graceful poses like those in Greek sculpture, or a drawing such as *Groupe de cinq danseuses avec paysage classique* in the Arthur Peto Collection, with its Acropolis-like setting, we realize why, on this level, too, the often mediocre ballet at the Paris Opera of his time could nevertheless hold him in thrall.

There were, no doubt, other reasons than those already given for Degas' life-long fascination with the dance; with an artist of his complexity, a single explanation is rarely adequate. The female dancers (he never painted the male ones) were youthful, graceful, charmingly dressed, and may well have had a sentimental appeal for him, one that remains unacknowledged in his unidealized and largely unerotic images of them. Certainly he was closely acquainted with the many dancers who posed for him and whom he helped to improve their positions at the Opera; and according to a studio legend that need not be true to be revealing, he followed one of them across the ocean to New York. He himself hints at a sentimental, though somewhat disillusioned, attitude to them in a letter to the sculptor Paul-Albert Bartholomé; lamenting his loneliness and lack of affection, he adds: "And even this heart (his own) is somewhat artificial. The dancers have sewn it into a bag of satin rose, of slightly faded satin rose, like their dance slippers." Later he concealed such feelings beneath a benevolent paternalism, indulging the young dancers' whims, enjoying their pranks, and supporting their efforts. But not entirely; for in pictures such as *Danseuse: Scène de ballet* he continued to juxtapose very suggestively the dark scroll of a double bass thrusting upward from an unseen orchestra and the light form of a dancer hovering on stage, as he had in several earlier ballet scenes—a juxtaposition whose meaning is made more explicit in Lautrec's poster of Jane Avril at the Jardin de Paris, also of the early 1890s. But we have already considered enough reasons for Degas' interest in the ballet, enough theories and arguments; for no one believed more strongly than he that "there is no arguing among the muses. They work all day, very much on their own. In the evening, work finished, they get together and dance."

(1978)

IV

Genre and Style

The American humorist Robert Benchley once said that there are two categories of people: those who believe that people can be divided into two categories and those who don't. Robert Benchley notwithstanding, most critics and historians of the dance remain firmly committed to the practice of categorization. Indeed, throughout most of this century, they have routinely divided Western, theatrical dancing into two sometimes antagonistic genres, ballet and modern dance. More recently, during the last fifteen or twenty years, a third major designation, that of post-modern dance, has been added. (Non-theatrical dancing—that is, social and ritualistic dance—will be considered in the final section of this book.)

Of course no one—not even the most overzealous pigeonholer—pretends that every individual example of theatrical dance can be easily and unambiguously assigned to one of these three genres. Where, for example, does one put the work of Twyla Tharp? Or Merce Cunningham, who is a transitional figure between modern and post-modern dance, not belonging wholly or comfortably to either category.

Obviously, a serious "taxonomy" of the dance will require that we further divide these genres into subgenres (within the genre of ballet, for example, we will have to distinguish between classical ballet and post-Fokine "modern" ballet). Granted, an attempt to accommodate every difficult case may lead us in the convoluted direction of Shakespeare's Polonius who speaks of "tragedy, comedy, history, pastoral, pastoral-comical, historical-pastoral, tragical-historical, tragical-comical-historical-pastoral," etc.

But does the very existence of "difficult cases" mean that the classification process itself is of little or no value? Some—most prominently, the Italian aesthetician Benedetto Croce—argue that every work of art is a "difficult" case, and that even to think in terms of genre or style is to misrepresent the unique and irreducible nature of each aesthetic object. For Croce, the ideal art criticism would consist almost entirely of monographs about individual works of art.

But are individual works of art that much more resistant to classification than living things? Few would deny the value of biological categories such as family, genus, and species (in fact, Darwin might never have formulated his theory of evolution had it not been for the classification of plants and animals in the eighteenth century). The only danger in subjecting works of art to a similar system of classification is that the critic may evolve a purely mechanical approach for arriving at critical judgments (for instance, "modern dance is such and such; therefore, the work before me is a 'good' modern dance to the extent that it possesses these characteristics . . .")

Yet far from blinding us to the uniqueness of an individual work of art, familiarity with the general category to which a particular work belongs may, in some instances, be an indispensable aid in fully appreciating that work. For example, as we have already seen, David Michael Levin argues that Balanchine's formalist dances all reveal the hidden essence of classical ballet and it is difficult to imagine someone fully appreciating certain works of Balanchine's without a knowledge of the genre to which they belong. Twyla Tharp's original "Deuce Coupe" for The Joffrey Ballet also takes a familiarity with the genre of ballet for granted when it examines the "syntactical" similarities between classical ballet and contemporary social dances.

Assuming then that considerations of genre are more than just critical conveniences, we still face the problem of deciding which sets of shared characteristics constitute genres. There are, after all, an almost unlimited number of ways in which individual dances might be classified. We could, for example, distinguish between dances that are purely formal in nature and those that are representational or expressive, those that project some sort of illusion and those that are rigorously anti-illusionistic, those that rely heavily on costumes, scenery, and lighting and those that do not.

All of these distinctions are important and all enter into critical discussion at some time or other, but most dance writers prefer to consider these differences subsidiary to more fundamental discriminations based on the nature and quality of the movement itself. Does that imply that the basic movement "vocabularies" of ballet, modern, and post-modern dance possess some sort of natural or objective status? Is there, in other words, any sort of direct aesthetic equivalent for the biological genus or species?

The literary critic Northrop Frye, in his influential study *The Anatomy of Criticism*, argues that there are four fundamental literary genres: comedy, romance, tragedy, and satire, and that they correspond to the four seasons: spring, summer, autumn, and winter respectively. (For example, the weddings that conclude many Shakespearian comedies are literary residues of ancient fertility rites associated with the coming of spring.) Can similar claims be made for dance?

Certainly, the early proponents of modern dance believed that they had discovered (or more correctly, re-discovered) the natural way of dancing. But what about ballet, which the early moderns rejected as arbitrary and unnatural? One of the major contentions of those who write about ballet in this section is that the classical ballet "vocabulary" is not arbitrary, that it constitutes the "natural" way of dancing on a proscenium stage. For example, Lincoln Kirstein, the American writer and General Director of the New York City Ballet, insists that "The root of ballet training in the five academic foot positions established some three centuries ago is not arbitrary. These determine the greatest frontal legibility and launch of the upper body in silhouette, framed in a proscenium." The classical ballet vocabulary, he adds, "depends on muscular and nervous control deriving from four centuries' research into a logic combining gross anatomy, plane geometry, and musical counterpoint." "Legibility" is a word that occurs again and again in Kirstein's writings. He sees ballet as the dance form most fully committed to the values of theatrical legibility, and the fundamental principle promoting this goal of maximum visibility is that of *en dehors*, the balletic turnout.

"Turning out," writes Adrian Stokes, the British art critic and balletomane, "means that the dancer, whatever the convolutions of the dance, continually shows as much of himself as possible

to the spectator." Stokes goes on to examine the intimate connection between *en dehors* and the five academic positions upon
which all balletic training rests. These basic positions allow the
dancer to move freely to the left and right without compromis-
ing the body's openness.

Ballet, argues Stokes, is the most "externalized" form of dance,
and consequently the most peculiarly European and Western.
Elaborating on a distinction first established by André Levinson,
Stokes contrasts the externalized, open nature of ballet with the
progressive, inward spirals of Spanish dancing, which betray its
non-Western, Oriental origins. The inwardness of such dancing
creates an intensification of mystery, an intimation of something
unknowable; but the openness of ballet by contrast, connotes
perfect clarity and intelligibility. (Kirstein carries this impulse
toward extroversion and outwardness even further, arguing that
the classical dancer simulates a conquest of aerial space. The dancer in other words, not only turns out from the center of his or
her being, but moves actively up and away from that center.)

Akim Volinsky, who wrote about dance and painting at the
turn of the century in Russia, attaches both a metaphysical and
an evolutionary significance to the verticality of classical ballet.
According to Volinsky, it is the human being's upright posture
that distinguishes him most noticeably from those lesser animals
that walk on all fours. "With the vertical," notes Volinsky,
"begins the history of human culture and the gradual conquest
of heaven and earth." Verticality is endowed with moral connotations as well: to be "upright" or "straight" is to be open and
virtuous. Furthermore, a vertical line "aspires upwards." When
we witness the vertical line of classical ballet, we experience a
peculiarly human feeling of exultation.

Unlike Kirstein and Stokes, Volinsky emphasizes the potential
"expressivity" of classical technique. That makes him a direct
counterpart of his countryman, Michel Fokine, the great Ballets
Russes choreographer and father of what we now think of as
"modern ballet." But Volinsky argues that the classical vocabulary itself is already deeply expressive, whereas Fokine believed
that expressivity could only be achieved through internal
reform. His best known manifesto of reform is probably his 1914
letter to the London *Times* in which he argued that mechanical,
ready-made combinations of steps should be replaced by choreography freshly designed for each occasion, that the corps de
ballet should not be used merely as a backdrop for the pyrotech-
nics of the soloists, that the ballet dancer's mimetic and expres-

sive capabilities not be limited to the face and the hands ("man can and should be expressive from head to foot"), and that dancing should be integrated with the other arts. (Fokine re-formulated the ideal of the Wagnerian *Gesamtkunstwerk* for the Ballets Russes.)

Despite the far-reaching nature of these proposed reforms, Fokine remained an advocate of evolution, not revolution. Unlike Isadora Duncan and the forerunners of modern dance, he did not repudiate the classical vocabulary outright: "If I do not agree with this style of dancing," he wrote in his essay "The New Ballet," "it does not mean that I ignore the school. On the contrary, I think that in order to create anything of value, one must study and pass through a proper school which, however, should not be confined to the study of fixed poses and steps."

This helps explain why both Stokes and Kirstein agree that there is no inherent incompatibility between Fokine's quest for a greater expressivity and the academic substructure of classical ballet. For example, when Nijinsky turns his feet "in" rather than "out" in Fokine's "Petrouchka," the choreographer is, in effect, acknowledging (rather than merely ignoring) the foundations of classicism. Stokes in fact writes that " ... it was because of the power exhibited by this wider expressiveness that we learned to love its source, the classical ballet."

The same, of course, cannot be said of Isadora Duncan and the other forerunners of what we now refer to as modern dance. To Duncan, the classical "vocabulary" was merely an arbitrary and unnatural assortment of poses wholly unsuited to the expression of personal emotion. (In the excerpt from his book *The Modern Dance* contained in Section I, John Martin argued that "to attempt to express dramatic ideas and personal experience while standing with the feet in fifth position, moving the arms in arbitrary arcs, is likely to be absurd.")

Echoing Noverre, Duncan insisted that to find the original source of the dance, "we must go to nature"; and she came to the odd conclusion that the solar plexus is the natural, "central spring of all movement." By contrast, "The ballet school," she writes in her autobiography, "taught the pupils that this spring was found in the centre of the back at the base of the spine. ... This method produces an artificial, mechanical movement not worthy of the soul."

"Soul" is a key concept in Duncan's vocabulary. In fact, she often seems to proceed on the assumption that the dancer need only nourish her soul and the body will automatically follow in good stead. And despite all her talk about "natural" ways of moving, Duncan's vision of the body remains peculiarly refined, upright, and highly sublimated. The "true" American dance, she writes, "will contain no jazz rhythm, no rhythm from the waist down. . . . This dance will have no hint in it either of the servile coquetry of the ballet or the sensual convulsion of the South African Negro. It will be clean."

Rayner Heppenstall, the British essayist and balletomane, criticizes Duncan for failing to find a theatrically legible form through which her soulful feelings could be objectified and externalized: "None of her movements," he writes, "is precise, sharp, clean, bright. There is no control. There is no line. Everything is fluid, formless, natural, free, without style, melting away. . . ." This may sound suspiciously like the knee-jerk reaction of any die-hard balletomane confronted with a form of dance not based upon the classical vocabulary. But Heppenstall's reservations about Duncan cut considerably deeper than that; for they are moral as well as aesthetic in nature. Duncan's brand of "self-expression" connotes for Heppenstall an unhealthy exhibitionism and self-centeredness. He believes that the emotional life of a healthy culture, by contrast, is regulated by impersonal forms and conventions. Thus the inability or unwillingness of dancers like Isadora Duncan to work within the impersonal, objective, inherited conventions of ballet is evidence of a dangerous egocentrism, a rejection of the shared, public nature of society itself.

Lincoln Kirstein makes the closely related argument that modern dance is inherently more limited and ephemeral than ballet because it lacks the transcendent, "timeless" element of an inherited, classical foundation. It depends too heavily on the "personality" of its creator. Noting that few modern dance companies have survived the death or retirement of their founders, he maintains that "self-expression triumphed without providing either a cohesive teaching method or a repertory past individual utterance." (Heppenstall, Stokes, and Kirstein all proceed on the assumption that ballet is the only form of theatrical dance that can achieve the degree of impersonality they advocate; but it is worth remembering that Mallarmé and many of the figures that Frank Kermode discusses in "Poet and Dancer Before Diaghilev" credited the pioneer modern dancer Loïe Fuller with a comparable transcendence of personality.)

Needless to say, the formlessness and theatrical illegibility that Heppenstall associates with Isadora Duncan does not characterize modern dance as a whole. Indeed, it makes perfect sense that the work of Duncan and her contemporaries was originally described not as modern dance, but variously as "free dance," "expressive dance," or even "barefoot aesthetic dance." The designation "modern dance" is usually and more properly reserved for choreographers such as Mary Wigman, Martha Graham, and Doris Humphrey who emerged during the period between the two world wars.

In "Mind and Medium in the Modern Dance," Katharine Everett Gilbert, the American aesthetician, examines the nature of the transition between these two stages in the evolution of modern dance. Gilbert shares Heppenstall's reservations about Duncan and all that she represented, but restates them in language derived from Lessing, suggesting that Duncan failed to pay proper attention to the *medium* in which she worked. Duncan, she suggests, was more concerned with "inspiration" and with the origin of movement than with the actual, physical movement that resulted. "Isadora's soul," she writes, "expressed itself fiercely without systematic submission to the conditions of a medium."

Gilbert credits the Hungarian-born choreographer and pioneer of dance notation, Rudolf von Laban with having formulated the necessary "grammar of motion" that enabled modern dance choreographers to channel their private emotions into objectified form. In contrast to Duncan, who emphasized the organic flow of energy undisciplined by any sort of constraint or physical restriction, Laban introduced the all-important principle of tension and opposition. (Similarly, Graham stressed the tension between contraction and release, and Doris Humphrey the opposition between "fall" and "recovery.")

Mary Wigman, his most celebrated pupil and the principal pioneer of modern dance in Europe, says that Laban taught her "to keep the balance between my emotional outburst and the merciless discipline of a superpersonal control." Of course, the fact that Wigman attached more importance than Duncan to formal conventions does not mean that she attached any less importance to the communication of emotion. In fact, Wigman's essay "The Philosophy of Modern Dance" is a straightforward version of the expression theory discussed in Section I:

> The primary concern of the creative dancer should be that his audience not think of the dance objectively . . . in other words, separate itself from the very life of the dancer's experiences;—the audience

should allow the dance to affect it emotionally and without reserve. It should allow the rhythm, the music, the very movement of the dancer's body to stimulate the same feeling and emotional mood within itself, as this mood and emotional condition has stimulated the dancer . . . the expression without the inner experience in the dance is valueless.

(Wigman, by the way, was a close friend and associate of the expressionist painter, Emile Nolde.)

Is there any single characteristic shared by those choreographers who created "modern" dances between the late 1920's and the 1940's—something that might enable us to speak of a *genre* of modern dance? Many critics would cite a common emphasis on the externalizing and communicating of inner experience. John Martin, for example, defined modern dance in precisely this way. Graham spoke of "making visible the interior landscape" and Doris Humphrey described modern dance as "moving from the inside out." (Remember that Stokes, Kirstein, and Heppenstall by contrast, all argued that ballet is unconcerned with inner experience.)

But Merce Cunningham, a former member of the Graham company, rejected this reliance on inner experience and emotional expressivity, thereby initiating yet another stage in the evolution of modern dance. Cunningham purged his choreography of expressive and symbolic elements, making movement once again an end in itself (an attitude that brings him closer in many ways to Balanchine than to the earlier practitioners of modern dance). And indeed, Cunningham's choreography possesses many balletic qualities that earlier modern dance strenuously avoided: lightness, verticality, fast, tricky footwork, a cool, often ironic tone. Rather than moving subjectively "from the inside out," Cunningham's choreographic decisions are often dictated by impersonal devices (tossing coins, rolling dice, consulting the I Ching).

Surely Cunningham's most radical innovation was to "free" choreography from any dependence on music. Movement and sound simply occupy the same space and the same time without directly affecting one another. But Cunningham is no "purist" attempting to reduce the art of dance to its minimalist essence. In fact, no one since Diaghilev has persuaded so many leading composers and painters to create musical scores, costumes, and scenery for the dance. But as Roger Copeland points out, Cunningham's collaborations are Brechtian and dissociated, whereas Diaghilev's were Wagnerian and unified. (The movement, the sound, and the decor in Cunningham's works are all conceived independently of one another and are not intended to "fuse" into a seamless whole. The space between them is essential.)

Copeland also examines the similarities between Cunningham's sensibility and those of the painters and sculptors with whom he has collaborated most often. Jasper Johns and Robert Rauschenberg, both of whom served at various times as artistic directors of the Cunningham company, were the painters most instrumental in repudiating the inward, subjective nature of abstract expressionism, substituting a more impersonal and objective mode of image-making. Cunningham's rejection of the expressionistic and subjective elements in modern dance is directly analogous. Unlike Mary Wigman, he places a high premium on objectivity.

"Objectivity" is an even more important concept for Yvonne Rainer, a founding member of the Judson Dance Theater and one of the most influential practitioneers of what has come to be known as "post-modern" dance. Like Merce Cunningham, the post-modern choreographers were deeply influenced by the objective, impersonal theories and practices of the contemporary art world (particularly the work of so-called minimalists and conceptualists).

In her essay, "A Quasi-Survey of Some Minimalist Tendencies . . . ," Yvonne Rainer examines a number of parallels between her own choreography and the work of minimalist sculptors. Rainer coins the term "found movement" to describe the pedestrian, un-stylized movement vocabulary that distinguishes post-modern dance from other forms of theatrical dance. Like their art world equivalent, the mass-produced "found object," found movements are not subjectively "shaped" by the artist's personality; they are merely transplanted from their everyday, utilitarian environment into an "art context" (where their sole function is to be perceived).

Another parallel between Rainer's choreography and much contemporary painting and sculpture is that she avoids certain time-honored modes of illusionism (in her case, this means refusing to conceal effort, or to make the body appear either lighter or heavier than it actually is). We might compare her attitude toward the physical materials of the dance medium with that of Susanne Langer who argues that

> in watching a dance, you do not see what is physically before you—people running around or twisting their bodies; what you see is a display of interacting forces . . .

Rainer on the other hand, insists that "it is important to distinguish between real energy and what I shall call apparent
energy." (We might also compare Rainer's attitude toward illusion in dance with the modified illusionism that David Michael
Levin claims for Balanchine whose work, he says, acknowledges
the actual, physical weight of the body, but only for the purpose
of then rendering it magically weightless.)

One of the concepts that appears most often in discussions of
post-modern dance is that of "the task" or "task-like" movement.
Tasks are found movements of a distinctly goal-oriented variety
(in Rainer's "Parts of Some Sextets," the task was to carry bulky
mattresses from one point to another; in Trisha Brown's "Walking on the Wall," performers in body harnesses undertook the
task of walking across the walls of a room parallel to the floor).
The "dance" in each of these instances consists of whatever
movements are needed to accomplish the task and the length of
time the performer takes to complete the task is determined by
objective conditions beyond the performer's (or the choreographer's) subjective control. In these situations, says Rainer,

> action or what one does, is more interesting and important than the
> exhibition of character and attitude, and that action can best be
> focused on through the submerging of the personality; so ideally,
> one is not even oneself, one is a neutral doer.

Tom Johnson's "Running Out of Breath," first performed by
Kathy Duncan, is included here as an illustration of the way in
which these ideas about found movement, impersonality, anti-
illusionism, and tasks actually function in performance. Here,
the task is to literally (not figuratively) run out of breath while
reciting a verbal text that focuses the audience's attention on the
actual, physical changes the performer undergoes in the process.

"Running Out of Breath" is typical of post-modern dances in
a number of ways: it does not require a "trained" performer, its
movement is pedestrian, it takes place in objective or clock time,
it is rigorously anti-illusionistic, the choreography is dictated by
the task assigned to the performer, and as with much conceptually oriented art, the essence of the work can be appreciated in
verbally paraphrased form (or from reading Johnson's scenario).

The post-modern emphasis on "impersonality" might seem in
a sense to bring us full circle, back to the balletic virtues extolled
by Stokes, Heppenstall, and Kirstein. But most balletomanes find
post-modern dance too austere and lacking in virtuosity for their
tastes. One understands why that is so after reading Yvonne Rai-

ner's postscript to her description of "Parts of Some Sextets" from 1965:

> NO to spectacle no to virtuosity no to transformations and magic and make-believe no to the glamour and transcendence of the star image no to the heroic no to the anti-heroic no to trash imagery no to involvement of performer or spectator no to style no to camp no to seduction of spectator by the wiles of the performer no to eccentricity no to moving or being moved.

Clearly, post-modern dance—at least in its early minimalist manifestations—ran the risk of purifying itself right out of existence. This sort of austere puritanism led the composer Steve Reich to quip that "For a long time during the 1960's, one would go to the dance concert where no one danced, followed by the party where everyone danced."

"What is needed now," Reich writes, "is not a return to the modern dance of the 1930's, or 1940's, or 1950's, but rather a return to the roots of dance as it is found all over the world; regular rhythmic movement, usually done to music." Reich demonstrates how the same minimal components of post-modern dance can become the building blocks for a more expressive, kinetically exhilarating form of choreography. He sees Laura Dean (who has choreographed to his music) as a possible harbinger of this new movement. (Twyla Tharp's evolution from minimalist austerity to balletic virtuosity suggests yet another way out of this cul-de-sac.)

Thus far, we have been proceeding on the assumption that most Western theatrical dances can be assigned with a fair degree of accuracy to one of three major genres. But as Selma Jeanne Cohen points out, contemporary developments have greatly complicated the problem of classification. Many major ballet companies now include modern dance works in their repertories, and today's dancers have usually trained in a variety of techniques, both balletic and modern. Certainly it is no longer possible to define as "ballet" any work performed by dancers who have been trained in an academic method based on the five positions. Consider a dance like *The Moor's Pavane*. Is it a modern dance when it is performed by the Limón Company and a ballet when it is performed by the Joffrey?

Then there is the troublesome concept of style. Ballet and modern dance, Cohen points out, are frequently referred to as styles; but she prefers to regard them—as we have in this anthology—as genres (which may then encompass any number of

styles). "Style" may describe the way an individual dancer interprets a work or it may connote characteristics shared by members
of a company. Collective styles are often attributed to national or
racial determinants. For example, we routinely speak of British
"reserve," Russian "flamboyance," or American "athleticism."

Ballet companies and their styles often become objects of
national pride and in the last generation a number of distinguished figures, Lincoln Kirstein preeminent among them,
devoted themselves to the development of an American ballet
tradition with a distinctive American style. For him, and for
many others, the New York City Ballet is the quintessence and
triumph of that style.

R. P. Blackmur, the renowned literary critic, agreed that the
New York City Ballet is a quintessentially American phenomenon, but he took a much less favorable view of what that style
represents. He accuses the dancers of being cold, bloodless tech-
nicians, all too representative of American culture as a whole.
"We Americans," he complains, "have the technique to bring
something to performance so well that the subject is left out."

Anna Kisselgoff, chief dance critic of the *New York Times,* characterizes style succinctly as "an attitude imposed upon technique." But she insists that the style we associate with the dancing of particular companies derives from the individuals who
have shaped the artistic identities of those companies and not
from some dubious national stereotype. Rejecting the claims
made by Kirstein and Balanchine, she argues that there is no
peculiarly American style in classical ballet. Our three major ballet companies all dance in distinctively different styles. The New
York City Ballet dances the way it does not because it is in New
York or the United States, but because it is headed by George
Balanchine. If Balanchine had formed his company in England
she suggests, it might well be dancing the very same way.

One of the most perplexing questions related to the issue of
style in dance derives from the confusion surrounding the terms
"classicism" and "romanticism." In all the other arts, classicism
and romanticism are sharply contrasted with each other. Romanticism is defined as an early nineteenth-century reaction against
the smug rationalism and formal rigidity of eighteenth-century
neo-classical art. By definition, romanticism comes after, and
attempts to repudiate, the assumptions of classicism. But dance
historians tell us that the great "classical" ballets of Petipa
("Swan Lake," "The Sleeping Beauty") follow, chronologically,

the great "romantic" ballets ("La Sylphide," "Giselle"). How is this confusion to be resolved?

Lincoln Kirstein offers the most persuasive solution. "The classic dance," he writes, "is not merely a department of theatrical dancing opposed to the 'romantic,' but rather a central line, or governing attitude which links the purest developments in traditional stage practice, whatever the epoch." Classicism thus refers to the vocabulary and underlying structure of the dance, not its subject matter or historical period. This approach allows us to view romanticism as a stylistic development of classicism rather than as an opposing style. Ballets such as "La Sylphide" and "Giselle" are very much a part of the more general romantic movement in early nineteenth-century Europe. (The denial of gravity and the rejection of Newtonian mechanics are leading romantic themes in many of the arts.) But these ballets utilized the classic dance vocabulary. Of course, they also made new contributions to that slowly evolving vocabulary. Dancing on pointe for example, which originally embodied the romantic ballerina's quest for the ethereal, has now become a basic attribute of classic dancing.

Ballet

LINCOLN KIRSTEIN
CLASSIC BALLET: ARIA OF THE AERIAL

A recent writer in a counter-culture weekly suggests (more in sorrow than anger) that, for our 'Seventies, dancing as a popular cult overtakes rock-music of the 'Sixties. This may or may not be as true of regional as of urban America, but on a grass-roots level, local proliferation of holiday *"Nutcrackers"* on some professional basis is astonishing. Parallel to this is the increased presence of "Dance" in colleges with residencies for well-known companies. The number of young people now aspiring to become dancers approaches actors, singers or musicians, a condition unthinkable twenty years ago, while there is a new paying public which hopefully organizes economic support, even state and civic aid.

Dance includes separate families for teaching and performance: "ballet," "ethnic," "social" and "modern." For ballet, there is a single canon of instruction comparable to that which equips pianists, violinists and singers in fingering or voice control. Different emphases obtain but the alphabet taught is universally legible from long tradition, demanding the same criteria. "Ethnic," which includes social styles (more for fun than show), encompasses folk-dance, recreation for amateurs and source-material for theater. Formerly "national" dances, stage-versions of Spanish, Slav or "oriental" were instructed, but today these, as balance or alternative to academic ballet, are largely replaced by "modern."

During the 'Thirties when "modern-dance" first asserted itself, an inheritance from Ruth St. Denis and Ted Shawn fragmented into main lines of apostolic succession. Forty years later, energy is lodged in the repertory of Martha Graham, her immediate heirs and theirs. Increasingly, with a use of the ballet *barre* and borrowings from ballet-trained instructors, "modern-dance" has lost some of its early antagonism to classic ballet. Stylistic lines blur and fuse. However, important polarities exist, so it may be useful to fix parameters of Ballet and Modern. Cursory definition involves oversimplification; generally it can be stated that ballet-training and performance accentuates the area of air, denial of gravity by leg-work in beats and jumps; brilliant multiple turns; speed in the stage-traverse; *pointe* (toe)-shoes; virtuoso acrobatics (attracting large audiences to opera-houses) accompanied by orchestras of symphonic dimensions.

"Modern-dance" came into being partly as a reaction against such factors, with a basic rationale accentuating the solar-plexus as source of contraction and release; a response to earth's gravity and pull; "psychology-through-movement" with ideas from myth and social-protest. Stemming from Bennington College, then spreading to state normal-schools where it began to replace "Phys. Ed" (physical education) as a more aesthetic body-building, "modern-dance" acquired the fervor of a crusade, vaunting ethical superiority over "mere" (mindless) entertainment.

Along with such protestant policy, there were other determinants. Ballet instruction was then not widely available nor performances visible. Conditions of labor and production costs were prohibitive for unpaid volunteers. A modesty of visual and musical accompaniment made virtues of necessity, fast elevated into articles of faith. It was proclaimed that main differences between "modern" and ballet were between "principles" and "technique," as if one lacked skill, the other morality. Both had both. Rather, difference was and is between accidental idiosyncrasy against tradition, personalism versus collectivity, discontinuity as opposed to an unbroken line. "Modern-dance" opted for self-expressive "originality," defined by a few notable heterodoxies. Self-expression triumphed without providing either a cohesive teaching method or a repertory past individual utterance. "Modern-dance" lies among the minor verse of theater. When one counts how few "major" poets (or anything else) there are, how "major" so many "minor" ones, this seems no aesthetic limitation, although it may prove both a temporal and popular one.

No matter how close "modern-dance" approaches widespread acceptance, however flexible or eclectic its expanded idiom, essential contrareity remains. "Modern-dance" choreographers can compose for ballet-trained professionals with few limitations, but "modern-dancers" cannot slip from one technique to the other, lacking academic classic training. Few modernists start aged eight or nine, which is mandatory for ballet as for piano or violin virtuosi. Admittance to ballet-schooling (at its most responsible), is not licensed by simple ambition, but through expert opinion. Severe physical preconditions determine the ultimate chances of a classical professional; such "elitist" limitations need not deter "modern." In ballet, as far as doing-one's-own-thing goes, there is little scope for "originality" or improvisation. "Modern-dancers," since they start so much later, with minds more developed, are free to intellectualize impulses which have no bearing on acrobatic efficiency depending on synthetic method. "Modern-dance" training is based on a few isolated concepts tailored first to their unique inventors and restricted by such stylization, then adapted by a more or less liberated succession to their own peculiar needs and possibilities.

Ballet's vocabulary, by which strong executants magnetize big audiences, depends on muscular and nervous control deriving from four centuries' research in a logic combining gross anatomy, plane geometry and musical counterpoint. Its repertory is comparable to opera, symphony and classical drama. "Modern-dance" may be equated with the collected works of contemporary prose or verse writers. It has still to be proven that subsequent performances lacking their originators may long hold the intensity of their originals. "Modern-dance" is no longer a vanguard of reform. Far livelier in its current effect on both ballet and "modern" are influences from popular music, jazz and its mutations. Here, its risk lies in the very timeliness of novelty; transient slang fixated on a given epoch.

The root of ballet-training in the five academic foot-positions established some three centuries ago is not arbitrary. These determine the greatest frontal legibility and launch of the upper body as silhouette framed in a proscenium. Ballet-repertory was calculated for opera-houses with orchestra-pits, and balconies rendering the stage-floor a virtual backdrop for half the public. It is not the only form of theatrical dance; it is the most spectacular. Extreme acrobatism entails hazard which, overcome, sparks the most ardent audience detonation. Its filigrain of discrete steps; its speed, suavity, and flagrant tenderness; its metrical syncopation and asymmetry make visual superdrama on the broadest spectrum. In "modern-dance," focus is elsewhere. From its start, it was on and in central somatic areas of the body, rather than extension of peripheries. A prime distinction exists between occidental and oriental dancing: open against closed, centripedal against centrifugal; kinetic against (dominantly) static; fast against slow. This is oversimplification, but a like parallel might be set for ballet against "modern": aerial versus terrestrial.

From Denishawn down to today, the orient, both in movement and morality, strongly influenced "modern-dance." From ideas via Emerson, Whitman and Nietzsche invoked by Isadora Duncan, with Denishawn's experience of Japan and India, first intellectual, then ethical superiority was claimed from religious precedent and temple practice. Ballet, with its vulgar connotations of frivolous luxury, sexual-toy or musical bagatelle (until Diaghilev) offered a likely target for self-educated amateurs. Isadora was a puritan; she feared seduction of her students by the charms of Russian ballet. In the wake of war and disaster, German and Austrian poets, painters, musicians and dancers of the 'Twenties and early 'Thirties proposed valid experiment which gained prestige as a passionate vanguard. Serious ballet had been lacking in their countries for nearly a century. American tours by Mary Wigman, Kurt Joos, Harald Kreutzberg corroborated and encouraged our own modernists. But, as Diaghilev himself said—the Germans had learned how to move as they forgot how to dance.

At the same time, classic ballet received fresh impetus with the arrival in New York of Diaghilev's heirs. America had seen no Russian dancers since 1917. Through painting by Matisse and Picasso, concerts by Stravinsky and Prokoviev, audiences were eager and prepared for "modern" ballets by Massine, Nijinska and Balanchine. This repertory was as much novelty as "modern-dance" and bore slight kinship to Pavlova's *Dying Swan*. However, the new ballets spoke with a Parisian accent and further spurred an opposition which was not only struggling for progressive form, but also a nascent national expression. From such tensions "American Ballet" was born.

It is not too much to claim that its present popularity began in commercial theater, on Broadway and in Hollywood. The strongest exterior influence on the development of the academic dance has derived (and still does, largely through Stravinsky) from jazz rhythm, beat, the shifting pulse and syncopation of styles and steps from ragtime to rock. "Modern-dance" unquestionably extended possibilities. Unorthodox use of the body in ballet, from Nijinsky and his successors was more an inversion of academic positioning than any radical extension of technique. The

Nijinsky in "Petrouchka" (1911). "Unorthodox use of the body in ballet, from Nijinsky and his successors, was more an inversion of academic positioning than any radical extension of technique." (Kirstein)

rehabilitation of theatrical elegance from commonplace habit came through Kern, Gershwin and Rodgers. Balanchine's insistence on the then-unknown credit "Choreography by" in 'Thirties musicals gave a new coinage to the classical line, at once sleek, rangy, athletic and modish, whose prototypes were more Ginger Rogers and Fred Astaire than ex-imperial ballerinas.

That ballet has gained a mass-audience is evident. That "modern-dance" has its own is plain. What continues to distinguish the two are elements which have always been present and do not change. In ballet what attracts its public is a sharper focus on the execution of steps, clear components of dance-speech, not necessarily at top speed nor unbroken flow, but which proclaim capacity in flexibility, lightness, power, brilliance *off the floor.* Ballet simulates a conquest against gravity of aerial space. Grace and elegance are involved but in unwavering control, the convincing wizardry in ease which at once conceals and demonstrates effort. In "modern-dance" the torsion of exertion, the moist anguish of psychological contest supplies pathos. The style in its tragic or mythic aspect stays agonized and intimate. Ballet is open, broad, grandiose, courtly and considerate, not of the exposed self, but of skill in steps and partners in a company. Psychic nuance, the visceral unconscious, upon which "modern-dance" depended remains its prime self-limiting material. However, as it has developed through a third or fourth generation, present champions are prompted by pop-music as well as Bach and Handel, for satire and comedy, increasingly a reaction from the solemn tyranny of their progenitors. But lacking any absolute acrobatic proficiency, it is doubtful whether continued use of the term "modern" holds much permanent contemporaneity. Its attraction becomes time-bound, a nostalgic mode, like "art-nouveau," "art-deco," "modern-art."

Dame Marie Rambert proposes that classic ballet offers a service parallel to *bel-canto* voice-production for trills and roulades. For her, *"La Bella Danza"* is not a nineteenth-century stylization nor a period fashion, but a steadily expandable vocabulary of spectacular action, propelling unique and extreme capacities of the dancer's instrument. For the ballet-artist, mastery of steps infers domination of space, as much above the floor as upon it. Limits-explored are not those of extreme emotion, but of expressive motion. Determined and defined, ballet is a continuous aria of the aerial.

(1976)

ADRIAN STOKES
From TONIGHT THE BALLET

THE CLASSICAL BALLET

The classical technique may not provide the reader's chief interest in the modern ballet: but he will now see that the classical technique underlies, and indeed defines, dancing which is ballet dancing. And it follows that anyone who has taken sustenance from the ballet spectacle and who, by the same token, cannot stomach the German schools of the "free" dance, will have interest and reverence at least for the classical technique. Moreover, it is probable that the frequenter of the ballet, in the process of becoming an enthusiast, will choose, rather than avoid, the nights on which *Swan Lake* or *Sylphides* or *Casse-Noisette* or *Coppelia* or *Giselle* are performed, the five classical ballets which have been constantly performed in London during the last few years.

The bearing of the classical dancer, we have said, is characterized by compactness. The thigh muscles are drawn up, the torso rests upon the legs like a bust upon its base. This bust swivels and bends but, in most *adagio* movements at any rate, the shoulders remain parallel to the pelvis bone. Every bend, every jump is accomplished with an effect of ease and of lightness. Perhaps nothing is more typical of the brilliancy of ballet than the manner in which the ballerina turns her head in a pirouette. Her eyes are fixed upon a point in space; as she turns, her head revolves last and comes round first with the eyes fixed on the same point. Thus by the fixed eyes that revolve in a flash back to the same position and fix the audience again, the volition as well as the actuality of speed, accuracy and brilliance is expressed.

The "turning out" of the classical dancer's thighs, legs and feet, give the broad base-line for jumping and turning and enable a balance that could not otherwise be attained. All the five positions are "turned out": the second and fifth positions allow the dancer to move sideways easily without turning the body. "Turning out" is the essence of ballet and we must pause to examine its aesthetic significance. Hitherto I have attempted to argue on general grounds that ballet is the most "externalized" form of the dance, an embodiment of the ideals of the European theatre. It will now be possible to make the conception more precise by treating it in terms of "turning out." For "turning out" means that the dancer, whatever the convolutions of the dance, continually shows as much of himself as possible to the spectator. When he stands in the first position facing the front, we see his feet and his legs in profile. The ballet dancer is, as it were, extended. We realize it best in the *adagio*, a supreme test for the ballerina. When, facing us, she bends forward over her front leg in an *arabesque*, the foot of the raised rear leg is turned out and tilted upward. A downward pointing foot not only would make an ugly line but would spoil the effect of openness, of disclosure and of that suspension slightly above the ground by which objects are best defined. Again, when the free leg is extended in front and is brought round in the execution of a *grand rond de jambe* to the second position *en l'air*, leg and foot are once more turned outwards. The late Monsieur André Levinson, famous as a ballet critic, had a special affection for this position. It typified for him the openness of the dance. In all such convolutions of the *adagio* the ballerina is showing the many gradual planes of her body in terms of harmonious lines. While her arms and one leg are extended, her partner turns her slowly round upon the pivot of her straight point. She is shown to the world with the utmost love and grace. She will then integrate herself afresh, raise herself on the points, her arms close to her body in the fifth position *en bas*, her feet close together, the one slightly in front of the other. It is the alighting of the insect, the shutting of wings, the straightening into the perpendicular of feelers and of legs. Soon she will take flight and extend herself again. Meanwhile she shows us on the points what we have not seen in the *arabesque* or *développé*, two unbroken lines from toes to thighs.

Compare this sublime fulfilment, this perfect intercourse expressed in planes, with the progressive spirals of Spanish dancing that betray its oriental ancestry or with the coils of mesmeric tension which the Indian or Javanese dancer builds up and with the same form expends. The uniform outwardness of ballet avoids such alternations. If it is less intense, it is no less profound: for ballet is adjusted to the planes of the stage, composes into a precise picture, a precise sphere of feeling which the imagination grasps entire.

As a rule, the dances of other civilizations seem to us to express foremost the absorption of strength, the building up of a reserve of vitality, a kind of inner recreation. There are dances that denote the expenditure of energy: but one is still conscious that behind the movements of such dances the dancer is drawing to himself the strength of the outside world, appropriating the life of animals or of the fields, or feeding upon a cultural heritage, himself its god. Such dances symbolize an intensification of the human mystery, the rapt human power of absorption alternating with expenditure. The more typical European forms of the dance are exactly the opposite: they show a dissolution of mystery, they express passion in terms of an uniform corporeal outwardness. The ballerina's body is etherealized. She seems scarcely to rest upon the ground. She is, as it were, suspended just slightly above the earth so that we may see her better. She seems cut off from the sources of her being, or rather, those dark internal sources are shown by her as something light and white, brittle as are all baubles, all playthings that we can utterly examine; yet, at the same time, so perfect is her geometry that we feel this plaything which our minds may utterly possess, to be as well the veriest essence. Her partner guides and holds her. And he—he then watches her *pas* with upraised hand, he shows her off. He has the air of perpetual triumph, and when the time comes for his own *variation* he bounds, leaps, bounces and rejoins the ballerina in the wings amid applause. Such is the abstract of the *pas de deux*, the crux of ballet.

In the *allegro*, ballet dancers move, and they move lightly and fast. Outside of ballet there is no true *allegro* in dancing, no fast travels that are executed with the utmost lightness and ease. All the same, a similar corporeal outwardness, we have said, is characteristic of the most typical European dances. As well as in the stately measures of palaces, ballet has its origin in dances of the people. The English country dances, dances for the village couples (whereas Morris dances, probably of oriental or Moorish ancestry, were performed by a squadron of men), some hundred years after reaching the English court, invaded the continent at the beginning of the eighteenth century. These *contredanses* as they were called in France, have a good deal to do with the development of ballet. It is probable that they assisted the growth of *allegro*. Certainly, except for the minuet, and for the gavotte which was considered scandalously vivacious when first introduced, slowly-trodden measures began to decline.

But apart from any historical proof, I would claim that ballet is the stylized, cultural form of the European dance (if one may entertain that conception for a moment) because ballet expresses through the agency of the human body, the very same mode of projecting feeling that characterizes all the greatest European

visual art. The same fixity without distortion and without stern-
ness, the same outwardness, is the hall-mark of our art, a steady
revelation that calls to mind the open face of the rose or smooth
mountains in unbroken sunlight. All art is the conversion of
inner states into outward objective form. But whereas the objective form is the constant in art, the degree of outwardness
thereby expressed varies a good deal. It is the pleasure of many
visual arts to *intimate*, by means of the objective form, an inner
state: whereas, in the highest achievements of European visual
art, that same inner intensity is entirely transposed into something smooth, gradual yet immediate: time and succession are
converted into spatial forms, not merely symbolized by spatial
forms. We like to have the mystery cleared, to see our feelings
laid out as something concrete and defined. We would win for
self-expression the homogeneity and the soft light of stone,
stone with its gradual, even-lighted surfaces. Watching the classical ballet I am constantly reminded of Agostino di Duccio's low
reliefs in the Tempio Malatestiano at Rimini, figures seemingly
pressed from the round into relief, preserving many values
which could be seen in a statue only if we walked round it. The
values of the round are expressed frontally by these gradual surfaces. Like the limbs of the dancer, those of these fifteenth century figures are turned outwards; otherwise no synthesis could
have been made of their various facets. And again, as in ballet,
none of these forms are abrupt or contorted. We witness at Rimini the gradual and glowing face of the stone. In ballet the
human passions are expressed by the gradual uncontorted curves
and straight lines of the extended human body. There is no
residuum, no veil. The human body is purged of atmosphere. All
is shown. When the ballerina extends her leg in a *développé* we
contemplate the essence of the European stage, a form of the theatre that is wedded to such display. This exhibition of graduated
limbs is an act of virtuosity; for "turning out" is not "natural"
but is accomplished by the dancer with an air of exuberant ease.
Ballet is full of virtuoso effects. The male dancer performing *tours
en l'air* like an animated helicopter. So be it.

The character that I have called typical of European visual art
and of the European theatre, is, of course, primarily a Mediterranean product which the Renaissance consolidated. For better
or for worse modern Europe is the inheritor of the Italian Renaissance. We now know how greatly and how long a typical
invention of that time in the visual arts like perspective, can be
misused or used meaninglessly. But perspective in the first place

was developed by the Renaissance artist to allow him to represent those many facets of the human form and of landscape and to order them in space. It may be objected that subsequent developments in the visual arts of Europe do not emphasize the non-contorted, if virtuoso, outwardness by which I lay so great store. Nevertheless, though it pass from one art to another, somewhere it always exists. There are many virtues in Baroque and Rococo architecture, but superficially, at any rate, these architectures do not exhibit the extreme spatiality noted above. All the same, it was from the attitude of seventeenth and eighteenth century deportment that the five positions of ballet dancing were taken. In Rameau's eighteenth century handbook we may read how to make a bow and why it would be ill-bred to turn in the foot. In making his salutations the eighteenth century gentleman gracefully showed himself, not only his front, but the sides of his legs and part of the back in the obeisance. He steps forward and he steps backwards, he shows himself in different perspectives. Such were the origins of the classical ballet as we have it today. "When you are able to make a graceful bow," says Rameau, "you unconsciously acquire a taste for dancing."

It may seem that these cultivated artificialities are not a very intense expression. That is true. Nor was there much intensity in ballet before 1780. Ballet is the last integral manifestation of the Renaissance spirit. . . .

There is now in London a large and enthusiastic ballet audience. It was created by Diaghilev himself or by the esteem which, since his death, ballet still holds. This audience would not enjoy classical ballet as they do had they not been introduced to it *via* the modern ballet or the prestige which Diaghilev gave it. Pavlova's company, it is true, never departed far from classical ballet. The public at large, however, went to see Pavlova, not her ballets. But whatever Diaghilev put on the stage heightened our awareness of ballet in general. First of all there was Fokine who re-created in his ballets and concentrated the classical *pas*, harnessed them to a direct expressiveness hitherto reserved for mime.

All the same the Fokine ballets and the ballets of Diaghilev's later periods as well, were, in a sense, a diffusion of pure dancing, a diffusion that embraced the painters, particularly the great Bakst, and the composers. Both in the choregraphy and in these other arts the classical ballet with its abstract, self-contained dances, was harnessed to a wider expressiveness. It was in terms of this wider expressiveness that a contemporary content could be treated: and it was because of the power exhibited by this wider expressiveness that we learned to love its source, the classical ballet. Diaghilev, not Pavlova, taught us to love classical ballet, to appreciate fully Pavlova herself.

And then there was Stravinsky. *Oiseau de feu!* What can we conceive to provide a more comprehensive image of the ballet, the classical ballet! Fire and bird-like movements (the *pointe* is like the tip of a wing) are in combination an extract of the ballet soul: it was in the music, in the décor as well. Then *Petrouchka,* the animated marionette, not the object of farce as *Coppelia,* but the figure of a great and profound tragedy. The music is a masterpiece. Some critics have complained that the music overwhelms the dancing. There are ballet purists who always would have music subservient to dancing, commissioned to supply a very definite rôle as a mere accompaniment to the dance. These purists have much in common with Mary Wigman. There is room in ballet for every kind of relationship between music and dancing: the one kind enhances the others, just as the modern and classical ballets enhance one another. A well-devised ballet programme today gives us at least three varieties of this relationship: and that variety is part and parcel of our pleasure.

In *Schéhérazade* and *Sacre du Printemps,* Diaghilev showed that symphonic music itself could be employed for ballet. There was no moonlight in the later ballets. A lyrical content was preserved with the help of the wry yet exuberant tricks of the music of *Les Six.* In *Les Matelots,* for instance, a ballet which has suffered so many unfortunate imitations at the hands of English choreographists, the more lyrical passages are entrusted to the wheezings of the trombone: but remember that the stage above is full of sunlight. This music and Massine's choregraphy provided that element of toughness, of wryness, necessary as fibre to the modern lyrical mood, a plant that extracts a soft brilliance from the glare and brass of full daylight.

In Massine's and Balanchine's ballets the classical *pas* are sometimes used, less to interpret a general idea as in Fokine's work, more to express character or situation. It is a half-ironic use of classical *pas* which yet retain the loveliness of their emblematic geometry. This characterization in really good ballets is swift and witty, profound, memorable. It is not a travesty so long as even the simplest classical *pas* are used to delineate a situation expressively. In *The Good-Humoured Ladies,* one of Massine's earliest works, the ladies course round the stage with *grands jetés,* thus expressing their confusion, their sense of imbroglio. Lifar's characteristic *variation* in *Les Matelots* (Lifar's part was taken by Lichine in the 1933 season) was at root a classical dance. In *La Pastorale*, the tall Doubrovska as the queen of film stars used to pass her *développés* over the head of her cavalier. That was a witty and memorable movement, a disdainful adjustment of a classical *pas* to current vulgarity, a complete expression of Hollywood situations in terms of ballet. By itself such a movement might seem a travesty of ballet; but the serious beauty of dancing and of the classically trained dancers, the beauty and brilliance of the décor and much of the music, existed as well in these ballets. It was ballet, the ballet style. And then, perhaps, after the interval we were treated to *Swan Lake* or to *Sylphides*. We enjoyed each of them, *Matelots* and *Swan Lake*, to the full, and each of them partly because of the other. They were entirely different variations upon the same theme; and we realized how fruitful, how vital was that theme, the ballet style. Thus Diaghilev could employ ballet to realize the most improbable conception: there was so much glory behind him. At the same time the purists grumbled. Still, Levinson admitted that the 1925 season was saved because in the midst of these innovations Diaghilev recalled Maestro Cecchetti, most famous of teachers, and put him again in charge of the troupe. The dancers performed their classical exercises each day with renewed vigour. "Diaghilev makes pebbles with gold," Levinson complained after watching *Les Biches* or some such ballet. And if Diaghilev did so, what a relief it was, what a proof of omnipotence, since everyone except the very best artists is always trying to make gold with pebbles. (Though to attempt to make gold with pebbles is a preferable activity in my view to the one of those London choregraphists, who, mistakenly endeavouring to emulate this period of Diaghilev's ballets, imagine that they contrive art in their making pebbles from pebbles.)

There are many fine old royalists—and I am not at all sorry that it is so—who will quarrel with me for not having dealt with the classical ballet at the beginning of this book and for not having confined myself to the classical ballet. Well, I have given my explanations. But let me now express again an unqualified love for the classical ballet. There is something hellenic about it, all the more noticeable seeing that the classical ballet is the form imposed upon a northern romanticism. This hellenism is deeply founded and therefore entirely unlike the superficial hellenism of Isadora Duncan's dancing. Ballet tends to revert to the treatment of classical subjects with which it started. The open, *physical* and graceful attitudes of the marble Greek gods in whom emotion is shown as an outward-turned body, was dramatized by the classical technique. One witnesses in ballet the release of power, not its integration, just as in the eighteenth century a man introduced himself, showed himself, by turning his feet outwards and by the wide sweep of his arm and by the slow inclination of his body. But the classical ballet as we know it today, the ballet in which the classical technique, and particularly the *allegro* which is so lacking in other forms of the dance was developed to its uttermost, dates from the Romantic Age.

La Sylphide, a ballet which provided Taglioni with her most famous part, was first produced in 1832. Tights had been adopted some thirty or forty years before, freeing the dancers' legs for leaps. About the same time the power to turn out the foot and the whole leg up to the thigh at an angle of ninety degrees became *de rigueur*. Before 1780 or so dancers had been content to turn out at an angle of forty-five degrees only.[1] The successes of Camargo, however, have been attributed to the fact that she was exceptionally well 'turned out' for that period. . . .

Marie Taglioni was, so to speak, the product of the same line of thought as had produced these developments, just as Liszt, the unrivalled pianist, was the product of the age which perfected the piano and produced the quintessential piano music. *La Sylphide* was both the first Romantic ballet and the first ballet in which most of the classical technique was exploited as we know it today. The romantic ballet *is* the classical ballet, we have said.

"Another point of interest concerning this ballet" (*La Sylphide*), writes Mr. Beaumont in his *A Short History of Ballet*, "is that the white muslin costume designed by Eugène Lami for Mlle. Taglioni—tight-fitting bodice leaving the neck and shoulders bare, bell-shaped skirt reaching midway between the knee and the ankle, pale pink tights and satin shoes—became the accepted uniform for the dancer of the pure classical ballet." This is the *ballet blanc* of pale tights and white ballet skirts, indicating to some people a rather faded mythology, especially if they have never seen a proper ballet but only some of the semi-ballet interludes of pantomime or of music-hall. This mythology, in classical ballet at any rate, will not seem faded to those who come to it from the modern ballet; for the latter will have taught them to appreciate the ageless and always emblematic qualities of ballet's geometry, seen at its purest when performed in the traditional costume.

Amid the glories of the Russian Imperial schools, amid the snows of the North, served by the tumultuous glint of Russian art, the classical ballet reached its height. Would that we might see the three acts of *Swan Lake* instead of a one-act résumé! Petipa, a Marseillais by birth who in his early days danced in Paris with Carlotta Grisi, the original Giselle, and with Fanny Elssler, was the choregraphist in chief of this great period in Russia during the last half of the nineteenth century. According to Levinson, however, it is an entire mistake to attribute *Swan Lake* to Petipa as the programmes always do, at any rate that part of the ballet which we are accustomed to see. The choregrapher was Petipa's understudy, Ivanov, who was responsible also for *Casse-Noisette*.

I have stated that in classical ballet the music was composed to order at the precise directions of the choregrapher. This is not necessarily anything against it as music. The requirements of particular dances have inspired the best composers at all periods. In the early days there were the gaillarde, pavane, volte, courante, canaries, allemande, gavotte, bourrée, passepied, rigaudon, passecaille and sarabande. Indeed, these court measures provided forms for a considerable part of seventeenth and eighteenth century music. Handel and Gluck wrote gavottes and sarabandes as songs in their operas. The minuet which Haydn and Mozart introduced as the third movement of a symphony, was a dance invented by Beauchamps, Louis XIV's ballet master and the original formulator of the five positions. He is believed to have evolved the minuet from a folkdance from Poitou.

An interesting treatise might be written on the influence of European dancing upon European music. Early nineteenth century music in particular reflects the vast influence of national and peasant dances, and it was at this time too that the waltz spread like fire. The waltz obtains an apotheosis in ballet. All these dances and the music they inspired added greatly to the variety of the ballet spectacle. For side by side with the dances evolved out of the classical exercises, the intrinsic ballet so to say, there has always existed in classical ballet many popular dances which could be added at will and which, in varying degrees, were translated into terms of the ballet technique. Popular and folkdances, especially since the time of Taglioni, have often served as the basis of a ballet. Upon such a basis, as upon its own intrinsic movements, classical ballet builds an architectonic that closely resembles the structure of a symphony. Modern ballet is constructed in a similar way. One of the great pleasures of a good ballet is therein to witness symphonic structure as something plastic.

Some popular steps like the ancient *pas de basque* belong to the intrinsic ballet. One cannot make any absolute distinction since nearly all the movements of classical ballet may be derived from some popular or court dance, two categories which are interrelated in their turn. No definition of a living art can be absolute. The obvious adapted importation, however, is generally called a "character" dance in classical ballet: such, for instance, are the frequent Spanish, Hungarian, Polish and Russian dances. For these dances, though they be reduced to terms of the stage, still retain their national style. The waltz, on the other hand, which, upon its first inception from the Bavarian *ländler*, grew rapidly into a cosmopolitan dance, has become part and parcel of ballet.[2]

Even the French classical-romantic ballet, like the earlier theatre ballet and like the court ballet that preceded it, was largely composed of 'character' dances. Moresque or grotesque dances, too, have existed in ballet since the earliest days, since the seventeenth century masques and the earlier Italian *intermedi*.

And so, when all is said and done, it is impossible to isolate the "intrinsic classical ballet." Yet the great style itself which orders each assimilation is immediately recognizable, and we find it just as much in those modern ballets which, from the old point of view, are composed very largely of "character" dances. We possess a great definition of this style in the ballet music of Tchaikovsky, a definition that can never be obscured. If music owes a great deal to dancing, the ballet style itself, the style of an evanescent art, owes its one and only permanent consolidation to Tchaikovsky, composer of the scores for *Swan Lake*, *The Sleeping Princess* and *Casse-Noisette*. A Tchaikovsky ballet is ballet twice over, ballet redoubled. For this music, apart from its context, that is to say, apart from any particular dance upon which Petipa or Ivanov had decided, is always impregnated with the spirit of the classical dance in general. More than anything else it has made that conception, the classical ballet, a definite and unescapable thing.

If you prod a piece of liver preparatory to cooking, it seems to bite back on the fork with a curious stringy bite. I can think of no sensation more different than the one Tchaikovsky's ballet music inspires. It is something white, firm yet crisp, which you cannot prod with the mind. It contains a white or silvery languor, a vast silvery thunder, stage thunder perhaps, though not the stage thunder of tea-trays but of the Tsar's packed sideboards of silver. *Ballon* is for ever enshrined in this music, so are the ephemeral, cygnet dart-points of the *fouettés* in the *pas de quatre* of *Swan Lake*, and a host of other movements. A Tchaikovsky waltz emits that glaucous brilliance by which this dance is glorified in ballet. There is something almost terrible in the climax of such music. But watch the stage: dancers never totter: at this moment they are more superb than ever: the final note reveals an attitude, an universal precision, a closure of virtuosity that is itself an acclamation.

With what fierce springs this music unwinds itself, how superbly it dawdles and fondles the *adagio* of the *pas de deux*, how brisk yet tender are the variations, and overwhelming to all but the dancers are the *coda* and the *presto!* This music of the severely classical dance is itself a modern ballet: for, just as in modern ballet everyday movements are englamoured, defined by synchronization as well, so in the ballet music of Tchaikovsky the very noises of the streets, the very tooting of horns, every noise and music that stumbles, is raised to the crystal pitch of the *ballet blanc*, translucent and transparent, clear yet refractive.

The *ballet blanc* of Tchaikovsky! As I write I see the *corps de ballet* of *Casse-Noisette* in steel-blue ballet skirts amid a snow ten times more profuse than the fall *Petrouchka* can command. They are waving branched sticks with baubles at their ends. This *corps de ballet* is the snow itself which Clara must traverse with the Nut-cracker before she can gain the kingdom of the Sugar Plum fairy. The light, silent yet careering flakes spread and mass with a continuity unusual in ballet, and therefore insistent, running to the stiff notes of wood-wind and brass: then, at the conclusion of this exhausting dance, the *corps de ballet* stand or lie piled up, waving still their white brilliant blobs as the curtain descends and rises and descends.

One has watched at twilight an almost invisible and ghostly winter's rain become illumined and compact. The rain had turned to snow. Flakes whirled and then fell slowly, for they were light.

Ballet etherealizes movement: the undulations, never tortuous, are those of snow or the swan's white neck.

(1935)

Notes

[1]They were content also with raising their straightened legs at not more than an angle of forty-five degrees for classical *pas*. Indeed, it is doubtful whether Camargo found it necessary to wear knickers when

dancing. By 1800 dancers raised their legs ninety deggrees for a movement such as the *développé*. This advance is to be associated with a change of costume. As long as for their classical *pas* ballerinas were wearing voluminous eighteenth century skirts, a greater agility was impossible. The earlier history of ballet can be most tersely written as a history of costume. It was Camargo who, in the first place, somewhat shortened the skirt and adopted the heelless shoe.

²Sometimes the *variations* in a ballet take their names from the music alone. Thus the naming of the Waltz and Mazurka in *Sylphides* refers solely to Chopin's music and not to the dances set to this music.

A. K. VOLINSKY
From THE BOOK OF EXULTATION

THE VERTICAL: THE FUNDAMENTAL PRINCIPLE OF CLASSIC DANCE

In ballet, ballerinas commonly dance on their toes. At first sight this deportment seems both unnatural and senseless. To understand so important an aspect of ballet, one must investigate the nature and meaning of the vertical in human life.

What is a vertical line? It is an upward-aspiring straight line. Things lie and stretch themselves along the earth, horizontally; or they soar away from it and free themselves of unnecessary supports. Man is so formed that impressions take shape in his mind in different ways, depending on whether he sees something lying or standing, horizontal or vertical. In the first case, the psychic sensation is restful and regular, without strong emotion; in the other, his soul is made to feel exalted. If I were to see a tree trunk floating in a river, in my mind's eye I would swim alongside it, as it does, quietly and still. One has only to see the same trunk set upright, aspiring from earth to the sky, and the soul is grasped by an involuntary impulse in a heavenward striving. A slithering snake awakens one impression; when it raises itself, another. A bear, too, changes when it rises swiftly and fearlessly confronts a menacing danger; and a gorilla ceases to resemble an ape when, staggering with exertion, it holds itself upright on its hind legs. High churches, obelisks, columns, mountains draw the soul upward. As man's eyes glide from below to above, earthbound and often pressingly heavy feelings and thoughts follow irresistibly.

Once man crept on all fours and lived in the trees as the apes do now. He lived horizontally then, without raising his glances to the stars, and he thought horizontally, too, about hunting his helpless prey over trees and ground. After a development process of many thousands of years, he came down from the trees, stood upright and straight on his legs and freed his arms for a deliberate battle with his environment. This was the moment of the greatest bloodless revolution in the history of mankind. Man ceased to be horizontal and became vertical. From this time on he is identified as a man, not an ape or a primate resembling man. At the same time, he acquires dominion over nature and becomes its master. This lordship is the result of the fact that man becomes conscious of his liberated arms and hands, he engages them usefully, and perfects his means of battle. He sharpens stone, manufactures arrows, stretches the bow, tosses boomerangs, which return to him, after birds, employs a lever, builds a hut, entices animals into traps, and so on. With the vertical begins the history of human culture and the gradual conquest of heaven and earth.

This is how the problem was viewed, too, by the Italian physician Moscatti, who lectured on the natural superiority of horizontality to verticality. Women, he maintained, would give birth more easily were they to move on all fours. Moscatti's discourse was taken up sympathetically by Immanuel Kant, the founder of modern critical philosophy. He agreed with Moscatti's supposition that to crawl is more natural, but emphatically asserted standing upright as an act of the spirit that overcomes the natural state and raises man above nature. . . .

The Greeks clearly set the vertical in opposition to the bent and crooked, not only in the geometrical but in the comprehensive spiritual meaning of the word. To see straight, to speak straight—all this is at once pictorially sensible and heroic. An upright city is a city of good and high morals that rests firmly on its foundation in a state of political and economic welfare. . . .

This is the meaning of the vertical in its widest sense. All peoples agree about its worth. In their languages the way of saying "straight" always means "honest." With every step the English take, they appeal to the "upright"; the Romans demanded that the heart burn as a flame, high and heavenward. Mountainward tend our souls—that is the sense of the Latin *sursum corda*. Ancient and modern are one in this perception of life. Antiquity understood all this even more deeply than we do. In our times, this type of word usage all too often is turned to allegory, that is, to a picturesque but not full-toned manner of expression.

Only in ballet do we possess all aspects of the vertical in its exact mathematically formed, universally perceptible expression. Everything in ballet is straight, upright, as a taut string that sounds a high note. Of course, I'm speaking of classic dance and not character or social dance, which purposefully and in keeping with their character permit all manner of crookedness. But in ballet, everything—the dances on the ground and in the air—is the direct heritage passed down to us by the sublime, proud, and pure antiquity. . . .

(1925)

MICHEL FOKINE
LETTER TO "THE TIMES," JULY 6TH, 1914

To the Editor of "The Times."

Sir—I am extremely grateful to the English Press for the attention which it has given to the "Russian Ballet," now appearing at Drury Lane Theatre, but at the same time I should like to point out certain misconceptions which exist as to the history of the ballet and the principles on which it is founded.

The misconceptions are these, that some mistake this new school of art, which has arisen only during the last seven years, for the traditional ballet which continues to exist in the Imperial theatres of St. Petersburg and Moscow, and others mistake it for a development of the principles of Isadora Duncan, while as a matter of fact the new Russian ballet is sharply differentiated by its principles both from the older ballet and from the art of the great dancer.

THE OLD CONVENTIONS

The older ballet developed the form of so-called "classical dancing," consciously preferring to every other form the artificial form of dancing on the point of the toe, with the feet turned out, in short bodies, with the figure tightly laced in stays, and with a strictly-established system of steps, gestures, and attitudes. Miss Duncan rejected the ballet and established an entirely opposite form of her own. She introduced natural dancing, in which the body of the dancer was liberated not only from stays and satin slippers, but also from the dance-steps of the ballet. She founded her dancing on natural movements and on the most natural of all dance-forms—namely, the dancing of the ancient Greeks.

The new ballet, which also rejects the conventions of the older ballet, cannot nevertheless be regarded as a follower of Miss Duncan. Every form of dancing is good in so far as it expresses the content or subject with which the dance deals; and that form is the most natural which is most suited to the purpose of the dancer. It would be equally unnatural to represent a Greek Bacchic dance with ballet-steps on the point of the toes, or to represent a characteristic Spanish national dance by running and jumping in a Greek tunic and falling into attitudes copied from paintings on ancient Greek vases. No one form of dancing should be accepted once and for all. Borrowing its subjects from the most various historical periods, the ballet must create forms corresponding to the various periods represented. I am not speaking of ethnographical or archaeological exactitude, but of the correspondence of the style of the dancing and gestures with the style of the periods represented. In the course of the ages man has repeatedly changed his plastic language and expressed his joys and sorrows and all his emotions under a great variety of forms, often of extreme beauty. For man is infinitely various, and the manifold expressiveness of his gestures cannot be reduced to a single formula.

The art of the older ballet turned its back on life and on all the other arts and shut itself up in a narrow circle of traditions. According to the old method of producing a ballet, the ballet-master composed his dances by combining certain well-established movements and poses, and for his mimetic scenes he used a conventional system of gesticulation, and endeavoured by gestures of the dancers' hands according to established rules to convey the plot of the ballet to the spectator.

THE NEW IDEAS

In the new ballet, on the other hand, the dramatic action is expressed by dances and mimetic in which the whole body plays a part. In order to create a stylistic picture the ballet-master of the new school has to study, in the first place, the national dances of the nations represented, dances differing immensely from nation to nation, and often expressing the spirit of a whole race; and, in the second, the art and literature of the period in which the scene is laid. The new ballet which recognizing the excellence both of the older ballet, and of the dancing of Isadora Duncan in every case where they are suitable to the subject to be treated, refuses to accept any one form as final and exclusive.

If we look at the best productions of sculptural and pictorial art from the point of view of a choreographer of the old school thoroughly versed in the rules of traditional gesticulation and of dancing with the toes turned out we shall find that the marble gods of Greece stood in entirely wrong attitudes; not one of them turned his toes out or held his hands in the positions required by the rules of ballet dancing. Equally faulty from the old-fashioned ballet-master's point of view are the majestic statues of Michael Angelo and the expressive figures in the paintings of the Renaissance, to say nothing of the creations of Raphael and of all modern art from Rodin down. If we are to be true to the rules of the older ballet we must turn our backs on the treasures of beauty accumulated by the genius of mankind during thousands of years, and declare them all to be wrong.

If we look from the point of view of the natural dancing of Miss Duncan, the fantastic attitudes of statues which adorn the temples of India, the severely beautiful figures of ancient Egypt, Assyria, and Babylon, the poetic miniatures of Persia, the watercolours of Japan and China, the art of prehistoric Greece, of the popular chap-books and broadsides of Russia—all alike are far removed from the natural movements of man, and cannot be reconciled with any theory of free and natural dancing. And yet they contain an immense store of beauty, an immense variety of taste, and are clear expressions of the character and ideals of the various nations which produced them. Have we any right to reject all this variety for the sake of adherence to a single formula? No.

THE FIVE PRINCIPLES

Not to form combinations of ready-made and established dance-steps, but to create in each case a new form corresponding to the subject, the most expressive form possible for the representation of the period and the character of the nation represented—that is the first rule of the new ballet.

The second rule is that dancing and mimetic gesture have no meaning in a ballet unless they serve as an expression of its dramatic action, and they must not be used as a mere divertissement or entertainment, having no connection with the scheme of the whole ballet.

The third rule is that the new ballet admits the use of conventional gesture only where it is required by the style of the ballet, and in all other cases endeavours to replace gestures of the hands by mimetic of the whole body. Man can be and should be expressive from head to foot.

The fourth rule is the expressiveness of groups and of ensemble dancing. In the older ballet the dancers were ranged in groups only for the purpose of ornament, and the ballet master was not concerned with the expression of any sentiment in groups of characters or in ensemble dances. The new ballet, on the other hand, in developing the principle of expressiveness, advances from the expressiveness of the face to the expressiveness of the whole body, and from the expressiveness of the individual body to the expressiveness of a group of bodies and the expressiveness of the combined dancing of a crowd.

The fifth rule is the alliance of dancing with other arts. The new ballet, refusing to be the slave either of music or of scenic decoration, and recognizing the alliance of the arts only on the condition of complete equality, allows a perfect freedom both to the scenic artist and to the musician. In contradistinction to the older ballet it does not demand "ballet music" of the composer as an accompaniment to dancing; it accepts music of every kind, provided only that it is good and expressive. It does not demand of the scenic artist that he should array the ballerinas in short skirts and pink slippers. It does not impose any specific "ballet" conditions on the composer or the decorative artist, but gives complete liberty to their creative powers.

These are the chief rules of the new ballet. If its ideals have not yet been fully realized, its purpose has at any rate been declared plainly enough to split not only the public and the Press but also the members of the St. Petersburg ballet, into two opposing groups, and has led to the establishment of that "Russian Ballet" which visits all foreign countries and is often mistaken for the traditional Russian Ballet which still continues its existence in Moscow and St. Petersburg.

No artist can tell to what extent his work is the result of the influence of others and to what extent it is his own. I cannot, therefore, judge to what extent the influence of the old traditions is preserved in the new ballet and how much the new ideals of Miss Duncan are reflected in it. In accordance with the principles of the new ballets which (together with the old ballet, *Le Lac des Cygnes*) constitute the repertory of the "Russian Ballet" at Drury Lane I was not only under the influence of the artists of the historical periods represented, but deliberately sought that influence. When I composed an ancient Greek ballet I studied the artists of ancient Greece; when I produced *Le Coq d'Or* I studied the old Russian chap-books and broadsides; and when I produced *Schéhérazade, Cleopatra, Le Spectre de la Rose,* and the Polovtsian dances in *Prince Igor,* in each case I made use of different materials appropriate to the ballet in hand.

Yours faithfully,

MICHEL FOKINE

(1914)

Modern Dance

ISADORA DUNCAN
THE DANCE OF
THE FUTURE

A woman once asked me why I dance with bare feet and I replied, "Madame, I believe in the religion of the beauty of the human foot." The lady replied, "But I do not," and I said, "Yet you must, Madam, for the expression and intelligence of the human foot is one of the greatest triumphs of the evolution of man." "But," said the lady, "I do not believe in the evolution of man"; at this said I, "My task is at an end. I refer you to my most revered teachers, Mr. Charles Darwin and Mr. Ernst Haeckel." "But," said the lady, "I do not believe in Darwin and Haeckel." At this point I could think of nothing more to say. So you see that to convince people, I am of little value and ought not to speak. But I am brought from the seclusion of my study, trembling and stammering before a public and told to lecture on the dance of the future.

If we seek the real source of the dance, if we go to nature, we find that the dance of the future is the dance of the past, the dance of eternity, and has been and will always be the same.

The movement of waves, of winds, of the earth is ever in the same lasting harmony. We do not stand on the beach and inquire of the ocean what was its movement in the past and what will be its movement in the future. We realize that the movement peculiar to its nature is eternal to its nature. The movement of the free animals and birds remains always in correspondence to their nature, the necessities and wants of that nature, and its correspondence to the earth nature. It is only when you put free animals under false restrictions that they lose the power of moving in harmony with nature, and adopt a movement expressive of the restrictions placed about them.

So it has been with civilized man. The movements of the savage, who lived in freedom in constant touch with Nature, were unrestricted, natural and beautiful. Only the movements of the naked body can be perfectly natural. Man, arrived at the end of civilization, will have to return to nakedness, not to the unconscious nakedness of the savage, but to the conscious and acknowledged nakedness of the mature Man, whose body will be the harmonious expression of his spirtual being.

And the movements of this Man will be natural and beautiful like those of the free animals. . . .

The school of the ballet of today, vainly striving against the natural laws of gravitation or the natural will of the individual, and working in discord in its form and movement with the form and movement of nature, produces a sterile movement which gives no birth to future movements, but dies as it is made.

The expression of the modern school of ballet, wherein each action is an end, and no movement, pose or rhythm is successive or can be made to evolve succeeding action, is an expression of degeneration, of living death. All the movements of our modern ballet school are sterile movements because they are unnatural: their purpose is to create the delusion that the law of gravitation does not exist for them.

The primary or fundamental movements of the new school of the dance must have within them the seeds from which will evolve all other movements, each in turn to give birth to others in unending sequence of still higher and greater expression, thoughts and ideas.

To those who nevertheless still enjoy the movements, for historical or choreographic or whatever other reasons, to those I answer: They see no farther than the skirts and tricots. But look—under the skirts, under the tricots are dancing deformed muscles. Look still farther—underneath the muscles are deformed bones. A deformed skeleton is dancing before you. This deformation through incorrect dress and incorrect movement is the result of the training necessary to the ballet.

The ballet condemns itself by enforcing the deformation of the beautiful woman's body! No historical, no choreographic reasons can prevail against that! . . .

. . . My intention is, in due time, to found a school, to build a theatre where a hundred little girls shall be trained in my art, which they, in their turn, will better. In this school I shall not teach the children to imitate my movements, but to make their own. I shall not force them to study certain definite movements;

I shall help them to develop those movements which are natural to them. Whosoever sees the movements of an untaught little child cannot deny that its movements are beautiful. They are beautiful because they are natural to the child. Even so the movements of the human body may be beautiful in every stage of development so long as they are in harmony with that stage and degree of maturity which the body has attained. There will always be movements which are the perfect expression of that individual body and that individual soul; so we must not force it to make movements which are not natural to it but which belong to a school. An intelligent child must be astonished to find that in the ballet school it is taught movements contrary to all those movements which it would make of its own accord.

This may seem a question of little importance, a question of differing opinions on the ballet and the new dance. But it is a great question. It is not only a question of true art, it is a question of race, of the development of the female sex to beauty and health, of the return to the original strength and to natural movements of woman's body. It is a question of the development of perfect mothers and the birth of the healthy and beautiful children. The dancing school of the future is to develop and to show the ideal form of woman. . . .

(1902 or 1903)

ISADORA DUNCAN
I SEE AMERICA DANCING

In one of his moments of prophetic love for America Walt Whitman said,

"I hear America singing," and I can imagine the mighty song that Walt heard, from the surge of the Pacific, over the plains, the Voices rising of the vast Choral of children, youths, men and women singing Democracy.

When I read this poem of Whitman's I, too, had a Vision: the Vision of America dancing a dance that would be the worthy expression of the song Walt heard when he heard America singing. This music would have a rhythm as great as the undulation, the swing or curves, of the Rocky Mountains. It would have nothing to do with the sensual tilting of the Jazz rhythm: it would be the vibration of the American soul striving upward through labour to Harmonious life. No more would this dance that I visioned have any vestige of the Fox Trot or the Charleston—rather would it be the living leap of the child springing toward the heights, toward its future accomplishment, toward a new great vision of life that would express America. . . .

I often wonder where is the American composer who will hear Walt's America singing, and who will compose the true music for the American Dance; which will contain no Jazz rhythm, no rhythm from the waist down; but from the solar plexus, the temporal home of the soul, upwards to the Star-Spangled Banner of the sky which arches over the great stretch of land from the Pacific, over the Plains, over the Sierra Nevadas, over the Rocky Mountains to the Atlantic.

I pray you, Young American Composer, create the music for the dance that shall express the America of Walt Whitman, the America of Abraham Lincoln.

It seems to me monstrous for anyone to believe that the Jazz rhythm expresses America. Jazz rhythm express the South African savage. America's music will be something different. It has yet to be written. No composer has yet caught the rhythm of America—it is too mightly for the ears of most. But some day it will gush forth from the great stretches of earth, rain down from the vast sky spaces of stars, and the American will be expressed in some mighty music that will shape its chaos to Harmony.

Long-legged strong boys and girls will dance to this music—not the tottering, ape-like convulsions of the Charleston, but a striking upward tremendous mounting, powerful mounting above the pyramids of Egypt, beyond the Parthenon of Greece, an expression of Beauty and Strength such as no civilization has ever known. That will be America dancing.

And this dance will have nothing in it either of the servile coquetry of the ballet or the sensual convulsion of the South African negro. It will be clean. . . .

(1927)

ISADORA DUNCAN
RICHARD WAGNER

It seems to me that the compositions of Wagner cannot be considered as the work of one artist or as the expression of one country. They are rather the entire revolt and all the feeling of an epoch, expressed through the medium of Richard Wagner.

That is why it seems so petty to have wished to abandon this music during the war; for the work of Wagner flows through every drop of blood in every artist of the world, and his mighty rhythm has become part of every heart-beat of each one of us. For Wagner is more than an artist: he is the glorious far-seeing prophet, liberator of the art of the future. It is he who will give birth to the new union of the arts, the rebirth of the theatre, tragedy and the dance as one.

He was the first to conceive of the dance as born of music. This is my conception of the dance also, and for it I strive in the work of my school. For in the depths of every musical theme of Wagner, dances will be found: monumental sculpture, movement which only demands release and life.

It is of this music that critics are wont to say, "It is not written for the dance"; but it is from this music that the dance, so long lifeless in the embryo, is being born again. In comparison with this new-born dance, the posed attitudes of the dancers of the Opera appear to us like the figures in the wax-works museums.

The theatre will live again in all its glory only when the dance once more takes its true place, as an integral and inevitable part of tragedy. It is because I believe this that I have dared to dance to the music of Wagner—yes, that I have raised my hands, vibrant with ecstasy, to the harmonious chords of *Parsifal*.

Do you understand the gigantic task that is imposed on us, before we can wrench from this music the torrential movement that must come—the glorious child-birth of the Dance?

(1921)

RAYNER HEPPENSTALL
From APOLOGY FOR DANCING

THE SEXUAL IDIOM

I never saw Isadora Duncan dance. That, I believe, may well be my best qualification for writing about her. For it seems that nobody who did see her was able to tell about her sanely. I know the music she interpreted. There are hundreds of photographs and drawings of her interpreting that music. Her autobiography is there, and her many articles on the Art of the Dance, for anybody to read. There are the many writings of those who saw and knew her, varying in waftiness and hysteria, from those of Mary Desti and Sewell Stokes to the brief obituary panegyric of Max Eastman. Above all, there are the many new schools of dancing which derived their forms and their energy from Isadora and which are, for the present day, much more important than she.

These I have watched and read, heard and seen, and I have seen Nicolas Legat (who was asked, in 1905, to join Isadora) frisk about with imaginary skirts, lift up swooning arms and speak the word "pornographique" most expressively. Evidently, if I had seen Isadora Duncan dance, there would have been no chance of critical sanity. With such a woman, you must either be outraged, or laugh, or fall cataclysmically in love; and find yourself in Jericho, anyway. I fancy I should have fallen in love. With such a woman and therefore with the art of such a woman. . . . It was all one. The art was the woman. It was the embellishment and justification of her extraordinary womanhood.

And the woman—which is to say, the little girl—was born under Aphrodite. She says, into the bargain:

> If people ask me when I began to dance I reply, "In my mother's womb, probably as a result of the oysters and champagne—the food of Aphrodite."

She was born, too, beside the sea, and her 'first idea of movement, of the dance, certainly came from the rhythm of the waves'—from which Aphrodite rose. Her antecedents were just what they should have been: American Rationalism, of the

plains and the skyscrapers, the America of Walt Whitman, entangled round a hot core of renegade Irish Catholicism. The family
was poor. There were three brothers and sisters, Augustin, Elizabeth and Raymond. The mother was a grass widow. Conditions
which make, altogether, for an oddly passionate family unity. . . .
And the mother played Schubert and Chopin, and they read
romantic poetry.

Isadora danced, as we say, from the cradle. Growing up, there
was local enthusiasm and misfortunes, provincial tournées,
Augustin Daly, New York, and then the whole family betook
itself to Europe, on a cattle-boat, to London, first, with Chelsea
garrets and all the proper appurtenances of struggling art. Days
spent in the British Museum, copying figures from the Grecian
urns, from which Raymond Duncan eventually worked out a
system of eight positions as seemingly fundamental as the five
positions of Ballet. . . . Encounters, gradually, with the great:
with Mrs. Patrick Campbell, Ellen Terry, Sir Henry Irving. . . . A
tour with Sir Frank Benson playing the first fairy in *A Midsummer Night's Dream*, for it "seemed that theatre managers were
unable to understand. . . ."

> In fact, at that time, it was difficult for me to understand why,
> when I had awakened a frenzy of enthusiasm and admiration in
> such men as Andrew Lang, Watts, Sir Edwin Arnold, Austin Dob-
> son, Charles Hallé—in all the painters and poets whom I had met
> in London—the theatre managers remained unmoved, as if the
> message of my Art were too spiritual for their gross materialistic
> comprehension.

Thence to Paris, to similar unremunerative or insufficiently
remunerative frenzies of enthusiasm and admiration. . . . And
Isadora, though fluttered by the great Rodin's sculpturous
advances, tried herself out, there, with remarkably elaborate
deliberation, for so young a virgin, on two lovers, both of whom,
however, were scared and fled.

Off to Germany, then, to Berlin, and to Vienna, with Loie
Fuller; to Hungary, where the first more or less satisfactory lover
was found, in a young actor, Romeo; and back to Germany, to
Munich, to start the legend of "die göttliche, heilige Isadora";
away to Florence, back to Berlin and its pseudo-Hellenism, away
to Venice. . . . And then to Greece, the Glory that was Greece, the
home of sea-born Aphrodite and the kin of Aphrodite, Apollo,
Dionysus, greater than Apollo, and the haven of Isadora's most
expansive visions and yearnings. . . .

I urge a high admiration for the energy and consistency with which Isadora sustained the phantasy of that Grecian excursion (with the presence of the family, who must have been rather nice, though they were evident humbugs, to keep up the necessary semblance of a sense of humour). She was a whole woman, most whole, perhaps, in her grand-manner follies and vulgarities, and she responded wholly to her blood's images of Aphrodite and Apollo, Dionysus, Minerva, Zeus. The pictures of her, with arms straining aloft, at the Parthenon, are never altogether cheap, however ridiculous they may seem. Stupidly, perhaps, and certainly with a great deal of confusion, she was submitting herself with all the profundity of her womanhood, to a real if forgotten splendour. She was seeking contact, in the deep passivity of racial experience, with the energies that had produced, as well as some of the greatest art, the richest and most satisfying of all our mythologies. But Isadora Duncan was the complete eclectic. She had no intellectual control over her experience, to keep it, in a possible metaphor, from evaporating. And a new phantasy presented itself, as the old one came to a circumstantial end. Isadora studied Glück, read Kant (just as though an Isadora might have something to do with Pure Reason) and Nietzsche, who drew the diffuse and incoherent mass of Grecian images to the focus of the single myth of Dionysus; and then went off to Bayreuth, to replace the satin slipper with the transparent tunic, in Wagner's heavily languorous Venusberg.

It would be difficult to find two divinities more essentially remote from each other than the Hellenic Aphrodite and Wagner's sonorously lavish Teuton Venus; but the name, the cognate persons of Love Incarnate in Woman's Form, was enough for Isadora, and she shifted her allegiance with no great effort. Her own erotic state changed as easily. In Bayreuth, she was adored by Heinrich Thode, with a cerebral passion to which her response, as she records it, is illuminating.

> The rehearsal at Bayreuth began. With Thode I sat in the darkened theatre and listened to the first notes of the Prelude of *Parsifal*. The feeling of delight through all my nerves became so poignant that the slightest touch of his arm sent such thrills of ecstasy through me that I turned sick and faint, with the sweet, gnawing, painful pleasure. It revolved in my head like a thousand whirls of myriad lights. It throbbed in my throat with such joy that I wanted to cry out. Often I felt his slight hand pressed over my lips to silence the sighs and little groans that I could not control. It was as if every nerve in my body arrived at that climax of love which is

generally limited to the instant; and hummed with such insistence
that I hardly knew whether it was utter joy or horrible suffering.
My state partook of both, and I longed to cry out with Amfortas, to
shriek with Kundry.

Each night Thode came to Philip's Ruhe. He never caressed me
as a lover, never sought even to undo my tunic or touch my breasts
or my body in any way, although he knew that every pulse of it
belonged only to him. Emotions I had not known to exist awoke
under the gaze of his eyes. Sensations so ecstatic and terrible that I
often felt the pleasure was killing me, and fainted away, to awaken
again to the light of those wonderful eyes. He so completely possessed my soul that it seemed it was only possible to gaze into his
eyes and long for death. For there was not, as in earthly love, any
satisfaction or rest, but always this delirious thirst for a point that I
required.

I completely lost my appetite for food, and even for sleep. Only
the music of *Parsifal* brought me to the point where I dissolved into
tears and wept, and that seemed to give some relief from this exquisite and terrible state of loving which I had entered.

The obvious comment, I suppose, is that Heinrich Thode's
behaviour, in keeping the proudly sensual Isadora, for so long,
in that feverishly and pervertedly heady state of being, was
almost unbelievably naughty: excusable, if at all, only on the
ground that Thode was, at the time, working on his St. Francis
and, quite evidently, needing his inspiration for Santa Clara.
More interesting, though, is the fact that Isadora could suffer this
state, gladly, for so long, and that she could still write it up with
such evident relish, twenty years after. Isadora Duncan was a
powerful and rich being, if ever any woman was, but her power
and her richness were essentially passive. Her essential nature
was rather to draw in, to absorb and assimilate—a kind of passional as well as intellectual Eclecticism—than to expand, to give
out abundantly, as her extravagance and her thoroughly uncon-
trolled dancing seem to show. The catalogue of her lovers is not,
in itself, uninteresting. But the significant thing is the infinite
variety of her total response to them. For each of her lovers, she
changed colour; she changed form, completely. She was altogether fluid and able to be transformed by any powerful man's
will, transformed wholly. Yet she was choosing her submissions.
Each submission was a manifestation of the passive female
power. She was absorbing and assimilating the rich wills of her
men.

At the same time, there is a curious unreality about all her
accounts. I have spoken of phantasies. I should have spoken

rather of the forms of one great polymorphous phantasy: which was Isadora Duncan's most substantial reality. Her nature never took form. It was as vast and changing and as finally unchangeable as the sea. It was a phantasy which Isadora sustained throughout her life, which endures in her legend and which she herself never understood at all. Even after the death of her children and after a run of loves which would have served to mature any half-dozen normal women, there is still, to the end, an extraordinarily adolescent flavour about Isadora's erotic nature and understanding. Her lovers, certainly, were never real men. From Romeo to Sergei Essenin, from Gordon Craig to the inexhaustible spring of wealth, to Lohengrin, and from Walter Rummel to the last stevedore, they were all visions and phantasies themselves and fuel to feed the one great phantasy. Isadora Duncan was a woman of amazingly rich and open erotic nature. She was also, very definitely, a sensationist. She was also an exemplarily glamorous mother. She was also an exhibitionist in the grand manner. In her schools, where the bodies of young girls were to be wrought to a beauty the world had not known, there was also something of Sappho and the Isle of Lesbos. But it is the phantasy which dominates. The phantasy embraces and assimilates all these things. They are facets, only of the phantasy.

And Isadora's life was Phantasy throughout. It never came to any true form at all, though Isadora was a whole being, and responded wholly, in each one of her phases. Her transformations were whole transformations. But the whole pattern of her life is as extravagant, as flamboyant, as lawless, as its substance, its single incidents. If it flowered, its flowers were of nothing more substantial than the stuff of methyl flames, wavering, disappearing in the light, evanescent in the haze through which Isadora looked out on the world and never able to achieve, or even to conceive, the peace, the stillness, into which life must subside when it will form into the round assurance of bloomed fruit. Evidently, Isadora Duncan was a beautiful woman, but even her own physical woman's beauty seems unformed, hazy, fluid: the kind of beauty that is frail in all its heavy lushness, changing from moment to moment and open, vulnerable, to every brief mood.

What has all this to do with the Dance, though? Evidently, a great deal. . . . Quite evidently in Isadora's own case and quite as much, if less evidently, with every form of the Dance. . . . Isadora's dancing is the restless physical movement of her phantasy. But a phantasy is not only a fluid, a formless thing, rejecting clarity. It is also a private thing. It is also an internal thing. As soon as it loses its private nature, by formulation and communication, and becomes externalised and takes form, it ceases to be a phantasy. It becomes a myth. And a myth is a verbal entity. The communication of phantasies, their translation into Myth, is the origin of Literature. The Dance can have nothing to do with phantasies. It can have nothing to do with anything private and internal. Nor can it have any honest commerce with verbal entities. And the Dance's end is always to be precise in its forms. Its desire is Clarity. Isadora Duncan was not concerned to dance, not concerned with any clarity of plastic forms. She was concerned with the Dance only as part of her primarily sexual phantasy.

She was concerned, also, as she thought, with Expression. She thought she was expressing herself, her fluid self, in the Heraclitean flux of restless half-forms. But the Dance cannot express a phantasy. Its first end is not Expression at all, or expression only of itself, of certain general qualities of style and of a passionate clarification. She thought she was recreating, for her self-expression, the forms of the Greek Dance. But forms of the Dance have force only for the community in which and by which they were evolved and created. They themselves become phantasy and formless to an age in which they need to be recreated, nostalgically, yearningly, from museum images. She thought, after reading Nietzsche, that her art was Dionysian. But the Dance of Dionysus, before and above everything else, was a free expression of the ecstasy of the whole community, not an exhibition, to the rest of the community, of one member's private ecstasy. Its forms are valid only as communal ritualia. In the rhythmical movements which Isadora Duncan executed in public, she was not even articulating, expressing, communicating a phantasy. A phantasy is not capable of communication, except by translation into myth and by relation with precise forms. She was only exhibiting signs of the ecstasy she felt in her private contemplation of the phantasy. Which, of course, excited the onlookers enormously. . . . They wanted to share the ecstasy itself.

Isadora's Art was, in effect, then, merely an art of sexual display, and I would stress the "merely." Isadora was not conscious of the fact. Nor, I suppose, were most of the spectators. She and they thought they were enjoying a spiritual experience. Perhaps they were, but it was only in the mass stimulation of private phantasies. There was no communication, or no communication in terms exact enough to be terms of art. Isadora thought she served all the gods, both ancient and modern: Apollo and Dionysus, the power-gods of European Royalty, the freedom-gods of America and the compassion-gods of Revolutionary Russia. In reality, she remained faithful to her stars. She served Aphrodite only. Her art was aphrodisiac.

But all art is aphrodisiac, surely? No, all art is antiaphrodisiac. All art engages sexual impulses (if only by deliberately eliminating them). It may even be that art is greater or lesser art according, precisely, to the strength and range of sexual impulses that it engages. But its function, as art, is to neutralise, to release, its engagements. In a Freudian term, art is always Sublimation. The need of the artist is to bring some intolerable pressure of passional experience—which will always be experience sexually charged, if not itself primarily sexual, since the passional being is primarily sexual—to the condition that I tried to describe, after Walter Pater, as the Condition of Music. A configuration of sexually charged experience is brought to the condition in which it can be contemplated as pure form, and a Catharsis is effected, a purgation of precisely those impulses or passions most strenuously engaged. The apparent process is usually a substitution of symbols for the passional realities, hypnotic and magical symbols to which the passional charge can be transferred, leaving no loose unresolved emotion, and which can be contemplated as formalised outward entities.

This is the mechanism of dreams according, more or less, to Freud. It is also the mechanism by which myths are produced, out of the intolerable pressure of primitive man's passional experience, out of pure erotic Phantasy. Initiation, the adventure of virginity, becomes an adventure, a dark and difficult entry, to the jewelled cave, ablaze with light, the Trophonian cave, Aladdin's cave; and modern man will endorse the myth's compulsion, its relation to his own phantasy. This is art, which transforms a surplus of sexual impulses into aesthetic contemplation. The materials of art may, however, be used in a contrary way. Stories, novels, pseudo-myths, are written and published, in vast quantities, weekly, whose sole function is in the stimulation of jaded or repressed sexual impulses. There are pictures, sometimes very finely painted pictures, whose intention and effect is the stimulation of sexual impulses, where these are jaded or repressed. There is the music of Wagner and Scriabin. But that which excites, instead of transforming and releasing, is Pornography, not Art, according, precisely, to the extent of its capacity for excitation. And it derives from feeble or stifled impulses, which need aggravation, instead of over-powerful impulses, which need redirection and release. This distinction between Art and Pornography is not an academic one; and it need not be stressed, I hope, that it is a distinction of which the censor, who bans James Joyce and encourages Ethel M. Dell, is not aware. Nor is it, of course, a distinction which disallows Pornography under all circumstances.

All this shows up more clearly in the Dance than elsewhere. I have already said something, in dealing with Tradition, about what I am calling the Sexual Idiom of Ballet. I pointed out, for instance, that a woman on her points, "because of change in significant line and stress and action, ceases to be significantly a woman. She becomes an idealised and stylised creature of the Theatre." And there is a kind of eternal virginity about her. She is inaccessible. She remains unravished. Or, in another light, another metaphor, I said:

> Major works of art, in any medium, are epicene. The Condition of Music is a Neutralisation. And this shows clearer . . . in Ballet, because the elements, the artistic material, is human bodies. In Ballet, the human organism is not only producer and consumer, but the goods, also, and aesthetic goods, like the angels, have no sex. . . . Aggressive masculinity or aggressive feminity is as destructive of the essential stylistic conditions of Ballet as flaunted inversion is. . . . Appeal, of any kind, . . . is out of place. Style—with Ripeness—is All.

And Style, in human movement, is fundamentally that substitution of symbols for realities, the production of ideal forms out of the natural animal movements of the human body. To dance, to move flauntingly and with potent rhythmical compulsion, is to project a state of organic excitement which, by the nature of the organism, is necessarily sexual or sexually charged. Ballet, by the force and technique of Tradition, by its intricate channels of convention, makes these states of organic excitement impersonal and transforms them, through its precise plastic forms, to states of artistic creation, the vicarious excitement of onlookers to states of aesthetic contemplation. Ballet is supremely the negation of Phantasy. Ballet is altogether concrete, outward, precise and sheer.

But Isadora Duncan would have none of these precise forms, this transformation. She wished to retain, as valuable in itself, the primary state of excitement, the personal ecstasy, and exhibit her state—communicating nothing but the excitation itself and perhaps something, vaguely, of its quality, its general tone—in movements which, she clamoured, must be free, their only semblance of form proceeding from the actual phase of her master phantasy. Look at the countless drawings and photographs of her. . . . She leaps along, knees thrusting upward in an agitation of the loins, head either plunging down to knees or flung back in taunting pride or turned in the glad terror of amorous flight. In her more serious dances, her arms cease to float caressingly but strain upward, trembling, in the infinity of desire or are flung wide in the infinite welcome of the matriarchal bosom, or are turned in, hands pressed over breast in spiritual hurt. Or she glides onward, in a tranced *lento cantabile*, in the plangent dream of fulfilment. And always, to end the exhibition, she strains herself upward, again, at the heavens, the hazy Cosmos, the ether streaming behind the stars. Or she falls in ecstatic swoon to the floor and lies panting, in a flaccid lush supinity. None of these movements is precise, sharp, clean, bright. There is no control. There is no line. Everything is fluid, formless, natural, free, without style, melting away, "with its own excitation, momently to mist." The only dancing is the dancing of a mist of loose drifting emotion. It was not an exhibition of dancing. It was a display of Womanhood, of the female principle as a hovering gaseous abstraction, as Womanhood might be before it crystallised into functions and social forms, seeking, swooning into, and yet resisting forms.

And that is what Isadora was concerned with, not the Dance. This is not authoritative. I did not see Isadora dance. The material is there for anybody's reconsideration. This case is an imaginative reconstruction, only, not dogmatic statement. It is so overwhelmingly evident, though. With the amazing physical and passional energy that she had, she wished to create, not new forms for the Dance, but new glamours for Womanhood; not finer art for the Theatre, but finer theatrical means for heightening the Female Mystery. She was not a dancer, but a sort of prophet. She thought she was both. She thought the Dancer was the greatest prophet. She speaks, always the "message" of her Art, and she speaks of her Art as "spiritual." She was concerned with the inward ineffable content. She was the glamorous matriarch, affirming, in herself, the glory of the primeval womb. She was, in fact, a bit of a feminist, a good deal of a suffragette. She wasted a lot of enthusiasm, for instance, on Emancipation, on "the right of women to bear children outside marriage," and so on. All of which, evidently, has rather more to do with Mrs. Pankhurst and the Masculine Protest than with dancing (or, for

that matter, with children). . . . But Isadora was of her generation, and her generation acclaimed her. She attracted to herself
all the frustrations, yearnings, hysterias, of her generation. Many
were found to acknowledge her prophetic nature. And that is
where she ceases to be a great woman, an amazing femme fatale,
a cause célèbre, a case, and becomes a nuisance. For, since her
death, in the Dance, the Prophetic Nature has acquired an alarm-
ing popularity.

Isadora Duncan was—so—the female counterpart of David
Herbert Lawrence, in Literature. Whether she was as great a person, it is difficult to say. Also, Lawrence often attempted art, as
well as grim and cosmic Pornography. And it is certain that Isadora's work was inferior, as well as less durable. Lawrence used
a medium which forced him to some precision. In Isadora's
medium, of free movement, there was no range of such precise
symbols as words to limit the glamorous-ineffable-vague. But the
similarity between the two cases is close.

> I spent long days and nights in the studio seeking that dance
> which might be the divine expression of the human spirit. . . . For
> hours I would stand quite still, my two hands folded between my
> breasts, covering the solar plexus. My mother often became
> alarmed to see me remain for such long intervals quite motionless
> as if in a trance—but I was seeking, and finally discovered, the cen-
> tral spring of all movement, the crater of motor power, the unity
> from which all diversions of movement are born, the mirror of
> vision for the creation of the dance—it was from this discovery that
> was born the theory on which I founded my school. The ballet
> school taught the pupils that this spring was found in the centre of
> the back at the base of the spine. From this axis, says the ballet mas-
> ter, arms, legs, and trunk must move freely, giving the result of an
> articulated puppet. This method produces an artificial mechanical
> movement not worthy of the soul. I, on the contrary, sought the
> source of the spiritual expression to flow into the channels of the
> body, filling it with vibrating light—the centrifugal force reflecting
> the spirit's vision. After many months, when I had learned to con-
> centrate all my force to this one Centre, I found that thereafter
> when I listened to music the rays and vibrations of the music
> streamed to this one fount of light within me—there they reflected
> themselves in Spiritual Vision, not the brain's mirror, but the
> soul's, and from this vision I could express them in Dance.

This is Isadora (wherever she borrowed her terms) finding her
way to the deep centre, the core, the dark source of all being,
which Lawrence, also, demanded that we seek and live by. Both
these modern prophets had the most unflinching belief in the

positive power of the solar plexus and the unabateable flame in the womb. Each of them was concerned, above all, to assert the ideal ultimate of his own sexual principle, though both, sexually, were unhappy and forced to retreat into a phantasy: Isadora the matriarch (would-be) and Lawrence the would-be patriarch, the Masculine Protest and the Oedipus Complex. Both travelled over the world, endlessly seeking self-fulfilment in alien images of the self-ideal. Both found their only conceivable images in dead races, in museums: Isadora among the monuments of the Glory that was Greece, and Lawrence, with his wider field of reference, among the Etruscans.

Both, in their questing, were anarchists, preachers of chaos, of a return to the gaseous mindlessness of the world's uncreated state. Both were anti-social. Both hated the conditions which had produced them and sought, not to change Civilisation's forms, but to escape into the primeval womb of Civilisation. Yet both returned to their place of birth. Lawrence came, at the end, to know that the only place of his salvation was his place of birth. He could not altogether desert the womb. And, after embracing every revolution and aristocratic counter-revolution in the world of her time and of the old world, Isadora yearned back to her origin and clamoured for the Dance of America.

In one of his moments of prophetic love for America, Walt Whitman said, "I hear America singing," and I can imagine the mighty song . . . from the surge of the Pacific, over the plains, the Voices rising of the vast Choral of children, youths, men and women singing Democracy. . . . I, too, had a Vision: the Vision of America dancing a dance that would be the worthy expression of the song. . . . It would have nothing to do with the sensual lilting of the Jazz rhythm: . . . no rhythm from the waist down; but from the solar plexus, the temporal home of the soul, upwards to the Star-Spangled Banner of the sky which arches over that great stretch of land from the Pacific, over the Plains, over the Sierra Nevadas, over the Rocky Mountains to the Atlantic.

I pray you, Young American Composer, create the music for the dance that shall express the America of Walt Whitman, the America of Abraham Lincoln. . . . It is too mighty for the ears of most. But some day it will gush forth from the great stretches of earth, rain down from the vast sky spaces of stars, and the American will be expressed in some mighty music that will shape its chaos to Harmony.

And this dance will have nothing in it either of the servile coquetry of the ballet or the sensual convulsion of the South African negro. It will be clean. I see America dancing, beautiful, strong, with one foot poised on the highest point of the Rockies, her two hands stretched out from the Atlantic to the Pacific, her fine head tossed to the sky, her forehead shining with a crown of a million stars.

Why should our children bend the knee in that fastidious and servile dance, the Minuet, or twirl in the mazes of the false sentimentality of the Waltz? Rather let them come forth with great strides, leaps and bounds, with lifted foreheads and far-spread arms, dancing the language of our pioneers, the fortitude of our heroes, the justice, kindness, purity of our women, and through it all the inspired love and tenderness of our mothers.

When the American children dance in this way, it will make of them Beautiful Beings worthy of the name of Democracy.

That will be America dancing.

It will, indeed. It does seem, often, as though America has no antiseptic, at all, against the Bigger and Better, the Louder and Funnier. The important point is, though, that Isadora's Vision is paralleled with visions of New Britain, everywhere in Lawrence, till Mellors, Lady Chatterley's game-keeper lover, put the British Proletariat into scarlet tights, that would show the curve of leaping buttocks and the endless rippling of male muscle. But was it not, in both cases, personal regression to the womb? Salvation in the Derbyshire game-keeper, mastering the British Aristocracy, was the vision of David Herbert Lawrence, envisaging, from the womb, his own rebirth among his own people. And Isadora's was the Dance of America. America Dancing was the vision of Isadora Duncan Reborn. The two of them embodied, finally, the whole regressive lassitude of their generation.

They were types of the lassitude. Their generation found a focus in them, for all its own regressive phantasies, and yearned to them, with their greater fullness and courage and heaviness. Both attracted to themselves great numbers of hysterical people. Both lived in a haze of adulation. Both were hunted down, at first, as pornographers (which they were, but in my special sense, only). Both have subsequently become text-books of sexual behaviour, Mrs. Grundies of the days before the Deluge. The similarity extends into the minutest details of the legend. Lawrence is remembered as one who healed the commonplace. People have rhapsodised on his way of washing dishes. Isadora, according to Sewell Stokes, was lovely, perhaps most lovely, when she snored, and Mary Desti sees her getting drunk as a lovely slow flowering into heavenly beatitude and beneficence, expanding, "like a flower, showering love on the whole world."

Both, in fact, were more significant, finally, as persons than as artists. Both were archetypal persons, incarnating and thereby alleviating major dissatisfactions of their age. Lawrence is the more compelling. And the cause is almost wholly in his medium. I do not know—nobody will ever know—whether Isadora Duncan may not have had as delicate sensibility, as great a spiritual nature, as D. H. Lawrence. Perhaps she had. But the significant thing is that the use of words, symbols more or less exact, forced Lawrence to clarification of his vision and phantasy and spiritual perception. Whatever the value of his message, he did "put it across." But what has a message to do with the Dance? What has physical movement to do with expressing the spiritual? If "spiritual" means anything, it can only be used of dancing which is as formally clear as Music must always be, of bodily movement which has attained the final clarity of spirit. Spiritual values are the gradual distillation of a long process of Tradition. Isadora Duncan wanted to manufacture them impromptu, out of brief ecstasies, trailing clouds of loose emotional glory. She was striving to recreate the Light that Never Was through a body that all too substantially is.

In their negative significance, also, in the efficiency of their anti-Traditionalism, Lawrence and Isadora are set apart by the nature of their media. Lawrence rejected the Intellect. Isadora rejected Ballet. And, in the two fields of Literature and the Dance, the two things are cognate. Ballet, as pure technique and as pure stylistic employment of technique, is very like what pure Intelligence is in Literature, what pure syntactical and metrical logic and form are in the making of Literature. Lawrence, in rejecting Intellect, used Intellect. He denounced pure Intelligence, renounced its possibilities for evil, in the most admirable employment and enjoyment of pure Intelligence. Finally, he did great service to Intellect, enriching it, and so to Literature, as a whole and with all it touches. Isadora could use no such means. She denounced Ballet, verbally, and danced her own way. If she had mastered Ballet, as Lawrence mastered pure Intelligence, she could have enriched it and done service to the Dance as a whole. Merely rejecting Ballet, she remains irrelevant to the Dance, except in negative senses.

But perhaps we should look more closely at Isadora's relations with Ballet. The actual detail of Isadora's life has not been retraced beyond the return from the Grecian excursion to Bayreuth. Apart from the first Russian excursion, the direct confronting of Ballet, it is not necessary to retrace it any further. On the

one hand, it is fairly familiar: the various lovers, the death of the
children, the pitiful long mother-lover relation with the adolescent hooligan and rare poet, Sergei Essenin, the defection and
final timely-tragic true femme-fatale death with her dancing
shawl. On the other hand, it is irrelevant. In 1905, when she first
went to Russia, Isadora Duncan was as nearly formed as she ever
would be: which is to say, she was entered into the thick of her
phantasy. And her art did not change, afterwards, so far as one
can see. She relinquished it and returned to it, only, grew fat and
grew thin, abandoned to it one new grief or joy and another and
all the final lassitude. And she tried, continually, to form great
schools, which never took the form she wanted them to. Contact
with Isadora seemed to be enough to set her pupils off, having
discovered their solar plexus, to vaunt their own prophetic
natures and spiritual missions. And that is all. But the direct confronting of Ballet is important, to an Apology for Dancing. Isadora Duncan's objections to Ballet are pattern-objections for
nearly all the modern world. This whole chapter should be read
as a general defence of the Dance against the "spiritual" dancers,
the inward dancers, the free, the natural, the prophetic and the
aesthetic dancers, the personal phantasists and exhibitionists. We
can look at Isadora's protest against Ballet, and then we can
come, casually enough, to those mushroom forms of the Dance
which were fertilised by her or in any of many ways reflect her
significance.

The arrival in St. Petersburg was well timed. On January 5th,
1905, Nicolas II, cowering in the Winter Palace, permitted his
guard to shoot down a mass of workers who had gathered without weapons, in the square below, to petition His Imperial Majesty for bread. Isadora Duncan arrived at dawn the following
day, and was greeted by a long procession of coffin-bearers, up
so early to bury their comrades before the disaffected city was
awake. Isadora wept, in the black Russian dawn. If she had not
seen it, she says, all her life would have been different. There,
before this seemingly endless procession, this tragedy, she
vowed herself and her art to the service of the people and the
down-trodden. Ah, how small and useless now seemed all her
personal loves and sufferings! How useless even her art, unless
it could help this. . . . So Isadora Duncan drove on to her palatial
suite at the Europa and cried herself to sleep. Soon her room was
filled with flowers. Two nights later, she appeared before the
élite of St. Petersburg, in the Salle des Nobles, and was acclaimed
by the Grand Duke Michel. Kchessinskaya called on her, to wel-

come her, on behalf of the Russian Imperial Ballet, and then Pavlova. Isadora was ravished by the artistry of these two heavenly beings, creatures of the Classical Tradition, the Dancer at his highest pure glamour. Then Pavlova took her to supper, after *Giselle*, with Bakst, Benois, Diaghilev and all the elect spirits of the Russian Intelligentsia. And Isadora (forgetting everything but her line of talk) proceeded to inveigh against Ballet.

She wanted Nature. She wanted the surge and lapping of the waves. She wanted the sapling trees, swaying in the breeze. She wanted to express—to be—these. She believed that the dawn and the sunset and the infinite wastes of the stars were lovelier, more rich in significance, than the choregraphic forms of Ballet. And so they are. In themselves they are more beautiful and more richly significant—at any rate, more impressive—than anything to be seen in a theatre. But that is hardly the point. To strive to recreate them, in human movement, in the Theatre, is not greatly different from wanting to recreate oak panelling in glazed wallpaper, silk hats in ash-trays or votive candles in the glowing of electric-light bulbs. The beauty of any natural happening or natural thing is its identity, its particularity, its unique and inimitable quality. And in its native context. . . . We don't want a classical Adagio on the high hill. We don't want the movement of lapping waves in the Theatre. In the Theatre, the theatrical—and only the theatrical—is natural. If you wish to reject the theatrical, then you must reject the Theatre. That is what Isadora did not understand. It is what the innumerable schools of free, soulful, natural and prophetic dancing do not understand. It is also, I am afraid, what a good many contemporary choreographers, within Ballet, do not understand. They want to run everything into a formless whole. They want to run together the natural glamours of the Open Air (the poetical glamour of situation) and the artificial glamours of the Theatre and make themselves one comprehensive Fairyland.

So, while enjoying in the highest degree the glamours of the Theatre, Isadora Duncan was able to turn out this line of talk. She was able to say that

> The school of the ballet to-day, vainly striving against the natural laws of gravitation or the natural will of the individual, and working in discord in its form and movement with the form and movement of nature, produces a sterile movement which gives no birth to future movements, but dies as it is made.

> The expression of the modern school of ballet, wherein each action is an end, and no movement, pose or rhythm is successive

or can be made to evolve succeeding action, is an expression of
degeneration, of living death. All the movements of our modern
ballet school are sterile movements because they are unnatural:
their purpose is to create the delusion that the law of gravitation
does not exist for them.

And so on. . . . And finally this . . .

> To those who nevertheless still enjoy the movements, for histor-
> ical or choreographic or whatever other reasons, to those I answer:
> They see no farther than the skirts and tricots. But look—under the
> skirts, under the tricots are dancing deformed muscles. Look still
> farther—underneath the muscles are deformed bones. A deformed
> skeleton is dancing before you. This deformation through incorrect
> dress and incorrect movement is the result of the training necessary
> to the ballet.
> The ballet condemns itself by enforcing the deformation of the
> beautiful woman's body! No historical, no choreographic reasons
> can prevail against that!
> It is the mission of all art to express the highest and most beau-
> tiful ideals of man. What ideals does the ballet express?
> No, the dance was once the most noble of all arts; and it shall be
> again. From the great depths to which it has fallen, it shall be
> raised. The dancer of the future shall attain so great a height that
> all other arts shall be helped thereby.
> To express what is the most moral, healthful and beautiful in
> art—this is the mission of the dancer and to this I dedicate my life.

When, in fact, they were not merely temperamental, Isadora's
objections to Ballet were moral, not aesthetic. At her most serious
(getting out of her phantasy), she was concerned with what is
humane, what ought to be, what improves and uplifts, in the
most obvious senses; and, if you have moralistic feelings first,
whether particularly, about dancing, or generally, about living,
then you must, ultimately, reject Ballet and follow on from Isadora. If you are concerned, however, with beauty and sheerness
and the subduing power of movement that is superhuman
enough to be slightly terrifying, then Ballet will seem to you the
only dancing. Supposing Isadora—on "deformation"—to be
right in more than an infinitesimal degree (which, of course, she
is not), it will seem to you proper that human bodies should
sweat and ache, in the Classroom, and even become, for ordinary
human purposes, constricted, reduced, perhaps, even ugly, so
long as movement in the Theatre is more beautiful, sheer and
compulsive. Reverting, again, to Tradition. . . . A definitely
"immoral" aspect is heightened in all art—in all life, for that

Isadora Duncan in "La Marseillaise" (1915). "The school of the ballet of today, vainly striving against the natural laws of gravitation or the natural will of the individual, and working in discord in its form and movement with the form and movement of nature, produces a sterile movement which gives no birth to future movements but dies as it is made." (Duncan) "When, in fact, they were not merely temperamental, Isadora's objections to Ballet were moral, not aesthetic . . . if you have moralistic feelings first, whether particularly about dancing, or generally, about living, then you must, ultimately reject Ballet and follow on from Isadora. If you are concerned, however, with beauty and sheerness and the subduing power of movement that is superhuman enough to be slightly terrifying, then Ballet will seem to you the only dancing." (Heppenstall)

matter—by the strong operation of Tradition. Tradition is something, always, of its own nature, to be struggled against. That is a large part of its function. The value of Tradition is fundamentally in the rich and fruitful conflicts and tensions set up between itself and the free human being. That is why continuous Religious Tradition, for instance, is spiritually necessary. And when either side yields or is violated, life becomes very poor and weak. By a violation of Tradition, we get Hollywood ethics and the welter of nasty Nonconformist sects. On the other hand, when the free individual life lets Tradition drain off all its energies, we get the hideous spectacle presented, almost unanimously, by the older generation in polite society. We get the incredible symbolic figure—it still exists, though!—of the withered old lady, with her scrutinising lorgnette. In Religion, we get a self-contained and inwardly sufficient churchy pietism which must certainly be as distasteful to God as it is to the unwithered creature. We get the Royal Academy. We get the verse of Mr. Alfred Noyes. And these things, also, have their equivalents in the Dance.

But, even in purely physical terms, there is no strong beauty without strong tensions and conflicts. The leaping of a powerful animal is beautiful, but it is a beauty which soon reduces, when repeatedly presented, in different sets of conditions, to a commonplace. Its trajectory, for instance, is not much different from that of an alighting bird, a javelin or a cannon-ball. I think the loveliest single movement I ever saw—certainly the most "unnatural," certainly terrible, certainly immoral—was that of a chained and ravenous animal. The chain being equated, I suppose, with Tradition. . . . On a very hot day, in the Schwarzwald, it was a lean and exasperated Great Dane, sheltering and sweltering in the barn-door of an inn, with its unusually long chain coiled by it. As two of us, tired and thirsty, came up to the inn (we had not seen the dog), it came out at us with a terrific howl, four or five yards out, two or three yards up, was caught and swung round in mid-air, at the length of its chain, and dragged back, by the tremendous recoil of its own power, with an amazing luscious planetary curve, crashing and shrieking against the barnwall, making the whole building and the baked earth shudder. No doubt, it was painful for the dog. It was also frightening for two human beings. But the pain and the fright did not last long. The moment's grip and rip of terrible beauty is indestructible.

Or is that only "the curious local callousness of the artist"? Am I, in any case, taking too much trouble over Isadora? Was she not just a rather silly, rather vulgar, rather adorable woman, possessed of enormous energy? She is dead and done with. Let her rest. And so on.... But Isadora Duncan's importance for the present situation in the Dance cannot be exaggerated. It is not so much her direct influence, though the young Michel Fokine was given a tremendous initial impetus by her theories. It is rather that the same vicious demands of the age which brought her to the surface are also dominating Ballet, independently. Ballet people, when they speak of her now, and of her successors, laugh at her and at them, heartily enough. But it remains fact that, for the most part, they themselves are demanding, from the Dance, just the same kinds—and sometimes, even, inferior kinds—of extrinsic and illegitimate satisfactions. Pure Style is at a discount, everywhere, in Ballet no less than in the innumerable kinds of Free Dancing.... In the meantime, the schools of Free Dancing themselves are numerous enough and dangerous enough. Every small-town teacher of dancing has her own particular brand of Freedom. And I believe that there are even more small-town teachers of dancing in America than in this country.

America, certainly, produced Ted Shawn, and, if you do still think that Ballet is cabin'd, cribb'd, confin'd and bound up with dead conventions, or suspect that Free Dancing may be either dancing or free; if you believe that Sturm und Drang is nobler than Moonlight and Muslin, or can argue that self-expression is different from exhibitionism; if, in fact, you would assert the claims of the Soul ... then you should not miss the earliest opportunity that presents itself of watching this gentleman dance. Ted Shawn and his Ensemble of Men Dancers, done up in jock straps and shaven chests, almost fulfil, I should imagine, Isadora's vision of America Dancing. It is true that these limber lads, when they came to London, did not impress the Great British as they have impressed the Great American Public, so that to be heartily rude about them is unnecessary, as well as not cricket. But what our surprisingly sceptical critics did not well understand is that the perspiration of these young huskies is the ultimate essence of all Freedom in the Dance. If you want precision, speed and beautiful line—which is to say, if you will have dancing—then you must get it through all the rigours of the classical Ballet technique. Reject these, in favour of no matter what Romanticism, and, finally you will get Mr. Shawn, standing up and lying down, suffering, agonising inwardly, sweating, with cumulative profusion, for twenty minutes or so, to communicate, through his eyes and hair, the intestinal passion of a spurious John Brown in the face of an altogether non-existent or at least invisible Glory. Even within the apparent confines of Ballet, sweat down a monster like *Union Pacific*, and you will get something like Mr. Shawn's *March of the Proletariat*, repeated later, with the addition of hats and an impression of clothes, as *Cutting the Sugar Cane*.

That dancing is no concern of the Ted Shawns of this world is shown clearest, perhaps, in the one important Ballet movement these dancers have adopted: a leaping circle of grands jetés—in which, however, the arms, pressed romantically back, behind the face (which they should frame), would break the heart of the most indifferent sculptor, let alone any Master of Ballet. And this, I suppose, is what all criticism of Free Dancers reduces to; that they do not dance. But let me not be thought to be blind to admirable effort. I have the greatest respect for the work of Margaret Morris, for instance, though she derives from Isadora more directly than any other school. Her remedial work, her work in athletic training, is, some of it, excellent. And I should be happy to see her courses substituted in public elementary schools, for the physical jerks—all too literally, jerks—of the present Government syllabuses. More than that. . . . Isadora Duncan was partly right in her argument that the Ballet training has a tendency to deform, at least, the bodies of children. A too early start in Ballet is vicious, in the case of all but the strongest children. Yet, if we are to have great dancers, there must be some training from the earliest years. And, if a national scheme were worked out, incorporating a good deal of Margaret Morris's work, there would, at the school-leaving age, be such a wealth of material for the true schools of the Dance as has never been dreamt of. Even Dalcroze Eurhythmics has its pedagogic justification. Only, these kinds of work, in practice, are useless for the Theatre.

And the work of Kurt Jooss—to some extent, also, that of the Central Europeans proper—escapes most of my criticisms of Free Dancing. The Jooss Dancers are fundamentally concerned to evolve a technique for the Theatre, not to exhibit themselves. Though there is not the cumulative force of centuries of Tradition, yet there is, here, something of the impersonality of Ballet itself. The basic argument against Kurt Jooss is, simply, that he has not made up his mind whether it is Drama or the Dance that he is concerned with. And that is an argument against most specifically modern work in the World of Ballet, too. . . .

A certain Impersonality—which means, in essence, Responsibility—must also be allowed to such as La Argentina (Antonia Mercé), though they dance alone and are celebrated, primarily, as unique theatrical personalities. Dancers of markedly national character cannot be accused of exhibitionism. However individual their techique, they have, behind them, a Tradition older than that of true Ballet, which preserves their work from the indulgence of private Phantasy. Argentina is quite spurious, in some senses. The work she arranges to the music of Granados, Albeñiz, de Falla (themselves rather spurious composers), is not nearly what it pretends to be. But she has, I think, a finer sense of the Theatre than any other dancer I have seen. Her personality has been worth all that miraculously careful stage-management. And her tricks cannot cover over that impressive strangeness of the forms of the Spanish Dance, which consists in an intricate fusion of Eastern and Western characteristics: the incoiling castañet-hypnotic incantatory structure of the Eastern Dance overlaid, as it seems, with the flaunting outwardness of the West, of the Bases of Ballet, with the two interplaying as intimately as the elements of a split personality. Still, failing a real Flamenco on his native heath, I prefer my Spanish entirely Westernised and stylised, in Ballet, where it entered in Petipa's hey-day and where, more recently, it has found a new importance as the evident basis of Massine's peculiar heroic manner.

But then the whole simple truth about Free Dancing, is that there can be no such thing as Free Dancing. The human body is one mass of resistances, which are only partially broken down by a life's devotion to sustained principles of muscular technique. The Dancer must always be concerned, supremely, with muscle, not soul, not expression, not literary significance. Let me repeat the most fundamental grounds of my position.

Man, in his natural state, plainly, is a thoroughly unsatisfactory piece of work: in form, in moving, far from express and admirable, as a rule, and much less like an angel, in action, then a well-bred whippet is. . . . And Ballet, fundamentally, is an attempt to defeat this fact, to reveal Man as, also, "an infinite reservoir of possibilities," which, however, needs Tradition and Organisation, as the commoner kind of reservoir needs filters and drain-pipes. . . . It is a struggle between a wastefully complex muscular system, designed for a limited range of animal acts and offices, and the economy, the simplicity, in line and mass, of the postures and movements—the Physical Ideas—to which his body, as a material of Art, aspires. And the result is not a triumph of Mind over Matter, but the emergence of non-cerebral Matter into such a condition of subtlety and sensibility that it can itself be called Mind.

For all Art, all Creation, is the end of a powerful and sustained love-pact between the Artist and his Material: his words, his musical tones, his pigments. There is courtship, long and difficult and delicate wooing, and the final-seeming creative act of love, which is never final. It shows clearest, perhaps, in Sculpture. The sculptor has to know every grain, every fibre, every substantial principle—the textures, the hot and cold, the humidities, the masses, the qualities of biting back on the chisel: all the resistances and all the potentialities—of the single block of wood or stone, before he can be fully ready and fit for the fruitful act of loving rape which satisfies himself and fulfils the material. It is the pattern of sexual love. It is the pattern of religious experience, where the soul is possessed and enjoyed and fulfilled by God.

The Dancer is hermaphrodite, in this. He commits rape and begets lovely forms in his own body, with continual increase of power. His material, the field of his creative experience, is his own muscular and nervous being. And his fulfilment is in the externalised joy of movement, the release, the building up of inherent tensions into a powerful system of release. This is the only true freedom. It is the kind of joy and freedom we call dancing. Not the joy of an inward, an unprojected ecstasy, which can only be communicated through erotic empathy and sympathy between the Dancer and the onlooker. . . . This is not Freedom. It may be a good kind of licence, but Freedom is a more difficult thing. It has to be achieved, as the end-product of a long and usually painful process. . . .

(1936)

KATHARINE EVERETT GILBERT
MIND AND MEDIUM
IN THE MODERN DANCE

Comparing small things with great, we may say that the renaissance of the modern dance resembles in various general
respects the classical Renaissance in Italy. One of these respects
is the emphasis on *humanism* and *a return to nature*. At both times
humanism has almost implied in itself a return to nature because
man was thought of as in harmony with the physical universe,
enjoying, reflecting, and focussing the world around him. Setting forth the first principles of the modern dance, Mary Wigman (born 1886) says: "Since I am expected to speak of the dance
as I perceive, love, and understand it, I do not wish to start with
art. . . . I wish to speak of him on whom art depends for sustenance, who portrays and demands art. I refer to the human
being." The verbal opposition in this sentence between art and
the human being is intended merely as an opposition between
an art that has cut itself off from its human root and so has
become academic and mechanical, and an art that acknowledges
and even claims its human root and is therefore vital. Dead art
has meant to the pioneers of the modern dance "impersonal and
graceful arabesques," "the superstitious execution of a mere formula," the "servile coquetry" of the academic ballet, a decorative
schema or abstract design, in a word, the exploitation of a repertory of clichés. The living art which these pioneers advocate
and teach must express human emotion and speak the language
of natural feeling.

Already as early as 1760 the French *maître de ballet* and writer
on the dance, Noverre, had stated the need of restoring the
dance to man and nature. He thus furnished, a century and more
in advance, certain features of the program of the choreography
of 1900. He says:

> Steps, the ease and brilliancy of their combination, equilibrium,
> stability, speed, lightness, precision, the opposition of the arms
> with the legs—these form what I term the mechanism of the dance.

> When all these movements are not directed by genius and when feeling and expression do not contribute their powers sufficiently to affect and interest me, I admire the skill of the human machine, I render justice to its strength and ease of movement, but it leaves me unmoved. . . .
>
> Dancing is possessed of all the advantages of a beautiful language, yet it is not sufficient to know the alphabet alone. But when a man of genius arranges the letters to form words and connects the words to form sentences, it will cease to be dumb; it will speak with both strength and energy; and the ballets will share with the best plays the merit of affecting and moving.

The book from which this excerpt is taken, *Letters on the Imitative Arts in General and on the Dance in Particular,* is the first item in the select bibliography of the founder of the systematic theory of the modern dance, Rudolf von Laban, for his work, *Die Welt des Tänzers.* In a sense, Noverre might himself be called the founder of the modern movement.

The general demand for a return to natural human feeling, common to all the moderns, shows various phases. These phases can be distinguished and will here be evaluated on the basis of the treatment of mind and medium.

The first extreme reaction from the frigidity of the ballet is sufficiently represented by the views of Isadora Duncan (1878–1927). She put "soul" back into the dance at approximately the moment when William James was deleting it from psychology. "Soul" signified to her two things: (a) a value, raising to the dignity of a major art what had dropped to the level of mere virtuosity and amusement; and (b) an *arché* or principle, i.e., the authentic basis for an art-form built out of the stuff of movement.

(a) In the simple philosophy, more mythology than science, guiding her reform, Isadora Duncan at times placed soul as the bearer of worth in contrast to the body, the heavy element pulling man down to earth. The highest class of dancers, she writes, understands that

> the body, by force of the soul, can . . . be converted to a luminous fluid. The flesh becomes light and transparent. . . . When, in its divine power, it completely possesses the body, it converts that into a luminous cloud and thus can manifest itself in the whole of its divinity. This is the explanation of the miracle of St. Francis walking on the sea. His body no longer weighed like ours, so light had it become through the soul.

At such moments she thinks of the perfecting of her art as involving the conquest of body with its crassness and slavery to the force of gravity. After the necessary preliminary discipline of the gymnasium, she writes, "the body itself must be forgotten." As a great dancer, she believed, of course, in the glory of the body. But she confusedly associated the feeling of soaring and of dominating her physical medium with the virtue of holiness. She seems often to overlook the beauty of the body *per se* and to find beauty in expression of soul.

(b) In the second place, Isadora Duncan, here reflecting from afar the Plato whom she admired, identified the spring of motion with the soul. In outlining the proper instruction of the child in the dance, she says that first attention must be given not to drill in patterns of movement but to the cultivation of the soul, which will then naturally express itself in appropriate movement. "The only power that can satisfactorily guide the child's body is the inspiration of the soul." Isadora's language is vague, but she obviously envisaged a line dividing man's spiritual inside, quick and energetic, from his derivative and instrumental outside. She sought not only value and dignity for her art (the dance, she said, must choose between being religion and merchandise), but spontaneity and creativeness. She charged that those who tried to adopt her method, copying the mere externals of her movements, failed—"not understanding that it was necessary to go back to a beginning." The analogy between her views of the primacy of the soul in movement and the teaching of the *Phaedrus* and the *Laws* in this respect is too obvious to escape notice. "Self-motion is the very idea and essence of the soul. . . . For the body which is moved from without is soulless." It will be recalled that the first illustration given by Ernst Cassirer in his *Philosophie der Symbolischen Formen* of a notion wavering in ancient Greek thought between the twilight of mythology and the clear light of reason is that of the *arché*. It stands, he says, for the moment of transition from the mythical notion of "beginning" to the philosophical notion of "principle." Isadora's "soul" is such a twilight symbol.

The mythical habit appears also in Isadora's references to the bond connecting humanity and nature. The human soul was, she thought, a mirror and symbol of the World-Soul. "Where," she inquires, "are we to look for the great fountainhead of movement?" And she answers that since a moving human being is not apart from organic and inorganic nature, "his movement must be one with the great movement which runs through the universe; and therefore the fountainhead for the art of the dance will be the study of the movements of nature." The dancer moved by spiritual stirrings has heard, she says, an inward music, "an expression of something out of another, a profounder world." The "holy" dancer, Isadora's ideal, mirrors cosmic motion: "her movements will become godlike, mirroring in themselves the waves, the winds, the movements of growing things, the flight of birds, the passing of clouds, and finally the thought of man in his relation to the universe." She once declared that the gestures of Duse elevated the actress to participation in the circling of the spheres.

The free improvisations of Isadora Duncan (to quote Serge Lifar) "had a word to say" to the world of dance, but did not inaugurate a new era. The conception she advocated was too tightly bound to her own fascinating personality for transmission, and exhausted itself in lyrical effusion. She had insisted on the beginning of movement without providing sufficiently for the middle and end. She perhaps fertilized the Russian ballet, but she had no lineal descendants in her own manner.

In the second phase of the modern dance movement, attention shifts from mind to medium. In the floating dream and unavailable ecstasy of Isadora Duncan, there was no work of art with determinable ratios and proportions, no universal language with grammar and vocabulary, no method or technique that could be taught to others, allowing the art to be propagated and so start or join a tradition. The German pioneer of the modern dance movement, Rudolf von Laban (born 1879), undertook to formulate a grammar of motion and a system of notation. For him the value of the new form could not be located in soul alone. A system of intelligible relations was indispensable, a firm frame for creativeness in this new kind.

Von Laban's grammar of motion deals with both the content and form of dance movements. First, as to the content. Now on any theory, ancient or modern, the movement of living bodies is the material out of which the dance is constructed, but the will to restore the dance to "nature" and the "human being" makes movement in the modern dance teleological instead of mechanical. The ballet is condemned for being a combination of senseless motions—spins as of a top, bounces as of a ball, ascents and floatings as of a balloon; the reformed dance, on the contrary, is to be developed out of mind-informed and goal-directed movements, in a word, out of gestures. Von Laban defines the dance as a sequence of gestures rounded into an artistic whole. Instances of gesture would be the greeting of friendship or the withdrawal of indignation.

Gesture in its turn breaks down for our modern analyst into parts; but intention and significance must be present in the parts as they animate the whole. A gesture, then, may be divided into tensions, or *Spannungen*, or rather it is the passage from tension to release, or from release to tension. A *Spannung* appears to be like what the psychologist Bentley calls a *"vital indicator,* which announces the position of the organism upon matters at issue." It is the minimum act by means of which a mind or psyche asserts the fact and mode of its distinction from death, or brute matter. *Spannung* is obviously a correlative term—it always stands over against the moment of release or conciliation. As thus part of a polar situation, *Spannung* recalls the dimensions of feeling worked out by Wundt. Wundt noted that feeling swings between *Spannung* and *Beruhigung,* also between *Spannung* and *Lösung.* Von Laban's thinking is not scientific, so that the parallel with the terms used by these psychologists cannot be pressed. It is true, however, that modern dancers voluntarily raise the "vital indicator," or sense of life and force, so that a movement's defiance of gravity and the earth-drag can be clearly shown.

To illustrate the rise of the tensions that constitute gesture and which are, therefore, close to the formative influence of the human dance, von Laban describes the alteration in a man's posture, when, after sleep or inattention, he suddenly becomes charged through and through in a joyous upward swing. The head lifts, the facial muscles tense, expression breaks, as it were, through a veil, the whole body, repudiating its submission to gravity, accents its own power, arching the feet and rounding the chest. One arm is raised, as if to contradict gravity, the other arm and a backward-thrust leg maintaining the delicate balance. If now, a motivated passage occurs by means of which this *Spannung* is exchanged for another in which the extended arm is placed athwart the chest, the head slightly lowered, the balance of the body eased backward, an expression of thoughtful benevolence substituted for that of dynamic assertion, a gesture pattern, that is, the germ of the dance, has been exhibited.

The sequence of gestures, or again, the sustained rhythm of tension and swing, requires a proper receptacle to contain it. This receptacle is the so-called *Raumkörper.* The spatial body, which is to be the place of a meaningful sequence, must itself harmonize with the expression of opposition and reconciliation; it must even take part in that expression, for it functions in the dance as well as contains it. Not thus functional is the three-dimensional space in which the ballet dancer cuts his figures.

What surrounds him is an indifferent environment, not a plastic partner. Order in space means for him a track on the floor, a collection of linear figures, the so-called five positions orienting the only accepted relations of his two feet to each other, and his own three dimensions. How, for the modern dance, the spatial body joins in, becomes internal to, the choreic process may be clarified by a comparison. In discussing the drawing of mammoths in the prehistoric caves of France and Spain, Baldwin Brown notes the very great importance of the first attempt to accommodate a sketched animal to the space which includes it. When, as in the Dordogne caves, the interest was confined to the presentation of the mammoth only, with no feeling for the relation of its form to the proportions of the wall or ceiling, art did not yet exist. With conscious proportioning of the animal to fit nicely into the shape and size of the field, genuine aesthetic concern begins.

The proportions and relations of the total space, then, are made real for the dancer by the way in which, within it, groups are balanced, or swept toward, or away from, each other. Diagonal lines tracked out are oriented in respect to indicated right lines and angles. A solo dancer sometimes appears to make lines roll around his body. He remains constantly aware of the axes around which planes are shifting or masses revolving. "The *Raumkörper*, the space-body," says Elizabeth Selden, "is to the dancer as substantial and real as his physical body."

But the formal part of medium is defined by von Laban not only through the organization of total space, but in terms of the system of motions anatomically possible to the individual dancer. This system he determines as a twenty-faced crystal, or icosahedron. Von Laban reckoned that the obliquely extended arms and legs of a dancer placed within the three planes that contain him, first, the vertical, up-down plane, second, the lateral, right-left plane, and third, the suspended, front-to-back-at-waist plane, would trace the axes of this twelve-cornered die. If one, then, thinks of the dancer's movement as rotating on these axes, one deduces the desired serial order. Since this geometrical form was to be interpreted, not primarily as the boundary of a body in repose, but as the law of the dancing process, von Laban developed quasi-musical scales, one of six double swings for men (the B scale), and one of twelve single swings for women (the A scale). One scale embodied in the icosahedron is identical with the sequence of parades in fencing. . . .

The directions in which the crystallized human thrusts himself forth have their intrinsic emotional charges. As the larger space was made pathic and organic by men and women wheeling and counterpointing within it, so, for one man, upward implies lightness and merriment; downward, strength and heaviness; inwardizing, bashfulness or tightness; expansion, happiness and confidence; motion backward expresses fear or self-defense; and a forward march, attack, greeting, or welcome.

A dance script is not external to the formal aspect of medium, because the demand that movement relations be identifiable by fixed signs reacts upon the choreographer. He must make a clear and distinct form, if the pattern is to be converted into sign-language. Von Laban devised a system of notation by means of which dance forms could be preserved and passed from group to group for repetition and criticism. The simple signs he uses indicate direction, extent, intensity, and time-value of movements of specific parts of the body. The script is recorded on a staff of five lines and four spaces, like that of music. The movements of the lower part of the body and the legs are indicated by signs *within* the staff; the movements of the upper part and the arms by signs *outside*. The staff is further parcelled out: the position of the feet is indicated in the two inner or middle spaces, the movements of the legs in the air by the two outer spaces. Immediately outside the staff are recorded the movements of the torso; signs for arm movements are to be found a slight distance away. Wedges tell the dancer whether to go forward or backward, right or left. Every lengthening of signs retards, every abbreviation accelerates, the movement; proportion of length of signs indicating whether two, three, or four fold. Variations and combinations of these basic signs give the dancer the necessary instructions for the turns, transfers, gestures, jumps, amount of stress and expansion of movements, repetitions, parts of the floor to be used, etc.

Thus far we have attempted no more than historical exposition of the initial forms assumed by two elements indispensable to all arts, mind and medium, at the beginning of the modern dance movement. America made mind lyrical, but attempted no structural analysis of medium. . . .

There is a close connection between the interpretation of the dancer as "complete" and the interpretation of him as a "communicant." One might call the dancer the typical speaker, or user of language, if speech and language did not normally connote exclusively words read and spoken. Gesture is for von Laban the original and archetypal language, of which all other languages are later and more limited branches. The ideal pattern according to which the mind gives and receives meaning is total bodily gesture—expressive movement. The dancer, then, may be defined as the one who has the maximum power of exchanging meaning with the rest of the world. He might be named the *communicant, per se*. To every level of living creature belongs a typical pattern of movement, symbolizing the cognitive relation set up between speaking center and responding environment. The hard cohesion of a stone speaks self-concentration and world-exclusion. We might perhaps say that the stone has the typically Forsytean (von Laban's word is *nehmend*) disposition. The linear up-stretching and down-drooping of a plant symbolize the desire for light and the droop of sorrow. Its mood is supplication. The lower animals move, on the whole, horizontally, seeking nourishment on their own flat and earthly level—hunters. Man's motions are typically centripetal; they pass out in all directions from a center—loving and giving, like Friday's child. The dancer's intelligence is aware of, and reacts to, every variant of approach and withdrawal, swinging and reaching, pushing and pulling, folding and unfolding, that makes up the world process. He stands at the cross-roads of in-working and out-going streams of power.

The two chief properties of the dancer's mind are brought together by von Laban in the sentence: "The phenomena of the world are to the dancer crystallizations of gesture-might." Less competent perception, he believes, stops with limiting surfaces, inert masses, and surface relations. But the gesturing man reads off the true nature of things in the manifold transformations of tension-form. The dancer as such, then, being the supreme agent of gesture, classifies entities according to their content of gesture-power.

The philosophy of Mary Wigman, the first and chief follower of von Laban, has much in common with her master's. She emphasizes the *Raumkörper*, the determinant tensions and crystallizations in the choreic medium, the unitary mode of apprehension, the archetypal language power of the dancing being. Surely in all this body of ideas there is more concern for pattern and medium than in the rhapsodies of Isadora Duncan. . . .

We noted that Mary Wigman roots the dance in living experience, but "experience" immediately becomes cosmic in scope for her. On the other hand, John Martin also invokes experience as the matrix of the art. But his conception of experience is akin to John Dewey's—the development of all the elaborations of human behavior out of crude beginnings in the satisfaction of survival needs. Biological truth is what we must study. The process of eating, for example—the assault upon the environment for the satisfaction of hunger, the appropriation of food, and the subsequent assimilation of it to the bodily tissues—furnishes the type we require. Our organs exist to keep us alive and happy.

In this "radically empirical" doctrine of the basic nature of the dance, what is mind and what is medium? The medium is "experience"—experience as human movement, because, as Martin says, the movement of behavior is only another name for experience. The parts of this material often listed in the manuals of the modern dance are as follows: "walking, strutting, running, leaping, hopping, skipping, galloping, turning, sliding, rolling, crawling, bending, stretching, balancing, folding, unfolding, soliciting, repelling, etc." This is a selection from the complete series of significant human movements, coined in the mint of the necessity of man's adaptation to his environment. For a more comprehensive study of the range of expressive movement, the empirical student would turn to Darwin's *The Expression of the Emotions* or the psychologist Allport's recent work, *Studies in Expressive Movement.*

The *mind* for the empiricist—*it* is itself almost the same as motor experience. The dancer is he who feels the primary human urges and knows how to move for satisfaction and expression. As we all know, the empiricists of Dewey's faith object to a radical separation of the mind from its object, or its environment, or from the material on which it works. At the beginning of his book, *Art as Experience,* Dewey takes the position, for example, that the Parthenon is not so much the embodiment of architectural beauty shining on a hill as the fulfillment of the civic and religious needs of the Athenian citizens. In other words, mind and medium here tend to lose their clear distinction from each other, as they did in the earlier mystic forms of dance theory.

For the theory of the modern dance the mind has thus far played three distinguishable roles: (1) that of soul, value-bearer and spring of motion; (2) the complete man and the archetypal communicant; (3) the empirical self—or better, biological organism. Medium has assumed two forms (since Isadora's "soul" expressed itself freely without systematic submission to the conditions of a medium): (1) the *Raumkörper* and icosahedron, and (2) the complete set of empirical motion-modes. Let us now try to bring these two elements into relation to each other. While both concepts, mind and medium, are indispensable in aesthetic analysis, they must come together in the crucial aesthetic fact: the work of art. Not mind and not medium alone, but the result of the operation of the artist's mind on the artist's medium produces the thing of value. It is the dance-form brought into independent being by the interaction of the two elements, and showing the characters of both, which puts to the proof the interpretation of mind, medium, and their mutual relations. Art is that activity, Aristotle says, which produces something distinct from the act of producing it. Unlike moral prudence, which is an activity continuous with its issue—wise human conduct—art realizes itself in something other than itself. Doubtless, Aristotle was thinking in this particular context of a craftsman such as the builder of a house, where it is easy to interpose a space between the mind that makes and what it produces. But his principle suggests one valuable general criterion of aesthetic excellence. The dance as work of art must be, among other things, an artificial creature, which will poise itself in external space-time to be looked at. It must be able to be the object of *theoria*. The function of art, Ruskin said, acknowledging the Aristotelian origin of the idea, is to secure man the happiness that may be defined as the energy or fulfillment of contemplation. But Aristotle's total treatment of the arts is flexible and sensitive to the various situations in which art finds itself. He even sets a definite problem suggested by the tendency of self-subsistence to disappear in the art of music. The relation between music and its soul-intention, we may paraphrase him as saying, is immediate; that between painting and its soul-intention is mediate, because painting employs external signs—figure and color. Figure and color are a stage removed from emotion, because not motion, he implies. The figurative arts employ a somewhat arbitrary language; music is almost communication purified of a medium, because music is motion and the feelings or ideas imitated (as Aristotle says) are also motion. Like knows like intuitively. "Why do rhythms and tunes, which after all are only voice, resemble moral characters, whereas savours do not, nor yet colors and odours? Is it because they are movements, as actions also are?" There is, as it were, for Aristotle, an underground passage connecting the mobile energy of the soul and the mobile energy of music that gives the one quick access to the other. He is interested apparently in the problem of what he calls the differences of imitative capacity, or what we should probably call natural expressiveness in the different arts. Of course, he is also interested in showing what arts are most useful in moral education.

Thus Aristotle set a standard for critical justice to the inevitable double orientation of art—toward independent status as analyzable structure, the object of *theoria,* and toward *psychic* expression, with a leaning toward practical involvement. "In any art, the more artistic [the work] is, the more form is there, i.e., the more measurable, definable, calculable, is it—the more rational or intellectual. Yet on the other hand, everybody since the world began has associated with art strength of feeling and unconsciousness of effort. A great piece of music can be taken to bits like a clock; a great poem, compared with any other piece of language, is intensely artificial; yet the amount of feeling which they represent is stupendous when compared with the song of a bird or a simple story." The complete loss of either pole for any alleged art or case of art is fatal to its specific value as art.

Now the arts vary intrinsically in the distance they normally interpose between the object and the human response, and so in their satisfaction of the obligation to *theoria.* As Aristotle said that music made an immediate transit to the hearer, without delay by signs, so Mr. Edward Bullough treats the dance as (to use his phrase) running a special risk of a loss of distance, because of the physical presence of living human beings as vehicles. He even hints that the decline of the status of the dance among the arts since Greek days may be due to its tendency to let distance disappear.

To measure the total resistance of the dance to "distancing" it is necessary to add together the factor pointed out by Aristotle in music, motion, to that pointed out by Bullough, presentment of the actual living body. In the dance the *contemplative* attitude is retarded by the constitution of the medium, namely the rhythmic movements of the actual human body. To the testimony leading to this conclusion of the ancient philosopher and the contemporary psychologist may be added the professional word of a *maître de ballet,* Serge Lifar. He declares that the dance is the most *bête* (dependent on the exploitation of the full animal body) of all the arts.

If immediacy is one characteristic property of the dance as such, the problem before us is: Is this general property augmented in the modern dance? The first answer would seem to be No. Certainly both von Laban and Wigman lay stress on the requirements of the dance as a work of art, and on the distinction between dance as an inclusive human type and as formed structure. Moreover, the trend toward abstraction in the modern dance would, it would seem, weaken the sense of a moving human presence. For example, Mary Wigman might be said perhaps to lose *qua* dancer her specific human character and to metamorphose into a bare space-tension. She is, one might suggest, a sort of animated brush stroke, painting in three dimensions the interesting intelligible constitution of a spatial volume. Or to use another figure, one might say that the dancer demonstrates effectively the processes of crystallization. The formulae of certain geometrical relations are through art made visible and vivid by active instruments—instruments which happen also to be living bodies. Indeed, such an idea is actually stated by Merle Armitage in a book on Martha Graham: "[In the dance] Mathematics, Geometry, and Numbers become neural and are projected as emotive patterns which live in space as well as in time."

Abstraction not only minimizes the sense of human presence, it might be argued, but also substitutes pattern for passion. The abstract pattern of the dance is built as an architect builds, it would seem, with something of the cool attitude of the architect. A figure or phrase being devised, this may then be repeated, reversed in direction, accumulated by the employment of further parts of the body, and by contrasts in tempo. It becomes, again, we might say, such an architectonic whole as a fugue or a sonata, which we think of as built up by similar methods out of voices, themes, and movements. The modern theorists, being interested in the autonomy of their art, do not, on the whole, admit that a dance, which they might name "Counterpoint" or "Canon," is an interpretation of a musical composition. Rather they insist that the choreic counterpoint or canon or arabesque is a parallel phenomenon, constructed by combining in proportionate ways the original "music" of the body. In this attitude they have the support, of course, of the history of the interrelations of music and the dance. Much of the liveliness and variety which gives charm to the sonata and symphony is the result of the assimilation of dance measures—the minuet, polonaise, sarabande, etc., so that the dance may claim equal primacy with music. Bach's C Minor Passacaglia, for instance, derived from a dance form. Doris Humphrey has recently constructed a modern dance which she calls by this name and which uses a two-piano arrangement based on Bach's music. It is easy to point out the large use of pre-classic forms among the moderns. Though obviously the substance of even these formal dances is a vehicle of some general mood, as is a fugue or a sonata, still because pantomime—realistic suggestion—is practically ruled out, these dances may illustrate what "abstraction" in the modern dance means. It means essentially the deletion of mimicry.

We recur to the problem of degree of distance. While abstract modern dances evoke emotion very little compared with a second large group of modern dances, immediately to be noted, they are more moving than the classical ballet, and thus increase the "risk" of the general dance beyond its already considerable tendency to allow "psychical distance" to disappear. It is easy to see why this is true. The general spirit of the modern dance, being a "return to nature" and "common humanity," even a pavane or a polonaise becomes through it recharged with our contemporary attitudes and with natural human sentiment. Again, abstraction in the sense of realization through bodily movement of space-relations is almost a stripping of human behavior to its primitive dynamic elements. If space is to be re-created by the dancer in terms of tensions and resolutions, let us suppose, if we will, that the dancer evaporates into a space tension. He will, even so, be a fighter or a lover, an embodiment of fear, or a builder of group solidarity. Let a choric group work together to show how a python-soul constructs a labyrinth, a spell-binding will draws a magic circle, witchery makes zig-zag intercrossing lines, as a result the line, circle, network, or diagonals created may actually be more starkly pathic than the confessed dramatic pantomine, because the simplified meaning of movement may be revealed without the dilution of associative content. This reminds us of Aristotle's description of music, music as a motion awakening soul as motion, like to like, without a detour through representation of objects.

The modern dance, however, uses pantomime or dramatic action as well as abstraction. In this latter favored form the intrinsic emotional appeal of the dance leaps to new heights. The material preferred is religious ritual, particularly primitive, and political, even revolutionary comment. Witness the titles: by Wigman: Dance to the Virgin Mary; Sacrifice, which includes (a) Dance for the Sun, (b) Summons of Death, (c) Dance for the Earth, (d) Dance to Death; The Celebration, which includes (a) The Temple, (b) The Mark of Darkness, (c) Festive Clamour;— these by Martha Graham: Vision of the Apocalypse; A Project for a Divine Comedy; Primitive Canticle; Primitive Mysteries, which includes (a) Hymn to the Virgin, (b) Crucifixes, (c) Hosanna: Bacchanalia; Dithyrambic; Incantation; Satyric Festival Songs; and American Provincials, which includes (a) Act of Piety, and (b) Act of Judgment. Under social comment, we may list the following by Graham: Immigrant, including (a) Steerage, (b) Strike;

Sketches from the People; Frontier; by Margaret Sage: Song of Labor and Revolutionary Hymn; by Jooss: The Green Table and The Big City; and by Doris Humphrey: With My Red Fires. In this phase of the modern dance, the powerful passions linked with religion, revolt, war, and lust are fully exploited by the present-day choreographers. That in these cases distancing would tend to be cut down is obvious.

To all those who emphasize the life-furthering aspect of art, its Dionysian element, and who distrust its formalism and artificiality, its Apolline element, the drift of the modern dance would seem a desirable aesthetic tendency, an accentuating of its already prerogative position among the expressive arts. Such persons are more interested in what mind—especially feeling— contributes than what medium demands. These make the dance a full-bodied and forceful communication about the social fundamentals. All other arts are taken, in this view, as specialities of gesture-language—poetry, for example, is fundamentally the behavior of the tongue, larynx, etc. Loss in force, but gain in delicacy of idea, accompanies for them the rise of painting, sculpture, music, and literature. The return of the dance, then, to primal urges is no more than the recollection and reaffirmation of all art's birth-right. . . .

(1941)

MARY WIGMAN
MY TEACHER LABAN

. . . Laban started to work intensely on his dance notation, the one thing to which he was absolutely faithful and for which he wrestled like Jacob with the angel. No error, no disappointment, no failure could ever keep him from pursuing this work. His gymnastic system based on the function of the joints and on the tension and relaxation of the human body's musculature was the first result of his research. His swing scales, by then properly defined, were the basis for his "Theory of Harmony of Movement."

I became the first victim to help prove his theoretical findings. Each morning he knocked on the door of my room: "Here comes the choreographer!" Laban stood there carrying an old-fashioned valise stuffed full with drawings and notes. When the wobbly kitchen table did not provide enough space for his papers, he spread them around the floor: from crosses to tiny human bodies and back again to crosses, stars and curves, signs and hastily scribbled notes were all over the room, leaving only a small space for my practical demonstrations. This was his great dream to be realized: an analysis of movement and the experiment of translating it into signs as a cross-, bar-, or point-system, in a series of lines or curves. He repeatedly designed, and rejected, always starting again from the beginning.

When the deep-breathing exercise was over, never quite to Laban's satisfaction, we turned to the development of his movement scales. They were most exactly tested for their relationships to each other, to be later demonstrated in their unshakable oneness of force, time, and space. The first of these scales consisted of five different swinging movements leading in a spiral line from downward to upward. The organic combination of their spatial directions and their natural three-dimensional qualities led to a perfect harmony. The different movements not only flowed effortlessly from one to the other, they seemed to be born of each other.

It also was hard work for me! Every movement had to be done over and over again until it was controlled and could be analyzed, transposed, and transformed into an adequate symbol. I have always had a pronounced sense for rhythm and dynamics, and my belief in *living* a movement and not just doing it was strong. Therefore my individual way of expression and reaction must have been as much torture to Laban as his indefatigable attempts to achieve objectivity were to me.

To point out the dynamic value of these movements they were given by him names like pride, joy, wrath, and so on. I needed little more than to hear the word "wrath" and I immediately threw myself into a colossal rage. The swinging virtually exploded in space. The endlessly repeated movements became more or less mechanical. I was simply delighted to do them once in a different, more personal way. Laban's wrath was even more vehement than mine. He jumped up as if bitten by a tarantula, hammered with his fists on the table so that the papers whirled around the room. He shouted: "You clown, you grotesque monster, with your terrific intensity you ruin my whole theory of harmony!" He was furious about what he called my super-self-expression, declaring that the movement itself *was* wrath and needed no individual interpretation.

Did I comprehend at all at that time what Laban had in mind? I was young and impatient, I wanted to dance, I wanted to create and communicate something that concerned other people too. What was a theory to me?

I believe the foundations of my career as a dancer as well as a dance pedagogue were laid in those few weeks. Objectivity and responsibility, patience, endurance, and self-discipline! How I needed them when I worked on my solo program, when my enthusiasm, my impatience, my passion for expression carried me away; when I was tempted to ignore all difficulties and complications; when it was so easy and seemed so right to jump over empty spots, to glide around dangerous corners, or to fill unexpected holes with hastily improvised movements, so I might go on and lose no time on the necessary but often so tiresome transitions. Or, when I was working with a group of young dancers, fascinated and absorbed by the dance idea I wanted to work out with them, their far too individual reaction and interpretation, their misunderstanding of my intentions, even their spontaneous enthusiasm, might have made me lose track of what I had in mind. If I were to get impatient or lose my temper, they would be terrified, would not react any more, and I could not go on with my work.

Only then I understood Laban's fury and my own terror of it, and also understood the young dancers who believed they were doing their best, just as I had done and felt when I was Laban's pupil. What a struggle, what an inner fight! But what a wonderful fight from beginning to end! I *had* learned my lesson. I knew that, without killing the creative mood, I had to keep the balance between my emotional outburst and the merciless discipline of a super-personal control, thus submitting myself to the self-imposed law of dance composition.

I remember my first solo program at the civic theatre in Zürich. After many trials and failures, it turned out to be a great success. Laban came backstage to congratulate me. He smiled and, being the great improviser he was, bent his knee: "Dear Wigman, though there was only one really harmonious movement in your whole program, I admit that you are a dancer, you may even be a great dancer." Today I would like to bend my knee before him and thank him for what he was to me and for what he gave me.

(c. 1970)

MARY WIGMAN
THE PHILOSOPHY OF
THE MODERN DANCE

The dance is one of many human experiences which cannot be suppressed. Dancing has existed at all times, and among all people and races. The dance is a form of expression given to man just as speech, philosophy, painting or music. Like music, the dance is a language which all human beings understand without the use of speech. Granted, the dance is as little an everyday expression as music: the man who begins to dance because of an inner urge does so perhaps from a feeling of joyousness, or a spiritual ecstasy which transforms his normal steps into dance steps, although he himself may not be conscious of this change.

In short, the dance, like every other artistic expression, presupposes a heightened, increased life response. Moreover, the heightened response does not always have to have a happy background. Sorrow, pain, even horror and fear may also tend to release a welling-up of feeling, and therefore of the dancer's whole being.

There is something alive in every individual which makes him capable of giving outward manifestation (through the medium of bodily movement) to his feelings, or rather, to that which inwardly stirs him.

Our own times confirm this definite principle.

We speak of the rediscovery and the reconquering of the body. We cannot deny that there is a definite cult of "body-consciousness" today. The interest in body-movement from sport to the art of dancing is wakened, keen and living.

It behooves us now to inquire whether this interest is merely an ephemeral mood, a transient fad, or whether it is actually a timely expression reflecting our own artistic life.

I believe that the latter is true. Do we not already speak of the technical age of the machine? And paradoxical as it may sound, between that which we designate as "technical," and that which we call the "modern dance," there is a definite correlation which is not fortuitous. It should not be a matter of wonderment or confusion to say that our technical age engendered the dance-motivated being. When we now consider that the primitive force or rhythm is behind the motor; that every machine breathes and symbolizes harnessed rhythmic force, and at the same time, when we recall that the impetus of the dance is also rhythm, we then have a definite foundation, a common nexus between the seemingly opposed expressions of life and forms of art.

It is this rhythmical expression in, and toward, life, which inculcates within the young people of today a positive consciousness for the dance. The use of rhythmical bodily movement as a medium of art-expression has become natural to, and is taken for granted by, the dance-conscious people of today. . . .

The primary concern of the creative dancer should be that his audience not think of the dance objectively, or look at it from an aloof and intellectual point of view,—in other words, separate itself from the very life of the dancer's experiences;—the audience should allow the dance to affect it emotionally and without reserve. It should allow the rhythm, the music, the very movement of the dancer's body to stimulate the same feeling and emotional mood within itself, as this mood and emotional condition has stimulated the dancer. It is only then that the audience will feel a strong emotional kinship with the dancer: and will live through the vital experiences behind the dance-creation. Shock, ecstasy, joy, melancholy, grief, gayety, the dance can express all of these emotions through movement. But the expression without the inner experience in the dance is valueless.

A definite change in dancing, particularly in Germany, has been taking place these past twenty years. The revised mode of terpsichorean expression we designate as the "modern dance" in contrast to the "classic dance" or the ballet.

The ballet had reached such a state of perfection that it could be developed no further. Its forms had become so refined, so sublimated to the ideal of purity, that the artistic content was too often lost or obscured. The great "ballet dancer" was no longer a representative of a great inner emotion (like the musician or poet), but had become defined as a great virtuoso. The ballet-dancer developed an ideal of agility and lightness. He sought to conquer and annihilate gravitation. He banned the dark, the heavy, the earthbound, not only because it conflicted with his ideal of supple, airy, graceful technique, but because it also conflicted with his pretty aesthetic principles.

Times, however, became bad. War had changed life. Revolution and suffering tended to destroy and shatter all the ideals of prettiness. Traditions, aged and cherished, were left behind. How could these old and broken-down traditions remain firm throughout this awful period of destruction? . . .

(1933)

ROGER COPELAND
MERCE CUNNINGHAM
AND THE POLITICS
OF PERCEPTION

"You wonder what to look at. I wonder how to live. Same thing."

Michelangelo Antonioni, "Red Desert"

"The history of the arts is tantamount to the discovery and formulation of a repertory of objects on which to lavish attention."

Susan Sontag, "The Aesthetics of Silence"

"Now that Rauschenberg has made a painting with radios in it, does that mean that even without radios, I must go on listening even while I'm looking, everything at once in order not to be run over?"

John Cage, "On Robert Rauschenberg, Artist, And His Work"

In 1950, the filmmaker Hans Namuth persuaded a reluctant Jackson Pollock to execute one of his famous "action paintings" on a canvas of glass while the camera recorded Pollock's frenzied gyrations from underneath. Although neither of them realized it at the time, their collaboration had resulted in one of the world's most significant *dance* films. For it demonstrated (in a way the paintings alone rarely do) that the fundamental impulse behind abstract expressionism was *the desire to transform painting into dancing.* Pollock wasn't the only abstract expressionist who thought of his art in "dancerly" terms: Arshile Gorky hired a Hungarian violinist to inspire his students while they painted. One of Franz Kline's masterpieces from 1950 is called "Nijinsky (Petrushka)."

Still, it's only after watching Namuth's film of Pollock painting that one can fully comprehend the truth of Harold Rosenberg's assertion that at the dawn of the abstract expressionist movement:

> the canvas began to appear to one American painter after another as an arena in which to act—rather than as a space in which to reproduce, re-design, or "express" an object, actual or imagined. What was to go on the canvas was not a picture but an event.

Abstract expressionism can be thought of as the culminating phase of modern art's love affair with the primitive. Ecstatic dancing is, of course, a central element in many of those rituals we think of as "primitive." And Pollock's conception of painting-as-dancing evolves directly out of those works he executed in the 1940's, works which took their primary inspiration from images of primitive ritual and mythology. But now, rather than reproducing the iconography of primitive art, he attempted to work himself into a virtually "primitive" state of consciousness.

Pollock wanted to express himself (his innermost self) in the most spontaneous, unmediated manner possible. His conception of painting-as-dancing could well have been inspired by Havelock Ellis who wrote "dancing . . . is no mere translation or abstraction from life, it is life itself." Yeats, in *Among School Children,* alluded to that same sacred bond between the dancer's life and the dancer's art when he asked, "How can we know the dancer from the dance?" Pollock wanted us to ask the very same question of *his* work: "How can we know the painter from the painting?"

Ecstatic dancing provides a provisional solution to the "problem" of steadily increasing self-consciousness as well as the fear of becoming too "civilized" for one's own good. Jacob Wasserman exaggerates only slightly when he writes in *The World's Illu-*

sion, "To dance means to be new, to be fresh at every moment, as though one had just issued from the hand of God." (Nor should we ignore the purely "therapeutic" and cathartic possibilities of dance. Dancing is a relatively safe form of intoxication. The harrowing private lives of Pollock, Gorky, and Rothko illustrate that they were all too familiar with the less healthy varieties.)

Ultimately, Pollock discovered the wisdom of Martha Graham's oft-quoted aphorism, "Movement does not lie."

Needless to say, no one watching Namuth's film has ever mistaken Pollock for a Graham dancer; but Graham's variety of modern dance has much in common with abstract expressionism: both were Jungian, gravity-ridden, and emotionally overwrought. Compare the titles of the major works that Pollock and Graham created in the 40's. Pollock painted "She Wolf," "Pasiphae," "Guardians of the Secret," and "The Totem, Lesson I." Graham danced works bearing equally incantatory titles: "Cave of the Heart," "Errand into the Maze," and "Night Journey."

Nor were they alone in rejecting the rational niceties of modern civilization. In the late 40's and early 50's, Existentialism— with its emphasis on "risk"—was emerging as a fully fledged philosophy of life. Brando, James Dean, and Montgomery Clift were creating screen characters full of inner anguish and inarticulate sensitivity. Mailer was just beginning a career devoted to the proposition that violent action is more authentic than polite, rational discourse. And Dylan Thomas was drinking himself to death in public.

Then in 1953, Robert Rauschenberg, a student of Josef Albers, created his "Erased DeKooning" in which he literally *erased* a painting by the famed abstract expressionist. Rauschenberg's gesture was probably too playful to be considered a passionate declaration of war on abstract expressionism; but it was, at the very least, an ironic dismissal of all that existential angst and public airing of matters more appropriately dealt with on the analyst's couch (Pollock often communicated with his Jungian analyst by painting for him). In 1957 (less than a year after Pollock's death) Rauschenberg created "Factum"—his notorious "double paintings"—one of which was created spontaneously in the manner of an abstract expressionist work, the other a meticulously recreated duplicate. His point: the product is not necessarily dependent on the process.

It's not surprising that Rauschenberg received very little encouragement from the art world at this time, immersed as it was in the abstract expressionist ethos. What is surprising though, is that one of his earliest admirers was a former Graham dancer with whom he became associated at Black Mountain College in 1953. The dancer's name was Merce Cunningham and the most significant thing about his association with Graham was the fact that it had ended. The dances Cunningham was now choreographing were much more balletic than Graham's; they were fast, light, ironic in tone, and virtually devoid of "expressive" or symbolic elements.

Even more unusual was Cunningham's insistence on "freeing" choreography from a dependence on music. In Cunningham's work, movement and sound existed independently of one another; choreography and music were both performed in the same space and time, but without affecting (or even acknowledging) one another. And most eccentric of all was Cunningham's use of chance procedures to "dictate" his choreographic sequences. Beginning in 1951 with his "16 Dances for Soloist and Company of Three," Cunningham decided to determine the arrangement of sequences by tossing coins, thereby invoking a wholly "impersonal" (and more objective) sense of order, rather than digging deeper and deeper into some subjective inner sanctum.

Thus Cunningham's repudiation of Graham and modern dance directly paralleled Rauschenberg's repudiation of abstract expressionism. And appropriately, Rauschenberg designed the majority of Cunningham's settings and costumes for the next 16 years (in 1966 Jasper Johns, another painter who was instrumental in forging a cooler, more impersonal style of object making, became Cunningham's artistic director).

All the while Cunningham's chief musical collaborator was, of course, John Cage. Much has been written about Cunningham's career-long collaboration with Cage. But despite Cage's undeniable influence on Cunningham (especially concerning his use of chance), the fact of the matter is that Cunningham's sensibility is actually much closer to that of Rauschenberg's and Johns'. Cage sees chance as a means of negating the ego and ultimately of overcoming the separation that the mind creates between itself and the world. But Cunningham's art, like Rauschenberg's, always insists on maintaining an ironic detachment from the world, especially from the "natural" world. Discussing the role of ecstasy in dance, Cunningham wrote in 1955, "What is meant is not license, but freedom, that is, a complete awareness of the world and at the same time a detachment from it."

Now, at this point we should probably pause to ask ourselves why Cunningham, Rauschenberg, and Johns felt compelled to reject this ethos of personal commitment and involvement. Why this emphasis on detachment, playing it cool, this aversion to intoxication? Again, it's necessary to compare Cunningham and Rauschenberg with Pollock and Graham. Both abstract expressionism and modern dance proceeded from Freud's belief that below the "cultural" ego lies the "natural" id (or in Jung's version, "the collective unconscious"). In order to re-establish contact with the natural and uncorrupted regions of the self, one must suspend rationality. But as de Chirico was among the first to point out, even the subconscious is in danger of becoming fully "acculturated" amidst the sensory overload environments of 20th century consumer society. It's no coincidence—I don't think—that Cunningham's aesthetic was forged in the mid-50's when the new medium of television was rapidly becoming an American institution. In an environment designed to stimulate wholly artificial desires—the "needs" of a consumer society—we have no way of knowing that what *feels* natural isn't really the result of subliminal cultural conditioning. This is the intellectual climate in which semiological studies have thrived in recent years; the semiologist proceeds on the assumption that "naturalness" is a bourgeois myth and that mass media have conditioned us to accept culturally-created needs as natural desires.

Especially in an age of abundance, the danger exists that we will confuse purchasing power with real freedom, while all the while our most fundamental perceptual habits have been conditioned by forces we neither recognize nor control. Or so the argument goes. (Marcuse's *One Dimensional Man* and Jacques Ellul's *The Technological Society* provide what are probably the most persuasive presentations of this potentially paranoid idea.) Amidst this climate of suspicion, artists like Cunningham and Rauschenberg have set out to critically examine that which "feels natural" rather than simply surrendering to it. Their motivations may not be as overtly political as those of a Jean-Luc Godard, but their attitude toward "naturalness" is much the same. And I suspect they would both endorse Ad Reinhardt's direct challenge to the abstract expressionist ethos: "One must never let the influence of evil demons gain control of the brush."

Modern dance is especially relevant here; for the pioneers of this form—from Isadora Duncan through Martha Graham—have always considered themselves apostles of freedom. To them, being free meant liberating oneself from the stuffy conventions of Puritanical culture. But for Cunningham, Rauschenberg, and the extraordinary community of composers, painters, and dancers with whom they collaborated, true freedom has more to do with seeing (and hearing) clearly, than with moving freely. Likewise, social mobility—regardless of whether it's horizontal or vertical—does not, in and of itself, constitute "freedom." (Oscar Wilde and Gertrude Stein both realized this when they advocated "doing nothing"—a detached contemplation of the world, rather than active involvement in it.)

But can we really extract a "politics" of perception from Cunningham's work? I think so. Here's a quote that tells us more about Cunningham than almost everything that's been written about him in the last 20 years:

> So long as the expression "*Gesamtkunstwerk*" (or "integrated work of art") means that the integration is a muddle, so long as the arts are supposed to be "fused" together, the various elements will all be equally degraded, and each will act as a mere "feed" to the rest. The process of fusion extends to the spectator who gets thrown into the melting pot too and becomes a passive (suffering) part of the total work of art. Witchcraft of this sort must of course be fought against. Whatever is intended to produce hypnosis, is likely to induce sordid intoxication, or creates fog, has got to be given up. *Words, music, and setting must become more independent of one another.*

The writer is none other than Bertolt Brecht; and his is perhaps the last name one would expect to arise in connection with Cunningham. Yet Brecht, in 1930 had anticipated Cunningham's revolution in his essay, "Notes on the Opera."

Brecht is here rejecting Wagner's theory of the integrated art work; and for Brecht it was no coincidence that Wagner occupied such a privileged place in the cultural life of Nazi Germany. To Brecht, the Nuremberg Rallies were one great Wagnerian opera: the masses mesmerized, the Führer unified with his followers. Brecht's alternative is intentional dis-unity, a separation of the elements which ultimately serves to keep the audience at a respectful distance, to prevent them from passively absorbing (or being absorbed into) the spectacle around them.

No one—and that includes Brecht himself—has carried this principle of separation as far as Merce Cunningham. In Cunningham's work, every collaborative element maintains its autonomy. The choreography, the score, the settings are all created in isolation and often don't encounter one another until the

© James Klosty

Merce Cunningham's "Tread" (1970, decor by Bruce Nauman). "Often the setting, lighting, or even the score for a Cunningham work serve to impede our more direct, 'uncomplicated' perception of the choreography." (Copeland)

very first performance. This is the aesthetics of peaceful co-existence: sound, movement, and setting all inhabit the same space without affecting what one another do.

Note that for Brecht, the ultimate goal of this dis-unity is to preserve the spectator's perceptual freedom.[1] And often, the setting, lighting, or even the score for a Cunningham work serve to impede our more direct, "uncomplicated" perception of the choreography. For "Tread" (1970), Bruce Nauman designed a row of standing fans lined up downstage directly *between the audience and the dance*. In "Walkaround Time" (1968), Jasper Johns designed a series of moveable plastic boxes which served a similar function. Ditto for Frank Stella's brilliantly bright rectangles of colored cloth moved around on aluminum frames for Cunningham's "Scramble" (1967).[2] In "Winterbranch" (1964), Rauschenberg's lighting plot contained chance elements which often left large areas of the stage in almost total darkness.

Cunningham was the first choreographer to achieve (or even attempt to achieve) the aims of the Russian Formalist Victor Shklovsky (a major influence on Brecht) who wrote that art is the effort to "remove the automatism of perception, to increase *the difficulty and length of perception.*" No one would hesitate to discuss the political implications of Shklovsky's statement (produced in 1917, in the wake of the October Revolution) or the political implications of Brecht's theory of opera: so why are we so wary of attributing similar motives to Cunningham? The problem is twofold: On the one hand, we're so eager to credit Cunningham with having liberated dance from the burden of having to project various sorts of meaning (narrative, symbolism, personal expression, etc.) that we fail to properly consider the *meaning* of this liberation. And the second part of the problem derives from the fact that even our most accomplished dance critics continue to employ an essentially descriptive approach to dance writing which is blissfully ignorant of the intellectual traditions that converge in Cunningham's work.

Here for example is Marcia Siegel on Cunningham's concert at The Brooklyn Academy of Music in 1972.

> Two of his three new works ("Landrover" and "TV Rerun") . . . involved a minimum of pop-art gadgetry, and they looked so bare and complete that I really got involved in them. Bizarre decors and sonic environments lend theatricality and sometimes fun to Cunningham's dances, but his unadorned works are as starkly satisfying to me as a tree against a February hillside.

After this audible sigh of relief (which is shared by all those who prefer trees in February to the "pop-art gadgetry" of America's most advanced visual artists), Ms. Siegel goes on to complain about the third work on the program:

> "Borst Park", the last of the new works, seems of lesser importance, containing less dancing and more tricks than I care for.

Even Arlene Croce, by far the most perceptive and erudite of America's working dance critics, had this to say about a recent work, "Exchange":

> I wish I had been able to watch it more closely, but my concentration broke about halfway through under the battering of David

Tudor's score. . . . How can you watch a dance with V2 Rockets whistling overhead?

She concludes by criticizing the non-dance elements of Cunningham's work for often being so "interfering and dictatorial." Several weeks later, Croce elaborated on this complaint when she made a passing reference to an older Cunningham work in which John Cage reads aloud from his writings while Cunningham dances:

> When Merce Cunningham and John Cage combined forces in "How to Pass, Kick, Fall, and Run" . . . they kept the words and the dancing on separate planes, and the result was that Cage distracted us every time he opened his mouth.

As Brecht once put it, this is reproaching the linden tree for not being an oak.

To many people, there's something downright *unnatural* about this perverse desire to complicate or postpone the more immediate sensory pleasure that dance can provide. After all, don't people dance (and watch dance) to re-establish contact with their bodies, to reassert the "natural" part of their being? And what troubles them about Cunningham is his critique of "the natural," his desire *to root the natural out of his dancing.*

I have no way of proving that Cunningham has been directly influenced by Shklovsky or Brecht, but Cunningham himself willingly acknowledges his debt to another great negator of the natural, Marcel Duchamp. In fact, the setting for his "Walkaround Time" was an outright homage to Duchamp—an assemblage of clear plastic rectangles imprinted with the iconography of Duchamp's masterpiece, "The Large Glass." In addition, the section of "Walkaround Time" in which Cunningham crouches down, stripping off one set of tights and pulling on another, was conceived as a visual allusion to Duchamp's "Nude Descending a Staircase"; and Cunningham has referred to those portions of the choreography adapted directly from his technique class as "readymades." (And of course, Duchamp is generally considered to be *the* primary influence on both Rauschenberg and Johns.)

Duchamp was the great grand-dada of what we now call "conceptual art"; and it was Duchamp's readymades which first illustrated the truth of Shklovsky's and Brecht's contention that art is essentially a matter of dislocating the perceptions. Put another way, the experience of art is not dependent upon physical labor, craft, inspiration, or self-expression; it may consist of nothing more than the act of estranging a familiar object from its *natural* context. (Duchamp's famous urinal ceases to be functional in its new museum context: it now exists only to be looked at.) The notion that art is not a matter of "making," but of "looking" is especially difficult to apply to dance—for most people still think of dancing as something one does, rather than something one looks at. Of all the arts, none remains as rooted in ritual as dance; and ritual, by definition, is a purely participational activity which is not designed to be looked at by detached spectators.

Significantly, it was also Duchamp who anticipated Rauschenberg's and Johns' repudiation of abstract expressionism when he derisively dismissed as "olfactory" those artists who wallow in the aroma of wet paint and wield their brushes in a sort of spacey stupor. To Duchamp, this sort of impulsive, spontaneous behavior was "animal like." And he wrote that "the direction in which art should turn is to an intellectual expression, rather than to an animal expression."

Now, it's one thing to expunge natural or "animal" expression from the inanimate arts of painting and sculpture (that was Rauschenberg's and Johns' central achievement); it's infinitely more difficult to expunge it from the bodily art of dance. But this is precisely what Cunningham has accomplished.

His critique of the natural begins by severing the traditional link between music and choreography. Schopenhauer saw in music an objectification of those blind, instinctual forces that animate behavior. And for a pioneer of modern dance like Isadora Duncan, dance was conceived of as the art of responding intuitively to musical inspiration:

> "Listen to the music with your souls," she told her students. "Now while listening do you not feel an inner self awakening deep within you—that it is by its strength that your head is lifted, that your arms are raised, that you are walking slowly toward the light?"

It is not the force of musical inspiration that sets Cunningham's dancers in motion, but rather an act of deliberation. In fact, sometimes in works such as "Variations V" (1965), the traditional relationship between music and dance is exactly reversed. Here the stage is wired with electronically sensitive antennae and photoelectric cells which produce sounds as the dancers sweep past them. Not only do Cunningham's dancers not perform *to* music; they must concentrate in such a way so as not to be affected by it. No doubt, this is part of what the renowned Cunningham dancer, Carolyn Brown, meant when she said that Cunningham technique is "designed to develop flexibility in the mind as well as in the body."

An equally important aspect of Cunningham's critique of the natural is his much misunderstood use of chance procedures for dictating choreographic sequence. Although the two are often confused with one another, Cunningham's use of chance is diametrically opposed to the sort of improvisation which lies at the heart of abstract expressionism. Cunningham is not attempting to break through the resistances of the intellect so as to unleash "natural" impulses buried within him. Quite the contrary: he utilizes utterly impersonal mechanisms (coins, dice, the I Ching, etc.) so as to avoid what might otherwise "come naturally." This is why so many dancers complain that Cunningham's choreography is often excruciatingly difficult—if not impossible—to perform: it doesn't *come naturally* to the human body.

And here lies another major distinction between Cunningham and the early modern dancers—from Duncan through Graham—who repudiated what they perceived to be the unnatural (and orthopedically unhealthy) postures of ballet in favor of movements more in keeping with the natural inclinations of the body. Cunningham was among the first modern dancers to cross the ideological picket lines in order to study ballet with George Balanchine. When everyone else in the Graham-dominated world of modern dance was carrying the weight of the universe on his or her shoulders and affirming the elemental force of *gravity* (modern dance can be thought of as a love affair with the floor), Cunningham was perfecting his lightness and speed.

Cunningham often initiates movement with an abrupt and ferocious intensity, only to reverse directions just as suddenly. Duchamp once wrote, "I force myself to contradict myself to avoid conforming to my own taste." And Cunningham's style— with its remarkably rapid reversals of direction, its continual *arresting of impulse*—probably comes as close as anyone ever will to embodying the principle of self-contradiction in movement. "The trouble is," says Cunningham, echoing Duchamp, "we all tend to fall back on our old habits. Dancing is very tiring: and when you're tired you just do the easy thing, the thing you know" (the thing that *feels natural*).

In addition, the Graham dancer was often taught to view the

floor metaphorically as "the earth." "Your spine," Graham told
her students, "is the line connecting heaven and earth." According to Tony Smith, Pollock conceived of his canvases in much
the same way:

> His feeling for the land had something to do with his painting can-
> vases on the floor. I don't recall if I ever thought of this before
> seeing Hans Namuth's film. When he was shown painting on glass,
> seen from below and through the glass, it seemed that the glass was
> the earth, that he was distributing flowers over it, that it was
> spring.

But in Cunningham's work, the stage space never seems even
metaphorically natural. If anything, it resembles the cool, ultra-
clean, impersonal environment of the modern museum. Like the
art objects which inhabit the space along with them (for "Rainforest" in 1968 Andy Warhol designed free-floating, silver-
mylar, helium-filled pillows), Cunningham's dancers are discreet
and self-contained, pure *surfaces*. If Pollock sought to transform
painting into dancing, then Cunningham sought to transform
the dancer into an art object.

Partnering is usually impersonal and asexual. Dancers are
often handled by one another like inanimate objects (this is especially true in works like "Tread" and "How To Pass, Kick, Fall,
and Run"). The effect often suggests a speeded-up, deadpan parody of "touchie-feelie" encounter group exercises.

Edwin Denby has described Cunningham's style as "extreme
elegance in isolation." One senses in Cunningham more than a
trace of that "air of coldness, that determination not to be
moved" which Baudelaire once cited as a chief characteristic of
the dandy. And his own dancing—even at its most frantic—
always exudes a slight aura of aloofness, an almost prissy stiff-
ness which resists any sort of "natural" Dionysian abandon. In
fact, Cunningham savagely parodies Graham's Dionysian pretensions in the hilarious "Bacchus and Cohorts" section of "Antic
Meet" (1958). (Even when Cunningham's movement seems
unmistakably "animal-like"—in "Rainforest" or the famous
"cat" solo—he never appears to be representing an animal, but
rather borrowing its heightened powers of sensory alertness.)

In "Crises" (1960), the dancers wore elastic bands around various parts of their bodies. By inserting a hand or an arm through
the stretch band around another dancer's wrist or waist, the performers could temporarily link themselves together without sac-

rificing their freedom as individuals. Freedom is the key word here. As Carolyn Brown has noted, everyone on stage in a Cunningham piece is always a *soloist*.

Not only is everybody a "soloist" in Cunningham's choreography, every section of every *body* can become a soloist as well; for Cunningham often sets the head, arms, torso, and legs moving in opposition to one another. As early as 1953, Cunningham had choreographed a piece ("Untitled Solo") in which the movement for each of several subdivisions of the body was determined separately and by chance. Thus the atomized body became a microcosm of the company-at-large.

The "isolation" (of one part of the body from another) is to Cunningham technique what the contraction (based on the more organic rhythm of breathing) is to Graham. These are the two fundamental building blocks out of which their respective styles are constructed. Simone Forti, a dancer whose natural and organic inclinations are at odds with Cunningham's, writes in her *Handbook in Motion:*

> I started going to the Merce Cunningham school. I remember watching my teachers, and feeling that I couldn't even perceive what they were doing, let alone do it . . . An important element of the movement seemed to be the arbitrary isolation of the different parts of the body. I recall a statement I made in exasperation one day in the studio. I said that Merce Cunningham was a master of adult, isolated articulation. And that the thing I had to offer was still very close to the holistic and generalized response of infants.

Note too her nostalgia for the spirit of abstract expressionism: in response to the emergence of artists like Rauschenberg, she notes mournfully:

> . . . at just this same time Abstract Expressionism seemed to stop. I've always wondered at its sudden end. Like a sudden death. Or a sudden glimpse of a precipice, and then everybody stopped. And no one talks about it. It's like a collective blind spot. Yet even to this day the sight of a De Kooning can radically change my breathing.

Cunningham may be a master of "isolation," but ironically, he has also managed to mastermind some of the most glamorous *collaborations* between celebrated painters, composers, and dancers since the days of Diaghilev's Ballets Russes. In addition to Cage, Rauschenberg, Johns, and Warhol, Cunningham has persuaded Robert Morris, Frank Stella, Christian Wolff, La Monte Young, and Earle Brown to compose scores and design settings for his company. They are the Picassos, Cocteaus, Stravinskys, and Saties of our era. But the similarities between Cunningham and Diaghilev end there. Diaghilev was animated by the Wagnerian dream of synthesizing the separate arts into a unified whole. Camille Mauclair, a Parisian art critic, wrote this rhapsodic praise of the Ballets Russes in 1910:

> This dream-like spectacle beside which the Wagnerian synthesis is but a clumsy barbarism, this spectacle where all sensations correspond, and weave together by their continual interlacing ... the collaboration of decor, lighting, costumes, and mime, establishes unknown relationships in the mind.

But just as Brecht rejected the Wagnerian melting pot, so does Cunningham repudiate Diaghilev's synthesis. By contrast, Martha Graham speaks for both Diaghilev (whose productions had assimilated the influence of Isadora) and the pioneer modern dancers when she writes (in her *Notebooks*): "What is the beginning? Perhaps when we seek wholeness—when we embark on the journey toward wholeness." Cunningham's rejection of "wholeness" initiates the era of *post-modern dance*[3] (in much the same way that Robert Venturi's rejection of "the international style" in modern architecture—which also promoted unity and wholeness—initiated a post-modern movement there as well). What I'm calling post-modernism effectively marks the end of that longstanding tradition in modern art and poetry which sought to transcend dualities—a Dionysian tradition that extends from Nerval and Nietzsche through D. H. Lawrence and Artaud. "Only connect!" wrote Forster in *Howard's End*. To which Cunningham might respond, "It's more important—at this point in time—that we dis-connect, at least as long as we live in a society whose perceptual habits have been conditioned by commercial television where the boundaries between the most diverse phenomena begin to break down and become blurred." According to this line of reasoning, any sense of "wholeness" experienced in the modern world is nothing more than a dangerous illusion. Wholeness, like innocence, cannot be regained. Rather than lamenting fragmentation and Eliot's "dissociation of sensibility," Cunningham encourages us to savor the experience of "non-relatedness." And how significant that a *dancer* would celebrate the potential virtues of fragmentation, for dance has always been thought of as a sort of universal language which transcends the impurities and dualities of speech. That's one reason both Mallarmé and Yeats were so infatuated with the pioneer modern dancer Loie Fuller. And to reject "the whole" is (etymologically speaking) to reject "the holy." Cunningham was the first choreographer to fully secularize the dance, to "de-primitivize" it.

Throughout his career, Cunningham has made a practice of excerpting fragments from different works in his standard repertory and "splicing" them together in a form he calls "Events." ("Splicing" strikes me as the most appropriate word for describing Cunningham's relation to the raw material of these events because he approaches his older works the way a film editor approaches his daily rushes: cutting, assembling, and re-assembling the fragments at will.) For almost ten years now, the vast majority of Cunningham's public performances have been devoted to these events, rather than to his titled, finished works. The events provide perhaps the ultimate example of Cunningham's determination to avoid completion and "wholeness."

It is precisely this aspect of Cunningham's achievement which makes him so much a creature of the intellectual moment we are now living through. In a very real sense, the most sophisticated French critical thought now finding its way into English (the work of Barthes, Deleuze, Derrida) is just beginning to catch up with the revolution Cunningham pioneered over twenty years ago. A recent work of literary criticism like Barthes' S/Z (with its emphasis on keeping the text open, on avoiding a unified, definitive reading) could just as easily be a description of Cunningham. "The goal of literary work (of literature as work) is to make the reader no longer a consumer, but a producer of the text," writes Barthes. This is an excellent description of what happens to us when we experience a piece by Cunningham. The on-stage activity does not respect the traditional hierarchies of organization according to which dancers located downstage center automatically command our attention in a way that the dancers upstage left or right do not.[4] Cunningham refuses to tell us what to look at or listen to. We may decide to "background" or "turn off" a sound so as to focus more intently on the movement. (Perhaps it's significant that Mark Lancaster's setting for one of Cunningham's most recent pieces, "Tango," is a television set broadcasting a live picture, but with the sound turned off.) Or we may cultivate a skill John Cage calls "polyattentiveness"—

the simultaneous apprehension of two or more unrelated phe-nomena. (David Tudor, who's composed many scores for Cun-ningham, often listens to several radios while he practices at the piano.)

Above all, the relations we establish between diverse stimuli are flexible; we can radically alter our mode of perception several times in the course of a single performance.[5]

Cunningham provides us with a do-it-yourself survival kit for maintaining our sanity, or at least perceptual clarity (which may be the same thing) in the modern city where everything seems to clamor for attention. This is the *moral* dimension of Cun-ningham's work; for there's a profound connection between what we choose to look at and the way we live our lives. It's precisely this aspect of Cunningham's accomplishment that most dance critics have not yet come to terms with. In 1968, Arlene Croce wrote about the difficulties that Cunningham's work poses for her:

> I thought, watching Merce's dances, that I was being subjected to a theory about dancing. I was too worried about the theory to look at the dancing . . . I don't remember just when it was that I stopped making a terrific mental effort to understand Merce and just began enjoying him. Today it seems just as preposterous to make a mental effort over Merce as it does over Fred Astaire.

No one sees movement more clearly than Croce; and she has provided us with some wonderfully precise descriptions of what Cunningham's dances look like. Applied to the work of some choreographers, this essentially descriptive approach is perfectly adequate. Unfortunately, it doesn't even begin to convey the sig-nificance of someone like Cunningham. True, Cunningham's work may not *symbolize* anything; but it does serve an end beyond itself: that of *perceptual training*. The importance of Cunningham's work lies not only in what we're given to see and hear, but in *the way we see and hear what we're given*. In the words of Peter Brook, the work of Merce Cunningham is "a continual preparation for the shock of freedom."

(1979)

Notes

[1]Brecht, of course, is primarily concerned with what he considers to be the undesirable consequences of emotional identification, illusion-

ism, and the willing suspension of disbelief—conditions that rarely arise in the (inherently) more abstract world of dance. The brand of empathy that most directly unites the dancer and his or her audience is kinetic responsiveness. John Martin, for example, writes of "the inherent contagion of bodily movement which makes the onlooker feel sympathetically in his own musculature the exertions he sees in somebody else's musculature." It's precisely this sort of kinetic empathy which is "interfered with" in much of Cunningham's work.

[2]It's especially instructive to compare the visual obstacles in these works with the setting for Alwin Nikolais' "Gallery" which also constitutes a barrier of sorts between the dancers and the audience. But Nikolais' barrier serves an illusionistic end; it promotes the trompe l'oeil from which the dance derives its effect. Cunningham's settings, on the other hand, promote an analytical scrutiny that is anti-illusionistic.

[3]There's a genuine problem of terminology here. The term "postmodern" usually refers to the next generation of post-Cunningham dancers: Steve Paxton, Yvonne Rainer, Trisha Brown, Lucinda Childs and a number of other choreographers who were associated with the experimental dance workshops at the Judson Memorial Church in the mid 60's. And what distinguishes many of the choreographers I've just mentioned from Cunningham is their ambivalence—if not outright hostility—toward technical virtuosity (which remained a sine qua non of Cunningham's work). One of the messages that emerged from the Judson years was that no movement—no matter how "pedestrian," is, in and of itself, "dancey" or "undancey." So for many of the Judsonites, the difference between dance and non-dance has nothing to do with the movement itself, but depends rather on the context in which the movement is perceived. Dance might thus be defined as *any movement designed to be looked at*. And this concern with the movement's perceptual context is a direct outgrowth of Cunningham's insistence on the perceptual detachment of the audience. Perhaps I'm still abusing the term postmodern by applying it to Cunningham; but it seems to me that the Judson generation's break with Cunningham is much less drastic than Cunningham's break with Graham—in fact, it's more like an organic evolution.

[4]It's entirely appropriate that one of Jasper Johns' target paintings appears on the famous poster he designed for the Cunningham company. Johns asks us to distribute our visual attention evenly throughout each circular band of the image, despite the fact that we've been conditioned to zero-in on the target's bullseye. Writing about Johns' painting "Target with Four Faces," Leo Steinberg suggests that "Johns puts two flinty things in a picture and makes them work against one another so hard that the mind is sparked. Seeing then becomes thinking"—a description that applies equally well to Cunningham's separation of the elements.

[5]Those eager to explore the many parallels between Cunningham's collaborations and the "de-constructive" theories of Barthes, Derrida,

and Lacan might begin by comparing the arbitrary, malleable relationship between auditory and visual stimuli with the equally arbitrary nature of the linguistic sign, the freely "floating" signifier. Furthermore, Cunningham's egalitarian distribution of bodies and objects throughout the performance space corresponds quite closely to Barthes' de-constructed text with its interchangeable fragments or "lexias," its "multiple entrances and exits," and its cacophony of separate "voices."

Post-Modern Dance

YVONNE RAINER
A QUASI SURVEY OF SOME "MINIMALIST" TENDENCIES IN THE QUANTITATIVELY MINIMAL DANCE ACTIVITY MIDST THE PLETHORA, OR AN ANALYSIS OF TRIO A

Objects	Dances
	eliminate or minimize
1. role of artist's hand	phrasing
2. hierarchical relationship of parts	development and climax
3. texture	variation: rhythm, shape, dynamics
4. figure reference	character
5. illusionism	performance
6. complexity and detail	variety: phrases and the spatial field
7. monumentality	the virtuosic movement feat and the fully-extended body
	substitute
1. factory fabrication	energy equality and "found" movement
2. unitary forms, modules	equality of parts
3. uninterrupted surface	repetition or discrete events
4. nonreferential forms	neutral performance
5. literalness	task or tasklike activity
6. simplicity	singular action, event, or tone
7. human scale	human scale

Although the benefit to be derived from making a one-to-one relationship between aspects of so-called minimal sculpture and recent dancing is questionable, I have drawn up a chart that does exactly that. Those who need alternatives to subtle distinction-making will be elated, but nevertheless such a device may serve as a shortcut to ploughing through some of the things that have been happening in a specialized area of dancing and once stated can be ignored or culled from at will.

It should not be thought that the two groups of elements are mutually exclusive ("eliminate" and "substitute"). Much work being done today—both in theatre and art—has concerns in both categories. Neither should it be thought that the type of dance I shall discuss has been influenced exclusively by art. The changes in theatre and dance reflect changes in ideas about man and his environment that have affected all the arts. That dance should reflect these changes at all is of interest, since for obvious reasons it has always been the most isolated and inbred of the arts. What is perhaps unprecedented in the short history of the modern dance is the close correspondence between concurrent developments in dance and the plastic arts.

Isadora Duncan went back to the Greeks; Humphrey and Graham[1] used primitive ritual and/or music for structuring, and although the people who came out of the Humphrey-Graham companies and were active during the thirties and forties shared sociopolitical concerns and activity in common with artists of the period, their work did not reflect any direct influence from or dialogue with the art so much as a reaction to the time. (Those who took off in their own directions in the forties and fifties—Cunningham, Shearer, Litz, Marsicano, et al.—must be appraised individually. Such a task is beyond the scope of this article.) The one previous area of correspondence might be German Expressionism and Mary Wigman and her followers, but photographs and descriptions of the work show little connection.

Within the realm of movement invention—and I am talking for the time being about movement generated by means other than accomplishment of a task or dealing with an object—the most impressive change has been in the attitude to phrasing, which can be defined as the way in which energy is distributed in the execution of a movement or series of movements. What makes one kind of movement different from another is not so much variations in arrangements of parts of the body as differences in energy investment.

It is important to distinguish between real energy and what I shall call "apparent" energy. The former refers to actual output in terms of physical expenditure on the part of the performer. It is common to hear a dance teacher tell a student that he is using "too much energy" or that a particular movement does not require "so much energy." This view of energy is related to a notion of economy and ideal movement technique. Unless otherwise indicated, what I shall be talking about here is "apparent" energy, or what is seen in terms of motion and stillness rather than of actual work, regardless of the physiological or kinesthetic experience of the dancer. The two observations—that of the performer and that of the spectator—do not always correspond. A vivid illustration of this is my *Trio A*: Upon completion two of us are always dripping with sweat while the third is dry. The correct conclusion to draw is not that the dry one is expending less energy, but that the dry one is a "non-sweater."

Much of the western dancing we are familiar with can be characterized by a particular distribution of energy: maximal output or "attack" at the beginning of a phrase,[2] followed by abatement and recovery at the end, with energy often arrested somewhere in the middle. This means that one part of the phrase—usually the part that is the most still—becomes the focus of attention, registering like a photograph or suspended moment of climax. In the Graham-oriented modern dance these climaxes can come one on the heels of the other. In types of dancing that depend on less impulsive controls, the climaxes are farther apart and are not so dramatically "framed." Where extremes in tempi are imposed, this ebb-and-flow of effort is also pronounced: in the instance of speed the contrast between movement and rest is sharp, and in the adagio, or supposedly continuous kind of phrasing, the execution of transitions demonstrates more subtly the mechanics of getting from one point of still "registration" to another.

The term "phrase" can also serve as a metaphor for a longer or total duration containing beginning, middle, and end. Whatever the implications of a continuity that contains high points or focal climaxes, such an approach now seems to be excessively dramatic and, more simply, unnecessary.

Energy has also been used to implement heroic more-than-human technical feats and to maintain a more-than-human look of physical extension, which is familiar as the dancer's muscular "set." In the early days of the Judson Dance Theatre someone wrote an article and asked "Why are they so intent on just being themselves?" It is not accurate to say that everyone at that time had this in mind. (I certainly didn't; I was more involved in experiencing a lion's share of ecstacy and madness than in "being myself" or doing a job.) But where the question applies, it might be answered on two levels: 1) The artifice of performance has been reevaluated in that action, or what one does, is more interesting and important than the exhibition of character and attitude, and that action can best be focused on through the submerging of the personality; so ideally one is not even oneself, one is a neutral "doer." 2) The display of technical virtuosity and the display of the dancer's specialized body no longer make any sense. Dancers have been driven to search for an alternative context that allows for a more matter-of-fact, more concrete, more banal quality of physical being in performance, a context wherein people are engaged in actions and movements making a less spectacular demand on the body and in which skill is hard to locate.

It is easy to see why the *grand jeté* (along with its ilk) had to be abandoned. One cannot "do" a *grand jeté*; one must "dance" it to get it done at all, i.e., invest it with all the necessary nuances of energy distribution that will produce the look of climax together with a still, suspended extension in the middle of the movement. Like a romantic, overblown plot this particular kind of display—with its emphasis on nuance and skilled accomplishment, its accessibility to comparison and interpretation, its involvement with connoisseurship, its introversion, narcissism, and self-congratulatoriness—has finally in this decade exhausted itself, closed back on itself, and perpetuates itself solely by consuming its own tail.

The alternatives that were explored now are obvious: stand, walk, run, eat, carry bricks, show movies, or move or be moved by some *thing* rather than onself. Some of the early activity in the area of self-movement utilized games, "found" movement (walking, running, etc.), and people with no previous training. (One of the most notable of these early efforts was Steve Paxton's solo, *Transit*, in which he performed movement by "marking" it. "Marking" is what dancers do in rehearsal when they do not want to expend the full amount of energy required for the execution of a given movement. It has a very special look, tending to blur boundaries between consecutive movements.) These descriptions are not complete. Different people have sought different solutions.

Since I am primarily a dancer, I am interested in finding solutions primarily in the area of moving oneself, however many excursions I have made into pure and not-so-pure thing-moving. In 1964 I began to play around with simple one- and two-motion phrases that required no skill and little energy and contained few accents. The way in which they were put together was indeterminate, or decided upon in the act of performing, because at that time the idea of a different kind of continuity as embodied in transitions or connections between phrases did not seem to be as important as the material itself. The result was that the movements or phrases appeared as isolated bits framed by stoppages. Underscored by their smallness and separateness, they projected as perverse *tours-de-force*. Everytime "elbow-wiggle" came up one felt like applauding. It was obvious that the idea of an unmodulated energy output as demonstrated in the movement was not being applied to the continuity. A continuum of energy was required. Duration and transition had to be considered.

Which brings me to *The Mind Is a Muscle, Trio A*. Without giving an account of the drawn-out process through which this 4½-minute movement series (performed simultaneously by three people) was made, let me talk about its implications in the direction of movement-as-task or movement-as-object.

One of the most singular elements in it is that there are no pauses between phrases. The phrases themselves often consist of separate parts, such as consecutive limb articulations—"right leg, left leg, arms, jump," etc.—but the end of each phrase merges immediately into the beginning of the next with no observable accent. The limbs are never in a fixed, still relationship and they are stretched to their fullest extension only in transit, creating the impression that the body is constantly engaged in transitions.

Another factor contributing to the smoothness of the continuity is that no one part of the series is made any more important than any other. For four-and-a-half minutes a great variety of movement shapes occur, but they are of equal weight and are equally emphasized. This is probably attributable both to the sameness of physical "tone" that colors all the movements and to the attention to the pacing. I can't talk about one without talking about the other.

The execution of each movement conveys a sense of unhurried control. The body is weighty without being completely relaxed. What is seen is a control that seems geared to the *actual* time it takes the *actual* weight of the body to go through the prescribed

motions, rather than an adherence to an imposed ordering of
time. In other words, the demands made on the body's (actual)
energy resources *appear* to be commensurate with the task—be it
getting up from the floor, raising an arm, tilting the pelvis, etc.—
much as one would get out of a chair, reach for a high shelf, or
walk down stairs when one is not in a hurry.[3] The movements
are not mimetic, so they do not remind one of such actions, but
I like to think that in their manner of execution they have the
factual quality of such actions.

Of course, I have been talking about the "look" of the movements. In order to achieve this look in a continuity of separate
phrases that does not allow for pauses, accents, or stillness, one
must bring to bear many different degrees of effort just in getting
from one thing to another. Endurance comes into play very
much with its necessity for conserving (actual) energy (like the
long-distance runner). The irony here is in the reversal of a kind
of illusionism: I have exposed a type of effort where it has been
traditionally concealed and have concealed phrasing where it
has been traditionally displayed.

So much for phrasing. My *Trio A* contained other elements
mentioned in the chart that have been touched on in passing,
not being central to my concerns of the moment. For example,
the "problem" of performance was dealt with by never permitting the performers to confront the audience. Either the gaze was
averted or the head was engaged in movement. The desired
effect was a worklike rather than exhibitionlike presentation.

I shall deal briefly with the remaining categories on the chart
as they relate to *Trio A*. Variation was not a method of development. No one of the individual movements in the series was
made by varying a quality of any other one. Each is intact and
separate with respect to its nature. In a strict sense neither is
there any repetition (with the exception of occasional consecutive traveling steps). The series progresses by the fact of one discrete thing following another. This procedure was consciously
pursued as a change from my previous work, which often had
one identical thing following another—either consecutively or
recurrently. Naturally the question arises as to what constitutes
repetition. In *Trio A*, where there is no consistent consecutive
repetition, can the simultaneity of three identical sequences be
called repetition? Or can the consistency of energy tone be called
repetition? Or does repetition apply only to successive specific
actions?

All of these considerations have supplanted the desire for dance structures wherein elements are connected thematically (through variation) and for a diversity in the use of phrases and space. I think two assumptions are implicit here: 1) A movement is a complete and self-contained event: elaboration in the sense of varying some aspect of it can only blur its distinctness; and 2) Dance is hard to see. It must either be made less fancy, or the fact of that intrinsic difficulty must be emphasized to the point that it becomes almost impossible to see.

Repetition can serve to enforce the discreteness of a movement, objectify it, make it more objectlike. It also offers an alternative way of ordering material, literally making the material easier to see. That most theatre audiences are irritated by it is not yet a disqualification.

My *Trio A* dealt with the "seeing" difficulty by dint of its continual and unremitting revelation of gestural detail that did not repeat itself, thereby focusing on the fact that the material could not easily be encompassed.

There is at least one circumstance that the chart does not include (because it does not relate to "minimization"), viz., the static singular object versus the object with interchangeable parts. The dance equivalent is the indeterminate performance that produces variations ranging from small details to a total image. Usually indeterminacy has been used to change the sequentialness—either phrases or larger sections—of a work, or to permute the details of a work. It has also been used with respect to timing. Where the duration of separate, simultaneous events is not prescribed exactly, variations in the relationship of these events will occur. Such is the case with the trio I have been speaking about, in which small discrepancies in the tempo of individually executed phrases result in the three simultaneous performances constantly moving in and out of phase and in and out of synchronization. The overall look of it is constant from one performance to another, but the distribution of bodies in space at any given instant changes.

I am almost done. *Trio A* is the first section of *The Mind Is a Muscle*. There are six people involved and four more sections. *Trio B* might be described as a VARIATION of *Trio A* in its use of unison with three people: they move in exact unison thruout. *Trio A'* is about the EFFORTS of two men and a woman in getting each other aloft in VARIOUS ways while REPEATING the same diagonal SPACE pattern throughout. In *Horses* the group travels about as a unit, recurrently REPEATING six different ACTIONS. *Lecture* is a solo that REPEATS the MOVEMENT series of *Trio A*. There will be at least three more sections.

There are many concerns in this dance. The concerns may appear to fall on my tidy chart as randomly dropped toothpicks might. However, I think there is sufficient separating out in my work as well as that of certain of my contemporaries to justify an attempt at organizing those points of departure from previous work. Comparing the dance to Minimal Art provided a convenient method of organization. Omissions and overstatements are a hazard of any systematizing in art. I hope that some degree of redress will be offered by whatever clarification results from this essay.

(1966)

Notes

[1]In the case of Graham, it is hardly possible to relate her work to anything outside of theatre, since it was usually dramatic and psychological necessity that determined it.

[2]The term "phrase" must be distinguished from "phrasing." A phrase is simply two or more consecutive movements, while phrasing, as noted previously, refers to the manner of execution.

[3]I do not mean to imply that the demand of musical or metric phrasing makes dancing look effortless. What it produces is a different kind of effort, where the body looks more extended, "pulled up," highly energized, ready to go, etc. The dancer's "set" again.

TOM JOHNSON
RUNNING OUT OF BREATH

INTRODUCTION

Considering the difficulties of communicating a dance on a printed page, it may be helpful if I explain where *Running Out of Breath* came from. Several of my pieces deal with similar situations, but they have usually been designed for musicians rather than dancers. One example is the "Unaccompanied Aria" from

The Four Note Opera. In that case a mezzo must sing for several minutes, without any accompaniment, and has to try to stay exactly on pitch. In the lyrics to the aria the singer explains the problem and expresses her trepidation. Ultimately she must sing the final note, at which point the piano comes in and everyone finds out whether she is still on key. Singers are a cautious lot, and generally they end up right on, but the risk is always there.

More recently Jon Deak asked me to write a piece for him, and I came up with *Failing: A Very Difficult Piece for Solo String Bass.* Here the problem is that the performer must play difficult, specifically notated music on his instrument, while simultaneously delivering a spoken monologue. Even a performer as fine as Deak is likely to miss a few notes or become a little tongue-tied once in a while. As the text explains, that is why the piece is called *Failing,* and that is what it is about.

In the summer of 1976 I saw a way of putting a dancer in a similarly precarious position, so I worked out a text (which may also be considered a score) for Kathy Duncan that I called *Running Out of Breath.* Like the other pieces, it sometimes seems manipulative, if not actually diabolical, and I used to question the ethics of such pieces. But the effect of actual performances is always a stimulating joining of art and life, and the performer always comes off as an admirable, courageous soul, rather than a tool, so I stopped worrying about it. Meanwhile the bulk of my work has been much more abstract, frequently formalistic, and more or less unrelated to this approach.

STAGING NOTES

In Kathy Duncan's original performance at the Byrd Hoffman Studio in New York, on November 19, 1976, she wore a tank top, gym shorts, and sneakers. She adhered to the basic image of simply running, though her changes of direction were often unpredictable. It is helpful if the dancer has good stamina and can maintain a brisk pace throughout, as Duncan does, but that is not essential. The important thing is that the dancer push to the limits of his/her energy, as suggested by the text. The comments in the final paragraph should be adjusted to fit whatever symptoms the performer is actually experiencing. If due to a cramp, injury, or complete exhaustion, the performer is unable to finish the dance, he/she should simply stop, say "I'm sorry, that's as far as I can go," and exit. The dance will then end in defeat rather than triumph, but its most important feature, literal truth, will be preserved.

TEXT-SCORE

In this dance solo I am required to run quickly around the space while delivering this memorized text. Naturally, if I continue running and reciting, I am gradually going to run out of breath. And that's what the piece is about, and that's why it's called, *Running Out of Breath.*

Of course, there is nothing unusual about running out of breath. Everyone knows what it feels like. It happens in almost any dance and any strenuous physical exercise. It is a universal experience, common not only among humans, but among all mammals. Birds, reptiles and amphibians all seem to run out of breath too. Maybe even fish and insects know what it feels like to run out of breath. So why am I wasting your time and my energy, just to run out of breath?

Well, I have some ideas of my own about that, but for the moment I must continue to deliver this memorized text, and according to it, the purpose is simply to observe someone else run out of breath. Of course we have all done that before, too, but in this context, where there is really nothing else to watch, or listen to or think about, it is possible for the audience to focus its entire attention on the act of watching someone run out of breath. How long does it take? Does it happen quickly or rather gradually? Do we tend to breathe faster and harder ourselves when watching someone else breathe faster and harder?

Maybe you will find these questions interesting, maybe you won't. Anyway, on a sort of philosophical level, that's what the piece is about. Meanwhile, there are other considerations. Particularly for me. For instance, will I be able to make it though the dance? So far, I am about half way through my memorized text. If I have been moving at a moderately fast pace, I should still be able to deliver complete phrases without breathing. Gradually, however, it will get harder and harder. If I don't pace myself about right, I may get a cramp or something, and have to stop. If I take it too easy, on the other hand, I may not really run out of breath.

Of course my vanity is at stake here. I don't want to appear weak or short-winded, and I am tempted to cheat a little in order to make a better impression. There are several ways of doing this.

For instance, turning, flailing movements may look like they take more energy than just running back and forth. So if I do mostly movements that look more strenuous than they are, I can get through the piece fairly easily. Another way to cheat would be to deliver the text at a fast pace. If I talk fast enough, the piece will only last four or five minutes, and I won't have time to get really out of breath. Another way to cheat would be to sneak two or three breaths between sentences. With enough practice I could learn to do that without anyone noticing, and I would get through in fine shape, and the audience would be quite impressed at my endurance.

But there is an obvious problem with all of these methods of cheating. Johnson slyly inserted a paragraph in the text describing all of the most obvious ways to cheat, so that the audience is going to be checking up on me. And if they catch me moving too easily or talking too fast or sneaking extra breaths, they will know immediately that I am cheating and will decide that I didn't do a good, honest performance of the piece.

So the only way to perform this piece really effectively is to go all out, set a brisk pace, and hope I make it to the end. Actually there is not much danger now, for I am close to the end of my text already. It is a challenge to deliver the final sentences of the text and make them comprehensible, when I have to pause so often to take a breath. But I can make it to the end. I will make it to the end.

By now you're probably wondering why I'm going through this struggle. My lungs ache. My legs feel like lead. My body feels like jelly. After all, it's not my piece. I'm only the performer. But there are a number of reasons why I wanted to do it. It works on a number of levels, most of which have been outlined above. But perhaps most important, I am proving to myself that I can meet the challenge.

(1976)

STEVE REICH
NOTES ON MUSIC
AND DANCE

For a long time during the 1960s one would go to the dance concert where no one danced followed by the party where everyone danced. This was not a healthy situation. Usually rock and roll in a dance concert is not the answer though it might be (and actually was) the first superficial answer one might come up with. The real answer is to create a genuinely new dance with roots that go back thousands of years to the basic impulse at the foundation of all dance; the human desire for regular rhythmic movement, usually done to music.

The avant-garde dance of the 1960s focused on non-dance movements to be performed in concert situations. Walking, running, working with objects, and performing specific tasks were among the genuinely new alternatives to the modern dance of expressive movements of an earlier generation. The basic idea of the Judson dance group (Steve Paxton, Yvonne Rainer, et al.), as well as the contribution of Simone Forti, could be summed up as: any movement is dance. This is the precise equivalent to the basic idea of the composer John Cage: any sound is music.

There is, however, another and primary sense of these words where one can say that all sounds are obviously not music, all movements are not dance, and most children can usually tell the difference.

What is needed now it not a return to the modern dance of the 1930s, 1940s, or 1950s, but rather a return to the roots of dance as it is found all over the world; regular rhythmic movement, usually done to music.

While the Judson group was the dance equivalent to the music of John Cage (even more so, curiously, than Merce Cunningham—think of Paxton's "Satisfyin' Lover," the walking piece; and Cage's 4'33", the silent piece), presently what is needed is the dance equivalent to recent music composed exclusively with the regular rhythmic repetition of a single musical pattern. Laura Dean is the first choreographer/dancer to work exclusively with such extreme regular rhythmic repetition as a fundamental technique, and soon, hopefully, there will be others.

Somehow in recent years movements in music have preceded similar developments in dance. Hopefully in the future they will occur simultaneously.

In the last few years there have been and still are a number of dance performances (largely by those formerly associated with the Judson group) based on improvisation and group dynamics. The momentary state of mind of the individual or group during performance creates or strongly influences the structure of the dance. Now we have an alternative to this where the pre-determined rhythmic structure of the dance creates or strongly influences the state of mind of the performers while performing. While this alternative is new for us at this particular time it has existed in other cultures for thousands of years.

Unfortunately there may soon be a number of choreographers who will present imitation Oriental, African or American Indian dances. This exoticism will be as vulgar and inappropriate as its musical equivalent (sitars in the rock band, "Indian style" melodies over electronic drones, etc). What is needed is not exoticism but rather a return to the roots of dance common to all cultures performed by members of this culture within the context of our own high-art tradition.

When I was in Ghana in 1970, I found there was a clear distinction between social popular dances and high-art religious dances. These obvious differences were in the formal or informal movement and dress of the performers as well as the location, time of day, and social-religious context of the performance, but all of the dances, popular and classical, had a strong rhythmic pulse.

For music and dance to go together they must share the same rhythmic structure. This common rhythmic structure will determine the length of the music and dance as well as when changes in both will occur. It will not determine what sounds are used in the music nor what movements are used in the dance.

In 1944 John Cage wrote, " . . . a dance, a poem, a piece of music (any of the time arts) occupies a length of time, and the manner in which this length of time is divided . . . is the work's very life structure. . . ." In the same article he said, "Personality is a flimsy thing on which to build an art." Cage understood that rhythmic structure was impersonal and thereby universal, i.e. understood by all. He also understood that a rhythmic structure did not dictate particular sounds for a piece of music, nor a set

of movements for a dance. *Those* elements *were* the manifestations of personality. What Cage put less emphasis on in the
1940s, and apparently still less as time went on, was the underlying impetus for dance; the natural human desire for regular
rhythmic movement. He also turned away from the reality that
people do in fact dance *to the music*—that music can and does
supply rhythmic energy for dance.

What is needed is a genuinely new Western high-art dance
with movements natural to the personality of someone living
here and now, organized in the clear (i.e. universal) rhythmic
structure, and satisfying the basic desire for regular rhythmic
movement that has been and will continue to be the underlying
basic impetus for all dance.

(1973)

Style

SELMA JEANNE COHEN
From NEXT WEEK, SWAN LAKE: REFLECTIONS ON DANCE AND DANCES

PROBLEMS OF DEFINITION

... Although the primary element involved with stylistic distinctions in dance is, and should be, the nature of the movements performed by the dancers, another set of factors tends to enter in—types of plot, relative importance of decor and costumes, kind of staging, among the most obvious. But even when writers pay lip service to these various components, discussions of styles of dance have been most often grossly oversimplified. We had romantic ballet in the early nineteenth century and classical ballet in the later nineteenth century. What we had in the seventeenth and eighteenth centuries was called ballet then, though some now try to view it as a kind of "pre-ballet," thus avoiding the curious situation of having a classic style both precede and follow a romantic one.

In the twentieth century we have had ballet and modern dance. The latter, once conceived as applying to almost anything that was not ballet, has now been given a reprieve by being divided into modern and post-modern, while Cunningham, who belongs chronologically between the two, seems to be left in limbo as belonging to neither (though the art historians would have saved him with the designation of "late modern"). Now, however, the post-modern label, which originally covered the aesthetic of the Judson Dance Theatre and their followers of the 1960s, is applied to a most heterogeneous assemblage of choreographers, who sometimes seem to have only the label in common.

The easy way to see contemporary dance is in terms of broad categories: ballet, modern, and (often with a slight sneer) Broadway-musical-type dance. This has frequently been done, and it has caused considerable distortion and confusion, raising my favorite question of recent years: Where do we put Twyla Tharp? Attempts at more specific formulations have not always succeeded either; for example the designation of "multi-media artist." This certainly applies to Alwin Nikolais, whose works of movement, sound, shape, and color utilize electronic sound devices, films, slide projections, a varied assortment of stage properties (e.g., masks, screens, ropes), and dancers. . . .

Nelson Goodman has noted that "an obvious style, easily identified by some superficial quirk, is properly decried as a mere mannerism. A complex and subtle style, like a trenchant metaphor, resists reduction to a literal formula. . . . The less accessible a style is to our approach and the more adjustment we are forced to make, the more insight we gain and the more our powers of discovery are developed."[1]

But caution is necessary here. Ballet and modern dance have often been considered as styles, the former simple and the latter complex (or vice versa). They are not styles at all in Goodman's sense of the term, which refers to properties manifested by a work that are characteristic of an author, period, region, or school. Rather, they are genres, broader categories, or types, that may encompass a number of styles, any of which may then be found simple or complex. Once such styles have been defined, we must still beware of the possibility of borrowings among them and even of the potentiality of a style taking on some of the properties previously linked exclusively to a genre other than the one with which it is usually associated. This does not necessarily result in a "merging" of the genres; that would occur only if their respective qualities should exist in the new work in such an ambiguous balance that they negate one another. Any real genre is usually characterized by the presence of more than a single quality, though conceivably some one quality may be discovered to be its sine qua non, while others may be somewhat modified without endangering the identity of the type. Perhaps the time has come for a test.

Ballet seems the logical place to start because on the surface it is so clearly accessible; we start children with ballet before we take them to operas or symphony concerts. T. S. Eliot was aware of a paradox: "The ballet is valuable because it has, unconsciously, concerned itself with a permanent form; it is futile because is has concerned itself with the ephemeral in content." He found it "a liturgy of very wide adaptability" that had not been used to its full potential.[2] But we may take his clue and look for the form that underlies the obvious specifics.

By "ballet" let's say we mean what is usually considered its quintessential style, classical, if by "classical" we mean pure. Lincoln Kirstein once defined style as a moral virtue manifested in the conquest of untidy egotism; ballet as "a clear if complex blending of human anatomy, solid geometry and acrobatics, offered as a symbolic demonstration of manners. . . ."[3] To John Martin it was "a glorification of the person as person, the presentation of its ideal essence freed from the encumbrances of a rationalistic universe of cause and effect."[4] Adrian Stokes suggested deftness and economy or neatness; Edwin Denby cited lightness, elevation, and ease. Kirstein qualified: "clean and open, grandiose without affectation, noble without pretension."[5] All of which sounds suspiciously like our old friend grace. But we should try to be more specific.

The answer is simple, of course; we've known for many years that classical style is movement based on the five positions of the feet. But we are looking for the principle that is manifested in the five positions, and that is the principle of outwardness, of *en dehors*. Generally this is taken to refer to the rotation of the legs in the hip socket, popularly known as "the turnout," and it is logical to consider this first, not only because it accounts for those five positions, but because it constitutes the major physical task to be accomplished by the ballet student. Without the rotation a great part of the classical vocabulary is out of reach, its major feats—shoulder-high extensions that do not disturb the equilibrium, multiple pirouettes, intricate entrechats—are difficult if not impossible to execute.

If this outwardness were limited to the legs, however, the body as a whole would look incongruous. In the full classical style, the entire person appears in extroversion—open to other bodies, open to the surrounding space. But not vulnerable, because the rib cage is held erect, confidently; the arms seem buoyantly lifted away from the body, the head appears to float atop a long, vertical, relaxed spine.

Outwardness is not practical for the affairs of everyday life. It does not facilitate progress in a direct, forward line, as in running to catch a bus; it makes the body occupy more space, which is inconvenient in a crowded elevator. Yet it is quite reasonable for a style that developed in a royal court, where to move in an ordinary manner would have been considered demeaning. The idea was to look noble rather than serviceable. The *en dehors* facilitates useless actions; it creates a state of dancing. The classical ballet style—brilliant and elegant—does not exist without it.

Yet the *en dehors*, while it is essential to classical ballet, is not unique to it. Outwardness also characterizes India's Bharata Natya where the legs are fully turned out and the torso is held high as in ballet, but contrary to ballet the dancer remains almost constantly in demi-plié, her whole foot on the floor, often stamping into the floor. The acknowledgment of weight in the lower body seems to contradict another classical balletic quality, which is a prevalent upward thrust. For Volynsky, "with the vertical begins the history of human culture and the gradual conquest of heaven and earth."[6] The ballerina raises herself to greet the gods. The Hindu view is different; its gods come down to visit mortals.

In classical ballet if the supporting knee is bent, it is usually only as a preparation for a rising movement. Most often the entire body is stretched; the variety and range of jumps are tremendous, and they are often extended by lifts. Pointe work, a natural extension of the upward thrust, was originally developed to enhance the portrayal of the ethereal sylph, but—like the aristocratic association of the turnout—the connotation is dispensable. Length of line and brilliance are enhanced by the use of pointes. Yet we can recognize classical style even when there are no jumps or lifts and no pointe work. We would not recognize it, though, if it failed to exhibit that sense of upward reaching, if it failed to stress verticality, which Volynsky called the line of exultation.

Lightness, so frequently considered an attribute of classical style, is often associated with verticality and with reason, since it relates to the height of the placement of the center of gravity in the body. It was essential for the fairy creatures of the romantic ballet and to some other character types in dramatic works (the slippery Younger Sister in *Pillar of Fire* is an example). There are also more abstract contexts where allegro movement is exploited for its own sake, and the impression of speed is enhanced—and also made physically possible—by the accompanying lightness of the body, the feet seem to flutter in the air (as Merrill Ashley's do in *Square Dance*).

Male dancers, including those who excel in elevation, seldom produce an appearance of sheer lightness, for the man more often stresses vigor and a firmness of stance and tread that show him to be in command of the situation. Yet we do not find him unballetic; he is not a stevedore type. The attack is strong but not heavy. Further, it never intrudes on, never distorts, the clean line of the movement. Actually, the emphasis was not always quite so far on the side of strength. Bournonville, in the mid-nineteenth century, included among his virtues as a dancer a manly joie de vivre. Today the Bournonville jump, a model of elasticity and lightness, stands as a charming souvenir of another era. Nowadays even the woman does not always want to exhibit lightness. Sometimes the reason is dramatic—as in the case of the vicious females who exult in their prowess in Robbins' *The Cage*—but sometimes it is simply a matter of desired movement quality—as the opening of the Balanchine/Stravinsky *Symphony in Three Movements* where even the girls' long flowing hair accentuates their sensuous weightedness.

Is virtuosity necessary? That may be going too far; skilled movement might be sufficient if by virtuosity we mean the all-out, knock-'em-dead kind. Nor need ballets be works of virtuosity, exhibiting the skills that are their subject matter. But evidence of skill, of control beyond the ordinary, must—I think—be visible in the performance. André Levinson wrote that "the very illusion of this enchanting art—which seems to ignore all natural laws—depends on an intelligent ordering of physical effort. The [classical] dancer then is a body moving in space according to any desired rhythm."[7] That intelligent ordering, manifested in every move, signifies the dancer's mastery; it creates the illusion that he is exempt from the restrictions of natural laws. Such laws account for the basic incompetence of the untrained body; it is seldom capable of maintaining an exact rhythm or following a completely straight line or moving in exact coordination with a group. All dancers have to do these things, but classical style demands them more stringently. It evokes Valéry's idea of another state of existence.

An additional quality that has been assigned to classical style is clarity. No extraneous actions detract our attention from the shape the dancer wants us to see, from the rhythm he wants us to feel. Frequently, this entails movement that is goal-oriented: reaching the exact point in space at the exact point in time is important; the resulting shape is frequently held for a while so that it can be fully enjoyed. This does not mean that movements have to be simple; they may be extraordinarily complicated, full of intricacies and surprises (the Bournonville dancer bounces along a circular path to the left and suddenly reverses direction in a diagonally-directed grand jeté). The richest styles have a clarity that is not immediately perceivable, which is true in all the arts but is especially challenging in dance, since—until video discs become common property—we cannot keep looking back at the work to discover the structural secret that illuminates it all. Still, an underlying kinetic logic tends to make itself felt, even when it resists conscious definition.

Clarity is relevant, not only to the movements of an individual dancer, but to the configurations of an ensemble as well. Balanchine's *Le Tombeau de Couperin* depends for much of its effectiveness on the dancers' precision in maintaining a series of intricate designs of lines and semi-circles and waving paths. The Rockettes present a similar case of reliance on accurate formations, which means that we have another instance in which a property is essential, but not unique, to ballet.

Concomitant to clarity is the self-revealing nature of classical style; it may, of course, reveal something beyond itself (though some theorists wish that it would not), but it always calls attention to its kinetic qualities; the ballerina's eye follows her flowing arm or looks down at her nimble feet; the man admires his partner's pirouettes or extends the line of her arabesque with his arms. Movement is displayed. Sometimes what is displayed is fantastic virtuosity, but not always. Balanchine's dancers sometimes, as in *Chaconne*, just walk—simply, and not at all simply, they walk. How beautiful a walk can be when it is not trying to get somewhere! Luminous, Volynsky would call it. Valéry said of the dancer (who was surely a ballet dancer) that "she teaches us that which we do, showing clearly to our souls that which our bodies accomplish obscurely."[8] This seems essential to the classical style.

One more factor may be considered. "A machine for manufacturing beauty," said André Levinson of the ballet dancer, provoking a good deal of indignation from those who wanted to preserve her humanity. But Levinson was not alone in his conviction that the discipline undergone by the performer resulted in her forgoing a natural method of functioning in order to take on an aesthetic mode: "To discipline the body to this ideal function, to make a dancer of a graceful child, it is necessary to begin by dehumanizing him, or rather by overcoming the habits of ordinary life. . . . The accomplished dancer is an artificial being, an instrument of precision. . . ."[9] Most theorists, disliking the term "dehumanize," prefer "impersonal," but I suspect they mean approximately the same thing. Martin spoke of an "ideal essence." That the exercises of the ballet dancer have been likened to ritual is no accident. Kirstein recalls Colette's Cheri, taunting his icy wife: "It's as if I'd married a ballet-dancer. Nine o'clock sharp, the Class: it's sacrosanct."[10] Or Violette Verdy commenting on Rudolf Nureyev and the first position: "It's like the Sign of the Cross everyday."[11] This is curiously reminiscent of that other dance form characterized by *en dehors*: Bharata Natya was designed for use in the temple. Such techniques mold the dancer to conform to the image—long, lithe, and with hidden strength—regardless of his real personality. The dancer always appears as a persona.

These qualities the classical dancer embodies with grace. Grace makes steps appear effortless, and—as if to prove that these incredible turns and extensions are really no trouble at all—grace connects them in a seamless flow, with no stops for determined preparations, and throws in a few broderies for good measure. Any sign of the practical, of the merely utilitarian, is forbidden. The classical style may be the highest manifestation we know of the image of grace.

If we look closely at all these properties no one appears to be sufficient in itself to qualify the style as classical ballet and no one is unique to this style. Nevertheless, their combination does create something unique. How many of them must be present and in what proportion should, I believe, be left unspecified. Why restrict possibilities? Apart from *en dehors* which, I suspect, must dominate any manifestation of classicism, the other qualities can, and certainly have, fluctuated considerably in the extent of their pervasiveness. I would hesitate, however, to term any of them completely optional, and I have not listed them (again excepting *en dehors*) in an order that I consider indicative of their relative importance. In fact, the degree of importance assumed by any of them might be taken as a key to the definition of a ballet style.

A choreographer who wants to work within the classical style accepts these constraints, which still offer him a considerable number of choices regarding relative emphasis. Many areas of choreographic choice remain free, undefined. Classical rhythms tend to be regular but are not necessarily so. Unison movement and symmetry tend to characterize ensembles, though any balanced and ordered arrangement would be consistent with the other elements of the style. The nature of some works makes them more demanding of such uniformity. Some of our younger critics, observing the Bournonville festival in Copenhagen in

1979, found that they tired of poses which were always repeated or reversed symmetrically; it was all so predictable. But for Bournonville dancing is joy, and joy means that life is in harmony with nature and society; it is symmetrical. The balletic genre can take on a number of divergent qualities without violating its essential nature, but not an unlimited number of divergent qualities.

As yet nothing has been said about the ballet vocabulary, that codified collection of steps with French names that many little girls and some little boys learn after school. Appropriately performed, the vocabulary displays the qualities of classical style. But style is a matter of structure and quality that can be manifested without the use of particular steps—though not without the use of particular kinds of steps. On the other hand, some steps can be performed in terms of other styles. There is nothing irrevocably balletic about *failli-assemblé*, as Humphrey proved in her Bach *Partita*, where it is performed with the stress on the landing into the floor instead of the rising from it.

Which brings us to the question of "modern dance." An easy way out is to say that it lacks the balletic qualities; but so do many other forms of dance—tap, for example, and hula. Furthermore, some works labelled modern dance exhibit some of the qualities we have just assigned to ballet.

The latter was not always true, for the genre was founded at the end of World War I in a spirit of revolt. Mary Wigman stated her position: "Mannered and stilted [the ballet] could never tell what I had to say which was purely personal."[12] Miriam Winslow elaborated, defining the enemy form as "an attitude of impersonal presentation of movements designed by other persons to express beauty and truth (emotions and ideas) with the object of pleasing the onlookers." Modern dance, on the contrary, made the individual the center; it was "based upon the dancer's relationship to time and space, to life itself."[13] The object was not to please, but to provoke and enlighten.

If modern dance is so truly personal, then it is bound to be heterogeneous. Can we find any common qualities? It depends on where we look.

For Humphrey it was "moving from the inside out"; for Graham it was "visualizing the interior landscape." Martin called it "the materializing of inner experience." Clear enough— for the 1930s and 1940s. Then in the 1950s Cunningham came along to negate the very core of identity claimed by his immediate predecessors. He denied that dance was about personal experience; it was, rather, about movement in time and space. Then came the defection of the Judson group, who agreed with Cunningham's disdain of representation but added their own rejection of skilled movement. The fragmentation accelerated: conceptual dance, multi-media productions, a return to Graham's archetypal images but without her narrative structures, a return to Humphrey's lyricism but with even, balletic flow replacing her irregular breath rhythms. All these have been called "modern dance."

What is modern dance? When I first worked on this problem of genres I read a paper on the subject at a conference where I first, rather neatly, defined ballet. When the moment came to do the same for modern dance, I was happily able to say that my time was up. Now, I fear, my time has come.

Lincoln Kirstein defined modern dance as "a loose idiom of idiosyncratic, free-form movement, identified with careers and contributions of half a dozen individuals, all in their prime in 1935."[14] José Limón, who had just begun to choreograph in 1935 and who considered himself a modern dancer, wrote in 1966 that the modern dance is "a state of mind, a cognizance of the necessity of the art of the dance to come to terms with our time."[15] But "free-form movement" is too vague to be useful, and Jerome Robbins' Age of Anxiety (1950), an exploration of the insecurity of the individual in contemporary society, certainly endeavored to cope with "our time" though it was called ballet.

Let's go back to movement. Watching ballet dancer Paolo Bortoluzzi in Limón's The Moor's Pavane, Anna Kisselgoff commented that his performance appeared "very much like kicking a football on a baseball diamond."[16] She attributed the stylistic failure to lack of both proper technical training and conviction in the ideology that sparked the birth of modern dance. Graham had once told Kisselgoff that the nature of the problem was indeed twofold: the ballet dancer lacked the necessary state of mind, but also tended to "learn by line instead of volume." Paul Taylor also suggested the latter kind of problem: "Ballet dancers are trained to concentrate on making shapes, rather than on what produced the shape."[17] Laura Dean remarked that what she is concerned about is "not what the body does, but where the energy goes, with what quality it goes."[18] Erik Bruhn had also essayed The Moor's Pavane, but drew a somewhat different conclusion about the kind of adjustment he had to make to meet the requirements of a modern dance role: "It's a question of manipulating your weight. As the movements are generally earth-

bound, you have to find a different 'center.' You have to feel
downwards, without looking as if you are digging into the
ground."[19]

Effort as opposed to the ballet dancer's ease? That may be part
of if, but more broadly it might be viewed—and this is what
some of the early moderns preferred—as an admission of
humanity. Unlike the depersonalized ballerina—her struggles in
the classroom stored away so that only the happy results are
seen—the modern dancer reveals the process behind the movement. Limón used to speak of the drama of the modern dancer's
jump. The ballet dancer soared without apparent effort—lovely!
But how much more moving was the sight of a man, heavy and
tense, raising himself, with willful determination, into the realm
of the spirit.

Further possibilities have been suggested, the most common
of them, perhaps, the negation of *en dehors,* the stress of turning
inward, of the body folding in on itself. But insistence on this
would eliminate most of the happier moments of the modern
dance—Graham's ecstatic *Diversion of Angels,* for example, where
a contraction sometimes leads not to an agonized closing but to
a rapturous extension of body and limbs into aerial space. Senta
Driver has suggested the addition of off-balance movements,
twisting, and spiraling as elements much used by the modern
dance.[20] She does not, however, urge that these be considered
essential to modern dance; only that they are characteristics
sometimes found in modern dance and hardly ever found in
ballet.

In movement we seem to find a broadening of the scope of the
acceptable palette, a kind of permissiveness that in turn allows a
greater range of qualities of being represented, of feelings
expressed. Limón spoke with grandeur of saints and demons;
now, Trisha Brown matter-of-factly tells the audience how she
went about composing the dance as she performs it. Perhaps this
is not a single genre . . .

If we do want to try to find a continuum, we must remember
that any rigidity of formulation would contradict the outlook of
the founders of the modern dance and immediately eliminate
them as proper exhibitors of its qualities. We must also resist the
temptation to make modern dance simply counter the properties
of classicism, point by point. After all, ballet has been around for
more than 300 years, and the full extent of the qualities by which
it is known now evolved only gradually. The earliest date usually set for the modern dance is the beginning of the twentieth

century, when Duncan with her natural movement and Denishawn with its exoticism broke with the forms of conventional
ballet. Some, however, would trace the origin of the genre that
we now recognize back no further than the expressionism of
Graham and Humphrey that emerged in the late 1920s. Around
1950 the nature of the modern dance changed radically with the
advent of the chance techniques of Cunningham, and again a
decade later with the ordinary movement presentations of the
Judson group, and yet again with the appearance of such symbolist choreographers as Meredith Monk and Kenneth King.
Today even the "post-modern" designation is risky, since we
seem already to have a second generation of innovators, many of
whom have adopted some of the qualities associated with the
Rainer aesthetic but rejected others. Sally Banes suggests that the
new virtuosity is nonillusionistic, "the gulf between artist and
spectator has been irrevocably bridged."[21] But I would not dare
claim that anything about the modern dance is irrevocable; the
future may hold many surprises. Meanwhile we have a past and
a present diverse and rich enough to occupy our minds for quite
some time. Can we identify the modern dance as a single entity?

If we cannot define a core, perhaps we can distinguish some
outer limits, and we might try to do this in terms of tendencies
that veer more in one direction than another. Generally, these
tendencies might be viewed as an emphasis on path rather than
goal in space; on weight rather than lightness in the body; on
sharpness of accent rather than flow; on asymmetrical rather
than balanced design; on exposure rather than concealment of
process. But the situation has evolved with the years. The use of
weight was far more important to the expressive phase of the
modern dance than it is to the formal styles of today. The exponents of everyday movement continue to stress weight, but for
non-dramatic reasons: they want to call attention to the shapes
of the ordinary. Taylor often combines weight with flow that seldom stops at a defined position in space; Tharp juxtaposes weight
and agility. Percussive accent and asymmetry have been submerged in Dean's repetitive spinning of matched figures, but she
maintains the sense of weight and concern for path. We have
various species of modern dance.

We also have modern ballet, a style that Deborah Jowitt once
described as prettier than early modern dance but less polite
than early ballet.[22] However, she wrote this around 1970 when
the prevalent type consisted of a basically classical vocabulary
attacked with some of the qualities associated with modern

dance, especially weight and sharpness. The altered dynamic was frequently justified by dramatic content, for early modern ballet took after early modern dance in its concern for expressiveness, though its themes tended to be less cosmic.

By 1980, however, modern ballet was something else again. Jennifer Dunning defined the school of Glen Tetley, Jiri Kylian, and Choo San Goh as "fast-paced, streamlined exercises in perpetual motion."[23] The new style uses balletic turnout but scorns its traditional lightness for aggressive rather than delicate speed. Virtuosity, which was often highlighted at climactic points by the classical style, is now pervasive, thrilling chiefly by its accumulations—more dancers leaping higher and faster and stronger until the momentum wears itself out. Volynsky's exultation is replaced by exhaustion. Calling this a hybrid form clarifies nothing; it is a style of its own.

We are also developing a new kind of company, one that performs works drawn from the repertories of both ballet and modern dance choreographers. And why not? A symphony orchestra does not limit itself to playing only a single musical genre. But in dance such diversity has seldom worked. Bodies trained in one manner of moving find it difficult to break long-standing habits. Also it seems that the cultivation of physical habits engenders psychological attitudes as well. This was most apparent in the early days of the modern dance when a real dichotomy existed: the ballet dancers felt themselves disciplined instruments of precision; their counterparts considered themselves freely creative and self-expressive individuals. They moved differently, felt differently.

The way the human being moves exemplifies certain manners of dealing with time, space, and energy—which amounts to exhibiting manners of dealing with the world in which we live, since those elements constitute the system of constraints with which we all have to cope. In this sense we necessarily relate to the dancer as a person. He displays a way of dealing with the world that we find congenial or admirable or distasteful. But if the manner is neutral, bland, the style is dull, we feel no involvement. For the dancer to execute the visible dimensions of the prescribed steps is not enough; that is only part of the style. The style lies also in the attitude toward the movement, which is also an attitude toward life.

Rayner Heppenstall stated that the classical style of ballet reflects what is "thought most significant in the culture of the West." He specified the qualities he considered distinctive: extroverted, expansive, centrifugal, objective. With these properties, he asserted, ballet needs no representational interest; it need not compete with drama. In itself, the style is "one epitome of the total history of the West," with its respect for tradition, for order, for "clarity of spirit." Ballet, he noted, "expresses only itself, which is to say, certain general qualities of style."[24]

Still he found these qualities metaphorically representational, an attitude that led David Michael Levin to assert that Heppenstall was pleading for a limited formalism, that of semantics, rather than for a "sweeping formalism in syntax." For Heppenstall the tensions of ballet subsist in the struggle between tradition and the free human being, between the demands of impersonality and precision and the individual free will; these reflect the tensions of life. For Levin, on the countrary, the opposing drives are self-referring. Stressing the tension between weight and weightlessness as "the essence of the ballet art," Levin found that when this essence is "properly isolated, exhibited, and—in a word—released, it can be exquisitely expressive entirely on its own."[25] Without mimesis, without "symbolic convention," the style is significant. Such arguments were not advanced with regard to the early modern dance, though they have become prevalent with regard to its later manifestations.

Does this mean that eventually, as the talk was going a few years ago, the two genres might merge? Certainly we have seen signs of growing similarity as both ballet and modern dance concentrate on themes of pure movement. We find such titles as Choo San Goh's *Momentum*, Glen Tetley's *Circles*, Douglas Dunn's *Gestures in Red*, and Molissa Fenley's *Energizer*, the first two called ballet, the last two modern dance. But representation or lack of it is a critical determinant, not of a genre of dance, but of a species within such a genre. The central factor must relate to the movement; can the movement qualities be merged?

In the 1970s Clive Barnes called attention to the trend in modern dance of incorporating elements of technical display, which had always distinguished the ballet. Now, while no style can be simultaneously predominantly light and weighted, goal-oriented and path-focussed, there is nothing in the nature of modern dance that invariably prohibits the exhibition of technical skill. However, skill does weaken a dramatic work when it detracts attention from emotional expressiveness (which is also true of ballet) or when it is used with qualities that are antithetical to the genre. The trouble with some recent performances of early modern dance works stems especially from the latter of

these: the lithe bodies of today's dancers fail to attack their movements with sufficient force, with sufficient weight, for that particular style. The result is not a merging but an incongruity.
Aware of the danger, Graham changed the costumes for her
revival of *Primitive Mysteries,* adding a ruffle to the formerly plain
skirt, a softening that would have clashed with the austere, angular performance of 1931, but that was entirely appropriate to the
milder approach of the dancers of 1964. Lightness and the early
modern dance simply cannot be merged.

Lightness, however, suits Cunningham, though he uses it in
an unballetic way. Arlene Croce has suggested that, for aerial
movement, he substitutes "incredibly rapid shifts of weight and
direction, and packed staccato changes of pace on the ground."[26]
He modifies other classical qualities as well. The dancer establishes a still, vertical center but quickly moves off it into perilous
off-balance positions, into asymmetrical configurations. Sometimes the Cunningham phrase takes on some of the smoothness
of balletic flow; at other times, like a good image in metaphysical
poetry, heterogeneous movements seem linked together by violence; at still other times the flow appears simply discursive.
Cunningham dancers tend to be balletically precise, skilled,
impersonal. When a critic admitted that he was confused by
David Vaughan's apparently equal enthusiasm for Cunningham
and Ashton, Vaughan remarked that he found their work
equally marked by purity, austerity, clarity, and rigor.[27] Perhaps
we would be better off in describing dance works if we looked
for such qualities instead of grabbing for the nearest available
label. Labels are useful when they lead the viewer to what is
actually present in the dance, but misleading when they call
attention exclusively to traits that it shares with others of somewhat the same ilk, often to the detriment of the very properties
that distinguish it as an especially important creation. . . . At
their greatest, both ballet and modern dance comprise a number
of subtle and complex styles that urge us to relinquish our neat,
comfortable havens of fixed categories for the hazardous but
rewarding shores of the aesthetically unknown. . . .

(1982)

Notes

[1]Nelson Goodman, *Ways of Worldmaking* (Indianapolis: Hackett, 1978),
p. 40.

[2]T. S. Eliot, "A Dialogue on Dramatic Poetry," in *Selected Essays 1917–1932* (New York: Harcourt, 1932), p. 34.

[3]Lincoln Kirstein, "What Ballet Is About," in *Three Pamphlets Collected* (Brooklyn: Dance Horizons, 1967), pp. 6–7.

[4]John Martin, *Introduction to the Dance* (New York: W. W. Norton, 1939), p. 212.

[5]Lincoln Kirstein, "Ballet Alphabet," in *Three Pamphlets*, p. 20.

[6]Akim Volynsky, "The Book of Exultation," *Dance Scope* 5, no. 2 (1971), 18.

[7]André Levinson, "The Spirit of the Classic Dance," in Selma Jeanne Cohen, ed., *Dance as a Theatre Art* (New York: Dodd, Mead, 1974), p. 116.

[8]Paul Valéry, "Dance and the Soul," in *Dialogues*, trans. William McCausland Stewart. Bollingen Series 45, vol. 4 (New York: Pantheon, 1956), 38.

[9]Levinson, "The Spirit of the Classic Dance."

[10]Kirstein, "What Ballet Is About," p. 32.

[11]Violette Verdy, "Speaking of Nureyev," *Ballet Review* 5, no. 2, 47.

[12]Mary Wigman, *The Mary Wigman Book*, ed. and trans. Walter Sorell (Middletown, Conn.: Wesleyan University Press, 1975), pp. 28, 30.

[13]Miriam Winslow, "A Dancer's Critique of Dance," in Frederick Rand Rogers, *Dance: A Basic Educational Technique* (New York: Macmillan, 1941), p. 85.

[14]Kirstein, "What Ballet Is About," p. 53.

[15]José Limón, "An American Accent," in Selma Jeanne Cohen, ed., *The Modern Dance* (Middletown, Conn.: Wesleyan University Press, 1966), p. 20.

[16]Anna Kisselgoff, *New York Times,* 24 August 1975.

[17]Paul Taylor interviewed by Deborah Jowitt, *Village Voice,* 23 April 1979.

[18]Laura Dean interviewed by John Gruen on "The Sound of Dance," WNCN, New York, 11 May 1980.

[19]Erik Bruhn quoted in John Gruen, *Erik Bruhn* (New York: Viking, 1979), p. 218.

[20]Senta Driver interviewed by Jack Anderson, *New York Times,* 25 February 1979.

[21]Sally Banes, "'Drive,' She Said: The Dance of Molissa Fenley," *The Drama Review* 24 (1980), 14.

[22]I have used Ms. Jowitt's apt remark a number of times, but neither of us can now remember exactly when it appeared in the *Village Voice.*

[23]Jennifer Dunning, *New York Times,* 11 February 1980.

[24]Rayner Heppenstall, *Apology for Dancing* (London: Faber and Faber, 1936), pp. 145, 113, 195.

[25]David Michael Levin, "Balanchine's Formalism," *Dance Perspectives* 55, 30.

[26]Arlene Croce, untitled contribution in Merce Cunningham et al., "Time To Walk in Space," *Dance Perspectives* 34, 25.

R. P. BLACKMUR
THE SWAN IN ZURICH

Standing alone in the bar of Covent Garden at the second interval (my companion was elsewhere for the moment) I found myself filling with the warmth made by the Sadler's Wells Ballet: warmth and sweetness and ease, nowhere embittered by any redundant sauce of expertness and nowhere laid waste by efficiency, and altogether I felt very free. Freedom is what one feels in intimacy when there is no need to worry about any of the labors of translation we call understanding; and here I had been made intimate with a style—in this case a style of theatrical dancing—so that it became a part of my own meaning. I had known the skills of this dancing all my life, and from the belated presence of past lives as well. My mind ran to Tokyo and the great Kabuki theatre where just a month before I had seen a day of plays with the sense of intimacy and little chance for the labor of understanding but had been pressed by color and movement, especially in the dance scenes (as in the whole fourth act of a play called, for short, "Onna Seigen"). In the Kabuki theatre there was clearly style; the style assaulted and intruded on me, with knives that left no wounds; the style was its own meaning, but like everything which, being unfamiliar, seems stylized, was no part of *my* own meaning. I knew only what I missed, just as one may be aware only of what has been forgotten. It was a world of brilliant impersonations where since I did not know the persons I could enjoy chiefly the alien brilliance. Here in Covent Garden I was at home—rather an older one than Hawthorne thought of—but there were other and more expert Americans than I here, who were at home only in the sense of being abroad together. Two of them stood behind me, pressing their opinions into the form of reactions: " . . . and the ensemble has no technique—or what there is, is sloppy. Fonteyn is all right, but for

the rest—these people should see the City Center a few times."
His friend answered in mollifying confirmation.

Hearing this—something to the effect, "Yes; it is true they
have no style"—I wondered what they would think of the Russian ballet with its ragged and athletic exuberance, and indeed I
wondered how I felt about it myself—aside from the great noise
of it with which London burred and bristled. Would I say of the
Russians, Yes; it is true they are a fortress state and they have no
style?—But the second bell had sounded, just as my companion
returned with her English warmth—which no doubt in expert
American opinion might also have been called sloppy—and
with its aid I was able to recover in good part the warmth and
sweetness of the Sadler's Wells Ballet—but only in good part, for
there was a triangular piece of my mind which retained the
prompting of opinion and fussed with what style was and particularly what American style was. It fussed and bored so
brownly, and kept on so, that at dinner afterward—as I remember, it was a Greek dinner with egg-lemon soup, vine leaves, and
resinous wine at the Akropolis restaurant, surely all appropriate
to the subject—I got myself sworn at least to surround, if I could
not define, American style, and I supposed, so swearing, that I
might be surrounding my own otherwise indefinable self. At
any rate, for six months afterwards, and with the pressure of the
three previous months, I set against everything American I could
remember and see and be, whatever luck and travel threw in my
way which might surround—which might illuminate—the limits and scope of American style. I was an American self-conscious
because of the rest of the world, a thought which seemed a little
too characteristic until I remembered that Hazlitt had defined
the Englishman best in his "Notes of a Journey through France
and Italy." When we are abroad we bring with us the conspicu-
ous part of what we left behind, and can sometimes learn to see
it, as in Cairo when I found that the Cairenes had no difficulty
in singling me from the British by my American walk, I got a
sight of my own legs going ahead of me never since lost. One's
gait, when not an oppression, is a part of one's perfectible role.
In harness racing there is a difference in gait between the 2:12
and the 2:15 horses which is radical but not unequal. In ballet,
then (and if so, of course in other things as well), might there
not be a radical difference in gait between the City Center and
the Sadler's Wells company which would be one indication of
the difference between the American and the British national
styles?

In London, with only memories of New York, Boston, and Bar Harbor to prompt me, I knew only there was a difference in speed: the Americans were much faster than the British ever wanted to be. The Americans kept their eyes on the ball, and were stripped for nothing but action. The British were rather absent-minded because they had so much else than the ball to attend to, and gave no effect at all—not even the slenderest ballerina—of being stripped. In them, stripping would have depleted the quality of their action. In the Americans, only the stripping made action possible. In Zurich—where I went to lecture the following week—these sentiments were fortified and developed, for it happened I got there on the afternoon of the last night of a series of performances of the City Center Ballet, and of course (at a price which annoyed and in pretense outraged him) the concierge procured me a seat on the aisle in the seventh row. It seemed to me, but not from the almost entirely Swiss audience, that I was about to confront a company of very old friends, of whom I might therefore find a sudden distrust— a distrust which might sharpen my eyes through the double blur of London and Zurich. . . .

. . . Of European theatre audiences there is none so incurious as the Swiss; which is perhaps an effect of their keeping history so in its place (say with Zwingli and Calvin) as almost to do without it. Even the Swiss houses do not give you curious regard; they seem to have no history in conduct of their own; and if you find the Swiss watching you in public it is not from curiosity or practical interest but out of that decorum which requires an exercise of the eyes. If Balanchine should look through the peephole in the curtain, though he might be pleased with the solid occupancy, he must surely shudder—it was so far from a warm house.

The question of warmth disappeared with the Bach-Balanchine "Concerto Barocco" into the terrifying vision of proficiency beyond conceivable impulse, and exactly equal to the reason which propelled it. One felt like tap dancing in a smaller and smaller space until one's self disappeared, and one understood at last what Kirstein and Balanchine must have been up to, sometime around 1935, when they had Paul Draper at work tapping to Bach. It is not necessary to think of the Dehumanization of Art but it is advisable to take a sidelong look at that thought; the dehumanization was an international game, but America in New York had her own development of that game. It was a magnificent technique for expunging the psyche—who is slow, and stubborn, and always purposeful with however much uncertainty—from the body which danced. I saw at once (or in the intermission after I had seen what this company could do with Britten-Robbins' "Fanfare") that here was high art (which may as well ignore as affirm the psyche) made out of American habits and predispositions into an almost totally characteristic, and indeed almost "closed" performance. We Americans have the technique to bring something to performance so well that the subject is left out. There is nothing we throw away so quickly as our *données*; for we would make always an independent and evangelical, rather than a contingent, creation. This is why other people in the world in part take us up and in part repudiate us; and it is why they find us both abstract and hysterical: we throw away so much and make so much of the meager remainder. We make a great beauty, which is devastated of everything but form and gait.

... The Americans did not like the softness of the Sadler's Wells girls. They missed the hardness of the American girls, hardness of flesh, of face, and the scrupulousness of motion so hard it inched on the brittle—as if every gesture were secretly fractured, but finely joined. There was also the hardness of pace or gait. What is so hard as hysteric exactness, unless it be abstract exclusiveness? And what, when one has learned them, comes so to be the habit of demand? My American friends were out of their habit and thought the intimate order they saw was sloppiness where rather it might be called a different optimum of precision. In their habit they were used to American hardness and no doubt thought the London bobbies too gentle for effective police-work; they expected to be bitched instead of welcomed. This hardness of ours runs along the whole road: an external hardness which comes from wearing our cultural skeletons on the outside. The English are soft on the outside (they call it being empirical, or making arrangements) and complain of the French logic that misses so much of what is sweet and gets into an external muddle; but French logic has nothing in the capacity of missing compared to the American logic of hysteria. What the City Center lacked in its excess of virtue was what I missed in them. There were all those beautiful legs and no one in the company who could walk except Diana Adams and none but her with a proper face. All the rest of the girls made up a ballet of pinheads. I do not speak of what these girls actually were off stage, which is very attractive, or what they would be like in love, but of what they really were under the transforming powers of their technique or—so far as it is the same thing—their style in the dance.

In that reality they had no faces and no legs that were inhabited. Some kind of sex was missing here—the tenderness—the predatoriness—the sexuality itself. To look at their faces was to look at what under other circumstances they would be if only the technique of the psyche echoed in the technique of their bodies. The men were a little better than the girls, as if their technique required some stigma—some echo—reflected in the face. But the girls were echoless technique. This was not so in Covent Garden. Of those girls I knew many faces, and of all of them I knew what their legs did as a grand exercise of all my sentiments—the very exercise, as it is the very knowledge, which can never be made perfect by any technique of body or any technology of sensibility. Technique has ultimately to do only with performance, and to the degree that a particular stage of technique is depended on alone it will exclude, because it thinks it stands for, what ought to be performed. We Americans—and in our ballet as much as anywhere—tend to stop when we have reached "technical" perfection; that is, we decide on our perfections ahead of time. This should, I think, be called whoring before the arts with only half our natural skills and wiles. What is forgotten is that all true techniques draw on the chthonic for their substance—as the best carpenter scribes with his eye and knows his square is in its live part a magical instrument; as a gesture comes to birth beyond, and *with*, every skill of nerve and muscle—and likewise draw on the heavenly only for the last form: which is the other end of the chthonic—But how shall the great initial beauty of the City Center be brought so far?

Only, I suppose, by meditations analogous to those which prompted the question. My way to bed—after going backstage for a moment to admire the private beauty of the American girls: and so to reassure myself of *all* possibilities—led from the foot of the lake along the Limat Quai to the third bridge where across the river stands the Hotel zum Störchen. The night was soft September with only the inner articulate skeleton of chill. I could not see the snowy mountain which I saw every clear day from my balcony up the river and far beyond the head of the lake, but it was enough in me from this day and from others in other years so that I knew it was there, and it gave me a remote resistless strength. I could not tell what it might not do to me. I could not see. I could not tell. Below the rail along the parade I could not see nor tell but knew the quiet swift sweep of the Lamat River: "wide water without sound," as Wallace Stevens says, but here also all a-flowing. By a pair of steps to a float stood a man all dark

but his face, which gathered darkness to its white, his shoulders
in the last stages of irresolution. At any moment he will go away,
I thought, as I passed to leeward of him. The airs were soft that
blew around him. A hundred yards down river they blew round
me, leaving a caress of chill on cheek and shoulder. Below me
was one of the swan pens, and a swan, head under wing, drifting
swiftly on the current that eased through the outer half of the
pen. As the body came just short of the lower barrier, the head
came nearly erect from under the wing, the renerved swan gave
two thrusting paddle strokes—enough to carry it almost to the
upper barrier. There, already drifting, the head went under the
wing again for four or five seconds of sleep. Of the hundred odd
swans who live on the Limat Quai, this one alone, at least on this
night, was with skill deeper than any technique rehearsing in
gesture the quality of its life in the quantity of the element it
lived in. In the meaning was the precision, in repetition never
altogether the same, always a little loose, unique only in the
instance. As hysterical, as abstract, as anything New York ever
happened on, yet a progressive echo of nature and of herself in
nature, this swan was in analogy a model of how the break-
through into style might be accomplished, without loss of quantity or quality of the impact of what was meant to be controlled.

But there is no sense exaggerating the value of a swan, least of
all in Zurich. In Berlin ten days later there was again the City
Center Ballet and a very different foil to put against them, in the
same theatre on successive days, the Ximenez-Vargas Spanish
Ballet from Madrid, which I have heard spoken of as very low
stuff indeed as ballet goes. The same theatre, but you would not
have thought so from the feeling of the house. For the Americans the house was bland, friendlier than Zurich and more aristocratic than bourgeois, but on the whole more correct than wel-
coming; hospitality was a grace one had learned to practice solo,
on either side of a barrier, nothing mutual. For the Spanish all
was heat and rejoicing of participation and release into (not
from) common action. People pounded and yelled, not for admiration of technical energy, but for the deep skills of life bursting
into momentary form; and indeed the audience had to be dark-
ened out of the house into the light rain. The contrast is worth
making clear. There was no lack of admiration for the Americans
and it was in no way perfunctory, but one was not related to
what one admired, and very little of the self was involved in the
admiration. As in the kinds of love, the Americans might express
a form of eros and might even reach for agape but there was in

their dancing none of the warm vibrancy of philia, of which the Spanish had so much, and without which eros is hysterical and agape abstract and hence persuade something less than the full self. Thus seen in the Spanish contrast, the sense of American hardness was reinforced with the sense of American abstractness: as if Lincoln Kirstein's boys and girls danced in organized abstraction fits. Again, only Diana Adams kept enough warmth in her while dancing to supply her face with life. If there was unity in their dancing it was the American unity which is achieved by cutting away; unity by privation or deprivation; unity by technique—by action precipitated in the kaleidoscope and learned in the muscles which could operate without the pressure of the person. Where other faces than Adams' were visible it was by intrusion—as the boys looked like college boys with crew cuts and the girls showed as puny in the face. Yet the legs were very beautiful in abstraction, quite beyond participation, with movements that could be repeated endlessly the same. . . . We are like a complex of new physical and spiritual forces let loose with our laboratory managers always a little behind in the understanding of the forces, in either their likely behavior or their possible aspirations. That we run to abstraction and hysteria is almost appropriate in the present phase of our natures. The ballet is only one extreme. Abstraction is where we ignore behavior and hysteria is where we replace it; both are modes appropriate for daily creation but there is more than the usual uncertainty about them that their creations, however beautifully articulated and however technically—even technologically—exact, will conform to anything like enough of the native impulses which taken in balance—in experience together—lead to purpose or choice or the delineation of these. There is no conformity which is exclusive, no order which is complete, and there is no conforming order worth mustering which does not invite, for its life, the constant and random supply of fresh disorder. Chaos is not what we must exclude; it is what we do not know, or ignore, of the behavior which, in all the versions of space and time we can manage, forms our lives, and order is how we arrange them with the behavior of lives past or to come. This is why society is immortal and immoral, and in the stature of our genius we give forms to how it is that this is so to the individual mortal and moral man. This is the role of man as virtuoso as it is the role of nature as herself, for she is nothing but the play of that role just as we are much less than ourselves if we do not play it.

It is in this high language that I would have us look at the ballet and its styles in the present western world, and it is similarly that I would have us look at our other arts and faculties. If we cannot or will not from some superior compulsion correct ourselves to common experience we can at least understand ourselves in terms of the behavior we believe not to be ours; and if we cannot be intimate with ourselves (short of some new dispensation on intimacy) we can look at the swan in Zurich. . . .

(1958)

ANNA KISSELGOFF
THERE IS NOTHING
"NATIONAL" ABOUT
BALLET STYLES

One idea that dies hard is that there are national styles of ballet. Within this line of thinking, the English are reserved in their dancing, the Russians are dramatic, the French have flair if not form, the Danes are charming and the Americans infuse their ballet dancing with an ingrained athleticism and exuberance.

No one will deny that distinctions of ballet style exist country to country. Certainly, Britain's Royal Ballet dances with reserve. The startling, high leg extension of the Bolshoi's Nadezhda Pavlova or the New York City Ballet's Colline Neary will never be found in a Royal Ballet ballerina.

But whether the Royal Ballet's reserve stems from so-called British understatement is open to debate. National stereotypes of any sort are an unreliable basis for generalization. Is "prim and proper" still the image of a Britain with a self-described dissolute upper class and a much-advertised mod explosion. As for charming Denmark, it boasts the most liberal pornography laws in the world.

Nonetheless, traditional ballet literature has suggested that national characteristics always make themselves felt in the high art of classical ballet: subconsciously, the gait of a young Italian sunning himself in the piazza is bound to suffuse the dancing of an Italian prima ballerina.

Yet, such determinist formulas fail to recognize that style in ballet, as in any art, is a direct result of creative influence. Rather than fall back upon dubious national stereotypes to explain why one ballet company accents its movements differently from another, why not admit that each style derives from the individuals who have shaped that company?

Indeed, there is no "American style" in classical ballet; the three major American companies all differ in their styles. The New York City Ballet, for example, dances the way it does because that is how George Balanchine wants it to dance; had he formed a company in England, it might be dancing the same way. Similarly, the Joffrey Ballet's style was fashioned by Robert Joffrey, and American Ballet Theater's by its early creative influences—that is Michel Fokine and Antony Tudor. And although Ninette de Valois was the organizing force behind the Royal Ballet, it was Frederick Ashton who molded its style. Elsewhere the esthetic of the Royal Danish Ballet was indelibly marked by one man, the 19th-century choreographer, August Bournonville. Human rather than mystical national forces have also molded Soviet ballet; its style was shaped both by a political policy that required dramatic realism and by a heritage of classical training that was modernized by such teachers as Agrippina Vaganova.

It could be argued, of course, that Ashton's work looks "English" because he is a product of his English upbringing. As it happens, Ashton was born in Ecuador and educated in Peru. Like Ninette de Valois, Margot Fonteyn, Alicia Markova and Robert Helpmann, the other figures crucial to the Royal Ballet's early history, he spent his formative years outside England. In 1934, Ashton's choreography for the Gertrude Stein-Virgil Thomson opera, "Four Saints in Three Acts," proved how easily he would have found a place in the American avant-garde of the 1930's. It is doubtful that Ashton, had he remained in the United States, would have seemed more British to Americans than Antony Tudor, an English choreographer whose works became the mainstay of American dramatic ballet.

These is no question that Ashton's sensibility is English as far as the *content* of his works is concerned. But the Ashton *style*— that is, the way he wanted dancers to move—is something else. Style is essentially an attitude imposed upon technique.

The Ashton style, for example, can be traced to a two-tiered Russian model. On one level, the very "British" Royal Ballet considers itself the heir to the old Maryinsky tradition. On another plane, it sees itself in the line of descent from Diaghilev's Ballets Russes. From the Maryinsky, it drew a stylistic ideal—the style that Pavlova and Karsavina brought to the West before the Soviet era expanded the old Russian classical style into a more flamboyant one with a greater acrobatic plastique.

The typical British fidelity to the "correct" Russian style was recently voiced again in the June issue of the British magazine *Dance and Dancers*. Reviewing Suzanne Farrell in Balanchine's "Chaconne," John Percival wrote: "Balanchine apparently encourages Farrell to concentrate on speed and on those incredibly high extensions. In the process, some disconcerting things happen. . . . I imagine many people would be horrified at the way strict academic style is distorted for the particular virtues emphasized."

At the same time that the Royal kept faith with the Maryinsky model, Ashton also made clear his dislike for rigid classicism. The way he loosened up an academic style is close to what was done by such Diaghilev choreographers as Fokine and Bronislava Nijinska. Ashton is closer to Nijinska, his mentor, than to Balanchine.

This difference exists, quite simply, because Balanchine has gone beyond the "correct" style in classical ballet. But rather than distort it, he has extended it. Those who believe in national styles will tell you that the special attack, speed and heightened silhouette of Balanchine's style reflect the vitality and rhythms of American life. Yet, by Balanchine's own account, the crucial artistic encounter of his career was his meeting with Stravinsky in Europe in 1928. The neoclassicism and pared-down style of the Stravinsky of that time determined the neoclassic, streamlined look that Balanchine developed later in his own work.

Undoubtedly, this is the direction his style would have taken wherever he settled. The sun in the piazza does not always filter into the theater.

(1976)

LINCOLN KIRSTEIN
From BALLET ALPHABET

CLASSIC AND ROMANTIC BALLET

CLASSIC BALLET

The classic dance is not merely a department of theatrical-dancing opposed to the "romantic," but rather a central line, or governing attitude which links the *purest* developments in traditional stage practice, whatever the epoch. To be sure, purity is comparative. In the vocabulary of step and gesture accumulated over the last five hundred years, there have been many "impure" influences, affecting the idiom from individual personalities, from exotic or national dances, from circus, music-hall and ballroom. But in the large residual body of expression, there is a basic-speech, founded on the five absolute *positions*, which demonstrate the human body on the stage in its grandest development by activity which is possible only in terms of dance, without reference to mimetic or associative gesture. As the residual information of medical practice is *materia medica*,—so in dancing it is *materia choreographica*. Its basic kinetic speech praises the body as free agent in air whose broadest extensions or highest leaps are its extreme lyric definition. The classic style is clean and open, grandiose without affectation, noble without pretension. Any idiosyncratic comment on it appears as offensive mannerism, which, however charming in a character-dance, destroys the linear purity of classicism.

"Classicism," wrote André Levinson, speaking of the ballerina Trefilova (ca. 1929), "tends towards geometric formula, but at the supreme moment, breaks and avoids it." Experiments in optics show that the line of least visual resistance is not necessarily the shortest distance between two points, but rather a long, easy curve which the eye may pursue with a gentle flow. This extended line is the property of every classic ballet position from *arabesque* and *attitude* to the more freely plastic *ports de bras*.

The classic dance may be rapid, but never brusque, jagged or broken. The classic line is sustained, serene and melodic, whose mercurial grace never disturbs its formal consistency unless it is dissolved on the metallic surface of technical incompetence or instinctive bad taste.

ROMANTIC BALLET

The term "romantic" as applied to ballet is a misnomer. Familiarly, it is a style of dancing as exemplified by revivals of *Giselle* (Coralli: 1841) or *Les Sylphides* (Fokine: 1909). Yet both ballets are familiarly labeled *ballets classiques*, although Fokine's is subtitled "a romantic revery" and is indeed an atmospheric pastiche of Taglioni's *La Sylphide* (P. Taglioni: 1830). In each case romanticism becomes not an opposition to, but a stylistic department of, classicism.

By "romantic" we generally understand an attitude in reaction to neo-classic Greek revivals of the late-eighteenth century and the republican Roman frigidity of Directory and Empire. Under Napoleon, dancers in Paris and Milan wore "Greek" tunics, not far from what Isodora Duncan would have considered "natural." But neo-classicism exhausted itself as a merely decorative style without reference to the life of its time. It was replaced by what came to be known as the "Gothick," but which was no more Gothic, as we understand it, than was its predecessor essentially antique. In philosophy, it was a shift from the finite, rational, orderly and demonstrable based on arbitrary archaeological precedent to the vague, atmospheric, warm, remote and infinite. The novels of Walter Scott and Monk Lewis, with their wild and loosely constructed plots, the tortured compositions of the painters Delacroix and Gericault, the verses of Byron and Victor Hugo, the dancing of Taglioni and Elssler on their elevated toe-points, were the facts of this revolution in action.

Taglioni embraced the colder aspect of romantic dancing, the marble maiden, the virgin lover, the human angel, the pure evanescent, ephemeral longed-for-eternal-feminine. Elssler embodied the warmer rôle; the exotic gypsy-hearted dashing earthforce of vague Central Europe, mysterious Spain, forbidding Scotland. National dances were the decorative frames for her characterizations. Romantic ballet did not forswear reality, since the neoclassic theatre itself had had little pretensions to realism. It merely denied logic, reason or formal design. Its principle was without ethic,—emotional and decorative. It disappeared (ca. 1850) because it could not survive the departure of its original exponents, and since it had even less connection with the life of its epoch than its predecessor, and was as well completely lacking in moral ideas. It had become instead of a comment on life through art, merely an outworn theatrical parody or pastiche of literature, painting and itself.

Hence the so-called Romantic ballet is not a department of the dance, but merely a localized theatrical echo of a transient influential literary and artistic movement.

(1939)

V

Language, Notation, and Identity

Dance writers frequently refer to "movement vocabularies" or to the "language of dance." But do various dance forms really constitute "languages" in any sort of rigorous sense? The answer to that question will of course depend upon how we define "language." Another question: do we possess, or are we capable of developing, a system of notation that will permit us to record the essential features of individual dances? These are some of the major issues examined by the articles in this section. R. G. Collingwood, the distinguished English exponent of the expression theory of art, argues that all art is a form of language. In his view language is any controlled and expressive bodily activity. Every kind of language, including verbal language (to which he assigns no primacy or priority), is a specialized form or offshoot of an original language of total bodily gesture. In this sense dance is the mother of all language and all other "languages" are merely subdivisions of this original language. Collingwood, one of the most sophisticated exponents of the expression theory of art, also holds that "the [linguistic] expression of emotion is not, as it were, a dress made to fit an emotion already existing, but an activity without which the experience of that emotion cannot exist." He takes it to follow that there is no way of expressing the same emotion in two different media. What is expressed in "dance" can be expressed only that way.

Joseph Margolis, the contemporary American philosopher, challenges the thesis that art is linguistic or quasi-linguistic in nature. Margolis plainly takes discursive, verbal language as the model and argues that in order to show that dance or any of the other arts is a language we would have to demonstrate that it meets the minimal requirements for being a language. In his opinion one would have to establish that these arts generate meanings by the use of rule-like or rule-governed conventions and that they include among their features a relatively stable vocabulary, a finite grammar, and criteria for identifying well-formed "sentences." If these characteristics are not present there is little point in claiming, as Collingwood does, that art is language, or dance the mother of all languages. Margolis notes that those who argue that art is a language frequently fail to distinguish between the natural sequences and correlations that a language might conventionally exploit and those that it actually does exploit. Another confusion is especially important for the issue of artistic expression. From the fact that works of art have expressive qualities, comes the tendency to infer that they express (that is, convey as language meaningfully conveys) some experience or quality.

Margolis concludes by discussing the issues involved in Nelson Goodman's having called his book *Languages of Art*. Margolis points out that Goodman's concern is "more with the properties of a musical score by which Beethoven's Fifth could be identified than with the properties of Beethoven's Fifth." That is, in his opinion, Goodman is more interested in the problem of whether there is a kind of language or notation in which it is possible to characterize the essential features of works of art than he is in the question whether the works are themselves linguistic in nature. In fact, Goodman does not believe that art is a language or even that art is a symbol system. He does suggest that works of art are symbols that function in linguistic and nonlinguistic systems. But it is to the problem of notation that we now turn.

Fernau Hall is concerned mainly with the aesthetic consequences of ballet's historic failure to develop an adequate and generally accepted notation. Ballet's illiteracy is responsible, he thinks, for the poverty of ballet's traditions. Although painting's traditions go back tens of thousands of years, the earliest ballet to survive more or less intact goes back to 1786 and our knowledge of ballet's past even after that date is profoundly impoverished and uncertain (we have no works of Sallé, Noverre, Vigano). In this situation choreographers must more or less create from scratch and (in marked contrast to music) there is no regular progress. Hall believes that a decisive contribution to the development of an adequate dance notation was made by Joan and Rudolph Benesh, with important consequences for the art of dance. A library of choreographic scores can be created in which dance students and choreographers will be able to study the history of their art and analyze the features of particular works of art. Hall proposes an attitude toward the past comparable to the one T. S. Eliot advocated in "Tradition and the Individual Talent": the truly original choreographer is more likely to find inspiration in traditional figures than he is in the work of his contemporaries. In addition, by incorporating notation into the creative process, the choreographer, like the composer, can view his entire composition at one time. This will permit him to say things that would be impossible if he had to work entirely from memory. The advent of a usable choreographic notation should encourage the development of an art of greater subtlety, complexity, and originality.

Nelson Goodman is less concerned with the aesthetic consequences of a dance notation than with the question whether it is in principle possible to develop such a notation. He asks whether dance is more like painting, for which there could be no such notation, or more like music, for which we possess a relatively adequate one. Goodman distinguishes between autographic and allographic arts and works of art. A work is autographic if, as in painting, printmaking, and sculpture, its genuineness depends upon the history of its production; allographic if genuineness is independent of the history of production. For example, a genuine impression of an etching must have been printed from the creator's original plate. There is no alternative. In contrast, a genuine instance of a novel need only be "spelled" correctly. A copy of a cheaply produced, unauthorized edition is as genuine an instance of a novel as the author's original manuscript. For allographic arts a test to determine the genuineness of an instance of a work is available, a test which does not require determining how and by whom the work was produced. A test of this sort is provided by a suitable notational system. For texts (like those of a novel) or for scores (musical or choreographic) the test of genuineness is correct spelling in this notation; for performance, the test is compliance with what is correctly spelled. In Goodman's view the definitive identification of works is possible only where a notation has been established. Goodman has no sympathy with those pessimists who think that because of its subtlety or complexity there is no hope of notating dance or with those optimists who think that a notation can be devised for almost anything. The significant theoretical issue is whether we can provide in terms of notational language real definitions that will identify a dance in its several performances and independently of any particular history of production. It seems clear to Goodman that the requisite classification exists. For, prior to any notation, he thinks that we make reasonably consistent judgments as to whether performances by different people or companies are instances of the same dance. We say that both Martha Graham and Janet Eilber have given performances of Graham's "Lamentation" or that both the New York City Ballet and American Ballet Theater have danced Balanchine's "Theme and Variations." Since we already make this distinction between what is constitutive and what is contingent in such performances the essential presupposition for the possibility of a dance notation is met. Whether such a notation is practically feasible is another question to which Goodman's answer is less decisive. But it seems to him that Labanotation meets the main syntactic and semantic requirements of a notational system, and he is especially impressed by the newer Eshkol-Wachsman system. Of course some writers have greater doubts than Goodman about the possibility of an adequate dance notation (see, for example, "The Identity Crisis in Dance" by Adina Armelagos and Mary Sirridge, cited in the Bibliography).

Jack Anderson, the journalist and dance critic, suggests that there may be less agreement than Goodman supposes about which features of dance are constitutive and which are contingent. Anderson makes a distinction between "materialists" and "idealists." For the materialist, and Anderson (like Goodman) is plainly sympathetic to the materialist, a dance is an assemblage of specific steps, and these steps are the essence of the dance. The ideas or interpretations that animate a performance of "Giselle" may differ widely, but we witness an authentic performance of "Giselle" if, and only if, the standard choreography is observed. For the idealist, however, dances exist, or at least can exist, as scenarios or as generalized production notions, and the specific dance movements may be altered so long as the essential conception of the dance is expressed or its essential effects achieved. For the idealist, the crucial thing is not that the ballerina perform the thirty-two fouettés in "Swan Lake," but that she do something that creates a similar effect of brilliant and haughty virtuosity. It is clear that the materialist will generally be sympathetic to the ideal of notating choreographic texts and preserving what he takes to be the essence of the dance. For the idealist, notation may be objectionable because from this point of view it confuses the inessential with the essential and conspires to perpetuate the one along with the other. Anderson is not sufficiently clear about whether he thinks all ballets are materialist by nature or whether some are in fact idealist. His main practical aim is, however, to warn us against the growing tendency to treat materialist ballets as idealist ones. The ballerina who omits the thirty-two fouettés has omitted something essential.

ROBIN G. COLLINGWOOD
From THE PRINCIPLES OF ART

LANGUAGE AND LANGUAGES

We have been using the word "language" to signify any controlled and expressive bodily activity, no matter what part of the body is involved. There is a tendency to think that there is only one such activity, or at least one which enormously outdistances any other in expressiveness, namely speech, or the activities of the vocal organs. Sometimes it is suggested that there is a physiological reason for this supposed fact, namely, that by using our vocal organs we can perform a variety of actions more subtly differentiated, and therefore more suitable for development into a language, than by using any other combination of organs. It seems more than doubtful whether either the original belief, or the reason given for it, it true. Probably any one of a number of kinds of bodily action is as suitable for expressive use, intrinsically, as any other; and the pre-eminence of one over the rest would seem to depend on the historical development of this or that civilization. All speakers do not use all parts of the vocal machinery alike. Germans speak more with the larynx, Frenchmen more with the lips. It is very probable that, because of this difference, Frenchmen have a finer control over lip-movements and Germans over throat-movements; but it is certainly not true that the difference itself is based on a physiological difference independent of it and prior to it, a difference of organic structure in virtue of which Germans are more sensitive in the larynx and Frenchmen in the front of the mouth. Had that been the case, these special sensitivities would be biological characteristics, inherited like skull-shape and pigmentation; and the ability to speak French or German in the proper way would depend on the speaker's pedigree. This is notoriously not the case. The groupings recognized by physical anthropology do not coincide with those of cultural anthropology.

If Frenchmen find lip-movements more expressive than throat-movements, and Germans the opposite, the same kind of difference may exist as between movements of the vocal organs and various other kinds of movements. A dispute between Italian peasants is conducted hardly more in words than in a highly elaborated language of manual gesture. Here again, there is no physiological basis for the difference. Italians do not possess more sensitive fingers than northern Europeans. But they have a long tradition of controlled finger-gesture, going back to the ancient game of *micare digitis*.

Vocal language is thus only one among many possible languages or orders of languages. Any of these might, by a particular civilization, be developed into a highly organized form of emotional expression. It is sometimes fancied that although any one of these languages might express emotion, vocal language has an exclusive, or at least a pre-eminent, function in the expression of thought. Even if these were true, it would not be of interest at the present stage in our discussion, for we are now dealing with language as it is before being adapted to serve the purposes of thought. As a matter of fact, it is probably not true. There is a story that Buddha once, at the climax of a philosophical discussion, broke into gesture-language as an Oxford philosopher may break into Greek: he took a flower in his hand, and looked at it; one of his disciples smiled, and the master said to him, "You have understood me."

Speech is after all only a system of gestures, having the peculiarity that each gesture produces a characteristic sound, so that it can be perceived through the ear as well as through the eye. Listening to a speaker instead of looking at him tends to make us think of speech as essentially a system of sounds; but it is not; essentially it is a system of gestures made with the lungs and larynx, and the cavities of the mouth and nose. We get still farther away from the fundamental facts about speech when we think of it as something that can be written and read, forgetting that what writing, in our clumsy notations, can represent is only a small part of the spoken sound, where pitch and stress, tempo and rhythm, are almost entirely ignored. But even a writer or reader, unless the words are to fall flat and meaningless, must speak them soundlessly to himself. The written or printed book is only a series of hints, as elliptical as the neumes of Byzantine music, from which the reader thus works out for himself the speech-gestures which alone have the gift of expression.

All the different kinds of language have a relation of this kind to bodily gesture. The art of painting is intimately bound up with the expressiveness of the gestures made by the hand in drawing, and of the imaginary gestures through which a spectator of a painting appreciates its "tactile values." Instrumental music has a similar relation to silent movements of the larynx, gestures of the player's hand, and real or imaginary movements, as of dancing, in the audience. Every kind of language is in this way a specialized form of bodily gesture, and in this sense it may be said that the dance is the mother of all languages.

This is what justifies the paradox of the behaviourists, that thought is nothing but the movements of the vocal organs which are commonly said to express it. For thought we must read in the present context emotion, and emotion at the imaginative level, not the merely psychic. For the vocal organs we must read the entire body; since speech is only one form of gesture. As thus corrected, the doctrine is true in this important sense: that the expression of emotion is not, as it were, a dress made to fit an emotion already existing, but is an activity without which the experience of that emotion cannot exist. Take away the language, and you take away what is expressed; there is nothing left but crude feeling at the merely psychic level.

Different civilizations have developed for their own use different languages; not merely different forms of speech, distinguished as English from French and so on, but different in a much deeper way. We have seen how Buddha expressed a philosophical idea in a gesture, and how the Italian peasant uses his fingers hardly less expressively than his tongue. The habit of going heavily clothed cramps the expressiveness of all bodily parts except the face; if the clothing were heavy enough, only those gestures would retain their expressiveness which can be appreciated without being seen, such as those of the vocal organs; except so far as the clothes themselves were expressive. The cosmopolitan civilization of modern Europe and America, with its tendency towards rigidly uniform dress,* has limited our expressive activities almost entirely to the voice, and naturally tries to justify itself by asserting that the voice is the best medium of expression.

But different languages are not related to one and the same set of feelings like his different suits of clothes to one and the same man. If there is no such thing as an unexpressed feeling, there is no way of expressing the same feeling in two different media. This is true both of the relation between different systems of speech and of the relation between vocal language and other forms of language. An Englishman who can talk French, if he reflects on his own experience, knows very well that he feels differently when he talks a different tongue. The English tongue will only express English emotions; to talk French you must adopt the emotions of a Frenchman. To be multilingual is to be a chameleon of the emotions. Still more clearly is it true that the emotions which we express in music can never be expressed in speech, and vice versa. Music is one order of languages and speech is another; each expresses what it does express with absolute clarity and precision; but what they express is two different types of emotion, each proper to itself. The same is true of manual gesture. Contempt may be expressed by shouting an insult at a man or by snapping your fingers under his nose, as joy may be expressed in a poem or a symphony; but with a difference; the

---

*Even so, dress is a kind of language; but when it is rigidly uniform the only emotions which it can express are emotions common to those who wear it. The habit of wearing it focuses the attention of the wearer on emotions of this kind, and at once generates and expresses a permanent "set" or habit of consciously feeling in the corresponding way. Rupert Brooke noticed that Americans "walk better than we; more freely, with a taking swing, and almost with grace. How much of this," he adds, "is due to living in a democracy, and how much to wearing no braces, it is very difficult to determine" (Letters from America, p. 16). Dropping the uniform carries with it a curious breach in the emotional habit; Mulvaney found that on discarding his trousers and donning a loin-cloth he began to feel like an Indian native (Kipling, The Incarnation of Krishna Mulvaney). The consciousness of sharing uniform dress with a circle of others is thus a consciousness of emotional solidarity with them; and this, on its negative side, takes the form of emotional hostility towards persons outside that circle. To illustrate this from the history of parties and classes is superfluous. It may be worth while to point out that in the liberal political theory, where rivalry between policies is dissociated from emotional hostility between the persons supporting them, it is essential that parties should not be distinguished by uniforms. Put your parties into uniform, and the difference of their policies becomes at once a less important division between them than their emotional hostility.

precise kind of contempt which is expressed in the one way cannot be expressed in the other.

Now, if a person acquires the ability to express one kind of emotions and not another, the result will be that he knows the one kind to be in him, but not the other. These others will be in him as mere brute feelings, never mastered and controlled, but either concealed in the darkness of his own self-ignorance or breaking in upon him in the shape of passion-storms which he can neither control nor understand. Consequently, if a civilization loses all power of expression except through the voice, and then asserts that the voice is the best expressive medium, it is simply saying that it knows of nothing in itself that is worth expressing except what can be thus expressed; and that is a tautology, for it merely means "what we (members of this particular society) do not know we do not know," except so far as it suggests the addition: "and we do not wish to find out."

I said that "the dance is the mother of all languages"; this demands further explanation. I meant that every kind or order of language (speech, gesture, and so forth) was an offshoot from an original language of total bodily gesture. This would have to be a language in which every movement and every stationary poise of every part of the body had the same kind of significance which movements of the vocal organs possess in a spoken language. A person using it would be speaking with every part of himself. Now, in calling this an "original" language, I am not indulging (God forbid) in that kind of a priori archaeology which attempts to reconstruct man's distant past without any archaeological data. I do not place it in the remote past. I place it in the present. I mean that each one of us, whenever he expresses himself, is doing so with his whole body, and is thus actually talking in this "original" language of total bodily gesture. This may seem absurd. Some peoples, we know, cannot talk without waving their hands and shrugging their shoulders and waving their bodies about, but others can and do. That is no objection to what I am saying. Rigidity is a gesture, no less than movement. If there were people who never talked unless they were standing stiffly at attention, it would be because the gesture was expressive of a permanent emotional habit which they felt obliged to express concurrently with any other emotion they might happen to be expressing. This "original" language of total bodily gesture is thus the one and only real language, which everybody who is in any way expressing himself is using all the time. What we call speech and the other kinds of language are only parts of it which have undergone specialized development; in this specialized development they never come altogether detached from the parent organism.

This parent organism is nothing but the totality of our motor activities, raised from the psychical level to the conscious level. It is our bodily activity as that of which we are conscious. But that which is raised from the psychical level to the conscious level is converted by the work of consciousness from impression to idea, from object of sensation to object of imagination. The language of total bodily gesture is thus the motor side of our total imaginative experience. This last phrase was used in Chapter VII, § 6, as a name for the work of art proper. We are now beginning to see that the theory of art which is going to emerge from Book II will either consist in, or at least involve, the identification of art with language.

(1938)

JOSEPH MARGOLIS
ART AS LANGUAGE*

The elementary question posed by the thesis that there are languages of art or that works of art are linguistic or quasi-linguistic utterances of some sort is just this: What are the minimal requirements of a language? Admittedly, the question is controversial—as may be seen in trying to decide whether Wittgenstein's sketches of seemingly minimal languages are viable and if so, what they entail. Be that as it may, there are some relatively indisputable features of a genuine language; which, once canvassed even informally, threaten the thesis in question. For example, languages are conventions of some sort: whatever the vehicles of meaning may be, they are said to have meaning, or to mean what they do, by virtue of rule-like or rule-governed conventions.[1] This consideration alone rules out the tantaliz-

---

*Professor Margolis has adapted his essay for inclusion in this anthology.

ingly appealing thesis that art is "the language of emotions," in the sense in which, because of natural causal connections, a work of art produces in an audience a sense of emotional experience the artist himself originally grasped as capable of being excited in himself and others by the work he has devised. There are variations on the thesis, but by and large it trades on some theory of "natural meanings" construed in causal terms. It was apparently the view of Roger Fry[2] and is variously described (and partially but not completely dismissed) by E. H. Gombrich[3] as a theory of mere "natural resonance" or "emotional contagion." The ulterior question of whether artists may rightly be said to create in the manner indicated is an important one, which we may waive here, since the difficulties concerning conventionality are of a deeper sort.

Now, in the sense that languages are conventional, their distinctive structures and processes are conventional as well. But any minimal language contains at least a vocabulary and a grammar and provides for some form of selectively linking elements of a vocabulary and other morphemic components, in accord with grammatical rules in order to form admissible sentences. We may be as generous and as open as we please here regarding surrogates of vocabularies, grammars, well-formed sentences; but there can be no point to speaking of a *language* without some explicit attention to these features or to arguably suitable surrogates. It was, in fact, Susanne Langer's inability to specify a vocabulary, conventionally sorted, recognizable and teachable that finally washed out her otherwise interesting thesis.[4] It is not in this connection necessary, it should be said, that the putative vocabulary of art be fixed, as in the manner of discursive languages; what *is* necessary is that there be designata for relevant symbols or symbolic forms marked. Even for what Langer chooses to call "presentational" symbols, however, in terms of which, say, musical forms are taken to be symbolic of the emotions with which they are isomorphic—or, "morphologically similar"[5]—two essential difficulties remain: one, that isomorphism is not a sufficient condition of anything's functioning symbolically; and two, that isomorphism (or even resemblance) cannot even be specified without the provision of a rule in terms of which relevant correspondences may be sorted. The point has been elaborately made by Nelson Goodman[6] and, earlier, in a more informal way, by C. L. Stevenson.[7] In fact, as Stevenson very usefully implies, it is only by assuming the extraordinarily generous (but very nearly vacuous) sense of a 'sign' that Charles

Morris once favored that the theory of presentational symbols (in the form sketched) has any prospect of being confirmed—the sense, namely, in which anything discriminated may be a sign (even as iconic sign) of itself, and the sense in which, in any "sign situation," *whatever* leads us to take account of something, existent or not, itself or something else, thereby functions as a sign.[8] Again, despite their obvious appreciation of the pitfalls of Langer's thesis, it is rather difficult to be sure that E. H. Gombrich and Ruth Saw have—in their respective, recent efforts to support some version of the theory of art as language—actually managed to escape it. What Gombrich confuses, following C. E. Osgood's notion of "semantic space"—no matter how cautiously he proceeds—is the difference between there being natural associations (as by testing among alternatives to be matched—say, gay and sad sensations and bright and dark colors) that may serve as the basis of a conventional idiom of emotions and the specification of a vocabulary that conventionally exploits such associations. Ruth Saw seems to have followed Gombrich in neglecting this point as well.[9]

It is, ironically, just the inventiveness of art forms that betrays the hopelessness of the thesis. For, works of art are not simply novel expressions of some sort *in a language;* they institute new conventions that are not readily collected as admissible expressions formed from a relatively stable vocabulary and finite grammar. It is one of the firmest contributions of the new linguistics that a so-called natural language (that is, a language that is spontaneously learned by children growing up in a human society, from the fragmentary linguistic behavior they confront) must have a finite grammar capable of "generating" (in effect, describing or accounting for the grammatical structure of) an infinite set of eligible or well-formed sentences.[10] Nothing remotely like a finite and common grammar has ever been plausibly formulated for the various arts—certainly not for the whole of the fine arts, or for any of the arts distinguished by medium, period, school, style, artists, or in any other comparable way. The best that we have been able to do in this regard is to specify the relatively *common properties* of any constellation of works of art that have been thought worth discussing together. Only if such common properties could, in addition, be construed in terms of the features of a common language could the thesis in question hope to be supported.

There are, then, at least two sorts of confusion that infect the art language theory. One, already remarked, fails to distinguish between what a language might exploit among natural sequences, by way of a convention, and what conventionally is provided for in an actual language. To appreciate the point is to see at a stroke that it hardly supports the claim merely to show that conventional symbols are often used *in* works of art—for instance, to *represent* the Passion of Christ. Here, a rudimentary linguistic complex—or, at any rate, a complex that is a fair analogue of a linguistic element—has actually been incorporated into a work of art. No one would wish to deny this.[11] But it goes no distance at all toward showing that all works of art, even when they lack such representational functions, may properly be construed in terms of a vocabulary, a grammar, and determinate and well-formed sentences. The other confusion is important for a different reason—because it goes to the heart of the issue of artistic expression. There is an understandable, but not for that reason defensible, tendency to construe the fact *that works of art have expressive qualities* as signifying or entailing *that works of art express* (that is, convey, as language meaningfully conveys) *utterances about some experience* or quality or the like. Here, the sensitive language theorist is likely to insist that *this* concept of art fails to do justice to the claim that art is the language of the emotions. Thus, Ruth Saw rightly insists: "A language of the emotions, then [that is, speaking of the fine arts] is not a language devised to convey information about emotions.... What is decidedly and undoubtedly 'good enough' in the attempts of human beings to communicate their emotional states to one another is the whole world of poetry, plays, music, painting, dancing, and sculpture." She continues, searching for the correct formula:

> A communicates emotion to B in these circumstances: A makes an object, visible or audible, that seems to him an appropriate expression of his emotional state, presents it to B who takes it as the appropriate correlate of the emotional state into which it causes him to pass. A and B each assumes that he is experiencing an emotion similar to the other's.[12]

Now, Saw is quite clear that to describe "art as communicating emotion" in this sense is not sufficient to entail that "art is language."[13] But what she apparently fails to see is that she has not even adequately provided for art's communicating emotion in any way that could possibly support the thesis that art is language or symbolic system. For, since there are no governing conventions to which A and B subscribe, they can only *discover* (by means other than "reading" the work of art) that they have similar emotions under relevantly given conditions *and then decide* (in a way that parallels representation) to regard the work as signifying this or that emotion. So the work can be *made* to symbolize a given emotion and thus come to be used linguistically or quasi-linguistically; and a work of art may be said to "communicate" emotion if, in suitably causing an emotion in one, it causes an emotion somehow appropriately similar to the emotion the artist intended to provide a correlate for—but that is the sense in which artists may, if they wish, exploit mere "natural signs". There seems, therefore, no way to recover the original claim in an interesting way.

Here, we may add the observation that, in construing works of art as expressive, as having expressive qualities, we are doing no more than attributing *intentional properties* of a certain sort to works of art. In holding, for instance, that cats have a certain characteristic way of expressing annoyance, we are by no means holding that the expression is *conventional*, though of course it will be intentional in the sense that a certain bit of cat-behavior may rightly be said to express annoyance or have the property of expressing annoyance. Similarly, though perhaps unexpectedly, even a work of art, which essentially depends on exploiting conventions of various sorts, many conceivably have an expressive property that is *not* conventional. It seems perfectly possible, for example, that a given piece of music (if the theory of natural resonance has any plausibility at all) may exhibit a certain natural expressiveness—for instance, natural gaiety; it will do so because it is a conventional object but not necessarily because the property it possesses it possesses only conventionally. This shows, then, the important difference between conventionally representing emotions and being a natural sign of emotions—in speaking about which we regularly equivocate when we speak about expression. The theory of expressive qualities is not, as such, a theory about language at all, though it may (or may not) be a theory about communciation; and the theory of the language of art is not, as such, a theory about properties in the usual sense, though it must be a theory about communciation. For these reasons, it is also quite possible that a work of art exhibit an expressive quality of a conventional sort without serving a linguistic or quasi-linguistic function in so doing. For instance, a dance step may exhibit a certain characteristic romantic languor without *representing, referring to, exemplifying,* or *symbolizing* such languor. Finally, a work of art may represent or symbolize given expressive qualities or the like without *having* or *possessing* congruent expressive qualities.[14] For example, a drama might well be a representation of Christian piety without possessing the expressive quality of Christian piety.[15]

Without doubt, the principal theory of art that conflates the distinction between a (minimal) language and the (semilinguistic) sign or semiotic function of bodily expression (whether natural or conventional) is that of R. G. Collingwood.[16] Since his theory leads him to hold that "the dance is the mother of all languages,"[17] he both obscures the potential importance of the natural expressiveness of the body for the development of natural language—a connection most influentially explored by Wittgenstein[18]—and conflates the distinction between language proper and either natural signs (as of grief or pain or hunger) or conventional signs (symbols) that may even employ natural signs intermittently within a system of conventionalized movements. It is not to the point that a sustained use of bodily movements to which we may assign relatively determinate designative and referential functions (symbols) presupposes genuine linguistic ability. Sometimes, as in the case of the chimpanzee, the linguistic competence of human trainers may be sufficient to account for first providing representational symbols that the chimpanzee can then acquire and use; also, the chimpanzee may thereby proceed, to some extent at least, to acquire the barest rudiments of language; and it may also be possible (as David Premack seems to believe) that the chimpanzee is natively capable of producing relatively discrete symbols prior to the development of anything that could be characterized as fully linguistic behavior.[19] In any event, Collingwood does not address such distinctions at all. Instead, he merely says that he is using "the word 'language' to signify any controlled and expressive bodily activity"; that *any* form of expressive bodily gesture is to be counted a language, and that, in that sense, "dance is the mother of all languages."[20] On the strength of this *passage* from expressive gesture (symbolic, because "controlled" or deliberate) to language, Collingwood concludes that "Art must be language."[21] His remarks, therefore, hardly bear on the thesis here advanced; they merely recommend a peculiarly loose and generous use of the term "language."

It is also important, in speaking of the minimal conditions of language, to make provision for the performance of speech acts of distinctive kinds—as of asserting, querying, commanding, advising, and the like; and, consequently, to make provisions for assigning truth values or compliance values or the like to sentences or utterances used in performing such acts.[22] But there seems to be no plausible sense in which the artist "uttering" his work of art straightforwardly performs a speech act or an act suitably analogous to a speech act. In the context of a wide-ranging discussion of problems of meaning in the arts, Göran Hermerén, for one, is candidly puzzled by the issue. Thus Hermerén says:

> Personally, I am inclined to deny that an artist in a painting can state beliefs or promise to do things in the same sense of "state" and "promise" as he can state or promise to do things by uttering certain words in certain kinds of situations. However, this is a complex issue, and it cannot be discussed here. . . . It is controversial how far the analogy between art and languages is illuminating, but the concepts of art, language, proposition, stating, etc., are still too unclear to permit a rational discussion of this problem at the present moment.[23]

But, of course, apart from our intuitions—which must simply be ranged against those who are willing to construe art as language—the very concept of a speech act (that is, of illocutionary acts, of full-fledged speech acts that require the use of language) presupposes that we have at our disposal sentences formed from a lexicon of expressions and facilitating morphemes and the like, in accord with a grammar; for, otherwise, there simply are no utterances to be used in performing any speech acts. This avenue of defense, then, also proves to be a dead end.

Another way of viewing the bearing of speech acts (or analogues of speech acts) on the analysis of works of art is this. Construe *expression* as the performance of some suitably characterized speech act by a speaker; and a work of art, as the *vehicle* of what the speaker expresses. Thus, for instance, on Ernest Jones's interpretation of *Hamlet*, Shakespeare may be said to have expressed a good deal about his Oedipal feelings *in* writing *Hamlet*. *On* the thesis that the artist has expressed himself or his feelings or the like, to say that the *work* expresses the man or his feelings or the like justifies us in inferring from the properties of the work to the feelings of the artist. In that sense, the work may be said to "imply" what we properly infer. This is a vexed thesis that trades on G. E. Moore's well-known use of 'imply'; it also underlies John Hospers's thesis about implied truths in fiction and Morris Weitz's thesis about works of art embodying truth claims.[24] The trouble, in a nutshell, is that the expressive function (no matter how it is articulated) is an ulterior function that, under certain circumstances, may be assigned to works of art, that need not, qua art, exhibit such function. That is, works of art are not as such "utterances" used in performing speech acts or analogous acts of expressing oneself; they are distinctive objects possessing what properties they possess (including expressive qualities) that, on an ulterior theory, we may interpret further as "utterances" so used. Whatever the internal difficulties of accurate interpretation along these lines, the thesis does not show that works of art are essentially, as such, the vehicles of acts of expression but only that, within limits and for ulterior purposes, they may be so viewed. Also to admit this much is not to admit that art is language; only that a work of art may provide evidence about an artist's state of mind and that the relationship of evidence to inference may be reversed, *on an imposed theory,* and put in terms of the implications of initial acts of expression.[25]

Finally, reference to the current literature occupied with our issue cannot possibly be complete without some mention of Nelson Goodman's recent book. Though he speaks of "languages of art," Goodman cautions us, on the opening page of his Introduction, that "'Languages' in any title should, strictly, be replaced by 'symbol systems'. But the title, since always read before the book, has been kept in the vernacular. The nonreader will not mind, and the reader will understand . . ."[26] So Goodman does not hold that art is language. He holds, rather, that the arts are symbol systems and that languages are symbol systems "of a particular kind", that satisfy at least the "syntactic requirements of disjointness and differentiation"[27]—roughly, the requirement that replicas of given marks or inscriptions (what, more familiarly but by way of an ontology unacceptable to Goodman, is expressed by the type-token distinction) are syntactically equivalent to one another and that, as a consequence of being "character-indifferent", "no mark may belong to more than one character";[28] and the requirement that it is theoretically possible that, for any given mark or inscription that does not belong to two given characters, it may be determined that the mark does not belong to the one character or does not belong to the other.[29] I waive here all discussion of the difficulty of applying Goodman's criteria of notationality to actual languages and bodies of art.[30]

Now, the odd thing about Goodman's account is that Goodman goes to great lengths to explicate the nature of notational schemes, that is, symbol systems of a special sort that permit us to identify works of art and their properties; but he has very little to say about works of art *as themselves symbols of some sort.* It is almost as if Goodman's concern is more with the properties of a musical score by which Beethoven's *Fifth* could be identified than with the properties of Beethoven's *Fifth*. He does, however, hold that the arts do function as symbols and supports the thesis by claiming that "works of art or their instances perform one or more among certain referential functions: representation, description, exemplification, expression."[31]

A word first about Goodman's views regarding the notation of artworks, an issue of some complexity that we cannot fully explore in the present context.[32] It is Goodman's contention that the dance is (what he calls) an allographic rather than an autographic art, that is, an art specimens of which (in accord with two rather different, by no means coextensive, accounts that he offers) are either incapable of forgery or numerically identifiable without reference to their "history of production."[33] The use of the term "forgery" may mislead us, since it is etymologically linked to a certain kind of manufacture, as by forge. What Goodman clearly has in mind, however, is that, in music and dance, as opposed to the so-called autographic arts (painting, for instance), it is not true that "the most exact duplication" of a given work can still be counted as not "genuine."[34] Nevertheless, just as an exact copy of a Dürer print, pulled from the original plate as accurately as you please, may still be unauthorized by Dürer—hence, not genuine (forged, or pirated)—so, too, a dance may be unauthorized, pirated, ungenuine intended, say, to be performed only by authorized, ritually clean dancers. There is *no* plausible way in which if the one is conceded, the other can be denied (except *ad hoc*, to confirm the very thesis at stake). But then, the relevance of the "history of production" for allegedly allographic art cannot be denied. In fact, *all* the arts have autographic features, both with respect to genuineness and history of production; *no* arts can be satisfactorily individuated on Goodman's allographic grounds—not even music;[35] and *no* conceptual problems arise regarding individuating works in ways that depend on intentional factors and factors bearing on the history of production.

The fact is that Goodman himself insists that autographic works (paintings and sculptures, for instance) *are* capable of being systematically sorted in terms of numerical identity, in the absence or on the inapplicability of allographic constraints— essentially, in the absence or on the inapplicability of employing a notation like a score. So the applicability of scoring (Labanotation, say) does not altogether preclude ascriptions of the ungenuine and does not provide (without autographic adjuncts) sufficient grounds for the individuation and reidentification of would-be allographic works. Perhaps, bearing in mind music and dance, a better way of putting the point is to say that natural notations that *do* effectively individuate artworks do not meet Goodman's extraordinarily strict conditions of "notationality"— no natural language or notation does or can[36]—*and* such notations invariably incorporate *some* reference to productive intent or origin.[37]

The trouble regarding Goodman's second issue is that, although in performing the functions mentioned, works of art are admittedly performing certain symbolic functions, it is by no means obvious that every work of art (or, characteristic works of art) must, because it is a work of art, perform any particular such function. We must be careful here. Goodman both acknowledges and insists that "a symbol may be a representation even if it denotes nothing at all."[38] So he is not holding that, as symbols works of art need be denotative in any sense—or, correspondingly, need perform any other particular symbolic function. If, on the other hand, he concedes (he does not seem explicitly either to affirm or deny) that a work of art may be such though it perform no symbolic function whatsoever, then he must be holding that, in addition to what minimally makes a work of art what it is, works of art may perform certain distinctive symbolic functions.[39] If, then, it could be shown that these functions cannot convincingly be taken to be essential to (or even strongly characteristic of) art, Goodman's entire thesis collapses. This, of course, is not at all to deny the importance of analyzing such symbolic functions wherever they occur; it bears only on the thesis that art is language or symbolic in nature.

As it happens, the counterargument is quite straightforward. About representation, Goodman says, "Nothing is intrinsically a representation; status as representation is relative to symbol system. A picture in one system may be a description in another; and whether a denoting symbol is representation depends not upon whether it resembles what it denotes but upon its own relationships to other symbols in a given scheme."[40] Since the question of whether a given work of art is or is not a representation or description is alway eligible and may well be decided, on the evidence, in the negative, it cannot be supposed that works of art always or characteristically perform such functions. But the decisive difficulty of Goodman's account lies in what he has to say about the nature of expression: "what is expressed is metaphorically exemplified," "whereas almost anything can denote or even represent almost anything else, a thing can express only what belongs but did not originally belong to it. The difference between expression and literal exemplification, like the difference between more and less literal representation, is a matter of habit—a matter of fact rather than fiat."[41] But Goodman has already held that "exemplification is possession plus reference. To have without symbolizing is merely to possess. . . . [A] swatch [of cloth] exemplifies only those properties that it both has and refers to."[42] So, although a work of art may be *made* to exemplify any suitable property that it possesses, it surely possesses any such property regardless of whether or not it is construed as exemplifying it, say, in being—rather like a swatch of cloth—a sample of such property. Hence, although Goodman holds that expression and not merely exemplification is referential in nature (and, as such, depends on a symbol system), there is no good reason to deny that works of art often simply possess expressive qualities—without representing, describing, or exemplifying anything—and, in possessing expressive qualities, may be said (elliptically) *to express those qualities.* For example, a dance movement may be naturally expressive and, because it is, it may be deliberately used ("controlled," in Collingwood's terms) as expressive, or used even to designate some expressive mood or other. In the first case, it may fairly be said to function in a symbolic way, as expressive, without in the least involving a referential, or exemplificatory, function of any sort. The quibble is important, because in accommodating Goodman's distinction, we see that, for an enormous range of so-called expressive qualities, the distinction does not apply, would be utterly gratuitous if insisted on, and in being applied falsifies the nonreferential nature of much art. In effect, Goodman has conflated the possession of properties with the performance of certain linguistic or symbolic acts or functions.[43] For, it is not the same thing to hold that a work of art that possesses certain (expressive) qualities may, if we wish, thereupon be construed as expressing those qualities and to hold that, in possessing certain (expressive) qualities, a work of art cannot but express those qualities, But if so, his original thesis, that works of art are symbols, fails. *A fortiori,* the thesis cannot be made to entail that an artwork must exemplify its own expressive qualities.

There seems to be no other promising way in which to defend the claim that art is language or that works of art are linguistic or symbolic utterances of some sort—which is not to deny that works of art may be made to perform linguistic or symbolic functions or that particular works may possess the property of serving some linguistic or symbolic function. We must conclude on the evidence, then, that the thesis is false. Also, nothing need be added regarding those fine arts that use language as a medium, simply because the medium is language: novels and poems are language or characters in symbol systems not because they are works of art but because they are formed in and of language. Their existence complicates the analysis of the thesis but does not require adjustment on essentials.

(1974)

Notes

[1]Cf. H. P. Grice, "Meaning," *Philosophical Review*, 66 (1957), 377–88. Grice has adjusted his theory of meaning many times to accommodate serious internal difficulties. Nor is it clear that his essential thesis regarding speakers' intentions is ultimately tenable. I have discussed this in "Meaning, Speakers' Intentions, and Speech Acts," *Review of Metaphysics*, XXVI (1973), 681–95. But, in any case, Grice's emphasis on distinguishing the conventionality of meaning ("meaning$_{NN}$"; that is, "nonnatural meaning") is useful.

[2]Cf. *Art History as an Academic Study* (Cambridge: Cambridge University Press, 1933).

[3]"Art and the Language of Emotions," *Proceedings of the Aristotelian Society*, Suppl. Vol. XXXVI (1962), 215–34.

[4]Cf. Ernest Nagel's review of Susanne Langer, *Philosophy in a New Key* (Cambridge: Harvard University Press, 1942), *Journal of Philosophy*, 40 (1943), 325–26.

[5]Cf. *Philosophy in a New Key*.

[6]*Languages of Art: An Approach to a Theory of Symbols* (Indianapolis: Bobbs-Merrill, 1968).

[7]"Symbolism in the Nonrepresentational Arts," in *Language, Thought, and Culture*, ed. Paul Henle (Ann Arbor: University of Michigan Press, 1958); also, Monroe C. Beardsley, *Aesthetics: Problems in the Philosophy of Criticism* (New York: Harcourt, Brace, 1958), chap. 7.

[8]Cf. C. W. Morris, "Aesthetics and the Theory of Signs," *Journal of Unified Science*, 8 (1939), 131–50.

[9]Cf. E. H. Gombrich, *Art and Illusion* (New York: Pantheon, 1960), chap. 4; also Ruth L. Saw, "Art and the Language of the Emotions," *Proceedings of the Aristotelian Society*, Suppl. Vol. XXXVI (1962), 235–46; and Ruth L. Saw, *Aesthetics* (Garden City: Anchor Books, 1971), chap. 6.

[10]The force of this thesis of so-called generative grammar is one of the principal concerns of Noam Chomsky, for instance; cf. *Language and Mind*, enlarged edition (New York: Harcourt Brace Jovanovitch, 1972).

Thus formulated, the thesis does not (yet) broach the much-disputed issue of innatism.

[11]The issue is explored further, below.

[12]*Aesthetics*, pp. 158–59.

[13]Ibid., p. 168.

[14]But see, below, remarks on Nelson Goodman's thesis.

[15]The distinction required is, it should be said, adumbrated in Stevenson, "Symbolism in the Nonrepresentational Arts." Cf. also Göran Hermerén's discussion of Beardsley's view of depicting, *Representation and Meaning in the Visual Arts* (Lund: Läromedelsforlagen, 1969), pp. 29–33.

[16]R. G. Collingwood, *The Principles of Art* (Oxford: Clarendon Press, 1938), chaps. 11–12.

[17]Ibid., p. 244.

[18]Ludwig Wittgenstein, *Philosophical Investigations*, trans. G. E. M. Anscombe (New York: Macmillan, 1953).

[19]David Premack has argued persuasively, though cautiously, that chimpanzees do appear to be capable of rather developed symbolic activity and understanding; and that they clearly are able to master certain significant preconditions of genuine language—in particular, "same"-"different" predicative contrasts, representations as such, "relations between relations" (syntactic relations). He is inclined (now), having confirmed this much empirically, to resist exaggerated linguistic claims for chimps. Cf. David Premack, *Intelligence in Ape and Man* (Hillsdale, New Jersey: Lawrence Erlbaum Associates, 1976), particularly, pp. 133–34; and David Premack and Guy Woodruff, "Does the Chimpanzee Have a Theory of Mind?" *The Behavioral and Brain Sciences*, I (1978), 515–26; also, Thomas A. Sebeok and Jean Umiker-Sebeok (eds.), *Speaking of Apes* (New York: Plenum Press, 1980). The linguistic ability of chimpanzees is still not entirely clear.

[20]Collingwood, *The Principles of Art*, pp. 241–44.

[21]Ibid., p. 273. His clearest statement on language is the following: "Bodily actions expressing certain emotions, in so far as they come under our control and are conceived by us, in our awareness of controlling them, as our way of expressing these emotions, are language . . . language is simply bodily expression of emotion, dominated by thought in its primitive form as consciousness" (p. 235).

[22]Cf. for instance J. L. Austin, *How To Do Things with Words* (Oxford: Clarendon Press, 1962); and William Alston, *Philosophy of Language* (Englewood Cliffs: Prentice-Hall, 1964).

[23]*Representation and Meaning*, p. 96. It may be mentioned that, although any theory of language must provide for speech acts, a speech-act model of a theory of meaning is inherently weak. Cf. Joseph Margolis, "Meaning, Speakers' Intentions, and Speech Acts."

[24]See Joseph Margolis, *Art and Philosophy* (Atlantic Highlands: Humanities Press, 1980), chap. 12, for a detailed discussion of these views.

²⁵This view is not unsympathetic to Alan Tormey's recent remarks about acts of expression; cf. *The Concept of Expression* (Princeton: Princeton University Press, 1971), chap. 3, particularly p. 93. Tormey's own theory of expression, in chap. 5, is justifiably restricted to expressive properties, which, as we have seen, do not concern the question of art as language.

²⁶Goodman, p. xii.

²⁷Ibid., pp. 40n., 225f.

²⁸Ibid., pp. 131–33.

²⁹Ibid., pp. 135–36.

³⁰See, however, Margolis, *Art and Philosophy.*

³¹Ibid., p. 256.

³²I discuss the issue at some length, specifically with respect to the dance, in "The Autographic Nature of the Dance," *Journal of Aesthetics and Art Criticism,* XXXI (1981), 419–27.

³³Goodman, pp. 113–98.

³⁴Ibid., p. 113.

³⁵The point is that, in music, it is conceptually impossible to specify distinctions of pitch independently of distinctions of tempo; nevertheless, Goodman claims the first services numerical identity, but the second does not (p. 185).

³⁶Cf. Goodman, chap. 4.

³⁷.This, for example, is the upshot of Adina Armelagos and Mary Sirridge's "The Identity Crisis in Dance," *Journal of Aesthetics and Art Criticism,* XXXVII (1978), 129-39. They explicitly note: " . . . dance is a process-art. At least part of the creative process is crucial to the identification of the work." (130). Cf. also Margolis, "The Autographic Nature of the Dance."

³⁸Ibid., p. 226.

³⁹Cf. Joseph Margolis, "What Is When? When Is What? Two Questions for Nelson Goodman," *Journal of Aesthetics and Art Criticism,* XXXIX (1981), 266–68.

⁴⁰Ibid., p. 226.

⁴¹Ibid., pp. 85, 89.

⁴²Ibid., p. 53.

⁴³A somewhat fuller account of these and related distinctions is provided in my "Numerical Identity and Reference," *The British Journal of Aesthetics,* 10 (April 1970), 138–46.

FERNAU HALL
DANCE NOTATION AND CHOREOLOGY

To anyone approaching the study of ballet with knowledge of other arts, what stands out most clearly is the poverty of its traditions. In painting the artist of today is aware of predecessors going back tens of thousands of years to the anonymous geniuses who worked in the caves of Lascaux and Altamira. Traditions are not so long in arts dependent on notation, but an epic poem like *Gilgamesh* takes us back about 5,000 years, and even in music we are aware of a European tradition going back over five hundred years and incorporating scores of masterpieces in an enormous variety of styles.

What we find in ballet is pathetic by comparison. The earliest ballet to survive more or less intact dates from 1786—Galeotti's *Amors og Ballet-mesterens Luner;* unfortunately this is no more than a suite of *divertissements.* (In fact Galeotti, over a very long lifetime, composed a large number of ballets with ambitious themes such as those of *Dido* (1777) and *Romeo and Juliet* (1811); but his successor in Copenhagen—Bournonville—took care that all of these were dropped, and only one trifle preserved.) Then there are fragments of *La Fille Mal Gardée,* also choreographed in 1786 (by Dauberval in Bordeaux). A version of this by Didelot was preserved in Russia and various versions of the latter are still to be seen from time to time in Russia and elsewhere, though unfortunately the staging of a completely new version of this ballet by Ashton for the Royal Ballet makes the fate of what survives in old dancers' memories very precarious. (Ashton's version has many merits: the trouble is that it may well replace the historic one, instead of taking its place alongside it.)

We have to move forward many years before we meet any further ballets surviving into the twentieth century. The work that launched the Romantic Ballet was *La Sylphide,* choreographed by Filippo Taglioni in 1832; this was lost, but by a lucky chance the great Bournonville staged his own version in Copenhagen in 1836—a version probably much better than the original—and this has been preserved with remarkable fidelity (along with a number of other Bournonville ballets) by the Royal Danish Ballet.

Of all the works of Bournonville's great contemporary Perrot only one survives—*Giselle*—and that was his very first major work. (He first worked on this ballet anonymously, composing the title role for Carlotta Grisi, but the ballet we know is derived from a version entirely revised by him in Russia.) *Giselle* has been preserved with great fidelity in Russia; no matter how far-reaching the changes in other ballets, *Giselle* was always regarded as sacrosanct and even the Bolshoi version is remarkably faithful. An Italo-Russian version of *Coppélia* survives—we have no way of knowing how much (if any) of the original French choreography of 1870 remains—but only two other important ballets survive from the nineteenth century, *The Sleeping Beauty* and *Swan Lake*, both with music by Tchaikovsky. (*The Nutcracker* is only of musical interest: choreographically it is a nullity, apart from the great *pas de deux*.) *Don Quixote*, which survives in Gorsky's version of the Petipa original, is little more than a series of bravura entrées, with little relation to the Cervantes novel; and the surviving Petipa ballets such as *Raymonda* and *La Bayadère* are very conventional. There we have the sum total of the so-called "classics" surviving into the twentieth century: nothing by such geniuses as Sallé, Noverre and Vigano, and very little by anyone else but Bournonville and Petipa.

Even in ballets produced in the twentieth century—in fact within living memory—the losses have been very serious; for ballets which have in them choreography worthy of the name (*i.e.* freshly composed dance-images, as distinct from *enchaînements* of classroom steps) suffer very badly in transmission. Any dancer working without guidance from the choreographer tends to change the choreography insensibly from week to week, moulding the line and the rhythms into patterns which are comfortable for him to perform; and when the role is handed over (usually by one dancer teaching it to another) the changes are often enormous; moreover they are cumulative, so that after a few years the choreographer (if still alive) can hardly recognize his handiwork. The ballet-master getting to work on the results of this transmission from dancer to dancer, and seeking to liven up something which seems to him rather pointless (because badly danced, or untrue to the original), is very likely to make further changes. One can see the end-product of this process very clearly in a ballet like *Les Sylphides*, for the versions of the various solos and group dances differ a good deal from company to company. (Here we have a combination of many factors: faulty transmission from dancer to dancer, alterations by ballet-masters, and a muddled heritage from various versions by Fokine.) In the great Tudor ballets—above all in *Dark Elegies,* composed from start to finish in imaginative dance-images—the changes in the absence of the choreographer have been particularly debilitating, though some very fine artists like Gillian Martlew and Anna Truscott do wonders with what survives.

The losses caused by imperfect transmission (or complete failure of transmission) are serious enough; but perhaps even more serious is the depressing effect on new choreography of the weakness of the balletic heritage at any time. In fact every so often the art of ballet has to be re-created almost from scratch after a period of decadence in which people almost forget that ballet ever was a major art. (We are just now emerging from such a period; fortunately it has been a relatively short one because in ballet as in the other arts the pace of change has speeded up.) Any artist (and above all any artist working in the theatre, where problems of co-ordination between the arts are unusually exacting) needs a wide background of knowledge: in fact if he is really original, he is more likely to find the sort of stimulus he needs in the work of artists who lived centuries ago than in that of his immediate predecessors, whose work will in all probability seem to him impossibly dreary and stale. But in ballet this can happen only to a very small extent: the works which survive are those which happened to suit the widely varying tastes of a series of generations, not the tough, spiky masterpieces— the equivalents of the poems of Donne, the late quartets of Beethoven, the paintings of Bosch. A young composer, for example, can learn a great deal about orchestration by studying the scores of a composer like Rimsky-Korsakov: not so the young choreographer.

In the absence of a notation choreography has inevitably failed to achieve the same sort of development in subtlety and complexity that has been going on in music ever since it has been written down: working on paper the composer can keep the whole of his composition in view at one time, both horizontally and vertically, and so he can say things that would be impossible if he had to work entirely from memory. Of course great things are possible without notation, as is proved by the achievements of Indian classical instrumentalists, singers and dancers who improvise within strict rules; but these artists are inevitably confined to what is possible within the range of their own achievements as executants, and also to what is possible in collaboration with a drummer. Western ballet has muddled through to a strange position half-way between the Western and Eastern modes: like Eastern music and dancing it is transmitted by memory only, but it is not improvised and like Western music it relies to a major extent on the composer passing on his ideas to others for execution.

The harsh facts of time and money are here of crucial importance. In fact there is the most extreme and crippling conflict between the artistic needs of the choreographer and almost any ballet company's available resources of money and rehearsal time. Tudor took two years to create *Dark Elegies*, gradually evolving the new kind of dance-image needed to express what he had in mind; and even at the first night (in 1937) the ballet was by no means complete. He was only able to work in this way—a way necessary to him, and in fact to any choreographer attempting something comparable—because the company with which he worked (the Ballet Club, or Ballet Rambert as it was known at its annual West End seasons) was not run on commercial lines: the dancers who appeared at the Mercury Theatre twice a week were paid only their fares. This could not go on indefinitely and when Tudor set up his own company he was quite unable to stage the ambitious new works he had in mind. A generation earlier Diaghilev was able to allow Nijinsky the scores of rehearsals he needed for his revolutionary works *L'Après-Midi d'un Faune* and *The Rite of Spring*, because of the availability of large subsidies from wealthy patrons; but that, too, could not and did not last.

Nowadays a company like the Royal Ballet's touring company or the Ballet Rambert, giving seven performances a week, can manage only a relatively small number of hours of studio work each week—and most of that goes in classes and rehearsals needed to fill gaps in ballets in the repertoire; a choreographer working on a new ballet is lucky if he is given half-a-dozen hours a week—and possibly not one of those hours with his full cast. A company based on Covent Garden, giving about four performances a week, is somewhat better off, but even here the time available is extremely limited. In fact a choreographer is likely to spend at least half the very limited time available to him simply teaching the steps and has not much time for polishing them and producing the dancers. This puts a great premium on choreography so conventional (*i.e.* based on familiar classroom patterns) that dancers can pick it up quickly and build it up in ways familiar to them from class work and from other equally conventional ballets, so that it will look effective on stage. In fact it is hard to imagine anything remotely equivalent to *Dark Elegies* being staged in England today: a choreographer might dream about it, but he would be unwise to put too much of his creative energies into the dream. (It is significant that Tudor never staged the Proust ballet he dreamed about for a long time: after he had been working for Ballet Theatre for several years, and might have been able to stage it, he had moved on a long way artistically and the project repelled him.)

All the factors crippling the development of ballet with which we have been concerned are connected in one way or another with ballet's illiteracy. It remained illiterate not because choreographers and ballet-masters were unaware of the importance of notation: on the contrary, attempts to invent a satisfactory system of dance notation can be traced back to the beginning of the fifteenth century—in fact to the very beginnings of ballet. Some inventors showed a great deal of ingenuity and their inventions were used for a time, mainly by themselves; but they did not survive the death of their inventors and there was no regular progress. Meanwhile music notation became standardized and gradually developed from century to century in harmony with the development of music—and in fact it made this development possible. Music notation took its place at the very core of all study of music and all composition, whereas dance notation remained on the fringe of ballet. In the late eighteenth century we find the great choreographer and theoretician Noverre rejecting notation out-of-hand, because it provided no record of many important aspects of choreography.

Noverre was quite justified in his attitude: the notations developed up to then could not record any of the subtleties which made his choreography dramatically expressive and in fact they assumed the use of conventional classroom steps in a conventional way, so that they were no more than an aid to the ballet-master's memory. In the nineteenth century various attempts were made to develop more comprehensive systems—among them the Stepanov system, an adaptation of music notation, which Sergeyev used to jog his memory when he revived Russian ballets for the Vic-Wells Ballet and the International Ballet. Then in the middle twenties of the present century Laban developed a system which incorporated his theories about modern dance; based on the icosahedron, it used symbols to represent various directions in space (up, forward, down, etc.). This was suited to the dance of the period, but in recent years attempts to adapt it to ballet have come up against great obstacles; for here great precision is needed and even the simplest poses and steps are in fact of great complexity.

The problem which baffled the inventors of systems of dance notation, century after century, was that they had to record something far more complex than music or speech: they had to set down in two dimensions, on paper, the movements of all parts of the body in three dimensions of space and one of time. It is possible to invent a system of notation giving a complete record of all movement, and also to invent one which is simple and practical. What seems impossible is to reconcile these two contradictory requirements. To achieve completeness a great many symbols are needed, and these make any such notation very slow to write and read—in fact quite unsuited to the tough conditions of work in a ballet company where time is always in short supply. Such complexity makes the notation useless for choreographers (who need something which suggests in a clear and simple way the actual movement in space) and makes it intolerable to dancers (who are rarely intellectuals). In the early years of this century, the Stepanov notation was taught at the Maryinsky, but the dancers hated it, and forgot it as soon as possible.

This was the situation which confronted Joan and Rudolf Benesh in 1947 when they set to work on dance notation. That they succeeded where so many other brilliant people had failed was probably due to two things: they started with a correct understanding of the very complex nature of the problem, and they brought together a wide variety of talents and experience (in addition to inventiveness and originality): in fact the problems they faced were (like many others which have baffled scientists for years) too complex for any one person to solve. Joan Benesh was a dancer, producer and choreographer; Rudolf Benesh was a very unusual combination of painter (with a special feeling for line and a fondness for drawing dancers) and musician.

They adopted two principles as fundamental. First, the system of notation had to begin and remain essentially visual (without the efflorescence of symbols which made previous systems impractical); and, second, it had to be integrated with music notation, taking advantage of the centuries of development of the latter and simplifying the work of relating the dancing to the music. They held fast to these guiding principles through all the years of development as they moved on from recording the movements of one dancer to the scoring of complete ballets. In fact the two principles helped them to maintain the essential combination of simplicity and completeness and at the same time to make the whole system homogeneous. (Any one problem could be solved in a variety of ways—but only one solution was true to the basic pattern, and to find this solution often demanded months or even years of work.)

But the germ-invention came very quickly to Rudolf Benesh after the problem had been posed to him by Joan Benesh. The germ-invention had the simplicity of genius: as with so many great inventions, it looks quite obvious by hindsight. Rudolf Benesh took the five-line stave of music, and imagined a dancer standing in front of it, as if it were a wall. Simple marks on the stave recorded the positions of the hands and the feet and made it possible to reconstruct the line of the body very accurately so long as the dancer remained in the plane of the "wall" and did not bend his arms or legs. If he bent his arms or legs, crosses indicated the position of elbows or knees. And if he moved out of the plane of the "wall," simple changes in the signs indicated extension in the third dimension, in front of or behind the "wall."

This was only the beginning. The Beneshes then found that they could draw movement-lines, uniting an infinite number of positions of the limbs and showing the exact path of movement in space: this was something completely new in notation, making it possible to compress an enormous amount of information into one simple line easily drawn and easily read; in fact the movement-lines were just as important as the original germ-invention. Now it was possible to make a single but precise and complete record of the dancing of a single person no matter what technique or style was used or how unconventional the dance-images; and this in turn made it possible to build up a full score without generating a mass of symbols so complex that no one could read them. In fact the Beneshes had to develop systems for showing, at each moment in time, the movements of the limbs, trunk, head, etc. of each person on the stage; the rhythm of his movements, and their relationship with the rhythm of the music; his position on the stage; the direction he faced and the direction he moved—two quite distinct things; his spatial relationship to the other dancers; and many other things. By this time Joan Benesh had joined the Royal Ballet, and she tried out all their solutions of the various problems on ballets in the repertoire (which covered a variety of styles).

A great deal has happened since those early pioneering days. The Benesh Notation is now established as an important element within British ballet, and is spreading to other countries. It is taught to the students in the schools associated with the two leading British companies (the Royal Ballet and the Ballet Rambert) and notators are at work in companies in eight countries apart from Britain. The work is naturally most advanced in the Royal Ballet, which has two staff notators.

From the point of view of a company like the Royal Ballet notation is of vital importance because it speeds up and makes far more accurate the revival of a ballet that has been dropped from the repertoire or has to be transferred to another section of the company. In fact the scores are so accurate and so easily read that notators who do not know a ballet can produce it from the score—as happened recently when a staff notator of the Royal Ballet's touring company produced *Sylvia* for this company. In future years, when enough dancers trained in notation have joined a company, the producers will be able to hand out parts for the dancers to learn in the same way that producers of plays hand out scripts to the actors.

The eventual impact on choreography is likely to be of great importance and is bound to be a complex one. The choreographer can work out his ballets on paper before reaching the rehearsal room, trying out various ways of making his effects and evolving structures in space and time far more complex than those possible when (as in the past) he had to rely on his memory and that of the dancers. One thing at least is certain: he is likely to make a more subtle use of music. Already one can see some possibilities for the future in the compositions of students at the Royal Ballet school, produced as an integral part of their studies of notation itself and based on close analysis of the music by means of a rhythm notation developed for this purpose. The choreographic score taken to rehearsal can incorporate the results of trials on dancers and the choreographer can concentrate on production, using assistants to teach the movements: this will make it possible for a choreographer to achieve far more original and expressive images within the time available.

But the indirect results of the rise of notation are likely to be equally far-reaching. Now, at last, it is becoming possible for young choreographers to master their craft by analysing the works of the great masters of the past and present, just as young film directors do at great film schools such as the one at Lodz, cradle of a number of great Polish directors. At present young choreographers show a sadly limited notion of the nature and potentialities of choreography and their attempts at producing original work, breaking away from what they know, tend to be pathetically empty—being no more than experiments for the sake of experiment.

What we are concerned with here is something so new that when an Institute was formed to foster its development a new name had to be coined: choreology. The Institute of Choreology was, in fact, formed in July of 1962, with a number of objects— among them the formation of a library of choreographic scores (not only of important ballets, but also of traditional classical and folk dances of the East and West); study and analysis of scores; and the fostering of training in composition.

Choreology—the study of all forms of dance through nota- tion—is still only in its early stages; but enough work has already been done to give hints of the sort of discoveries that will be made. When Joan Benesh notated *Petrushka* she discov- ered aspects of Fokine's choreography which had never been suspected before, because they could only emerge when the "polychory" (choreographic counterpoint) was spread out on a page. Looking at the score of the Finale of the dance of the nurses, coachmen and grooms in Scene 4, she found this pattern:

Bar	1	2	3	4	5	6	7	8	9	10	11	12	13	14
Men	a	a	b	c	d	d	e	f	g	g	h	i	a	a
Women			A	B	C	C	D	D	E	F	g	g	A	B

Against musical phrases of fourteen bars the men and women dance in phrases of twelve bars, but the men start two bars ahead of the women and keep this separation through this section of the dance. Though the men and women have different steps fit- ted to the music in different ways, their dances combine together in a delightfully satisfying manner, partly because they have the same structure within the phrase (apart from the choreographic cadence *h, i* which is not found in the women's dance). What is more (and this is a stroke of genius) Fokine unites the two phrases with a repeated pattern of steps *g, g* which is performed both by the men and the women at relatively the same point in their respective phrases.

The importance of this sort of analysis for aspirant choreographers is obvious: by combining their studies with exercises in composition (on paper and with dancers) they can move forward towards a professional mastery of their art which up to now has been possible only for the isolated genius. Knowledge and training cannot, of course, provide a substitute for talent; what they can do is help the choreographer to make the most of his talent—and this is what the art of ballet desperately needs at the present time, when the fashionable styles of recent decades are clearly moribund and there is a real chance of new and creative styles emerging.

(1964)

NELSON GOODMAN
From LANGUAGES OF ART

THE ROLE OF NOTATIONS

1. A problem concerning authenticity is raised by the rather curious fact that in music, unlike painting, there is no such thing as a forgery of a known work. There are, indeed, compositions falsely purporting to be by Haydn as there are paintings falsely purporting to be by Rembrandt; but of the *London Symphony*, unlike the *Lucretia*, there can be no forgeries. Haydn's manuscript is no more genuine an instance of the score than is a printed copy off the press this morning, and last night's performance no less genuine than the premiere. Copies of the score may vary in accuracy, but all accurate copies, even if forgeries of Haydn's manuscript, are equally genuine instances of the score. Performances may vary in correctness and quality and even in 'authenticity' of a more esoteric kind; but all correct performances are equally genuine instances of the work.[1] In contrast, even the most exact copies of the Rembrandt painting are simply imitations or forgeries, not new instances, of the work. Why this difference between the two arts?

Let us speak of a work of art as *autographic* if and only if the distinction between original and forgery of it is significant; or better, if and only if even the most exact duplication of it does not thereby count as genuine.[2] If a work of art is autographic, we may also call that art autographic. Thus painting is autographic, music nonautographic, or *allographic*. These terms are introduced purely for convenience; nothing is implied concerning the relative individuality of expression demanded by or attainable in these arts. Now the problem before us is to account for the fact that some arts but not others are autographic.

2. Why, then, can I no more make a forgery of Haydn's symphony or of Gray's poem than I can make an original of Rembrandt's painting or of his etching *Tobit Blind?* Let us suppose that there are various handwritten copies and many editions of a given literary work. Differences between them in style and size of script or type, in color of ink, in kind of paper, in number and layout of pages, in condition, etc., do not matter. All that matters is what may be called *sameness of spelling:* exact correspondence as sequences of letters, spaces, and punctuation marks. Any sequence—even a forgery of the author's manuscript or of a given edition—that so corresponds to a correct copy is itself correct, and nothing is more the original work than is such a correct copy. And since whatever is not an original of the work must fail to meet such an explicit standard of correctness, there can be no deceptive imitation, no forgery, of that work. To verify the spelling or to spell correctly is all that is required to identify an instance of the work or to produce a new instance. In effect, the fact that a literary work is in a definite notation, consisting of certain signs or characters that are to be combined by concatenation, provides the means for distinguishing the properties constitutive of the work from all contingent properties—that is, for fixing the required features and the limits of permissible variation in each. Merely by determining that the copy before us is spelled correctly we can determine that it meets all requirements for the work in question. In painting, on the contrary, with no such alphabet of characters, none of the pictorial properties— none of the properties the picture has as such—is distinguished as constitutive; no such feature can be dismissed as contingent, and no deviation as insignificant. The only way of ascertaining that the *Lucretia* before us is genuine is thus to establish the historical fact that it is the actual object made by Rembrandt.

Accordingly, physical identification of the product of the artist's hand, and consequently the conception of forgery of a particular work, assume a significance in painting that they do not have in literature.[3]

What has been said of literary texts obviously applies also to musical scores. The alphabet is different; and the characters in a score, rather than being strung one after the other as in a text, are disposed in a more complex array. Nevertheless, we have a limited set of characters and of positions for them; and correct spelling, in only a slightly expanded sense, is still the sole requirement for a genuine instance of a work. Any false copy is wrongly spelled—has somewhere in place of the right character either another character or an illegible mark that is not a character of the notation in question at all.

But what of performances of music? Music is not autographic in this second stage either, yet a performance by no means consists of characters from an alphabet. Rather, the constitutive properties demanded of a performance of the symphony are those *prescribed in* the score; and performances that comply with the score may differ appreciably in such musical features as tempo, timbre, phrasing, and expressiveness. To determine compliance requires, indeed, something more than merely knowing the alphabet; it requires the ability to correlate appropriate sounds with the visible signs in the score—to recognize, so to speak, correct pronunciation though without necessarily understanding what is pronounced. The competence required to identify or produce sounds called for by a score increases with the complexity of the composition, but there is nevertheless a theoretically decisive test for compliance; and a performance, whatever its interpretative fidelity and independent merit, has or has not all the constitutive properties of a given work, and is or is not strictly a performance of that work, according as it does or does not pass this test. No historical information concerning the production of the performance can affect the result. Hence deception as to the facts of production is irrelevant, and the notion of a performance that is a forgery of the work is quite empty.

Yet there are forgeries of performances as there are of manuscripts and editions. What makes a performance an instance of a given work is not the same as what makes a performance a premiere, or played by a certain musician or upon a Stradivarius violin. Whether a performance has these latter properties is a matter of historical fact; and a performance falsely purporting to have any such property counts as a forgery, not of the musical composition but of a given performance or class of performances.

The comparison between printmaking and music is especially telling. We have already noted that etching, for example, is like music in having two stages and in being multiple in its second stage; but that whereas music is autographic in neither stage, printmaking is autographic in both. Now the situation with respect to the etched plate is clearly the same as with respect to a painting: assurance of genuineness can come only from identification of the actual object produced by the artist. But since the several prints from this plate are all genuine instances of the work, however much they differ in color and amount of ink, quality of impression, kind of paper, etc., one might expect here a full parallel between prints and musical performances. Yet there can be prints that are forgeries of the *Tobit Blind* but not performances that are forgeries of the *London Symphony*. The difference is that in the absence of a notation, not only is there no test of correctness of spelling for a plate but there is no test of compliance with a plate for a print. Comparison of a print with a plate, as of two plates, is no more conclusive than is comparison of two pictures. Minute discrepancies may always go unnoticed; and there is no basis for ruling out any of them as inessential. The only way of ascertaining whether a print is genuine is by finding out whether it was taken from a certain plate.[4] A print falsely purporting to have been so produced is in the full sense a forgery of the work.

Here, as earlier, we must be careful not to confuse genuineness with aesthetic merit. That the distinction between original and forgery is aesthetically important does not, we have seen, imply that the original is superior to the forgery. An original painting may be less rewarding than an inspired copy; a damaged original may have lost most of its former merit; an impression from a badly worn plate may be aesthetically much further removed from an early impression than is a good photographic reproduction. Likewise, an incorrect performance, though therefore not strictly an instance of a given quartet at all, may nevertheless— either because the changes improve what the composer wrote or because of sensitive interpretation—be better than a correct performance.[5] Again, several correct performances of about equal merit may exhibit very different specific aesthetic qualities— power, delicacy, tautness, stodginess, incoherence, etc. Thus even where the constitutive properties of a work are clearly distinguished by means of a notation, they cannot be identified with the aesthetic properties.

Among other arts, sculpture is autographic; cast sculpture is comparable to printmaking while carved sculpture is comparable to painting. Architecture and the drama, on the other hand, are more nearly comparable to music. Any building that conforms to the plans and specifications, any performance of the text of a play in accordance with the stage directions, is as original an instance of the work as any other. But architecture seems to differ from music in that testing for compliance of a building with the specifications requires not that these be pronounced, or transcribed into sound, but that their application be understood. This is true also for the stage directions, as contrasted with the dialogue, of a play. Does this make architecture and the drama less purely allographic arts? Again, an architect's plans seem a good deal like a painter's sketches; and painting is an autographic art. On what grounds can we say that in the one case but not the other a veritable notation is involved? Such questions cannot be answered until we have carried through some rather painstaking analysis.

Since an art seems to be allographic just insofar as it is amenable to notation, the case of the dance is especially interesting. Here we have an art without a traditional notation; and an art where the ways, and even the possibility, of developing an adequate notation are still matters of controversy. Is the search for a notation reasonable in the case of the dance but not in the case of painting? Or, more generally, why is the use of notation appropriate in some arts but not in others? Very briefly and roughly, the answer may be somewhat as follows. Initially, perhaps, all arts are autographic. Where the works are transitory, as in singing and reciting, or require many persons for their production, as in architecture and symphonic music, a notation may be devised in order to transcend the limitations of time and the individual. This involves establishing a distinction between the constitutive and the contingent properties of a work (and in the case of literature, texts have even supplanted oral performances as the primary aesthetic objects). Of course, the notation does not dictate the distinction arbitrarily, but must follow generally— even though it may amend—lines antecedently drawn by the informal classification of performances into works and by practical decisions as to what is prescribed and what is optional.

Amenability to notation depends upon a precedent practice that develops only if works of the art in question are commonly either ephemeral or not producible by one person. The dance, like the drama and symphonic and choral music, qualifies on both scores, while painting qualifies on neither.

The general answer to our somewhat slippery second problem of authenticity can be summarized in a few words. A forgery of a work of art is an object falsely purporting to have the history of production requisite for the (or an) original of the work. Where there is a theoretically decisive test for determining that an object has all the constitutive properties of the work in question without determining how or by whom the object was produced, there is no requisite history of production and hence no forgery of any given work. Such a test is provided by a suitable notational system with an articulate set of characters and of relative positions for them. For texts, scores, and perhaps plans, the test is correctness of spelling in the notation; for buildings and performances, the test is compliance with what is correctly spelled. Authority for a notation must be found in an antecedent classification of objects or events into works that cuts across, or admits of a legitimate projection that cuts across, classification by history of production; but definitive identification of works, fully freed from history of production, is achieved only when a notation is established. The allographic art has won its emancipation not by proclamation but by notation.

3. The possibility of a notation for the dance was one of the initial questions that led to our study of notational systems. Because the dance is visual like painting, which has no notation, and yet transient and temporal like music, which has a highly developed standard notation, the answer is not altogether obvious; and ill-grounded negatives and irresponsible affirmatives have been put forth about equally often.

The ill-grounded negatives rest on the argument that the dance, as a visual and mobile art involving the infinitely subtle and varied expressions and three-dimensional motions of one or more highly complex organisms, is far too complicated to be captured by any notation. But, of course, a score need not capture all the subtlety and complexity of a performance. That would be hopeless even in the comparatively simpler art of music, and would always be pointless. The function of a score is to specify the essential properties a performance must have to belong to the work; the stipulations are only of certain aspects and only within certain degrees. All other variations are permitted; and the differences among performances of the same work, even in music, are enormous.

The irresponsible affirmative answers consist of pointing out that a notation can be devised for almost anything. This, of course, is irrelevant. The significant issue is whether in terms of notational language we can provide real definitions that will identify a dance in its several performances, independently of any particular history of production.

For such real definitions to be possible there must, as we have seen, be an antecedent classification of performances into works that is similarly independent of history of production. This classification need not be neat or complete but must serve as a foil, a scaffolding, a springboard, for the development of a full and systematic classification. That the requisite antecedent classification exists for the dance seems clear. Prior to any notation, we make reasonably consistent judgments as to whether performances by different people are instances of the same dance. No theoretical barrier stands in the way of developing a suitable notational system.

Practical feasibility is another matter, not directly in question here. The antecedent classification is so rough and tentative that the decisions to be made are many, intricate, and consequential. And inadvertent violation of one of the syntactic or semantic requirements can easily result in a non-notational language or a system that is no language at all. Bold and intelligent systematization is called for, along with a good deal of care.

Among notations that have been proposed for the dance, the one called *Labanotation*[6] after the inventor, Rudolf Laban, seems deservedly to have gained most recognition. An impressive scheme of analysis and description, it refutes the common belief that continuous complex motion is too recalcitrant a subject-matter for notational articulation, and discredits the dogma that successful systematic description depends in general upon some inherent amenability—some native structural neatness—in what is described. Indeed, the development of Laban's language offers us an elaborate and intriguing example of the process that has come to be called "concept formation".

How far, though, does the system meet the theoretical requirements for a notational language? I can answer only tentatively, from an inadequate knowledge of the system. That the characters

are syntactically disjoint seems clear.* Satisfaction of the requirements of finite differentiation is less easily ascertained; but Laban
avoids a good many pitfalls here. For example, one naturally
looks for a violation in the directional indications, since if every
different angle of a line stands for a different direction, neither
the syntactic nor the semantic requirement of differentiation is
fulfilled. But in Labanotation, direction of facing is indicated by
a "direction pin" in any of eight positions disposed at equal
intervals around the full horizontal circle (Figure 1); and a direction halfway between any two proximate directions among these
eight is indicated by combining the signs for the two (e.g., as in
Figure 2).

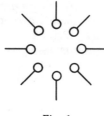

Fig. 1   Fig. 2

This device admits of no further iteration to indicate directions
between two proximate directions among the sixteen. Elsewhere
in the system, differentiation is often achieved just as decisively
as here. One is alerted for trouble by such a statement as: "The
relative length of the direction symbol shows its time value"; but
here, as in music, time is divided into beats, and the least difference in duration provided for in the language is presumably the
same as in standard musical notation.[7]

*The reader need not be fully conversant with the several technical terms
occurring in these paragraphs. Briefly, features of a symbol system apart from
its interpretation are *syntactic*; features dependent upon interpretation of the
system are *semantic*. An alphabet is normally 'syntactically disjoint and differentiated'—that is consists of distinct characters; a column of mercury on the
other hand does not thus divide into distinct characters. The numbers on the
dial of a pill counter are 'semantically disjoint and differentiated' as well, while
an ungraduated thermometer is not. Language—e.g., English—is syntactically
but not semantically 'disjoint and differentiated'; its words are made up of letters from the alphabet but there is no like segregation of its field of application.
For further explanation, see *Languages of Art*, chapter 4.

Like standard musical notation, Labanotation provides for more and less specific scoring, and so violates the condition of semantic disjointness. The *ad lib* signs and the explicit license to describe in detail or leave open certain aspects of a movement[8] have much the same effect as do the free-cadenza and figured-bass notations in music. The result is that identity of a work will not be preserved in every chain of alternating steps between scores and performances. The flexibility offered may be welcomed by the choreographer or composer, and does not affect score-to-performance steps; but it leaves the performance-to-score steps insufficiently determined until the specificity of the scoring is stipulated. Labanotation as a whole is a discursive language comprising several notational subsystems; and in some cases, a class of performances may be a work relative to one but not another of these notational systems.

So far, I have been considering only the basic vocabulary. Some of the other symbolism introduced cannot be embraced in any notational system. A prime example is the use of words or pictures to indicate physical objects involved in the dance.[9] If object-words in general are admitted, then semantic disjointness and differentiation are sacrificed and we have a discursive language. If object-sketches in general are admitted, then syntactic differentiation goes by the board, too, and we do not even have a language. One remedy would be to restrict the admitted words or pictures very severely in appropriate ways. Another, suggested earlier for tempo-words in music and stage directions in the drama, would be to treat these characters not as integral parts of a score at all but as supplementary and nondefinitive. Whether this is fitting depends upon whether (as seems fair enough) a performance employing different objects or even none is an instance of the same dance, just as a performance of *Hamlet* in modern dress and without scenery or accessories is an instance of the same play.

All in all, Labanotation passes the theoretical tests very well—about as well as does ordinary musical notation, and perhaps as well as is compatible with practicality. I am not saying that we have here a good or effective notational system for the dance, that the decisions embodied in it are sound or happy or consistent. Such an appraisal by a layman would be impertinent and worthless. By extensive use, the language may be found unsatisfactory or become traditional enough to acquire authority. If this or another language becomes standard enough, its underlying analysis of movement into factors and particles will prevail; arbitrary decisions will blossom into absolute truth, and expedient units for discourse ripen into the ultimate components of reality—awaiting revolution.

Laban conceived his system as a notation not merely for dance but for human movement in general, and went on to develop and supplement the system as a means for analyzing and classifying all human physical activities. The need for some such system is especially apparent, for example, in industrial engineering and in psychological experimentation. Whether the experimenter or the subject repeats his behavior on a second occasion depends upon the criteria of identity of behavior that are applied; and the problem of formulating such criteria is the problem of developing a notational system. As for nonhuman movement, a zoologist has recently proposed an entertaining and illuminating method of codifying the various gaits of horses.[10]

(1968)

Notes

[1]There may indeed be forgeries of performances. Such forgeries are performances that purport to be by a certain musician, etc; but these, if in accordance with the score, are nevertheless genuine instances of the work. And what concerns me here is a distinction among the arts that depends upon whether there can be forgeries of works, not upon whether there can be forgeries of instances of works. See further what is said in section 2 concerning forgeries of editions of literary works and of musical performances.

[2]This is to be taken as a preliminary version of a difference we must seek to formulate more precisely. Much of what follows in this chapter has likewise the character of an exploratory introduction to matters calling for fuller and more detailed inquiry in later chapters.

[3]Such identification does not guarantee that the object possesses the pictorial properties it had originally. Rather, reliance on physical or historical identification is transcended only where we have means of ascertaining that the requisite properties are present.

[4]To be original a print must be from a certain plate but need not be printed by the artist. Furthermore, in the case of a woodcut, the artist sometimes only draws upon the block, leaving the cutting to someone else—Holbein's blocks, for example, were usually cut by Lützelberger. Authenticity in an autographic art always depends upon the object's having the requisite, sometimes rather complicated, history of production; but that history does not always include ultimate execution by the original artist.

[5]Of course, I am not saying that a correct(ly spelled) performance is correct in any of a number of other usual senses. Nevertheless, the composer or musician is likely to protest indignantly at refusal to accept a performance with a few wrong notes as an instance of a work; and he surely has ordinary usage on his side. But ordinary usage here points the way to disaster for theory.

[6]Laban was working on the matter in Vienna as early as the 1920's. He published *Choreographie* (Jena, Eugen Diederichs, 1926); *Effort*, with F. C. Lawrence (London, MacDonald & Evans, Ltd., 1947); and *Principles of Dance and Movement Notation* (London, MacDonald & Evans, Ltd., 1956). A convenient and well-illustrated exposition by Ann Hutchinson is available in a paperback book, *Labanotation* (Norfolk, Conn., New Directions, 1961), which is cited in the next three footnotes. One of the competing systems has been proposed by Rudolf and Joan Benesh in *An Introduction to Dance Notation* (London, Adam & Charles Black, Ltd., 1956). I leave it as an exercise for the reader to compare the Laban and Benesh systems in the light of the principles set forth in the present book.

A very impressive system of notation for dance and movement in general has been developed by Noa Eshkol and Abraham Wachsman at the Research Center for Movement Notation in Tel Aviv. This system seems to offer important advantages, and deserves close study. It is set forth in *Movement Notations* (Weidenfeld & Nicolson, London 1958) and in a number of other publications. [I was not familiar with this system when I wrote *Languages of Art*.]

[7]Or less. The least duration indicated by any of the characters actually presented or mentioned in *Labanotation* (p. 52) is one-sixteenth of a beat, probably because at even the slowest normal tempo, that is the shortest time in which a dancer can be expected to execute a distinct and recognizable unit of movement. But so long as a limit is set, just where does not matter.

[8]For use of the *ad lib* signs, see *Labanotation*, pp. 88, 187. On permitted variance in specificity of scoring, see e.g., pp. 59, 262. In such passages we find, I think, the significance of the introductory statement: "Labanotation allows for any degree of specificity" (p. 6). Read as meaning that the system allows for specification to within any given degree of precision whatsoever, this statement would imply lack of differentiation.

Incidentally, Labanotation seems to be redundant, although whether alternative symbols are actually coextensive is not always clear from the exposition (e.g., see p. 144). We have seen that coextensive characters in music sometimes differ in meaning through entering into parallel compounds that differ in extension; so far I have not discovered any analogue of this in Labanotation.

[9]*Labanotation*, pp. 179–81.

[10]See Milton Hildebrand, "Symmetrical Gaits of Horses," *Science*, vol. 150 (1965), pp. 701-78.

Eshkol and Wachsman (see note 6 above) have applied their system of notation to animal movement in *The Golden Jackal* (Movement Notation Society, Holon, Israel).

JACK ANDERSON
IDEALISTS, MATERIALISTS, AND THE THIRTY-TWO FOUETTÉS

"If in the Black Swan pas de deux the ballerina cannot adequately perform all thirty-two fouettés, may she replace them with other brilliant steps?"

Balletgoers occasionally ponder this question after performances and, for practical reasons, dancers must ponder it, too. A scholarly friend once observed that more than practicality is involved here, for behind the question lies the whole problem of the identity of a dance.

Like a poem, a dance is something everyone can recognize, but no one can define. The definitions advanced often seem commonplace, even banal: thus, almost everyone would agree that a dance is an art work involving movement through space and time. From all the possible movements of which persons are capable, someone selects the limited number of movements which comprise a particular dance. But having summarized the obvious, difficulties still arise, since one can regard the movements in any dance in two distinct—and, at their extremes, nearly irreconcilable—ways. For convenience, I shall call these positions the Idealist and the Materialist, and I use the terms solely in the sense I define here, without reference to other meanings they may possess in philosophy or theology.

Idealist dancegoers regard a dance as the incarnation in movement of ideas or effects; typically, Idealists may not mind that in different productions of what is ostensibly the same ballet steps are changed, provided that the alterations express the same idea, produce the same effect, or illumine the work's central concept. The Materialist, in contrast, regards a dance as an assemblage of specific steps (or, in the case of improvisatory or indeterminate pieces, specific instructions for deliberately unforeseeable steps) from which ideas or effects may be derived. Therefore the Materialist can maintain that it is possible for two productions of the same work to employ identical steps and yet be different in effect—a familiar example being the way in which some ballerinas offer a birdlike Odette, while others emphasize her humanity. To cite a more recent example, there is Emilia in Limón's "The Moor's Pavane." In conversation, Pauline Koner, the role's creator, said that she deplores those dancers who stress what one critic admiringly calls Emilia's "evil abandon," for both she and Limón wanted Emilia to be a warm-hearted confidante. But a Materialist spectator might countenance such an interpretation, provided that steps remain unaltered, for the interpretation would suggest that the steps are capable of many emotional colorations, just as in the theater Hamlets have ranged from pale neurasthenics to stalwart men of action.

In the past, choreographers and balletmasters were frequently Idealists in practice, staging for local companies their own versions of ballets which other choreographers successfully mounted elsewhere. Necessity may have been partly responsible: before the age of air travel, choreographers could not whiz from city to city. Nor did there exist any compact record of a ballet comparable to a score or a playscript. So Bournonville staged his own "La Sylphide" in Copenhagen, while early "Giselle"'s were produced in Italy and America which apparently did not employ the Paris choreography.

However, following the rise of the Diaghilev Ballet and modern dance came emphasis upon the Materialist position. A dance was increasingly regarded as a sequence of specific steps chosen by a specific choreographer. Fokine might tinker with his steps from season to season, modernist exponents of "self-expression" might alter their choreography nightly, but all would rage if they caught someone else trying to do his unauthorized version of "their" dances. Conscientious balletmasters started sorting out their memories with the result that, despite emendations, several older works came to be viewed in Materialist terms—among them the Bournonville "La Sylphide," the Coralli-Perrot-Petipa "Giselle," the Ivanov-Petipa "Swan Lake," and the Petipa "The Sleeping Beauty." Interest developed in notation—and in the copyright laws.

Nevertheless, Idealism again flourishes. As before, expediency may be partly responsible. There exist many fine companies and star performers. What we lack are fine choreographers. We do, though, possess adroit second-rank choreographers, while several top stars also interest themselves in stage production. Consequently, companies find it convenient to produce ballets derived from existing sources which may attract audiences because of the familiarity of their theme or score and which contain big leading roles which can be performed by the local stars and can also be learned by any guest stars who come to town. While the results may be pleasant, the practice may conceivably threaten the integrity of choreographic works.

Before indulging in dire speculations it might be useful to examine how works exist in repertoires. Most contemporary ballets are regarded in Materialist terms. Who would think of doing "his own" version of, say, "Undertow" or "Ballet Imperial"? Tudor and Balanchine themselves may constantly fuss with their ballets: Tudor may assign one ballerina a double role in "Undertow," while Balanchine may redo the mime and scrap the décor and even the very title of "Ballet Imperial." But, as the authors of the works, their changes are comparable to a poet's revisions. No one else, though, would dream of touching these ballets.

In total contrast are works which exist not as carefully preserved choreography, but as scenarios or generalized production notions. The most familiar example of this sort of ballet is "La Fille Mal Gardée." Dauberval's choreography was forgotten long ago. What survives is the idea of a certain kind of ballet in which certain kinds of things happen and, in our time, the Ashton, Balachova, and Mordkin-Nijinska-Romanoff versions have fleshed out that idea in different ways. Yet even when the accompanying music varies, the results are identifiable as "Fille."

More common are works which exist because of an idea which is coupled with a musical score, particularly when no single treatment of these ballets has managed to supersede previous versions (as the Ivanov-Petipa "Swan Lake" superseded Reisinger and Hansen) or to intimidate other choreographers from attempting their own versions. Examples include "Sylvia," "Daphnis and Chloë," "The Rite of Spring," "Romeo and Juliet," "Cinderella," "The Miraculous Mandarin," "Don Juan," and "The Prince of the Pagodas." Related to this type of production are hypothetical reconstructions of older ballets (such as anyone's "Pas de Quatre" and the Gsovsky and Lacotte restorations of Taglioni's "La Sylphide"), as well as "Coppélia" and "The Nutcracker," for which, in effect, no standard choreography now exists, although it should be theoretically possible to find people who could produce older versions of both.

Significantly, most examples of Idealist principles in dance are narrative or thematic, since these works can be summarized in verbal concepts which any choreographer can ponder. Yet, even though abstract dance is almost inevitably the product of Materialist thinking, there have been instances of an Idealist approach to abstraction: after the success of Balanchine's "Agon" several European choreographers did their own "Agon"s, using Stravinsky's music and the general concept of a contest, and certain basic categories of abstraction seem to be dominant from season to season. Presently, the ballet of dreamy-lovers-and-Romantic-music has largely replaced the neat-geometrics-to-Baroque-concerti which flourished a few seasons back.

Judging from European critics and the few works shown here, it would seem that among current choreographers John Neumeier is emphatically Idealist. His ballets often employ existing scenarios, or Neumeier will take a familiar scenario and twist it to emphasize fresh, but thematically related, ideas, as when (according to reports) in his "Daphnis and Chloë" schoolchildren visit the archaeological site where the events of the legend may have occurred and then become involved in a reenactment of the legend. Neumeier's speculations sometimes presuppose considerable audience sophistication. His "Baiser de la Fée" virtually assumes familiarity with the sensibilities of Tchaikovsky and H.C. Andersen, the scenario of Balanchine's "Baiser," and the characteristics of Balanchine's choreographic style. It is refreshing when a choreographer assumes that an audience is intelligent. But what we have seen of Neumeier's works are more interesting for their ideological superstructure than for their actual choreography.

Whatever one thinks of them, their existence poses no threat. But Idealist principles can menace works which have heretofore occupied an honored place in a repertoire. The classics—first "Swan Lake" and "The Sleeping Beauty," and now "Giselle"— are gradually eroding. The influence of Soviet ballet may be partly responsible, for the Russians since Gorsky have stressed ideas for dancing and remain fond of separating the functions of scenarist and choreographer. Such modern ballets as "Spartacus" and "The Stone Flower" have been repeatedly rechoreographed, each time by someone who tries to reveal more clearly than his predecessors the essence of the scenario and score. Similarly, the Soviets use the classics as though they were the dance equivalents of Greek myths, the stories of "Swan Lake" and "The Sleeping Beauty" serving each new choreographer in the same way that the Electra myth has served playwrights from Aeschylus to O'Neill.

A few non-Soviet modern ballets have also been so regarded. Some years ago when Festival Ballet revived Fokine's "Scheherazade" with moderate success, a critic wrote that he thought greater success might have been possible if the ballet had been rechoreographed, the critic apparently considering "Scheherazade" not as steps by Fokine, but as an idea for a ballet. For several years the Royal Danish Ballet tried to get Ashton to rehearse his "Romeo and Juliet." When attempts failed, the company this season presented a totally new "Romeo" by Neumeier. My point has nothing to do with the strengths or weaknesses of Neumeier's ballet (several Danish critics admire it): what does fascinate me here is that the company seems to treat "Romeo and Juliet" not as a specific ballet by Ashton (or by Neumeier either, for that matter), but as an idea for a certain kind of ballet (by any appropriate choreographer) which the Danes ought to produce.

Idealists often accuse Materialists of pedantry for their concern with the establishment of a choreographic text. They like to remind Materialists that choreographers change their ballets and that many old ballets are works by several choreographers (or by a choreographer and his assistants), and they will argue that since certain variations were designed to feature the specialties of particular dancers, it should therefore be permissible for other dancers to introduce their own specialties into these passages.

Idealists are correct in claiming that in watching dance we do not always notice steps as detachable entities. As a dancegoer, I confess that I cannot supply the technical names for most of the steps I see, and I can describe few passages of choreography from memory in elaborate detail. Nor can I recall many passages from Shakespeare by memory. But if substantial changes were made during a performance of Shakespeare's language or someone's choreography, I might feel uneasy. For the changes would suggest that, for whatever reason, a particular work was being remade.

Several Idealist arguments appear less weighty when one examines how the other arts deal with comparable issues. Certain poets have constantly rewritten poems, and their revisions are often included by publishers in variorum editions. Choreographers have likewise changed their dances; frequently, these changes are small, but they can also be extensive. Which version is the "true" version? Since all are by the same choreographer, they might all be called "true." A greater problem is that of determining which is "best," especially since dance companies (and theatrical and musical organizations) cannot publish alternate readings in a variorum. If the choreographer is also the company director, he will probably declare that, despite possible protests to the contrary, his latest version is best. But if the choreographer is not in charge of the company—or, more drastically, if he happens to be dead—then the artistic director, like a scholar studying quartos and folios, must pick and choose among alternates.

That some variations were designed to display their original performers should not deter anyone else from preserving their steps. Artists are inevitably inspired, or limited, by the interpreters they have at hand and tailor their works accordingly. Some passages in Shakespeare are probably phrased as they are because of Burbage's abilities, while the operatic repertoire contains several roles for decidedly odd voices: in "The Magic Flute" alone are such curiosities as the Queen of the Night and Sarastro. But if the creative artist happens to be talented, he does more than devise stunts: from the idiosyncrasies of his performers he invents steps which are both appropriate and beautiful. It is, after all, Odile, not Odette, who does the fouettés. Therefore the choreography's very peculiarities may constitute a genuine artistic challenge to succeeding interpreters.

As for multiple authorship, only obdurate upholders of the purist view that an art work is necessarily the product of a single genius should find it troublesome that ballets may have passages by several choreographers. Many old master paintings contain the brushstrokes of both the master and his students, and successful theatrical collaborations extend from Beaumont and Fletcher to Kaufman and Hart.

However, the performing arts must resolve problems related to a particular kind of multiple authorship. During some, but by no means all, past periods, performers could add ornaments to the music they played or the choreography they danced. Should performers today add comparable ornaments? If so, how many? And of what kind? In dealing with these questions one should remember that the personal touches were only ornaments: decorations added to an existing structure, not a substitution for that structure—an extra trill in the music or turn in the choreography, but no wholesale rewriting. The story is told of the soprano who auditioned for Rossini by singing a heavily ornamented version of one of his own arias. "Very nice," the composer remarked. "Who wrote it?" Rossini later explained that, while he expected his music to be embroidered, he did not want it distorted out of recognition.

At least, since that soprano was Rossini's contemporary, her ornamentations probably contained no gross anachronisms. Adding ornaments becomes more difficult today when one has to make sure that they harmonize with the original. Among the peculiarities of Cranko's "Swan Lake" was the fact that the new choreography did not always blend with the bits retained from Ivanov-Petipa. To avoid comparable discrepancies, musicians study tables of ornamentation and sometimes, instead of inventing their own ornaments or cadenzas, play the conjectural ones suggested by scholars. Therefore, perhaps dancers today ought to be chary about embroidering steps, even where dancers of an earlier generation might have embroidered freely.

A related problem of authorship is peculiar to dance. Since dances are passed down by memory and memories are faulty, gaps exist in some ballets which have to be filled. Thus parts of our Bournonville stagings derive from Hans Beck and Harald Lander. If Beck and Lander, why not Nureyev or MacMillan? The question admits of no conclusive reply, but several factors may be taken into account. Obviously, if gaps exist, they must be filled—preferably with style and taste. In some circumstances, totally new dances may be added to expand a ballet, but they should not displace old choreography. The Royal Ballet was reprehensible when it supplanted Petipa's "Swan Lake" pas de trois with an Ashton pas de quatre (attractive though it was); it is no longer reprehensible now that it dances both divertissements.

Yet even when old choreography is retained, too many interpolations may destroy the character of a work; and the more time that elapses between the date of the original and the date of the interpolations, the greater danger there is of this occurring, since gaps in time also imply gaps in sensibility. Take Bournonville's "La Sylphide," for example. Modern producers wonder whether there should be a solo for Effie. Adding one probably does no mischief, since it can never take more than a few minutes. But what about a full-scale duet for James and the Sylph? A *Dance*

Magazine critic writes that "La Sylphide" is "unsatisfactory" because it lacks "a proper pas de deux." But is what would be proper for Petipa or Balanchine also proper for Bournonville? The very lack—indeed, the impossibility—of physical contact between the principals is part of Bournonville's conception and contributes to the individuality of his ballet. To add a pas de deux might blunt that individuality: when Lander added such a duet for his Ballet Theatre production, some viewers thought the results, though tasteful, made the ballet ponderous. In the same way, despite the arguments that heroes in classical ballets should get chances to dance, the melancholy solos which recently have been devised for the princes in the Tchaikovsky classics not only look disquietingly alike, they usually look uninteresting. Curiously, cutting scenes entirely often produces less artistic trouble than replacing old choreography with new or adding extra choreography to an existing scene: almost nobody pines for the restoration of "Giselle"'s happy ending, while the supposedly complete Russian "La Bayadère" lacks the fifth act which Petipa originally choreographed.

Staging ballets might be less vexing if dance possessed a universally accepted system of notation. Yet there are dancegoers who may secretly rejoice that such a system does not exist. These fans insist that, rather than consisting of steps which may produce effects, a dance consists primarily of effects embodied in steps. Therefore steps may be altered if comparable effects are gained. According to this theory, one might contend that while Camargo, in her time, astounded audiences with entrechat quatre, any revival of a Camargo ballet (granting, for purposes of argument, the possibility of such a thing) should contain not entrechat quatre, which no longer astounds, but some other flashy step. This would then be called preserving the ballet's spirit, if not its letter.

But would it be? For who today can view the eighteenth century so unaffected by the artistic and social upheavals which have transpired since then that he can create choreography which would in all ways be equivalent to genuine choreography of the period? And just what shall our modern Carmago do, if not entrechat quatre? Thirty-two fouettés, perhaps? An obvious anachronism! Yet what step would not be? However, in our Camargo revival, if all the steps were preserved as they existed in her time, then the entrechat quatre—simply for being unlike the others—might still possess theatrical potency of a kind.

It is dangerous to believe that we know for sure what the "real" effects of a dance are supposed to be, for the kinds of effects we treasure may be partially determined by the taste of our age. Not long ago, sincere commentators argued that because Bach was hampered by the provincial musical forces he had at hand, the best way to achieve the true effects of the Bach cantatas was to utilize symphony orchestras and huge mixed choirs. Today, the vogue is for chamber orchestras, ancient instruments, and small all-male choirs, as we now consider sweet radiance more important than massive solemnity. Who knows what we shall feel a decade hence?

Similarly, in dance we have at different times prized different effects. At one time Odette's mimed account of her tribulations was dropped from the second act of "Swan Lake," perhaps because producers considered it stilted. Now it is back, possibly because the sheer multiplicity of Odette's gestures (even if one cannot literally "read" them all) conveys a sense of dramatic urgency. To achieve another effect, Benno no longer participates in the "Swan Lake" adagio. This traditional bit was changed only recently—but the change is well-nigh universal. Presumably the reason for dropping Benno is that it seems odd for a third person to intrude upon a love scene; besides, Benno was only put there in the first place to assist the aging Pavel Gerdt in handling the ballerina. Yet Ivanov, being a genius, made Benno's presence part of the beauty of that scene, for Odette was then able to swoon in a more ecstatic manner than she has been able to do now that a single man must hold her, let her go, and then also catch her.

Perhaps, someday, someone will want to rehabilitate Benno. (He has already turned up in the Ballets Trockadero de Monte Carlo travestie production.) But will people remember the choreography? At least, despite vagaries of taste and textual corruptions, scores exist for Bach. Still, some Idealists would regret the development of dance notation, since they fear that notation might stunt the organic growth of dance by making dance become cut and dried and, finally, mummified.

Arid choreography is always deplorable, but notation need not bring it about. Notation might even encourage individuality. With the standard repertoire notated, producers could feel free to stage that traditional choreography as they pleased—setting "Swan Lake," for instance, in any historical period or in outer space—for the Materialist approach to production implies that at various times the same choreography can be used to produce quite different effects, just as Shakespeare's words have been subjected to Christian, Freudian, Marxist, and existentialist interpretations. Moreover, with standard choreography notated, a choreographer might be emboldened to create a totally new and different ballet based upon a classic story, just as a playwright might reinterpret a classic myth. One trouble with even our most radical revisions of the classics is that they seldom are radical enough. Thus every "Swan Lake" contains a semblance of Ivanov's second act as an obeisance to tradition. But with Ivanov notated, an innovator could choreograph a "Swan Lake" which in no way resembled Ivanov stylistically, just as O'Neill's conception of Electra is stylistically different from that of Sophocles.

Our present willingness to tolerate extensive changes in extant works may be a hangover from the old attitude that dance is not really an important art—that, finally, it does not matter what is danced, provided the results are diverting. Yet in our century dance has gained enormous artistic significance, and so what is danced surely matters as much as how it is danced. If no two productions of any work in the performing arts can ever be exactly the same, the work itself should possess some sort of solid identity and integrity.

Until the time when dance acquires a sense of its own identity, we are left with our original question about the Black Swan: To fouetté or not to fouetté?

Idealists will not hesitate to permit the ballerina to substitute steps, while Materialists would caution against the substitution. Conceivably, the ballerina, reluctant to look less than dazzling, might go ahead and change the steps anyway. Even so, her artistic conscience ought to be reminding her that she still remains at least thirty-two fouettés short of perfection.

(1975)

VI

Dance Criticism

The word "criticism" is commonly applied to many different sorts of writing about the arts. Some of this writing is primarily theoretical and some primarily historical. But in the context of this chapter, we shall define criticism as writing that emphasizes the description, interpretation, and evaluation of particular works of art—which is not to imply that the theoretician and the historian won't also refer to particular works of art, but they do so for significantly different reasons.

The theoretician's primary task is to formulate underlying principles, general rules that apply to broad categories of aesthetic experience. Individual works of art may well prove indispensable to the theoretician, but he will employ them chiefly to illustrate and test these general principles. The historian may focus more directly than the theoretician on particular works of art, but his chief objective will be to reconstruct the work in its original historical context, evaluating it according to the prevailing standards of its own period, rather than the historian's personal standards or those that obtain during his lifetime. The critic, by contrast, will often be called upon to evaluate older works according to his personal standards which originate in the present.

By distinguishing criticism from theory and history in this way, we do not mean to imply that criticism can (or should) ever be wholly divorced from the concerns of history or theory. The critic who writes about a revival of "Giselle" without any knowledge of the historical conventions that inform the ballet is at an obvious disadvantage. (The suggestion that the critic should approach every work of art as "innocently" as possible is very difficult to defend.)

Similarly, if a critic intends to use words such as "represent," "express," or "symbolize" in a responsible manner, he should (at least ideally) be fully aware of the theoretical issues they raise and the questions they beg. Indeed, most of the "abstract" issues raised in other sections of this book (questions about whether or not the dance medium is defined by some essential limitation, the criteria used for assigning individual dances to genres, the difficulties of deciding whether or not a reconstruction of an older work constitutes an authentic instance of that work)— these and countless other theoretical issues have immediate, practical consequences for the working critic. But the critic will raise these issues for the purpose of illuminating particular works of art, rather than as ends-in-themselves.

Of course, the differences in method and philosophy that distinguish individual critics from one another are just as significant (and numerous) as the differences that distinguish critics from historians and theoreticians. In their classic study *Theory of Literature*, René Wellek and Austin Warren distinguish between "intrinsic" and "extrinsic" criticism. Intrinsic critics (most prominently, the so-called "new critics" who dominated literary scholarship in this country during the 1940's and 50's) sought to concentrate the critic's attention on the formal properties of the art object itself rather than on the life of its creator or the subjective responses of its perceiver.

By concentrating on what they took to be the work itself (the actual words of the text) rather than on the historical context in which it was created or the "intentions" of its creator, the new critics sought to ensure that the work retained its aesthetic autonomy, and that it not become merely a tool for illuminating the private life of the artist or the social history of his era. Extrinsic critics, by contrast, argue that information about the work's sources, the historical conventions it utilizes, or the intentions of its creator do not necessarily distract attention from the aesthetic properties of the work. Quite the contrary: knowledge of this sort is often essential to an adequate understanding of the art object.

Critics also differ according to the relative degree of emphasis they assign to description, interpretation, and value judgment. Some critics strenuously resist the temptation to "rank" works of art, believing that such exercises amount to little more than subjective expressions of taste and that preferences of this sort are ultimately beyond dispute ("de gustibus non est disputandum").

Northrop Frye has written derisively of "the literary chit-chat which makes the reputations of poets boom and crash in an imaginary stock market." But many critics argue that judgments of value are unavoidable and that they constitute the ultimate responsibility of the critic. (The English word "criticism" is, after all, derived from the Greek word *krinein* which means "to judge.") Evaluation, such critics argue, is not a hopelessly subjective enterprise. Hierarchies can be erected in a spirit of "disinterestedness" that transcends purely private preferences. Matthew Arnold, for example, defined criticism as "the disinterested endeavor to learn and propagate the best that is known and thought in the world."

Critics often differ widely in their approach to interpretation as well. Some critics conceive of their task as a form of "speculative play" and encourage highly personal, sometimes willfully extravagant "readings" of works, provided that these readings are not at odds with the empirical properties of the art object. Others approach interpretation by way of a hermeneutical system (the Marxist, the Freudian). But those who wish to keep the critic's attention focused more squarely on the "objective" properties of the work, will argue, as did T. S. Eliot, that "interpretation . . . is only legitimate when it is not interpretation at all, but merely putting the reader in possession of facts which he would otherwise have missed."

The function of criticism also varies widely depending on the publication (and public) the critic writes for. Some people insist on a distinction between criticism and reviewing. Walter Kerr, for example, has argued that the reviewer writes for an audience that has not yet seen the work under discussion, whereas the critic addresses a more specialized audience already familiar with the work. The reviewer thereby functions to a greater extent than the critic as a "consumer guide"; his primary responsibility is to describe the work in question and to offer an opinion of its worth. The critic, because he is less burdened by the purely "journalistic" responsibilities of the marketplace, is freer to interpret the work and to discuss the issues that it raises.

These distinctions—between reviewers and critics, between intrinsic and extrinsic approaches to criticism, between critics who interpret works in unabashedly subjective ways and those who don't—apply as much to dance criticism as to the criticism of any other art. But there is no denying the fact that dance criticism is younger and less diversified than the criticism of most of the other arts. Certainly, the student of twentieth-century dance criticism is not confronted with anything even vaguely comparable to the rather bewildering array of "schools"—Freudian, Marxist, Mythic, Formalist—that characterize the criticism of an art such as literature (and dance criticism is virtually untouched by more recent critical methodologies in the other arts based on interpretive strategies imported from linguistics, structuralism, and semiology).

Thus, compared with the labyrinthine complexities of recent literary or art criticism, the existing body of dance criticism appears either embarrassingly naïve or refreshingly straightforward. These differences are not difficult to account for. Unlike painting, literature, and sculpture, dances do not "sit still," permitting the critic to scrutinize them in a spirit of leisurely detachment. The literary critic can stop at will to re-read a difficult passage; the art critic can examine a painting from various distances or walk all the way around a work of sculpture. But the dance critic must make do with a fleeting burst of sensory impressions.

Of course, this is the situation that prevails, to a greater or lesser extent, in all of the performing arts (which are, by definition, temporal and perishable). The theatre critic John Mason Brown once remarked that "to many people, dramatic criticism must seem like an attempt to tattoo soap bubbles." But the drama critic, unlike the dance critic, often has access to a text; and when the time comes to provide the reader with a sense of this text, he need only quote directly from it. (The critic of the visual arts has even fewer problems in this regard, since his commentary can be accompanied by a photograph of the object under discussion.)

Perhaps these difficulties explain why dance criticism places as much emphasis as it does on description (often at the expense of interpretation and evaluation). To the critic of literature or painting, "mere" description may seem rather pedestrian and unambitious. But for the dance critic, "mere" description is not only the most difficult task; it is also one of the most valuable— in so far as the dance critic is helping to establish the physical reality of the dance (or, at the very least, lending some degree of permanence to an otherwise elusive and ephemeral event).

The challenge facing the dance critic is threefold: the enormously difficult task of *seeing* the movement clearly in the first place; then, the almost equally challenging task of remembering what he sees; and, finally, the nearly impossible task of describing what he has seen in a manner that will be comprehensible to the reader (especially one who hasn't already experienced the work being discussed). Lincoln Kirstein once lamented the fact that "even the most detailed and rhapsodic appreciations are usually unintelligible unless you have seen the ballet." Indeed, one of the cruel paradoxes of dance writing is that a literal, moment-by-moment account of what strikes the eye and ear is destined to lose the reader in a thicket of undifferentiated detail. "To write descriptions of dancing," notes Kirstein, "is even more aimless than to paint pictures of music."

And yet, all of the writers anthologized in this section have managed to surmount these considerable obstacles. Significantly, almost all of them are, or at least have worked as, journalists (which is to say, they must address a broad-based public of non-specialists, many of whom have not seen the dance under discussion). Here we encounter another notable difference between dance criticism and the criticism of literature or painting (where the most influential and widely respected critics have been scholars rather than journalists). No doubt, this is a consequence of the high premium good dance criticism places on description, the journalist's forte.

The essays in this section have been arranged chronologically so as to illustrate what we believe to be the general direction contemporary dance criticism has travelled (one that closely parallels the development of "new criticism" in literature). In the course of the last fifty years, dance criticism has developed a steadily improved capacity for precise descriptions of the body in motion. To observe this evolution, one need only compare the writing of Théophile Gautier, probably the most highly regarded dance critic of the nineteenth century with his twentieth-century counterparts, Edwin Denby and Arlene Croce.

Gautier, a renowned poet and novelist, an accomplished journalist, an amateur painter, and the librettist for both "Giselle" and "La Péri," would appear to be ideally suited for the job of dance critic. And at least by nineteenth-century standards, he was. Gautier provides the reader with extremely vivid visual analogies for the dance—images the work evokes in his mind's eye—but alas, he gives us very little sense of what the dance actually looked like (for instance, "Mlle. Taglioni reminded you of cool and shaded valleys, where a white vision suddenly emerges from the bark of an oak to greet the eyes of a young, surprised, and blushing shepherd").

The virtual absence of precise physical descriptions in nine-teenth- and early twentieth-century dance criticism is particu-larly disappointing to dance historians who must rely upon eye-witness accounts of choreography as an aid to reconstruction. This is especially true of works choreographed prior to the exis-tence of film, videotape, or adequate notational systems. All too often, today's criticism becomes tomorrow's history.

Gautier may tell us less than we would like to know about nineteenth-century choreography, but he never disguises the fact that he is primarily interested in writing about the dancers, rather than the dances they perform. In his review of Fanny Elss-ler in "The Tempest," he candidly admits "the literature of legs [that is, choreography] is hardly a subject for discussion; let us come at once to Fanny Elssler." But when he does, Gautier offers us some extraordinarily perceptive comments about the differ-ences between Elssler and her rival, Marie Taglioni:

> Mlle. Taglioni is a Christian dancer, if one may make use of such an expression in regard to an art proscribed by the Catholic faith: she flies like a spirit in the midst of transparent clouds of white muslin with which she loves to surround herself; she resembles a happy angel who scarcely bends the petals of celestial flowers with the tips of her pink toes. Fanny is a quite pagan dancer; she reminds one of the muse Terpsichore, tambourine in hand, her tunic, exposing her thigh, caught up with a golden clasp; when she bends freely from her hips, throwing back her swooning, volup-tuous arms, we seem to see one of those beautiful figures from Her-culaneum or Pompeii. . . .

Unlike most of Gautier's dance criticism, André Levinson's essay about Isadora Duncan is not a review of a particular per-formance, but rather an overview of Duncan's career, an attempt to trace her lineage and assess her ultimate significance. Levin-son began writing about dance in Russia around the turn of the century, but emigrated to Paris after the revolution. He is one of the few dance writers who deserves to be called a "scholar-jour-nalist." (The short reviews he published in Parisian dailies con-stitute some of the most erudite dance journalism ever written.)

Levinson, whose formalist views were discussed in the introduction to Section I, is usually thought of as a die-hard classicist who resisted the innovations of Fokine and Diaghilev. One would therefore expect him to come down equally hard (or harder) on the anti-balletic ambitions of Isadora Duncan; but his attitude toward her in this essay is more complicated than that. He credits her with having created a "new beauty," but he argues that the sources of this beauty are not to be found, as is commonly believed, in antiquity. Rather, Duncan generates an aura that owes more to the English Pre-Raphaelite artists than to those of ancient Greece. Levinson also emphasizes the mimetic and figurative nature of Duncan's dances as well as her ability to endow movement with an illusionistic power of suggestion: "the figurative strength of her gestures is such that the audience can see the sacrificial flowers and vessels in her hands." His descriptions of Duncan in performance help us to understand Susanne Langer's theory that dance creates an illusion of "virtual forces."

Carl Van Vechten is often referred to as the father of American dance criticism, and his work is included here not for its enduring influence, but rather for the key role it played in the development of dance criticism in America. Until quite recently, journalistic dance criticism was not written by specialized dance writers like André Levinson in Paris, but rather by music critics. Van Vechten's career is emblematic in this regard. He was hired by the *New York Times* in 1906 as an assistant music critic, and most of his earliest dance assignments came to him by default. (This is still the situation that prevails at many American newspapers.)

But Van Vechten educated himself "on the job" and quickly became known as America's foremost dance journalist, a reputation that he maintained throughout the 1920's. His concise, five-hundred-word portrait of Anna Pavlova illustrates just how much a superior journalist can accomplish in a (very!) limited amount of space. To Van Vechten, writing in 1920, Pavlova constituted the last of the great classic dancers, a living link to the pre-Fokine era. As for her association with Diaghilev, Van Vechten notes that "with the modern movement in dancing, with which she mistakenly allied herself at one time in her career, she has nothing whatsoever to do."

After Van Vechten, the next important figure to emerge in American dance criticism was John Martin, who wrote for the *New York Times* between 1927 and 1962, seminal years in the history of modern dance. Martin was the very model of the partisan critic. His flag-waving efforts on behalf of modern dance were instrumental in winning wider audiences for this new American art form (in this sense, he anticipates the equally partisan campaign on behalf of post-modern dance conducted by Jill Johnston at the *Village Voice* in the mid 1960's).

Both Martin and Van Vechten made enormous contributions to the early stages of dance criticism in this country, but it is not until the advent of Edwin Denby that American dance criticism achieves a level of distinction comparable to that which prevails in criticism of the other arts. The poet Frank O'Hara once said of Denby, "He sees and hears more clearly than anyone else I have ever known." And indeed, the first thing one notices about Denby's criticism is the unprecedented clarity and precision with which he describes the exact contours of the body in motion. Denby's celebrated description of the adagio section in Balanchine's "Concerto Barocco" is probably the most frequently quoted passage in contemporary dance criticism; and it illustrates, quite vividly, his critical method:

> The correspondence of eye and ear is at its most surprising in the poignant adagio movement. At the climax, for instance, against a background of chorus that suggests the look of trees in the wind before a storm breaks, the ballerina, with limbs powerfully outspread, is lifted by her male partner, lifted repeatedly in narrowing arcs higher and higher. Then at the culminating phrase, from her greatest height he very slowly lowers her. You watch her body slowly descend, her foot and leg pointing stiffly downward, till her toe reaches the floor and she rests her full weight at last on this single sharp point and pauses. It has the effect at that moment of a deliberate and powerful plunge into a wound, and the emotion of it answers strangely to the musical stress.

Note that Denby provides us with a "close reading" of the dance (a precise description of what the bodies are actually doing) as well as a much more subjective description of the feelings and images the movement evoked in him. It is probably no coincidence that so much of Denby's best writing was evoked by the choreography of Balanchine. Balanchine's choreography facilitates "seeing" and Denby rises admirably to the challenge. In other words, a connection exists between Balanchine's desire to focus the audience's attention on the complexities of movement itself (which he accomplishes by eliminating the theatrical "inessentials") and Denby's ability to pay such close attention.

But Denby's approach to dance writing is anything but strictly formalist. In fact, he is particularly good at describing the ways in which a choreographer like Balanchine can explore a subject or tell a story obliquely, without resorting to the literalness of mime. For example, he says of a section in "Agon": "It recalls court dance as much as a Cubist still life recalls a pipe or guitar." Clearly, for Denby, even a cool, formalist ballet like "Agon" has a subject—in this case, "young people competing for fun at the brief height of their power and form."

Although Denby wrote about all varieties of theatrical dance, he remained principally a balletomane. Deborah Jowitt on the other hand, who has been writing dance criticism for the *Village Voice* since 1967, responds sympathetically (and perceptively) to modern and post-modern dance as well as to ballet. Unlike the other articles in this section which focus either on particular works or particular performers, Jowitt's essay about Martha Graham is a more specialized analysis of the choreographer's movement "vocabulary," of its sources, and of the way it has evolved over the years. Jowitt stresses the bold eclecticism with which Graham draws on the straight, narrow look of American Indian dancing, the archaic style of Egyptian friezes, Siamese and Cambodian knee-walks—combining and transforming these influences so as to produce a style that looks "wildly original."

Jowitt is, by her own admission, reluctant to rank or "grade" works of art hierarchically. By contrast, Arlene Croce, founder of *Ballet Review* and dance critic for the *New Yorker*, proceeds on the assumption that evaluative judgments are the sacred responsibility of the critic. The criteria by which she declares that some dances are superior to others are especially evident in her reexamination of Balanchine's "The Four Temperaments," written almost thirty years after the work was premiered. Croce appeals to what is sometimes called "the verdict of the ages," the assumption that the best work is the most lasting work. (And critics like Croce, when evaluating new work, will attempt to think and feel beyond their immediate reactions to the work in an effort to predict whether or not it will last.)

Thus Croce compares "The Four Temperaments" with another, and for her, lesser, Balanchine work of the 40's, "Danses Concertantes." "A masterpiece," she writes, "doesn't so much transcend its time as perpetuate it; it keeps its moment alive. In 'The Four Temperaments' . . . the moment is luminously there. In 'Danses Concertantes,' the moment eludes me."

In what she calls the opening "statement" of the ballet, Croce describes the way in which a ballerina "lifts and lowers the free foot, curls it around the standing leg, and carefully flexes it before arching to full point. We see in short, a foot becoming a point—nature being touched to artificial life." And for Croce, this moment sums up the "story" of "The Four Temperaments": the molding of the classical dancer's body as a symbol of the process by which human beings are transformed into archetypes. This is, of course, an unabashedly "subjective" interpretation of "The Four Temperaments," but Croce is always careful to buttress her "reading" of the ballet with a detailed and more impersonal description of what the dancers are actually doing.

Croce's interpretation of "The Four Temperaments" may help explain why she has not been particularly sympathetic to postmodern dance, a genre that often eschews the very process that Balanchine seems to be celebrating, the transformation of the natural body by classroom technique. But Croce *has* written enthusiastically on numerous occasions about Twyla Tharp, who began her choreographic career as a post-modernist unsympathetic to technical virtuosity, but then gradually re-incorporated technically based dancing (without sacrificing the braininess and conceptual rigor of those early, minimalist works).

Croce particularly admires Tharp's ability to transform "nontheatrical" subject matter so as to make it theatrically legible (a process similar to that depicted in "The Four Temperaments"). In her review of the original version of "Deuce Coupe," Croce discusses Tharp's use of contemporary teenage social dancing and concludes, "no one but Twyla Tharp would have known how to make these dances legible in the theatre. A hundred kids going berserk at a school prom is a powerful but not necessarily a theatrical spectacle. To be realized on the stage, such potency has to be objectified. . . . In the process, it becomes beautiful, but 'beauty' isn't the choreographer's object—clarity is."

And clarity—the ability to *see* clearly—is (clearly) what distinguishes critics like Denby, Jowitt, and Croce from the rest of us. They exemplify what John Ruskin must have meant when he wrote:

> The greatest thing a human soul ever does in this world is to *see* something and tell what it saw in a plain way. Hundreds of people can talk for one who can think, but thousands can think for one who can see. To see clearly is poetry, prophecy, and religion—all in one.

THÉOPHILE GAUTIER
FANNY ELSSLER IN "LA TEMPÊTE"

Mlle. Fanny Elssler has made her reappearance in the part of Alcine in *La Tempête*. The ballet *La Tempête* is a ballet, that is the most favourable remark that can be made about it. Furthermore, it has the advantage of spoiling one of the finest themes for an opera that could ever be imagined. It is not quite clear in this piece why Prospero should be replaced by Oberon; Oberon is inseparable from *A Midsummer Night's Dream,* he cannot move without his wife, Titania; Alcine, that bewitching creation of Ariosto, appears quite out of her element in the isle of *The Tempest,* beside Caliban, and I doubt very much whether Fernando can make him forget that brilliant knight, Roger. But we shall not prosecute too far our observations regarding the intrinsic merit of the theme; the literature of legs is hardly a subject for discussion; let us come at once to Fanny Elssler. Much applause bursts forth and the gauze curtain parts to reveal the captivating enchantress, and no one has any doubt but what the virtuous Fernando will soon be unfaithful to the memory of Lea, Oberon's ward.

Fanny Elssler's dancing is quite different from the academic idea, it has a particular character which sets her apart from all other dancers; it is not the aerial and virginal grace of Taglioni, it is something more human, more appealing to the senses. Mlle. Taglioni is a Christian dancer, if one may make use of such an expression in regard to an art proscribed by the Catholic faith: she flies like a spirit in the midst of the transparent clouds of white muslin with which she loves to surround herself, she resembles a happy angel who scarcely bends the petals of celestial flowers with the tips of her pink toes. Fanny is a quite pagan dancer; she reminds one of the muse Terpsichore, tambourine in hand, her tunic, exposing her thigh, caught up with a golden clasp; when she bends freely from her hips, throwing back her swooning, voluptuous arms, we seem to see one of those beautiful figures from Herculaneum or Pompeii which stand out in

Marie Taglioni and Fanny Elssler. "Mlle. Taglioni is a Christian dancer
... she flies like a spirit in the midst of the transparent clouds of white
muslin with which she loves to surround herself ... Fanny is quite the
pagan dancer; she reminds one of the muse Terpsichore ... (Gautier)

white relief against a black background, marking their steps with resounding cymbals; Virgil's line:

Crispum sub crotalo docta movere latus,

involuntarily springs to the mind. The Syrian slave whom he loved so much to see dancing beneath the pale arbour of the little inn would have had much in common with Fanny Elssler.

Undoubtedly, spiritualism is a thing to be respected; but, as regards dancing, we can quite well make some concessions to materialism. After all, dancing consists of nothing more than the art of displaying beautiful shapes in graceful positions and the development from them of lines agreeable to the eye; it is mute rhythm, music that is seen. Dancing is little adapted to render metaphysical themes; it only expresses the passions; love, desire with all its attendant coquetry; the male who attacks and the female who feebly defends herself is the basis of all primitive dances.

Mlle. Fanny Elssler has fully realised this truth. She has dared more than any other dancer of the Opera; she was the first to transport to these modest boards the audacious Cachuca, without its losing any of its native zest. She dances with the whole of her body, from the crown of her head to the tips of her toes. Thus she is a true and beautiful dancer, while the others are nothing but a pair of legs struggling beneath a motionless body!

(1837)

THÉOPHILE GAUTIER
REVIVAL OF "LA SYLPHIDE"

It must be stated that the Opera lacks ballets and does not know how to find employment for its army of dancers and pretty supers; it appears that the literature of legs is the most difficult of all styles, for no one can succeed at it.

The revivals of *La Fille Mal Gardée, La Somnambule,* and *Le Carnaval de Venise* have only attained a comparative success, without any effect on the box-office receipts.

To see these old-fashioned pieces which delighted our fathers, and whose melodies, ground out by barrel-organs at every street-corner, lulled us to sleep in our earliest years, one became conscious of a kind of bitter-sweet emotion, as though, in rummaging in a corner of some dusty drawer, one came across some iridescent skirts, a few pieces of discoloured lace, a broken fan, with an episode from Rousseau's *Confessions* painted on one side and a pastoral on the other, forgotten relics of a grandmother or a great-aunt, long since departed.

But this altogether poetic sentiment, although not without its fragrance, does not suffice to fill the auditorium at the Opera; besides, the shabbiness of the scenery, completely faded and torn in every fold, forbade the exhumation of these mummies of ballets which, twenty years ago, perhaps, had fresh and youthful bodies and charming features with happy smiles, but which will always seem to us somewhat ridiculous, out-of-date, and old-fashioned.

For some time past there has been talk of Mlle. Fanny Elssler's reviving Mlle. Taglioni's parts in *La Sylphide* and *La Fille du Danube;* the Taglionists gave vent to cries of sacrilege and the abomination of desolation—one would have thought that it was a question of laying hands on the Ark of the Covenant. Mlle. Elssler herself, with that modesty which so well becomes her talent, shrank from encroaching on parts in which her illustrious rival had shown herself to be perfect, but it was not right that so charming a ballet as *La Sylphide* should be struck out of the repertory because of exaggerated scruples; there are a thousand ways of playing, and, above all, of dancing the same character, and the pre-eminence of Mlle. Taglioni in comparison with Mlle. Elssler is a matter than can quite well be contested.

Mlle. Taglioni, tired out from her interminable travels, is no longer what she was; she has lost much of her lightness and her elevation. When she appears on the stage, you always see the white mist bathed in transparent muslin, the ethereal and chaste vision, the divine delight which we know so well; but, after some bars, signs of fatigue appear, she becomes short of breath, perspiration bedews her brow, her muscles seem to be under a strain, her arms and chest redden; formerly, she was a real sylphide, but now she is merely a dancer, the first dancer in the world, if you will, but nothing more. The princes and kings of the North have so applauded her, so wearied her with compliments, they have caused so many showers of flowers and diamonds to fall upon her, that they have weighed down her tireless feet, which, like those of the amazon Camilla, could run over blades of grass without bending them; they have loaded her with so much gold and so many precious stones that Marie full of grace has not been able to take to flight again, and only timidly skims the ground like a bird with wet wings.

Mlle. Fanny Elssler to-day is in the full flower of her talent, she can only vary her perfection and not transcend it, because above very good is too good, which is nearer to bad than may be thought; she is the dancer for men, as Mlle. Taglioni was the dancer for women; she has elegance, beauty, a bold and petulant vigour, a sparkling smile, an air of Spanish vivacity tempered by her German artlessness, which makes her a very charming and very adorable creature. When Fanny dances, one thinks of a thousand pleasant things, in imagination one wanders into marble palaces flooded with sunlight and silhouetted against a deep-blue sky, like the friezes of the Parthenon; you feel yourself leaning on your elbow on the balustrade of a terrace, with roses round your head, a cup full of Syracusan wine in your hand, a white greyhound at your feet, and beside you a beautiful woman with a plumed head-dress and robe of crimson velvet; you hear the thrum of tambourines and the silvery tinkle of small bells.

Mlle. Taglioni reminded you of cool and shaded valleys, where a white vision suddenly emerges from the bark of an oak to greet the eyes of a young, surprised, and blushing shepherd; she resembled unmistakably those fairies of Scotland of whom Walter Scott speaks, who roam in the moonlight near the mysterious fountain, with a necklace of dewdrops and a golden thread for girdle.

If one may make use of the expression, Mlle. Taglioni is a Christian dancer, Mlle. Fanny Elssler is a pagan dancer—the daughters of Miletus, beautiful Ionians, so celebrated in antiquity, must have danced in the same manner.

Hence Mlle. Elssler, although not fitted by temperament for Mlle. Taglioni's parts, can replace her in every way without any risk or danger; because she has sufficient versatility and skill to adapt herself to suit the particular style of the part.

The theme of La Sylphide is one of the most delightful themes for a ballet that could possibly be encountered; it includes an idea at once moving and poetic, a rare thing in a ballet, and we are delighted that it is to be staged again; the action is self-explanatory and can be understood without any difficulty, and lends itself to the most graceful pictures—in addition, there are hardly any dances for men, which is a great comfort.

Mlle. Elssler's costume was of a delicious freshness; her dress might have been fashioned of dragon-flies' wings and her feet shod with satin made from lilies. A garland of convolvulus of an ideal shade of pink encircled her beautiful brown hair, and behind her white shoulders quivered and trembled two little wings made of peacocks' feathers, superfluous with such feet!

The new Sylphide was frantically applauded; she invested the rôle with an infinity of delicacy, grace, and lightness—she appeared and vanished like an intangible vision; when you believed her to be in one place she was in another. She surpassed herself in the pas with her sister; it is impossible to see anything more perfect or more graceful; her miming, when she is caught by her lover in the folds of the enchanted scarf, expresses with a very poetic regret and pardon the feeling of disaster and of error beyond repair, while her last long look at her wings which have fallen to the ground is full of a great tragic beauty.

At the beginning of the ballet, there took place a little accident which, fortunately, had no serious consequences, but which at first alarmed us: at the moment when the Sylphide disappears through the fireplace (a strange exit for a sylphide) Mlle. Fanny Elssler, being carried too quickly by the counter-weight, knocked her foot violently against the frame of the chimney-piece.

Fortunately, she did not hurt herself; but we take this opportunity of inveighing against these "flyings" which are a tradition of old opera. We see nothing graceful in the spectacle of five or six unfortunate girls almost dying of fright from being suspended in mid-air by iron wire which may quite well give way; these poor wretches who distractedly move their arms and legs like toads out of their element involuntarily remind one of stuffed crocodiles hung from a ceiling. At the performance given for Mlle. Taglioni's benefit, two sylphides remained suspended in mid-air, it was impossible to pull them up or lower them down; people in the audience cried out in terror; at last a machinist risked his life and descended from the roof at the end of a rope to set them free. Some minutes later, Mlle. Taglioni, who only spoke this once in all her life (at the theatre, of course), went towards the footlights and said: "Gentlemen, no one has been hurt." The following day two sylphides of the second class received a present from the real Sylphide. It is not unlikely that another difficulty of this sort will soon recur.

(1838)

ANDRÉ LEVINSON
THE ART AND MEANING
OF ISADORA DUNCAN

Thanks to the fact that, up to recent times, ballet has been the exclusive domain of a closed circle, it was isolated from the general public by prejudices which have not yet been overcome. The individual form in which the art of dance first reached us, exciting and troubling us, was the dance of Isadora Duncan. This powerful artist did not immediately arouse our sympathy; her widespread recognition came later, coinciding with a decline in her style. Consequently, evaluations of her dancing have been as enthusiastic as they have been superficial.

Instinctively reacting to the new beauty Miss Duncan reveals, friends of her art in the public and in the press created a completely false and unsuitable criterion for evaluating her talent: they compared her dancing to ancient dance.

Little is known about ancient dance; its living tradition is irretrievably lost. We do know of its deep ties to forms of cult worship. In acknowledging the absence of a religious basis in her explorations of dance, Miss Duncan herself denies that her art is a direct organic perpetuation of antiquity; her dance, she asserted in a public lecture, is not a dance of the past but a dance of the future. But if there is not a genuine link to the little-known essence of ancient dance in her art, then its ideological, I would say even moral, base coincides in part with the themes of the somewhat simplified and vulgarized Hellenism of our day. Its slogans are: freedom of the body, the cult of plastique, palpable beauty—a cult nourished by the beautiful relics of museums. But it seems to us that there is no need to mix our current Hellenism with the already difficult-to-comprehend character of ancient culture.

Fans of Duncan's art, hoping to find a measure of support for their arguments and to justify their enthusiasm before the judgment of skeptics, greatly overestimate the significance of such museum pieces. There is no question that one must credit Miss Duncan with a serious study of the monuments of ancient art— of reliefs, and especially of vase painting, all of which develop and enrich her dance. But it would be quite erroneous to perceive this as her innovation or as the "focal point" of her art. The fact is that by reconstructing antiquity through documents which have been preserved, it is possible to recreate the tradition not only in choreography but on the contemporary stage as well. Perhaps many have not been able to discern, through the veil of her creative individuality, the unprecedented evocation of antiquity which is one of the main attractions of Sarah Bernhardt's interpretation of Racine's *Phèdre*. The *création* of this image is preceded by an extensive study of museum treasures right up to the Attic treasures in our own Hermitage. The basic inability of plastic arts, sculpture, and painting to give movement to each instant has been fatal in attempts to restore ancient forms of dance. These art forms can only fix one instant of movement, chiefly its beginning or end. Plastic art is especially static, as it is tied to rules of equilibrium. Therefore, ancient art can give us only a whole series of poses and positions. It is not within its powers to give us an entire presentation of the dynamics of dance or movement itself. Even the most consistent and resourceful attempts to recreate ancient dance are inevitably characterized by inadequacy and arbitrariness.

But Duncan's art is not tied genetically to antiquity. It is supported (to a greater degree) by the contemporary Hellenic slogan of the body's freedom from clothing and the cult of the body reborn. The contemporary ideal of nudity, which only censorship prevented Duncan from achieving, does not at all agree with ancient aesthetics, which valued the choreographic meaning of clothing and draperies. Consequently, one generally cannot relate the slogans supporting nudity purely to aesthetics. But the overemphasis on slogans is in protest against false shame, against the hermetically sealed philistinism of Duncan's moralizing critics. In a word, the slogan offers a conventional lie as opposed to the attacks of the naive.

A socially significant issue raised by Duncan is our deep concern for the physical development of the younger generation, and our own struggle against approaching degeneration. Duncan's innovation in the area of dance naturally added to the blossoming of various types of sports. This was seen in the development of every imaginable kind of gymnastic group during the past decade. Duncan's dancing appeared to affect choreography in the same way that the sudden appearance of the natural corset affected dress reform in the world of fashion. It is completely natural that Isadora Duncan sought not so much to create a new phalanx of refined artists as to make her pedagogical goal the general dissemination of her message to the masses. It is not without reason that A. G. Kornfeld noted, in his "small eulogy" to the artist, the significance of her art as "the possibility for all of us to be beautiful."

The cult of athleticism, of the strong, lithe, healthy body, gave rise to talk not only of the influence of contemporary society on her dancing, but of the "racial" quality evidenced in Duncan's art. The aesthetic character of her dance carries this typically *anglo-saxon* impression. This characteristic is best described by a term already in use for another aspect of English artistic culture—"Pre-Raphaelitism."

Pre-Raphaelitism is a reactionary movement which brings overrefined classical and post-classical forms back to the level of primitive artistic concepts. It is a compromise movement—one not quite strong enough. Although it finally breaks with the academic tradition, it does not then return to the initial stages of development of the art but timidly stops short. English Pre-Raphaelite artists broke from the powerful maturity of the cinquecento thanks to Botticelli and Verrocchio; none of them approached Giotto.

Duncan has that vividness of form, that absence of chiaroscuro, that concreteness of art which characterized the quattrocento. In her *Ange avec violon,* in her poetic *Primavera,* there is all the healthy strength of the good Lorenzo di Credi, softened by the fragile intellectualism of Botticelli. Duncan has that romantic yet not overly profound *nostalgie du passé* which developed in the treatment of antiquity during the quattrocento, that idyllic note, that inability to capture the monumental such as one sees in the work of Pietro di Cosimo, whose Venus sits among the little multicolored flowers in a melancholy field while a fleeting butterfly alights on her bared knee.

In essence Duncan's dance is *mimetic*—figurative. She draws her forms from imitations of natural, common poses and movements, and with her spontaneous mimicry she conveys emotional experiences. It is true that there is not an exact duplication, but there is a deep *analogical* resemblance to antiquity. In the *Ange avec violon* she imitates, with the movement of her arms, the motions of playing a real violin; in *Primavera,* choreographed according to Botticelli's painting, she drops countless flowers; in the *Lullaby* of Gretchaninoff, she bends just so over the infant's cradle, and when her Narcissus bends his beautiful knee over the imaginary stream into which he gazes, the audience can feel the moisture and transparency of the current, the trembling and the sudden coldness going through his body. As, in Goethe's ballad, water drawn from the palm of the hand by Brahmane's wife turns into a crystal ball, so Duncan's imitative gesture scoops imaginary objects from the surrounding atmosphere revitalizing them with actual palpable life. That is why her use of various props—palm branches, golden leaves in Tchaikovsky's *Romance*—seems to be an unnecessary infringement on her original purity.

In her dancing she extracts mimetic, even dramatic content from the music's impressions. This has elicited many opinions as to whether she dances Chopin, Grieg, Beethoven authentically, but even a whole crusade of musicians could not arrive at the truth. Since this or that image or mood are created by irrational forces within our minds, they cannot be identical for everyone, and therefore cannot be considered universal.

I am convinced of music's power to inspire moods and movements by the extraordinary example of the somnolent Madeline—who dances under hypnosis. Her will is paralyzed, and the only source of her movement is the musical rhythm, that insurmountable imperative, spontaneously acting upon her imagination and surrogate will. From it comes the diversities of her dance and the sometimes frenzied rise of dramatic experience.

In depicting her spiritual moods, Duncan does not go beyond the boundaries of realistic movement. Her dance—free from the constraints of clothing, is a free, broad run; leaps are not characteristic of her (although they are a primary element of classical ballet), nor is dancing on point, which is practiced by all ballerinas whose heads and arms, in addition, are guided by specific rules of equilibrium. Duncan's head is freely thrust back or is bent forward; her hands, independent of the movement of her arms, live as a free expression of life. In this there is yet another analogy to ancient dance. Lulled by the rhythm, passive and indecisive, her head, arms and torso sway right and left at the beginning of a Strauss waltz. Her impatient leg simply beats time.

Impressions of Duncan's latest performance take shape in a more definite and concrete form, which I venture to describe here. Here she performed plastic and dramatic creations like Gluck's *Orpheus* and the songs of Richard Wagner.

After the orchestra's overture, a mournful Orpheus appears from a dark corner of the stage, flooded with crimson light. The head is tilted back, the hands are at his sides. In this long funeral moment, his mood is revealed only by the agonizingly slow movement of his footsteps. His costume, which is too long, falls in straight, rigid pleats, as if a body were dragging behind him, hindering his movement. This material constraint expresses Duncan's impotent despair until she extends an invoking arm upward, with fingers outstretched. Then, as a violin intones Orpheus' repeated cry, "Eurydice! Eurydice!" she bends over an imaginary grave and with gestures of tenderness breaks the solemn, stern ritual of funereal rites. This action, executed by Duncan with the absolute minimum of figurative means, lacks the distinctive mark of ancient funereal mimicry. The ancient mourner invariably feigns the gesture of pulling out his hair by placing his crooked arm over his head. Duncan's portrayal is not based on archaeology but on spontaneous experience. True, this experience is not sufficiently deep, because the sublime conception is not within the dancer's means. The second scene—a chorus, and the dances of the Furies spellbound at the end of Orpheus' lyre—is less attractively conceived. It is true that Duncan skillfully manages to evoke the impression of a moving chorus with many people represented. She is able to communicate the orchestra's anxious dissonances by sudden breaks in her plastic line; but the dance itself fails because of the lack of technical means. This "flat-footed" or, as the Romans called it, "planipes" dance did not use leaps or movements on point, but allowed for great variety of certain kinds of runs and steps. Her knee thrusts forward, billowing the light cloth of her tunic, or she throws her legs back, breaking the pleats in her garments, pleats which consistently fall back into place. Often during her dance Duncan throws back her head and thrusts forth her arms with extended, pointing fingers; the typical gesture of an ancient "dactylology." In general, the artist only uses material from ancient dances in measure with her amateur technical capabilities.

On the stage of the Elysées Theatre, Duncan relates to the image of Orpheus' drivers a blissful shadow, a nuance of the fragile grace of the eighteenth century. In the final glorification of the gods, her extended hands, trembling with joy, bring the Olympians generous and beautiful gifts of thanks. The figurative strength of her gesture is such that the audience can see the sacrificial flowers and vessels in her hands.

Of course, Duncan's mimetic paraphrase in no way exhausts the contents of *Orpheus*. The artist herself knows that gesture is conditioned by and dependent on meaning. As the sweet voice of the real Orpheus, accompanied by a solo violin, sings in self-forgetfulness, a mute dancer moves across the stage. But even with her naive and limited concept of Orpheus, Duncan's performance was distinguished by nobility and deep tenderness.

The Brahms waltz suite, which formed the second half of the program, answers to a great degree to Duncan's talent. At the base of her art lies an unconscious sense of formal creation and a particular musical sensitivity. Her dance is *impressionistic* and calls forth a feeling of involuntariness, of sudden improvisation. The Brahms waltzes are an example of this. In the first measure, the dancer seems to be already rocking and even resisting the inspiration of the music until her movement begins to become more defined and full and the whirlwind of the dance totally carries her away. More than anything else, Duncan's art is *reproductive*: it is a sound turned into movement. Often her gestures remind one of the instinctive dancing movement of a conductor at his music stand.

The Brahms was followed by a Schubert encore. Somewhat naive, but noble and penetrating, the fully realized artistry of these dances had a lyric charm which dispersed the uncertain and sometimes painful impressions of *Orpheus*.

On the second evening, in Wagner's *Four Poems*, from the epoch of *Tristan*'s creation, the psychological *passivity* of Duncan's art was once again revealed. In *L'Ange* her arms cross in supplication and her lips shine with gratitude; she coils her arms and bends her torso in exhaustion beneath the sweet charms of the music. She intertwines her arms in a gesture of torment and self-defense—*Suffering*. In *Dreams*, the dancer, lying on the ground, actually seems to be a sleeping person—symbolism is always important in her dance and, raising herself on her elbow, she joyfully gazes at images of a magic dream.

These *Poems* serve as Duncan's prelude to *Isolde's Death*. Here again, her strength is focused on the mimicry of the face and hands: her legs are motionless: only occasionally does a swift gust carry her ahead a few paces. Again, as in *Orpheus*, the artist in a white chlamys with wide sleeves, and with gestures of lamenting tenderness, bends beneath the body of her beloved until the storm of ecstasy straightens her bent back and turns her clouded gaze upward.

With each crescendo of the orchestra, she shakes her uplifted arms and finally throws them vigorously to and fro. Her least effort is accompanied by smooth and sinewy movements of her horizontally extended arms, exactly like an unseeing soul. It goes without saying that this was not a tragic and majestic ascension of Isolde: the dancer's movements are the echo of her imagination—her voice.

In the *Bacchanale* from *Tannhäuser*, the dance in Venus' grotto, the dancer does not succeed at all. She is not capable of communicating a multifaceted musical image in which melodic figures at first stand out distinctly and then slip back into the sea of orchestral polyphony: the representation of bacchanalia cannot be realized without the counterpoint opposition of separate groups within a mass of dancers. This is why the artist, who is usually so mindful of the rhythm, here sometimes reinterprets it. Her whole appearance, uniting full-grown maidenliness with young masculinity, is alien to the music's spontaneous charms. The violet stage lighting and the blood-red tunic are powerless.

The Three Graces (this was the preparatory study for Botticelli's *Primavera* performed by Duncan on a previous occasion) is the height of her art. The dancing nymph reaches out her hand to an unseen friend, and then she herself is suddenly the friend, a new dancer joining in to the music; after this a third one springs up. Here, elements of banal transformation (a quick change of clothing) are side by side with sudden and full metamorphosis. This brings us to the very essence of the artist's creative ability.

The psychological elements are joyfulness, light intoxication with the spring sun, free strides, a gentle breeze, and the playful pleats of her tunic. There is something bucolic about her. There is no tragedy. No eroticism. There is no real femininity in her essence. In her there is a simple grace, strength, the joy of youth. And this is why this artist-androgyne can be at once Orpheus and Eurydice, Narcissus and Daphne, Pan and Echo, and L'Ange avec Violon. These two evenings defined for us Duncan's significance. Undoubtedly, her art form has become familiar, and its emotion will only sometimes reflect our experiences; her excitation will often be fruitless. Because we see in it the appearance of an unusual personality, all her art is valuable, but its content exhausts itself. A phenomenon like Duncan is a frequent occurrence, appealing but not remarkable. Placing her within the general evolution of theatrical dance is a precarious business. . . .

(1917)

CARL VAN VECHTEN
ANNA PAVLOWA, 1920

It may seem a little unprecise to describe a personality so vivid as that of Anna Pavlowa as old-fashioned. Yet she is old-fashioned, in the delightful sense of that epithet; not old-fashioned like things of the day before yesterday, the slang of 1910, the bicycle, or "ballroom dancing," but like the lambrequins, waxflowers, shell-baskets, glazed chintzes, and mezzotints of our grandmothers, which the Baron de Meyer has so pleasantly revived.

She is the last of the great school of classic dancers, a fragrant reminiscence of the early nineteenth century, born of the same tradition as Taglioni and Fanny Elssler and Carlotta Grisi, and as great as these, perhaps greater than these. With the modern movement in dancing, with which she mistakenly allied herself at one time in her career, she has nothing whatever to do. Save in such a divertissement as *Les Sylphides,* she was entirely out of place in the Russian Ballet, into which the more nearly contemporary art of Karsavina fitted so neatly. Even less appropriately can Pavlowa be identified with Isadora Duncan and the so-called revival of the dances of the Greeks. The Russian has, to be sure, assumed character rôles, but she is only supreme as the exponent of the classic ballet in works like *Coppélia,* in the true Italian tradition, or Adolphe Adam's *Giselle.* In Glazunow's *Bacchanale,* which she and Mordkin performed with so much abandon, she may have appeared to commit herself to the new freedom, but it was to be observed that even in this number she preserved the conventions of the classic school by wearing tights and balletslippers.

Her only rival in coeval choreographic history, Adeline Genée, a far inferior performer, was practically vanquished from the day that Pavlowa first set foot on the London stage, Genée, who had enjoyed her hour, was roguish, witty, twinkling, and saucy. (Saucy is a word that has almost fallen into disuse because no new girls are born to fit it. Perhaps Marie Tempest was the last. She *was* saucy. Another epithet, piquant, frequently applied to *sauces* for steaks, might with equal justice be applied to *her.*) But the Scandinavian not only lacked the finished technique of

the Russian, she also wanted her tragic grace. For the mask of
Pavlowa is truly tragic, a face of haunting intensity and hurt
loveliness. It may be that with her passing the school of toe-
dancing will also pass, but it may also be remarked that nothing
dies so long as any one is great enough to keep it alive.

(1920)

EDWIN DENBY
THREE SIDES OF *AGON*

ONE

Agon, a ballet composed by Igor Stravinsky in his personal
twelve-tone style, choreographed by George Balanchine, and
danced by the New York City Ballet, was given an enormous
ovation last winter by the opening night audience. The balcony
stood up shouting and whistling when the choreographer took
his bow. Downstairs, people came out into the lobby, their eyes
bright as if the piece had been champagne. Marcel Duchamp, the
painter, said he felt the way he had after the opening of *Le Sacre*.
At later performances, *Agon* continued to be vehemently
applauded. Some people found the ballet set their teeth on edge.
The dancers show nothing but coolness and brilliantly high
spirits.

Agon is a suite of dances. The score lasts twenty minutes, and
never becomes louder than chamber music. On stage the dancers
are twelve at most, generally fewer. The ballet has the form of a
small entertainment, and its subject—first, an assembling of contestants, then the contest itself, then a dispersal—corresponds to
the three parts into which the score is divided.

The subject is shown in terms of a series of dances, not in terms
of a mimed drama. It is shown by an amusing identity in the
action, which is classic dancing shifted into a "character" style
by a shift of accentuation. The shift appears, for example, in the
timing of transitions between steps or within steps, the sweep of
arm position, in the walk, in the funniness of feats of prowess.

The general effect is an amusing deformation of classic shapes due to an unclassic drive or attack; and the drive itself looks like a basic way of moving one recognizes. The "basic gesture" of *Agon* has a frank, fast thrust like the action of Olympic athletes, and it also has a loose-fingered goofy reach like the grace of our local teenagers.

The first part of the ballet shows the young champions warming up. The long middle part—a series of virtuoso numbers—shows them rivalizing in feats of wit and courage. There is nothing about winning or losing. The little athletic meet is festive—you watch young people competing for fun at the brief height of their power and form. And the flavor of time and place is tenderly here and now.

TWO

Agon shows that. Nobody notices because it shows so much else. While the ballet happens, the continuity one is delighted by is the free-association kind. The audience sees the sequence of action as screwball or abstract, and so do I.

The curtain rises on a stage bare and silent. Upstage four boys are seen with their backs to the public and motionless. They wear the company's dance uniform. Lightly they stand in an intent stillness. They whirl, four at once, to face you. The soundless whirl is a downbeat that starts the action.

On the upbeat, a fanfare begins, like cars honking a block away; the sound drops lower, changed into a pulse. Against it, and against a squiggle like a bit of wallpaper, you hear—as if by free association—a snatch of *Chinatown, my Chinatown* misremembered on an electric mandolin. The music sounds confident. Meanwhile the boys' steps have been exploding like pistol shots. The steps seem to come in tough, brief bursts. Dancing in canon, in unison, in and out of symmetry, the boys might be trying out their speed of waist, their strength of ankle; no lack of aggressiveness. But already two—no, eight—girls have replaced them. Rapidly they test toe-power, stops on oblique lines, jetlike extensions. They hang in the air like a swarm of girl-size bees, while the music darts and eddies beneath them. It has become complex and abstract. But already the boys have re-entered, and the first crowding thrust of marching boys and leaping girls has a secret of scale that is frightening. The energy of it is like that of fifty dancers.

By now you have caught the pressure of the action. The phrases are compact and contrasted; they are lucid and short. Each phrase, as if with a burst, finds its new shape in a few steps, stops, and at once a different phrase explodes unexpectedly at a tangent. They fit like the stones of a mosaic, the many-colored stones of a mosaic seen close-by. Each is distinct, you see the cut between; and you see that the cut between them does not interrupt the dance impetus. The novel shapes before you change as buoyantly as the images of a dream. They tease. But like that of a brilliant dream, the power of scale is in earnest. No appeal from it.

While you have been dreaming, the same dance of the twelve dancers has been going on and on, very fast and very boring, like travel in outer space. Suddenly the music makes a two-beat cadence and stops. The dispersed dancers have unexpectedly turned toward you, stopped as in a posed photograph of athletes; they face you in silence, vanish, and instantly three of them stand in position to start a "number" like dancers in a ballet divertissement.

The music starts with a small circusy fanfare, as if it were tossing them a purple and red bouquet. They present themselves to the public as a dance-team (Barbara Milberg, Barbara Walczak, Todd Bolender). Then the boy, left alone, begins to walk a "Sarabande," elaborately coiled and circumspect. It recalls court dance as much as a cubist still life recalls a pipe or guitar. The boy's timing looks like that of a New York Latin in a leather jacket. And the cool lift of his wrong-way-round steps and rhythms gives the nonsense so apt a turn people begin to giggle. A moment later one is watching a girls' duet in the air, like flying twins (*haute danse*). A trio begins. In triple canon the dancers do idiotic slenderizing exercises, theoretically derived from court gesture, while the music foghorns in the fashion of *musique concrète*. Zanily pedantic, the dance has the bounce and exuberant solemnity of a clown act. The audience laughs, applauds, and a different threesome appears (Melissa Hayden, Roy Tobias, Jonathan Watts).

For the new team the orchestra begins as it did for the previous one—first, the pushy, go-ahead fanfare, then the other phrase of harmonies that keep sliding without advancing, like seaweed underwater. (The two motifs keep returning in the score.)

The new team begins a little differently and develops an obvious difference. The boys present the girl in feats of balance, on the ground and in the air, dangerous feats of lucid nonsense. Their courage is perfect. Miss Hayden's dead-pan humor and her distinctness are perfect too. At one point a quite unexpected flounce of little-girl primness as in silence she walks away from the boys endears her to the house. But her solo is a marvel of dancing at its most transparent. She seems merely to walk forward, to step back and skip, with now and then one arm held high, Spanish style, a gesture that draws attention to the sound of a castanet in the score. As she dances, she keeps calmly "on top of" two conflicting rhythms (or beats) that coincide once or twice and join on the last note. She stops and the house breaks into a roar of applause. In her calm, the audience has caught the acute edge of risk, the graceful freshness, the brilliance of buoyancy.

The New York audience may have been prepared for *Agon's* special brilliance of rhythm by that of *Opus 34* and *Ivesiana*, two ballets never shown on tour. All three have shown an acuteness of rhythmic risk never seen and never imagined outside the city limits. The dangerousness of *Agon* is as tense as the danger of a tightrope act on the high-wire. That is why the dancers look as possessed as acrobats. Not a split-second leeway. The thrill is, they move with an innocent dignity.

At this point of *Agon* about thirteen minutes of dancing have passed. A third specialty team is standing on stage ready to begin (Diana Adams, Arthur Mitchell). The orchestra begins a third time with the two phrases one recognizes, and once again the dancers find in the same music a quite different rhythm and expression. As the introduction ends, the girl drops her head with an irrational gesture more caressing than anything one has seen so far.

They begin an acrobatic adagio. The sweetness is athletic. The absurdity of what they do startles by a grandeur of scale and of sensuousness. Turning pas de deux conventions upside down, the boy with a bold grace supports the girl and pivots her on point, lying on his back on the floor. At one moment classic movements turned inside out become intimate gestures. At another a pose forced way beyond its classic ending reveals a novel harmony. At still another, the mutual first tremor of an uncertain supported balance is so isolated musically it becomes a dance movement. So does the dangerous scoop out of balance and back into balance of the girl supported on point. The dance flows through stops, through scooping changes of pace, through differences of pace between the partners while they hold each

© *Martha Swope*

Diana Adams and Arthur Mitchell in Balanchine's "Agon" (1957). " ...
a pose forced way beyond its classic ending reveals a novel harmony."
(Denby)

other by the hand. They dance magnificently. From the start, both have shown a crescendo and decrescendo within the thrust of a move, an illusion of "breath"—though at the scary speed they move such a lovely modulation is inconceivable. The fact that Miss Adams is white and Mr. Mitchell Negro is neither stressed nor hidden; it adds to the interest.

The music for the pas de deux is in an expressive Viennese twelve-tone manner, much of it for strings. Earlier in the ballet, the sparse orchestration has made one aware of a faint echo, as if silence were pressing in at the edge of music and dancing. Now the silence interpenetrates the sound itself, as in a Beethoven quartet. During the climactic pas de deux of other ballets, you have watched the dancer stop still in the air, while the music surges ahead underneath; now, the other way around, you hear the music gasp and fail, while the two dancers move ahead confidently across the open void. After so many complex images, when the boy makes a simple joke, the effect is happy. Delighted by the dancers, the audience realizes it "understands" everything, and it is more and more eager to give them an ovation.

There isn't time. The two dancers have become one of four couples who make fast, close variations on a figure from the pas de deux. The action has reverted to the anonymous energy you saw in the first part. Now all twelve dancers are on stage and everything is very condensed and goes very fast. Now only the four boys are left, you begin to recognize a return to the start of the ballet, you begin to be anxious, and on the same wrestler's gesture of "on guard" that closed their initial dance—a gesture now differently directed—the music stops, the boys freeze, and the silence of the beginning returns. Nothing moves.

During the stillness, the accumulated momentum of the piece leaps forward in one's imagination, suddenly enormous. The drive of it now seems not to have let up for a moment since the curtain rose. To the realization of its power, as the curtain drops, people respond with vehement applause in a large emotion that includes the brilliant dancers and the goofiness of the fun.

The dancers have been "cool" in the jazz sense—no buildup, inventions that did not try to get anywhere, right after a climax an inconsequence like the archness of high comedy. But the dramatic power has not been that of jokes; it has been that of unforeseeable momentum. The action has had no end in view—it did not look for security, nor did it make any pitiful appeal for that. At the end, the imaginary contestants froze, toughly confident. The company seems to have figured jointly as the off-beat hero,

and the risk as the menacing antagonist. The subject of *Agon*, as
the poet Frank O'Hara said, is pride. The graceful image it offers
is a buoyance that mystifies and attracts.

THREE

A program note says that "the only subject" of the ballet is an
interpretation of some French seventeenth-century society
dances. The note tells you to disregard the classic Greek title
(Agon) in favor of the French subtitles. It is a pity to. The title
and the subtitles are words that refer to civilized rituals, the former to athletics, the latter to dancing. Athletic dancing is what
Agon does. On the other hand, you won't catch anyone on stage
looking either French or Greek. Or hear musically any reason
they should. French Baroque manners and sentiments are not
being interpreted; elements or energies of forms are.

The sleight-of-hand kind of wit in the dancing is a part of that
"interpretation." You see a dancer rushing at top speed, stop
sharp in a pose. The pose continues the sense of her rush. But
the equilibrium of it is a trap, a dead end. To move ahead, she
will have to retract and scrounge out. She doesn't, she holds the
pose. And out of it, effortlessly, with a grace like Houdini's, she
darts away. The trap has opened in an unforeseen direction, as
music might by a surprising modulation. At times in *Agon* you
see the dancer buoyantly spring such traps at almost every step.
Or take the canonic imitations. At times a dancer begins a complex phrase bristling with accents and a second dancer leaping
up and twisting back an eighth note later repeats it, then suddenly passes a quarter note ahead. The dissonance between them
doesn't blur; if you follow it, you feel the contradictory lift of the
double image put in doubt where the floor is. Or else you see a
phrase of dance rhythm include a brief representational gesture,
and the gesture's alien impetus and weight—the "false note" of
it—make the momentum of the rhythm more vividly exact.
These classic dissonances (and others you see) *Agon* fantastically
extends. The wit isn't the device, it is the surprise of the quick
lift you feel at that point. It relates to the atonal harmonies of the
score—atonal harmonies that make the rhythmic momentum of
the music more vividly exact.

At times you catch a kind of dissonant harmony in the image
of a step. The explosive thrust of a big classic step has been deep-
ened, speeded up, forced out farther, but the mollifying motions
of the same step have been pared down. In a big step in which

the aggressive leg action is normally cushioned by mildly rounded elbows the cushioning has been pared down to mildly rounded palms. The conciliatory transitions have been dropped. So have the transitional small steps. Small steps do not lead up to and down from big ones. They act in opposition to big ones, and often stress their opposition by a contrariness.

The patterns appear and vanish with an unpredictable suddenness. Like the steps, their forms would be traditional except for the odd shift of stress and compactness of energy. The steps and the patterns recall those of Baroque dancing much as the music recalls its Baroque antecedents—that is, as absurdly as a current Harvard student recalls a Baroque one. Of course, one recognizes the relation.

Agon shifts traditional actions to an off-balance balance on which they swiftly veer. But each move, large or small, is extended at top pitch. Nothing is retracted. The ardent exposure is that of a grace way out on a limb.

The first move the dancers make is a counteraccent to the score. Phrase by phrase, the dancers make a counterrhythm to the rhythm of the music. Each rhythm is equally decisive and surprising, equally spontaneous. The unusualness of their resources is sumptuous, like a magnificent imaginative weight. One follows the sweep of both by a fantastic lift one feels. The Balanchinian buoyancy of impetus keeps one open to the vividly changeable Stravinskian pressure of pulse and to its momentum. The emotion is that of scale. Against an enormous background one sees detached for an instant, the hidden grace of the dancer's individual move, a chance event that passes with a small smile and a musical sound forever into nowhere.

(1957)

EDWIN DENBY
A BALANCHINE
MASTERPIECE
(CONCERTO BAROCCO)

Concerto Barocco, the Balanchine novelty of the current Monte Carlo season at the Center, is an unpretentious and good-tempered little ballet and it is also the masterpiece of a master choreographer. It has only eleven dancers; it is merely straight dancing to music—no sex story, no period angle, no violence. It does not seem to be trying to win your interest, but before you know it it has absorbed your attention and doesn't let it go. It has power of rhythm and flow; in a wealth of figuration it is everywhere transparent, fresh, graceful and noble; and its adagio section is peculiarly beautiful.

Concerto Barocco was recognized as a masterpiece at once when it was shown here in dress rehearsal four years ago by Lincoln Kirstein's American Ballet. It had just been created then for the Rockefeller-sponsored South American tour of that company. And though this ballet tour has recently been spoken of as one of Mr. Rockefeller's inter-American mistakes, as a ballet critic I can say that in showing *Concerto Barocco*, he was showing our neighbors choreography of the best quality in the world—showing a United States product that no country of western Europe could have equaled. A mistake such as that does anyone honor.

It is a pleasure to report that the Monte Carlo production of *Barocco* is excellent both in the dancing on stage and in the playing in the orchestra pit. Unfortunately though, the piece has in the present production been given a backdrop of meager, dirty blue and a set of harsh black bathing suits for the charming girls. Meagerness and harshness are not in its spirit; some of the wonderful clarity in its spacing is dimmed; and in so poverty-struck a frame, the rich title of the ballet strikes one as absurd.

But *Concerto Barocco* comes by its fancy title quite honestly. The name might lead you to expect an evocation of Baroque dancing or Baroque mannerisms; still what the title actually promises is a Baroque concerto, and this is just what you get. Balanchine has set his ballet so happily to Bach's *Concerto for Two Violins* that the score may be called his subject matter. The style of the dance is pure classic ballet of today, and the steps themselves follow the notes now strictly, now freely. But in its vigorous dance rhythm, its long-linked phrases, its consistent drive and sovereign articulation, *Concerto Barocco* corresponds brilliantly to this masterpiece of Baroque music.

The correspondence of eye and ear is at its most surprising in the poignant adagio movement. At the climax, for instance, against a background of chorus that suggests the look of trees in the wind before a storm breaks, the ballerina, with limbs powerfully outspread, is lifted by her male partner, lifted repeatedly in narrowing arcs higher and higher. Then at the culminating phrase, from her greatest height he very slowly lowers her. You watch her body slowly descend, her foot and leg pointing stiffly downward, till her toe reaches the floor and she rests her full weight at last on this single sharp point and pauses. It has the effect at that moment of a deliberate and powerful plunge into a wound, and the emotion of it answers strangely to the musical stress. And (as another example) the final adagio figure before the coda, the ballerina being slid upstage in two or three swoops that dip down and rise a moment into an extension in second— like a receding cry—creates another image that corresponds vividly to the weight of the musical passage. But these "emotional" figures are strictly formal as dance inventions. They require no miming in execution to make them expressive, just as the violin parts call for no special schmalz. And this modesty of stage presence combined with effects so strong and assured gives one a sense of lyric grandeur.

The adagio section is the only movement with a lyric expression. The introductory vivace is rather like a dance of triumph, strong, quick and square; while the concluding allegro is livelier and friendlier, with touches of syncopated fun and sportive jigging. Both these sections have sharply cut rhythms, a powerful onward drive and a diamond-like sparkle in their evolutions. There are, for instance, many lightning shifts in the arm positions and yet the pulse of the dance is so sure its complexity never looks elaborate. The ten girls who execute the little chorus and the two girl soloists are precise and quick and their grace is wonderfully natural. They are all so earnestly busy dancing, they seem more than ever charmingly young, and their youth gives an innocent animal sweetness to their handsome deportment.

(1945)

DEBORAH JOWITT
MONUMENTAL MARTHA

As a choreographer, Martha Graham is also a brilliant archeologist. Or is it psychologist? At any rate, during her long career, she has been adept at exposing famous old scars of the Western world and making them bleed significantly.

Paradoxically, although we consider her one of the creators of "American Modern Dance," she has made comparatively few dances with specifically American subject matter or themes: and her extraordinary movement vocabulary developed, it seems to me, not only from her own motor impulses, but from shrewd borrowings from the dance styles of other, more ancient cultures. Her work provides an object lesson in the uses of the past, for her style has never looked eclectic, has never looked anything but authentic and wildly original.

This isn't the serious article that ought to be written on the evolution of Graham's style. I think I'm in the business of throwing out teasers. Martha Graham began to work with Ruth St. Denis and Ted Shawn in 1916 and stayed with the Denishawn Company until 1923. (In 1919 she got her first big part—as the fierce heroine of Shawn's Aztec ballet, "Xochitl.") Seven years of Denishawn. The influence had to be profound; Graham utilized it profoundly.

St. Denis and Shawn were interested in exotic genre pieces— evocations of various oriental, archaic and primitive styles, or what they imagined these styles to be. (In spite of their earnest research, I suspect that they viewed even the American Indian exotically or, at any rate, romantically.) Many of Graham's own early dances—which she has since denounced in print—seem to have been little antique studies. But as early as the late twenties, she began her important process of exploration, assimilation and transformation.

For one series of works, among which is the 1931 masterpiece, "Primitive Mysteries," she created a "primitive" style based in part on the straight, narrow look of American Indian dancing. This early Graham style had the purity of an earth-sky rite, with its rooted look, pounding feet, stiffly vertical posture, arms that branched occasionally into angular gestures. Austere, hopeful, unambiguous dancing that reflected her ruthless asceticism and her desire to purge dance of all trivialities of movement. Graham has returned occasionally to elements of this style—especially for male figures like the Christ in "El Penitente," the Creature of Fear in "Errand into the Maze," the Revivalist in "Appalachian Spring." Among other things, it conveniently turns men into living phallic pillars.

Graham also utilized—beginning I'm not sure when—features of the so-called "archaic" style derived from Egyptian friezes. Perhaps she liked this style originally for the simple strength of its designs. But, as performed by a living human body, the artificial stance—feet walking in one direction while the upper body twists open against that base—can easily become, and eventually did for Graham, a metaphor for a kind of ardent ambivalence. She kept the twist, increased it, bent the body in several places, tipped it slightly off center, until in her famous fall sequences, she arrived at a position in which the arms opened in one direction, while the knees remained pressed together, hips averted from the focus of the reaching arms. An agonized and somehow reticent posture and one ideally suited for the dire predicaments of those Greek heroines she dealt with from the late forties on, when she began to become the unhappy high priestess of our collective unconscious.

Elements of various Far Eastern styles have also enriched Graham's vocabulary, but these, too, she restructured. Frantic, beating arm gestures or a bowed head made decorative Cambodian knee-walks look anything but decorative. She added a twist to a flex-footed attitude (also Cambodian or Siamese), so that her head could look backward—away from where her feet were going. A position reminiscent of Lord Shiva drawing his bow (Indian Bharata Natyam) looks entirely different when the dancer's spine pulls away from the direction of the gesture. Tiny, smooth Japanese steps; arm gestures like oppositely curving half moons; hands bent stiffly at the knuckle: Graham pressed all these oriental movements and poses into violence and ended up with something startlingly expressive of all of our illustrious Western dilemmas, like the polarity of spirit and flesh.

Just as some Eastern styles do, Graham made us aware of the shape of the dancing body in still positions, but she linked those poses together not with flowing transitional steps, but with tense little runs, or by a process which involved unmaking the pose for a second and then abruptly reforming it one step further on in space. Although the long, breathing stillnesses that punctuate

Graham dancing are very Eastern, little else about the dynamics of her style relates to the controlled fluidity of much oriental dancing. Graham, until very recently anyhow, wanted her movement performed with tremendous tension. One set of muscles inhibited or restricted another. In many of her important works of the forties and fifties, you felt the dancing shuddering along in huge jerks, propelled by the violently contracting and expanding bodies. When I first saw Graham in 1955, I was stunned by the whiplash of her spine; by the way, as Medea in "Cave of the Heart," she writhed sideways on her knees—simultaneously devouring and vomiting a length of red yarn; by the elegantly neurotic quivers that went through her Emily Brontë in "Deaths and Entrances." What she did wasn't like any dancing that I knew; it was more like a body language consisting solely of epithets.

Conventions of Eastern theater have merged with gleanings from Jung, Einstein and cinema in Graham's art. In the course of one dance sequence, characters can jump back and forth in time—acting, meditating on the results of that action, expressing their feelings in relation to it. They can be both narrators and protagonists. Two people can portray one or one portray two. Everyone can be her own grandma. In "Seraphic Dialogue," three aspects of Joan of Arc wait, immobile as decor, for an agonized fourth Joan-who-remembers to call them to life. Symbolic props not only create devastating images—think of the vast red cloak in "Clytemnestra" which spreads like blood over everything—but also free Graham from the anathema (to her) of impressionism. In "Dark Meadow," for example, a little branch pops out from a pillar, and we know it's spring and don't need anyone being a flower, or even smelling the air. The dancers can get on with the business of peopling that spring.

Recent Graham works have often approached a kind of exoticism, almost as if the style were reflecting a morbid nostalgia for Graham's own lost-dance-power, or else as if the physical weakness that comes with age had imparted a flabbiness to her dances that she was too overwrought to notice. I don't know how else to explain the voluptuous profusion of movement, the beautiful, limber, half-naked dancers sinking into the movement phrases as into a warm bath, the absence of the old percussive force. Sometimes things looked pretty, dreamlike, absentminded; sometimes wilfully decadent. And she herself remained on stage at the heart of many of her compositions, portraying any number of unhappy ladies remembering their flaming pasts. The works had to be shaped around this almost immobile central figure, whose brave attitudes had no muscle power behind them, who seemed driven by a blaze of nerves.

Now in her 70's, Martha Graham has finally retired as a dancer. But other dancers have taken her roles successfully before and will again. (Mary Hinkson and Pearl Lang will alternate in the title role in the revival of "Clytemnestra.") Let's hope, selfishly, that she reconstructs some of her great works for us. Perhaps too, through the act of retiring as a dancer, of reaffirming herself as a choreographer, she can again make works for the company that will have the vitality of "Diversion of Angels" or "Canticle for Innocent Comedians."

I hope she outlasts her imitators.

Goodbye Martha. And welcome back.

(1973)

ARLENE CROCE
MOMENTOUS
(THE FOUR TEMPERAMENTS)

A masterpiece by definition transcends its time, but even masterpieces are created in response to some need of the moment. Perhaps it would be more true to say that a masterpiece doesn't so much transcend its time as perpetuate it; it keeps its moment alive. In *The Four Temperaments,* revived at the New York City Ballet after some years out of repertory, the moment is luminously there. In *Danses Concertantes,* the moment eludes me. Although Eugene Berman's frontcloth says 1944, the program says "New choreography by George Balanchine," and what Balanchine in part created and in part reconstructed for his revival in 1972 doesn't add up to a major work either of the forties or of the seventies. To read about the original *Danses Concertantes,* which starred Alexandra Danilova and Frederic Franklin with the Ballet Russe de Monte Carlo, is to anticipate a joyous tease of a ballet—modest, light, and playful. The new *Danses Concertantes* is clearly modest, but it's also remote and sourish, and the Berman décor, much praised in its day, is something of a shock. (At the last performance of the ballet's run this season, the unaccountably gloomy backdrop had been removed.) Of the pas de deux for the two stars, I can only assume that it has been entirely rechoreographed, and indifferent casting from 1972 onward hasn't helped me see what Edwin Denby in 1944 described as a "happy flirtation." The much improved Robert Weiss and the highly promising Daniel Duell both danced the man's role this season, but neither as yet has the impact of a star or the quality that Denby said Franklin projected in the part—"the fatuousness of a happy male." Even if they'd had those things, that's still only one half of a flirtation.

Yet if there is a time capsule embedded in this remade *Danses Concertantes*, I would guess it to be the third pas de trois (which Berman dressed in lavender). With one man supporting two storklegged women in double arabesques penchées, it has the robust chic and the rippling erotic tension we associate with high-style Balanchine, and it has also a kind of systematic visual punning, an intertwining of echoes and cross-references, that distinguishes his greatest work of the forties. What a monumental decade it was! Balanchine by then was established in America, but not solidly established; from *Concerto Barocco* and *Ballet Imperial* on through *The Four Temperaments* to *Theme and Variations* and *Symphony in C* he is on the attack. His objective: to make plain to American audiences the dynamics of classical style. In each of these ballets, the dancing grows from simple to complex structures, and every stage of growth is consequentially related to every other. It is partly because of their structural logic that his ballets make such great sense—or such vivid nonsense—to us years after they were completed, but it's also because such logic isn't the featured attraction; it's only the means by which a particular kind of entertainment is elucidated. What *is* featured is human variety.

This is true even of *The Four Temperaments*, one of the earliest works in which the elements of logic are arrayed in a form so brilliantly consequential that they nearly become the whole show. The relation between the continuity of the piece and its subject, which is the four varieties of human temperament (melancholic, sanguine, phlegmatic, choleric), is truly a magical one, consisting of a dance logic Balanchine has made look uniquely ritualistic. It isn't ritualistic in an exotic sense, it is ritual achieved by the most radical exposure of classical style Balanchine has provided to date. *The Four Temperaments*, created in 1946, marks one of Balanchine's several "beginnings," and, like *Apollo*, his first collaboration with Stravinsky, and *Serenade*, his first ballet for American dancers, it is a messianic work, which conveys to this day the sense of a brilliant and bold new understanding. Hindemith's score, subtitled "Theme with Four Variations (According to the Four Temperaments) for String Orchestra and Piano," was written to Balanchine's commission in 1940, but it was not until the formation of Ballet Society, following the Second World War, that Balanchine composed his choreography. After years of working on Broadway, in Hollywood, and for ballet organizations not his own, he was again in charge of a company, and in his first ballet for Ballet Society (the direct predecessor of the New York City Ballet) he made a fresh start, reestablishing the bases and the directions of American dance. Nowadays, *The Four Temperaments* (carelessly billed without the *The*, as if there could be more than four) doesn't appear novel in the way it did to observers of that time; its "distortions" and "angularities" have been absorbed into one important stream of Balanchine ballet and have been imitated the world over. But its style, in both root and blossom, is so consistent and so consistently keen to the eye, and the scale on which it flowers is so active in its leaps from tiny to enormous and back again, that one follows the progress of the ballet in wonder; it never fails to surprise and to refresh, and so it is new every time.

Going back to basics in 1946, Balanchine concentrated his attention equally on the smallest details and the largest resources of classical dance and on making transitions from one to the other clearer, perhaps, than they'd ever been before. When, in the opening statement of the ballet—the first part of the Theme—we see a girl, supported on her points, turning from side to side and transferring her weight from one foot to the other as she turns, we see her do it with a finicky grace: she lifts and lowers the free foot, curls it around the standing leg, and carefully flexes it before arching to full point. We see, in short, a foot becoming a point—nature being touched to artificial life. The detail looms for an instant, then quickly takes its place in the grand scheme of the ballet. The Theme is full of elementary particles, jostling, caroming, crisscrossing space in strokes that define the boundaries of the territory Balanchine will invade. In the Theme's second statement (there are three such statements, each a pas de deux), the side-to-side turns have become full revolutions, rapid finger-turns marked off by the girl's point as it taps the floor. In the third statement, the finger-turns are taken in deep plié with one foot held off the ground in passé position. The weight on that one supporting point looks crushing, but, as we have seen, there is something about a woman's point that makes it not a foot—that makes it a sign. The image created by the third girl as she is spun is blithe, even comical; could Balanchine have been thinking of the bass fiddle the forties jazz player spins after a chorus of hot licks?

The developing sense of the passages I've cited is analogous to the process that takes place in the molding of a classical dancer's body. The "story" of *The Four Temperaments* is precisely that story—the subjection of persons to a process and their re-emergence as human archetypes—but these citations may make it seem as if that process happened all in closeup, and if that were true we would be in a crazy man's world. The world of *The Four Temperaments* is wide and swarming with possibilities, yet if we could pass the choreography through a computer to see how many core gestures there actually are, there would probably not be more than six—maybe eight. Balanchine has built a large and dense composition on a handful of cellular motifs, and it's this economy that allows us to perceive the ballet and survive it, too. There are gestures that seem to cluster in family relationships and that recur subtly transformed. How many elaborations are there on grand battement en balancoire? How many derivations from, adaptations of, combinations with? Some of these we see clearly, others hang just at the edge of vision. There are gestures that do not change at all—they're like stabilizing props that keep back the tide. One of these is the "Egyptian profile" with squared elbows; another is the women's splits across the men's thighs (but this, too, is an evolution—from the first pas de deux: the girl dropped in a split to the floor and slid into the wings). Balanchine's control of the action's subliminal force allows us the most marvellous play in our minds; we're torn in an agony of delight between what we see and what we think we see. Metaphoric implications flash by, achieve their bright dazzle of suggestion, and subside into simple bodily acts. The way the women stab the floor with their points or hook their legs around men's waists or grip their partners' wrists in lifts—images of insatiable hunger, or functional necessities? Balanchine gives us a sharp pair of spectacles to see with, but he occasionally fogs one of the lenses. If he didn't we'd perish from the glare.

And that lens we see with—isn't it a moving lens, a camera eye? Darting in for details, withdrawing to lofty heights, it views the dance from as many perspectives as the body can indicate in its manifold placements within space. Space itself is liquefied, and planes on which we observe the dance rise, tilt, descend. Sometimes we are launched and roving in this liquid space; sometimes we are pressed, riveted, to the floor. Out of these volatile perspectives drama is made. In the first variation (Melancholic), we have an expansive field of vision, but the solo dancer does not seem to know how much room he has. His space is penetrated by menacing diagonals for the entries of the corps. The corps is a few small girls, a small menace. But they are enough to block and frustrate his every attempt to leap free. He leaps and crumples to earth. We recognize this man: his personal weather is always ceiling zero. (It's a nineteenth- rather than a seventeenth-century conception of melancholy—Young Werther rather than Robert Burton.) In the Sanguinic variation, for a virtuoso ballerina and her partner, the vista is wide, the ozone pure and stinging. The ballerina is an allegro technician; she is also a character. She enters and pauses. Her partner is expectant. But she pauses and turns her gaze back toward the wings. For a moment she seems to wear a demure black velvet neck ribbon, and then she is bounding like a hare in the chase, an extrovert after all. The Sanguinic variation takes us to the top of the world, and twice we ride around its crest, its polar summit (a circuit of lifts at half-height). In these two thrilling flights, the camera eye pivots on the pinpoint of a spiral, once to end the trajectory, once to start it. We see, as in some optical effect of old cinema, a scene spread from the center of its compass, then respread in reverse.

The topography of the ballet shrinks in the Phlegmatic variation to the smallest it has been since the Theme. Phlegmatic is indolent, tropical, given to detached contemplation, to pretentious vices. The male soloist languishes, and loves it. Slowly he picks up invisible burdens, lifts them, and clothes himself in their splendor. Slowly, self-crowned, he picks up his right foot and studies it. His little dance with the corps includes cabalistic gestures toward "his" floor, and he hovers close to the ground, repeating his mumbo-jumbo (a syncopated time step) as if he expected the ground to answer him. The confined, floor-conscious world of Phlegmatic and Melancholic returns redeemed in the next section, when Choleric, that angry goddess, executes her climactic ronds de jambe par terre. Here we have the traditional dénouement of an eighteenth-century ballet (or such a nineteenth-century one as *Sylvia*), in which Mount Olympus hands down a judgment on the mess mortals have made. Chol-

eric enters in a burst of fanfares and flourishes, kicking the air.
Her fury must be appeased, assimilated by the ballet's blood-
stream. The entire cast collaborates in the process. Key motifs are
recapitulated in tempi that charge them with new vitality. We
are racing toward the finality of a decision, and then it comes.
Those ronds de jambe are a space- and air-clearing gesture. Three
circles traced on the ground: it is the most wonderful of the ballet's magic signs; the vastness of it incorporates all bodies into
one body, all worlds into one planet. After a silence in which
nobody moves, the great fugue of the finale begins its inexorable
massed attack. All the parts the ballet is made of are now seen at
once in a spectacle of grand-scale assimilation. Apotheosis. We
see a succession of sky-sweeping lifts; we see a runway lined by
a chorus of grands battements turned to the four points of the
compass. The lifts travel down the runway and out as the curtain
falls.

As a conception for a ballet, the four temperaments, or humors
of the blood, have been realized with a profundity that doesn't
depend on the intellectual powers of either the audience or the
dancers. Balanchine has interpreted the subject in the form of a
dance fantasy, but never so literally or so schematically that we
need fear, if we miss one element, having missed all. We can
trust the ballet in performance because it is built of the things
that dancers as a race know about. No small part of its moral
beauty comes directly from the dancers, from their fastidious
concentration, their ghetto pride. Yet in *The Four Temperaments*,
as in every ballet, casting does make a difference. This season,
the perfect cast was Bart Cook in Melancholic, Merrill Ashley in
Sanguinic, Jean-Pierre Bonnefous in Phlegmatic, and Colleen
Neary in Choleric—all of them new to their roles, and all hitting
new highs in their careers. For dancers and audience alike, the
ballet represents the cleansing and healing that Robert Frost
speaks of in "Directive" when he says, "Here are your waters and
your watering place./Drink and be whole again beyond
confusion."

(1975)

ARLENE CROCE
JOFFREY JAZZ
(DEUCE COUPE)

As its name indicates, *Deuce Coupe* is a vehicle for two companies, and as a joint presentation of Twyla Tharp's company and
the City Center Joffrey Ballet it was the hit of the entire spring
season. Now it's back, in repertory, with much the same cast as
before (a very smiley Nancy Ichino has gone in for Starr Danias,
and there are one or two other minor replacements) and in even
better performance condition. The audience loves it; I love it. But
Deuce Coupe is more than a big hit, more than the best thing the
Joffrey Ballet has ever done—it's the outstanding accomplishment to date of the ballet year.

For excitement and originality, none of the new works by
major choreographers compare with it—not even Merce Cunningham's *Changing Steps*, which was included in a series of
Events given last March at the Brooklyn Academy. I say "not
even Cunningham" because there may well be a genealogical
link between him and Twyla Tharp. I won't attempt to trace
Twyla Tharp's line of descent—she seems to have absorbed
something from nearly everybody who moves well—but, like
Cunningham, she is routinely classified as an "avant-garde" choreographer, and only a few years ago she was one of those choreographers who were working without music and in nontheatrical and open spaces—either out-of-doors or in museums and
gyms. The only element that she did not eliminate was dancing
itself, and in this she was unique—defying the exponents of
nondance and antidance. The way she danced was unique, too.
The open-space movement in choreography goes on, and Twyla
Tharp now has her imitators, but at that time nothing like her
had ever been seen before. The finest of the post-Cunningham
generation of choreographers, up until *Deuce Coupe*, she was
thought to be also the most forbiddingly idiosyncratic. Even
when, with her own small company, she started choreographing
in more conventional surroundings to eighteenth-century music
and to jazz, the burn of her intensely personal style didn't wear
off, and her dancers seemed to be moved by a form of private

communication which made them unlike any other dancers that
one could see. I believe that the dances she has done for them—
especially the great jazz ballets *Eight Jelly Rolls* and *The Bix Pieces*
and *The Raggedy Dances*—are her best work. But *Deuce Coupe* is a
good work, too. It isn't a great ballet, but it fills to abundance
every need it was meant to fill, and, as far as ballet audiences are
concerned, nothing like *it* has ever been seen before, either.

Deuce Coupe is a pop ballet and a great gift to the Joffrey company. Since 1968, when Robert Joffrey put his company on the
cover of *Time* with a mixed-media/rock ballet called *Astarte*, it
has been polishing its reputation as America's great swinging
company. This is one half of the Joffrey company's Janus profile;
the other is the image of custodian of modern-day classics from
the international repertory. But the Joffrey's dual policy
stretched the capacities of its dancers too far and broke them.
Dancers live and progress on roles that are created for them. All
those slick, empty, and violent ballets by Gerald Arpino that
slammed the audience with the Dionysian ecstasy of dance or
appealed to the audience's political convictions and hunger for
"relevance" certainly did contribute to the shaping of a style, but
it was a style that rendered Joffrey dancers unfit for anything
better. As classical dancers, the Joffreys have no touch; they look
squat, badly placed, hectic, and unmusical. When Joffrey, who
has excellent taste in non-Joffrey ballets, imports a classic Danish
ballet like *Konservatoriet*, his dancers can hardly get through it.
At the moment, they are having serious problems with a production of Frederick Ashton's *The Dream*. (What dream is this?
Their tendency to broaden and coarsen is like a bad dream of
American ballet.) After seven years in residence at the City Center, the company had grown so unattractive that serious dance
lovers stopped attending everything but the classic revivals—the
choices were always interesting, even if the actual performances
were not. What this withdrawal of attention meant was that the
structure by which the company made its dancers grow was
dead. Generally speaking, you can't feed dancers on imports and
revivals. Imports and revivals please audiences; they seldom
help the dancer, who can't be at his best in somebody else's old
part.

It would be too much to claim that *Deuce Coupe* has saved the
Joffrey, but it does give the dancers something genuine to
respond to—something that's exactly suited to their talents—
and it tidies up the company's self-image. It's just as if Twyla
Tharp had said, "So you want pop? I'll give you pop," but what

she has given the Joffrey is so close to the real thing that part of the audience—the part that has decided what contemporary, orgiastic, youth-spirited, with-it ballet looks like—is taken by surprise. *Deuce Coupe* astounds by the utter unfamiliarity of familiar things. Its music is a tape collage of fourteen Beach Boys hits, starting with "Little Deuce Coupe" and ending with "Cuddle Up"—probably the last jukebox pop that *was* pop, and not Pop Art. Its décor is spray-can graffiti applied to a rolling backcloth while the ballet is in progress. And its dancing—that which gives it life and joy—is a peculiar Tharpian combination of classical ballet and the juvenile social dancing of the past decade. The ballet steps are like a primitive's-eye view of classical style, fascinating in their plainness and angularity, and the social dances are rich with crazy, campily corny suggestion. Neither type of dancing is what it would be in the hands of any other choreographer, and yet neither is what it ordinarily appears to be in its raw state—in the classroom, or in school gyms, ballrooms, and discothèques. Whatever the Tharp eye sees, it changes. (Even the graffiti, with their characteristic stilted lines, curly serifs, and locked edges, look as it they were intended for *Deuce Coupe*. And, oh, New York! Isn't it nice to see the stuff in a place where it belongs?) As a result, the whole ballet has this low-contrast choreographic weave that knits its separate scenes together, but there's so much action going on, and the action is so complicated and delicately timed, that the effect is never one of monotony. (There is one moment when the ballet seems to slump. At the end of "Don't Go Near the Water," we get one more roiling group instead of something we haven't seen before.) This complexity and delicacy can be undervalued. Most of the time in *Deuce Coupe*, the dancers appear to be behaving with such realism that we could believe they were making it up as they went along. People who don't often go to the ballet might recognize the validity of these dances at once and wonder why such a fuss was being made over them. People who go more regularly fall into the trap of their expectations, and *Deuce Coupe* looks formless to them—just taken off the street and thrown onto the stage. Actually, no one has put contemporary American popular dancing of quite this intensity and freedom on the stage before, and I am sure no one but Twyla Tharp would have known how to make these dances legible in the theatre. A hundred kids going berserk at a school prom is a powerful but not necessarily a theatrical spectacle. To be realized on the stage, such potency has to be objectified; the material has to be changed and heightened. In the process, it becomes beautiful, but "beauty" isn't the choreographer's object—clarity is. And Twyla Tharp does something that people dancing for recreation don't do: she makes a theatrical translation of the music. In "How She Boogalooed It," she doesn't give us the Boogaloo—she gives us something that looks more like snake dancing at top speed. "Alley Oop," "Take a Load Off Your Feet," "Long Tall Texan," and "Catch a Wave" are based as much on the lyrics as on the music, and include several obvious, Broadway-style jokes. In "Papa Ooh Mau Mau," the dancers mime smoking pot and freaking out. When the music isn't interesting enough, it's speeded up or two tracks are run side by side. We do get a long way from the school prom. The spontaneity and naturalness of the dances are a marvelous illusion, a secret of professional style. Everyone has had the experience in the theatre of the happy occurrence— some fantastically accurate inflection or bit of punctuation, so like a moment in life we think it couldn't happen again. Twyla Tharp's choreography is full of such moments that do happen again. In *Deuce Coupe*, I think of Nina Wiener's freak-out or Glenn White landing in fifth position right on the *pow!* of the downbeat in "Wouldn't It Be Nice." (The surprise is partly that you hadn't seen him jump.)

Deuce Coupe makes rather a special point of ballet versus pop dancing. In this, it's an extension of *The Bix Pieces*, which was composed two years ago for the Tharp company's formal Paris début. (Its most recent performances took place this past summer at Jacob's Pillow and a few weeks ago on the CBS Sunday-morning program *Camera Three*.) *The Bix Pieces*, named for Bix Beiderbecke, is based on jazz-band dance music of the 1920's. The dancing is a moody synthesis of the tap-toe-baton-acrobatic routines that millions of American children have been heirs to, and in the course of the work a narrator informs us, "The fundamental concepts can produce infinite combinations and appearances. For example, 'slap, ball, change' is 'chassé' in ballet, or 'slap' ('tendu'), 'ball' ('piqué'), 'change' ('plié')." This is demonstrated, and the narrator goes on to say, "So, you see, all things can be profoundly and invisibly related, exactly and not at all the same." *Deuce Coupe* deals in a similar technical paradox—sometimes at too great a length. For example, it has a ballerina (Erika Goodman) performing a classical solo virtually all through the piece. Sometimes she's alone onstage and sometimes she's the eye of the hurricane, but she never stops dancing, and since there are other ballet dancers on the stage, I have sometimes wondered why she's there. She is eternal, the others are temporal? But I have never wished Miss Goodman off the stage while watching her on it. I like what she does, and she's doing it this season with unusual beauty. Erika Goodman is chubby and neckless, with big legs that wave in disproportionately high extensions. With her large-scale gesture and demonstrative warmth, she's becoming a baby Struchkova. But, like most of the Joffrey girls, she lacks something as a classical stylist, and her role—a taxing one, which consists of the ballet vocabulary performed alphabetically—is so Tharpian in conception that it really doesn't resemble classical ballet enchaînements at all. What we see in her random provocative movements is a parallel to the dislocated, familiar-unfamiliar movements that dominate the main action of the ballet. The two dance forms—ballet and popular—remain technically distinguishable but become stylistically fused. It's a Tharpian fusion, and the didactic point of *The Bix Pieces* disappears. All things are no longer so invisibly related.

There's a sense in which *Deuce Coupe* would be better if the Joffrey members of the cast were better classical dancers. Twyla Tharp has asked a lyricism of them, and a precision of épaulement, that they can't consistently supply. Yet in "Wouldn't It Be Nice," the most exhilarating of the Beach Boys songs, the steps are entirely classical, and this is the number I love best. From the opening port de bras to the quietly held preparations in fifth—held so long that when the jetés into attitude-front start popping like molecules around the stage the pressure appears to blow them into the air—there is a tender mystery to the dancing which seems equal to the best of *The Bix Pieces* and to the best classical ballet I know. *Deuce Coupe* makes the Joffrey dancers look human (at the first performance I had trouble recognizing most of them); it rescues them from the curse of pseudo ballet and gives them back their natural grace of movement. They look very much as they might have looked as children—which is right for the preteen, presexual world that the ballet invokes—and they are magically divested of their customary hard-sell performing style. Besides Miss Goodman and Mr. White, the Joffrey dancers who shine most vividly in this new light are (in order of their appearance): Rebecca Wright, William Whitener, Beatriz Rodriguez, Larry Grenier, Gary Chryst, Donna Cowen, and Eileen Brady.

As for the Tharp dancers, they always do what comes naturally. Their stage personalities are so alive that we can follow them from ballet to ballet like characters in the Sunday comics. Twyla Tharp herself, with her sorrowful-baleful semihallucin- ated stare, is the Krazy Kat of the bunch. Sara Rudner is the Mys- terious Lady (her *Deuce Coupe* solo "Got to Know the Woman" is ironically seductive, like an adolescent's vision of sexuality), and Rose Marie Wright, the "Long Tall Texan," has an instantaneous impact on the audience—it applauds her on sight. Kenneth Rinker, the lone male, is a brotherly, somewhat taciturn cordu- roy-cap type, and the two other girls, Isabel Garcia-Lorca and Nina Wiener, have a fashion-model elegance. The group dancing of the Tharp company suggests a federation of individuals, and you can see the same kind of freedom in the group dancing of *Deuce Coupe*. But the restlessness and pain of American children are in it, too. The end of the ballet—the long, slow crescendo of tossing arms, lunges in plié, and backward bourrées on point, with here and there a fall to the floor—is half truth, half myth. It sums up a kind of schmaltzy romanticism that young people love to wrap themselves in, and it is absolutely true to our expe- rience of their world. The crescendo is ingeniously stage-man- aged, gaining might not by mass but by intensity, like a hum that gets louder, and it ends in a masterstroke—a freeze-pose black- out into silhouette. The cliché is the only possible schmaltz-cli- max. Then, gradually, it loosens, Miss Goodman takes a few hops forward, and *Deuce Coupe* continues somewhere in space as the curtain falls.

Deuce Coupe is fresh and exciting because it is closer to its source in popular culture than most pop or "jazz" ballets ever care to be. The music is the kind of music for which a dance idiom already exists. The choreography is in part a parody of that idiom, but it is authentic. In two other ballets in the Joffrey rep- ertory, Eliot Feld's *Jive* and Arpino's *Trinity*, the music is concert- hall jazz and evangelical rock, respectively: two forms for which the dancing has to be invented, and in both ballets the chore- ography is more synthetic than the music. *Jive* is set to Morton Gould's "Derivations for Clarinet and Jazz Band"—the same score that Balanchine used for a piece called *Clarinade*, which is remembered solely because it was the first ballet he created at Lincoln Center. The music doesn't work any better for Feld, who transforms it into a tight, cheerless, and ambivalent pastiche of the fifties, the period of Jerome Robbins wearing sneakers. It ends with the dancers lurching at the audience and crying "Jive!" *Jive* (a forties title) represents a good choreographer working below his form. *Trinity* represents a bad choreographer working at the very top of *his*. The work is all big jumps and running lifts, and it is consumed with the fake piety of the beads-and-amulets era. At the end, the dancers place peace candles all over the stage. In the context of these two ballets, and of the Joffrey repertory generally, *Deuce Coupe* is a masterpiece. Not only is it musically sound and poetically convincing—its emotions are the kind that make civilized contact in the theatre possible. It doesn't bludgeon us for a response; when it throws out a manipulative net, it does so with a grin. It doesn't pretend that we share the life it depicts, or make us feel that we should. It is completely objective, but, beyond that (*Jive* is objective, too, and dead), it respects its material. *Deuce Coupe* is an adult ballet about kids.

(1973)

VII

Dance and Society

Paul Valéry's definition of dance—useful though it may be in helping us to distinguish dance from similar-looking activities in nature—is nonetheless limiting in at least one respect: it excludes all non-theatrical dances, those ritualistic and social dances which have historically performed a variety of practical functions. These non-theatrical dances are often the creation of many individuals, whose contributions are made anonymously over long periods of time. Unlike contemporary works which may reflect nothing more than the individual attitudes of their choreographers, these non-theatrical dances are often viewed by anthropologists and sociologists as sensitive cultural barometers of the societies that produce them.

In the view of Havelock Ellis, famous as a sexologist and social theorist, dance functions in all the major manifestations of human life: religion, love, art, work, morals. For the primitive to dance is to worship and pray, and to take part in controlling the world, including the social world. Among primitive people dancing is a way of courting and constitutes "a novitiate for love." Since it encourages sexual selection it may also be viewed as a kind of unconscious eugenics that aids the highest development of the race. In the modern world dancing is known mainly as a profession, an amusement, and an art. But at all times dancing has been customary and has decisively influenced the socializing and moralizing of the species. Ellis thinks that savage dancers stirred by a single influence exhibit a wonderful unison as they fuse into a characteristic style. He is one of those celebrants of primitive wholeness to whom we alluded in the Introduction to Section II. It is precisely this feeling of unity that advocates of the Wagnerian *Gesamtkunstwerk* were attempting to re-capture. Indeed, apart from war, dancing is the chief factor making for social solidarity in primitive life. The value of dance as a method of individual and national education was recognized as civilization became increasingly self-conscious. In the *Laws* Plato remarked that a good education includes knowing how to dance and sing well. Ellis felt that this function of the dance was no longer generally appreciated and that dance ought to figure more prominently in a modern education.

For Ellis the ultimate significance of dancing lies in the fact that it manifests a general rhythm which marks not only life, but the entire universe as well. A notable manifestation of this view was current among the Elizabethans who, according to the Shakespearean scholar E. M. W. Tillyard, often pictured universal order as a dance. The angels or saints dance to the music of heaven as the planets and stars dance to the music of the spheres. Social dances, in their original manifestations, often imitated these heavenly movements, as did the court ballets of the sixteenth and seventeenth centuries, which adapted their intricate floor patterns from the social dances of the period. Today, many of these dances might strike us as purely formal, geometrical configurations—no more "representational" than an elaborate football halftime show. But in fact, they often enacted a version of the cosmic drama that Tillyard describes. Earthly things duplicate these planetary dances and the dance is, in fact, the very foundation of human civilization and of political and moral order. Davies's long poem, *Orchestra*, which Tillyard discusses at length, gives expression to this view and in it Queen Elizabeth is seen as the central point in the dance pattern exhibited by her court. As such she is the symbol and guarantor of order and natural unity in a perilously poised social world.

Ellis noted the gradual transition from dancing as a sacred function to dancing as an art or profession. The English scholar of ancient Greek religion and art, Jane Harrison, suggests, more specifically, that in Athens it is the decay of religion, the loss of faith in the magical efficacy of the Spring Rite, that provides the impulse to art. So long as people believe that by excited dancing they can induce the coming of spring and achieve the practical end of guaranteeing their food supply and securing their lives, ritual survives. But when this faith weakens, they drift away and become mere spectators of a rite established by custom. The rite dies, but its mould persists and, in the case of the *dromenon* of Dionysus, it blossomed into drama. Art succeeds religion and contemplation replaces action. This change is reflected in the development of the Greek theatre. The *orchestra* with its chorus of dancing worshippers yields in importance to the seats for spectators which finally give their name "theatre" to the entire structure. Our word "theatre," Harrison reminds us, is derived from the Greek word *theatron* which means, literally, "seeing place" (a place set aside for spectators). Ritual, by contrast, is a more purely participatory activity. This linguistic connection between our word "theatre" and the act of watching helps explain why writers such as Stokes, Heppenstall, and Kirstein refer to classical ballet as the quintessentially "theatrical" variety of dance, the one most committed to complete "legibility."

Ross Wetzsteon, the *Village Voice* critic and editor, examines ritual dancing and aesthetic contemplation from a contemporary point of view. Reflecting on a performance of the Whirling Dervishes in Austin, Texas, he wonders how the Dervishes can go on performing their rituals for an eclectic and largely secular audience. Will the spirit be ready at curtain time? Will they achieve ecstasy at every performance? He also wonders what access non-believers can have to an unfamiliar religious ritual they witness for their ecumenical and aesthetic purposes. Can one review the Pope performing the Mass? Is it relevant that some New York dancers can whirl better than the Dervishes? Wetzsteon reports that the Dervishes think that non-believers, as well as believing non-participants, can share the ecstatic experience: this dancing is not purely aesthetic in its effects.

The political functions and implications of the striptease are examined by Roland Barthes, the late French critic who wrote extensively about popular culture as well as about literary works. He argues paradoxically that the dance which accompanies the striptease is in no way erotic. Rather, it constitutes the last and most efficient barrier to nudity, which in fact it hides. The social role of the striptease is to inoculate the public with a touch of Evil, the better to plunge it afterwards into a permanently immune Moral Good.

Roger Copeland calls attention to the fact that the modern arts have pursued the goal of minimalist self-purification. But he argues that the arts cannot pursue what Ortega y Gasset called "dehumanization" or what Clement Greenberg called "self-criticism" forever. He thinks that at some point it becomes a purely practical, if not an ideological or spiritual necessity, for art to reestablish relations with the world and to reclaim human experience. If art is to perform its traditional function it must reestablish its connection with the human body and with what John Crowe Ransom called "the world's body." This is in fact what dance and photography did in the 60's and 70's and it accounts in large part for the immense popularity and prestige of these arts in that period. Unlike those minimalist arts that progressively eliminated the human form, choreography like that of Balanchine's modernist ballets progressively reveals the human form even as it pursues its minimalist goals.

In the essays we have discussed so far, the emphasis has been on the social role and functions of dance, although Roland Barthes also hints at the way in which French striptease reflects French, and specifically French bourgeois, culture. In the remaining essays the emphasis shifts decisively to the way dance reflects the society in which it is created. As Ruth Katz, the Israeli musicologist, suggests, the dance of the day is a good reflection of the values of a given time and she writes of the moment after the French Revolution, when "everyone" danced the waltz. In her view the triumph of the waltz reflects the values of liberty and equality that were celebrated by the Revolution as well as the uncertainties that attended the new social dispensation. In contrast to the social and geometrical formalities of its predecessor, the minuet, the waltz permitted individual variations and interpretations. (For a fuller discussion of the social context of the minuet, see Shirley Wynne's article "Complaisance, an Eighteenth-Century Cool," listed in the Bibliography.) The waltz allowed different kinds of individuals and members of different social classes to come together on an equalitarian basis. Katz observes, however, that despite the new equalitarianism the individual lost his sense of having a proper place in a predictable society after the Revolution, and she finds this social factor reflected in the new individualism and sense of self that characterized the post-revolutionary period. For Katz this aspect of social experience finds expression in the "letting go" characteristic of the waltz, in the experience it gives of an "escape" from reality through the thrilling dizziness of whirling one's way into a world of sensuality.

It is generally conceded that dances like the minuet and the waltz reflect the culture and sensibility of a particular time and place. But writers on classical ballet have generally viewed it as an international form of universal aesthetic validity. Joann Kealiinohomoku, an anthropologist of dance, rejects this claim and the ethnocentricity that lies behind it. For her, ballet is simply another form of ethnic dance. She also points out that many apologists for ballet, and for Western dance more generally, have a wholly inadequate conception of what they alternately describe as folk dance, ethnic dance, or primitive dance. For these are often not the manifestations of collective impulse or inspiration, or the expression of unhistorical tribal unities that writers like Ellis suppose. Certainly, there is no specific form or quality that characterizes the primitive in dance. Kealiinohomoku subscribes to the cultural relativism that inspires most cultural anthropology, and calls for a more enlightened investigation of non-Western dances and of the way they reflect the cultural traditions of the societies in which they develop.

Elizabeth Kendall, the American social historian and dance critic, shows how the birth of the Modern American Woman gave rise to the first generation of American solo dancers, who, in fact, became prime symbols of the new phenomenon. Kendall notes that the New Woman appeared as America emerged in world politics (and typically, the dancers' merits were first appreciated in Europe). Social reformers and feminists had been attempting for decades to free women's bodies and minds through spiritual and physical panaceas: dress reform, open air, aesthetic exercise, artistic pursuits. Physical culture and art came into vogue at the same time in the 1890's, and occupied women in a country where women had more time, more money, and more space to be individuals than in any other country at any other time in history. In fact, "the physical" and "the artistic" were the two realms in which the American woman's supposed new capacities for self-expression were exercized. Dancing was the synthesis of these two realms.

HAVELOCK ELLIS
From THE DANCE OF LIFE

THE ART OF DANCING

ONE

Dancing and building are the two primary and essential arts. The art of dancing stands at the source of all the arts that express themselves first in the human person. The art of building, or architecture, is the beginning of all the arts that lie outside the person; and in the end they unite. Music, acting, poetry proceed in the one mighty stream; sculpture, painting, all the arts of design, in the other. There is no primary art outside these two arts, for their origin is far earlier than man himself; and dancing came first.[1]

That is one reason why dancing, however it may at times be scorned by passing fashions, has a profound and eternal attraction even for those one might suppose farthest from its influence. The joyous beat of the feet of children, the cosmic play of philosophers' thoughts rise and fall according to the same laws of rhythm. If we are indifferent to the art of dancing, we have failed to understand, not merely the supreme manifestation of physical life, but also the supreme symbol of spiritual life.

The significance of dancing, in the wide sense, thus lies in the fact that it is simply an intimate concrete appeal of a general rhythm, that general rhythm which marks, not life only, but the universe, if one may still be allowed so to name the sum of the cosmic influences that reach us. We need not, indeed, go so far as the planets or the stars and outline their ethereal dances. We have but to stand on the seashore and watch the waves that beat at our feet, to observe that at nearly regular intervals this seemingly monotonous rhythm is accentuated for several beats, so that the waves are really dancing the measure of a tune. It need surprise us not at all that rhythm, ever tending to be moulded into a tune, should mark all the physical and spiritual manifestations of life. Dancing is the primitive expression alike of religion and of love—of religion from the earliest human times we know of and of love from a period long anterior to the coming of man. The art of dancing, moreover, is intimately entwined with all human tradition of war, of labour, of pleasure, of education, while some of the wisest philosophers and the most ancient civilisations have regarded the dance as the pattern in accordance with which the moral life of men must be woven. To realise, therefore, what dancing means for mankind—the poignancy and the many-sidedness of its appeal—we must survey the whole sweep of human life, both at its highest and at its deepest moments.

TWO

"What do you dance?" When a man belonging to one branch of the great Bantu division of mankind met a member of another, said Livingstone, that was the question he asked. What a man danced, that was his tribe, his social customs, his religion; for, as an anthropologist has put it, "a savage does not preach his religion, he dances it."

There are peoples in the world who have no secular dances, only religious dances; and some investigators believe with Gerland that every dance was of religious origin. That view may seem too extreme, even if we admit that some even of our modern dances, like the waltz, may have been originally religious. Even still (as Skene has shown among the Arabs and Swahili of Africa) so various are dances and their functions among some peoples that they cover the larger part of life. Yet we have to remember that for primitive man there is no such thing as religion apart from life, for religion covers everything. Dancing is a magical operation for the attainment of real and important ends of every kind. It was clearly of immense benefit to the individual and to society, by imparting strength and adding organised harmony. It seemed reasonable to suppose that it attained other beneficial ends, that were incalculable, for calling down blessings or warding off misfortunes. We may conclude, with Wundt, that the dance was, in the beginning, the expression of the whole man, for the whole man was religious.[2]

Thus, among primitive peoples, religion being so large a part of life, the dance inevitably becomes of supreme religious importance. To dance was at once both to worship and to pray. Just as we still find in our Prayer Books that there are divine services for all the great fundamental acts of life,—for birth, for marriage, for death,—as well as for the cosmic procession of the world as marked by ecclesiastical festivals, and for the great catastrophes of nature, such as droughts, so also it has ever been among primitive peoples. For all the solemn occasions of life, for bridals and for funerals, for seed-time and for harvest, for war and for peace, for all these things there were fitting dances. To-day we find religious people who in church pray for rain or for the restoration of their friends to health. Their forefathers also desired these things, but, instead of praying for them, they danced for them the fitting dance which tradition had handed down, and which the chief or the medicine-man solemnly conducted. The gods themselves danced, as the stars dance in the sky—so at least the Mexicans, and we may be sure many other peoples, have held; and to dance is therefore to imitate the gods, to work with them, perhaps to persuade them to work in the direction of our own desires. "Work for us!" is the song-refrain, expressed or implied, of every religious dance. In the worship of solar deities in various countries, it was customary to dance round the altar, as the stars dance round the sun. Even in Europe the popular belief that the sun dances on Easter Sunday has perhaps scarcely yet died out. To dance is to take part in the cosmic control of the world. Every sacred dionysian dance is an imitation of the divine dance.

All religions, and not merely those of primitive character, have been at the outset, and sometimes throughout, in some measure saltatory. That was recognised even in the ancient world by acute observers, like Lucian, who remarks in his essay on dancing that "you cannot find a single ancient mystery in which there is no dancing; in fact most people say of the devotees of the Mysteries that 'they dance them out.'" This is so all over the world. It is not more pronounced in early Christianity, and among the ancient Hebrews who danced before the ark, than among the Australian aborigines whose great corroborees are religious dances conducted by the medicine-men with their sacred staves in their hands. Every American Indian tribe seems to have had its own religious dances, varied and elaborate, often with a richness of meaning which the patient study of modern investigators has but slowly revealed. The Shamans in the remote steppes of Northern Siberia have their ecstatic religious dances, and in modern Europe the Turkish dervishes—perhaps of related stock—still dance in their cloisters similar ecstatic dances, combined with song and prayer, as a regular part of devotional service.

These religious dances, it may be observed, are sometimes ecstatic, sometimes pantomimic. It is natural that this should be so. By each road it is possible to penetrate towards the divine mystery of the world. The auto-intoxication of rapturous movement brings the devotees, for a while at least, into that self-for-getful union with the not-self which the mystic ever seeks. The ecstatic Hindu dance in honour of the pre-Aryan hill god, after-wards Siva, became in time a great symbol, "the clearest image of the *activity* of God," it has been called, "which any art or reli-gion can boast of."[3] Pantomimic dances, on the other hand, with their effort to heighten natural expression and to imitate natural process, bring the dancers into the divine sphere of creation and enable them to assist vicariously in the energy of the gods. The dance thus becomes the presentation of a divine drama, the vital reënactment of a sacred history, in which the worshipper is enabled to play a real part.[4] In this way ritual arises.

It is in this sphere—highly primitive as it is—of pantomimic dancing crystallised in ritual, rather than in the sphere of ecstatic dancing, that we may to-day in civilisation witness the survivals of the dance in religion. The divine services of the American Indian, said Lewis Morgan, took the form of "set dances, each with its own name, songs, steps, and costume." At this point the early Christian, worshipping the Divine Body, was able to join in spiritual communion with the ancient Egyptian or the later Japanese[5] or the modern American Indian. They are all alike privileged to enter, each in his own way, a sacred mystery, and to participate in the sacrifice of a heavenly Mass.

What by some is considered to be the earliest known Christian ritual—the "Hymn of Jesus" assigned to the second century—is nothing but a sacred dance. Eusebius in the third century stated that Philo's description of the worship of the Therapeuts agreed at all points with Christian custom, and that meant the promi-nence of dancing, to which indeed Eusebius often refers in con-nection with Christian worship. It has been supposed by some that the Christian Church was originally a theatre, the choir being the raised stage, even the word "choir," it is argued, mean-ing an enclosed space for dancing. It is certain that at the Eucha-rist the faithful gesticulated with their hands, danced with their feet, flung their bodies about. Chrysostom, who referred to this behavior round the Holy Table at Antioch, only objected to drunken excesses in connection with it; the custom itself he evi-dently regarded as traditional and right.

While the central function of Christian worship is a sacred drama, a divine pantomime, the associations of Christianity and dancing are by no means confined to the ritual of the Mass and its later more attenuated transformations. The very idea of danc-ing had a sacred and mystic meaning to the early Christians, who had meditated profoundly on the text, "We have piped unto you and ye have not danced." Origen prayed that above all things there may be made operative in us the mystery "of the stars dancing in Heaven for the salvation of the Universe." So that the monks of the Cistercian Order, who in a later age worked for the world more especially by praying for it ("orare est laborare"), were engaged in the same task on earth as the stars in Heaven; dancing and praying are the same thing. St. Basil, who was so enamoured of natural things, described the angels dancing in Heaven, and later the author of the "Dieta Salutis" (said to have been St. Bonaventura), which is supposed to have influenced Dante in assigning so large a place to dancing in the "Paradiso," described dancing as the occupation of the inmates of Heaven, and Christ as the leader of the dance. Even in more modern times an ancient Cornish carol sang of the life of Jesus as a dance, and represented him as declaring that he died in order that man "may come unto the general dance."[6]

This attitude could not fail to be reflected in practice. Genuine dancing, not merely formalised and unrecognisable dancing, such as the traditionalised Mass, must have been frequently introduced in Christian worship in early times. Until a few centuries ago it remained not uncommon, and it even still persists in remote corners of the Christian world. In English cathedrals dancing went on until the fourteenth century. At Paris, Limoges, and elsewhere in France, the priests danced in the choir at Easter up to the seventeenth century, in Roussillon up to the eighteenth century. Roussillon is a Catalan province with Spanish traditions, and it is in Spain, where dancing is a deeper and more passionate impulse than elsewhere in Europe, that religious dancing took firmest root and flourished longest. In the cathedrals of Seville, Toledo, Valencia, and Jeres there was formerly dancing, though it now only survives at a few special festivals in the first.[7] At Alaro in Mallorca, also at the present day, a dancing company called Els Cosiers, on the festival of St. Roch, the patron saint of the place, dance in the church in fanciful costumes with tambourines, up to the steps of the high altar, immediately after Mass, and then dance out of the church. In another part of the Christian world, in the Abyssinian Church—an offshoot of the Eastern Church—dancing is also said still to form part of the worship.

Dancing, we may see throughout the world, has been so essential, so fundamental, a part of all vital and undegenerate religion, that, whenever a new religion appears, a religion of the spirit and not merely an anaemic religion of the intellect, we should still have to ask of it the question of the Bantu: "What do you dance?"

THREE

Dancing is not only intimately associated with religion, it has an equally intimate association with love. Here, indeed, the relationship is even more primitive, for it is far older than man. Dancing, said Lucian, is as old as love. Among insects and among birds it may be said that dancing is often an essential part of love. In courtship the male dances, sometimes in rivalry with other males, in order to charm the female; then, after a short or long interval, the female is aroused to share his ardour and join in the dance; the final climax of the dance is the union of the lovers. Among the mammals most nearly related to man, indeed, dancing is but little developed: their energies are more variously diffused, though a close observer of the apes, Dr. Louis Robinson, has pointed out that the "spasmodic jerking of the chimpanzee's feeble legs," pounding the partition of his cage, is the crude motion out of which "the heavenly alchemy of evolution has created the divine movements of Pavlova"; but it must be remembered that the anthropoid apes are offshoots only from the stock that produced Man, his cousins and not his ancestors. It is the more primitive love-dance of insects and birds that seems to reappear among human savages in various parts of the world, notably in Africa, and in a conventionalised and symbolised form it is still danced in civilisation to-day. Indeed, it is in this aspect that dancing has so often aroused reprobation, from the days of early Christianity until the present, among those for whom the dance has merely been, in the words of a seventeenth-century writer, a series of "immodest and dissolute movements by which the cupidity of the flesh is aroused."

But in nature and among primitive peoples it has its value precisely on this account. It is a process of courtship and, even more than that, it is a novitiate for love, and a novitiate which was found to be an admirable training for love. Among some peoples, indeed, as the Omahas, the same word meant both to dance and to love. By his beauty, his energy, his skill, the male must win the female, so impressing the image of himself on her imagination that finally her desire is aroused to overcome her reticence. That is the task of the male throughout nature, and in innumerable species besides Man it has been found that the

school in which the task may best be learnt is the dancing-
school. Those who have not the skill and the strength to learn
are left behind, and, as they are probably the least capable members of the race, it may be in this way that a kind of sexual selection has been embodied in unconscious eugenics, and aided the
higher development of the race. The moths and the butterflies,
the African ostrich and the Sumatran argus pheasant, with their
fellows innumerable, have been the precursors of man in the
strenuous school of erotic dancing, fitting themselves for selection by the females of their choice as the most splendid progenitors of the future race.[8]

From this point of view, it is clear, the dance performed a double function. On the one hand, the tendency to dance, arising
under the obscure stress of this impulse, brought out the best
possibilities the individual held the promise of; on the other
hand, at the moment of courtship, the display of the activities
thus acquired developed on the sensory side all the latent possibilities of beauty which at last became conscious in man. That
this came about we cannot easily escape concluding. How it
came about, how it happens that some of the least intelligent of
creatures thus developed a beauty and a grace that are enchanting even to our human eyes, is a miracle, even if not affected by
the mystery of sex, which we cannot yet comprehend.

When we survey the human world, the erotic dance of the animal world is seen not to have lost, but rather to have gained,
influence. It is no longer the males alone who are thus competing for the love of the females. It comes about by a modification
in the earlier method of selection that often not only the men
dance for the women, but the women for the men, each striving
in a storm of rivalry to arouse and attract the desire of the other.
In innumerable parts of the world the season of love is a time
which the nubile of each sex devote to dancing in each other's
presence, sometimes one sex, sometimes the other, sometimes
both, in the frantic effort to display all the force and energy, the
skill and endurance, the beauty and grace, which at this moment
are yearning within them to be poured into the stream of the
race's life.

From this point of view we may better understand the
immense ardour with which every part of the wonderful human
body has been brought into the play of the dance. The men and
women of races spread all over the world have shown a marvellous skill and patience in imparting rhythm and measure to the
most unlikely, the most rebellious regions of the body, all

wrought by desire into potent and dazzling images. To the vigorous races of Northern Europe in their cold damp climate, dancing comes naturally to be dancing of the legs, so naturally that
the English poet, as a matter of course, assumes that the dance of
Salome was a "twinkling of the feet."[9] But on the opposite side
of the world, in Japan and notably in Java and Madagascar, dancing may be exclusively dancing of the arms and hands, in some
of the South Sea Islands of the hands and fingers alone. Dancing
may even be carried on in the seated posture, as occurs at Fiji in
a dance connected with the preparation of the sacred drink, ava.
In some districts of Southern Tunisia dancing, again, is dancing
of the hair, and all night long, till they perhaps fall exhausted,
the marriageable girls will move their heads to the rhythm of a
song, maintaining their hair, in perpetual balance and sway.
Elsewhere, notably in Africa, but also sometimes in Polynesia, as
well as in the dances that had established themselves in ancient
Rome, dancing is dancing of the body, with vibratory or rotatory
movements of breast or flanks. The complete dance along these
lines is, however, that in which the play of all the chief muscle-
groups of the body is harmoniously interwoven. When both
sexes take part in such an exercise, developed into an idealised
yet passionate pantomime of love, we have the complete erotic
dance. In the beautiful ancient civilisation of the Pacific, it is
probable that this ideal was sometimes reached, and at Tahiti, in
1772, an old voyager crudely and summarily described the native
dance as "an endless variety of posturings and wagglings of the
body, hands, feet, eyes, lips, and tongue, in which they keep
splendid time to the measure." In Spain the dance of this kind
has sometimes attained its noblest and most harmoniously beautiful expression. From the narratives of travellers, it would
appear that it was especially in the eighteenth century that
among all classes in Spain dancing of this kind was popular. The
Church tacitly encouraged it, an Aragonese Canon told Baretti in
1770, in spite of its occasional indecorum, as a useful safety-valve
for the emotions. It was not less seductive to the foreign spectator than to the people themselves. The grave traveller Peyron,
towards the end of the century, growing eloquent over the languorous and flexible movements of the dance, the bewitching
attitude, the voluptuous curves of the arms, declares that, when
one sees a beautiful Spanish woman dance, one is inclined to
fling all philosophy to the winds. And even that highly respectable Anglican clergyman, the Reverend Joseph Townsend, was
constrained to state that he could "almost persuade myself" that

if the fandango were suddenly played in church the gravest worshippers would start up to join in that "lascivious pantomine."
There we have the rock against which the primitive dance of sexual selection suffers shipwreck as civilisation advances. And that
prejudice of civilisation becomes so ingrained that it is brought
to bear even on the primitive dance. The pygmies of Africa are
described by Sir H. H. Johnston as a very decorous and highly
moral people, but their dances, he adds, are not so. Yet these
dances, though to the eyes of Johnston, blinded by European civilisation, "grossly indecent," he honestly, and inconsistently,
adds, are "danced reverently."

FOUR

From the vital function of dancing in love, and its sacred function in religion, to dancing as an art, a profession, an amusement,
may seem, at the first glance, a sudden leap. In reality the transition is gradual, and it began to be made at a very early period
in diverse parts of the globe. All the matters that enter into courtship tend to fall under the sway of art; their aesthetic pleasure is
a secondary reflection of their primary vital joy. Dancing could
not fail to be first in manifesting this tendency. But even religious dancing swiftly exhibited the same transformation; dancing, like priesthood, became a profession, and dancers, like
priests, formed a caste. This, for instance, took place in old
Hawaii. The hula dance was a religious dance; it required a special education and an arduous training; moreover, it involved the
observance of important taboos and the exercise of sacred rites;
by the very fact of its high specialisation it came to be carried out
by paid performers, a professional caste. In India, again, the
Devadasis, or sacred dancing girls, are at once both religious and
professional dancers. They are married to gods, they are taught
dancing by the Brahmins, they figure in religious ceremonies,
and their dances represent the life of the god they are married
to as well as the emotions of love they experience for him. Yet,
at the same time, they also give professional performances in the
houses of rich private persons who pay for them. It thus comes
about that to the foreigner the Devadasis scarcely seem very
unlike the Ramedjenis, the dancers of the street, who are of very
different origin, and mimic in their performances the play of
merely human passions. The Portuguese conquerors of India
called both kinds of dancers indiscriminately Balheideras (or
dancers) which we have corrupted in Bayaderes.[10]

In our modern world professional dancing as an art has become altogether divorced from religion, and even, in any biological sense, from love; it is scarcely even possible, so far as Western civilisation is concerned, to trace back the tradition to either source. If we survey the development of dancing as an art in Europe, it seems to me that we have to recognise two streams of tradition which have sometimes merged, but yet remain in their ideals and their tendencies essentially distinct. I would call these traditions the Classical, which is much the more ancient and fundamental, and may be said to be of Egyptian origin, and the Romantic, which is of Italian origin, chiefly known to us as the ballet. The first is, in its pure form, solo dancing—though it may be danced in couples and many together—and is based on the rhythmic beauty and expressiveness of the simple human personality when its energy is concentrated in measured yet passionate movement. The second is concerted dancing, mimetic and picturesque, wherein the individual is subordinated to the wider and variegated rhythm of the group. It may be easy to devise another classification, but this is simple and instructive enough for our purpose.

There can scarcely be a doubt that Egypt has been for many thousands of years, as indeed it still remains, a great dancing centre, the most influential dancing-school the world has ever seen, radiating its influence to south and east and north. We may perhaps even agree with the historian of the dance who terms it "the mother-country of all civilised dancing." We are not entirely dependent on the ancient wall-pictures of Egypt for our knowledge of Egyptian skill in the art. Sacred mysteries, it is known, were danced in the temples, and queens and princesses took part in the orchestras that accompanied them. It is significant that the musical instruments still peculiarly associated with the dance were originated or developed in Egypt; the guitar is an Egyptian instrument and its name was a hieroglyph already used when the Pyramids were being built; the cymbal, the tambourine, triangles, castanets, in one form or another, were all familiar to the ancient Egyptians, and with the Egyptian art of dancing they must have spread all round the shores of the Mediterranean, the great focus of our civilisation, at a very early date.[11] Even beyond the Mediterranean, at Cadiz, dancing that was essentially Egyptian in character was established, and Cadiz became the dancing-school of Spain. The Nile and Cadiz were thus the two great centres of ancient dancing, and Martial mentions them both together, for each supplied its dancers to Rome.

This dancing, alike whether Egyptian or Gaditanian, was the expression of the individual dancer's body and art; the garments played but a small part in it, they were frequently transparent, and sometimes discarded altogether. It was, and it remains, simple, personal, passionate dancing, classic, therefore, in the same sense as, on the side of literature, the poetry of Catullus is classic.[12]

Ancient Greek dancing was essentially classic dancing, as here understood. On the Greek vases, as reproduced in Emmanuel's attractive book on Greek dancing and elsewhere, we find the same play of the arms, the same sideward turn, the same extreme backward extension of the body, which had long before been represented in Egyptian monuments. Many supposedly modern movements in dancing were certainly already common both to Egyptian and Greek dancing, as well as the clapping of hands to keep time which is still an accompaniment of Spanish dancing. It seems clear, however, that, on this general classic and Mediterranean basis, Greek dancing had a development so refined and so special—though in technical elaboration of steps, it seems likely, inferior to modern dancing—that it exercised no influence outside Greece. Dancing became, indeed, the most characteristic and the most generally cultivated of Greek arts. Pindar, in a splendid Oxyrhynchine fragment, described Hellas, in what seemed to him supreme praise, as "the land of lovely dancing," and Athenaeus pointed out that he calls Apollo the Dancer. It may well be that the Greek drama arose out of dance and song, and that the dance throughout was an essential and plastic element in it. Even if we reject the statement of Aristotle that tragedy arose out of the Dionysian dithyramb, the alternative suppositions (such as Ridgeway's theory of dancing round the tombs of the dead) equally involve the same elements. It has often been pointed out that poetry in Greece demanded a practical knowledge of all that could be included under "dancing." Aeschylus is said to have developed the technique of dancing and Sophocles danced in his own dramas. In these developments, no doubt, Greek dancing tended to overpass the fundamental limits of classic dancing and foreshadowed the ballet.[13]

The real germ of the ballet, however, is to be found in Rome, where the pantomime with its concerted and picturesque method of expressive action was developed, and Italy is the home of Romantic dancing. The same impulse which produced the pantomime produced, more than a thousand years later in the same Italian region, the modern ballet. In both cases, one is inclined to think, we may trace the influence of the same Etruscan and Tuscan race which so long has had its seat there, a race with a genius for expressive, dramatic, picturesque art. We see it on the walls of Etruscan tombs and again in pictures of Botticelli and his fellow Tuscans. The modern ballet, it is generally believed, had its origin in the spectacular pageants at the marriage of Galeazzo Visconti, Duke of Milan, in 1489. The fashion for such performances spread to the other Italian courts, including Florence, and Catherine de' Medici, when she became Queen of France, brought the Italian ballet to Paris. Here it speedily became fashionable. Kings and queens were its admirers and even took part in it; great statesmen were its patrons. Before long, and especially in the great age of Louis XIV, it became an established institution, still an adjunct of opera but with a vital life and growth of its own, maintained by distinguished musicians, artists, and dancers. Romantic dancing, to a much greater extent than what I have called Classic dancing, which depends so largely on simple personal qualities, tends to be vitalised by transplantation and the absorption of new influences, provided that the essential basis of technique and tradition is preserved in the new development. Lulli in the seventeenth century brought women into the ballet; Camargo discarded the complicated costumes and shortened the skirt, so rendering possible not only her own lively and vigorous method, but all the freedom and airy grace of later dancing. It was Noverre who by his ideas worked out at Stuttgart, and soon brought to Paris by Gaetan Vestris, made the ballet a new and complete art form; this Swiss-French genius not only elaborated plot revealed by gesture and dance alone, but, just as another and greater Swiss-French genius about the same time brought sentiment and emotion into the novel, he brought it into the ballet. In the French ballet of the eighteenth century a very high degree of perfection seems thus to have been reached, while in Italy, where the ballet had originated, it decayed, and Milan, which had been its source, became the nursery of a tradition of devitalised technique carried to the finest point of delicate perfection. The influence of the French school was maintained as a living force into the nineteenth century,—when it was renovated afresh by the new spirit of the age and Taglioni became the most ethereal embodiment of the spirit of the Romantic movement in a form that was genuinely classic,—overspreading the world by the genius of a few individual dancers. When they had gone, the ballet slowly and steadily declined. As it declined as an art, so also it declined in credit and in popularity; it became scarcely respectable even to admire dancing. Thirty or forty years ago, those of us who still appreciated dancing as an art—and how few they were!—had to seek for it painfully and sometimes in strange surroundings. A recent historian of dancing, in a book published so lately as 1906, declared that "the ballet is now a thing of the past, and, with the modern change of ideas, a thing that is never likely to be resuscitated." That historian never mentioned Russian ballet, yet his book was scarcely published before the Russian ballet arrived to scatter ridicule over his rash prophecy by raising the ballet to a pitch of perfection it can rarely have surpassed, as an expressive, emotional, even passionate form of living art.

The Russian ballet was an offshoot from the French ballet and illustrates once more the vivifying effect of transplantation on the art of Romantic dancing. The Empress Anna introduced it in 1735 and appointed a French ballet-master and a Neapolitan composer to carry it on; it reached a high degree of technical perfection during the following hundred years, on the traditional lines, and the principal dancers were all imported from Italy. It was not until recent years that this firm discipline and these ancient traditions were vitalised into an art form of exquisite and vivid beauty by the influence of the soil in which they had slowly taken root. This contact, when at last it was effected, mainly by the genius of Fokine and the enterprise of Diaghilev, involved a kind of revolution, for its outcome, while genuine ballet, has yet all the effect of delicious novelty. The tradition by itself was in Russia an exotic without real life, and had nothing to give to the world; on the other hand, a Russian ballet apart from that tradition, if we can conceive such a thing, would have been formless, extravagant, bizarre, not subdued to any fine aesthetic ends. What we see here, in the Russian ballet as we know it to-day, is a splendid and arduous technical tradition, brought at last—by the combined skill of designers, composers, and dancers—into real fusion with an environment from which during more than a century it had been held apart; Russian genius for music, Russian feeling for rhythm, Russian skill in the use of bright colour, and, not least, the Russian orgiastic temperament, the Russian spirit of tender poetic melancholy, and the general Slav passion for folk-dancing, shown in other branches of the race also, Polish, Bohemian, Bulgarian, and Servian. At almost the same time what I have termed Classic dancing was independently revived in America by Isadora Duncan, bringing back what seemed to be the free naturalism of the Greek dance, and Ruth St. Denis, seeking to discover and revitalise the secrets of the old Indian and Egyptian traditions. Whenever now we find any restored art of theatrical dancing, as in the Swedish ballet, it has been inspired more or less, by an eclectic blending of these two revived forms, the Romantic from Russia, the Classic from America. The result has been that our age sees one of the most splendid movements in the whole history of the ballet.

FIVE

Dancing as an art, we may be sure, cannot die out, but will always be undergoing a rebirth. Not merely as an art, but also as a social custom, it perpetually emerges afresh from the soul of the people. Less than a century ago the polka thus arose, extemporised by the Bohemian servant girl Anna Slezakova out of her own head for the joy of her own heart, and only rendered a permanent form, apt for world-wide popularity, by the accident that it was observed and noted down by an artist. Dancing has for ever been in existence as a spontaneous custom, a social discipline. Thus it is, finally, that dancing meets us, not only as love, as religion, as art, but also as morals.

All human work, under natural conditions, is a kind of dance. In a large and learned book, supported by an immense amount of evidence, Karl Bücher has argued that work differs from the dance, not in kind, but only in degree, since they are both essentially rhythmic. There is a good reason why work should be rhythmic, for all great combined efforts, the efforts by which alone great constructions such as those of megalithic days could be carried out, must be harmonised. It has even been argued that this necessity is the source of human speech, and we have the so-called Yo-heave-ho theory of languages. In the memory of those who have ever lived on a sailing ship—that loveliest of human creations now disappearing from the world—there will always linger the echo of the chanties which sailors sang as they hoisted the topsail yard or wound the capstan or worked the pumps. That is the type of primitive combined work, and it is indeed difficult to see how such work can be effectively accomplished without such a device for regulating the rhythmic energy of the muscles. The dance rhythm of work has thus acted socialisingly in a parallel line with the dance rhythms of the arts, and indeed in part as their inspirer. The Greeks, it has been too fancifully suggested, by insight or by intuition understood this when they fabled that Orpheus, whom they regarded as the earliest poet, was specially concerned with moving stones and trees. Bücher has pointed out that even poetic metre may be conceived as arising out of work; metre is the rhythmic stamping of feet, as in the technique of verse it is still metaphorically called; iambics and trochees, spondees and anapaests and dactyls, may still be heard among blacksmiths smiting the anvil or navvies wielding their hammers in the streets. In so far as they arose out of work, music and singing and dancing are naturally a single art. A poet must always write to a tune, said Swinburne. Herein the ancient ballad of Europe is a significant type. It is, as the name indicates, a dance as much as a song, performed by a singer who sang the story and a chorus who danced and shouted the apparently meaningless refrain; it is absolutely the chanty of the sailors and is equally apt for the purposes of concerted work.[14] Yet our most complicated musical forms are evolved from similar dances. The symphony is but a development of a dance suite, in the first place folk-dances, such as Bach and Handel composed. Indeed a dance still lingers always at the heart of music and even the heart of the composer. Mozart, who was himself an accomplished dancer, used often to say, so his wife stated, that it was dancing, not music, that he really cared for. Wagner believed that Beethoven's Seventh Symphony—to some of us the most fascinating of them and the most purely musical—was an apotheosis of the dance, and, even if that belief throws no light on the intention of Beethoven, it is at least a revelation of Wagner's own feeling for the dance.

It is, however, the dance itself, apart from the work and apart from the other arts, which, in the opinion of many to-day, has had a decisive influence in socialising, that is to say in moralising, the human species. Work showed the necessity of harmonious rhythmic coöperation, but the dance developed that rhythmic coöperation and imparted a beneficent impetus to all human activities. It was Grosse, in his "Beginnings of Art," who first clearly set forth the high social significance of the dance in the creation of human civilisation. The participants in a dance, as all observers of savages have noted, exhibit a wonderful unison; they are, as it were, fused into a single being stirred by a single impulse. Social unification is thus accomplished. Apart from war, this is the chief factor making for social solidarity in primitive life; it was indeed the best training for war. It has been a twofold influence; on the one hand, it aided unity of action and method in evolution: on the other, it had the invaluable function—for man is naturally a timid animal—of imparting courage; the universal drum, as Louis Robinson remarks, has been an immense influence in human affairs. Even among the Romans, with their highly developed military system, dancing and war were definitely allied; the Salii constituted a college of sacred military dancers; the dancing season was March, the war-god's month and the beginning of the war season, and all through that month there were dances in triple measure before the temples and round the altars, with songs so ancient that not even the priests could understand them. We may trace a similar influence of dancing in all the coöperative arts of life. All our most advanced civilisation, Grosse insisted, is based on dancing. It is the dance that socialised man.

Thus, in the large sense, dancing has possessed peculiar value as a method of national education. As civilisation grew self-conscious, this was realised. "One may judge of a king," according to ancient Chinese maxim, "by the state of dancing during his reign." So also among the Greeks; it has been said that dancing and music lay at the foundation of the whole political and military as well as religious organisation of the Dorian states.

In the narrow sense, in individual education, the great importance of dancing came to be realised, even at an early stage of human development, and still more in the ancient civilisations. "A good education," Plato declared in the "Laws," the final work of his old age, "consists in knowing how to sing and dance well." And in our own day one of the keenest and most enlightened of educationists has lamented the decay of dancing; the revival of dancing, Stanley Hall declares, is imperatively needed to give poise to the nerves, schooling to the emotions, strength to the will, and to harmonise the feelings and the intellect with the body which supports them.

It can scarcely be said that these functions of dancing are yet generally realised and embodied afresh in education. For, if it is true that dancing engendered morality, it is also true that in the end, by the irony of fate, morality, grown insolent, sought to crush its own parent, and for a time succeeded only too well. Four centuries ago dancing was attacked by that spirit, in England called Puritanism, which was then spread over the greater part of Europe, just as active in Bohemia as in England, and which has, indeed, been described as a general onset of developing Urbanism against the old Ruralism. It made no distinction between good and bad, nor paused to consider what would come when dancing went. So it was that, as Remy de Gourmont remarks, the drinking-shop conquered the dance, and alcohol replaced the violin.

But when we look at the function of dancing in life from a higher and wider standpoint, this episode in its history ceases to occupy so large a place. The conquest over dancing has never proved in the end a matter for rejoicing, even to morality, while an art which has been so intimately mixed with all the finest and deepest springs of life has always asserted itself afresh. For dancing is the loftiest, the most moving, the most beautiful of the arts, because it is no mere translation or abstraction from life; it is life itself. It is the only art, as Rahel Varnhagen said, of which we ourselves are the stuff. Even if we are not ourselves dancers, but merely the spectators of the dance, we are still—according to that Lippsian doctrine of *Einfühlung* or "empathy" by Groos termed "the play of inner imitation"—which here, at all events, we may accept as true—feeling ourselves in the dancer who is manifesting and expressing the latent impulses of our own being.

It thus comes about that, beyond its manifold practical significance, dancing has always been felt to possess also a symbolic significance. Marcus Aurelius was accustomed to regard the art of life as like the dancer's art, though that Imperial Stoic could not resist adding that in some respects it was more like the wrestler's art. "I doubt not yet to make a figure in the great Dance of Life that shall amuse the spectators in the sky," said, long after, Blake, in the same strenuous spirit. In our own time, Nietzsche, from first to last, showed himself possessed by the conception of the art of life as a dance, in which the dancer achieves the rhythmic freedom and harmony of his soul beneath the shadow of a hundred Damoclean swords. He said the same thing of his style, for to him the style and the man were one: "My style," he wrote to his intimate friend Rohde, "is a dance." "Every day I count wasted," he said again, "in which there has been no dancing." The dance lies at the beginning of art, and we find it also at the end. The first creators of civilisation were making the dance, and the philosopher of a later age, hovering over the dark abyss of insanity, with bleeding feet and muscles strained to the breaking point, still seems to himself to be weaving the maze of the dance.

(1923)

Notes

[1]It is even possible that, in earlier than human times, dancing and architecture may have been the result of the same impulse. The nest of birds is the chief early form of building, and Edmund Selous has suggested (*Zoologist*, December, 1901) that the nest may first have arisen as an accidental result of the ecstatic sexual dance of birds.

[2]"Not the epic song, but the dance," Wundt says (*Völkerpsychologie*, 3d ed. 1911, Bd. I, Teil I, p. 277), "accompanied by a monotonous and often meaningless song, constitutes everywhere the most primitive, and, in spite of that primitiveness, the most highly developed art. Whether as a ritual dance, or as a pure emotional expression of the joy in rhythmic bodily movement, it rules the life of primitive men to such a degree that all other forms of art are subordinate to it."

[3]See an interesting essay in *The Dance of Siva: Fourteen Indian Essays*, by Ananda Coomaraswamy. New York, 1918.

[4]This view was clearly put forward, long ago, by W. W. Newell at the International Congress of Anthropology at Chicago in 1893. It has become almost a commonplace since.

[5]See a charming paper by Marcella Azra Hincks, "The Art of Dancing in Japan," *Fortnightly Review*, July, 1906. Pantomimic dancing, which has played a highly important part in Japan, was introduced into religion from China, it is said, in the earliest time, and was not adapted to secular purposes until the sixteenth century.

[6]I owe some of these facts to an interesting article by G. R. Mead, "The Sacred Dance of Jesus," *The Quest*, October, 1910.

[7]The dance of the Seises in Seville Cathedral is evidently of great antiquity, though it was so much a matter of course that we do not hear of it until 1690, when the Archbishop of the day, in opposition to the Chapter, wished to suppress it. A decree of the King was finally obtained permitting it, provided it was performed only by men, so that evidently, before that date, girls as well as boys took part in it. Rev. John Morris, "Dancing in Churches," *The Month*, December, 1892; also a valuable article on the Seises by J. B. Trend, in *Music and Letters*, January, 1921.

[8]See, for references, Havelock Ellis, *Studies in the Psychology of Sex*, vol. III; *Analysis of the Sexual Impulse*, pp. 29, etc.; and Westermarck, *History of Human Marriage*, vol. I, chap. XIII, p. 470.

[9]At an earlier period, however, the dance of Salome was understood much more freely and often more accurately. As Enlart has pointed out, on a capital in the twelfth-century cloister of Moissac, Salome holds a kind of castanets in her raised hands as she dances; on one of the western portals of Rouen Cathedral, at the beginning of the sixteenth century, she is dancing on her hands; while at Hemelverdeghem she is really executing the *morisco*, the *"danse du ventre."*

[10]For an excellent account of dancing in India, now being degraded by modern civilisation, see Otto Rothfeld, *Women of India*, chap. VII, "The Dancing Girl," 1922.

[11]I may hazard the suggestion that the gypsies may possibly have acquired their rather unaccountable name of Egyptians, not so much because they had passed through Egypt, the reason which is generally suggested,—for they must have passed through many countries,—but because of their proficiency in dances of the recognised Egyptian type.

[12]It is interesting to observe that Egypt still retains, almost unchanged through fifty centuries, its traditions, technique, and skill in dancing, while, as in ancient Egyptian dancing, the garment forms an almost or quite negligible element in the art. Loret remarks that a charming Egyptian dancer of the Eighteenth Dynasty, whose picture in her transparent gauze he reproduces, is an exact portrait of a charming Almeh of to-day whom he has seen dancing in Thebes with the same figure, the same dressing of the hair, the same jewels. I hear from a physician, a gynaecologist now practising in Egypt, that a dancing-girl can lie on her back, and with a full glass of water standing on one side of her abdomen and an empty glass on the other, can by the contraction of the muscles on the side supporting the full glass, project the water from it, so as to fill the empty glass. This, of course, is not strictly dancing, but it is part of the technique which underlies classic dancing and it witnesses to the thoroughness with which the technical side of Egyptian dancing is still cultivated.

[13]"We must learn to regard the form of the Greek drama as a dance form," says G. Warre Cornish in an interesting article on "Greek Drama and the Dance" (*Fortnightly Review,* February, 1913), "a musical symphonic dance-vision, through which the history of Greece and the soul of man are portrayed."

[14]It should perhaps be remarked that in recent times it has been denied that the old ballads were built up on dance songs. Miss Pound, for instance, in a book on the subject, argues that they were of aristocratic and not communal origin, which may well be, though the absence of the dance element does not seem to follow.

E. M. W. TILLYARD
From THE ELIZABETHAN WORLD PICTURE

THE COSMIC DANCE

Ever since the early Greek philosophers creation had been figured as an act of music; and the notion appealed powerfully to the poetically or the mystically minded. As late as 1687 Dryden gave it its best known rendering in English poetry, keeping strictly to the old tradition.

> From harmony, from heavenly harmony,
>   This universal frame began:
>   When nature underneath a heap
>   Of jarring atoms lay
>   And could not heave her head,
> The tuneful voice was heard from high:
>   Arise, ye more than dead.
> Then cold and hot and moist and dry
>   In order to their stations leap
>   And music's power obey.
> From harmony, from heavenly harmony,
>   This universal frame began;
> From harmony to harmony
> Through all the compass of the notes it ran,
> The diapason closing full in man.

But there was the further notion that the created universe was itself in a state of music, that it was one perpetual dance. It was a commonplace in the Middle Ages and occurs in the works of Isidore of Seville, most popular of all medieval encyclopedists. He wrote

> Nothing exists without music; for the universe itself is said to have been framed by a kind of harmony of sounds, and the heaven itself revolves under the tones of that harmony.

The idea of creation as a dance implies "degree," but degree in motion. The static battalions of the earthly, celestial, and divine hierarchies are sped on a varied but controlled peregrination to the accompaniment of music. The path of each is different, yet all the paths together make up a perfect whole. Shakespeare's

> Take but degree away, untune that string,
> And hark, what discord follows,

together with Lorenzo's speech on music shows his knowledge of the general doctrine. Elyot shows the same when he says that the governor's tutor

shall commend the perfect understanding of music, declaring how necessary it is for the better attaining the knowledge of a public weal: which is made of an order of estates and degrees, and, by reason thereof, containeth in it a perfect harmony: which the governor shall afterward more perfectly understand when he shall happen to read the books of Plato and Aristotle of public weals, wherein be written divers examples of music and geometry.

Like the static notion of degree, the dance to music is repeated on the different levels of existence. The angels or saints in their bands dance to the music of heaven. Milton has his own beautiful version of this dance in *Reason of Church Government:*

The angels themselves, in whom no disorder is feared, as the apostle that saw them in his rapture describes, are distinguished and quaternioned into their celestial princedoms and satrapies, according as God himself has writ his imperial decrees through the great provinces of heaven. Yet it is not to be conceived that these eternal effluences of sanctity and love in the glorified saints should by this means be confined and cloyed with repetition of that which is prescribed, but that our happiness may orb itself into a thousand vagancies of glory and delight, and with a kind of eccentrical equation be, as it were, an invariable planet of joy and felicity.

Milton speaks poetically not explicitly, but he certainly means that the blessed in heaven resemble the planetary spheres in the variety of their motions and in the music to which those motions are set. Nor is the comparison derogatory to the angels, for of all the dances that of the planets and stars to the music of the spheres in which they were fixed was the most famous.

On the earth natural things, although they shared in the effects of the Fall, are pictured as duplicating the planetary dance. Milton in *Comus*, which as a masque would turn its author's thoughts to dancing, not only expresses his sense of the world's fullness, of the vastness of the chain of being, but passes from immobility to motion. He pictures all the seas dancing in obedience to the moon and allows Comus himself to make the impudent claim that he and his crew are duplicating the dance of the planets:

> We that are of purer fire
> Imitate the Starry Quire
> Who in their nightly watchfull Sphears,
> Lead in swift round the Months and Years.
> The Sounds, and Seas with all their finny drove
> Now to the Moon in wavering Morrice move.

The notion of the seas dancing is not Milton's but is an inherited commonplace. Here is Sir John Davies's* version in *Orchestra:*

> And lo the sea, that fleets about the land
> And like a girdle clips her solid waist,
> Music and measure both doth understand;
> For his great chrystal eye is always cast
> Up to the moon and on her fixed fast.
> And as she danceth in her pallid sphere
> So danceth he about his centre here.

Further than *Orchestra* I need not go, for this poem is the perfect epitome of the universe seen as a dance. Davies published *Orchestra* in 1596 when he was a student as the Inns of Court aged 27. Popularly reputed to be a work of pure extravagance, it is poetically one of the airiest and nimblest of Elizabethan poems, hovering with accomplished skill between the fantastic and the sublime. It is not for nothing that it is contemporary with *A Midsummer Night's Dream*. In subject matter it combines invention with a mass of cosmic commonplaces. The poet recounts how one night when Penelope at Ithaca appeared among her suitors Athena inspired her with special beauty. Antinous, most courtly of the suitors, begs her to dance or in his own words to

> Imitate heaven, whose beauties excellent
> Are in continual motion day and night.

Penelope refuses to join in something that is mere disorder or misrule, and there follows a *débat* between the two on the subject

---

*Not to be confused with John Davies of Hereford, poet and writing-master. Sir John Davies was poet, lawyer, Attorney-General for Ireland, and author of a prose work on the Irish question.

of dancing, Antinous maintaining that as the universe itself is one great dance comprising many lesser dances we should ourselves join the cosmic harmony. It was creative love that first persuaded the warring atoms to move in order. Time and all its divisions are a dance. The stars have their own dance, the greatest being that of the Great Year, which lasts six thousand years of the sun. The sun courts the earth in a dance. The different elements have their different measures. The various happenings on the earth itself

> Forward and backward rapt and whirled are
> According to the music of the spheres.

The very plants and stones are in some sort included.

> See how those flowers that have sweet beauty too
> (The only jewels that the earth doth wear,
> When the young sun in bravery her doth woo),
> As oft as they the whistling wind do hear,
> Do wave their tender bodies here and there;
> And though their dance no perfect measure is,
> Yet oftentimes their music makes them kiss.

> What makes the vine about the elm to dance
> With turnings windings and embracements round?
> What makes the loadstone to the north advance
> His subtile point, as if from thence he found
> His chief attractive virtue to redound?
> Kind nature first doth cause all things to love;
> Love makes them dance and in just order move.

In human existence dancing is the very foundation of civilisation. Penelope herself is full of the dance without knowing it:

> Love in the twinkling of your eyelids danceth,
> Love danceth in your pulses and your veins,
> Love, when you sew, your needle's point advanceth
> And makes it dance a thousand curious strains
> Of winding rounds, whereof the form remains,
> To show that your fair hands can dance the hey,
> Which your fine feet would learn as well as they.

Then, prompted by the God of Love, Antinous in final persuasion gives Penelope a magic glass to look in, where she sees first the moon with a thousand stars moving round her and then the mortal moon, Elizabeth, surrounded by her Court.

Her brighter dazzling beams of majesty
Were laid aside, for she vouchsaf'd awhile
With gracious cheerful and familiar eye
Upon the revels of her court to smile;
For so time's journeys she doth oft beguile.
Like sight no mortal eye might elsewhere see,
So full of state art and variety.

For of her barons brave and ladies fair,
Who, had they been elsewhere, most fair had been,
Many an incomparable lovely pair
With hand in hand were interlinked seen,
Making fair honour to their sovereign queen.
Forward they pac'd and did their pace apply
To a most sweet and solemn melody.

Davies never finished his poem, but presumably the sight of
Queen Elizabeth as the central point of the court's dance-pattern
"in this our Golden Age" would have persuaded Penelope to lay
aside her prejudice.

The introduction of Queen Elizabeth and her court is not mere
flattery; it shows the cosmic dance reproduced in the body poli-
tic, thus completing the series of dances in macrocosm body pol-
itic and microcosm. But it stands too for something central to
Elizabethan ways of thinking: the agile transition from abstract
to concrete, from ideal to real, from sacred to profane. And the
reason is the one given before for similar catholicity: the Elizabethans were conscious simultaneously and to an uncommon
degree of "the erected wit and the infected will of man." It was
thus possible for Davies to pass from the mystical notion of the
spherical music to the concrete picture of Elizabeth's courtiers
dancing, without incongruity.

Orchestra is a fine poem. It serves as pure didacticism, as perfect
illustration of a general doctrine. Yet it draws poetic inspiration
from the doctrine it propounds. And it has no qualms or doubts
about the order it describes. It testifies to the preponderating
faith the Elizabethans somehow maintained in their perilously
poised world. Not that Davies does not know the things that
imperil it:

Only the earth doth stand for ever still,
Her rocks remove not nor her mountains meet;
(Although some wits enrich with learning's skill
Say heav'n stands firm and that the earth doth fleet

And swiftly turneth underneath their feet):
Yet, though the earth is ever stedfast seen,
On her broad breast hath dancing ever been.

If Davies knew (as here he shows he does) the Copernican astronomy, he must have known that this science had by then broken the fiction of the eternal and immutable heavens. But he trusts in his age and in the beliefs he has inherited, and like most of his contemporaries refuses to allow a mere inconsistency to interfere with the things he really has at heart.

(1943)

JANE HARRISON
From ANCIENT ART
AND RITUAL

FROM RITUAL TO ART

The distinction between art and ritual, which has so long haunted and puzzled us, now comes out quite clearly, and also in part the relation of each to actual life. Ritual, we saw, was a re-presentation or a pre-presentation, a re-doing or pre-doing, a copy or imitation of life, but—and this is the important point—always with a practical end. Art is also a representation of life and the emotions of life, but cut loose from immediate action. Action may be and often is represented, but it is not that it may lead on to a practical further end. The end of art is in itself. Its value is not mediate but *immediate*. Thus ritual *makes, as it were, a bridge between real life and art*, a bridge over which in primitive times it would seem man must pass. In his actual life he hunts and fishes and ploughs and sows, being utterly intent on the practical end of gaining his food; in the *dromenon* of the Spring Festival, though his *acts* are unpractical, being mere singing and dancing and mimicry, his *intent* is practical, to induce the return of his food-supply. In the drama the representation may remain for a time the same, but the intent is altered: man has come out from action, he is separate from the dancers, and has become a spectator. The drama is an end in itself.

We know from tradition that in Athens ritual became art, a *dromenon* became the drama, and we have seen that the shift is symbolized and expressed by the addition of the *theatre,* or spectator-place, to the orchestra, or dancing-place. We have also tried to analyse the meaning of the shift. It remains to ask what was its cause. Ritual does not always develop into art, though in all probability dramatic art has always to go through the stage of ritual. The leap from real life to the emotional contemplation of life cut loose from action would otherwise be too wide. Nature abhors a leap, she prefers to crawl over the ritual bridge. There seem at Athens to have been two main causes why the *dromenon* passed swiftly, inevitably, into the drama. They are, first, the decay of religious faith; second, the influx from abroad of a new culture and new dramatic material.

It may seem surprising to some that the decay of religious faith should be an impulse to the birth of art. We are accustomed to talk rather vaguely of art "as the handmaid of religion"; we think of art as "inspired by" religion. But the decay of religious faith of which we now speak is not the decay of faith in a god, or even the decay of some high spiritual emotion; it is the decay of a belief in the efficacy of certain magical rites, and especially of the Spring Rite. So long as people believed that by excited dancing, by bringing in an image or leading in a bull you could induce the coming of Spring, so long would the *dromena* of the dithyramb be enacted with intense enthusiasm, and with this enthusiasm would come an actual accession and invigoration of vital force. But, once the faintest doubt crept in, once men began to be guided by experience rather than custom, the enthusiasm would die down, and the collective invigoration no longer be felt. Then some day there will be a bad summer, things will go all wrong, and the chorus will sadly ask: "Why should I dance my dance?" They will drift away or become mere spectators of a rite established by custom. The rite itself will die down, or it will live on only as the May Day rites of today, a children's play, or at best a thing done vaguely "for luck."

The spirit of the rite, the belief in its efficacy, dies, but the rite itself, the actual mould, persists, and it is this ancient ritual mould, foreign to our own usage, that strikes us today, when a Greek play is revived, as odd and perhaps chill. A *chorus,* a band of dancers there must be, because the drama arose out of a ritual dance. An *agon,* or contest, or wrangling, there will probably be, because Summer contends with Winter, Life with Death, the New Year with the Old. A tragedy must be tragic, must have its *pathos*, because the Winter, the Old Year, must die. There must needs be a swift transition, a clash and change from sorrow to joy, what the Greeks called a *peripeteia*, a *quick-turn-around*, because, though you carry out Winter, you bring in Summer. At the end we shall have an Appearance, an Epiphany of a god, because the whole gist of the ancient ritual was to summon the spirit of life. All these ritual forms haunt and shadow the play, whatever its plot, like ancient traditional ghosts; they underlie and sway the movement and the speeches like some compelling rhythm.

Now this ritual mould, this underlying rhythm, is a fine thing in itself; and, moreover, it was once shaped and cast by a living spirit: the intense immediate desire for food and life, and for the return of the seasons which bring that food and life. But we have seen that, once the faith in man's power magically to bring back these seasons waned, once he began to doubt whether he could really carry out Winter and bring in Summer, his emotion towards these rites would cool. Further, we have seen that these rites repeated year by year ended, among an imaginative people, in the mental creation of some sort of daemon or god. This daemon, or god, was more and more held responsible on his own account for the food-supply and the order of the Horae, or Seasons; so we get the notion that this daemon or god himself led in the Seasons; Hermes dances at the head of the Charites, or an Eiresione is carried to Helios and the Horae. The thought then arises that this man-like daemon who rose from a real King of the May, must himself be approached and dealt with as a man, bargained with, sacrificed to. In a word, in place of *dromena*, things done, we get gods worshipped; in place of sacraments, holy bulls killed and eaten in common, we get sacrifices in the modern sense, holy bulls offered to yet holier gods. The relation of these figures of gods to art we shall consider when we come to sculpture.

So the *dromenon*, the thing done, wanes, the prayer, the praise, the sacrifice waxes. Religion moves away from drama towards theology, but the ritual mould of the *dromenon* is left ready for a new content.

Again, there is another point. The magical *dromenon*, the Carrying out of Winter, the Bringing in of Spring, is doomed to an inherent and deadly monotony. It is only when its magical efficacy is intensely believed that it can go on. The life-history of a holy bull is always the same; its magical essence is that it should be the same. Even when the life-daemon is human his career is unchequered. He is born, initiated, or born again; he is married, grows old, dies, is buried; and the old, old story is told again next year. There are no fresh personal incidents, peculiar to one particular daemon. If the drama rose from the Spring Song only, beautiful it might be, but with a beauty that was monotonous, a beauty doomed to sterility.

We seem to have come to a sort of *impasse*, the spirit of the *dromenon* is dead or dying, the spectators will not stay long to watch a doing doomed to monotony. The ancient moulds are there, the old bottles, but where is the new wine? The pool is stagnant; what angel will step down to trouble the waters?

Fortunately we are not left to conjecture what *might* have happened. In the case of Greece we know, though not as clearly as we wish, what did happen. We can see in part why, though the *dromena* of Adonis and Osiris, emotional as they were and intensely picturesque, remained mere ritual; the *dromenon* of Dionysos, his dithyramb, blossomed into drama.

Let us look at the facts, and first at some structural facts in the building of the theatre.

We have seen that the orchestra, with its dancing chorus, stands for ritual, for the stage in which all were worshippers, all joined in a rite of practical intent. We further saw that the *theatre*, the place for the spectators, stood for art. In the orchestra all is life and dancing; the marble *seats* are the very symbol of rest, aloofness from action, contemplation. The seats for the spectators grow and grow in importance till at last they absorb, as it were, the whole spirit, and give their name *theatre* to the whole structure; action is swallowed up in contemplation. But contemplation of what? At first, of course, of the ritual dance, but not for long. That, we have seen, was doomed to a deadly monotony. In a Greek theatre there was not only orchestra and a spectator-place, there was also a *scene* or *stage*.

The Greek word for stage is, as we said, *skenè*, our scene. The *scene* was not a stage in our sense, i.e., a platform raised so that the players might be better viewed. It was simply a tent, or rude hut, in which the players, or rather dancers, could put on their ritual dresses. The fact that the Greek theatre had, to begin with no permanent stage in our sense, shows very clearly how little it was regarded as a spectacle. The ritual dance was a *dromenon*, a thing to be done, not a thing to be looked at. The history of the Greek stage is one long story of the encroachment of the stage on the orchestra. At first a rude platform or table is set up, then scenery is added; the movable tent is translated into a stone house or a temple front. This stands at first outside the orchestra; then bit by bit the *scene* encroaches till the sacred circle of the dancing-place is cut clean across. As the drama and the stage wax, the *dromenon* and the orchestra wane. . . .

Greek tragedy arose, Aristotle has told us, from the *leaders* of the dithyramb, the leaders of the Spring Dance. The Spring Dance, the mime of Summer and Winter, had, as we have seen, only one actor, one actor with two parts—Death and Life. With only one play to be played, and that a one-actor play, there was not much need for a stage. A *scene*, that is a *tent*, was needed, as we saw, because all the dancers had to put on their ritual gear, but scarcely a stage. From a rude platform the prologue might be spoken, and on that platform the Epiphany or Appearance of the New Year might take place; but the play played, the life-history of the life-spirit, was all too familiar; there was no need to look, the thing was to dance. You need a stage—not necessarily a raised stage, but a place apart from the dancers—when you have new material for your players, something you need to look at, to attend to. In the sixth century B.C., at Athens, came *the* great innovation. Instead of the old plot, the life-history of the life-spirit, with its deadly monotony, new plots were introduced, not of life-spirits but of human individual heroes. In a word, Homer came to Athens, and out of Homeric stories playwrights began to make their plots. This innovation was the death of ritual monotony and the *dromenon*. It is not so much the old that dies as the new that kills.

(1913)

ROSS WETZSTEON
THE WHIRLING DERVISHES:
AN EMPTINESS FILLED
WITH EVERYTHING

Circles . . . white circles . . . circles of light . . . I'm trying to find
the right words . . . but cliches are never more common than
when we're confronted by transcendence . . . I'm trying to find
something better than T-shirt Sufisms to describe the feelings
aroused by the swirling undulations of the Whirling Dervishes'
skirts . . . don't say "hypnotic" . . . don't say "parables of ecstasy"
. . . something about the relationship between movement and
meditation . . . the transfixing serenity of ceaseless motion . . . the
revolutions revealing, like the circles they describe, that the center is synonymous with the whole . . . that timelessness has its
own rhythms . . . I start to take notes on the pad in my lap,
watching the Whirling Dervishes last week in Austin, Texas, but
I immediately sense the shock of the elderly lady on my right,
my hostess and guide, a devotee of the Mevlevi Sufi order of
Islam, and smile as I realize I agree with her—how detached!
taking notes on ecstatic trances—then smile at the smile, as I also
realize that whatever *she's* feeling, I've fallen into the rational-
ist's prejudice against reason, our materialistic preference for
emotional participation over intellectual detachment, our naive
assumption, in fact, that immanence and abstraction are contradictory. Eastern thought has entered our consciousness without
having passed through our intelligence—even more western
than disengagement is our will and will-lessness, our self-loath-
ing decision to float with the self.

So I continue to take notes, mildly self-contemptuous, when I
suddenly realize I've already mentally accused the dervishes
themselves of the same kind of spurious duality—a kind of self-
observing, self-transcendence. On the plane from New York to
Texas, I'd decided that to mention that the Whirling Dervishes
had a press agent for their American tour would be to exploit a
glib paradox—the intelligentsia's easy scorn for America's tacky
eclecticism, the taco-burgers of cultural journalism—but still,

several troubling questions remained. Facetiously, if the Pope were to travel to Tokyo, expenses paid by Sushi University, to perform a high mass in a prosceniumed temple for the entertainment of 2000 Buddists at 50 yen a head, would the wine and wafer transubstantiate? More seriously, if one begins by wondering what access non-believers can have to an unfamiliar religious ritual they merely witness for their ecumenical edification, a kind of spiritual window shopping, one has to go on to speculate how the believers themselves can survive such circumstances. Would the spirit be ready at curtain time? Would not some violation of the soul be involved? Religious ritual, of course, is not performed for its own sake—which is the only way a non-believer can experience it (e.g., the mass as spectacle, or, in this case, the Whirling Dervishes as dance)—but as a means of reaching another level of being, as a way of releasing spiritual meaning. What you see, in short, is not what you get. A sacrament is merely the outwards of an inner grace, so, just as wine is fermented grape juice to a Turk, would not whirling be show biz to an American? And worse, from the point of view of the believers themselves, might the spectators, who can't follow, actually hold the participants back? To perform a religious ritual at the behest not of the soul, not of the communicants, but of an *audience*—wouldn't the altered purpose of the ritual debase the ritual itself?—vinegar instead of blood? vertigo instead of levitation?

But then—halfway across the circle I also remembered what had seemed at the time merely an amusing confusion with my hostess and guide an hour before the performance. Trying to communicate between English and Turkish in insecure French, I asked, thinking of avant-garde dance, of Robert Wilson and Andy de Groat in particular, how the Whirling Dervishes felt about the appropriation of spinning for non-religious purposes. Madame Atashi responded as she frequently did, with a smiling Sufi parable, which I ineptly translated as follows: "Man want to say prayer for he who died. Other man ask, who died? First man answer, he who put on the hat only for play." When I discerned that "the hat" referred to the sacred hat used by the Whirling Dervishes in their religious ceremonies, the meaning of the parable became clear—to adopt the surface appurtenances of the ritual (and, in answer to my question, for American dancers to spin) is to die. But as Madame Atashi went on to talk about the masters' love and tolerance for non-believers, I became increasingly unsure of my self-satisfied interpretation—until suddenly it dawned on me that to her the parable meant just the opposite, that one must pray for everyone, even for those "who put on the hat only for play." Relax, Bob and Andy.

Sufi parables, of course, are intended to yield multiple meanings, and even though the meaning I had found in this particular case was clearly false, its very falseness made me aware of another meaning—that one mustn't be too sure. If I had arrived at a different but equally valid interpretation from Madame Atashi, in short, I would have discerned one level of Sufi truth, the multiplicity of meanings. But having utterly missed the point, I was reminded of a deeper level of truth—the insecurity of even the multiplicity of meanings—the truth that you can learn from being wrong.

But what did any of this have to do with the spinning taking place on stage? Simply that this particular circle was now complete—something about the relationship between movement and mediation—but not so much a circle as a spiral, returning to the same point but on a different level. And now the issues of whether or not to take notes, of the Pope in Tokyo, of prayers and parables, of sacraments and Sufisms, didn't seem answered so much as irrelevant. Back to the stage, to the swirling skirts, now neither a detached witness, nor a Sufi convert, but at least willing to be unsure, and perhaps even—for all they ask is our openness—ready to levitate.

Arms crossed over their chests, each hand grasping the opposite shoulder—after the 10-minute opening chant by the Hafiz, the 10-minute prelude by the reed flute, after walking solemnly in a circle and kissing the Sheik's hand—each of the seven dervishes begins to turn slowly counter-clockwise. Two, three, four, five times—and at the first fluttering moment of spiritual quickening, each dervish feeling his own intimation of ascension, their hands slowly leave their shoulders and their arms slowly extend and rise, both meanings of grace, an inaudible hymn, the first bird unfolding its wings. Pivoting on their left feet and wheeling their right legs around "the pillar," their right palms up, their left palms down, as if in acceptance and dispensation, they continue to revolve slowly counter-clockwise around the pivots, which themselves rotate counter-clockwise around the stage, seven circles within a larger circle. Despite the common image, the last thing one feels in the presence of the dervishes is any sense of frenzy—their spinning evokes, rather, an effortless, tranquil, almost stately ecstasy. Four times they spin, approximately 10 minutes each time, followed by a brief recita-

The Whirling Dervishes. "Despite the common image, the last thing one feels in the presence of the dervishes is any sense of frenzy—their spinning evokes, rather, an effortless, tranquil, almost stately ecstasy." (Wetzsteon)

tion from the Koran and the concluding sound "Hu," all the names of God in one.

What's a theater critic to say? Some of the spinners are clearly more "talented" than others, and if the truth were known, many New York dancers I've seen are "better" spinners than most of the dervishes (though Dogan Ergin is surely one of the finest flute players in the world). But talent is beside the point—was Raphael closer to God than the daubers in his classes? The dervishes are less artists than priests, and the priest fulfills his function less through his talent than through our participation, less through private inspiration than through communal designation, as assent of which he is more servant than beneficiary. So "evaluation" is also clearly beside the point—one might "review" Raphael, but not the mass—an incompetent dervish might embrace his God more ecstatically than a master. But let's put on the hat for a moment, if only for play.

Madame Atashi, when I asked her to try to put into words the nature of the "experience" she kept talking about, said simply, "to feel it is better than to describe it." Well, yes, this is what critics always hear, and it always seems both self-evident and evasive. It's a little too convenient to believe in "mute Miltons" if your poetry is lousy. But then, one of the dervishes asked me after the performance for my reaction, and I found myself agreeing—to say anything at all is difficult, for to undertake the act of detachment necessary to describe is precisely to deny the feeling of the experience.

But having suffered the sloppy solipsism of non-verbalists none too gladly myself, I hastened to add, in embarrassment, that there are *some* questions I can now answer: The dervishes feel that non-believers, as well as believing non-participants, can share the ecstatic experience (if they are *disposés*, in Madame Atashi's word); they themselves don't invariably enter such a state at every performance *(individuel aussi)*; the circle, unlike the cross, is tolerant, the only form in which every part is equal; and spinning, like a circle, is an emptiness filled with everything.

On a Sunday afternoon, in the summer of 1961, on the island Paros, in the middle of the Cyclades in the middle of the Aegean, I sat on the shore and watched the waves. After about an hour, I gradually realized I was coming out of something. The only words I could find to describe the experience were hopelessly banal—the feeling of being outside of one's body, the oneness of the universe, etc., etc. But the banality of the words was utterly irrelevant—and since that day, I've never felt a moment's fear of death. Now like you, and you, I wince when people start to tell me about their extraordinary "mystical experiences." But the odd thing is, that hour on the beach didn't feel extraordinary at all— the only extraordinary thing about it was how matter-of-fact it felt—if I felt it was extraordinary, I'd lose it.

(1978)

ROLAND BARTHES
STRIPTEASE

Striptease—at least Parisian striptease—is based on a contradiction: Woman is desexualized at the very moment when she is stripped naked. We may therefore say that we are dealing in a sense with a spectacle based on fear, or rather on the pretence of fear, as if eroticism here went no further than a sort of delicious terror, whose ritual signs have only to be announced to evoke at once the idea of sex and its conjuration.

It is only the time taken in shedding clothes which makes voyeurs of the public; but here, as in any mystifying spectacle, the decor, the props and the stereotypes intervene to contradict the initially provocative intention and eventually bury it in insignificance: evil is *advertised* the better to impede and exorcize it. French striptease seems to stem from what I have earlier called "Operation Margarine," a mystifying device which consists in inoculating the public with a touch of evil, the better to plunge it afterwards into a permanently immune Moral Good: a few particles of eroticism, highlighted by the very situation on which the show is based, are in fact absorbed in a reassuring ritual which negates the flesh as surely as the vaccine or the taboo circumscribes and controls the illness or the crime.

There will therefore be in striptease a whole series of coverings placed upon the body of the woman in proportion as she pretends to strip it bare. Exoticism is the first of these barriers, for it is always of a petrified kind which transports the body into the world of legend or romance: a Chinese woman equipped with an opium pipe (the indispensable symbol of "Sininess"), an undulating vamp with a gigantic cigarette-holder, a Venetian decor complete with gondola, a dress with panniers and a singer of serenades: all aim at establishing the woman *right from the start* as an object in disguise. The end of the striptease is then no longer to drag into the light a hidden depth, but to signify, through the shedding of an incongruous and artificial clothing, nakedness as a *natural* vesture of woman, which amounts in the end to regaining a perfectly chaste state of the flesh.

The classic props of the music-hall, which are invariably rounded up here, constantly make the unveiled body more remote, and force it back into the all-pervading ease of a well-known rite: the furs, the fans, the gloves, the feathers, the fishnet stockings, in short the whole spectrum of adornment, constantly makes the living body return to the category of luxurious objects which surround man with a magical decor. Covered with feathers or gloved, the woman identifies herself here as a stereotyped element of music-hall, and to shed objects as ritualistic as these is no longer a part of a further, genuine undressing. Feathers, furs and gloves go on pervading the woman with their magical virtue even once removed, and give her something like the enveloping memory of a luxurious shell, for it is a self-evident law that the whole of striptease is given in the very nature of the initial garment: if the latter is improbable, as in the case of the Chinese woman or the woman in furs, the nakedness which follows remains itself unreal, smooth and enclosed like a beautiful slippery object, withdrawn by its very extravagance from human use: this is the underlying significance of the G-String covered with diamonds or sequins which is the very end of striptease. This ultimate triangle, by its pure and geometrical shape, by its hard and shiny material, bars the way to the sexual parts like a sword of purity, and definitively drives the woman back into a mineral world, the (precious) stone being here the irrefutable symbol of the absolute object, that which serves no purpose.

Contrary to the common prejudice, the dance which accompanies the striptease from beginning to end is in no way an erotic element. It is probably quite the reverse: the faintly rhythmical undulation in this case exorcizes the fear of immobility. Not only does it give to the show the alibi of Art (the dances in strip-shows are always "artistic"), but above all it constitutes the last barrier, and the most efficient of all: the dance, consisting of ritual gestures which have been seen a thousand times, acts on movements as a cosmetic, it hides nudity, and smothers the spectacle under a glaze of superfluous yet essential gestures, for the act of becoming bare is here relegated to the rank of parasitical operations carried out in an improbable background. Thus we see the professionals of striptease wrap themselves in the miraculous ease which constantly clothes them, makes them remote, gives them the icy indifference of skillful practitioners, haughtily taking refuge in the sureness of their technique: their science clothes them like a garment.

All this, this meticulous exorcism of sex, can be verified *a contrario* in the "popular contests" *(sic)* of amateur striptease: there, "beginners" undress in front of a few hundred spectators without resorting or resorting very clumsily to magic, which unquestionably restores to the spectacle its erotic power. Here we find at the beginning far fewer Chinese or Spanish women, no feathers or furs (sensible suits, ordinary coats), few disguises as a starting point—gauche steps, unsatisfactory dancing, girls constantly threatened by immobility, and above all by a "technical" awkwardness (the resistance of briefs, dress or bra) which gives to the gestures of unveiling an unexpected importance, denying the woman the alibi of art and the refuge of being an object, imprisoning her in a condition of weakness and timorousness.

And yet, at the *Moulin Rouge*, we see hints of another kind of exorcism, probably typically French, and one which in actual fact tends less to nullify eroticism than to tame it: the compère tries to give striptease a reassuring petit-bourgeois status. To start with, striptease is a *sport:* there is a Striptease Club, which organizes healthy contests whose winners come out crowned and rewarded with edifying prizes (a subscription to physical training lessons), a novel (which can only be Robbe-Grillet's *Voyeur*), or useful prizes (a pair of nylons, five thousand francs). Then, striptease is identified with a *career* (beginners, semi-professionals, professionals), that is, to the honourable practice of a specialization (strippers are skilled workers). One can even give them the magical alibi of work: *vocation;* one girl is, say, *"doing well"* or *"well on the way to fulfilling her promise,"* or on the contrary *"taking her first steps"* on the arduous path of striptease. Finally and above all, the competitors are socially situated; one is a salesgirl, another a secretary (there are many secretaries in the Striptease Club). Striptease here is made to rejoin the world of the public, is made familiar and bourgeois, as if the French, unlike the American public (at least according to what one hears), following an irresistible tendency of their social status, could not conceive eroticism except as a household property, sanctioned by the alibi of weekly sport much more than by that of a magical spectacle: and this is how, in France, striptease is nationalized.

(1957)

ROGER COPELAND
DANCE, PHOTOGRAPHY, AND THE WORLD'S BODY

In her influential book *On Photography*, Susan Sontag offers a rather uncharitable explanation for the current level of interest in the photographic arts:

> The seemingly insatiable appetite for photography in the 1970's expresses more than the pleasure of discovering and exploring a relatively neglected art form. . . . Paying more and more attention to photographs is a great relief to sensibilities tired of or eager to avoid the mental exertions demanded by abstract art. Classical modernist painting presupposes highly developed skills of looking, and a familiarity with other art and with certain notions about the history of art. Photography, like pop art, reassures viewers that art isn't hard; it seems to be more about subjects than about art.

But I'd like to suggest that the current enthusiasm for photography is evidence of something other than a growing perceptual and intellectual laziness, something much more positive (and necessary). Granted, we are at this moment experiencing a "backlash" against modernism (or more specifically, against two closely related manifestations of the "modern": formalism and minimalism). And yes, photography has benefited substantially from this shift in sensibility. But it's essential to recognize that this widespread dissatisfaction with two of the avant-garde's most celebrated projects was initiated in most instances by the artists themselves and not in response to a restless, fickle, and inattentive public.[1]

The fact of the matter is that the arts simply cannot pursue the goal of "self-purification" indefinitely. By "self-purification" I mean the two different varieties of radical surgery that the arts have performed on themselves during the last 100 years. First came the process that Ortega y Gasset called "dehumanization" in which the arts purged themselves of their "human content" or "lived reality." This resulted in a variety of "formalism." Art stopped serving as a "criticism of life" (Matthew Arnold's conception of art's function). Art turned its back on the world and refused to "hold the mirror up to nature."

Subsequently, the separate arts underwent an even more impoverishing variety of "purification" that Clement Greenberg calls "self-criticism":

> What had to be exhibited and made explicit was that which was unique and irreducible not only in art in general but also in each particular art . . . The task of self-criticism became to eliminate from the effects of each art any and every effect that might conceivably be borrowed from or by the medium of any other art. Thereby each art would be rendered "pure." ("Modernist Painting")

Less, in other words, is more. But surely, at some point in time, it becomes a purely practical, if not an ideological or spiritual necessity, for art to re-establish relations with "the world" and to reclaim for itself those aspects of human experience once rigorously excised in the name of modernist purity.

Some of the various activities loosely referred to as "conceptual art" provide a case (perhaps *the* case) in point. Here, the quest for self-purification led art to divest itself of its very object-hood.[2] And significantly (at least for my purposes here), the only factor lending many such experiences a semblance of "materiality" was photographic documentation. Oftentimes, the photograph not only lent a touch of "permanence" to an otherwise ephemeral event, it also served to "situate" the event in the larger context of "the world" (the same world that the event itself—in its defiantly self-referential way—often refused to acknowledge). The world, as it turns out, does not cease to exist simply because we refuse to acknowledge it.

And at approximately the same time (late '60's early '70's), photography began to achieve widespread acceptance as an art in its own right. I don't think it's coincidental that dance is the only other art to have flourished so visibly in the '70's. Both photography and dance help restore to us what John Crowe Ransom called "the world's body." Ransom complained that science had robbed the world of its body by concerning itself only with the abstract principles which underlie experience, rather than with the concrete immediacy of experience itself ("as science more and more completely reduces the world to its types and forms, art, replying, must invest it again with a body" wrote Ransom).

Siegfried Kracauer has written at great length about the extent to which the modernist arts unwittingly sustain this curse of scientific abstractness:[3] "Abstract painting," he argues, "is not so much an anti-realistic movement as a realistic revelation of the prevailing abstractness." Photography and the cinema, on the other hand, can help bring about what he calls "a redemption of physical reality" by "clinging to the surface of things" (rather than extracting their skeletal substructure or interior meaning).[4] Clearly, for Kracauer, abstraction equals subtraction, and art is left impoverished rather than purified.

But even the most abstract photograph is "connected" to the world beyond it in a way that a painting by, say, Ad Reinhardt or Frank Stella is not. Sontag makes this point deftly (even if she doesn't acknowledge its healthier implications):

> ... the identification of the subject of a photograph always domi-
> nates our perception of it—as it does not necessarily, in a painting.
> The subject of Weston's "Cabbage Leaf," taken in 1931, looks like a
> fall of gathered cloth; a title is needed to identify it. Thus, the image
> makes its point in two ways. The form is pleasing, and it is (sur-
> prise!) the form of a cabbage leaf. If it were gathered cloth, it
> wouldn't be so beautiful. We already know that beauty, from the
> fine arts. Hence ... what a photograph is *of* is always of primary
> importance. The assumption underlying all uses of photography,
> that each photograph is a piece of the world means that we don't
> know how to react to a photograph ... until we know *what* piece
> of the world it is. What looks like a bare coronet—the famous pho-
> tograph taken by Harold Edgerton in 1936—becomes far more
> interesting when we find out it is a splash of milk.

Kracauer makes the closely related argument that photography (and the cinema) are the only arts which continually re-direct the viewers' attention back to the pre-existing world.[5] The other arts—especially in their abstract, modernist phases—consume and transcend their raw materials.

What Kracauer says of photography is perhaps even truer of much contemporary dance. For example, George Balanchine is often accused of "dehumanizing" his ballerinas; and there are in fact a great many parallels to be drawn between his choreography and the proposals Ortega makes in his famous essay. Balanchine, at least in his formalist works, eliminates the narrative structure and the theatrical accessories (period costume and scenery) we associate with 19th Century classical ballet. But in contrast with those minimalists in the other arts who progressively eliminated the human form, the end result of Balanchine's paring-down process is to reveal the palpable physicality of the dancer's body more fully than it has ever been revealed before. Thus, perhaps ironically, the more "abstract" and the more "minimalist" the Balanchine ballet, the more it exhibits what Ransom called "the bodiness of the world."

We might go further and say that contemporary dance in the popular, stripped-down, Balanchinian mold has brought about the "de-sublimation" of the dancer's body. Even though we routinely define dance as the art of the human body in motion, it's only in our own time that choreographers have chosen to reveal rather than conceal the actual human form. As long as dance, like the other arts, was envisioned as a mode of sublimation (that is, the conversion of bodily energy into something more spiritual, something worthy of the soul), the dancer's body invariably served a "higher" end beyond itself. In the earliest court ballets for example, the body was allegorized; its significance lay in the allegorical meaning of the group pattern that enveloped it. In the romantic ballet, the body was etherealized; "spirituality" could only be achieved by transcending its materiality.

But in our own de-sublimating century, we have come more and more to believe (as D. H. Lawrence argued) that the soul is *in* the body. (Consider the way Afro-American street jargon has re-defined the word "soul.") Thus, choreographers such as Balanchine, Cunningham, Yvonne Rainer, and Lucinda Childs have created dances that are, in their own way, profoundly responsive to our new "spiritual" (as well as aesthetic) needs.

Ultimately, dance and photography offer at least a provisional solution to the problem Ortega y Gasset refers to as "the progressive dis-realization of the world":

> "The progressive dis-realization of the world" which began in the philosophy of the Renaissance reaches its extreme consequences in the radical sensationalism of Avenarius and Mach. How can this continue? . . . A return to primitive realism is unthinkable: four centuries of criticism, of doubt, of suspicion have made this attitude forever untenable. To remain in our subjectivism is equally impossible. Where shall we find the material to reconstruct the world? ("On Point of View in the Arts")

Dance, as we've seen, can never completely lose touch with the human form (as John Martin once wrote, "no movement can be made by the human body which is wholly non-representational"); and likewise, photography invariably reveals some aspect of the material world. But at the same time, neither dance nor photography is in any danger of lapsing into a naive, regressive realism. Dance is inherently "unrealistic" to the extent that the human figure is estranged from the world of speech. Analogously, photographic art (unlike cinematic art) remains for the most part uninterested in the "realism" of color. Despite the attention recently lavished on serious photographers who work in color (William Eggleston, for example), most photographic artists remain committed to the more "abstract" beauty of black and white (which is not to say that all color photography is necessarily "realistic").

Ortega thought that a formal appreciation of art was incompatible with a more directly empathic involvement in "lived reality":

> Perception of lived reality and the perception of artistic form . . . are essentially incompatible because they call for a different adjustment of our perceptive apparatus.

Commenting on Titian's portrait of Charles the Fifth on horseback, Ortega argues that in order to appreciate the painting properly

> . . . we must forget that this is Charles the Fifth in person and see instead a portrait—that is, an image, a fiction. The portrayed person and his portrait are two entirely different things: we are interested in either one or the other. In the first case, we "live" with Charles the Fifth, in the second, we look at an object of art. ("The Dehumanization of Art")

But this is precisely the sort of either/or dichotomy that photography transcends. When we look at André Kertész's "Railroad Station" (1937), we see *both* an arrangement of forms and lines reminiscent of Cubist painting *and* a "human reality" we readily recognize from our own mundane experience.

To Ortega, the mutual exclusivity of "formalism" and "realism" mirrored the unbridgeable nature of the gap between the avant-garde artist and "the masses." But today, the desire to "épater le bourgeois" appears to be on the wane; and what Lionel Trilling once called "the adversary relationship" between the avant-garde artist and middle-class society has transformed into something more closely resembling peaceful co-existence. This is the cultural ambience in which photography and dance now thrive.

(1977, 1981)

Notes

¹This desire to escape the minimalist cul-de-sac is evident in almost all of the arts, not just painting. In the mid-sixties, Twyla Tharp, for example, was creating minimalist dances for performers who were

rarely called upon to move, let alone "dance" in a virtuosic manner. Yet today, she choreographs for Baryshnikov. Composers like Steve Reich and Philip Glass have progressively "thickened" the textures of their once minimal music. And in the world of architecture, Robert Venturi has led the revolt against minimal "purity" by declaring "Less is a bore."

[2]Of course, the conceptualists were motivated by other concerns as well, chief among them being the desire to create "non-buyable" artworks. Thus, photography, while re-locating the conceptual event in the world, also re-implicated it in the dynamics of the marketplace (because photographic documentation is collectable).

[3]Ironically, Kracauer would dismiss as "abstract" the very sort of poetry that Ransom championed in his book *The World's Body*. Ransom felt that the poetic image (or "iconic sign") was more concrete than the abstract, scientific "concept" which gives us not the world's body, but the world's skeleton.

[4]The word "redemption" betrays the essentially "spiritual" nature of Kracauer's argument. Like Bazin (whom he resembles in so many ways) Kracauer saw modernism as the creation of an alternative world which further estranges an already alienated species from its natural habitat. So perhaps I should make clear the extent to which I'm appropriating the work of Kracauer and Bazin for my own (purely secular) purposes. Both of them are just as opposed to formalist abstraction in the photographic arts as they are in the other arts (in fact, even more so). But *my* point is that even the most "abstract" photograph still demonstrates their essential ideas about the special relation between the photograph and its subject (even if that subject is "pre-stylized").

[5]Furthermore, in *Theory of Film*, Kracauer insists that, unlike painting, the frame of the photograph "is only a provisional limit, its content refers to other contents outside the frame." Stanley Cavell expands on this idea nicely in his book, *The World Viewed:* "You can always ask, pointing to an object in a photograph—a building, say—what lies behind it, totally obscured by it. This only accidentally makes sense when asked of an object in a painting. You can always ask, of an area photographed, what lies adjacent to that area, beyond the frame. This generally makes no sense asked of a painting. You can ask these questions of objects in photographs because they have answers in reality. The world of a painting is not continuous with the world of its frame; at its frame, a world finds its limits. We might say: A painting *is* a world: a photograph is *of* the world."

RUTH KATZ
THE EGALITARIAN WALTZ

One need not be an anthropologist or a cultural historian to remark that social dancing these days seems to isolate the individual in a trance-like self-absorption which virtually disconnects him from the world and even from his partner. Indeed, the dance of the day—like other art forms—is often a good reflection of the values of a given time and place. Today's developments, both in the dance and in society, provide more than the usual scholarly justification for looking back to one of the earliest manifestations of individualism and escape in the dance and its association with the values of liberty, equality and uncertainty which followed upon the French Revolution. The dance was the waltz; the dancers, at first, were the middle classes, soon to be joined by both upper and lower classes; the time and place are Central Europe, and soon the whole Western world, at the beginning of the nineteenth century.

The history of the dance makes plain that the upper classes of Western society borrowed many of their dance forms from "the people," although the dances underwent various transformations in the course of their adaptation. Two forms of the same dance frequently existed side by side, the upper classes preferring the restrained and calmer version, while the country folk preferred the freer and wilder form.[1] Despite the apparent differences between court and folk dance, and the variations in the extent of similarity from dance to dance, and from time to place, the kinship is almost always discernible. Historically, the tie between the two forms was particularly close until the fifteenth century. From that time forward, there is an increasing gap.

We are told that dances tended to be quite simple until the fifteenth century, and their unwritten rules could be learned through observation and participation. The emphasis on both court and folk dance was primarily on their larger basic features, where the relatively few individual components of each dance were fused into an artistic whole. Beginning in the fifteenth century, however, this emphasis on simplicity and on the whole begins to be replaced by a liking for multiple elements, complexity and attention to small details.[2] Without entering into an

explanation of the underlying reasons for this new aesthetic outlook—a problem which is not really relevant to the present
paper—it will be recalled that this new "realism of particulars"
also found expression in other arts of the period such as the illumination of books, for example, or the importance attached to
detail in the weaving of tapestries, etc.

In the dance, the attention to detail gave rise to an elaborate
vocabulary of steps. For the first time, intricate features had to be
learned with exactitude and memorized carefully. This new
development led, eventually, to the establishment of a new
profession, the dance teacher, and to the crystallization of a "theory" of the dance to which the proliferation of dance manuals
attests. As a result, courtly dance and folk dance spread further
apart. They continued to influence each other, one may say, but
their aims and styles were different.[3]

The purpose of this paper, however, is not to analyze why the
cultural gap between the social classes widened, but rather to
point out a moment in history when they converged once again,
when "everybody" danced the waltz. This vantage point, perhaps, may also contribute to the clarification of why and when
high culture and popular culture diverge and converge.

THE UNIVERSALITY OF THE WALTZ

Popular imagery today has it that in the early decades of the
nineteenth century, kings and commoners, nobles and bourgeoisie whiled away their nights waltzing. Hollywood has contributed substantially to this image[4] and perhaps that alone is
enough to make it suspect, particularly when one recalls, from
cultural history in general, and from the history of the dance
alluded to above, that the homogeneity of cultural expression
had declined, as the class structure became more heterogeneous.
Yet, for all this, a close investigation substantiates the popular
image. Indeed, everybody seems to have been dancing the waltz.

No less interesting than the success of the waltz as a dance
form is its success from a purely musical point of view. Concert
performances of the waltz attracted audiences as significant as
those whose legs it propelled. The standing of Johann Strauss Sr.
among composers and among concertgoers was very high, and
in an era when Beethoven had just died (1827), the waltz was
admitted not only to the ballroom and to "pop" concerts, but to
the very halls in which Beethoven had resounded the night
before. We know that not only kings and queens lent their ears,

but that composers like Schumann, Mendelssohn, Wagner, Rossini, Meyerbeer, Bellini, Auber, Berlioz, Brahms, and even Cherubini, who had lived through the entire high classical era, were among those who praised and applauded Strauss.[5] Farga, with all his exaggerated enthusiasm, seems right when he says, "Nie vorher und nie nachher erreicht die Unterhaltungsmusik ein derartiges Niveau vie zur Zeit Strauss und Lanners."[6]

If one holds to the theory that every artistic creation is an expression of the world in which it was created, two questions immediately arise: 1. What social conditions account for this radical change? In particular, what changes had taken place in the relationship among the social classes that could be made manifest in this way? 2. Apart from the social basis which may explain the convergence of cultural behavior, one must inquire into the cultural expression itself: What is it about the waltz that made it suitable for this unique role? In what sense does the nature of the dance itself reflect the society which created it? Both of these sets of questions will occupy us in what follows.

THE MINUET AND THE WALTZ

To make the argument of this paper more tangible, it is interesting to compare the character of the waltz and its social setting with that of the minuet and its social setting. The major dance which immediately preceded the waltz, the minuet, is a courtly dance whose folk origins had been transferred from their initial unrestrained expressiveness into the classical ideas of clarity, balance and regularity. While outwardly simple, the minuet had to be "studied," a fact to which a great number of dance manuals devoted to its rules and regulations attest. Goethe's oft-cited observations, made at one of the carnivals he attended in Rome, substantiates this point even further. He remarks, "Nobody ventures unconcernedly to dance unless he has been taught the art; the minuet in particular, is regarded as a work of art and is performed, indeed, only by a few couples. The couples are surrounded by the rest of the company, admired and applauded at the end."[7] Thus, we also learn from Goethe something which is fully corroborated in the dance manuals: the minuet involves not only dancers but onlookers as well, and these latter are an important part of the spectacle.

The delicately planned geometry of the dance steps were the quintessence of dignity and formality. There was no room for individual variation, embellishment or creativity. All is as carefully planned and executed as the architecture of a Le Notre garden. The dancers' dress was costly but moderate, emphasizing an appreciation for the beauty of simplicity. Subdued half-tone colors predominated. The hoop skirt symbolized additional restraint and "distance."

But for all the simplicity and uniformity, social status considerations played an important part in the dance. Perhaps it was the presence of an audience which made it so tempting to incorporate into the dance symbols of the status of the dancers in the social structure; perhaps it was something else. But what we do know is that it took a great deal of research to determine who would open the ball, and in what succession each guest should enter the dance.[8] The minuet, it may be said, reflected and incorporated the wordly ranks which its participants brought with them when they entered the ballroom. Paradoxically, this was made possible by the very uniformity of the minuet.

Not so the waltz. The waltz emphasized not uniformity, but individual expression; there are no rules to be studied, save for a few basic steps; the individual is encouraged to introduce his own variations and interpretations. Here, the dancers surrender their worldly identities upon entering the "society of the dance" where individuals take on new roles and where recognition is accorded not by virtue of one's status in the larger society, but by virtue of one's performance in the dance. Often, in dances like the waltz where individual expression is encouraged, the best dancers are permitted to bring the dance to a close while the others encircle them to watch and applaud. Except in this latter sense, there are no onlookers or audience in the waltz. The emphasis is on the participation of all, and on the equality of all, while rewarding achievement within the dance itself rather than status one brings to the dance from "the world outside."

THE ACCEPTANCE OF THE WALTZ

If the minuet represented the separateness of the classes and retained social distinctions even within the dance, the waltz represents the breaking down of these distinctions. In trying to explain how this happened, the first thing to note is that the waltz, or something very much like it, had been rejected by the middle and upper classes not very long before.

About the middle of the eighteenth century the word "walzen" was introduced as the name of a whirling or revolving dance movement. Ultimately, the word is thought to derive from the Latin "volvere" (to turn around). From both verbal and pictorial documents dating as early as the sixteenth century, it can be deduced that the waltz as a dance movement is of much older date than that in which it received a definite name. The Weller, the Spinner, and the Volte—noted by sixteenth-century writers such as the Meistersinger, Kunz Has,[9] and Thoinot Arbeau in his Orchesographie[10]—show great resemblance to the later waltz in that the dancing couple whirl in close embrace, often revolving about the room, rather than dancing separately side by side in the form that predominated until after the minuet.

These precursors of the waltz were severely criticized by moralists and others. Thoinot Arbeau was concerned with the dizziness caused by the Volte,[11] while a variety of clergymen remarked on the young women who allowed themselves to be grasped anywhere by their partners and lusted to be thrown into the air and twirled about.[12] One such warning is sounded by Cyriacus Spangenberg in his publication of 1578 warning all pious young men against those "Jungfrauen die da Lust zu den Abendtanzen haben und sich da gerne umbdrehen, unzüchtig küssen und begreifen lassen."[13]

The upper classes, at least, heeded the warnings, although perhaps for other reasons. Under the influence of the ballet and the increasing distance between folk-dance and court-dance, during the seventeenth and greater part of the eighteenth century, courtly dance found little room for the sensual. The minuet, the most dignified representative of those dances the movements of which were conventionalized, was a conscious work of art, lacking that element of spontaneity which characterized the dances it replaced. While some of the whirling dances were "salonfähig" for a time, the dancing masters easily succeeded in substituting artistic skill and discipline for spontaneity and expressiveness.

The return to naturalness in the dance began in the eighteenth century, together with the renewed interest in folk song, and was part of a movement to recapture the vitality of the folk for the new nationalistic needs of society. Thus, the centuries-old German Dreher was rediscovered, and in a short time became a world-conquering dance which not only dominated dancing itself but succeeded in penetrating into compositions which had little to do with dancing.[14]

Of the many whirling dances, it is particularly the Landler from which the waltz derived. The couples in close embrace made a turn to each two measures while at the same time following a circular course. The three-four rhythm with the strongly accentuated first beat characteristic of most Landlers was adopted by the waltz.

The waltz attained its true character, however, by being danced like a Schleifer, having given up the skips and the turning under the arm of the Landler in favor of dragging the feet along the floor.[15] The skips unquestioningly represented a certain freedom of expression, but it is these smooth revolutions, the ecstatic gliding motion, which first made it possible to really "let go." Of course, this very "letting go" was the basis on which the ancestors of the waltz had been resisted.

THE WALTZ IN IDEOLOGICAL AND SOCIAL PERSPECTIVE

It is well known that the development of courtly art since the close of the Renaissance came to a standstill toward the middle of the eighteenth century and was superseded by middle-class subjectivism and romanticism. Arnold Hauser, discussing this development, distinguishes, however, between pre-revolutionary romanticism and that of the post-revolutionary period.

The French Revolution, argues Hauser, although it conceived of art as harnessed to the needs of the emerging "new" society, created an idea of artistic freedom which had no precedent. The revolution itself limited the freedom of the individual artist by focusing on art and not the artist. It declared that art must not be the privilege of the rich and the leisured, or an idle pastime, but that it must "teach and improve and contribute to the happiness of the general public and be the possession of every man." By creating a correspondence between the idea of artistic truth and that of social justice, the revolution challenged the dictatorship of the academies and the monopolization of the art market by the court and aristocracy.

The consequent romanticism denied that there existed objective rules of any kind to govern the production or consumption of art. It enshrined the concept of the uniqueness of individual expression and the struggle against the very principle of tradition, authority and rule. Whereas the pre-revolutionary middle class saw art as one means of expressing identification with the aristocracy and aloofness from the lower classes, in the post-revolutionary period it began to think of art as individualistic and idiosyncratic, a "matter of taste" which might vary among different people, different times and different places.[16] Thus, art which had previously been looked upon as possessing universal validity, in this over-all rebellion against authority of any kind, could no longer be judged by absolute standards. The continuous striving toward the goal of perfection, so characteristic of the eighteenth century, gave way to a kind of relativism in which it became possible to "like" both a Beethoven and a Strauss, not because they stand comparison, but because they need not be compared.

As the individual was "freed" from conventional standards and tastes, and the artist was "freed" from his royal patrons and a market developed in which the artist had to satisfy "public opinion" and its new leaders, the critics, the demand increased for lighter and less "complicated" music which led, ultimately, to a division into "serious" and "light" music which had not existed previously. The concert societies and later the large concert halls replaced performances at court and drawing rooms, and induced greater concentration on expressiveness and on individual style. "Individual style" in fact, now characterized the music of the nineteenth century. Emotionalism and sentimentalism now served the middle class as a means of expressing its intellectual independence of the aristocracy, but ultimately led to a cult of sensibility in which the aristocracy itself could join.

Along with nationalism, then, the newly-awakened concern with sensibility, the throwing off of traditional standards and the rise of relativism all cut across barriers to create an ideology of romanticism. This ideology began in the middle classes, but, in time, spread both upwards to the waning aristocracy and downwards to the industrial lower classes. These cohesive forces combined with the economic and political interaction which reduced the barriers between classes.

Yet, for all the equality which the newly-freed individual might experience with those about him, psychologically speaking, there is a loss involved: the sense of having some fixed and proper place in a stable and predictable society. The individual stood alone. This, of course, is the most famous dilemma of modern man, the roots of which are to be found in the post-revolutionary period.[17]

THE APPROPRIATENESS OF THE WALTZ

The attributes of the waltz are compatible with this social and ideological setting. This was a period of unity, as we tried to point out, in which nationalism, relativism and the over-all ideology of romanticism brought very different kinds of people into contact and sympathy with each other. The universality of the waltz gave expression to this unity and mutual accessibility. Furthermore, the period was one of individual assertiveness and achievement, and the waltz allowed for freedom of expression and provided an opportunity for proving oneself. The beautiful commoner, if she waltzed very well, would be invited to dance with the prince.

But with all of this the times were troubled too. Austria, for example, was at war no less than five times between 1792 and 1814, yet she was the leader in the crusade for Gemütlichkeit. The individual who had lost his sense of belonging since the revolution, who no longer had an idea of a proper place in a predictable society, became an object of importance and interest to himself at the expense of his commitment to other social roles. "Gemütlichkeit" is only one of the symptoms of this new state of being. Self-experiences now replaced the experiences of the world outside and were treated as though they were constantly slipping away and being lost forever. Losing oneself in the waltz is indeed one of the most symbolic cultural expressions of this new frame of mind, and the waltz craze of the first decades of the nineteenth century expresses so well this attitude to experiences and their temporality. It is interesting and amusing to mention in connection with this that the Apollo Palace in Vienna, where the waltz was danced with passion and verve by up to 6,000 persons in five large and thirty-one smaller dancing rooms, is supposed to have contained a hall for pregnant women who were eager not to lose even a moment of the dance, even though they preferred not to mingle with the general crowd.[18]

The waltz not only made it possible for different kinds of individuals to come together on an egalitarian basis, it also made possible a kind of "escape" from reality through the thrilling dizziness of whirling one's way in a private world of sensuality. The "letting go" function of the waltz seems relevant to a world without clear standards, in which the individual stood alone having to find his own way. Werther, Goethe's romantic hero, confesses to Wilhelm that while waltzing with Lotte, everything around him seemed to disappear. "Ich war kein Mensch mehr," he relates, "das liebenswürdigste Geschöpf in den Armen zu haben und mit ihr herumsufligen wie Wetter, dass alles ringsumher verging."[19]

Although the waltz seemed like a centrifugal force generated by rotation and threatening to hurl the dancers into space, the support given by each partner to the other was so strong that there was no "danger" in their abandonment. In other words, the waltz permitted additional "freedom," the kind of sexual contact which had heretofore been unthinkable in public. The greater physical contact between the sexes made possible by the waltz is cleverly illustrated in the following sarcastic verses written by Lord Byron on this subject:

> Round all the confines of the yielded waist
> The strongest hand may wander undisplaced:
> The lady's in return may grasp as much
> As princely paunches offer to her touch.
> Pleased round the chalky floor how well they trip;
> One hand reposing on the royal hip,
> The other to the shoulder no less royal
> Ascending with affection truly loyal!

> Thus all and each in movement swift or slow,
> The genial contact gently undergo;
> Till some might marvel with the modest Turk
> If "nothing follows all this palming work"?
> Something does follow at a fitter time;
> The breast thus publicly resign'd to man
> In private may resist him—if it can.

The waltz, it seems, not only made it possible to lose consciousness of time and space, but by introducing sensual thrills and encouraging free erotic expressions it also succeeded in providing the "desert island" to which one might escape. In this sense the waltz may have represented a world in which only the senses were operative, a world which was void of responsibility, an experience of self and self-involvement, an escape from reality and a surrender to the moment which can best be understood when contrasted with the element of objectivity and detachment so essential in the execution of the minuet.[20]

CONCLUSION

Everybody danced the waltz. The waltz, the dance of the middle class, was as expressive for the upper classes who now shared the world view of the middle classes as it was for the lower classes in urban centers who also shared the same world view, not yet having developed one of their own. As was pointed out, the different social strata could share the same cultural expressions because of the greater cultural mobility which resulted from the over-all endorsement of romanticism and its manifold aspects, which directly or indirectly encouraged such a development. The acceptance of some of the basic ideas of the early nineteenth-century philosophy of nationalism directly facilitated cultural mobility.

Louis Philippe with his bourgeois manners and clothes best portrays the changed world view of the upper class. He loved the waltz and paid tribute to one of his major composers. He invited Johan Strauss, Sr., and his orchestra to play some of the waltzes with which he was already familiar at his court.[21]

Louis Philippe is not the only one in whose court the waltz resounded. In 1834 Strauss played for King Friedrich Wilhelm III and the Prussian court. And Czar Nicholas and the Czarina of Russia, upon hearing Strauss in Vienna invited him to introduce his waltzes at St. Petersburg.[22]

The Vienna Congress, held in the years 1814–15, is not only important in modern European history, but also represents an important moment in the history of the waltz. The diplomats and delegates who attended the Congress represented their countries but not a particular social class. The Congress was composed of mixed groups. It consisted of aristocrats of the old regime who applied eighteenth-century diplomatic principles, as well as representatives of other classes who were imbued with post-revolutionary political ideas. The well-known saying "le Congrès ne marche pas, il danse" is certainly significant of the rage for dancing, but it is doubly significant for us that it was the waltz which propelled the legs of the delegates of all classes.

While the different social classes could share the same cultural expressions, the expressions themselves could now vary, since the new society was no longer guided by absolute values. This was a society for whom art became a matter of changing taste; a society for whom it was "natural" for varied artistic expressions to co-exist. Moreover, any individual of that society could respond favorably to a diversity of artistic expressions, no longer experiencing the need to rank them in a single continuum of merit.

This is what permitted Berlioz to take Johann Strauss as the starting point and climax of one of his essays for the *Journal des Débats*, to which he was a monthly contributor. With Strauss as his example, Berlioz demonstrated to the Parisians the supremacy of German music and set him on a plane with Gluck, Beethoven and Weber.[23]

Musically speaking, Berlioz is not the only well-known composer of that period to have accepted the waltz and to have praised one of its greatest composers. However, the main supporters of the waltz were the members of the audience who required lighter music and wanted to be entertained. This audience, which was continuously increasing, was catered to because music became a commodity on the free market and made adjustments to the new situation. The idea of making music accessible to the masses can be traced directly to the revolution which made art the possession of every man, and which in the process of democratizing art, lowered its standards. As will be recalled, the social reformers saw a correspondence between the idea of artistic truth and that of social justice. Indeed, the waltz, to this society, represented some kind of artistic truth because it was so socially just. The Congress of 1815, which in a way, tried to eliminate from history both Napoleon and the French Revolution, took over the new dance of the bourgeoisie as its own form of social expression, gazing once more at "Liberté, égalité, fraternité," with affection and approval, knowing that the dance, and more specifically the waltz, may have proven to be one of the very few areas where those great ideas could actually be manifested, an area where freedom did not impair equality and vice versa. What a wonderful world in which to get lost!

(1973)

Notes

[1]Curt Sachs, *World History of the Dance* (New York, 1937), p. 282.

[2]*Ibid.*, p. 298.

[3]*Ibid.*, pp. 299–302.

[4]One will recall Warner Brothers' "The Great Waltz" in this connection, as well as more recent offerings, such as a Walt Disney cartoon about Johann Strauss in which both cats and mice join together in the waltz.

[5]H. E. Jacob, *Johann Strauss, Father and Son* (Richmond, Va., 1939), pp. 79–108.

[6]Franz Farga, *Lanner und Strauss* (Vienna, 1948), p. 42.

[7]J. W. von Goethe, *Italien, Zweiter Aufenthalt in Rom*, 1788. Sachs uses this quotation in a somewhat different connection, primarily to emphasize the aesthetic values of the minuet, *op. cit.*, p. 399.

[8]The audience served as an integral part of the dance, the spectators, not only the audience, were saluted with ceremonial bows which preceded the actual dance. Ciambattista Dufort finds it necessary to devote two whole chapters of his manual *Trattato del ballo nobile* (Naples, 1728)

to this subject, Gottfried Taubert devotes sixty pages of his *Rechtschaffe-ner Tanzmeister* (Leipzig, 1717) to the same, and J. M. de Chavanne devotes almost his entire book *Principes du Minuet* (Luxembourg, 1767) to that crucial opening which so well expresses the atmosphere of the whole dance.

[9] See Edward Reeser, *The History of the Waltz* (Stockholm, n.d.), p. 1.

[10] Thoinot Arbeau, *Orchesography*, translated by Mary Stewart Evans (New York, 1967), pp. 119–23.

[11] *Ibid.*, p. 121.

[12] See Paul Nettl, "*Tanz und Tanzmuzik*," in Adler's *Handbuch der Musikgeschichte* (Berlin 1930), Vol. II, pp. 979–80.

[13] Cited in Reeser, *op. cit.*, p. 9.

[14] See Paul Nettl, *The Story of Dance Music* (New York, 1947), pp. 252–86.

[15] See Sachs, *op. cit.*, p. 433.

[16] For a suggestive discussion of the above see Arnold Hauser, *The Social History of Art* (London, 1951), Vol. II, pp. 622–710.

[17] For a relevant sociological study of the European drama see Leo Lowenthal, *Literature and the Image of Man* (Boston, 1957), pp. 136–220.

[18] Jacob, *op. cit.*, p. 24.

[19] J. W. Goethe, *Die Leiden des jungen Werther* in *Goethes Sämtliche Werke* (München, 1910), Vol. II, p. 265.

[20] Callois includes waltzing in the type of game to which he assigns the term *ilinx*—the Greek term for whirlpool—to cover "the many varieties of such transport . . . which consist of an attempt to momentarily destroy the stability of perception and inflict a kind of voluptuous panic upon an otherwise lucid mind." See Roger Caillois, *Man, Play and Games* (New York, 1961), pp. 23–26.

[21] Jacob, *op. cit.*, p. 91.

[22] Jacob, *ibid.*, pp. 80–81.

[23] See Hector Berlioz, *Memoirs* (New York, 1966), pp. 375–77. Also see Jacques Barzun. *Berlioz and the Romantic Century* (Boston, 1950), Vol. I, pp. 473–74.

JOANN KEALIINOHOMOKU AN ANTHROPOLOGIST LOOKS AT BALLET AS A FORM OF ETHNIC DANCE

It is good anthropology to think of ballet as a form of ethnic dance. Currently, that idea is unacceptable to most Western dance scholars. This lack of agreement shows clearly that something is amiss in the communication of ideas between the scholars of dance and those of anthropology, and this paper is an attempt to bridge that communication gap.

The faults and errors of anthropologists in their approach to dance are many, but they are largely due to their hesitation to deal with something which seems esoteric and out of their field of competence. However, a handful of dance anthropologists are trying to rectify this by publishing in the social science journals and by participating in formal and informal meetings with other anthropologists.

By ethnic dance, anthropologists mean to convey the idea that all forms of dance reflect the cultural traditions within which they developed. Dancers and dance scholars, as this paper will show, use this term, and the related terms *ethnologic, primitive* and *folkdance*, differently and, in fact, in a way which reveals their limited knowledge of non-Western dance forms.

In preparing to formulate this paper, I reread in an intense period pertinent writings by DeMille, Haskell, Holt, the Kinneys, Kirstein, La Meri, Martin, Sachs, Sorell and Terry. In addition I carefully reread the definitions pertaining to dance in *Webster's New International Dictionary*, the 2nd edition definitions which were written by Humphrey, and the 3rd edition definitions which were written by Kurath. Although these and other sources are listed in the bibliography at the end of this paper, I name these scholars here to focus my frame of reference.

The experience of this intense rereading as an anthropologist rather than as a dancer, was both instructive and disturbing. The readings are rife with unsubstantiated deductive reasoning, poorly documented "proofs," a plethora of half-truths, many out-and-out errors, and a pervasive ethnocentric bias. Where the writers championed non-Western dance they were either apologists or patronistic. Most discouraging of all, these authors saw fit to change only the pictures and not the text when they reissued their books after as many as seventeen years later; they only updated the Euro-American dance scene.

This survey of the literature reveals an amazing divergence of opinions. We are able to read that the origin of dance was in play and that it was not in play, that it was for magical and religious purposes, and that it was not for those things; that it was for courtship and that it was not for courtship; that it was the first form of communication and that communication did not enter into dance until it became an "art." In addition we can read that it was serious and purposeful and that at the same time it was an outgrowth of exuberance, was totally spontaneous, and originated in the spirit of fun. Moreover, we can read that it was only a group activity for tribal solidarity and that it was strictly for the pleasure and self-expression of the one dancing. We can learn also, that animals danced before man did, and yet that dance is a human activity!

It has been a long time since anthropologists concerned themselves with unknowable origins, and I will not add another origin theory for dance, because I don't know anyone who was there. Our dance writers, however, suggest evidence for origins from archeological finds, and from models exemplified by contemporary primitive groups. For the first, one must remember that man had been on this earth for a long time before he made cave paintings and statuary, so that archeological finds can hardly tell us about the beginnings of dance. For the second set of evidence, that of using models from contemporary primitives, one must not confuse the word "primitive" with "primeval," even though one author actually does equate these two terms (Sorell 1967:14). About the dance of primeval man we really know nothing. About primitive dance, on the other hand, we know a great deal. The first thing that we know is that there is no such thing as *a* primitive dance. There *are* dances performed by primitives, and they are too varied to fit any stereotype.

It is a gross error to think of groups of peoples or their dances as being monolithic wholes. "The African dance" never existed; there are, however, Dahomean dances, Hausa dances, Masai dances, and so forth. "The American Indian" is a fiction and so is a prototype of "Indian dance." There are, however, Iroquois, Kwakiutl, and Hopis, to name a few, and they have dances.

Despite all anthropological evidence to the contrary, however, Western dance scholars set themselves up as authorities on the characteristics of primitive dance. Sorell combines most of these so-called characteristics of the primitive stereotype. He tells us that primitive dancers have no technique, and no artistry, but that they are "unfailing masters of their bodies"! He states that their dances are disorganized and frenzied, but that they are able to translate all their feelings and emotions into movement! He claims the dances are spontaneous but also purposeful! Primitive dances, he tells us, are serious but social! He claims that they have "complete freedom" but that men and women can't dance together. He qualifies that last statement by saying that men and women dance together after the dance degenerates into an orgy! Sorell also asserts that primitives cannot distinguish between the concrete and the symbolic, that they dance for every occasion, and that they stamp around a lot! Further, Sorell asserts that dance in primitive societies is a special prerogative of males, especially chieftains, shamans and witch doctors (Sorell 1967:10–11). Kirstein also characterizes the dances of "natural, unfettered societies" (whatever that means). Although the whole body participates according to Kirstein, he claims that the emphasis of movement is with the lower half of the torso. He concludes that primitive dance is repetitious, limited, unconscious and with "retardative and closed expression"! Still, though it may be unconscious, Kirstein tells his readers that dance is useful to the tribe and that it is based on the seasons. Primitive dance, or as he phrases it, "earlier manifestations of human activity," is everywhere found to be "almost identically formulated." He never really tells us what these formulations are except that they have little to offer in methodology or structure, and that they are examples of "instinctive exuberance" (Kirstein 1942:3–5).

Terry describes the functions of primitive dance, and he uses American Indians as his model. In his book *The Dance in America* he writes sympathetically towards American Indians and "his primitive brothers." However, his paternalistic feelings on the one hand, and his sense of ethnocentricity on the other, prompt him to set aside any thought that people with whom he identifies could share contemporarily those same dance characteristics, because he states "the white man's dance heritage, except for the most ancient of days, was wholly different" (1956:3–4, 195–198, 3).

With the rejection of the so-called primitive characteristics for the white man, it is common to ascribe these characteristics to groups existing among African tribes, Indians of North and South America, and Pacific peoples. These are the same peoples who are labeled by these authors as "ethnic." No wonder that balletomanes reject the idea that ballet is a form of ethnic dance! But Africans, North and South Amerindians and Pacific peoples would be just as horrified to be called ethnic under the terms of the stereotype. Those so-called characteristics-as-a-group do not prevail anywhere!

Another significant obstacle to the identification of Western dancers with non-Western dance forms, be they primitive or "ethnologic" in the sense that Sorell uses the latter term as "the art expression of a race" which is "executed for the enjoyment and edification of the audience" (1967:76), is the double myth that the dance grew out of some spontaneous mob action and that once formed, became frozen. American anthropologists and many folklorists have been most distressed about the popularity of these widespread misconceptions. Apparently it satisfies our own ethnocentric needs to believe in the uniqueness of our dance forms, and it is much more convenient to believe that primitive dances, like Topsy, just "growed," and that "ethnological" dances are part of an unchanging tradition. Even books and articles which purport to be about the dances of the *world* devote three quarters of the text and photos to Western dance. We explicate our historic eras, our royal patrons, dancing masters, choreographers, and performers. The rest of the world is condensed diachronically and synchronically to the remaining quarter of the book. This smaller portion, which must cover all the rest of the world, is usually divided up so that the portions at the beginning imply that the ethnic forms fit on some kind of an evolutionary continuum, and the remaining portions at the end of the book for, say, American Negro dance, give the appearance of a post-script, as if they too "also ran." In short we treat Western dance, ballet particularly, as if it was the one great divinely ordained apogee of the performing arts. This notion is exemplified, and reinforced, by the way dance photos are published. Unless the non-Western performer has made a "hit" on our stages, we seldom bother to give him a name in the captions, even though he might be considered a fine artist among his peers (Martin is the exception). For example, see Claire Holt's article "Two Dance Worlds" (1969). The captions under the photos of Javanese dancers list no names, but you may be sure that we are always told when Martha Graham appears in a photo. A scholar friend of mine was looking over the books by our dance historians, and he observed that they were not interested in the whole world of dance; they were really only interested in *their* world of dance. Can anyone deny this allegation?

Let it be noted, once and for all, that within the various "ethnologic" dance worlds there are also patrons, dancing masters, choreographers, and performers with names woven into a very real historical fabric. The bias which those dancers have toward their own dance and artists is just as strong as ours. The difference is that they usually don't pretend to be scholars of other dance forms, nor even very much interested in them. It is instructive, however, to remind ourselves that all dances are subject to change and development no matter how convenient we may find it to dismiss some form as practically unchanged for 2,000 years (see DeMille 1963:48). It is convenient to us, of course, because once having said that, we feel that our job is finished.

As for the presumed lack of creators of dance among primitive and folk groups, let us reconsider that assumption after reading Martin's statement:

> In simpler cultures than ours we find a mass of art actually created and practiced by the people as a whole. (Martin 1939:15)

The first question which such a statement raises is what is a "mass of art"? Martin never really defines art, but if he means art as a refined aesthetic expression, then it can be asked how such could ever be a collective product. Does he mean that it appeared spontaneously? Does he really think there can be art without artists? And if he believes that there must be artists, does he mean to imply that a "people as a whole" are artists? If so, what a wonderful group of people they must be. Let us learn from them!

Doubtless, Martin probably will say that I have taken his statement to an absurd extension of his meaning, but I believe that such thoughtless statements deserve to be pushed to their extreme.

It is true that some cultures do not place the same value on preserving the names of their innovators as we do. That is a matter of tradition also. But we must not be deceived into believing that a few hundred people all got together and with one unanimous surge created a dance tradition which, having once been created, never changed from that day forward.

Among the Hopi Indians of Northern Arizona, for example, there is no tradition of naming a choreographer. Nevertheless they definitely know who, within a Kiva group or a society, made certain innovations and why. A dramatic example of the variety permitted in what is otherwise considered to be a static dance tradition is to see, as I have, the "same" dance ceremonies performed in several different villages at several different times. To illustrate, I observed the important Hopi "bean dances" which are held every February, in five different villages during the winters of 1965 and 1968. There were the distinguishing differences between villages which are predictable differences, once one becomes familiar with a village "style." But, in addition, there were creative and not necessarily predictable differences which occurred from one time to the next. The Hopis know clearly what the predictable differences are, and they also know who and what circumstances led to the timely innovations. Not only do they know these things, but they are quite free in their evaluation of the merits and demerits of those differences, with their "own" usually (but not always) coming out as being aesthetically more satisfying.

In Martin's *Introduction to the Dance* (1939) the first plate contains two reproductions of drawings of Hopi kachinas. Judging from its position among the plates, this must be Martin's single example of dances from a primitive group. DeMille also shows Hopis as examples of primitive dancers (1963:33,35. The latter is a "posed" photo). Let us see how well the Hopis compare to the generalities attributed to primitive dancers.

PARADIGM

Hopi dances are immaculately organized, are never frenzied (not even, in fact especially, in their famous snake dance), nor is there a desire to translate feelings and emotions into movement. The dances are indeed serious, if this is synonymous with purposeful, but many dances are not serious if that word negates the fact that many dances are humorous, use clowns as personnel, and contain both derision and satire. Hopi dance is also social if one is speaking as a sociologist, but they have only one prescribed genre of dance which the Hopis themselves consider "social" in the sense that they can be performed by uninitiated members of the society. Hopis would find the idea of "complete freedom" in their dance to be an alien idea, because much of the form and behavior is rigidly prescribed. Certainly they would never lapse into an orgy! Nor do they "hurl themselves on the ground and roll in the mud" after the rains begin (DeMille 1963:35).

Hopis would be offended if you told them that they could not distinguish between the concrete and the symbolic. They are not children, after all. They certainly understand natural causes. But does it make them primitive, by definition, if they ask their gods to help their crops grow by bringing rain? Don't farmers within the mainstream of America and Europe frequently pray to a Judeo-Christian God for the same thing? Are the Hopis more illogical than we are when they dance their prayers instead of attending religious services with responsive readings, and a variety of motor activities such as rising, sitting, folding hands and the like?

Once again assessing the Hopis in the light of the characteristics presumably found for primitive dancers, we find that Hopis don't dance for the three specific life events which supposedly are "always" recognized in dance. That is, Hopis don't dance at births, marriages, or deaths.

Obviously, it cannot be said that they dance on "every" occasion. Furthermore, the Hopi stamping would surely be a disappointment to Sorell if he expected the Hopis to "make the earth tremble under his feet" (1967:15). DeMille might also be surprised that there is no "state of exaltation" or "ecstasy" in Hopi dance (cf. DeMille 1963:34,67).

It is true that more Hopi dances are performed by males than by females, but females also dance under certain circumstances and for certain rituals which are the sole prerogative of females. What is more important is that women participate a great deal if one thinks of them as non-dancer participants, and one must, because it is the entire dance *event* which is important to the Hopis rather than just the actual rhythmic movement.

For the Hopis, it is meaningless to say that the primary dancers are the chieftains, witch doctors and shamans. Traditionally they have no real "government" as such, and every clan has its own rituals and societies which are further divided according to the village in which they live. Thus everyone will participate to some degree or another in a variety of roles. There is no shaman as such, so of course there cannot be shamanistic dances. As for witch doctors, they do not dance in that role although they dance to fulfill some of their other roles in their clan and residence groups.

I do not know what is meant by a "natural, unfettered society," but whatever it is I am sure that description does not fit the Hopis. In their dance movements the whole body does not participate, and there is no pelvic movement as such. The dances are indeed repetitious, but that does not interfere in the least with the real dramatic impact of the performance. Within the "limitations" of the dance culture, Hopi dance still has an enormous range of variations, and this is especially true because the dance "event" is so richly orchestrated.

Far from being an "unconscious" dance form, Hopi dancing is a very conscious activity. And I cannot believe that it is any more "retardative" or closed within its own framework than any other dance form, bar none. Finally, I find nothing in Hopi dance that can be called "instinctively exuberant," but perhaps that is because I don't know what "instinctive exuberance" is. If it is what I think it is, such a description is inappropriate for Hopi dances.

Lest someone say that perhaps the Hopis are the exception to prove the rule, or, perhaps, that they are not really "primitive," let me make two points. First, if they are not "primitive" they do not fit into any other category offered by the dance scholars discussed in this article. Their dances are not "folk dance" as described, nor do they have "ethnologic dances," nor "art dances" nor "theatre dance" as these terms are used in the writings under consideration. Clearly, in the light of these writers' descriptions, they are a "primitive," "ethnic" group with dances in kind. Secondly, I know of no group anywhere which fits the descriptions for primitive dance such as given by DeMille, Sorell, Terry and Martin. Certainly I know of no justification for Haskell's statement that "many dances of primitive tribes still living are said to be identical with those of birds and apes" (1960:9). Unfortunately, Haskell does not document any of his statements and we cannot trace the source of such a blatant piece of misinformation.

It is necessary to hammer home the idea that there is no such thing as a "primitive dance" form. Those who teach courses called "primitive dance" are perpetuating a dangerous myth. As a corollary to this let it be noted that no living primitive group will reveal to us the way our European ancestors behaved. Every group has had its own unique history and has been subject to both internal and external modifications. Contemporary primitives are not children in fact, nor can they be pigeonholed into some convenient slot on an evolutionary scale.

I suggest that one cause for so much inaccurate and shocking misunderstanding on the subject of primitive groups is due to an overdependence on the words of Sir James Frazer and Curt Sachs whose works have been outdated as source material for better than three decades. In their stead I would suggest that they read some of the works of Gertrude P. Kurath, whose bibliography appeared in the January, 1970 issue of *Ethnomusicology*. This and other suggested readings are given at the end of this article.

DEFINITIONS

It is disconcerting to discover that writers tend to use key words without attempting real definitions which are neither too exclusive nor too inclusive. Even the word *dance*, itself, is never adequately defined to apply cross-culturally through time and space. Instead of definitions we are given descriptions, which are a different matter altogether. I have been closely questioned as to the need for definitions "as long as we all mean the same thing anyway," and I have even been asked what difference it makes what we call something as long as we all understand how some term is being used. The answers are twofold: without the discipline of attempting to define specific terms we are not sure we do all mean the same thing or that we understand how a term is being used. On the other hand, the tacit agreement about frames of reference can distort the focus of emphasis rather than giving the broadly based objectivity which comes from using a term denotatively.

For seven years I pondered over a definition of dance, and in 1965 I tentatively set out the following definition which has since undergone some slight modifications. In its current form it reads:

> Dance is a transient mode of expression, performed in a given form and style by the human body moving in space. Dance occurs through purposefully selected and controlled rhythmic movements; the resulting phenomenon is recognized as dance both by the performer and the observing members of a given group. (1965:6, rev. 1970)

The two crucial points which distinguish this definition from others are the limiting of dance to that of human behavior since there is no reason to believe that birds or apes perform with the *intent* to dance. Intent to dance and acknowledgment of the activity as dance by a given group is the second distinguishing feature of my definition. This is the crucial point for applying the definition cross-culturally as well as setting dance apart from other activities which might appear to be dance to the outsider but which are considered, say, sports or ritual to the participants. *Webster's International Dictionary* shows much contrast in the definitions of dance between the 2nd and 3rd editions. The reason for the contrasts is clear when it is understood that a performer-choreographer of Western dance wrote the dance entries for the 2nd edition (Doris Humphrey), while an ethnochoreologist (Gertrude P. Kurath) wrote the entries for the 3rd edition.

We cannot accept Kirstein's contention that "it is apparent . . . that the idea of tension, from the very beginning, has been foremost in people's minds when they have thought about dancing seriously enough to invent or adapt word-sounds for it" (1935:1). Alber (Charles J. Alber 1970: personal communication) assures me that both Japanese and Mandarin Chinese have time-honored words for dance and related activities and that the idea of tension does not occur at all in these words. Clearly Kirstein's statement indicates that he has not looked beyond the models set out in Indo-European languages. Can we really believe that only white Europeans are "advanced" enough to speak about dance?

The notion of tension through the etymology of European words for dance does reveal something about the Western aesthetic of dance which is apparent from the Western dance ideals of pull-up, body lift and bodily extensions. Elsewhere these things are not highly valued. Indeed my "good" Western trained body alignment and resultant tension is a handicap in performing dances from other cultures. Martin seems to have the greatest insight in the relativity of dance aesthetics when he describes dance as a universal urge but without a universal form (1946:12). Further he states:

> It is impossible to say that any of these approaches is exclusively right or wrong, better or worse than any other. . . . They are all absolutely right, therefore, for the specific circumstances under which they have been created (1946:17).

Indeed Martin comes the closest to the kind of relativity which most American anthropologists feel is necessary for observing and analyzing any aspect of culture and human behavior (see Martin 1939:92–93, 108). It is true that Sorell and others speak of differences caused by environment and other pertinent circumstances, but Sorell also ascribes much of the difference to "race," to "racial memory," and to "innate" differences which are "in the blood" (1967:75–76, 275, 282, 283). These ideas are so outdated in current anthropology, that I might believe his book was written at the end of the 19th century rather than in 1967.

It is true that many cross-cultural differences in dance style and dance aesthetics are due to both genetically determined physical differences and learned cultural patterns. In some cases the differences are clear. For example, a heavy Mohave Indian woman could not, and would not perform the jumps of the Masai people of East Africa. Other differences are not clear because they are part of a chicken/egg argument until further research is done and until more of the right questions are asked. We do not know, for example, whether people who squat easily with both feet flat on the ground do so because their leg tendons are genetically different from non-squatters, or if anyone could have the same tendon configuration if they habitually assumed such postures (see discussion in Martin 1939:97). As for "innate" qualities, we have almost no real evidence. There is nothing to support claims such as "barefoot savages have an ear for rhythms most Europeans lack" (DeMille 1963:48). There is much we do not know about bodies and genetics and cultural dynamics, and in addition, we are especially ignorant about systems of aesthetics. It would be wiser for Western dance scholars to leave qualifying remarks and openendedness in their discussions of these things, or else these scholars may have a lot of recanting to do.

Two terms which now require discussion are "primitive dance" and "folk dance." These comments are to be understood against the framework of my definition of dance which I have already given.

British, and especially American, folklorists are concerned with defining the "folk" in order to know what "folk dances" are. Our dance scholars, on the other hand, usually use "folk dance" as a kind of catch-all term. For example, DeMille lists Azuma Kabuki under her chapter on folk dance companies (1963:74). To call this highly refined theatrical form "folk dance" doesn't agree with Sorell's argument that folk dance is dance that has not gone "through a process of refinement"; that has not been "tamed" (1967:73). Perhaps such discrepancies help to show why definitions are so important and what a state of confusion can exist when we presume we all "mean the same thing."

Rather than following Sachs' contention that the "folk" or the "peasant" is an evolutionary stage between primitive and civilized man (1937:216), I shall follow the more anthropologically sophisticated distinctions which are discussed by the anthropologist Redfield in his book *Peasant Society and Culture* (1969: see especially pp. 23, 40–41). In brief, a primitive society is an autonomous and self-contained system with its own set of customs and institutions. It may be isolated or it may have more or less contact with other systems. It is usually economically independent and the people are often, if not always, nonliterate. (Notice that the term nonliterate refers to a group which has never had a written language of their own devising. This is quite different from the term illiterate which means that there is a written language, but an illiterate is not sufficiently educated to know the written form. Thus DeMille's statement that the primitives are illiterate is a contradiction of terms [DeMille 1963:23].) In contrast, peasant or folk societies are not autonomous. Economically and culturally such a community is in a symbiotic relationship with a larger society with which it constantly interacts. It is the "little tradition of the largely unreflective many" which is incomplete without the "great tradition of the reflective few." Often the people in peasant societies are more or less illiterate. If one adds the word dance to the above descriptions of primitive and folk (or peasant) there might be a more objective agreement on what is meant by "primitive dance" and by "folk dance."

Another troublesome term is that of "ethnic dance," as I have already indicated. In the generally accepted anthropological view, ethnic means a group which holds in common genetic, linguistic and cultural ties, with special emphasis on cultural tradition. By definition, therefore, every dance form must be an ethnic form. Although claims have been made for universal dance forms (such as Wisnoe Wardhana has been attempting to develop in Java: personal communication 1960), or international forms (such has been claimed for ballet: see Terry 1956:187), in actuality neither a universal form nor a truly international form of dance is in existence and it is doubtful whether any such dance form can ever exist except in theory. DeMille says this, in effect, when she writes that "theatre always reflects the culture that produces it" (1963:74). However others insist on some special properties for ballet. La Meri insists that "the ballet is not an ethnic dance because it is the product of the social customs and artistic reflections of several widely-differing national cultures" (1967:339). Nevertheless, ballet is a product of the Western world, and it is a dance form developed by Caucasians who speak Indo-European languages and who share a common European tradition. Granted that ballet is international in that it "belongs" to European countries plus groups of European descendants in the Americas. But, when ballet appears in such countries as Japan or Korea it becomes a borrowed and alien form. Granted also that ballet has had a complex history of influences, this does not undermine its effectiveness as an ethnic form. Martin tells us this, although he probably could not guess that his statement would be used for such a proof:

The great spectacular dance form of the Western world is, of course, the ballet. . . . Properly, the term ballet refers to a particular form of theater dance, which came into being in the Renaissance and which has a tradition, technic and an aesthetic basis all its own (1939:173).

Further quotations could be made to show the ethnicity of ballet, such as Kirstein's opening remarks in his 1935 book (vii).

ETHNICITY OF BALLET

I have made listings of the themes and other characteristics of ballet and ballet performances, and these lists show over and over again just how "ethnic" ballet is. Consider for example, how Western is the tradition of the proscenium stage, the usual three part performance which lasts for about two hours, our star system, our use of curtain calls and applause, and our usage of French terminology. Think how culturally revealing it is to see the stylized Western customs enacted on the stage, such as the mannerisms from the age of chivalry, courting, weddings, Christenings, burial and mourning customs. Think how our world view is revealed in the oft recurring themes of unrequited love, sorcery, self-sacrifice through long-suffering, mistaken identity, and misunderstandings which have tragic consequences. Think how our religious heritage is revealed through pre-Christian customs such as Walpurgisnacht, through the use of Biblical themes, Christian holidays such as Christmas, and the beliefs in life after death. Our cultural heritage is revealed also in the roles which appear repeatedly in our ballets such as humans transformed into animals, fairies, witches, gnomes, performers of evil magic, villains and seductresses in black, evil step-parents, royalty and peasants, and especially, beautiful pure young women and their consorts.

Our aesthetic values are shown in the long line of lifted, extended bodies, in the total revealing of legs, of small heads and tiny feet for women, in slender bodies for both sexes, and in the coveted airy quality which is best shown in the lifts and carryings of the female. To us this is tremendously pleasing aesthetically, but there are societies whose members would be shocked at the public display of the male touching the female's thighs! So distinctive is the "look" of ballet, that it is probably safe to say that ballet dances graphically rendered by silhouettes would never be mistaken for anything else. An interesting proof of this is the ballet *Koshare* which was based on a Hopi Indian story. In silhouettes of even still photos, the dance looked like ballet and not like a Hopi dance.

The ethnicity of ballet is revealed also in the kinds of flora and fauna which appear regularly. Horses and swans are esteemed fauna. In contrast we have no tradition of esteeming for theatrical purposes pigs, sharks, eagles, buffalo or crocodiles even though these are indeed highly esteemed animals used in dance themes elsewhere in the world. In ballet, grains, roses and lilies are suitable flora, but we would not likely find much call for taro, yams, coconuts, acorns or squash blossoms. Many economic pursuits are reflected in the roles played in ballet such as spinners, foresters, soldiers, even factory workers, sailors, and filling station attendants. However, we would not expect to find pottery makers, canoe builders, grain pounders, llama herders, giraffe stalkers, or slash and burn agriculturists!

The question is not whether ballet reflects it own heritage. The question is why we seem to need to believe that ballet has somehow become acultural. Why are we afraid to call it an ethnic form?

The answer, I believe, is that Western dance scholars have not used the word *ethnic* in its objective sense; they have used it as a euphemism for such old fashioned terms as "heathen," "pagan," "savage," or the more recent term "exotic." When the term ethnic began to be used widely in the '30's, there apparently arose a problem in trying to refer to dance forms which came from "high" cultures such as India and Japan, and the term "ethnologic" gained its current meaning for dance scholars such as Sorell (1967:72), Terry (1956:187, 196), and La Meri (1949:177–178). (An interesting article by Bunzell on the "Sociology of Dance" in the 1949 edition of *Dance Encyclopedia* rejects the use of the word "art" for these dance forms, however. In the context of his criticism, his point is well taken [1949:437].) I do not know why La Meri chose to discard this usage and substituted the word "ethnic" for "ethnologic" in her 1967 version of the *Dance Encyclopedia* article. She did not otherwise change her article, and since it was originally written with the above mentioned dichotomy implicit in her discussion, her 1967 version becomes illogical. (For a critical review of the *Dance Encyclopedia* and especially of La Meri's entries see Renouf, *Ethnomusicology* May, 1969:383–384.)

It is not clear to me who first created the dichotomy between "ethnic dance" and "ethnologic dance." Certainly this dichotomy is meaningless to anthropologists. As a matter of fact, European cultural anthropologists often prefer to call themselves ethnologists, and for them the term "ethnologic" refers to the objects of their study (see Haselberger's discussion 1961:341). The term "ethnological" does not have much currency among American cultural anthropologists although they understand the term to mean "of or relating to ethnology," and "ethnology" deals with the comparative and analytical study of cultures (see entries in *Webster's New International Dictionary*, 3rd edition). Because "culture," in a simplified anthropological sense, includes all of the learned behavior and customs of any given group of people, there is no such thing as a cultureless people. Therefore, "ethnologic dances" should refer to a variety of dance cultures subject to comparison and analysis. Ethnic dance should mean a dance form of a given group of people who share common genetic, linguistic and cultural ties, as mentioned before. In the most precise usage it is a redundancy to speak of "an ethnic dance," since any dance could fit that description. The term is most valid when used in a collective and contrastive way.*

Apparently one pan-human trait is to divide the world into "we" and "they." The Greeks did this when "they" were called *barbarians*. Similarly, the Romans called the "they" *pagans*, Hawaiians call "they" *kanaka'e*, and Hopis call the "they" *bahana*. All of these terms imply not only foreign, but creatures who are uncouth, unnatural, ignorant and, in short, less than human. The yardstick for measuring humanity, of course, is the "we." "We" are always good, civilized, superior; in short, "we" are the only creatures worthy of being considered fully human. This phenomenon reveals the world view of the speakers in every language, so far as I know. Often the phenomenon is very dramatic. According to a scholar of Mandarin and Japanese languages, in Mandarin the "they" are truly "foreign devils," and in Japanese the "they" are "outsiders" (Charles Alber, personal communication: 1970).

I suggest that, due to the social climate which rejects the connotations with which our former words for "they" were invested, and because of a certain sophistication assumed by the

---

*Harper distinguishes between ethnic and theatrical dance on the basis of "integral function of a society" versus dance which is "deliberately organized" to be performed for a general, impersonal audience (1967:10). This dichotomy, which is based on genre rather than the society, provides a good working classification. However, the distinction fails when the terms are tested. Thus one can have ethnic dances of an ethnic society, but not theatrical dances of a theatrical society. It seems clear that "ethnic" is a more embracive category under which "traditional" and "theatrical" might be convenient sub-divisions. In any case, Harper's discussion is thought-provoking.

apologists for the "they," English-speaking scholars were hard-pressed to find designators for the kinds of non-Western dance which they wished to discuss. Hence the euphemistic terms *ethnic* and *ethnologic* seemed to serve that purpose.

It is perfectly legitimate to use "ethnic" and "ethnologic" as long as we don't let those terms become connotative of the very things which caused us to abandon the other terms. We should indeed speak of ethnic dance forms, and we should not believe that this term is derisive when it includes ballet since ballet reflects the cultural traditions from which it developed.

I must make it clear that I am critical of our foremost Western dance scholars only where they have stepped outside their fields of authority. Within their fields they command my great respect, and I would not want to argue their relative merits. Scholars that they are, they will agree with me, I feel confident, that whatever are the rewards of scholarship, comfortable complacency cannot be one of them.

(1970)

Sources Cited

Bunzel, Joseph H., "Sociology of the Dance," *The Dance Encyclopedia*, Anatole Chujoy, comp. and ed. New York: A. S. Barnes and Co., 1949, pp. 435–440.

DeMille, Agnes, *The Book of the Dance*. New York: Golden Press, 1963.

Frazer, Sir James G., *The Golden Bough*. New York: Macmillan Co., 1947.

Harper, Peggy, "Dance in a Changing Society." *African Arts/ Arts d'Afrique* 1:1, Autumn, 1967, pp. 10–13, 76–77, 78–80.

Haselberger, Herta, "Method of Studying Ethnological Art." *Current Anthropology* 2:4, October, 1961, pp. 341–384.

Haskell, Arnold, *The Wonderful World of Dance*. New York: Garden City Books, 1960.

Holt, Claire, "Two Dance Worlds." *Anthology of Impulse*, Marian Van Tuyl, ed. New York: Dance Horizons, Inc., 1969, pp. 116–131.

Humphrey, Doris, "Dance" and related entries, *Webster's New International Dictionary*, 2nd edition, unabridged. Springfield, Massachusetts: G. and C. Merriam Co., Publishers, 1950.

Kealiinohomoku, Joann Wheeler, *A Comparative Study of Dance as a Constellation of Motor Behaviors Among African and United States Negroes*, unpublished M.A. thesis. Evanston, Illinois: Northwestern University, 1965.

Kinney, Troy and Margaret West Kinney, *The Dance*. New York: Frederick A. Stokes Co., 1924.

Kirstein, Lincoln, *Dance*. New York: G. P. Putnam's Sons, 1935.

————, *The Book of the Dance.* Garden City, New York: Garden City Publishing Co., 1942.

Kurath, Gertrude Prokosch, "Dance" and related entries, *Webster's New International Dictionary,* 3rd edition, unabridged. Springfield, Massachusetts: G. and C. Merriam Co., Publishers, 1966.

La Meri, "Ethnic Dance," *The Dance Encyclopedia,* Anatole Chujoy and P. W. Manchester, comps. and eds. New York: Simon and Schuster, 1967, pp. 338–339.

————, "Ethnologic Dance," *The Dance Encyclopedia,* Anatole Chujoy, comp. and ed. New York: A. S. Barnes, 1949, pp. 177–178.

Martin, John, *Introduction to the Dance.* New York: W. W. Norton and Co., Inc., 1939.

————, *The Dance.* New York Tudor Publishing Co., 1946.

————, (John Martin's Book of) *The Dance.* New York: Tudor Publishing Co., 1963.

Redfield, Robert, *The Little Community* and *Peasant Society and Culture.* Chicago and London: Phoenix Books, The University of Chicago Press, 1969. (First published separately, 1956.)

Renouf, Renée, Book Review of *The Dance Encyclopedia,* Anatole Chujoy and P. W. Manchester, comps. and eds., *Ethnomusicology* 13:2, May, 1969, pp. 383–384.

Sachs, Curt, *World History of the Dance,* Bessie Schönberg, trans. New York: Bonanza Books, 1937.

Sorell, Walter, *The Dance Through the Ages.* New York: Grosset and Dunlap, 1967.

Terry, Walter, "Dance, History of," *The Dance Encyclopedia,* Anatole Chujoy and P. W. Manchester, comps. and eds. New York: Simon and Schuster, 1967, pp. 255–259.

————, "History of Dance," *The Dance Encyclopedia,* Anatole Chujoy, comp. and ed. New York: A. S. Barnes and Co., 1949, pp. 238–243.

————, *The Dance in America.* New York: Harper and Brothers Publishers, 1956.

Recommended Reading

Adriann G. H. Claerhout, "The Concept of Primitive Applied to Art." *Current Anthropology* 6:4, Oct. 1965; Peggy Harper, *op. cit.;* Herta Haselberger, *op. cit.;* Adrienne L. Kaeppler, "Folklore as Expressed in the Dance in Tonga," *Journal of American Folklore* 80:316, April–June 1967; Adrienne L. Kaeppler, *The Struture of Tongan Dance,* unpubl. doctoral diss., Honolulu, University of Hawaii, 1967 (University Microfilms, Ann Arbor); Joann W. Kealiinohomoku and Frank J. Gillis, "Special Bibliography: Gertrude Prokosch Kurath, "*Ethnomusicology* 14:1, Jan. 1970; Gertrude Prokosch Kurath, "Panorama of Dance Ethnology," *Current Anthropology* 1:3, May 1960; Renée Renouf, *op. cit.;* Armistead P. Rood , "Bete Masked Dance: A View from Within," *African Arts/Arts d'Afrique* 2:3, Spring 1969.

ELIZABETH KENDALL
From WHERE SHE DANCED

"A POSSIBLE GRACE"

One hundred years ago a kind of entertainment called spectacle-extravaganza flourished, and it was there that theatrical dancing as an art survived, no matter how tenuously, in this country. The dancing was called ballet, although it was a very different ballet from today's. Popular dancing of that time— square dancing, jigs, reels, vaudeville soft shoe—was not considered art, not until it began to borrow some of the fancy ballet look of the spectacle extravanganzas that were not plays or operas or musicals or ballets but blends of all these forms inside a loose fantastical pantomime plot geared to the display of theatrical marvels.

Every country in the Western world produced spectacle-extravaganzas, with variations according to nationality. Some of the classics of the genre have survived in the repertories of modern ballet companies because of their splendid music scores— Delibes' *Coppélia* (France, 1870), Tchaikovsky's *Sleeping Beauty* and *The Nutcracker* (Russia, 1890 and 1892). No American spectacle is extant, because this country's productions tended to be even more loosely structured and, in modern terms, far-fetched, than Europe's. They were vast tableaux with processions, displays of empires or of fairy kingdoms, featuring the latest theater technology—but they did not really represent a theatrical form with its roots in American culture the way the same spectacles in Europe recalled the old court masques and the pomp and hierarchical display of monarchies.

American spectacles with dancing are thought to date from the first production of *The Black Crook* (1866), a lavish show whose dance emphasis came about by chance. When the manager of a popular New York theater, Niblo's Garden, inserted into his theater's current melodrama a whole foreign corps de ballet he had just bought, the resulting hybrid was a monumental hit. The "crook" in the title was a learned hunchback, Herzog, who made a pact with the devil about the fate of three other characters, Aminta (whom he loved), Rudolfo (whom she loved), and Count

Wolfenstein. It was a familiar Faustian tale, with plenty of occasion for theatrical wonders to appear and disappear; flying scenery, clouds of golden mist, magic glades, gilded chariots, and the like—and, thanks to the manager, a stunning array of diminutive foreign ballerinas in gauze costumes and satin toeshoes.

America was dimly familiar with the look of ballet dancing from the tours of Europe's solo Romantic ballerinas of the 1840s—the most memorable of whom was Fanny Elssler with her famous *Cracovienne* and her *La Tarentule*. When Elssler and her counterparts came from Europe in the forties, their highly articulate art was almost nowhere taught in America, and Mlle. Elssler's ballet master, James Sylvain, had a desperate time trying to find girls just to fill the stage and stand correctly for her corps de ballet. This remained the general condition until twenty years later, when *The Black Crook* encouraged some teaching of ballet decorum: the original production and its many revivals required a corps of 150 girls along with demi-soloists and soloists (soloists in the first production, Marie Bonfanti and Rita Sangalli, were artists and set high standards from the beginning). No one in the American audiences, though, quite realized there was a *system* involved in this kind of dancing, and a highly exacting mode of study; that the ballerinas advertised from La Scala or from San Carlo had emerged from academies far stricter and more disciplined that any convent school for girls. Instead, for a good many years, they were seen as wildly exotic curiosities. During this time, scores and scores of new soloists and corps de ballet girls populated the countless *Black Crook* revivals and imitations. Indeed, the reason *The Black Crook* seems to have fascinated the public for so long was not merely the display of legs but the un-Americanness of the whole thing. Watching *The Black Crook* was to most people a form of ogling foreigners in their most exotic plumage. The importance of ballet and also its peculiarly non-sensical aura in America can be recognized in advertisements for subsequent spectacles, like this one for *Enchantment* (1879):

An Entirely New Grand Spectacle of 4 Acts and 20 Tableaux

First appearance in America of the renowned Terpsichorean artists: Mlles Casati, Conalba and E. Capelini (Europe's greatest premier danseuses assolutas from The Theater La Scala, Milan, and San Carlo, Naples, and the Grand Opera House, Paris)

Also appearances of Mlles Sallio, Camis, Ortoli (Theater National Bucharest), Mlles R. Carpelini, Pasta and Ciappa, together with extensive Corps of Coryphées

Miss Rose Lee (from the Covent Garden Theater, London)
Miss Jessie Greville (of the Alhambra, London)
Miss Eugenie Nicholson (from the Crystal Palace, Southampton)
Mr. C. T. Campbell (of the Opera Comique, London)
Les Vantoches Vallotte, Human Automatons
Molva, most graceful of all gymnasts
La Troupe Rajade, Comic Eccentrics
& Occarinistes, who play upon an entirely new instrument

The featured ballet dancers—Italian, French, English (the Russians hadn't come out of their dark continent yet)—might as well have been creatures from the moon for all the public knew or cared—they seemed more like contortionists than actresses (and actresses were foreign enough). At any rate, if they were viewed as people, as women at all, they were condemned as absolutely outside the pale of normal American social intercourse. It is fascinating to think how many of them must have been crisscrossing America in the 1880s and 90s in spectacle after touring spectacle—*La Surprise* (after *Lucia di Lammermoor*), *La Nymphe de Diane* (after *Sylvia*), *Ali Baba*, *Aladdin's Lamp*, *The Black Venus*, *Excelsior*, *Columbus and the Discovery of America*, *Railroads on Parade*, *Turco the Terrible*—to name only a few.

While the soloists toured, the corps de ballet never travelled from city to city; instead it was assembled in each new territory by an advance ballet master. He drew on collections of American girls of the humblest social order, country girls just come to the city, factory girls, runaway girls who read in a newspaper that a corps of 150 was needed. They called at the stage door and were fitted into tutus and drilled in lines to stand obediently, or walk or turn as coryphées, without having the least idea of what ballet dancing was about. This race of girls did not give ballet a very high standing—and in fact ballet was considered synonymous with the leg shows that also featured ranks of girls in tights. One was a San Francisco production of the late 1860s called *The Female Forty Thieves, or, The Golden Legion of the Fairy Region*. The San Francisco *Bulletin's* comment about it could have served for many leg shows and the spectacle-extravaganzas:

> The bountiful display of Amazonian limbs, and the number of revolving tableaux introduced without any particular reason, pleased the spectators.

The American "pick-up" ballet girls, even the high-class ones with some training, were if anything more suspect than the incomprehensible foreigners—they couldn't dance as well *and* they had presumably chosen to throw away all respectability and a normal life. Whether or not it was true, all were assumed to be at the disposal of gentlemen who hired them for club celebrations and bachelor dinners. A former ballet girl could not enter domestic service or work in a shop once she had been in that sort of theater work. The only way for her to advance in her profession was laterally, over to a vaudeville solo spot or from show to show. Many girls did go to vaudeville, starting in the 1890s as solo acts came to prominence, and a whole new genre—skirt dancing, a cross between jigs and clogs and the formal pseudo-ballet steps of spectacles—arose for girl solo dancers. Those who were chorines, ballet girls, and skirt dancers of the late-nineteenth century are mostly invisible to us now: they rarely wrote their memoirs. But by searching old magazines and programs it is possible to follow a few of them from show to show and to learn what training they had, if any.

In New York at least, some training was available. All along, certain of the foreign ballerinas in those American spectacles married in this country or simply retired, and taught privately in their homes—usually girls already in the theater. Gradually by the 1890s a relaxation of moral standards for women meant that these Mesdames attracted more pupils, amateur *and* professional, and could afford studios—especially when some of the smart ones added dance fads such as physical culture exercises, aesthetic posing, or risqué serpentine motions to the classical techniques they had been taught and were still trying to propagate. The Metropolitan Opera didn't open a ballet school until 1909, but earlier, Marie Bonfanti, original star of *The Black Crook*, maintained a studio near Union Square and then one next to the Palace Theater on Broadway. Léon Espinosa and members of his family taught dancing at Madison Square Garden after he was appointed ballet master there in 1890. Mme. Elizabetta Menzeli, former Berlin colleague of Marie Taglioni, also trained in Paris, St. Petersburg, and Vienna, had a professional school on East 16th Street in the 1880s and 90s, the Conservatoire de Chorégraph Classique. There she taught a few girls with serious dance ambitions and coached many amateur ladies for "all kinds of acts, plays, sketches, etc."

The existence of these schools was one reason for the rise in the late 1890s of the first generation of American solo dancers whose names are remembered today—Loie Fuller, La Belle Dazié, Gertrude Hoffman, Bessie Clayton, Isadora Duncan, Ruth St. Denis. All of them began as ballet girls, but they are remem-

bered now because they came out of the corps de ballet to
become soloists, on vaudeville stages or musical comedy stages
or on various art stages of their own devising. All of them were
strong-minded, original young women who were not happy in
a corps de ballet of a spectacle, nor were they willing to accept
the age-old taint of the American ballet girl, which had nothing
to do with their dreams and ambitions. They were of their time,
a time that saw the birth of a new social being, the Modern
American Woman. They, the dancers, would become one of her
prime symbols. The New Woman emerged as America emerged
into world politics. She happened after decades of reformers' and
feminists' trying to free women's bodies and minds through spiritual and physical panaceas: dress reform, open air, aesthetic
exercise, artistic pursuits. Physical culture and art came into
vogue at the same time, in the 1890s and occupied women in a
country where women had more time, more money, more space
to be individuals than in any other country at any other time. In
fact, "the physical" and "the artistic" were the two realms where
American women's new capacities for self-expression were exercised. Dancing was the synthesis of those two realms.

If there was a new American woman, it was not exactly clear
what was correct for her to do. Henry James, that constant
observer of women, said the American woman was the one in
the world who was the least afraid, "the most confidently grown,
the most freely encouraged plant in our democratic garden." Yet
he thought this kind of encouragement interfered with women's
learning true femininity in the age-old sense of that term. James
lived in Europe. By 1907, when he wrote two articles for *Harper's
Bazaar* on the speech and manners of American women following a long return visit to America, he saw that women here were
ignoring, had always ignored, the feminine qualitites that he
most admired in European women, which consisted of "definite
conceptions of duty, activity, influence; of a possible grace, of a
possible sweetness, a possible power to soothe, to please and
above all to exemplify."

In Europe a woman was trained to be a private being within a
complex social fabric. A European woman could shun wifehood
and motherhood and choose the life of nun, courtesan, artist, ballerina, joining a parochial feminine hierarchy whose values were
understood and needed by the whole society. An American
woman was trained for a cruder and more public purpose. Very
little true artistic discipline was offered her in the nineteenth
century. Girls were taught to sew and read and play the piano,

even to perform quadrilles and other social dances, insofar as these things helped them to be valuable members of families, wives and mothers and citizens of the Democracy. Even such staunch feminists as Catharine Esther Beecher, eldest daughter of the famous Calvinist Lyman Beecher and sister of Harriet Beecher Stowe, did not believe a woman should cultivate her personality for her own sake but for a larger, more selfless purpose. She described this in an 1871 address to the Christian Women of America.

> Women's great mission is to train immature, weak and ignorant creatures, to obey the laws of God; the physical, the intellectual, the social and the moral—first in the family, then in the school, then in the neighbourhood, then in the nation, then in the world—the great family of God whom the Master came to teach and to save.

There were a few examples in nineteenth-century America of unconventional educations producing women with bold minds of their own. Margaret Fuller, the sole female among the cabal of Transcendentalist writers in Concord and Boston, was one of these. She was specially tutored by her father in the "masculine" disciplines of logic, Latin, law, and oratory—but she did not learn the arts. She did not, for instance, study ballet, which was a discipline as articulate and civilized as logic or law, only in another realm, an artistic and wordless one that was not available to upstanding American women. To have seriously taught Margaret Fuller theatrical dancing or any art would have been more subversive than to discipline her mind—for it would have permitted her a private cultivation of her spirit, an artist's intense dialogue with self which in fact Margaret Fuller sought painfully all her life. An artist, a woman alone with a vigorous, disciplined imagination that she listened to over and above her husband, children, or neighbors, was *not* part of the American design. A woman like Margaret Fuller, over-trained in a consciousness of public morality, was.

Contemporary with Margaret Fuller lived several non-intellectual, seemingly immoral, Bohemian heroines who put *themselves* outside of the American design—*they* were supposed to be the artists. Lola Montez, the Irish dancer-courtesan who almost became a Californian, was a woman like this, or Adah Isaacs Menken, the Jewess from New Orleans, proclaimer of free verse and frequent star of the old pantomime *Mazeppa* (in which she always made her entrance costumed as a prince, "en travestie," in tights, strapped to the back of a white stallion who galloped down several runways to deposit his rider in the center of the drama). These women, unlike the fine and strictly professional actresses of nineteenth-century America, used the theater to advertise their personalities. They were in fact "artistes,"poseurs instead of real artists, for they suffered from the opposite malady from Margaret Fuller's—they had no discipline instead of too much; wild ideas, without any experience of artistic skill or structure. Adah Menken never could learn her dramatic lines, nor did she see the reason to—for her instincts in gesture and costume (a "one-piece yellow silk garment" sometimes replaced the tights) kept her audience captive. Although Adah Menken may be considered the first American spectacle-extravaganza star, she had no effect on the genre itself. She was an isolated legend. Her only real skill was equestrian. (She herself rode the horse onstage in *Mazeppa*, instead of the cardboard dummy that was standard for this galloping entrance.)

Extravagant and uncultivated "artistic" impulses troubled Henry James in his countrywomen fifty years after Adah Menken's career had peaked. And now these impulses were in style; they cropped up in numbers of high spirited modern girls who came of age in the 1880s and 90s. There was money to indulge an artistic bent, yet no one knew quite how to do this in a society where wives and mothers were still the only feminine models of good behavior. Only by going abroad could an American girl encounter the artistic discipline to guide her new-found instincts. Back home, professional training only occurred in exceptional cases in the theater and music or literature (a fine writer like Kate Chopin—*The Awakening*, 1899—was allowed to imitate modern French literature in her Catholic and cosmopolitan education in St. Louis). But dancing, the art that was scorned and misunderstood, the art that wasn't even an art, provided discipline.

American artistic dance was born of some American dancers' extravagant desires for self-expression, guided, no matter how unconsciously, by disciplines they had absorbed from the theater. An old fashioned corps de ballet, casual though that institution was in America, provided the only secular example of a disciplined feminine hierarchy based on Henry James's "conceptions of duty" and "a possible grace." These new dancers had been physically trained in these conceptions of duty; their bodies had learned to move to the rhythm, and to be still. Their minds raged against the confinement of a corps de ballet, yet their bodies had been taught harmony. They were ballet girls possessed

of those "unballetic" qualities of the new American woman—
her "great fund of life," her self-absorption, her fearlessness, her
unbounded imagination, and her often monstrous daring. It was
the combination of the ballet girl's body with the American
untamed spirit that produced our first solo dancers and our first
native art form.

The unskilled American ballet chorine did not disappear with
the advent of a new dance; she was more than ever present in
the expanded theater activity at the turn of the century. She was
needed in large numbers for the choruses of the musical comedies that were replacing the old spectacles as the most popular
theatrical genre. Her story has been told in uncanny detail in
Theodore Dreiser's great novel of 1900, *Sister Carrie*. But it is not
Dreiser's silent, helpless, and strangely elegant Carrie who concerns us in the story of American art-dance, nor is it Henry
James's high-strung but undisciplined heroines of the leisure
class who never thought of the theater as an arena for themselves—but a rarer kind of girl somewhere between those two.

A sort of pattern emerges, even from the strongly individual
stories of these first dancers. They were usually of genteel background but poor; they turned to the theater first for money and
then for adventure. Gertrude Hoffman, for instance, the first
"art" dancer in American vaudeville, received a strict convent
education in San Francisco; it included some social dancing, perhaps too much, for she ran away at fifteen to perform in the oper-
etta chorus of the Castle Square Theater, became a rehearsal
director, then moved up the theatrical ladder through sheer
dogged intelligence. Ethel Gilmore, one of the few trained ballerinas of her time, was the daughter of a widowed Irish Canadian ladies' tailor, Rachel Janet Gilmore, whose love of color had
brought her to theatrical costuming and to New York. She put
her three daughters into Elizabetta Menzeli's school—and all
three of them made their débuts in the ballet chorus of a Florenz
Ziegfeld show, *Miss Innocence* (1906). Ethel, the middle one, was
picked in 1908 to replace the great Danish-English ballerina Adeline Genée in Ziegfeld's *The Soul Kiss*, and Ray, the youngest,
became the top "picture girl" model in New York.

It was usually the mothers of these dancers who formed them,
who stood as bulwarks guarding the light-heartedness, the freedom needed for young dancers, yet who taught them the disciplines of poverty. They held on to certain defiant beliefs about
women's inner independence so they could teach their daughters things that weren't part of the American mission to save

"immature, weak and ignorant creatures." Through personal catastrophe—their husband's death or desertion—these mothers had been left outside the pale already, on the fringe of the big cheerful family of the democracy.

Mary Dora Duncan, mother of Isadora and of three older children, was a fascinating and brave woman who taught her children as much of the civilized arts as she knew how to—music, dance, and aesthetic exercise, poetry and ideas borrowed from more sensual civilizations—arts of no use in an orderly American existence. It was almost a European education she gave her youngest daughter, almost a courtesan's training, but with an American crusading edge. The Duncan clan was aggressive; their heroes and heroines were past and present California Bohemians (such as Adah Menken), and they wanted to be a guerrilla band of serious artists inside what they saw as a misguided and thoroughly inartistic America. The story of Isadora's art consists of her discovering the seriousness of it after she had declared it loudly to be there. And she had the physical and theatrical skills to find this. Skills and training explain how Isadora grew up to become not only a desperate, chaotic, bold, and grandly tragic personality (as in a Henry James novel about a too proud American girl), but an artist who fashioned a new form of dancing.

In terms of pure dance invention, Isadora was the most significant figure in her generation. Her bold self-questioning was connected at the root to her physical training—that is, her mind and her body were inseparable, which is probably true of all great dance innovators. However, Isadora, while remaining an American "character," became a world artist who influenced the art-dance of Russia and Germany and England as much as or more than she did American dance.

It is not Isadora Duncan but another self-created dancer, Ruth St. Denis, who began the lineage of modern dance in America. Because Ruth St. Denis was a more specialized artist than Isadora, because she could have emerged only in America and she appealed mostly to American audiences, her story is to a great extent the story of this book. For a few years at the start of the century, Americans who saw her found in her dancing something that satisfied them deeply: a pantomimic shorthand of spectacle-extravanganza with religious overtones. The child Ruth Dennis was unlike those other early American dancers in several ways. She was a Protestant, whereas most of them were

Catholics. Although her mother taught her some of the same aesthetic exercises Isadora's mother taught her, the intent behind Ruth's education was hygienic and spiritual not artistic. It was more in the American idiom. Ruth Emma Dennis was a highly religious and moral woman; her daughter's heroines were not the artistic ballerinas and actresses of Isadora's childhood but women reformers, aesthetics lecturers, Delsarte priestesses, and the pioneer women doctors of the nineteenth century, all of whom exhorted women to examine the conditions of their bodies as a manifestation of the conditions of their spirits. And besides her background of health reform, Ruth knew more than the other solo dancers about the popular theater and less about dance training, so that a significant part of her dance inventions derived from theater and the techniques of tragic actresses of her day.

Ironically, Ruth St. Denis became the mother of American art-dance because she never belonged completely to art, but believed equally in religion, hygiene, and the popular theater. She was a high-toned entertainer more than she was a schooled artist—and yet her imagination contained the freshness of an artist as well as the single mindedness of a crusader. Ruth St. Denis' art was half-conscious. It came from the natural performer's unerring instincts for putting herself and her audience into another time and place—Egypt, the Orient—simply by acting out that time and place with costumes and movements. Lacking a dance education, she invented one, a kind of dance pre-history culled from her visions of antique and sensual civilizations and some scraps of information from public libraries. But she believed it. She never doubted she was giving her audience an ideology as well as a performance.

It is striking that Ruth St. Denis and the other American dancers, who all found dance metaphors in other civilizations, appeared just as the Russian Ballet made its blinding entry into Western culture and began the twentieth-century revival of ballet as an art form. The Russians, led by choreographer Michel Fokine, had also rediscovered ancient pagan civilizations. They introduced a pagan abandon into the traditional language of classic ballet and thus made new dance forms based on the old. The Americans had little experience with living theater-dance forms that made sense to them, yet blindly, almost coincidentally, they found the right ones for their culture. It seems almost a sociological accident that the imaginations of some American women, on the periphery of American life, were so untamed and so fresh that they could divine something of what the Russians reached after decades of consummate tradition and education. It still appears sometimes as if American Modern Dance exists by accident. Ruth St. Denis, its accidental founder, set the tone of it by drawing ultimately on the stuff of her personality rather than on a system of theater discipline. How that personality emerged out of her unconventional early education, her entry into vaudeville, her years in the theater, her début as a cultural priestess, is an epic of her time. It is known today because her husband, Ted Shawn, built a learning institution, Denishawn, around her, and taught the students in it to re-enact—intently, systematically, at times grimly—the process by which the original Priestess had discovered her dance.

(1979)

BIBLIOGRAPHY

I. What Is Dance?

Armelagos, Adina, and Mary Sirridge. "The In's and Out's of Dance: Expression as an Aspect of Style." *Journal of Aesthetics and Art Criticism* 36, no. 1, Fall 1977, pp. 15-24.

Best, David N. *Expression in Movement and the Arts*. London: Harry Kampton, 1974.

Cohen, Selma Jeanne. "A Prolegomenon to an Aesthetics of Dance." *Journal of Aesthetics and Art Criticism* 21, no. 1, Fall 1962, pp. 19-26.

Gilson, Étienne. "The Dance," in *Forms and Substances in the Arts*. Trans. by Salvator Attansio. New York: Charles Scribner's Sons, 1966, pp. 184-209.

Hanna, Judith Lynne. *To Dance Is Human*. Austin: University of Texas Press, 1979, pp. 17-24.

Lange, Roderyk. *The Language of Dance*. London: Macdonald and Evans, 1975, pp. 1-27.

Langer, Susanne K. *Feeling and Form*. New York: Charles Scribner's Sons, 1953.

————. *Problems of Art*. New York: Charles Scribner's Sons, 1957.

Martin, John. *Introduction to the Dance*. New York: Dance Horizons, 1975.

Royce, Anya Peterson. *The Anthropology of Dance*. Bloomington: Indiana University Press, 1977, pp. 3-16.

Sheets, Maxine. *The Phenomenology of Dance*. Madison: The University of Wisconsin Press, 1966.

Straus, Erwin W. "The Forms of Spatiality," in *Phenomenological Studies.* Trans. by Erling Eng. New York: Basic Books, 1966, pp. 3–37.
Valéry, Paul. "Dance and the Soul," in *Dialogues.* Trans. by William McCausland Stewart. New York: Pantheon Books, 1956, pp. 25–62.

II. The Dance Medium

Arnheim, Rudolf. "Concerning the Dance," in *Toward a Psychology of Art.* Berkeley: University of California Press, 1966, pp. 261–65.
Bateson, Gregory. "Why a Swan?" in *Anthology of Impulse.* Edited by Marian Van Tuyl. New York: Dance Horizons, 1969, pp. 95–99.
Feibleman, James K. *Aesthetics.* New York: Duell, Sloan and Pearce, 1949, pp. 302–5.
Greenberg, Clement. "Modernist Painting," in *The New Art.* Edited by Gregory Battcock. New York: E. P. Dutton, 1973, pp. 66–77.
Greene, Theodore Meyer. *The Arts and the Art of Criticism.* Princeton: Princeton University Press, 1940, pp. 338–49
Levin, David Michael. "The Embodiment of Performance." *Salmagundi,* Autumn 1975/Winter 1976, pp. 120–42.
Lessing, Gotthold. *Laocoön: An Essay on the Limits of Painting and Poetry.* Trans. by Edward Allen McCormick. Indianapolis: Bobbs-Merrill, 1962.
Martin, John. *Introduction to the Dance.* New York: Dance Horizons, 1965, pp. 61–70.
Valéry, Paul. "Some Simple Reflections on the Body," in *Aesthetics.* Translated by Ralph Mannheim. New York: Pantheon Books, 1964, pp. 31–40.

III. Dance and the Other Arts

Anderson, Jack, ed. "The Dance, The Dancer, and the Poem: An Anthology of Twentieth Century Dance Poems." *Dance Perspectives* 52, Winter 1972.
Brakhage, Stan, Maya Deren, Parker Tyler, et al. "Cine-Dance." *Dance Perspectives* 30, Summer 1967.
Clark, Mary, and Clement Crisp. *Ballet Art: From the Renaissance to the Present.* New York: Clarkson N. Potter, 1978.
Copeland, Roger. "Perspectives on Dance and Cinema." *Dance Magazine,* April 1974, pp. 44–49.
Croce, Arlene. "Dance in Film," in *Afterimages.* New York: Knopf, 1977, pp. 427–45.
Cage, John, Norman Dello Joio, Martha Graham, Louis Horst, Alwin Nikolais, "Composer/Choreographer." *Dance Perspectives* 16, 1963.
Elsbree, Langdon. "The Purest and Most Perfect Form of Play: Some Novelists and the Dance." *Criticism,* Fall 1972, pp. 361–72.

Kim, Myung Whan, "Dance and Rhythm: Their Meaning in Yeats and Noh." *Modern Drama* 15, no. 2, September 1972, pp. 195–208.

Krauss, Rosalind E. "Mechanical Ballets," in *Passages in Modern Sculpture*. New York: Viking Press, 1977, pp. 201–42.

Munro, Thomas. "The Afternoon of a Faun and the Interrelation of the Arts," in *Toward Science in Aesthetics*. New York: Liberal Arts Press, 1956, pp. 342–63.

Olitski, Jules. "On Dance." *Partisan Review* 48, no. 3, Summer 1981, pp. 456–57.

Priddin, Deirdre. *The Art of Dance in French Literature*. London: Adam and Charles Black, 1952.

Roslavleva, Natalia. "Stanislavski and the Ballet." *Dance Perspectives* 23, 1965.

Sorrell, Walter. *The Dancer's Image*. New York: Columbia University Press, 1971.

Ter-Arutunian, Rouben. "In Search of Design." *Dance Perspectives* 28, 1966.

Tompkins, Calvin. *The Bride and the Bachelors*. New York: Viking Press, 1968.

Valéry, Paul. "Degas, Dance, Drawing," in *Degas, Manet, Morisot*. Trans. by David Paul. New York: Pantheon Books, 1960, pp. 5–18.

Yudell, Robert. "Body Movement," in *Body, Memory, and Architecture* by Kent Bloomer and Charles Moore. New Haven: Yale University Press, 1977, pp. 57–76.

IV. Genre and Style

Ballet

Aschengreen, Erik, "The Beautiful Danger: Facets of the Romantic Ballet." *Dance Perspectives* 58, Summer 1974.

Beaumont, Cyril. *Michel Fokine and His Ballets*. London: Beaumont, 1935.

Buckle, Richard. *Nijinsky*. New York: Simon and Schuster, 1972.

Copeland, Roger. "Balanchine: Ballet's First Modernist." *The New York Times*, January 15, 1978, section 2, p. 1.

Coton, A. V. *Writings on Dance, 1937–68*. London: Dance Books, 1975.

Eliot, T. S. "The Ballet." *Criterion*, April 1925, pp. 441–43.

Heppenstall, Rayner. *Apology for Dancing*. London: Faber and Faber, 1936.

Goldner, Nancy. *The Stravinsky Festival of the N.Y. City Ballet*. New York: The Eakins Press, 1973.

Kirstein, Lincoln, et al. *The Classic Ballet*. New York: Knopf, 1977.

———. *Dance: A Short History of Classic Theatrical Dancing*. New York: Dance Horizons, 1969.

———. *Movement and Metaphor*. New York: Praeger, 1970.

———. *Nijinsky Dancing*. New York: Knopf, 1975.

———. *Three Pamphlets Collected*. New York: Dance Horizons, 1967.

Levinson, André. "The Spirit of the Classic Dance." *Theatre Arts Monthly,* March 1925.

Noverre, Jean-Georges. *Letters on Dancing and Ballets.* Trans. by Cyril Beaumont. New York: Dance Horizons, 1966.

Poirier, Richard, "The American Genius of George Balanchine." *The New Republic,* 183, no. 15, October 11, 1980, pp. 21–31.

Stokes, Adrian. *Tonight the Ballet.* New York: E. P. Dutton, 1935.

Story, Alan. *Arabesques.* London: Newman, Wolsey, Ltd., 1948.

Modern Dance

Cohen, Selma Jeanne, ed. "Essays, Stories, and Remarks about Merce Cunningham." *Dance Perspectives* 34, Summer 1968.

————, ed. *The Modern Dance: Seven Statements of Belief.* Middletown, Connecticut: Wesleyan University Press, 1966.

Coton, A. V. *The New Ballet.* London: Dobson, 1946.

Cunningham, Merce. *Changes: Notes on Choreography.* Edited by Frances Starr. New York: Something Else Press, 1968.

Duncan, Isadora. *The Art of the Dance.* Edited, with an introduction by Sheldon Cheney. New York: Theatre Arts Books, 1969.

Graham, Martha. *The Notebooks of Martha Graham.* New York: Harcourt, Brace, Jovanovitch, 1973.

Horst, Louis. *Pre-Classic Dance Forms.* New York: Dance Horizons, 1968.

Humphrey, Doris. *The Art of Making Dances.* Edited by Barbara Pollack. New York: Grove Press, 1959.

Kirstein, Lincoln. "Martha Graham," in *Martha Graham.* Edited by Merle Armitage. Los Angeles: Lynton Kistler, 1937, pp. 23–33.

Klosty, James, ed. *Merce Cunningham.* New York: Saturday Review Press, 1975.

Martin, John. *The Modern Dance.* New York: Dance Horizons, 1972.

Mazo, Joseph. *Prime Movers: The Makers of Modern Dance in America.* New York: Morrow, 1977.

McDonagh, Don. *The Complete Guide to Modern Dance.* Garden City, New York: Doubleday and Company, 1976.

Shawn, Ted. *Every Little Movement: A Book about François Delsarte.* New York: Dance Horizons, 1974.

Wigman, Mary. *The Language of Dance.* Trans. by Walter Sorell. Middletown, Connecticut: Wesleyan University Press, 1966.

Post-Modern Dance

Anderson, Jack. "Yvonne Rainer: The Puritan as Hedonist." *Ballet Review* 2, no. 5, 1969, pp. 31–37.

Banes, Sally. *Terpsichore in Sneakers: Post-Modern Dance.* Boston: Houghton Mifflin, 1980.

Carroll, Noel. "Post-Modern Dance and Expression," in *Philosophical*

Essays on Dance. Edited by Gordon Fancher and Gerald Myers. New York: Dance Horizons, 1981, pp. 95–104.

Copeland, Roger. "The Neo-Classical Task." *New Performance* 2, no. 3, 1981, pp. 50–59.

———. "Post-Modern Dance and the Repudiation of Primitivism." *Partisan Review* 50, no., Winter 1983.

Forti, Simone. *Handbook in Motion.* Halifax: Press of Nova Scotia College of Art and Design, 1974.

Johnston, Jill. "The New American Modern Dance," in *The New American Arts.* Edited by Richard Kostelanetz. New York: Collier Books, 1967, pp. 162–93.

Kirby, Michael. "Objective Dance," in *The Art of Time.* New York: E. P. Dutton, 1969, pp. 103–13.

Kostelanetz, Richard. "Metamorphosis in Modern Dance." *Dance Scope* 5, no. 1, Fall 1970, pp. 6–21.

Livet, Anne, ed. *Contemporary Dance.* New York: Abbeville Press, 1978.

McDonagh, Don. *The Rise and Fall and Rise of Modern Dance.* New York: E. P. Dutton, 1970.

Michelson, Annette. "Yvonne Rainer, Part One: The Dancer and the Dance." *Artforum.* January, 1974, pp. 57–63.

———. "Yvonne Rainer, Part Two: 'Lives of Performers.'" *Artforum.* February, 1974, pp. 30–35.

Morris, Robert. "Notes on Dance." *Tulane Drama Review* no. 10, Winter 1965, pp. 179–86.

Pops, Martin L. "Some Remarks on Modern and Post-Modern Dance," *Salmagundi,* Fall 1980/Winter 1981, pp. 242–49.

Rainer, Yvonne. *Work 1961–73.* New York: New York University Press, 1974.

V. Language, Notation, and Identity

Armelagos, Adina, and Mary Sirridge. "The Identity Crisis in Dance." *Journal of Aesthetics and Art Criticism,* 37, no. 2, Winter 1978, pp. 129–39.

Benesh, Rudolph and Joan Benesh. *An Introduction to Benesh Dance Notation.* London: Black, 1956.

Eshkol, Noa, and Abraham Wachsman. *Movement Notation.* London: Weidenfeld and Nicholson, 1958.

Goodman, Nelson. *Languages of Art.* Indianapolis and New York: Bobbs-Merrill, 1968.

Hall, Fernau. "Benesh Notation and Choreology." *Dance Scope* 3, no. 1, Fall 1966, pp. 30–37.

Hanna, Judith Lynne. "Toward Semantic Analysis of Movement Behavior: Concepts and Problems." *Semiotica,* no. 25½, 1979, pp. 77–110.

Hutchinson, Ann. *Labanotation.* New York: Theatre Arts Books, 1977.

——. "Perspective on the Dance Notation Situation." *Dance Scope* 5, no. 1, Fall 1970, pp. 39–46.

Kleinman, Seymour. "Movement Notation Systems: An Introduction." *Quest*, no. 33, January, 1975, pp. 33–56.

Laban, Rudolph von. *Principles of Dance and Movement Notation.* London: MacDonald and Evans, Ltd., 1956.

Margolis, Joseph. "The Autographic Nature of the Dance." *Journal of Aesthetics and Art Criticism* 29, no. 4, Summer 1981, pp. 419–27.

Stone, Roslyn E. "Human Movement Forms as Meaning-Structures: A Prolegomenon." *Quest*, no. 23, pp. 10–17.

Turnbaugh, Douglas Blair. "Dance Notation: Potential and Problems." *Dance Scope* 4, no. 2, Spring 1970, pp. 34–47.

Ziff, Paul. "About the Appreciation of Dance," in *Philosophical Essays on Dance.* Edited by Gordon Fancher and Gerald Myers. New York: Dance Horizons, 1981, pp. 69–83.

VI. Dance Criticism

Aloff, Mindy, ed. "On Dance Criticism." *New Performance* 2, no. 1.

Brown, Carolyn, Arlene Croce, Nancy Goldner, Dale Harris, and David Vaughan. "Symposium: Writing about the Dance." *Ballet Review* 7, no. 4, 1978–79, pp. 108–24.

Cocteau, Jean. "Diaghilev and Nijinsky," in *Cocteau's World.* Trans. and edited by Margaret Crosland. New York: Dodd, Mead, and Company, 1972, pp. 257–60.

Croce, Arlene. *Afterimages.* New York: Knopf, 1977.

Denby, Edwin. *Dancers, Buildings, and People in the Streets.* New York: Horizon, 1965.

——. *Looking at the Dance.* New York: Horizon, 1968.

Gautier, Théophile. *The Romantic Ballet.* Trans. by C. W. Beaumont. New York: Dance Horizons, 1972.

Haggin, B. H. *Ballet Chronicle.* New York: Horizon Press, 1971.

Johnston, Jill. *Marmelade Me.* New York: Dutton, 1971.

Jowitt, Deborah. "A Private View of Criticism." *Arts in Society,* Fall 1976, pp. 204–9.

——. *Dance Beat: Selected Views and Reviews, 1967–76.* New York: Marcel Dekker, 1978.

Siegel, Marcia B. *At the Vanishing Point: A Critic Looks at Dance.* New York: Saturday Review Press, 1972.

——. *The Shapes of Change: Images of American Dance.* Boston: Houghton Mifflin, 1979.

——. *Watching the Dance Go By.* Boston: Houghton Mifflin, 1977.

Sontag, Susan. "On Dance and Dance Writing." *New Performance* 2, no. 3, pp. 72–81.

Van Vechten, Carl. *The Dance Writings of Carl Van Vechten.* Edited by Paul Padgette. New York: Dance Horizons, 1974.

VII. Dance and Society

Artaud, Antonin. "On the Balinese Theatre," in *The Theatre and Its Double*. Trans. by M. C. Richards. New York: Grove Press, 1958, pp. 53–67.

Boas, Franziska, ed. *The Function of Dance in Human Society*. New York: Dance Horizons, 1972.

Bourguignon, Erika. "Trance Dance." *Dance Perspectives* 35, Autumn 1968, pp. 8–19.

Copeland, Roger. "Towards a Sexual Politics of Contemporary Dance." *Contact Quarterly*, 7, no. 3/4, Spring/Summer 1982, pp. 45–50.

De Mille, Agnes. "Ballet and Sex," in *Dance to the Piper*. Boston: Little, Brown, and Co., 1952, pp. 54–60.

Harrison, Jane. *Ancient Art and Ritual*. London: Williams and Norgate, 1918.

Huizinga, Johan. *Homo Ludens*. Boston: Beacon Press, 1955, pp. 164–65.

Kendall, Elizabeth. *Where She Danced*. New York: Knopf, 1979.

Koegler, Horst. "In the Shadow of the Swastika: Dance in Germany 1927–1936." *Dance Perspectives* 57, Spring 1974, pp. 3–48.

Lawrence, D. H. "The Hopi Snake Dance," in *Mornings in Mexico*. New York: Knopf, 1927, pp. 141–79.

Leeuw, Gerardus van der. *Sacred and Profane Beauty*. Trans. by David E. Green. New York: Holt, Rinehart and Winston, 1963.

Rust, Frances. *Dance in Society*. London: Routledge and Kegan Paul, 1969.

Rahner, Hugo. "The Heavenly Dance," in *Man at Play*. New York: Herder and Herder, 1976, pp. 65–90.

Slonimsky, Yuri. *The Bolshoi Ballet*. Moscow: Foreign Language Publishing House, 1960.

Wolcott, James. "Dance Captures that Old Rock Magic." *The Village Voice* December 29, 1975, p. 66.

Wynne, Shirley. "Complaisance: An Eighteenth-Century Cool." *Dance Scope* 5, no. 1, Fall 1970, pp. 22–35.

renewed 1981 by Susanne K. Langer (New York: Charles Scribner's Sons, 1953). Reprinted with the permission of Charles Scribner's Sons and Routledge & Kegan Paul Ltd.

David Michael Levin. "Balanchine's Formalism" from *Dance Perspectives* 55, Autumn 1973. Reprinted by permission of Dance Perspectives Foundation.

David Michael Levin. "Philosophers and the Dance" from *Ballet Review* 6:2 (1977–78). Reprinted by permission of *Ballet Review*, published quarterly by The Dance Research Foundation, New York, N.Y. 10014.

André Levinson. Excerpt from "The Art and Meaning of Isadora Duncan," translated from the Russian by Susan Cook Summer and Debra Goldman, from *Ballet Review* 6:4 (1977–78). Reprinted by permission of *Ballet Review*, published quarterly by The Dance Research Foundation, New York, N.Y. 10014.

André Levinson. "The Idea of the Dance: From Aristotle to Mallarmé" originally appeared in *Theatre Arts Monthly*, August 1927, and is used by permission of Theatre Arts Books, 153 Waverly Place, New York, N.Y. 10014.

Stéphane Mallarmé. "Ballets" from *Mallarmé: Selected Prose Poems, Essays, and Letters*, translated by Bradford Cook. Copyright © 1956 by The Johns Hopkins University Press. Reprinted by permission of the publisher.

Joseph Margolis. Excerpt from "Art as Language" from *The Monist* 58:2, and subsequently revised by the author. Copyright © 1974 by *The Monist*, La Salle, Illinois. Reprinted by permission of the author and the publisher.

John Martin. "Dance as a Means of Communication," an excerpt from *The Dance* (1946); and "Metakinesis," "Extension of Range," and "Form and Metakinesis," excerpts from *The Modern Dance* (1972), are reprinted by permission of the author.

Jean-Georges Noverre. Letter 1 from *Letters on Dancing and Ballets*, translated by Cyril W. Beaumont. Reprinted by permission of the Imperial Society of Teachers of Dancing.

Yvonne Rainer. "A Quasi Survey of Some Minimalist Tendencies . . ." from *Minimal Art: A Critical Anthology*, edited by Gregory Battcock. Copyright © 1968 by Yvonne Rainer. Reprinted by permission of the author.

Theodore Reff. Excerpt from "Edgar Degas and the Dance" reprinted from *Arts Magazine* 53:3, November 1978, by permission of the publisher.

Steve Reich. "Notes on Music and Dance" from *Ballet Review* 4:5, (1973). Reprinted by permission of *Ballet Review*, published quarterly by The Dance Research Foundation, New York, N.Y. 10014.

Jacques Rivière. Excerpt from "Le Sacre du Printemps," translated by Miriam Lassman, from *Nijinsky Dancing*, by Lincoln Kirstein. Reprinted by permission of Lincoln Kirstein.

Bernard Shaw. Excerpt from "8 February 1893" from *Music in London 1890–94*, vol. 2. Reprinted by permission of The Society of Authors on behalf of the Bernard Shaw Estate.

Francis Sparshott. "Why Philosophy Neglects the Dance." Copyright © 1983 by Francis Sparshott. Reprinted by permission of the author.

Adrian Stokes. Excerpt from "The Classical Ballet" from *Tonight the Ballet*. Copyright © 1934 by Adrian Stokes; renewed 1963. Reprinted by permission of the Estate of Adrian Stokes and Da Capo Press, who have reprinted *Tonight the Ballet* and *Russian Ballets* together in one volume.

E. M. W. Tillyard. Excerpt from *The Elizabethan World Picture*. Copyright 1944 by Macmillan Publishing Co., Inc., renewed 1972 by Stephen Tillyard, Mrs. V. Sankaran, and Mrs. A. Ahlers. Reprinted by permission of Macmillan Publishing Co., Inc., Chatto and Windus Ltd., and the author's literary estate.

INDEX

Numbers in italics indicate material written by named author.